Starflacker

Starflacker

Inside the Golden Age of Hollywood

Dick Guttman

A Bedside Reader for People Who Love Movies

R Guttman
Associates, Inc.

R Guttman Associates, Inc.
118 S. Beverly Dr., Suite 201
Beverly Hills, CA 90212
www.starflacker.com

Printed in the United States of America

ISBN Paperback: 978-0-9864071-0-9
ISBN ebook: 978-0-9864071-1-6

Cover artwork: John Robertson
Interior Design and Layout: Ghislain Viau

To TCM and Robert Osborne who bear continuing
and loving witness to the great films and the great stars

Acknowledgments

I am grateful to Ghislain Viau of Creative Publishing Book Design for the interior design and distribution and to Ellen Reid for her guidance. Noted artist John Robertson for his painting, Starflacker, seen in the cover collage.

Gratitude to my wife, family, staff, clients, associates and everyone whose originality graced my life and is celebrated in this book. Notably excepted from these kind feelings are Baby Doc, the Shah of Iran, Generalissimo Francisco Franco and members of the Guatamalan facist junta.

Contents

Flack: *n.* A press agent; a publicist. — *v. intr.* To act as a press agent. *tr.* to act as a press agent for.

—*(American Heritage College Dictionary)*

Star-flack-er: *n.* One who acts as a press agent for stars [deriving from the transitive verb *flack,* to act as a press agent for]

—*(Monika Robertson)*

Preface

I thought I would write a book about my friend Warren Cowan who so powerfully shaped our business of independent entertainment publicity. Although he lived 90 years, Warren did not live long enough to tell the tale. My own escapades with the storied stars and the storied press agents of the Golden Age of Hollywood were impatient. They kept lining themselves up for my attention as I outlined the Warren Cowan story. The whole challenging and privileged adventure of being a press agent seemed to be the point, precisely because it's been told up to now primarily by writers who found flacks an easy target for satire and disdain.

Instead of speaking for one PR pro, I found myself speaking for all of them, all the publicity guys and gals of my brief 60 years on the job.

PR people lead essentially similar lives. It's just the improbable narrative anecdotes which vary from flack to flack. Here is an introduction to mine and to the rules of the game which I've recognized along the way. Many of the extraordinary people who enriched my career, people who made you love movies, are gone. I sifted through my experience to provide those stories which allow these remarkable personalities to introduce themselves to you and, in the process, justify the secret, improbable and wild-ride world of PR.

To set the mood:

Somewhere in the 1970s when we were all too young to think of death, at the most vulnerable wee hour of a deep sleep I was awakened by a phone call from an Associated Press writer in New York asking me to confirm a report that Michael Caine had been killed.. automobile accident. It was a Sunday morning, too, when I got the call about Sharon Tate, and so I mumbled, "What?" It couldn't happen twice. It would, in fact, happen on sad occasion over the years, but Michael… I rejected the thought. Maybe I misunderstood. However, he repeated it. "Where did this story originate?" I asked. "Radio station in Long Island." "Shouldn't they be getting the story from AP and not the other way around?" "Whatever, but we need your response or your checking it out." On a hunch, I asked if anyone else was injured. "No.. single vehicle accident, no passenger." "I can verify right now," I told him, "that Michael Caine was not killed in that accident." "Yeah? How's that?" he demanded skeptically. "Because Michael Caine does not know how to drive, so he doesn't."

A life in PR entails a lot of rude awakenings. With some of them, you actually can go back to sleep.

Within the thousand tales and many more in this writing is one which made it very clear to me why I undertook what proved to be a five year (I have a day job) venture in remembering and evaluating and sharing:

At one point in the wide-eyed year of 1956, I, an ingenuous 23 year old press agent working in Paris on Billy Wilder's romantic comedy "Love In The Afternoon," arranged for Gary Cooper to be interviewed one evening at the actor's Hotel George V suite.

Peer Oppenheimer, the editor of Family Weekly, a major American Sunday supplement magazine of the time, and I arrived at the appointed hour to the apparent consternation of Cooper's valet. After a half hour, the door to Cooper's bedroom opened and Coop, immaculately dressed for an evening… looking like Gary Cooper, super dooper… emerged preceded by two tall and gloriously beautiful women dressed as though they were about to step onto the Balmain runway. "Gentlemen," Coop said, 'I apologize. I recall having set the interview for tonight, ignoring that I had prior commitment. Peer, if you'll pardon the inconvenience, I'd love you and Dick to be my guests for a wonderful dinner tomorrow night, and I promise to make up something that will give you a good story."

Fifty-five years later, Cooper's two guests at that epicurean dinner at Calvados compared their recall of the events. The memory was a very warm one for Peer. 'I was very flattered that Gary knew that I would never reflect in my story the circumstances of the night before," Peer said. "He never mentioned it. He trusted me."

Peer's remark reminded me that in a time before blogs and Facebook when newspapers, magazines and radio were the sole and blindly trusted intermediaries, a very legit and independent media understood its function as one of the three conjoined sides of the basic triangle of stardom. An important connective tissue of shared society, stardom is compounded of *A. stars, B. media reportage of those stars and C. the public's image of the stars.* That long period's intense esteem and affection for movie stars, which helped power our optimism through wars and economic woes, was influenced to some degree by PR and by a media focused on building stars rather than exploiting them. To a greater degree, of course, those stardoms were constructed of the qualities and traits the public recognized in each of those stars, and of the dreams they invested in them. The stars did their part with winning and moving performances and by living up to the images and charm quite accurately ascribed to them.

That was it. That's why I began this writing… and continued with it and further continued with it until I was written out. With their wit and scalawag ways, those Golden Age legends illustrate the inner workings and delights of a Hollywood which exists no more. It's a story which was captured as well in the memories of my fellow flacks of the period, the other people who similarly connected those stars to the media and public or protected the stars *from* them. Far too many of those memories have already been laid to rest with a stone on top to secure the silence. So "Starflacker," the crowded recollections of one PR pro, speaks for them all, reflecting the strange but common experiences which entice every press agent through a day or through a career. And here's the driving premise… those indestructible , imperishable stardoms we flacks polished and brandished were a national treasure… and *Hollywood has sadly lost its ability to generate such legend.*

The Golden Age of Stardom was and no longer is. What made that time so different? What made its stars so bright and eternal? Those stars and their celebrity were, above all, the hallowed dreams of their audience. Today the public doesn't dream because it doesn't have to. It has the instant gratifications of digital babble and at-your-fingertips porn and worst-case scenarios. Every scabrous thing you want to know about anyone… true or probably and expectably not… is yours for the online asking. Today's public feeds on the miseries and foibles of its celebrities. Back in the golden day, nobody chortled over Judy Garland's struggles. They loved her.

If you've selected "Starflacker" for your reading, you will be joining me in the improbable adventures of life in a much-maligned and under-estimated business.

I think you'll find my all-star companions of the road as amusing and amazing as I did. This all is written with abiding affection for those with whom I traveled that road. Perhaps my peers, the people with whom I share this profession, will discover that my experiences correspond to their own. They share with me the intriguing challenge of *serving artists in an industry whose first purpose is no longer that of creating great stardoms*. Not that fine roles in fine films don't come along. But that's the problem. They no longer pour forth. They merely come along.

I particularly hope this PR diary's revelations meet the expectation and justify the devotion of that other intended audience, the people who share my love of the Golden Age and its stars and its films... people who, as do I, check the TV listings each morning to see what's on TCM.

These star-flacking experiences did actually occur as described... all quarter million and more words of them, all however many hundred pages of them, 600 or perhaps 800. This count in the e-book world varies with the type size you choose. Ask yourself what kind of deranged mind could possibly have *made up* all this stuff or imagined the thousands of dialogues? Every anecdote happened, however Kafkaesque some may seem. This is your visitor's pass to Hollywood with its hair down... the All-Access-Pass Hollywood of any press agent's existence, but in this case that of my own past six decades.

During the Oscar campaign for 'The Artist" I had insisted into its strategy that we emphasize the relevance of that admittedly-French film's being the only award contender that was made in Hollywood that year. I called for a double dose mention of that element in a TV promo. But Harvey Weinstein responded, "No, we'll say it once. We're not all ADD like Dick Guttman." An astute editor had once instructed me to "tell 'em what you're gonna say, say it, tell 'em that you've said it." *While that doesn't always work in the minimalism of a news story, it's a good general rule of effective communication.* And, since I don't have to have an editor for this diary (a circumstance I deeply cherish... this is just me talking to you, no editors' polish or contrivance) here is advance notice of some of the concerns you may find recurring in this, my unspooling of a life in PR:

Long Before Tabloids And Twitter, Stars Had Mystery, Stature And Staying Power. Hollywood publicists (press agents, PR gals and guys, flacks) were an important part of that equation... intimate witness to the hundreds of stars and stardoms whose glories remain undiminished by age or even death. *Stars then were built for style and built to last.* But Hollywood doesn't care about that anymore. They're happy with whoever is trending.

Gone Are The Days: but how and why and is it irreversible? We'll explore how THE NEW HOLLYWOOD, THE NEW PUBLIC AND THE NEW MEDIA HAVE REMOVED THE LADDERS NEEDED TO REACH LEGEND.

STARDOM THEN AND NOW: Reality TV has, of course, produced some true talents, but when select personalities peddling little more than their notoriety, are the priority appetite and focus of both public and media, it's time to rescue fame from its sorry devaluation. The legends of the past served us well, and we need to continue the tradition. "Starflacker" surveys not only the ingredients but also the how and the why of legendary stardom.

THE BAD BOYS (AND GIRLS) OF PR: This confessional memoir is the frank, funny and proud revelation of a derided profession which critically influences our obsessive interest in entertainment and its over-large influence on our lives. PR Hollywood style. Along with its capture of the wit and idiosyncrasies of legendary Hollywood figures, observations unique to a flack's eye view, *this diary reveals an unusual profession which shared and shaped the glory days of Hollywood and of its golden stars, a profession which flourishes still, swimming upstream against the changing and diminishing standards of fame and glamour.* Folded into this rich mulch are The Rules of Publicity which are also a guideline to the widely useful skills of persuasion.

Chapter 1

A Life In Pr

Cary Grant called one morning. He was the only person who could coax two syllables out of my first name. "Di-ick, this is Cary," he announced crisply. Never any danger of mistaking the voice we all knew better than our own. Funny how easy those stars were to imitate… and how impossible to replicate. I asked how I could help him. For a press agent… a flack, a publicity guy or gal,… three out of four calls are asks. How-can-I-help-you? cuts to the chase. "You know this fellow Vernon Scott, don't you? United something," Cary began. "United Press International." "That's the one. I wonder if he would write a story for you… something I'd like to clear up." Cary liked to clear things up. He'd called me early in our association to clear up the matter of the English muffins at New York's Plaza Hotel. It was widely rumored for decades that he once had called the manager of the hotel (in some reports it is Conrad Hilton whom he called) to find out what had happened to the other half of one of the two English muffins on which his eggs Benedict were supposed to have arrived. The rumor had it that he had requested that the other half be brought up to his room since he'd paid for it. That, he had told me on the prior call, was nonsense. He had merely inquired if the other half became part of someone else' eggs Benedict or if it was wastefully discarded. He was told it was put to good use, and he was fine with that. "Do you want me to quash that rumor?" I'd asked during the muffin call. "No, I just wanted you to know. It's too late now. That muffin has done its damage."

But this time, it was clear that he wanted me to take action. "What's the problem, Cary?" "One of those women's magazines," he said, "they've printed this story quoting me as having said that I never loved any of my wives." "That's pretty rude. Did you ever say that… or anything like it?" "LIKE it, yes… yes , I did. I once commented that I had never LEFT any of my wives. They all left ME. Do you think you can get friend Vernon to speak to me to tidy that up?" "Cary," I said, "this is one I think I can sell."

There's a winding road leading to almost every association in our business. Here's the one which led us to Cary Grant. I came clientless into my own business. My longtime boss and teacher, Warren Cowan, thought it would be rude if I departed his company, Rogers & Cowan, with some of his clients in my pocket. With my middleclass Midwest ethic, I actually agreed, although many of them were there because I was doing a good job on them. So naked came I to partnership with Jerry Pam. The distinguished writer and producer Leslie Stevens, taking pity lightly salted with belief, demanded that Warner Bros. hire the newly hatched, not quite fledged firm of Guttman & Pam to represent Leslie's new adventure series starring Hugh O'Brian and Sir John Gielgud. This led to our representing Hugh who, along with Cary Grant was on the board of Faberge which, as direct result of Hugh's intervention, we very shortly represented as well. Such are the domino forces of Hollywood good fortune, and so we came into the delightful custodianship of Cary Grant's publicity needs, underwritten by George Barry… Jerry developed a close bonding with George Barry, the head and driving force of the Faberge beauty products empire. My wife very early in the game cautioned me not to use the word "friend" to describe a business contact. In the first place, it presumed. More relevantly, she insisted that in any relationship in which money is exchanged, "association" is a safer assumption than friendship and a truer stone on which to stand. Since lasting relationship has been pretty much the theme of my life in PR, I think some friendships have crept in.

George Barry was bored when he wasn't doing at least twelve things at once. Energetic, restless, he was tasteful, eclectic, a song writer as well as beauty industry genius. We very shortly helped him get an Oscar nomination as a tunesmith. He was fascinated with film-making and glamour. The latter, of course was his business. Cary Grant and Hugh O'Brian were very active board members and closely involved in our work to build Barry and Faberge into real powers in the film world. We helped George market a number of good films, most notably the Oscar-nominated "A Touch Of Class." Other relationships developed from the

Faberge connection, particularly with that life force known as Glenda Jackson, who achieved the Best Actress Oscar for that light romantic comedy.

Occasionally a news story will refer to some press agent as being famous or even powerful. That is delusional. "Persuasive," "perceptive" and "persistent" maybe. They are the p-driven adjectives which feed a PR gal's or guy's family and put the kids through school. *Fame is what you sell, not what you seek.* The fame you help your clients achieve will enrich both their careers and yours. Content yourself with that. Power is the number of doors to which you acquire the keys. Your skill set must contain, above all, your up-to-date knowledge of the evolving media and whatever hard-won trust you have managed to get the media to accord you. Sharpen these with your audacity and polish them with techniques and instincts honed from campaigns triumphant or bitter. It doesn't hurt if you know how to write. You are judged by your batting average, although most often you will be the only one keeping count of your home runs. So don't fixate on those or on your strikeouts. Learn from each. if you help bring awareness, continuity and dignity to enough careers, a useful kind of reputation grows on you like ivy on college walls.

By those rules, to which I've always subscribed, writing a memoir is high treason. There is, on the other hand, the prospect of freeing up all the space these recollections occupy in the brain and the faint hope of offering reasonable explanation as to what might hold one to a profession so often and dismissively impugned, disdained and even distrusted. The writing, no small incentive, is also evidence that you have held off cerebral ravage for one more year and offers the possibility that you can revisit it all on paper when you can no longer revisit it in mind.

Being a press agent will infect your life, because people... even friends, even wives or husbands... will give your every utterance bitter analysis for sincerity, the old did-he-mean-that-or-is-he-just-*saying*-it? I love to compliment my wife. Gisela is in so many essential ways complimentable. Often I bring forth something from deep within my wonder, and she says, "PR." One night, driving home, I determined to bestow upon her an expression of love so deeply from the soul as to certify irrefutable devotion. At a proper moment when I thought I had her attention, I said, "Darling, there are other women with whom I could have spent my life, but you're the only woman I could not have spent my life *without*." There was a long pause. Naturally, I understood she was stunned by such protestation of love. Then she looked deep into my eyes and said with great and earnest intensity, "Who were they?"

At a Beverly Hills Hotel lunch event hosted by People Magazine, I was standing with three other veteran press agents, all well deserving of their superb reputations. Pat Kingsley (the once-and-always empress of the craft,) Stan Rosenfield (who has kept his clientele very starry and his sense of humor buoyant, each of which achievements qualifies as heavy lifting in our game) and Dale Olsen (who brought a lot of dignity, suave and journalistic skill to a steamy trade.) PR vets tend to hang together in the chatter part of an event because our experience is alien to that of everyone else in the room. We are as set apart from the world as hit men must be. Our shop talk would seem in code or, if comprehended at all, brutal to tender ears.

Our business, like that of the hit man, is immaculately clandestine if done well. You and your clients are best served if a story does not read or play like a press agent plant. The trick is to make publicity seem the natural consequence of the clients' accomplishments and talents, which by and large it is, while your having generated the story is nowhere evident. The fine Italian hand of the press agent should never be seen, although sometimes that is quite impossible. No one should know any stories about you... unless you are foolish enough to write a book to sum it all up or to justify your erratic experiences and the pleasure you took from them.

So, I was surprised when Stan said to me, "There's a story I've heard about you, and I always wanted to know if it's true." "What kind of story?" "That Paul Newman asked you to watch the latest cut of a new movie with him, just you and him. And when it was over, he asked you to tell him straight out what you thought of it, positive or negative. And that you did, and that when you got back to the office, you were told that you'd been fired off the film." He had me. I couldn't remember that, at least not until I realized WHY I couldn't remember it. The way Stan had heard it and related it made it sound as though Paul had gotten me fired, and that simply wasn't true. That wasn't Paul Newman. He was as straight-up and honest a guy as he was an actor. It was something about which I hadn't thought for decades, but it snapped into place and made me laugh. It's a PR guy's perverse sense of humor that gets him or her through. "'WUSA'," I said.

Paul was a vivid guy to be around. That was 1970, and he sort of trusted me or at least my judgment because a few years before that I'd done a pretty good job as PR point man on his directorial debut, "Rachel, Rachel," which meant a lot to him. It had received four Oscar nominations, including Best Film and Best Actress for his wife, Joanne Woodward. All of us working on it at Rogers & Cowan loved that film, and the publicity showed it.

It wasn't a big surprise that Paul asked to show this new film to me alone. We talked movies from time to time. When the lights came up, he said, "So give it to me straight... what you thought... no holds barred." Even though the film was packed with people I cared about... Paul, Joanne, Larry Harvey, Tony Perkins... I had problems with it, and I assumed he did, too, or why else the screening and the uncommon request? It was evident that he cared about "WUSA." The film had a lot on its mind, a powerful and prescient examination of the encroachments into our politics that right wing radio was about to introduce. The self-preservation part of my brain said "lie and then run." So I did the semi-honest thing and changed the subject. "Well, you know, Paul, what I think will really help us sell the film is all those songs by this Neil Diamond kid... 'Sweet Caroline' and... wow. And it captures the feeling and, hey, here's what we can do... I can have you and Joanne send out his album to all of the film critics saying how you..." By now my voice was high and fast like your voice gets when you're speeding out onto a limb. And Paul was looking at me with a kind of disgusted impatience. "Cut the crap," he said... "what you THINK about the film... straight... I won't get angry. I want to hear, and I don't want to hear what you think I WANT to hear." "Yeah?" "Yeah." "OK, who am I PULLING for in this film?" I said, and it was all I had to say. He nodded gravely. "Thanks."

It was twenty-five minutes from Paramount back to the Beverly Hills offices of Rogers & Cowan, the entertainment industry's pre-eminent public relations firm, the company Warren Cowan and Henry Rogers had made the daddy of all big Hollywood PR firms. and where I had worked the first 16 years of my career, with a couple of years off for bad behavior in Europe to find out who I was... As I walked in the front entrance, the receptionist said, "Mr. Cowan wants to see you." Warren Cowan was not merely my boss. He was my friend and he had been my mentor, but I was reaching that point where you start to perceive yourself as your own mentor henceforth. Warren looked up at me as I came into the office and he said dryly, "Congratulations. You're off the film." "Are you telling me that Paul…?" Clipped, controlled anger, "No, it wasn't Paul." "Then who…?" "It doesn't matter… one of the producers." OK, I was content that Paul had kept his word. He'd gone back to the production office and asked "Who am I pulling for in this film?" And then they'd checked who was the idiot he'd just shown the film to and called Warren to tell him they were bidding me goodbye. The company wasn't off the film… just I. "What the hell did you do?" Warren asked, putting spaces between the words… "Do? He showed me the film." "And because of that they called me to cut you loose from it? What the hell did you DO? " Warren insisted, his calm almost rigid now. "Paul asked me to tell him… well, insisted, really…" "What? He asked you what?" "To tell him exactly what I thought of the film." Warren sat there for several moments, looking at me as though I'd been speaking in tongues. "Asked me to tell him what I thought of the film," I repeated. Suddenly, Warren came up out of his seat like a rising fog, his hands waving at the ceiling, his fingers running scales on the air. It was an Elmer Gantry moment. "And… you… TOLLLLD… HIMMM?" he roared.

Postscript. I related the above story not too long ago to Peter Bart, the respected and sometimes feared (maybe because he tells it straight) editor of Daily Variety and the second in command to Bob Evans at Paramount at the time of "WUSA." It was at the Comic Con convention in San Diego, and I was having Frank Miller, the reigning and originating icon of graphic novel super-hero films, guest on one of the television interview shows Peter does with Peter Guber for Bravo. Bart listened to my tale and then said, "I never got so much flak for not liking a film as I did from the producers of 'WUSA." At least I was in good company. I did do a lot of work on the film… anonymously from my office… and we did have Paul and Joanne mail out the Neil Diamond album from the song soundtrack.

It hadn't occurred to me, until Stan mentioned having heard that story, that flack-related misadventures might be of interest to anyone but the mis-adventurers. Then I recalled my delight in Arthur Mayer's book "From The Long Chase To The Chaise Longue" in which that distinguished exhibitor recalled inspired PR stunts-that-went-wrong in the 20s, 30s and 40s like the plan to steal the Times Square New Year's Eve. The scam was for four tons of leaflets promoting some upcoming film to be dropped on the Times Square revelers just before midnight, perfectly timed to hit the crowd as a blinding blizzard of movie promo just as the ball started to drop. At the precisely-timed moment, the leaflets were poured into the void from the ramparts atop the highest building looming over Times Square. The crowd below didn't know what hit them because... nothing ever hit them... The torrent of leaflets had descended about ten feet from the point of release before catching a wind that gave them a free ride directly out to sea. Subtract the wind, and that would have been a winner. Publicity ideas that work are often counter-intuitive. Try to explain the rationale of a good idea, and you probably find that you can't. How do you describe a gut feeling?

Our planet should only be as green as I was behind the ears when I tried to explain movie star age to Audrey Hepburn. It was *her* birth year we were talking about, granted, but it was *my* professional judgment that was involved. Audrey Hepburn was the classic movie star. She would have been regal even if she hadn't first blossomed before our eyes as the escaped princess in "Roman Holiday," winning the Best Actress Oscar in her initial starring role. She had performed in a film first in 1951 with a single line, glowingly delivered, at the end of Alec Guinness' "The Lavender Hill Mob." Two years later she was on the Oscar stage accepting the Best Actress trophy, the queen of the western world or, as she was even more suitably swathed in our affections, the princess of the western world.

I worked with her two years later on the filming of Billy Wilder's "Love In The Afternoon" in Paris. That was 1956. Subsequent to her "Roman Holiday" ascension to the throne, her title role in Wilder's "Sabrina Fair" and her Natasha in "War And Peace" had further established her reign. There is no young actress currently functioning who begins to approach her starry perch. She was 26 and I had just turned an ingenuous 23, much lacking in worldly wisdom, newly arrived in Paris for a crash course. These numbers have some pertinence in this little parable about one of publicity's most important rules. The moral of the parable, in fact, is that age does count.

I was the assistant unit publicist, pretty much the most insignificant team member on a location shoot, but Audrey Hepburn treated me with the same generous, genuine and smiling cordiality she did her co-star Gary Cooper or a lighting technician, for that matter. My great good fortune was that my boss, the unit publicist, recoiled from dealing with the stacked deck of iconic legends who peopled that set... Wilder, Hepburn, Cooper, Maurice Chevalier, France's greatest international star. So I was the point guy, and I had just enough experience and more than enough audacity to do it. The "press book" on every film has to contain the bios, the summation of the life and career of each star. The writing of Audrey Hepburn's biography and the clearing of it with her fell to me.

So one morning I saw her in the cold, grey great hallway entrance of the Studios de Boulogne and I said, "Miss Hepburn, did you have a chance to read your bio?" "Yes, Dick, and it's fine. Oh, except you didn't put in my birthdate." "May 4? I didn't put that in?" "Well, yes, but not the year." "Miss Hepburn," I said, and you have to remember that I had just turned 23 and therefore 26 seemed pretty ancient to me, "You're twenty-six, which is, you know, a nice age. But someday… someday you're going to be THIRTY-six." I stopped, letting the full weight of that inevitability seep in. She was looking at me with a quizzical smile, a bit amused and willing to see where this went. "And?" she encouraged. "And let's say there's this role, Anna… and the script says 'Anna, 30, and some producer says 'Audrey Hepburn is 36'… you see what I mean?" "Well," she answered, "it seems very silly to me, but you do as you see fit."

Exactly twenty years later, she was promoting "Robin And Marion," teamed with Sean Connery in a mature telling of the Robin Hood romance But the producers didn't want it to be too mature, so when I read an interview with Audrey Hepburn, I was interested to see that she was the same age as I. It was nothing that she stated, just an age that must have been established in the press book. If she even knew that, which I sincerely doubt, I'm sure the producers had said "Audrey, audiences are getting younger and younger. Two middle-aged lovers getting all mushy?" To which I'm sure she would have said, "Well, it seems very silly to me, but you do as you see fit."

A little less than twenty years after that, she was the ambassador for UNICEF. Working for the endangered children of the world is what absorbed her, and not making films. Barbara Walters was interviewing her for one of her Oscar night specials, and it was established by Ms Walters that Audrey Hepburn was, once more (as only I might have noted,) three years older than I. As soon as she had escaped the tyranny of Hollywood's delusions as to what is important, Audrey Hepburn was very happy to shed things she found silly but that others thought fit. She was royalty until the day she died and right on into eternity.

Paparazzi are the guys who chase name stars and teeny boppers from store to store or who hide in lone wolf ambush to get some compromising or unattractive photographic or video shots. When I was appearing before the House Judiciary

Committee to urge passage of a bill protecting privacy of stars, I was asked why we tried to have it both ways... protect our clients from them in those coercive situations, but court paparazzi coverage on our red carpets. I had to explain that they are two different breeds. The feral shutter-clickers, the paparazzi, don't show when stars are glammed up and prepared, all smiles, coiffure and haute couture. The good guys, the "event photographers," look for the most complimentary shot, and without their flashing lights, big events would not feel like big events. Age is a big commercial consideration for paparazzi. They target the celebs du jour who are young enough and mindless enough to matter to the young and selectively mindless prowlers of the internet gossip world. Or they can always make a buck by grabbing a shot that makes a legitimate talent and star look cruelly more than his or her age. Or disappointingly his or her age.

In consideration of paparazzi/stalkerazzi hunting habits, I tried to talk a client out of throwing his big bash 50th birthday party on the beach in front of his house. Beaches can't be defended against the hoping-to-make-you-look-bad camera guys. Everything from the mean tide-line to the water is public property, so if the tide is out, so is a privacy-seeking star's luck. Hollywood movies and Hollywood careers each rely on the willing suspension of disbelief. Why tag some age label on yourself? The paparazzi got their shots, and the word "fifty" was in every story or caption. Not too long thereafter, age seemed a very key factor in the evaporation of a crucial project. Age doesn't need an invitation to your party... he knows where you live. On the other hand, I have never actually stipulated a false age. It was too easy to acquire the truth from the Department of Motor Vehicles before or, now, in eight thousand places on the internet. No lie ever held back time, but clean living habits, a good constitution and benevolent genes sometimes slow the impetuous passage of years. Anno domini is not always the most accurate reflection of one's age. Some lucky few of us have a painting growing old in the attic.

I take love for granted. I am, I think, a good press agent, but I've been a lousy matchmaker. At one of our earliest celebrity pro-am ski tournaments, I had Natalie Wood paired with the hot upcoming skier Spider Sabitch and Claudine Longet with Olympic silver medalist Billy Kidd. Claudine asked me if they could switch, and Natalie said it was fine with her. The first part of the trade worked out quite well. Photos of Billy Kidd skiing down the hill backwards instructing Natalie as she snowplowed her first trip down the course, these ate up the whole front page of the LA Times sports section and were widely syndicated. Claudine and Spider did well in the competition and not so well afterwards when their friendship and his life ended in an argument involving bullets. Less dire was the end of Kim Cattrall's friendship with and engagement to "Murder One" star Daniel Benzali which commenced when I arranged for Daniel to attend the premiere of Martin Scorcese's "Casino." I suggested he do so in the company of a beautiful actress and did I have the girl for him! It was love at first sight for these two clients and the opposite at first fight. End of an engagement for them and of two friends and two clients for me.

For a press agent, numbers add up to... news. Warren Cowan loved to employ promotable numbers relating to clients' careers. He never met an anniversary he didn't like. It was always good for a week or so of promo. Tony Curtis' 20th year as a top ten box-office star, Frank Sinatra's 30th gold album, Shirley McClain's 15th number one boxoffice hit. The one number Warren never celebrated was age. "Age closes too many doors," he reasoned...

I once sat in a casting meeting in which two venerated but just-turning-venerable macho stars were suggested for a new action film. "Great," the producer said dismissively. "You want to do the big chase scene with wheelchairs or walkers?"

I make a point of NOT knowing my clients' ages. I feel actors don't have age. They have *range*... I usually make that clear to a new client up front. Don't tell me your age, but let's agree on your age range. Jack is 38 to mid-forties, Jane is 26 to 33. That way, when a journalist calls and asks an age, I honestly can say I don't know, but I can give them the range appropriate to that performer. It widens role opportunities, and, amazingly, some of the press respect that an actor need not get carded for a role. The truth is that you are not necessarily your chronological age. Sissy Spacek was 38 years old when she won the Oscar for playing a 14 year old in a substantial portion of "Coal Miner's Daughter."

On the other hand, the number of years a client has been acknowledged as best, most attractive, biggest boxoffice, sexiest.... That isn't age. That's STATUS. Clint Eastwood was never too young or too old. He was always Clint Eastwood. Gable was Gable courting Mae West at the beginning or Marilyn Monroe at the end. Katharine Hepburn just went on being Katharine Hepburn. That process was perhaps easier in the 30s on through the 60s, those old-fashioned decades when you bought a chair to last. Now when obsolescence is built into everything, staying young is just a little more important. A performer has to take measures against letting nature's sunset clause abbreviate his or her career.

Media like to play gotcha with evidences of plastic surgery, but it is such a common recourse now that stars today sometimes feel they need to consider enhancement simply to maintain competitive equity, let alone advantage. Many feel that, since there is now such default assumption that it has been done, why not just go ahead and do it? I had a reflection of that when Clint Eastwood was preparing "The Bridges Of Madison County" and I asked him to consider Jacqueline Bisset. He said that it was already pretty much set with Meryl Streep. He added, "plus, I really want someone who's never done any 'work.'" Plastic, of course. "Jackie has never even thought of it," I said with certainty." "You're kidding," he commented in amazement. He said she had made and sent in her own screen test for it, but on the rote assumption that she couldn't possibly have let God play out his plan and still look that gorgeous, it hadn't been viewed. The Streep deal was done as had been pretty much ordained from the beginning, but Clint went back and looked at Jackie's tape, and he called and said it was great.

On a recent visit Bisset made to the Today Show following her winning a Golden Globe, the interviewer commented on Jackie's perpetual beauty and her well-known refusal to have plastic surgery. "I don't think it makes you look younger," la belle Jacqueline responded, "… just different." Her Golden Globe acceptance speech trended on twitter because she was rushed to the stage not knowing that she'd won… and it showed. People remembered it above all others because it was delightfully whacky, but what women remembered more was her comment that "forgiveness is the best beauty treatment." Coming from so renowned and unfading a beauty, a lot of effort to forgive issued forth among the nation's fair ladies.

Marlon Brando was a star who proved that being an icon is never bad. It paints age, when it eventually arrives, in more interesting colors. A performer of whichever gender is who he or she is now, but in a way he or she also is all of variations of self to which we had been attracted from the beginning on. One of Hollywood's great treasure chests is filled with Golden Age stars who acted their age across the years, the successive ages over successive decades of stardom…

Spencer Tracy, Henry Fonda, Fredrick March, John Wayne, Melvin Douglas, Bette Davis, Olivia de Havilland, Shirley MacLaine, Walter Huston, Anthony Quinn, Dietrich, Cagney, Nicholson, Lemmon, Martin Landau, Eli Wallach, Jimmy Stewart, certainly Clint in anything over the past few decades. "Gran Torino" was a kind of elegy to that idea. Or Gable summing up his whole career in "The Misfits," Hepburn and Bogart brandishing and culminating their ripe vintage in "The African Queen" summing up the rugged courage and style that coursed through their extraordinary careers. Gene Hackman certainly would be part of this awesome group, except that at the time he began his long hiatus from acting at the start of his seventies, he had retained the vigor of forty years before and still was getting roles that powered through movies. "The Royal Tannenbaums," one of his last, was one of his most vital, youthfully gleeful and age-defying roles of all. More than other actors, he seemed never to have had an age but was always what was appropriate to the character.

In many films these long reigning stars served the function which Francis Coppola described to Mssrs. Guttman and Pam as "the yardstick." During the pre-production stage of "Apocalypse Now.", Jerry Pam and I had front row seats on Coppola's and his long-time producing partner Fred Roos' casting process. Francis kept his eye firmly on his intention of locking in Brando to portray Kurtz, the maddened hero/villain of the Joseph Conrad novel "The Heart Of Darkness" on which "Apocalypse" was based. Brando, he told us, had been his 'yardstick" when he was casting "The Godfather," filling the other roles with young actors who over the years were to become yardsticks themselves for other people's films. But Coppola had needed them to go toe-to-toe with Marlon frigging Brando to prove their substance to the audience. With Pacino, Duval, Jimmy Caan, Talia Shire, Diane Keaton and John Casale holding their own in the company of Brando at the Oscar-winning top of his game, audiences could appreciate how big league Coppola's new young stars were. (DeNiro, who was in "Godfather II," had no scenes with Brando for the simple reason that they played the same character.) So Coppola was single-minded about having Brando serve the same function for Marty Sheen and Fred Forrest and all of his "Apocalypse" discoveries. Yes, that was Harrison Ford in a brief role, as was the case in Coppola's "The Conversation. Coppola and Roos were grooming him. Then Roos gave him a practice breakout role in Lucas' "American Grafitti" and a real one in "Star Wars."

Brando, fully understanding the function he was serving, got a lot of "Apolalypse" money for not a lot of time.

Kirk Douglas was another actor who was a giant measuring rod... as well as a LIGHTNING ROD...against whose skills terrific new talent would be placed in balance and because of whose talent, courage and charisma terrific new films could get green-lighted. If it is the combination of intensity and special presence, as much as talent, that makes a great star, Kirk was Exhibit A. When he walked into a room, you could practically hear him ticking. His every thought or look was vivid. And, amazingly, it still is. He stole a recent Oscarcast with two words. Kirk Douglas literally opened the door to what would become my career when I, in my brief passage as an office boy, was delivering an envelope stuffed with clippings. It had never occurred to me until that moment that this Rogers & Cowan company for which I was office-boying had anything to do with movies. It quickly became apparent to me that Kirk occupied a major part of the mind and attention of Warren Cowan, king of press agents.

I never got it straight... the part about whether they had been roommates or not, whether they had met before or if it happened that Warren, a kid just out of the Air Force after World War II, simply started doing publicity for another kid bound for stardom, Kirk Douglas. But they were close friends, which didn't mean Kirk was shy about saying what he wanted and what he thought he should have had. Maybe that's what sealed the friendship that spanned decades and vicissitudes, the fact that they were two hungry Jewish kids from New York, each pedal-to-the-metal into their elected orbits. In an interview I covered, Kirk was asked to name the most important film of his already long career, and he answered, "Something I haven't made yet, I hope." The two projects he cared about at any time were the one he was making or selling and the great one down the road that would make everyone forget all the others. He inculcated this sense of present and future urgency in Warren and, eventually, in me.

Kirk was a client whom Warren approached with the manic dedication of friendship, and the kid gloves of a pro who needed to serve a smart, demanding superstar client impatient of any error or unexplored opportunity. With Kirk as ravenous and inspired a producer as he was an actor, opportunities abounded. He made them, and Warren sold them with equally insatiable fervor.

I wasn't as directly involved with Kirk during the tumultuous period before and during production of that Douglas opus major, "Spartacus," as I was during the film's re-release. Yes, re-release. Executive Producer Douglas and his long-time associate, Producer Edward Lewis, had bent the nose of an industry still bloodied by the black-listings which had so completely colored the 50s for the movie community, the anti-communist hysteria fed by the House Committee On UnAmerican Activities and the rantings of Sen. Joe McCarthy. "Spartacus" meant so much to Kirk... a story that clearly reflected his own lifelong challenge of oppressive authority... that he had changed directors in early stream, supplanting Anthony Mann with Douglas' "Paths Of Glory" director and cohort Stanley Kubrick. Douglas had, from the start, risked not only the film and his Bryna Productions company but also his entire career in hiring the black-listed writer Dalton Trumbo to script "Spartacus." That decision very specifically spat in the face of the still resonating anti-red phobia that had such grasp on the fearful creatures of Hollywood. I had spent plenty of time on-set because of the involvement of other R&C clients including Tony Curtis and Peter Ustinov

Douglas loved the sheer engaged-battle of the experience, taking on the regressive spirit of the industry leadership and wrestling it to the mat. He didn't just need to prove his point... he needed to prove it again and again, to rub it in because the stakes had been so gloriously high. Two years later he and Eddie Lewis gambled Bryna Productions' very existence again by bringing Dalton Trumbo back in to write that tone poem to independent spirit, "Lonely Are The Brave." Even the title of that film tells you everything you had to know about Kirk Douglas... a cowboy of modern times defying a period that had rejected the independent spirit of the West. In some ways, that film, with which I was very much involved to the extent of having my office at Bryna Productions on the Universal lot for a long while, was as important to Kirk as was "Spartacus," and it was carrying the same message.

The decision to re-release "Spartacus" very shortly after the initial release was Kirk's alone, and all pressures were on to make it work. The betting was against it, which was in itself a delicious challenge to Kirk. This re-release was handed to us by Kirk as a major (and some thought impossible and maybe relationship-ending) challenge for Rogers & Cowan.

First we had to think through how to present such an audacious and unusual thing. Johnny Friedkin was the head of Rogers & Cowan's New York office. He was the guy on whom his friend Neil Simon had based the character of the dedicated cynic and slob, Oscar, in "The Odd Couple." Johnny came up with the idea of calling Kirk's venture not a re-release but a "second wave." It was like a battle strategy from the film itself, the slave uprising which shook Rome like Kirk was shaking Hollywood. That metaphor increased the pressure because it made the crazy idea of attempting two fairly consecutive releases of the same film seem sane. But we needed more than a home run to give this effort the juice it needed, actually the juice Kirk felt had not been sufficiently extracted from the first release run of "Spartacus."

Kirk had bet the farm on it and all of the potential farms of his future when he hired Trumbo. The brilliant and principled and notably black-listed writer's very name had become a battle-cry of the push-back against blacklist mentality just as Spartacus' name had been the battle-cry of the slave revolt against the Roman Empire. One thing supremely evident with Kirk was that his political courage matched all the other daring feats of athleticism and courage of his life. The right wing fervors of the Black List and the House Un-American Activities Committee had cleaved the industry down the middle. The fearlessness of Kirk Douglas was needed to jumpstart regeneration from the political purge

This particular audacity had personal meaning to me. When HUAC, the House of Representatives' high court of inquisition of anything suspiciously left-wing, was planning hearings concerning UCLA… or The Little Red School House as some on the HUAC bandwagon called it…… I was given to understand that I would be subpoenaed. I came to college a life-long Democrat because I was born that way as most middle class Jews were then, but I was politically unsophisticated. I wrote short stories for the school's literary/humor magazine and also for the UCLA Daily Bruin when the paper was doing a theme issue. A prominent Film Department professor, Norman Dyrrenfurth, had just been part of the team that first scaled one of the planet's highest mountains, Annapurna, and this was to be celebrated with a special issue of the Daily Bruin… I was asked to write a "mountain climbing story." What I dreamed up was a tale of an Alpine village that held as gospel that the nearby mountain could not be scaled. It scorned other hamlets where the inhabitants assisted and guided climbing attempts. A local shepherd of the village, however, thought he could reach the top of that peak. He disappeared for a week and everyone, including his fiancée, chose to believe that he'd drowned in the river rather than think that one of their own had headed up the impossible mountain. When he returned and proclaimed his victorious climb, he was ostracized and dumped by his fiancée who begged him to recant. But he held to his claim and lived the life of a pariah. As an old man, lying in the meadows with his flock, when the clouds cleared and he could see the peak, he was sure he could glimpse the mound of rocks he'd built there. So far so ok, but I needed a name for him… Engel… yeah, not bad… , Germanic, an angel trying to fly to heaven? Fine. First name? Friedrich sounded mountain-climby, Germanic as well, yodel-y, *and it had a certain familiar ring.* It didn't connect for me that Friedrich Engels co-authored The Communist Manifesto with Karl Marx. Even though the s of his last name was missing (a brilliant literary device some people assumed,) I was an instant celebrity. The left-leaners and fellow-travelers of my acquaintance thought I'd created a ringing indictment of right wing oppression. Some of my conservative friends thought I'd proven their point that Friedrich Engels was clearly delusional. People of either conviction loved or hated me according to their interpretation of the parable. What made it more inflammatory was that I had called it, for no reason whatsoever, "The Mound On Feather Peak." Maybe because it suggested a curved mountain, impossible to ascend. The symbol of student opposition to Joe McCarthy was a green feather. That seemed to have given it even greater political weight… The staff of the House Un-American Activities Committee, it seems, saw Red, and the Daily Bruin editor told me I was slated to be called before its kangaroo court because my story had proven what they felt was the commie-loving slant of the UCLA student newspaper… After a nervous few weeks during which I was afraid even to hint the matter to my parents, the editor called again to say I was off the hook. HUAC, it was concluded, hadn't been able to decipher if I was a raving commie or a right wing zealot patriot. There is something to be said for ambiguity.

But that gives you a slight sense of the times and the sheer gallantry and defiance of Kirk's choice of Trumbo. So "Spartacus" was coming around again, the idea of a "second wave" having been snapped up by Douglas and Universal. And we were about to launch it. The campaign had to have some giant, never-done-before linch pin, and it was Warren who decided to kick it off with a handprint ceremony for

Kirk in the fore-court of Grauman's Chinese Theatre. It was a powerful kickoff, but it wasn't entirely original because it had been done a hundred times before. Nobody was more aware of that than Warren, and he assigned me to think of something that would make it that most important word... "more." For Warren the whole world hung on each of these crucial challenges. That was his secret advantage... he never relinquished his sense of urgency or perhaps even jeopardy. . He and Kirk were so much alike in that. I went up to the Grauman's Chinese and walked around, studying the concrete footprints and handprints and signatures... all of those famous people... how to make this one special in the face of so much precedent. How do you make the precedented gesture unprecedented? When you're in your 20s, the world lies heavy on your shoulders.

I had not yet at that point in my life come up with the theory... the rule, the guideline... that would finally spark virtually every decision I would make in my career conduct and in every aspect of my life, "A PROBLEM IS AN OPPORTU-NITY IN DISGUISE." Turn a problem inside out and it's the solution. The creative person, whether he or she recognizes it or not, loves problems. Problem and solution are the steel and flintstone of creative ignition. That is one of the first and most difficult tasks of maturing... learning to love and to embrace the problem.

As I walked that fabled courtyard, the fact that a hundred had preceded Kirk seemed to be not the problem but rather the answer. I would gather as many of the prior footprint honorees as I could to participate in Kirk's commemoration. The event would honor them, too, but they also would honor and give weight to the event. It wouldn't be "just another" footprint ceremony. When I put this to Warren, he asked "Why would they come out for him?" Well, in the first place, who deserved that tribute more than Kirk? Apart from saluting his art, a lot of creative people admired his audacity, his visible resistance in standing up to the blacklists. In the second place, for many of them the footprint ceremony had been the career highlight, one recalled now in their minds only. It would be a great second curtain call, especially for those whose bright star may have slipped a bit behind the clouds, a reminder of honors and stature past.

In the midst of organizing this, we had to arrange the shooting of a new theatre trailer with Kirk explaining the special reason why this film was coming around the track a second time. It was agreed that it would be Kirk talking into camera, talking directly to people, about why he made this film and the special circumstance of the "second wave" for "Spartacus." The morning of the shoot,

Kirk turned down the studio's draft, and I had to write a new version… and get it right the first time. We were shooting in three hours.

When I got to Kirk's giant dressing room at Universal, he was already with his make-up man and simultaneously meeting with some other men about the next film. The make-up area was a long extension of the suite, what we called in my Missouri childhood, a sunporch. Kirk talked to my image in the mirror and put his hand up to be filled. You have to keep in mind that this was well over fifty years ago, so I was still "kid" to him. "(Is) that the immortal prose, kid?" "We'll see," I answered, not very certainly. He read it. The others watched. Accustomed to awaiting Kirk's decisions, they had habits of rapt attention. He looked up at my mirror image without expression and then he read it again. Finishing it, he swiveled his chair around and leveled a look at me. "Dick," he started… I knew it was serious because he used the actual name, and it was in that clenched-teeth, back-of-the-throat growl we all know so well, "how long have you been in this business?" A crew was already set up on the soundstage to shoot this. "Mr. Douglas," I answered with what sounded, at least to me, like an unwavering voice, "long enough to know better than whatever it is you have on your mind." The others were a little startled by that and were waiting for his reaction … or eruption… as uncertainly as I. His eyes never left mine. Finally it came, "Ok then. Go over to the stage and say I'll be right there."

Now all we had to do was to make the handprint ceremony come off like none had ever come off before. We sent out the invitations to each prior inductee. I got George Jessel, the mandatory master of ceremonies for any event of consequence at that time, to be the interlocutor for this PR production. I sent the invitations from Sid Grauman, Hollywood's exhibitor extraordinaire and the guy who had been so kind as to put them all in his cement. The acceptances started to roll in, at first from some stars whose accomplishments had, with time, faded from appreciation. Then from that superstars' superstar, Bette Davis, and from other heralded names including both Roy Rogers AND Trigger, the only hoof-print honoree in that cement garden of fame. It was a starry and nostalgic group… 27 of them showed up to be interviewed by an Oscar night type turnout of press especially considering that there were only seven TV channels and three networks then. I had stayed up all night mapping out the specific responsibility of the ten staff members we had there… probably my only executive blueprint ever, since

I'm much better winging it. And it came off as Warren Cowan had hired me to dream it. Kirk topped the evening with a first for that fore-court. He emplaced his handprints by doing a handstand. And the "second wave" rolled in on another substantial wave of strategized publicity.

Kirk Douglas is and was serene… if that's a word that could ever be attached to Kirk Douglas… as long as he has the reins in his hands… that has always been Kirk. When I speculated about the root of that determination once, his wife Anne commented, "The only thing that could destroy Kirk would be if someone could prove he'd been poorer as a kid then Kirk was." His autobiography was called "The Ragman's Son." There must have been shades of those memories just beneath that smooth patina of control the world knows as Kirk Douglas. One time we stood outside the entrance to the American Room at the Brown Derby on Vine St. just before he addressed a small group. He suddenly grabbed me by the lapels and said, "Sure, it's easy for you. You just open the door and push me through it. I've gotta face them." I said, "Kirk, it's thirty film students from UCLA… they're giving you an award." He straightened my lapels and went in and knocked them dead. Kirk Douglas.

Much more recently, after his stroke, we were doing a press conference at the dedication of a new million dollar playground the Kirk and Anne Douglas Foundation was donating to a charter school (also on Vine St., coincidentally.) It must have been during some brief split between him and Warren, because Kirk's son Peter had asked us to do it. Kirk's speech was slurred but his mind still clear, and he still had a clear sense of how to reach the kids and feed the cameras. He started doing chin-ups on the equipment he and his wife were giving schools all over L.A. The kids and the cameras loved it. Such civic generosity he does not consider charity. In the keynote speech at an Israeli fund-raiser which I attended with him during that period, he was brilliantly articulate through the slur of his stroke. He explained that Hebrew held no word for 'charity." The applicable word for such sharing, he said, is "zedakah" which means "the right thing." When Jewish immigrants arrived penniless in a new land, the zedakah they received, if their neighbors could gather it, was the tools of their trade. Isn't that what he did for Dalton Trumbo with "Spartacus," give him back the tools of his trade? Certainly, "zedakah" is a word Kirk Douglas chose to live by, boldly and without concern for consequence. Kirk Douglas… damn the torpedoes, full speed ahead.

Thanks to Kirk and his Bryna (his mother's name) Productions projects, I got to work on some of the greatest films of the fifties and sixties, "Lonely Are The Brave" and "Seven Days In May," among my favorites. I loved being part of the making of "Two Weeks In Another Town," too, because it re-gathered the artistic group that had created perhaps the best film ever made about Hollywood, "The Bad And The Beautiful." "Two Weeks" wasn't in the same league, but it was a class reunion.

I learned a lot from Kirk. In 1962, he had bought the rights to Ken Kesey's novel "One Flew Over The Cuckoo's Nest" before it was published. He gave Rogers & Cowan five thousand dollars cash and told us to buy up a thousand copies within two days of pub date. (Yes, a hard cover was five bucks then.) With that rush of sales, the booksellers thought they had a big hit on their hands and pushed it like mad in their store windows. It's hard to buy a thousand copies without buying large quantities at a time, which would have been a dead give-away that someone was priming the pump. So I asked my mom to have each of her vast collection of friends buy one book in each of ten different stores. They could keep the books and give them to their friends. Some booksellers might have been mystified that middle aged Jewish women were rushing in to buy a book about patient abuse in an insane asylum, but it worked.

Kirk starred as Randle P. McMurphy in the stage version on Broadway to rave reviews, but didn't get around to taking "Cuckoo's Nest" to film. That task fell to his son Michael about a dozen years later, and because Michael was a client (of my own firm Guttman & Pam) by that time and because his co-producer Saul Zaentz had become my friend and, I suppose, believer through another client, Bob Radnitz, we wound up handling one of the greatest films of all time, one of the few ever to win all five key awards, Best Film, Best Director, Best Actor, Best Actress and Best Screenplay.

It also afforded me the casual acquaintance of the novelist, Ken Kesey, in whose daring life and brilliant writing was reflected his experimentation with such hallucinogens as LSD. He'd already left a massive intellectual footprint on the sixties and seventies, both on its literature and on the spirit of the times. In a way, he WAS the Zeit-geist of that period. When he learned that I'd been one of the first guinea pigs in the CIA's testing of LSD, the agency's Cold War exploration of its "mind-control" possibilities, it engaged an unlikely kinship. Kesey had been introduced to the drug in the same test program three years after I was. This was before a class action lawsuit by survivors and congressional investigations brought the CIA/LSD program to wider and quite notorious attention. Some of its subjects, possibly quite a few, had committed suicide. Kesey's interest in the drug continued afterwards, while mine had stopped right after I'd tried to jump down an elevator shaft to get the demons out of my head. Kesey was intrigued that someone so resistant to any form of intoxicants as I had actually volunteered for the tests. Prior to taking that mind-bending jolt of lysergic acid with its two year hangover of horror and anxiety, I'd never sipped a beer, puffed a cigarette or had as much as a contact high. That I, a curious and evidently ignorant psych student, had wandered so wide-eyed into that blowout amused Kesey. I'd been told that the substance I would ingest was a "pseudo-psychotic," a ticket to the world of insanity... a return ticket, mind you. Manic/depressive, catatonic, schizoid, you name it, I tried each and every one of them on for size in that eternal eight or ten hours. Once you feel your mind buying into that chaos, you never really trust it again.

Learning From Your Clients

Actors are curious about how and why things work. In the process of doing the job, a press agent often shares with the client why a situation is approached in a specific manner. It is very constructive and instructive to have to articulate the "why" of things you do intuitively. And occasionally a client gives back to his publicist some insight into how and why publicity works. Here are a few good lessons clients have taught me:

Kirk Douglas provided a compelling illustration of A Problem Is An Opportunity In Disguise. Kirk and John Wayne were coming out in a film called "The War Wagon." Louella Parsons was the most affectionately regarded of the reigning triumvirate of female gossip columnists (Hedda Hopper and Sheilah Graham filling out the list) who ruled Hollywood, She had, on the specific morning in question, run a story about some nasty comments John Wayne was alleged to have made about Kirk. Louella and Hedda, especially, could undo a career or the prospects for a film with one negative item, and the rest of the media picked up from them. It was read-'em-and-weep for Warren Cowan when I laid Lolly's column of that day on his desk. He called Kirk and said he wanted to come over and talk about something, and then he and I drove up three blocks (three very long blocks, and time is more than money in PR... it is advantage) to Kirk's Beverly Drive home so tastefully lavished with Chagalls and Picassos.

"What's up? Kirk asked, entering the room. Warren handed him the column, and, while he was still reading, Warren said, "Kirk we have a good idea how to respond to Louella on this." We didn't really, but In Hollywood PR, you grab the bull by the horns or else he takes you for a ride on them. Kirk looked up, "Hmmm? Respond? Hold on." He dialed the phone and said to whoever answered, "Tell him it's Kirk. (a few moments of waiting and then) Duke, it's... yeah... no, I know it's bullshit... No, you don't have to tell her it's bullshit, she knew when she wrote it... No, here's what we do. (Suddenly there was that big gleeful Kirk Douglas grin all over his face) I call her, mad as hell and I tell her that no-good right-wing sonovabitch can jump in the lake, and then you come back... Yeah, that would be great. Who knows what a western's gonna do right now. We'll build a fire under it and, wait a second, we have to figure out why we're feuding... oh yeah, that's great, as long as we have all the reins in our hands. If it's good enough for Jack Benny and Fred Allen, it's good enough for us. Ok, let it rip... let's have some fun." Kirk was giving us a master class in how to conduct a feud to drive a blast of awareness into your sails. *The effective rule he was teaching was that there is far more energy, far more active thrust in a negative story than in a positive one as long as you're controlling the story and it's not controlling you. You don't undertake anything adventurous without command of the variables.*

Barbra Streisand with her insistence on truth and that it not be embellished is a good influence on a press agent who may lean a little to the flexible side of that noble dedication. No press agent ever met an embellishment he didn't like. But you always implement anyone's career publicity exactly as they call it. With Barbra it's" just the facts." And only after they're checked and rechecked. We recently were involved in a news release that a three-disc DVD package of some of her concerts and previously unseen archival footage had debuted at #1 in the Billboard charts. The draft release contained the obligatory career achievement information for such stories including, in this instance that she was the number one (a recurring statistical reference in her case) album-seller in the US among all female recording artists. It's an especially impressive achievement when you consider that she is the only album-seller of any gender in the top ten who was not primarily a rock and roll or country and western performer, the two forms of music which have dominated the past half century. The release was held up at her request until we checked and rechecked the RIAA listings to determine that this was still applicable, as it was by a very wide margin.

All other statistical mind-blowers, valid one and all, receive similar scrutiny. She also once requested removal of a line in her biography which pointed out that only Elvis Presley had achieved more gold records than she. That was and remains quite accurate, but she said that Presley's accomplishments were and always would be incomparable, that no artists could be compared to him because he had achieved them even though he died at age forty-two. It was a great reminder for me. *Facts can be true but misleading, and it is intrinsically wrong to cheat that.*

One of the most remarkable of these truth quests occurred upon the publication of one of the three dozen unauthorized Streisand biographies. These inventive works surface periodically. They tend to be so error-laden that comprehensive correction of each piece of misinformation would be a massive, even ludicrous, task. We had learned that by and large these books have a little flurry of publicity about their most outrageous unfounded tales, and that then they tend to sink under the weight of their deceptions and delusions. This one had some particularly nasty charges, and I asked Barbra if she wanted me to refute them. "Only one," she said, "where he says my stepfather beat me." I commented that it's very well known that her stepfather was very hurtful and mean to her. "But he never beat me," she said. "I would like that to be clarified."

Peter Ustinov enhanced my PR skills with a concept he passed along one day when I had him buried in interviews to sell his new book of short stories. I apologized for loading on so many face-to-face sit-downs with press. He insisted it was fine. "I love doing interviews," he said, "I find out what I think about things. I have all kinds of opinions I don't even know about until somebody asks me what I think about that subject. I look forward to new questions." What a powerful concept with which to prepare any client for the interview process! It has never failed me in orienting new clients to enjoy or, at the very least, endure with high spirits the interview process. You can't be very good at something you don't enjoy, and this is an approach to the task of being interviewed which makes it an exciting personal exploration. Thank you, Peter.

Gene Hackman is another legendary client who also was, for me, a pretty good teacher of my own craft. *The press agent equivalent of the shine on a salesman's shoes is the conviction in his sell. If you don't believe it, you can't sell it.* Gene was on location for a film on which no one was crazy about the script. When he came down to breakfast one morning, he found two other cast members batting some of the day's lines around, making fun of them, giving comic readings, and they invited him into the game and pressured when he declined. Finally, he said, "You know what? Those lines you're mocking? When you say them in a movie theatre, your face is going to be twenty feet high. You damn well better find something in that dialogue that you can believe." A lesson in acting, a lesson in press agenting... a lesson in whatever it is you do. *If you want to sell a line, a product or a news story, you damn well better find something in it you can believe.*

From watching Warren Beatty, I gathered that *the only guarantee of success is a solid creative vision in both the production and selling of a film... or in the accomplishment of anything.* It became a target I tried then to apply to any PR task. When I was invited into the family of such films as "Bonnie And Clyde," "Shampoo," "Reds," "Heaven Can Wait," "Bugsy" and "Dick Tracy," I observed how he drew the other artists into his vision and drew from their creative ideas responding to that vision. Any filmmaker on that kind of a roll is doing something right, and, more likely, doing everything right.

Working for decades with Jay Leno has been an education in the importance of humility in effective pr., however counter-intuitive that may seem. Humility in pr is not a contradiction. It's an essential. And if a flack doesn't understand that, the client is endangered. Knowing when enough is enough is primary. Jay dominated the late night talk/comedy scene for over 20 years, notwithstanding the number of times NBC sought to replace their enduring number one guy in that time slot. But Jay constantly rode the brakes on our undertaking publicity to stress or celebrate that unwavering dominance. I think this modesty is one reason the largest audience evidenced such loyalty. Up until its final decision to replace him, it was NBC that did the number one flag-waving, And in that lame duck last partial year, he drew a lot of his warmest laughter from allusions to his departure. At Thanksgiving, he noted that he wasn't buying a turkey, he was just going to fry a peacock. In George W. Bush's heralded final visit with Jay, the former President noted that he'd always had a good relationship with NBC, and Jay responded that he was happy that at least one of them did, Jay's jabs deliver truth without rancor, that rarest of public behaviors, grace.

Another factor is that, behind all of his more lethal jokes about the presumptions and foibles of the famous or anyone of degrading stupidity, you somehow understood that Jay is a very nice guy. If I had a hundred bucks for every time I had to turn down an award for him, I would be writing this book from Tahiti. He understood that none of that means as much as a good joke. If his unfailing and unending dominance was referenced in the media, it was almost exclusively the function of journalists' desire to acknowledge the overwhelming fact of his number one ratings, quarter after quarter, year after year and for an astounding period without a single interruption. It wasn't the by-product of intensive promotion. It was simply the choice honestly made by a vast public. Bruce Bobbins, of Dan Klores' office in New York with whom I shared work on Jay, and I understood that, and we didn't want to disturb it with any braggadocio, however due. It's not like publicity does not have subtle ways of confirming and maintaining status. That's what it's designed and engaged to do. A key accolade here, the occasional prestigious award there. It has worked for others, mostly for those who deserved them. Jay must have set a record for crackerjack awards politely declined, any one of which had been earned many times over.

The public understands that comedians who need new material every night have writers. Many, like Jay, often reference that in their monologues and celebrate their writers. A loyal guild guy, Jay closed the show down for a month during the Writers Guild strike a few years back, and he kept paying his staff (other than the writers) long past the million dollar mark. To keep them working, he finally resumed the show the only way he could within Guild rules, by writing all of the material himself. And the show very evidently kept its sharp edge of humor. Following the strike, the Guild contacted me to say they had determined that everything Jay did was well within the Guild rules and that they wanted to apologize to him because some Guild members had denigrated his decision. When I referred this to him, he said, "Ask them not to issue an apology." "Jay, they feel obliged to." "Whatever."

Validating the public's perception of Jay's easy-going nature, his default response to anything is "whatever." When Conan O'Brian was taking his victory laps coming into the Tonight Show and his sympathy laps on the way out, Jay simply did not comment, even to refute charges that simply contradicted the truth. When Jimmy Kimmel tried to foment a feud, Jay didn't rise to the insults, and a one man feud eventually runs out of credibility. When it became evident that Jay's turning over the show to Jimmy Fallon six months before his contract required would allow Fallon to launch powerfully out of the highly-rated NBC coverage of the Sochi Olympics, Jay agreed. But he required NBC to pay his staff for the remaining six months to ease the disruption of job loss. As it turned out, working on the show which nailed down the highest ratings for two decades made most of them top draft choices.

I think that one of the keys to Jay's enduring pre-eminence in one of the toughest ratings battlegrounds in television… even after the game ceased to be a three horse network race and became a network and cable marathon… was the fact that people saw that Jay was up to any moment he faced, the comedic with unfailing wit and the challenging with quiet dignity. The public has always perceived that he wasn't pr'd into his constant ratings eminence… and, even more importantly, that he could consistently stand on his own two feet without being wired for levitation. This came up when he was subpoenaed as witness in an excruciatingly public trial of a famous celebrity. The night before his appearance, we were talking in his dressing room, and he mentioned that the network wanted to send two very able public relations execs to accompany him. I told him that I had watched coverage of Larry King's arrival the previous day to testify at the same trial. "He had an entourage with him of six or eight guys. It looked like he was the defendant. I think the lesson is 'no frigging press agents,'" I said. It was apparent that Jay had already come to the same conclusion. The next day I was racing to the office to catch his arrival on the voracious TV news coverage, but an accident on Pacific Coast Highway had frozen traffic. The radio stations, however, were giving a play-by-play of everything TV was covering outside the court, and they reported a flurry of excitement when Jay arrived. "Look at that," the news anchor said with wonder, "he's walking in all alone, all by himself. What a guy!"

Chapter 2

Larger Than Life...

Over the past fistful of decades, the person who has been Larger Than Life in the walk-tall manner on which John Wayne had so long held the patent is, by unanimous decision, Clint Eastwood, who carved out a style all his own. I suddenly realize it's almost fifty years since the spaghetti westerns injected him into our feature film bloodstream. Seems like yesterday. It took Hollywood at least one of those decades, maybe two, to realize what a Renaissance hombre this guy was. They didn't see all the Oscars and films of substance coming, but the hints were there in all of his early work. Even when the product was strictly guns and saddles or guns and detective badges, he was giving it his own unique finesse. And he was doing so on both sides of the law and on both sides of the camera. Nobody carried a bigger badge or bigger gun than did Dirty Harry Callahan or a cooler, more laconic resolve than his Arizona sheriff Walt Coogan in "Coogan's Bluff."

And no one set his own nihilistic law or broke the conventional one more convincingly than his Man With No Name in the Sergio Leone horse operas or Will Munny, his killer for hire in "Unforgiven." Josey Wales was an outlaw only to the people who wanted him dead. The image of set jaw and steely stare through narrowed eyes is so powerful that it sometimes overwhelmed and delayed the acknowledgment of his acting range in "The Beguiled," "Honky Tonk Man," "Million Dollar Baby" and other films including most recently "Gran Torino," which was not grizzled grey Dirty Harry, but a deep and touching portrait of loneliness and estrangement and, finally, devotion. Clint so often was directing actors like Morgan Freeman, Gene Hackman, Hilary Swank, Sean Penn and Tim Robbins to Oscars and many more to nominations, that he diminished the focus on his own powerful work in front of the cameras.

The only time Clint and Wayne actually worked together was in an ad concerning a proposition on the California ballot about the registration of guns. I don't intrude myself into the politics of my clients, except when the dedications of liberal activists like Warren Beatty, Barbra Streisand and Paul Newman or the environmental concerns of many others so closely correspond to my own. Hollywood is a politically varied town, and knowledgeable publicity professionals of all stripes have opportunities to help cherished causes. When Jay Leno's wife, Mavis, bravely headed the Feminist Majority campaign against Gender Apartheid, trying to draw world attention to the brutal oppression of women under the Taliban regime in Afghanistan long before 9/11 belatedly directed the public's eyes to it, I was honored to be allowed along for the ride. She and the Feminist Majority deservedly were nominated for Nobel Peace Prize consideration for their work. Clint and I never talked politics.... with one very embarrassing exception, the ballot issue on the registration of guns.

Clint had called me out to his office at Universal to go over ads for an upcoming film. Shortly into the process, one of his associates came in and said, "Clint, John Wayne's waiting for you on Stage 19 for that Prop Ten (pick a number) commercial." As Clint set down the half avocado out of which he had been spooning his lunch, I felt I had to speak up. "Clint, I've never imposed any of my politics on you, right?" "Yeah?" he said in a dead voice, feeling it coming. "Well," I stammered on, "I just think that Dirty Harry and Rooster Cogburn doing an ad on this proposition is a step over the line." He gave me that steely stare and in the calm, slow, deadly, raspy make-my-day whisper said, "Well, that just shows what a dumb asshole you are, because we're pushing this thing the same direction you would." And then he laughed like hell and strode out of the room.

It was only on the drive back to my office that I developed the strong suspicion that it had been a set-up, that I'd been brought out there for the scam. Among other things, Clint is a great showman with an unerring sense of where the laugh will be. He had, rather than just telling me he was doing the ad, staged the scene, knowing full-well what my reflex response would be when the guy came in and said his line. As a life-long practical joker, I know you share the laugh even when you get stooged. It was worth driving all the way out there for the show.

A press agent is always trying to figure out what it is that makes popular artists, individually, connect with their public. What is the personal quality, quite apart from the talent and physicality, which so electrically engages and melds with the audience? With Clint over the years, I read that variously... the guy who takes care of things, the guy you can rely on, deadly force, lifeforce. But there's a constant element through all of the phases of his acting stardom and his directing stardom as he evolved from the someone's-gotta-do-it violence of the early films to the humanism in this great-director stage of his career, this constant trek to the Oscar stage and time of speaking out in film for important values. His half-time pep talk to America in the recent Super Bowl ad was the culmination of that, sending us all back onto the field with the prospect of hard-earned victory atop our to-do list. Here's the compelling constant.... *with Clint Eastwood, you always got... you always get... the straight goods.* Whoever he was at any stage in his evolution as an artist, as a man or simply tending the garden of his philosophy, he told you straight out who he was and how he thought. He never bent to fashion or marketplace or presumed popular attitude. You always got pure Clint.

Paul Newman had his own specific aura. Even the way he ate a hamburger. There was a burger on the menu in the Paramount commissary that was about three inches high, and it was his standard fare for an interview lunch. He was the only person I knew who could not only get his mouth around it, but also could eat it with no loss of gentility, all the while carrying on a serious conversation. He ate a hamburger like he approached a film or like he raced a car, vigorously. And he didn't chat, he conversed. He even told jokes vigorously and enjoyed them immensely, and they always got bigger laughs than they deserved because he enjoyed them so much. One sticks in my mind because we all roared and then had to figure out what was so excruciatingly funny about it. A reporter is sent to interview a bee keeper who has over four million bees, a world record or something. He goes to the guy's farm but there's only this little shed. He asks the beekeeper, "Is it true that you have four million bees that you...?"... "Yep." "But how do you know that it's exactly...?" "All very scientific, how many acres pollinated in how many hours." "But where do you keep four million..." "In that shed." He leads the guy in and as his eyes adjust to the dark the reporter sees an empty shed, and knows this is a gag. Still, he asks, "But where...?" "Right there," and the bee keeper points to a shelf on which there are four one gallon jugs.

"They're all in those jugs?" the reporter questions. "A million each." "But aren't they all just like... *crushed* together?" The beekeeper nods and says, "Fuck 'em."

I think that sticks in my mind because it was a joke about indifference which struck the funny bone of one of the least indifferent men I ever knew. Paul was engaged long before his Newman's Own philanthropy. Most conversations with him were about urgent issues. Late in the 60s when Vietnam and Civil Rights had the town galvanized, Paul Newman and Warren Beatty poured massive effort into producing an all-star Anti-ABM rally (opposing a massive step-up in the Cold War arms race) which they presented at the Palladium in Hollywood and which re-ignited the industry's liberal base for the peace issues of that divisive period. They turned out a star-base rivaling an Oscarcast. Gisela and I jumped into that up to the waist and with full passion. These stars didn't squander their influence. They thought deeply and acted decisively. Paul insisted that Joanne was the deep thinker in the family, which was probably true, but he had a mind that was engaged and curious and passionate, the goofball jokes notwithstanding.

This issue-focus was evident during the filming of "Butch Cassidy." John Foreman had been Paul's main guy at the Rogers & Cowan publicity firm, head of the company's Paul Newman think tank. He then became part of Paul's management team, and he was at this particular moment a producer of "Butch Cassidy and The Sundance Kid," the film that would finally prove Paul as successful at comedy as he was with drama. His comedies before then hadn't added up to much, at least not in the light of his limitless talent. So you would think he would give some attention to the film's promotional needs, but most of our meetings were dedicated to his support of the presidential campaign for Eugene McCarthy. The only press he allowed us to call to the set were to promo McCarthy. Politics was serious obligation for him. While driving to a promotional appearance one night, he and I were discussing Jefferson's statement that democracy needed to refresh itself with a revolution every twenty years. Paul suggested that maybe Jefferson thought democracy could evolve into something even more effective as it adapted to changing conditions. "More effective? Than democracy?" I challenged. "I'm sort of attracted to benevolent despotism..." he said with a straight face... and then that grin... "as long as I'm the benevolent despot." I had a feeling he wasn't entirely kidding.

On another occasion, we were heading for UCLA for a discussion with a film school class after they'd had a preview screening of "Rachel, Rachel." Curiosity is a dangerous indulgence for a press agent, but I was moved to blurt, "Paul, why do you do publicity?" "What do you mean?" "I mean you get first offer of almost every good role anyway." He thought about and then said , "Almost." It was a joke, but "almost" is powerful medicine and a reasonable basis of strategic motivation. My question wasn't quite as stupid as it may sound in this telling, because both Paul and I knew it was rhetorical. We both understood that Rogers&Cowan's prime area of service was to achieve the greatest possible success of each film to the greatest possible benefit of his career and the resultant awareness of this flow in the eyes of the industry, the public, the media… and, at least at the back of my mind, history.

The "Rachel, Rachel" screening was a hit with the film students, and Paul was a hit, but so was his VW with a Porsche engine which he'd parked just outside and which they wanted to see. The last quarter of the talk-around took place out by the car. They were all excited by the big engine, and I think Paul thought the wrong lesson was going down, because he said, "You know, you don't always have to show them everything you have inside. Sometimes it's best to let it out just on occasion… you know, surprise 'em?." I think he was letting them look at the motor inside of him, too, and the secret of why he was such a brilliantly economical actor and filmmaker. I felt like I was a student there again and damn glad I'd come to class that night.

Warren Cowan, the most superstar of all superstar press agents, was a larger-than-life-seeking missile. His genius was that he knew that his clients' stardom is what he *sold* and that their stardom is what sold *him*. His reputation for handling the biggest made him the biggest. Excepting the guys who head the major talent agency empires, there never was and never will be another career adjunct specialist handling as vast a chunk of the town's talent as he, and very often simultaneously. Just as an actor might feel rejected when someone else gets a role she or he wanted, Warren felt rejected if he couldn't land a massively big star. Well, he handled most of them, but it's always the ones that got away that keep you up at night. As a kid in New York, he collected baseball player autographs. For the ones he hadn't scored, he would track them to their hotels and slip into revolving doors with them, stopping the door-swing until he had it. The two star signatures he hadn't collected on a contract were Rock Hudson and Steve McQueen. Hudson was a yachting enthusiast, and Warren did everything but wear a sailing cap to get him.

He found rare boating books and sent them, but Hudson finally hired Dale Olsen who piloted him past the shoals and rogue tides of media in his final years, through the at-last-exposed waves of Hollywood homophobia and the countering nobility of those who fought it. This was evidenced in the manner in which Rock's tragic decline from HIV/AIDS engaged Hollywood in the struggle to achieve a cure under the inspired leadership of Hudson's close friend, Elizabeth Taylor.

Steve McQueen was equally elusive. He was very much in control of his own product and his own image. Finally, Steve's partner in Solar Productions, a company through which he wanted to make films with a conscience, gave us an appointed time to make a presentation to Mr. McQueen and his associates. We were told it had to be in writing (which was my job at R&C) and that the writer would have to read it. Aye, there's the rub. I read, even my own words, haltingly. So I set about putting as much of it as I could into blank verse. The meter of the verse can impose a certain clarity. But boring is boring, and I felt I was barely keeping them awake, even though I'd come up with some ideas relating to how Mr. McQueen's company was "solarizing'" the industry, whatever that means. At the end, it was very cordial, which usually means you didn't get the gig. On the way out, Mr. McQueen nodded me over to him. "Thanks for taking the stab at it," he said, "but let me ask you a question. Do I really look like a guy who doesn't know blank verse when I hear it?" "I'm dyslexic. I needed the edge." "OK, then," he said. But it wasn't ok, because we didn't get the job.

Warren didn't let me forget it. He was most often the good cop, liberally praising good accomplishment, but there was a prescribed incidence of bad cop, little or big nitpicks to keep the rest of it from going to your head or sparking visions in your mind of going it on your own. A frequent tool in this was his repeatedly educating me to the fact that "You know, Joanne Woodward never really liked you." It was entirely possible that this was true, but it was strange and finally funny how often Warren would slip it in when we were laying out some specific campaign for Paul and Joanne and he would just say it as a kind of mantra, sometimes just popping out of the silence when we were driving someplace. Another time, we were driving in the car with some other R&C staffers on board. I said, "Warren, you know what?" "What's that?" he responded. "Well," I said, "it's a fact that Joanne Woodward apparently does not like me." Warren glanced at the strangely surprised looks on the faces of the others and then he said with strong intonation of astonishment, "You're kidding."

When Yves Montand was making "Let's Make Love" I went to the set to have lunch and go over a few things with him. Yves was tall and toughened by his childhood in the Italian ghettos of rough-house Marseilles. But he was quiet in demeanor, and he carried himself with great dignity. We had lunch in the 20th commissary, always a very starry place, joined by Milton Berle and Tony Randall, also his co-stars in the film and also among my charges at Rogers & Cowan. For an actor who'd played some formidable tough guys, Yves had a striking elegance and decorum, and this was an irresistible target for Milton's monkey business. The conversation began pretty straight forward... "that line" this and "what the director meant" that. Milton suddenly went into an ecstasy over a pudding he had ordered. "Yves, you have to try this pudding." Yves gave a skeptical look at the plop of paste Milton extended to him on a teaspoon. "What eez that?" Yves asked with distaste. "Pudding. Milton said in obvious thrall. "Flan..." Tony offered, "... crème broule." "You HAVE to try it," Milton insisted. And with that he delicately inserted the spoonful into Yves' mouth... and then let go and turned to resume some point of discussion with Tony. Yves was left with a spoon sticking out of his mouth and, seemingly the entire room had been focused on the gag. Luckily, no one thought it funnier than Yves who, spoon still sticking out of his mouth, started to throttle Milton with a firm grasp around his throat. There was applause from nearby tables, and Tony orchestrated it with his hysterical high giggle. Milton had to recover the floor and started looking frantically under the table shouting "Where's my spoon? Who stole my spoon?" To which Yves added, "You better get up off the floor before you have eet steeking out of your esss."

The town just didn't know what to make of Simone Signoret and Yves Montand when they arrived in Hollywood together, each in his/her own vehicles of stardom. We knew them from the American sensation of two great thrillers by French director H. G. Clouzot. Simone took the town by main force in director Jack Clayton's "Room At The Top," wresting the 1959 Oscar from one of the starriest lists of nominees ever. It wasn't a complete surprise. We'd encountered her dazzling beauty and dazzling acting in "Casque D'Or" and "La Ronde." Everyone was into "foreign films" then, and her real impact had come in 1954 in Clouzot's classic thriller. "Les Diabolique." It was the kind of fare to which film school students took dates. At the film's most diabolical moment of horror, I felt someone grab onto me frantically and then I realized it wasn't my date, but some guy sitting on the other side of me, out of his mind in terror. The year before, the hot foreign film had been Clouzot's "Wages Of Fear," which put Montand on everyone's map, a masterful tough guy under-actor a la Bogart or John Garfield with a franco-italo flare and masculine grace. Who knew that he was also one of the greatest live variety artists in the world… singer, dancer, lyric mime, impressionist… he could do it all at a level that chilled you with surprise. Simone knew, so she pressured him to make his American live musical performance debut in Hollywood. She wanted him to be discovered in all of his talents before he assumed his Hollywood stardom. It was work to get the big star turnout for the premiere night because of the who-knew? factor, but they were all pressing through the stage door to get to him after the show. Simone just smiled because it was nothing she didn't expect and everything she had expected.

Simone had become a special friend of mine during the "Room At The Top" campaign. She and Yves, royalty in Europe as actors, as intellects and as bold political activists, arrived in Hollywood as the most doted-upon European artist couple since Olivier and Leigh. They generated constant media attention. So I was obliged to spend a large amount of time at the Montands' second story bungalow apartment above the gardens of the Beverly Hills Hotel. When media was in attendance, the door across the landing at the top of the stairs was always closed. But if I was there only to go over photos or to have a discussion, no media, that door would open and Marilyn Monroe would wander in, usually in a thick black bathrobe, beautiful in the absolute absence of make-up and with the soft confusion of unbrushed hair. Apparently, she never had in her and Arthur Miller's refrigerator whatever she could count on being in Simone and Yves'. As she ate from a bowl of cereal or a small carton of yoghurt, she would wander into their conversation or look at the photos and make pretty good choices. Miller would come in sometimes in slacks and sweater, and they seemed an informal melding of close friends. This is before Simone had to go back to Paris for work there and before Yves and Marilyn would start their work together on their ultimately unsuccessful musical comedy, "Let's Make Love."

Another couple frequently there was novelist Romaine Gary and Jean Seberg. The easy flow of intellectual affinities in those rooms made it feel like the Left Bank. The two apartments might just as easily have been looking out over Notre

Dame and the Seine or down Boulevard St. Germain. A lot of the media interest at that time and much of the conversation concerned the conflict raging in France over Algerian independence and the right wing's insistence on keeping Algeria a department (equivalent of a federal state in the US) of France. When I'd resided in Paris a half decade before, I was constantly stopped by police who would go over my papers because I looked somewhat middle eastern, thin, dark hair and eyes... of which attributes only the eyes remain... Simone and Yves and Gary and other French intelligentsia opposed de Gaulle's demands that the Arabs thusly conjoined with La Belle France continue to honor their obligations to the French flag. They would have had an easier time teaching them to dance the can can. One of the reasons Simone wanted to get back to Paris was to return to the frontlines of the ideological warfare, for the Montands' liberal opinions were viciously derided in the French press.

If you love the French, it was impossible not to love Yves Montand. Having spent such intense time with that earlier French cultural ambassador Maurice Chevalier, I could see that Chevalier was what Americans think a Frenchman is, bubbling personality, twinkling charm, and Yves was what a Frenchman actually is. He was a real guy, very straightforward about what he thought, a very basic charm, down to earth. I asked Simone once how Yves, the son of Italian immigrants to the Marseilles slums, got so French and how his name got so French. She said it was because Italian immigrant laborers (he was born Ivo Livi) didn't do well in the labor-competitive French seaport, so they had to live in the cheaper which is to say higher floor slum apartments. When his mom wanted him upstairs and Right Now!... she would lean out over the metal banisters and yell, "Ivo! Monta!" ("Yves! Get your ass up here!") His friends would always mimic her, but he defiantly gave the phrase the Gaelic glaze which became the professional name his talents carried to vast fame.

After Simone was away for a while and the rumors of the Montand and Monroe affair started to circulate, Simone would call me not to check up on what I might have heard or observed but to see how Yves was. I'm not telling tales out of school about that relationship. It was big news, and it's certainly on the record. I told Simone once that I really felt I should go off his account. I had too much loyalty to her. But she asked me to stay on and to take care of Yves for her. I did my best, and it was fine with Yves even though he knew I felt very protective of her. One time I was at the bungalow waiting to take him to a photo shoot… a Life Magazine story… and he was in the bathroom brushing his hair. I was standing outside the bathroom watching him as a press agent will do when his or her client is late for an appointment. It's like watching a pot to make it boil sooner? You know how you do that? To tell this story right, I have to explain what a French "puh!" is. It is a barely audible blowing out of the air through lightly conjoined lips, like blowing out a candle… that's it, like blowing out a candle, not with a "whuh" but with a "puh"… a French habit when they wish to express that something means nothing, that it's not even worth considering. It's not even a real puh because you don't actually hear the vowel sound, just the air percussion. At any rate I was just watching the back of Yves' head, not thinking anything that I was aware of, and he said, his eyes moving to another part of the mirror to gaze directly at me, "Why do you reproach me?" He wasn't angry… just a question. And the use of that word surprised me. In the first place, it's not that common in English, and it's sound-alike in French means something quite the opposite. But that's what he said, and I answered, "What do you mean? I don't reproach you. I wasn't even thinking about you… maybe that we're late is all." "No, I was watching your eyes. I know you admire her, protect her, love her… who doesn't? But you have no right to judge me. Simone and I have been married for all those years…. I have never… neVAIR! (his finger striking at the air)… had an affair. Puh! a prostitute here, a prostitute there." I couldn't help it. It was so damn French and self-exculpatory. I started to laugh. That made him smile, and he said "Eh bien (ok,)" and we went off to the photo session. Later when the pot had stopped boiling over and partners were restored to their rightful mates, Yves starred on the French stage in Arthur Miller's "After The Fall," which was the playwright's tribute to or exorcism of Marilyn Monroe. Monroe and Miller were two more of those people who, like Clint Eastwood and Paul Newman, like Cary Grant and Kirk Douglas, Gary Cooper and Audrey Hepburn, are… simply and significantly… larger-than-life.

It has to do in part with degree of fame and with what these set-apart few have come to symbolize in the public mind. They are so persuasively and uniquely themselves that they are unimaginable in any altered form. That doesn't mean they can't undertake a variety of roles. Henry Fonda's quintessential bad guy in Sergio Leone's "Once Upon A Time In The West" is all the more intense because we measure it against the everyman decency of the roles we most closely associate with him... Marilyn Monroe's sad exit confirmed that the fault-lines in her perfection were part of the desirability which had captured our imagination.

A Hollywood press agent has frequent encounters with such highest-plane personalities. Orson Welles, Brando, Groucho Marx, Charlie Chaplin, Marlene Dietrich, Streisand, Bergman, Grant, Cooper, Eastwood, Beatty, Taylor, Garson, Holden, Kaye, Garland, Hackman, Sinatra, Hepburn, Rooney, Stravinski, Hope, Leno, Carson, Newman, Olivier, Nicholson, Douglas, Lemmon, Laurence Harvey, Burton, Signoret, Montand, Berle, Monroe, the Schells (Maria and Max,) Christie, Bisset, Seymour, Connery, Caine, Natalie Wood, the Douglases (father and son,) Jimmy Woods, Aldrin, Hitchcock, Schwarzenegger, Reeve, as well as noted scientists, jurists, politicians and the top ranks of moguls and musicians and filmmakers have trickled through, glanced off of or played leading , even seminal, roles in my life. Similar and over-lapping lists play roles in the lives of other press agents. These opportunities have fallen to me, as they do to most Hollywood flacks, in the natural course of plying the trade. It's about as good as one can do without being Jay Leno, Merv Griffin or Mike Douglas, all three of which uber talk show hosts I've represented, each much larger-than-life himself. Some of the experiences a publicist enjoys or endures are tangential chats or merely interesting moments while some others are career-long associations or even... a dangerous assumption to make in Hollywood.... friendships.

George Sanders' patented brand of blasé distingue evolved into ennui and brought him to suicide, leaving a note that said, "I am leaving because I am bored." He should have taken lessons from James Mason who was never bored or boring. If a moment even hinted at becoming conventional, Mason would concoct some mischief to avert it. James' special above-it-all charm, distain and amusement made him vivid in life, work and ironic, biting humor. You never knew which way he would bounce. You knew only that it would be some way you didn't expect. When I first worked with James Mason, it wasn't as his press agent. We were in a scene together during the filming of Joseph Mankiewicz' "Julius Caesar" on stage 25 at MGM. (Press agent confession: "In a scene together" here is technically accurate but essentially a bald-faced lie.) While I was in my teens, after I started film school, I haunted unemployment offices for work as a "waver" in films. Wavers were not as exalted as extras. They were the guys who waved in the background of crowd scenes for, as I recall, about five dollars a day and lunch. But I was in the presence of movie-making. On "Julius Caesar" I was "discovered" while we wavers were standing in the line to the wardrobe department where we were to be handed our mini-skirted togas. I was plucked from oblivion because I had curly hair… or, as I call it now, the good old days. I was hauled off to the hair department to have my forehead plastered with ringlets, and then marched to a place fairly close to the Soothsayer who would inform Julius Caesar (Louis Calhern) to "beware the Ides of March." I wasn't exactly featured, but I was close enough to hear the immortal lines. Close enough to require some dramatic response. I did a pretty good gasp upon hearing this ragged nobody so address, one might even say threaten, our nation's greatest hero, but there isn't much more of me on screen than a ringlet.

I was within ogling distance of gods… Mankiewicz, Marc Antony (Marlon Brando,) Brutus (James Mason,) Calpurnia (Greer Garson, my mother's favorite actress and someone who would later become very dear to me) and Cassius (Edmond O'Brien who was to become a close personal friend even more than client.) I revered Brando, and who didn't? The pedestal on which film students placed him was Mount Olympus. He had done only three films, "The Men," "Streetcar Named Desire" and "Viva Zapata" but he was already in glory with evident promise of the glories to come. "Waterfront" and "Guys And Dolls" and "The Wild One" were a few years off, but he was The Man, especially since Jimmy Dean wouldn't do "East Of Eden" or "Rebel Without A Cause" for another two years. Dean was still in film school with us at UCLA.

The presence that most awed me was James Mason. The saints preserve us, "Odd Man Out" his very same self! With his immortal stumble toward his doom as Johnny McQeen, the dying Irish rebel in Carol Reed's dark tone poem of love and patriotism and death, Mason had taken a front row seat in my own personal pantheon of acting greats. And there he was, a hero incarnate. I never met an actor who doesn't hold in reverence that Masonian voice rumbling up from the back of his throat, so masterfully shaped for irony, the perfect tool for his self-deprecating wit and amused scorns.

The best kept secret to happiness in press agenting is that you have to be crazy about great acting and the men and women who can do it. That also applies to great writing, directing, comic invention and musicianship, instrumental, vocal or composition. Still a writer imagines and an actor becomes. Acting is a stronger magic. You have to venerate the larger-than-life characteristics of their special gift to be able to best serve their talent and your craft. The objective distance some press agents affect as a thick outer skin comes at a high price. They miss so much of the honor and so much of the fun. Just this afternoon I did a gallery shoot with Martin Landau, and the photographer said "Do what you want," and Marty held his tie in a certain silly way, canted his head and became Oliver Hardy before our eyes, and then he scratched his head and morphed into Stan Laurel. Everyone in the room stood in awe. He became both Laurel and Hardy at the same time. You can't even imagine that, can you?... because that's how great it was.

I started working with James Mason around the time of "North By Northwest," and I once lamented to him not having known him when he was doing "The Seventh Veil" and "The Man In Grey," those imperious, haughty, darkly romantic roles that brought out the excited masochisma in women all over the world and, thus, brought him to Hollywood. "Oh," he said, with that Mason huff of suppressed amusement, "you wouldn't have liked me then. I was almost a Beatle, and I didn't handle it very well. If you think I'm contentious and litigious now, you should have seen me then." His attitudes were charmingly bizarre, and he moved in a cool that was unlike that of anyone else. Some of the most vivid instances of memory relate to his divorce trial from Pamela, the conclusion of one of the most colorful, outrageous and publicly conducted marriages in a town famous for all of the above. I'm quite certain that the flip side, their romance, must have been equally volcanic. They had lived in a British enclave just north of the Beverly Hills Hotel, a verdant and palmy dead-end street they had shared for many years with Charlie Chaplin and other noted Brits. What a neighborhood of eccentrics. And the divorce trial was everything you would want a Hollywood divorce trial to be, media crowding every entrance and exit, nothing withheld, body blow charges that seemed never to exhaust the principals. They were two glorious personalities, with the divorce trial to prove it. At some point in it, Pamela, whose youthful beauty was still compellingly evident, began a rather public relationship with a local TV personality named Joe somebody. The day after some escapade in the press featuring Pamela and Joe somebody, James and I stepped out of the limousine into the stroboscopic flash of bulbs. The media, like a pack of border collies, started herding him down the hall at the end of which Joe somebody huddled over a cigarette he was smoking with the earnest intent of someone who did not wish to be seen. He heard the rumble of the approaching crowd following James toward him, cameras at the ready. He looked up just as James, that calm mask of a smile upon his face, drew within a step of him. Joe's stunned reaction was the wide-eyed stare of someone readying himself for a blow. Seconds of sustained suspense. At the raise of James' hand, Joe pulled back, shutter-fingers poised. "Joe," James said, and then his fingers merely tapped Joe's cheek in a love pat... "you scoundrel" followed by his little grunt of amused disdain. James' smile never wavered. The photographers were aghast. All they had were shots of two old friends saying hello. They looked like a bunch of guys whose pockets had just been picked.

But the memorable and cherished moment of the day came later when the limousine was cruising through Beverly Hills to drop me off at my office. In those days, there were actual newsstands, little kiosks where newspapers were peddled, their headlines all displayed and crying out "extry, extry, read all about it!" to passing cars and pedestrians. As we passed the Beverly Wilshire Hotel, we noticed such a stand emblazoned with the provocative front page banner headline of the Los Angeles Herald-Examiner. It read, for all in the car to see, "MASON ACCUSED OF HABITUAL ADULTERY." That came as a shock even to me whose life was lived headline to headline. I looked at James. There was a long silence, and then he exhaled the James Mason chuckle... the amused one... a quick spurt of levity, that "hmmpf" that could be compared only to Sydney Greenstreet's little snort of delight at Sam Spade's audacities in "The Maltese Falcon." "Hmmpf," James remarked again, "Well done, Guttman."

With Mason, it was always the unexpected. Even his anger emerged in terse irony rather than the explosive venting not uncommon in the movie business. As he got older, I felt we needed some new art (photos) to capture his more matured handsomeness, so I set a photo session with John Engstead, who reigned with George Horrell as the premiere portraitists of that star-studded moment in Hollywood history. It was, somehow, more a time of timeless stars than in this period of a-new-hottest-guy-or-gal-every-day instant stardom only occasionally sustained. The studios had done their job well in their contract-stars day, building giants, nourishing or banishing them by wit or by whim. And James was one of the most glorious. That, I felt, needed to be celebrated in new eight-by-tens. Engstead did his magic which was capturing the person inside. Both he and I were disturbed by the number of distracting wrinkles gathered by time on the Mason face. That's not how you saw James when you were with him. It all escaped perception in his imposing presence. But there they were, and we set about righting that. Of course, in such a pursuit, there is that inevitable one-too-many retouches. Oblivious to this, I sent the prints off to James in Southeast Asia where he and Peter O'Toole and Richard Brooks were making "Lord Jim." Back from there came a telegram from him. "Thanks for the photos. Very beautiful. The next time I'm there I would love to meet her."

His grand gestures were always ironic, too. The decade of the sixties was a time when the tabloid press was in gestation. There was not yet the gaggle of blaring national supermarket super-rags thriving on sad tidings real or imagined which we have now. Nor was there our current flood of digital entities, the anyone-can-play blogs, that internet "media" glut so immediate and therefore so often half-baked. No, there were then only one or two little publications which were just inventing the indelicate art of annoying stars with evil dream-ups. James and Pamela were constant targets and, as James had openly admitted, he (and, even more, they) had a history of being overly litigious. Except with these scammy little newspapers (think Danny DeVito in "LA Confidential,") there was nothing to sue. You can't sue a fly speck. There was one particularly such guerilla journalist who was especially annoying to Hollywood and a major pain in the ass for James. One fine day it was learned that this guy had been ambulanced to the hospital. James was not displeased to hear this, and he asked the circumstance. The story derived from the fact that this dirt peddler could bring desperate young performers to some industry attention. With such leverage, he had compelled a starlet to perform an act upon him and instead of doing what was intended, she had bitten down... hard. James sent a huge array of flowers to him at the hospital with a note reading, "Dear......, Congratulations. So few of us achieve our destinies. James Mason." In the light of that, it was very James that he also took delight in having me plant outrageous stories ascribing all kinds of infamous behavior to him as long as it was in sufficiently discredited outlets. There was one columnist back east whose nasty stories in one of the tabloid raglets had won him a special fame of hate. James dictated the stories for me to plant, all so loathsome that they couldn't possibly be true. The writer, such was his villainy, didn't get that fine point of *reducto ad absurdum*, and he printed them in all of their obvious fabrication. Each time one of these fairytales for the vacuous appeared, James would hoot with delight. This writer, whose affection I did not seek, thought me a fine fellow for passing such treacheries on to him. That enchanted James even more, and he referred to the guy as "Guttman's friend."

James had come into my office one day bearing a canvas that was three feet high and four feet wide, a sizable work of art. An artist of note, James had painted me sitting at a little, well-worn typewriter. You could almost hear its clacking as I pounded at it with evil glee writing lies about him. My alter ego, my better self, clad in the draped white sheets of heaven (proudly bald as compared to the sad toupee on the lesser me) stood behind me, smiling sadly in doleful impatience with my mendacity and the deceitful tricks of my trade. Thus had James lovingly explained the theme of the painting to me. That more perfect me was holding our family's late alligator, Wally, of whose demise I will speak in due course. He was petting Wally as they both awaited my arrival in the unlikely event that I would, at the appointed hour, be directed to the up escalator. Inscribed at the bottom was what James promised was an incantation to ward off the existential doubts that he hoped would haunt every flack, those crises of conscience which he felt must come even unto press agents. This dedication stated, "Mason done this for Guttman with affection and admiration." I loved that painting, and Gisela who has professionally presented some of the promising and anointed young artists, thought it was "a really good piece both in execution and theme, simultaneously loving and vicious." A number of years later, I took it home so that it could be properly framed. Three days later our house went down along with 270 other houses in the 1993 Malibu fire. My better angel and Wally went down with them. There was so much to mourn, but that one was sorely missed.

James always called me Guttman. I don't recall his ever addressing me as Dick except in times of extreme exasperation, as in "you dick!" James and Gene Hackman would often feed Gisela's convictions about the failing clarity of my intellect with such phrases as "that dick" or "he doesn't get it." Every time she disagrees with me she cracks, "Gene always says that you don't get it." It was, in fact, only one time in Paris when we were dining in a Chinese restaurant along the Seine and she and Gene were incapable of understanding some sophisticated point I was making. Gene looked at me, and then turned to Gisela and said, "He doesn't get it." That puny history notwithstanding, Gisela would and still does drag Gene's comment out like her best china on special occasions of our disagreement.

A rare but treasured compliment from James occurred when I learned that he had slipped into town and was in secret residence at the Bel Air Hotel. James' voice and speech were as distinctive and beautiful as any that ever graced the screen, not just that rich and edgy baritone but also the clear, determined enunciation of every syllable, the crisp hiss or percussion of every consonant. It was at a nightclub on the Sunset Strip once that I watched the Hip Hypnotist Pat Collins put a guy from the audience under and then tell him he was James Mason. She instructed him to do something and he responded disdainfully, "I dohhhhhhn't WAAAAANT to." It sounded just like James. All of the Ts had separate and derisive clarity. This fellow, under hypnosis, had caught the disdain that makes James' speech so singular. He had identified James' deft knack of lavishing upon each consonant and vowel the celebration and exactitude it so RICHly deSERVES. After that, I could imitate James' voice rather well. It was the stone-hard dismissal that characterized it. Armed with this mimicry, which I knew could be an instrument of rich payback for all of his wicked practical jokes, I called the Bel Air Hotel and asked for his room by number . "And whom may I say is calling?" the operator asked. "James MAson," I answered in what seemed to me perfectly good Mason. There was a long pause and then came James' real voice, exasperated, "Yes, Mr. Maaason?" with contemptuous emphasis on the "May…" I found I could feed his voice back to him in fairly precise imitation. He was getting more and more aggravated and finally he took a deep breath and growled , "Guttman… you PRICK!" Epiphany.

James was a guy who rejoiced in sending the worst postcards he could find from wherever he went, including Count Ugolino chewing off the heads of his nephews, this from Barcelona for some unknown reason. This sadistic practice culminated in one card which was a nocturnal study of a woman's beguiling behind on some Mediterranean beach, with something like "remembering the silken strokes of the warm wind and your hands" scrawled on the back. He sent this not to the office but to the house, addressed to me but for Gisela's eyes only. It was remarkable to me, and somewhat insulting, that Gisela did not immediately discern that this had to be from the mad mind of James Mason. An intense interrogation followed, including "If it was from James, why did she send it to the house?" She! He could never know how maliciously the card had accomplished its villainy.

James used the ruse of madness for the cruelest tortures, ringing me up once from Hong Kong at three AM to discuss his clothes for some layout. "James, it's three o'clock." "Yes, I thought I'd catch you before you left for dinner." "Three in the morning." "In the morning? How strange. I thought it would be afternoon." "Then why did you call me at home?" I growled. "Do I detect some slight tone of irritation?" he said with urbane surprise and absolute delight.

His last word came as I slammed the phone down. I just didn't want to hear that damn chuckle.

In "Sunset Boulevard," Gloria Swanson's Norma Desmond idealizes silent screen stars by observing the "we had FACES then." What I recall of the British invaders of Hollywood is that they had WORDS then... AND they had trained VOICES. It began of course with Chaplin as an advance scout, only minus the words. In the thirties with Leslie Howard, Robert Donat, Rex Harrision, Charles Laughton, Cary Grant, Ronald Coleman, George Saunders, Herbert Marshall and then for the 40s, Olivier and David Niven and that bunch and then James Mason and his group. They were all cocky and some were cockney, especially Michael Caine and the other sixties rebels. And what distinguished them from mere mortals was not the crisp perfection or distinctive accents of their speech, but their wicked way with words, both in selection and inflection. With the notable exception of Olivier, and almost without other exception in my long years of work with them, they were not afraid of but rather enjoyed interviews. Not only did these exercises in language skills "help me find out what I think about things," as Ustinov put it, but it gave them an opportunity to engage in wordplay... swordplay, really, the swordplay of wit... manipulating words and thoughts like Russian chess masters dispatch knights and pawns. James Mason could parry and thrust phrases with the best of them. In fact, he WAS the best of them. He was always up to taking his dogma for a walk, ready to do verbal magic tricks for media for whatever news angle required it. For him it wasn't the linguistic gymnastics but the chance to impart some logic that today would be called politically incorrect but then was viewed as insurrectionist. When the Profumo Scandal broke in England, that country and the world suddenly discovered that political power often tempts sexual excess. Surprise, surprise, egocentric politicos like sex and they have lots of favors to render in exchange for a little spice in that part of their lives. As you may recall, the downfall of top English power-player John Profumo had to do with British beauties like Christine Keeler and Mandy Rice-Davies' being dispensed as lollipops to influence British political decisions. Every other Brit actor in Hollywood was ducking TV and print requests for comments on the sexy scandal. Not James. I had cameras lined up to catch him on the tennis courts at the Beverly Hills Hotel as he expounded on the thought that politics required the occasional cleansing influence of some good prostitute revelations.

"That's how politics evolves," he said, *'throw the old scoundrels out, bring the new scoundrels in.* " It became a catchphrase of the Profumo news cycle. Did it hurt his career? In close order after that he did, "The Fall Of The Roman Empire," "Lord Jim," "The Pumpkin Eater" and 'Georgie Girl." It's not hard to love people who can throw words about like hand-grenades. *That has been perhaps my single most-treasured part of publicity. Or of my personal life, for that matter.* Gisela refuses to think or say anything the way anyone else would. In some dispute today, I advised her to stop complaining about whatever the issue was. "Complaining?" she cried, wounded. "I don't complain. I bitch." "Really?" I mused, "aren't they the same thing?" "Well, yes," she granted, "bitching IS complaining... but with ZEST." God help me, but I DO love zest.

James and I thought alike on publicity. It should be an instrument of fun. When he was promoting "The Deadly Affair," I booked him onto the Merv Griffin Show. The talent coordinator on the show, a friend of mine, had found a quote James had once made to the effect that he enjoyed acting because each role required him to learn some new skills. In "Deadly Affair," James does some pretty mean dart throwing in a pub scene. This fellow wanted to have Merv relate the quote, mention James' having had to toss darts for the role, and then they would wheel out this big dart board. James Mason, wicked wit or not, was a great actor. Throw darts on a talk show and wind up hitting a band member? I thought not. I said no. When we got to the show, I had the prescience to go backstage, and there, sure enough, was the dart board. I mentioned all of this to James. When James went out, second guest since Don Rickles had been first and would be sitting there, Merv shortly went into his intro that James had made this quote about learning skills for each new film. To which James responded, "No, I never said anything even remotely like that." Merv was never thrown, and he knew how to play out any impromptu moment, so he went into an act of consternation. "James, you said very specifically that you enjoyed that, like learning to throw darts for your upcoming film 'The Deadly Affair.'" "Who told you that?" James continued blandly, "I can't throw darts for shit. They had to get a dart *double.* Didn't you notice the terrible James Mason hairdo they gave him?" Now Merv was playing his discombobula-tion, and he held up his note cards, saying, "I don't get this. We have these highly paid people called talent coordinators, and they question the guests in advance and then give me these cards saying what the guests want to talk about." At which point Don Rickles reached over and took the cards from Merv's hands saying, "Let me see those things," and he started to read them, "See Dick and Jane. See Dick and Jane run." Then James and Don started a conversation about the immense enjoyment they had derived from the Dick and Jane books, breaking up Merv who knew a good "bit" when he was riding one. When we got back to James' suite at the Beverly Hills Hotel, there was already a beautiful basket of fruit waiting and a card from the talent coordinator saying, "Dear James, Thank you for the delightful appearance. We look forward to seeing you again soon."

Many people argued which actor had the greatest voice of that day… Richard Burton and James Mason were the most usual suspects. Some insisted Laurence Olivier, but Mason and Burton battled for the crown. God-given voices? Certainly in part, but James Mason took voice lessons almost every day of his acting life. One of the consequences of that intimidating timbre was that it held most people at a distance when they were with him. People seemed too intimidated, in fact, to offer to shake hands. James may have cultivated that vocal intimidation for just that purpose, even counted on it. While he embraced a friend warmly, he had contempt for the normal social convention like meaningless handshakes with strangers. Also, he had a skin condition on his hands that made them as rough as coarse sand paper, and he was very self-conscious of that, while being self-conscious about almost no other aspect of his extraordinary self . He did love to assault the expectations of his friends with his idiosyncrasies. Hearing that Gisela and I were in Madrid, he issued a command that we come up to Estoril to see the castle he'd just purchased while shooting "The Fall Of The Roman Empire." "You'll love how I've furnished it," he assured, alluding to Gisela's passion for antique furniture. From the outside, the castle (nestled into cobble-stoned streets) met and exceeded our expectations. Gisela was breathless to see the treasures that awaited within. We entered to find that it was…virtually empty. Finally James headed us to a room which he advertised as his *piece de resistance*, his bedroom. It had a single furnishing… a ridiculous pink tube iron bed… He must have stumbled upon the only garage sale in Spain. Gisela looked at it blankly. "I can see you're impressed," he smirked, pleased with her offended sensibilities. "I didn't want to overdo it." As we all left to go to lunch, Gisela said, "James, what you've done to this beautiful castle is the worst thing England has inflicted upon Spain since the sinking of the Spanish armada." James smiled and said, "Coming from you, I take that as a great compliment."

But I cherished James' brusque "Guttman," and I think it was his tip of the hat to the fact that that was Sydney Greenstreet's name and only form of address or designation in "The Maltese Falcon." In the credits it was Casper Gutman, with one t. Greenstreet's character came up the last time I saw John Huston. It was his final press conference which we held at the Beverly Hilton Hotel where we were announcing that Huston would be the honoree of the Santa Fe Film Festival which Guttman & Pam was handling. Huston still was imposing and inspiring even as he sat in a wheel chair with a tank of oxygen in his lap and tubes in his nostrils. The culmination of the film fest would be a masquerade ball at which everyone would have to come as a character of a John Huston film. As we waited backstage for his introduction to the press for what we didn't know would be the last time, he said, "And what, Mr. Guttman, will be your costume at the ball?" "My driver's license," I said. "Yes, yes," he smiled, nodding with polite consent, "of course." He died shortly before the festival took place.

John Huston was a great, grizzly bear, meticulously well-spoken and courteous, Irish charm masking iron will. Clint nailed Huston with his performance in "White Hunter, Black Heart." In his own on-screen performances, Huston rarely displayed the joyous sense of humor so evident in his conversation and in his films... the razor sharp quips and gesture of "Maltese Falcon," the mad narrative leaps and ironic nuttiness of "Beat The Devil," the subtle comedy and soaring affection of ineptly romantic characters of "African Queen." Comedy in his films always came out of character, and in Bogart he had a fine fiddle that could play in any elected voice. No single Bogart portrayal in their long partnership borrowed in any way from another. It was a director/star relationship rivaling John Ford and John Wayne or Frank Capra and Stewart, Cooper or Gable, take your pick. We handled a number of Huston films, and we usually freed Wally Beene from his client representation duties at our office to do unit publicity on them. He and Huston were cut from the same bolt of rough-hewn tweed, spoke the same language of adventurers, smoked the same cigars which Huston in his epicurean tastes bought (Wally said he didn't do the Huston films for the money but for the cigars.) Huston and Wally conducted the business of director and unit press guy over hard-fought poker hands. There was one actor, Wally reported, that Huston identified as an anti-Semite but whom he had hired for a particular film because he was a great actor and right for the role. Huston never punished him for that perceived prejudice on the set, only at the poker table. Huston played not only for himself to win but also for the actor to lose, nicking him constantly with little remarks that could be taken as jokes, but were understood without comment by all at the game as meant to draw blood. "I think that was the funniest movie John Huston never made," Wally delighted.

Clint Eastwood can't stand not being expert at anything he tries. When Gisela and I helped ski entrepreneur Chuck Dwight and Olympian Jimmy Heuga initiate the concept of celebrity pro-am ski tournaments at Bear Valley in 1968 and 69, Clint gamely came up for the ride even though he'd never been on skis. His first descent in gangly snowplow showed a long distance to go. First Gisela showed him a few basics and took one explanatory run down with him and then brought Jimmy Heuga in for real coaching. Clint was, in a few days, good enough to make an honorable showing in the competition. A few years later in a winter event Gisela and I did with Dwight and for Guttman & Pam's first big corporate clients, the fabled Sun Valley ski resort, Clint was hitting the moguls with the best of the skiers and even doing helicopter skiing in tough powder with Bill Janss who owned the joint. In other evidence of the kind of expertise he demands of himself, you may have caught an earful of his piano skills when he hosted his PBS series on jazz. And that was definitely Clint doing his own piano in "Honky Tonk Man."

Since that film had Clint making the long jump from pistols to pianos, I thought his personal skills at the 88 should be a key element in the film's promotion, and I talked him into rolling out some prodigious ragtime on a visit to Johnny Carson and The Tonight Show. I don't know what I was thinking to second guess myself on that, but I was concerned that Clint might evidence a little jolt of nerves laying his hands on a keyboard in public for the first time and for an audience of millions. Oh, ye of little faith. Clint just sat down and turned his fingers loose, and it was impressive in both its skill and its ease. You could see the wonder and delight in Johnny's grin all the way through it, and the shake of his head at the end when the big guy came through it unscathed and shining.

The same compulsion to excellence prevailed when he chose to learn to pilot helicopters. We had our first demonstration of this when we were Patty Hearst's guests at her annual week-with-friends at Wintoon, the William Randolph Hearst hideaway in the Northern California Sierras just south of Mount Shasta. It is

80,000 acres of redwoods, about 120 square miles. In the late 1920s, Hearst quite prophetically postulated that America would go to war with Japan at some point, and that it would be ignited by a Japanese air attack on some great symbol of American power. He was off only in his geography. Rather than Pearl Harbor, he was convinced that the point of attack would be his mind-boggling castle at San Simeon on the central California coast. The Hearst Castle, he reasoned, was (and maybe actually is) the greatest celebration of American capitalist accomplishment. He created a similar but far more reclusive monument to power in his redwoods escape, building a breathtaking Bavarian- village-cum-hunting-lodge along the most exquisite roaring turns of the McCloud River which rushed with the icy meltings of the Mr. Shasta ice cap. The racing river spurts out of natural underground tubes in the foothills on Wintoon land.

Clint owned a ranch on Hat Creek about 50 miles to the east, only a few minutes by helicopter. He choppered in, Clint at the stick, making a spectacular landing in a redwood-lined clearing on a bend of the McCloud. I'm sure it was perfectly safe, because one reason experts get away with the spectacular is that it is always within the wide scope of their skill and in adherence to the regulations and knowledge defining what the safety boundaries are. But it looked astonishing. I'm pretty sure this was the summer of 1992 because it was while we were swimming that Clint asked me to come aboard on the "Unforgiven" Oscar campaign. The next time we were to go up to Wintoon, Clint offered to pick us up in Redwood City, the closest major airport... south of Lake Shasta and far south of Wintoon... and to helicopter us to the Hearst estate. Gisela resisted. I argued that he was really an expert pilot. "Too expert," she said, and we drove the hour and a half up from Redwood City. She never went aerobatic flying with Gene Hackman, either, but, truth in advertising, neither did I. But I did send Mike Douglas up with him for a white knuckle segment on his talk show.

Clint Eastwood can match anyone larger-than-life for larger-than-life. But you don't really notice it because he's so down-to-earth. He talks anybody's language right back to them, whether it is a construction guy in a bar or talking jazz and piano styling with Errol Garner. Sure, he's a legend when he walks in, but he quickly subtracts that from the equation. His appeal is egalitarian, but his interests are sophisticated. In the mid-60s when it was assumed all food including potato chips was healthy as long as it tasted good, he introduced us to health food, turned Gisela into a health nut with his level of expertise, which probably added years to our lives and has kept him, in his 80s, directing several Oscar contending films a year, sometimes even simultaneously. An uncommon man with a common touch to all. One night Bridget Byrne, a film journalist who had done numerous Eastwood stories for me, and I bumped into each other at the Palomino, the mecca of country music in the San Fernando Valley, to which we had each repaired because Sondra Locke was appearing there as a guest star with Eddie Rabbit. No Eastwood in sight until Bridget said, "There he is, (nodding to the bar.} No wonder he's king." Clint was there yakking and laughing with casual connection with some guys. He was in jeans, a pack of cigarettes rolled up in the sleeve of his white tee shirt just like them. Come to think of it, in well over 40 years, I don't believe I've ever seen Clint smoke a cigarette. Maybe he does, or maybe we think he does because Sergio Leone always had him dripping those little dark cigars from the corner of his mouth in the spaghetti westerns.

I started working with Clint after "A Fistful Of Dollars," "The Good, The Bad And The Ugly" and "For A Few Dollars More" had morphed his "Rawhide" popularity into movie-going public pre-eminence. The thing was, the people knew it, but Hollywood hadn't yet caught on. When I started representing him at Rogers & Cowan, I was trying to acquaint columnist Louella Parsons with the public's wild enthusiasm for Clint Eastwood, and she had never heard of him. Hollywood lives in its own little world, even when some guy next door is whomping them at the box office. She was going to New York, and I suggested she ask every taxi driver who Clint Eastwood was. She came back singing…. and printing… his praises. The New York Times had wider view, and when I asked their west coast writer Aljean Harmetz to pitch Clint, that paper checked and saw a new big train coming down the tracks of American cinema.

It was a prominent front page story. The fundamental truism in PR, the very base of PR's efficacy, is that everyone has the courage of someone else' convictions, and the NY Times is a big someone else. Clint was very abruptly the same kind of superstar to the industry that he already was to the public. It was just when "Coogan's Bluff" was coming out, the film that would lay the ground work for the "Dirty Harry" franchise and the Clint Eastwood/Don Siegel actor-director partnership. There couldn't have been a better cross-over film, because Clint's Coogan was still in a oowboy hat, but he had come to the big city and knocked them dead and proven that his gunfighter cool worked just great in a contemporary setting. "Hang Em High, " Clint's first U.S. and Malpaso project, had already done exceedingly well, but it really was "Coogan's Bluff" that showed Clint Eastwood to be a star for all circumstances. He firmed up his Malpaso producing empire at Universal with some of the top action directors including John Sturges ("Joe Kidd") and Ted Post ("Hang Em High.") But most of all and most directly encouraging Clint to explore Clint's own directing style was Don Siegel ("Coogan's Bluff," "Two Mules For Sister Sara," "The Beguiled," "Dirty Harry" and "Escape From Acatraz.") Clint took it from there, with the blessing of Siegel who had always had him direct a few "Clintus shots" in each film.

Clint's great director period, which has now stretched nearly four decades and grown more profound with each, has shown that distinctive artists don't seek to surpass their masters, but rather they move along their own distinctive path from the base of those teachings. Eastwood has always honored those from whom he learned, and often with a twist. In the cow-town graveyard scene of "High Plains Drifter," particularly prominent among the wooden grave markers are those ultimate trail-blazers of the Old West, Sergio Leone and Don Siegel.

When we represented Siegel, I got Merv Griffin to devote an entire show to Don upon the opening of "The Black Windmill." My bargaining chips? Clint, John Cassavetes, Michael Caine and I believe Walter Matthau, all of whom showed up for him for that TV tribute. Afterwards, Merv hosted a dinner for them all in the back room of Musso & Frank, and a warmer and funnier and more raucous evening of guy affection for another guy I've never enjoyed. Merv should have taped that hour, too.

Clint's first film as a director was "Play Misty For Me," and he cast Siegel as a bartender in the first scene he shot. Not just a good luck charm, but also nail-on-the-head casting. Clint never wasted a frame. His female star, Jessica Walters, was nominated for the Best Actress in a Dramatic Film Golden Globe. It was a good omen for the start of a directing career, so I suggested he let me arrange for him to present the award. He would be presenting either to his star or to Jane Fonda, for "Klute," a very esteemed performance, I argued. I knew full well how Clint felt about her having been photographed in celebration on a North Vietnamese anti-aircraft gun emplacement shortly before, but I said this would be an occasion of honor for art, not political statement. When he opened the envelope, it said Jane Fonda, and he announced it with dignity and with a gracious smile.... until Jane sent a young man up to accept it, attired in military jacket and jeans with a very political statement, which I had promised would not be the case. I could see his eyes narrow into a Clint squint. I hurried backstage to rescue Clint from having to do photos with the guy, and as we were moving back to our seats he said simply and in his rumble-from-dark-heavens whisper, "Have I ever thanked you for all the good advice?"

Clint had the curiosity and the courage to put his initial action hero identification frequently to the test. Instead of repeating the action genre that had jumpstarted him to the head of the pack, he talked studio bosses into the adventurously noir romantic thriller, "Beguiled," which had a Civil War setting but had a lot more in common with the sexy French thriller "Les Diaboliques" than with "Gone With The Wind." When we had the first big screening for "the town" at the Directors Guild Theatre, it was generally concluded that he had removed the limits the industry places on any big box-office action star. He was suddenly free to fly wherever he wanted. He came up to Gisela after the film and said, "Weird flick, huh, Gi?" Yes, it was weird to Hollywood that someone who could hit a home run every time he put on a cowboy hat, and picked up a gun and set a new high bar for tough, would play a guy victimized by a group of sexually-repressed-and-not-happy-about-it women. But it established him as a guy who doesn't have to care about any studio's or even the industry's expectation. Clint had just escaped from Alcatraz... free as a bird, free even to do as a director his acclaimed jazz ode, "Bird." Clint had no limits, and he has used that carte blanche freely, dangerously and successfully ever since. When he showed me "Beguiled" the very first time, he wanted me to pay special attention a still photo during the title sequence, a shot of Clint as a wounded Union soldier among a sea of wounded in the carnage of a huge battlefield, hundreds of men moving or littered all about. It was actually a true photo from the period, and, technology not being then what it is now, I asked how they laid his face in. The shot, it turned out, was unretouched. A northern soldier who was the spitting, bleeding image of Clint Eastwood, face and figure, lay there on a field a century and a decade before, wounded exactly as the script called for Clint to be wounded. It was a good and remarkable omen for a guy who was about to take his first spin at a non-action dramatic role. And a gutsy role reversal, since, in this film, Clint was the victim.

It was films like that... and the gentle musical tone poem "Honky Tonk Man" and his homage to jazz greatness, "Bird"... which opened the door for him to be received and publicized as a star and filmmaker beyond genre. And "Bronco Billy" was a deft spin in Capra/Sturges mode. When Clint was filming "Space Cowboys" about four old astronauts (played by Clint, Jim Garner, Donald Sutherland and Tommy Lee Jones) who were being sent back into space, he asked me to find out if Jay Leno would, following the taping of a regular Tonight Show, film a sequence of these four over-the-hill space vets appearing on the show. Jay loved it, but stipulated that it had to be improv. At one point, Jay asked the four superannuated fly-boys if each had military background. All nodded their "oh yeahs" and "sures." "North or South?" Jay pressed. It cracked-up all of them and, of course, it stayed in the film.

Push was coming to shove in the Oscar campaign for his "Million Dollar Baby" when Clint called to ask if I thought it had a legit shot at Best Film. "Are you asking if you should do Jay on 'The Tonight Show?'" I queried, knowing that he was always a reluctant talk show guest... perhaps less the past few years, but certainly still the case then. "I suppose so. Yeah." "Absolutely, but you have to get the right night." He loved the film and wanted to support it. We worked over the dates the ballots would be mailed out and when one might expect them to be filled out, determining the right date for a booking." I called the show and, naturally, they were delighted at the prospect of having Clint on, but on that particular date they had already booked Thomas Haden Church, a Supporting Actor nominee for "Sideways," as the first guest. There are few absolutes in Hollywood, but one definitely is that there were certain degrees of stature which require a first-guest booking on The Tonight Show with Jay Leno, a kind of holy of holies. Anything else would be an affront to nature. I asked if they would check Mr. Church if he would move back to second guest if it meant doing the show with Clint Eastwood, and I wasn't surprised that he readily and graciously did so.

Sitting in Clint's dressing room before the show, I told him about Church's having surrendered the very coveted first guest position to accommodate him. "Really?" Clint said and then went down the hall to knock on Church's door, spending about twenty minutes there and, I supposed, starting a nice friendship. At the Oscars after Clint and "Million Dollar Baby" did win Best Film, I was riding up in the elevator to the photography and press rooms with him and Barbra Streisand who had presented the award. "Maybe it was the Leno show," he said with a grin, but then guys or gals who have just won the Best Motion Picture Oscar again will grin at just about anything.

If you think his unflappable cool means that his on-screen anger is not unleashed in real life, you'd be mostly right. In over forty years, I've seen him explode only twice… which, considering the frustrations that beset a director or a producer or a star, much less all three in one package, is moderation to the most improbable degree. Each was because of some injustice done not to him but to someone else who wasn't in position to stand up for herself (in one case) or himself (in the other.) The most amazing test of this equanimity I witnessed occurred when I went back with him to Harvard where he was presented with the Hasty Pudding Award. It required him, at one point, to be fitted with bra to dance with the in-drag chorus line, part of the time-honored nuttiness of the very honorable event. He submitted in good humor. I have never seen noblesse oblige more sorely tested or graciously accommodated.

He went along with some of my publicity ideas even when he didn't think much of them. When he was shooting "High Plains Drifter" on the eastern slopes of the Sierras near June Lake and Mammoth, he had a western town constructed along the shores of Mono Lake which is lined with large boulders of pumice. Pumice is a volcanic rock that is mostly air, veined… laced really… with tubes of air pockets. I had the cast members photographed tossing boulders apparently weighing hundreds of pounds back and forth, although ten pounds was probably the maximum weight. It got a lot of pickup because I neglected to include in the caption the matter of the actual weight. What got a big pickup was a shot of the distinguished Little Person actor Billy Curtis smiling into camera while holding what appeared to be a 500 pound boulder lightly on one shoulder. The film had an aspect of fable to it, and I think Clint figured the photos lent themselves to the mystic and mythic dimensions of the story.

One of the reasons Ciint was and is such a superlative director and producer is the great affection he has for his actors. I observed this particularly in the fondness he had for the octogenarian Chief Dan George. We had just done the press junket for "The Outlaw Josey Wales" in and around Santa Fe, New Mexico, all of the press events held at a huge ranch nearby where the press were moved about on hayrides, and the gathered press loved not only the film but the gregarious experience. Clint often portrayed loners, and many of his films were about the loneliness of isolation, but "Josey Wales" was about community and people supporting each other. So, too, was "Gran Torino," which was one of his most moving films because it, like "Josey Wales," beautifully blended two great Eastwood themes... the loner and the blended community. I fully understand why "Unforgiven" dominated its year and is in the pantheon of Hollywood's historic westerns, but I still feel "Josey Wales" challenges "Unforgiven" as Clint's greatest epic western. Upon completion of that successful Santa Fe launch, Clint, Chief Dan, Joe Hyams (one of the film business' greatest PR and marketing guys and Warner Bros.' vice president in charge of Clint Eastwood, a very exalted position) and Giscla and I flew in a Warner's jet directly to Sun Valley where "Josey" would be screened and promoted at a Heroes Film Festival Guttman & Pam had helped initiate as part of our work for the resort. Chief Dan, well into his eighties, was always attended by several very beautiful Native American young women. As Mel Brooks sort of said in "History Of The World," "It's good to be chief." The exposure there went well, especially the photographers' thrill in grabbing shots of Chief Dan and Iron Eyes Cody together and my thrill in setting it. And I frequently noticed Clint's enjoyment of Chief Dan's enjoyment. Like most original people, Clint admires originality in others as much as he appreciates great performances.

The junket for "Play Misty For Me," Clint's first film as a director, was to be held in some vicinity of Carmel, California since that was where the film was set and had been shot. It is also where Clint has home and businesses and where he would eventually be mayor. I interested the studio in holding the press junket at the famous Ventana Inn in Big Sur, on the central California coast near Carmel. I didn't hide the fact that we represented the Ventana Inn, and I did get the film company good rate breaks and my resort client great press breaks. We held one of the events at Clint's famous bar, The Hog's Breath Inn, but the accommodations and the main press events were at Ventana. The studio, of course, planned and managed the junket, and I was there only in a consultation capacity assisted by a female staff member (all but three of my executives have been women,) and she (as has been the case with all of the others... sheer happenstance) was very attractive. I soon realized, that she enjoyed inordinate popularity with all of the guys in the press corps. Well, that always helps. It was not until the end of the weekend's proceedings that I found that this derived in some part from the Ventana's spas. There were three large and separated thermal baths, any of which could be enjoyed with bathing suit or sans bathing suit. One was for women, one for men and the one in the middle one was not segregated by gender. That was her choice, and I think you can imagine why this was a source of her popularity. It was definitely a first for Guttman & Pam.

I don't know if fans today can begin to understand the dimension of Paul Newman's stardom in the 60s, 70s, 80s and beyond. There is no contemporary young star who is actually the equivalent of that. I remember the day Paul turned 40, and all of the press agents at Rogers & Cowan who were less than a decade his junior, suddenly confronted our own mortality and wondered if our days of prevailing were soon behind us. That "don't trust anyone over 30" stuff had really gotten to us.

Most stars upon whom such interest is imposed try to shun publicity, but Paul did what needed to be done to sell his films. He wore the crown almost apologetically. Or maybe he just shielded himself from any personal perception of it. There weren't a lot of movies shown on TV then…TV being only the seven VHF stations… so the series of films called Million Dollar Movies (a million dollars… whewwww!) that aired on Channel 9 in L.A. got a lot of viewership. With this in mind, I called Paul one day to warn him that his first film, the swords and sandals flick "The Silver Chalice," would be the million dollar movie the following week. I knew how embarrassed he was about that film, and I thought he should be prepared. He said, "I'll call you back." About fifteen minutes later he was on the phone. "What if we take an ad in the L.A. Times?" "Saying?" "Paul Newman apologizes, Channel 9 at 8 o'clock." "Paul, it runs every night, Monday through Friday." "Holy shit." "Yeah." "Ok, We take it on Monday… 'Paul Newman apologizes, Channel 9, 8 o'clock, every night this week.'" It received a terrific amount of attention, and some critics even rose to the defense of the film, especially its introduction to Paul's promise.

Paul went at everything with intensity and vigor… his driving, his interviews, his hamburgers. It amazed me each time how he could get his mouth around one of those things. Critics who didn't know characterized the Actors Studio stars, notably Paul, Marlon Brando, Jimmy Dean, Steve McQueen, as guys who "stared at their navels." Yes, they could get a lot of juice out of a quiet moment, a silent look, but who better than those stars could bring vigor and intensity to a scene, a role, a movie?

His wife, Joanne Woodward, was a constant in his interviews, even when they weren't co-starring in the film the interview was pushing. They made more films together than Tracy and Hepburn. They were as married as any couple I've ever observed in this business. I recall his discussion of how he came at a role from the inside out and she from the outside in, but the end results blended. During one interview, he alluded to Joanne as "the last of the great broads," one of those phrases that give insight into how and why two people click. It was a phrase of such affection that it actually passed into the common vernacular, and I've seen its use many times since. He occasionally discussed that they came at their political and social and humane passions differently, too, but always arrived at the same position. And if they didn't, he acceded to Joanne's point of view. He was so happily influenced by and in awe of her mind and spirit.

I recall one interview Vernon Scott was doing at a home they occupied for a while off Coldwater Canyon. This was in the late sixties when the confluence of such social afflictions as Vietnam and Richard Nixon and smog and other flagrant pollutions made some of us wonder if there might be a better place to raise kids. There wasn't, but the thought flitted through the mind. Vernon commented that he had been looking into New Zealand and he counted off the reasons. Paul thought about it a moment and then said, "No, there's too much to be done here."

Another time, when they had a rented house just off of Sunset and were, therefore, subject to map-of-the-stars'-homes lookicloos, the conversation was interrupted by the doorbell. Joanne opened the door and said, "Yes, his eyes really are as blue as they are in the movies." And we heard a woman say, "Thank you, Miss Woodward. Have a nice day." And Joanne returned to the conversation. That particular house had a little sign on the front lawn beside the path up from the sidewalk. It read "Please... They've moved. The Fergusons." But it didn't help.

I called her one morning with the reviews of "Paris Blues." She said, "Thanks, but I really don't want to hear them." "But they're great," I insisted. "If I believe the good ones, don't I have to believe the bad ones?" One evening when I took her to an interview at CBS, I was low on gas and asked if she would mind if I stopped at the station across Beverly Boulevard. It was at the very start of eco awareness. The attendant came to the window... attendants still came to your window and they still pumped the gas... and I said, "Fill her up, please... lead-free." Joanne nodded and said, "Well, that's a relief. Why don't people get it? It's their Earth? Why don't they understand?" It's forty years later and they are just starting to. But maybe too late.

Paul chose "Rachel, Rachel" as his directorial debut as an homage and a gift to Joanne. The beautiful and Oscar-nominated Stewart Stern script delved quietly and compassionately into a woman's psyche in ways that no script ever had before. It was "a labor of love" in all of love's meanings. I worked to incorporate that in the campaign. It's hard work to make a film appreciated as a "discovery film." You have to select and pursue exactly the right taste influencers, get them to discover it, build on that. This was before our instantaneous digital awarenesses were even imaginable. "Word of mouth" was the ballgame. Warren Cowan used to insist on word-of-mouth screenings for taxi drivers and hair-dressers, people who talked to people in the course of their daily chores.

Once we got that word cranking in the business, we made an outreach to saturate "Rachel, Rachel" on "the Bel Air circuit." Bel Air is one of the richest residential areas for the entertainment elite. The Bel Air circuit was the network of top industry people who had home screening rooms and who competed to get to screen the hot films first. They "knew" people at the studios, and I'm sure being on the Bel Air circuit was an expensive game, but it was a ready evidence of being wired within the industry. We made aggressive efforts to make "Rachel, Rachel" a prime and easy get for the circuit. The film quickly had the cache, and, most important of all they saw that it delivered beyond their expected delights. So it wasn't a surprise but rather a grand celebration when Paul Newman won the New York Film Critics award as best director. Pre-Oscar awards were not so proliferate then, and the New York Critics honor was a major harbinger of awards to come. So expectations were high on that morning in early February when the media and the expectant, fingers-crossed press agents gathered at the Academy for the announcement of the Oscar nominees for 1968

"Rachel, Rachel" had four… including the big one, Best Film, plus Joanne for Best Actress, Estelle Parsons for Best Supporting actress, and Stewart Stern for Best Adapted Screenplay… but not for Paul as director. We'd had a similar disappointment when Kirk Douglas won the New York Film Critics' prize and the Golden Globe for his performance as Vincent Van Gogh in "Lust For Life" but failed to win the Oscar. But Paul wasn't even nominated for the Oscar for "Rachel, Rachel." . With some regularity, motion pictures nominated for best film fail to get director nominations. But this was a major contender that was very strongly and generally characterized as "a director's film." Of course, all films are that, but some like "Rachel, Rachel" are received as the powerful realization of a director's vision, a vision that powered the film to life in spite of the industry's resistance to films of such fragile, delicate narrative where every brush stroke is meticulous and contributive. How could such a "director's film," already singularly honored for its direction, get nominated without the director along for the ride? The question really bothered all of the people involved with the film and in Paul's high-powered entourage...

Abe Greenberg was the entertainment editor of The Hollywood Citizen-News, which had industrial strength in what was then a six paper town (not counting the trade papers). Paul's omission from the best director fieldstuck in Abe's craw, too. I encouraged him not to let it lie, to get to the "why" of it. Each of the branches of the Academy... editors, actors etc..., selects the nominees in its category or categories, with all of the branches jointly selecting best picture nominees. The list of members of the directors branch was available, certainly for a top journalist, and Abe made up a mailing list (not difficult because many directors had studio deals) and polled the voting directors to find the answer to one simple question: how many of them had seen "Rachel, Rachel." The result was staggering. Even after its best film nomination, even after the official Academy screenings and all the studio screenings of "Rachel, Rachel" as a Best Film nominee, even after all the weeks at local theatres where their Academy card would admit them and a guest, only forty percent of the membership of the directors branch had seen Paul Newman's heralded film. For some reason, that brought closure to the Newman camp.

Until Abe published the story, the industry had pretty much assumed that Oscar voters, without question, saw the key contenders, and "Rachel, Rachel" had certainly been a key contender. It demonstrated to me and to a lot of others that the name of the game was making sure the voters saw your film. Abe's investigative poll very much changed the way Oscar campaigns were contemplated and conducted. No longer the bland assumption that the best films all will be viewed by this select electorate. With time and technology, it came to pass that videos and then DVDs of the films would be sent to Academy members . Guttman and Pam pioneered some of the innovations in this getting-the-eyes business, a few of them so effective that we kept them our own private edge for a few years until the town caught on.

A Conflict of Interest

Paul was represented at Rogers & Cowan by John Foreman who was very classy, delightfully acerbic and really more of a manager than a press agent. So most of the press agently tasks… writing releases, setting and working interviews, promoting films… fell to me. John eventually joined Freddie Fields in his management firm CMA where he served Paul in that capacity before moving into production to produce "Butch Cassidy And The Sundance Kid" and other films for Paul and some great films without him, including best film nominee "Prizzi's Honor." I worked on the release publicity for Paul on "The Hustler" in 1961. When Paul was nominated for that film, for what many thought his finest performance, and Maximilian Schell was nominated for "Judgment At Nuremberg," company policy dict atedthat I be recused from Paul's campaign, so that the two nominees could have completely independent campaigns. In such situations when the agency had multiple clients competing for the same awards, different account execs would be assigned to each, so each client would get the best possible campaign without any modification to benefit another. In a publicity agency with such a wide and powerful clientele, these conflicts arose often, and no one suffered or benefitted from any special preference. One year we repped four of the five best actor nominees, and none of them made… nor might they have… any complaints.

Max, being very specifically my account, a very close friend and our daughters' godfather, was my baby for the campaign. Paul, whose managerial and agency entourage was a who's-who of important "contacts" for Rogers & Cowan (power people who drive major stars to your firm or help keep them there), was much more the direct preoccupation of Warren Cowan and John Foreman. I was keeping Max visible and doing a subtle campaign because one of the other best actor nominees that year was Spencer Tracy, who also had been nominated for "Judgment At Nuremberg." Max did not have mere reverence for Tracy as man and as actor; he had awe. We agreed it would be unseemly for him to labor to win out over his and everyone else' hero. A balls-out, glad-handing campaign with Max showing up everywhere and milking every conceivable interview was definitely not Max's style. In the first place, Spencer Tracy had become a dear and idolized friend for Max. We were making good and respectful moves, one of which was that it wasn't an aggressive and visible striving.

We were both (as was Max's respected William Morris agent, Phil Kellogg) content with the nomination because it had already placed this young Swiss actor so firmly on the map. Brilliant, not yet 30, devastatingly handsome and attractive to women (as well as romantically involved with many of the most famous of them), how many brass rings do you need to grab? It was firmly understood that this was merely the first of many nominations or awards for Maximilian Schell, which certainly proved to be the case. He was doomed to be, perennially, a great actor in great roles in addition to being locked-in as a hot leading man... very much as his sister Maria (also a client) had done as a sure-thing great actress/ leading lady. Don't let people kid you that nominations are not campaigned for. The appearance of no campaign is, in fact, a very specific KIND of campaign.... Tactic # 12 in PR 101.

Max directed most of his interviews and appearances to lauding his competitors., and very sincerely so. I would not normally think that the best strategy, but in this case, it seemed to be. Specifically, he did often acknowledge the sheer brilliance of Paul's "Hustler" performance. I did not want Paul's devotees in the office or the vast and powerful part of the industry so massively invested in Paul to think of Max as a usurper. It was generally held that this was Paul's year, especially since "Judgment" had two competing Best Actor nominees to divide the film's "vote." Moreover, "Judgment," with seven great actors starring in a kind of mosaic narrative, each with killer plotlines and scenes, did not permit the kind of dominant tent pole performance with which Paul carried "Hustler." George C. Scott, Jackie Gleason and Piper Laurie were astonishing in "The Hustler," but Paul moved that film with a savage fury and determination. It was clearly HIS year, as the year before had belonged to Burt Lancaster's "Elmer Gantry" performance in another title-role.

For most years through the 70s, it was widely believed that films had "votes," meaning blocs of voters who had loyalties to vote in a specific manner. In particular, it was assumed that voters associated with one studio or another might vote their loyalties. Thanks to the secret ballot, that probably wasn't the case, and it definitely is not the case now, largely because so few employees these days are lifers at one studio or the other. There is clearly no longer the perceived self interest in a home team win.

We were so convinced and content that Max had already collected and banked his benefits from this performance with the nomination, Max had determined that he wouldn't make the trip to Hollywood for the awards, but would continue his skiing trip in Austria. with some dazzling beauty whose identity I knew not. I had surrendered his seats. At the rehearsal the day before the Oscarcast, there was no big picture of him in a seat so that the show's director and cameramen would know where to "pick him up." In the middle of the night preceding the awards, I got a call from Max saying that he had stored his skis and was about to drive down to Vienna or Zurich with only three hours to make the four-hour drive to jump on a plane which might, with luck, get him to Hollywood just as the awards were starting. More calls were exchanged that night as some avalanche on the road held him up or when he almost took a shortcut off some cliff. They were holding the plane for him at the airport. Oscar morning was a flurry of calls to retrieve his seat, to have a limo meet him, to have a tux there that might approximate his size and to lay aside a room for him to change in a Santa Monica motel near the Santa Monica Civic Auditorium, where the awards were held. No one thought Max's name was in the envelope, but the Academy parted the sea to make sure a nominee was there just in case... Although Warren Cowan and Rogers Cowan had vested interests in a Paul Newman win, Warren took a guiding hand in assuring the tricky logistics of getting Max to the Oscars in time. He told the Academy just to have the limo available to Max at the holding area and that we would take care of his pick-up. He had credentials messengered so that Sandy Friedman, office boy on his way to top PR pro and a driver of remarkable and stomach-clenching insanity, could collect Max at the airport and deliver him to the Awards. Meanwhile I was across from the Oscar site, overseeing preparations at the motel which the Academy took over for Bob Hope's and other dressing rooms and as a general staging area. Max' plane was, of course, late. Sandy had to do his speed maniac act on side streets to avoid the jammed freeway. Max arrived physically drained by the trans-oceanic mad dash, emotionally siphoned and hyped at the same time, given his acceptance that he didn't have a chance to win. He was one great massage shy of getting to the auditorium on anything other than a litter. A masseur? In the few remaining minutes? At which point, Bob Hope strode out of his suite, as only Bob Hope could stride, heading coolly towards his opening the show in about six minutes, and I asked if he had a masseur on him. He looked at Max and said, "Yeah, you look like you need it. Ralph!" And Ralph the masseur looked out of Bob's suite. Bob pointed to Max and said, "Take care of my son, will you?"

The show was an hour-and-a-half over by the time the limo raced Max across the street. I hadn't had time to dress or to get my credentials, so I hurried home to see Max lose with dignity, the ironic end to a crazy hunch. Gisela's parents were visiting from Germany, and they had a good sense of the tension Gisela and I were feeling. Max was family. All that subtle but exhausting campaign and all that rush... for nothing. A major actress/dancer was doing a stomach-pumping, bottom-bouncing dance of the period, and my mother-in-law was agonized that this poor girl had become so ill in front of millions of people. Then the award. A shot of Max slumped gloomily in his seat, physically beat, drained of hope. They announce his name. He stays frozen in his slump, overwhelmed with having lost, having made that crazy race for... but it slowly occurs to him that the sound of his name was not merely a mocking echo in his brain.

The next day I arrived at the office to a traitor's reception. The farm had been bet on Paul's handsome nose. The apple cart had been upset, and I was expected to clean it up. There were a lot of people-you-don't-want-to-make-mad who we would have been thrilled if mad at Rogers & Cowan was all they were. "Well, you really fucked up this one, Guttman," one staff member said. I don't believe he was speaking for all, but you could have built an igloo out of the welcome I was receiving... If anyone disagreed with the party line, they sure weren't going to do it in public. I went into Warren's office, and his look was not that of anger but rather disappointment. "You HAD to DO it, huh?" he said. "Do what, Warren? My job? You like Max, too." "I love him, but that's beside the point. Just lay low for a while with certain people". "Did Paul say anything to you?" "He and Joanne are the only ones who haven't." I started out of the office, but his voice caught me. "Richard..." He was the only one who called me that. I turned. "Good job."

I went over at midday to the Chateau Marmont hotel where Max always stayed. We had to work out a thank you ad he would take in the trade papers. As we were working on it, he said, "It costs more to win than to lose." I knew he was joking. We couldn't agree on what words of gratitude suited the occasion, and I told him we were getting too late for them to lay out the ad. He said they should just reproduce his handwriting, and he wrote, "No man is an island unto himself. Each is a part of the continent, a piece of the main. John Donne" and then he listed everyone he wished to thank and then "thank you for being part of my continent." "Max," I pleaded," they're going to think John Donne won the Oscar

We need your name." "They'll know." "Who'll know?" "They," he said, pointing to the names. Another big argument, and finally, at the very end, he wrote, "Max."

As I was leaving, I said, "You know, this changes the whole game." "It's just a line in my biography," he insisted. Well, he made sure of that by going off to do a play in Vienna and then shooting a "Hamlet" in German for German television. But even absence or indifference couldn't hold that talent down. He did have a point, though. All glory has its season, and the length of memory and heat varies. Once upon a June, barely three months after the Oscars, I asked an actress if she could name the four people who had won the recent Best Acting and Best Supporting Acting awards. She couldn't name any.... And she was one of them. Of course, it was Cloris Leachman, and she was, as likely as not, just having me on. But most people in Hollywood would have drawn a similar blank, including some winners.

Two stand-alone monuments to larger-than-life are, you will most certainly agree, Orson Welles and Sir Laurence Olivier.

Welles, who eventually and unfortunately matched his unbounded genius with his unbounded corpulence, entered movie-making at a time when it was assumed that all of the rules had been created and carved into concrete. So "Citizen Kane" and "Magnificent Ambersons" seemed like an alien intrusion. He had all of these wonderful new rules all his own, and he chose to do it the hard way... starting off with a film that was a lacerating critique of the most powerful man in the American media, William Randolph Hearst. So a lot of media cards were stacked against him. And he alienated much of the Hollywood establishment by being so brilliant and so unlimited by the age of twenty-two. Geniuses three times his age were limited by Hollywood superstructure rules, so why not he? But brilliant he stayed even after his appetites for food and for film freedoms ate him out of house and home. My rare experiences of him came toward the end when his girth gave him little else to be oyher than Orson Welles, but the talents were still expansive. Guttman & Pam long represented the Merv Griffin show, and I made a point to attend the tapings whenever Welles was there. It was like being in the proximity of Leonardo or Ludwig. I was always prepared for an epiphany... and one night it came.

Merv taped the show at his theatre and office complex on Vine Street. You could enter from the parking lot behind the building with direct access to backstage and the wings, which is what Welles did, because, sadly, he was so wide that it was difficult for him to manage the narrow hallway which led to the green room toward the front where all of the other guests gathered to watch the show and ready themselves for their own entrance. As result, Welles would do his waiting in a small room adjacent to the stage entrance, a room large enough to hold only one Orson Welles… and there most certainly was only one Orson Welles.

I arrived at the show late. Mr. Welles was already in his little room, busily distracted drawing sketches on a large pad of paper. Later, when Merv introduced him, I went into the theatre and stood at the back so that I could experience his appearance live. Merv was at ease with everyone, interested in everyone, but the two people who most commanded his interest and awe were Dr. Armand Hammer and Orson Welles. His personal office was definitely out of bounds if Dr. Hammer was visiting. We had to speak softly so as not to disturb them. This brilliant businessman and master of the world was Merv's guru. Merv, in turn or perhaps as result, was the brightest business man with whom I've ever worked… and with John Paul deJoria, Kathy Ireland, Wayne Rogers, Clint Eastwood and George Barrie in the mix, that's saying a lot. Merv also was like a kid at the feet of Orson Welles, particularly when the moment arrived, as it always did, that Welles did his magic. He picked an audience member at random who chose a name from a basket, everyone in the audience having scribbled his or her name into the collection. The man selected stood up, a professorial type whom Welles then engaged in conversation, instructing him to think of some public figure as they spoke.

Picking up the pad and sketching pen which had been placed before him, Citizen Welles began to draw as they chatted. Visibly, Orson Welles was having trouble. Finally, he put his pad down and said that the man's mind wasn't being very cooperative. "All I'm hearing is anger. Is this someone you don't like?" "Hate," the man said. "Well, just calm down and try to picture his face. The man did, and Orson Welles concentrated and then started to sketch in earnest. Finally he said, "Is this the object of your scorn?" And he held to the man and the cameras a very good caricature of Henry Kissinger. Yep, that was the guy. Much applause. Someone else' name was picked from the basket and Mr. Welles asked that woman to pick anyone else. She selected a heavyset woman in a sweatshirt. This lady was very nervous and had trouble concentrating when asked to think of a celebrity. Again, it wasn't coming through clearly. "You don't have to be so nervous, dear," Welles offered. "Why don't you come up here with me? Maybe you're just too far away." No, no, she couldn't. "I'm not dressed for… we were just shopping and then someone said there were tickets, and…" But he cajoled her to the stage, and indeed she was ill-clad for her weight in shorts and almost shaking when she arrived next to him. He patted her hand to calm her. "Now let's just talk, but you think about your celebrity, and I hope it's not someone you hate." "Someone I love," she offered, and he told her that was a great relief. He started to sketch as they spoke and she calmed. Finally he asked if this was the person she loved, and the sketch was of Bob Hope… and that's precisely whom she had in mind. To her delight, Welles signed the caricature for her. We were all in a thrall of mystification. We went to commercial for Mr. Welles to depart. Merv never showed Mr. Welles laboring on or off the set.

At the end of the program, I passed Mr. Welles' cubicle as I went to my car, and he had, of course, already left. But on the floor were perhaps a dozen of the drawings he had been doodling before. I went in and looked at them. They were all practice sketches of Henry Kissinger and Bob Hope. What we had seen was not magic but rather, and something much more to be treasured, a masterful theatrical production by that ultimate master of theatricality and controlled attention, Orson Welles. I had finally witnessed a production of the Mercury Theatre. It was a missing piece from the great scavenger hunt of my life, and I was thrilled. So thrilled that I forgot to take one of the drawings. What an idiot!

My only actual conversation with Mr. Welles came when he had miraculously agreed to present an award to Warren Beatty… miraculously in that he was not given to public appearances. But he and Warren were the only talents ever to be nominated for Best Actor, Best Director, producer of a Best Film nominee and Best Screenplay for the same film, Mr. Welles for "Citizen Kane" and Warren for "Heaven Can Wait" and "Reds." Mr. Welles arrived early and I tried to entertain him with my inexhaustible curiosity about every thought he'd ever had and every miracle he'd ever pulled from his hat. I was particularly interested as to why he had done his character in "The Lady From Shanghai" with such a pronounced Irish accent, and he said, "The Irish are a mystical people." The cutting of that film's final shoot-out in the funhouse hall of mirrors was a major subject for me, and he was amused that our final exam in film editing at UCLA had been for each to assemble his own cut of the raw footage from that sequence in which maintaining screen direction… cutting coherently so that an actor on the right side of the screen doesn't suddenly bounce over to the left side of the screen…. were thrown to the wind by the constant use of mirrored shots and the intention to confuse. Images that appeared to be at some specific "there" were actually at some multi-mirrored somewhere else. But I had my conversation with Orson Welles, Charles Foster Kane, Othello, Harry Lime, "Touch of Evil's" Hank Quinlan, all of the above. I'd spent a childhood sitting on the floor in front of the family radio, waiting in thrall to the very end of his Mercury Theatre broadcasts when he would say "I remain… your obedient servant" Serve us well he obviously did, often quite disobediently but always to our fascination.

How could anyone complain about an occupation so generous of brushes with greatness?

Another strange insight into Welles' deep but idiosyncratic talent came when a top lawyer had overseen the contract on a script sale for me. Instead of payment, he wanted me to track down the rights to an Australian novel called "Dead Calm." A dedicated seaman, he wanted to film the story of a couple whose sailing vessel is trapped in a dead calm on open seas when one morning a mysterious sailboat appears nearby, and no sign of life. When the husband rows over to see what the matter is, a young man from that vessel hijacks the husband's skiff, commandeers his boat and, sails off with the wife, leaving the husband on the sinking mystery ship with two murdered people and no means of giving chase. My research showed that the last rights resided with Orson Welles. Jerry Pam went off to Cannes shortly thereafter and made a trip to visit Welles' former assistant to find out what happened to the rights. "Oh," she said, "Mr. Welles made the movie." But it had never made it to exhibition. She told Jerry that Welles starred in it with Jeanne Moreau and Laurence Harvey. When I checked Larry, he confirmed it, saying that he had jumped at the chance to work with Orson Welles. "And it actually was filmed?" "About a half or a third of it." Larry recalled fondly that the experience had been everything he'd expected, including the abrupt and incomplete conclusion. "What, why, how?" I stammered. "He ran out of either money or belief." The film eventually was shot again as an Australian production which launched the acting careers of Nicole Kidman, Sam Neill and Billy Zane and propelled director Phillip Noyce to major Hollywood productions.

Welles' mind-reading was one thing, but I barely survived another instance of instant theatre, the contrivance of another maddening film genius, John

Carpenter. These guys are supremely sane, and it is we whom they make crazy as we wander fitfully through the nooks and crannies of their imaginations. John, that master of terror and the hallowed concocter of "Halloween" horror, was, by my arrangement, to receive the George Pal Career Achievement award from the Academy of Science Fiction and Horror. It was a big deal, and when I asked John who he wanted me to get to present it, he said he'd already taken care of that. It would be Frank Darabont who had established his own masters degree in film-making with "The Shawshank Redemption." What a great choice I thought… or at least up until Darabont took the podium to make his presentation speech. The gist of his introduction was that he'd been asked to hand John Carpenter this award bearing the name of George Pal, who, he said, was Hungarian and a great filmmaker, neither of which could be said for John Carpenter. A gasp from the audience which had gathered to honor Carpenter. The gasp did not dissuade Darabont. "Give John Carpenter an award with George Pal's name on it? If I had my choice, I wouldn't give Carpenter an *ashtray* with George Pal's name on it." A rush of audience dislocation surpassing "Springtime For Hitler." Darabont went on for fifteen minutes reading in detail every horrible review… who knew there could have been that many?… that John Carpenter ever received. The audience was roiling. I was in a state of shock, happy only that I had not made the presenter selection myself. I looked at John, and he had this mad smile on his face, and I was sure that the humiliation of it all had driven him out of his mind. It went on… it went on. Finally, it was Leonard Nimoy's bright and outspoken wife Susan who could stand it no more, and she yelled out… "OK, ok, we get the point… you hate John Carpenter… well, WE don't, so just shut up and hand him the goddam award." She spoke for us all. Darabont sighed with relief and explained that when he accepted giving this award, he had to swear to deliver exactly the speech that had been written for him by…… John Carpenter. Everyone was stunned, and then there was spontaneous applause for a great piece of theatre. Why I asked John afterwards about his reason for staging it, I can't imagine. His whole life and art has been given over to horrifying audiences. I asked if this was payback to me for some transgression, and he said that that certainly was a consideration. It was, everyone agreed in exhausted relief, great Grand Guignol.

Sir Laurence Olivier is rather a poster boy for larger-than-life. I'd seen him perform "The Entertainer" on the London stage, and at a certain point Rogers

& Cowan was engaged to sell the film version for the U.S. I flew to London to try to get Sir Larry to do something he hadn't done before... promote a film for the American domestic market. I checked into the Dorchester and was ushered to what was either their smallest room or their largest broom closet. But that was fine. Laurence Harvey had arranged for me to meet with Olivier (who was appearing on stage in "Rhinoceros,") so I left word where I could be reached and went off about other business there. When I got back to the hotel that evening, the doorman, who almost didn't let me in upon arrival, was suddenly aglow with great and empathetic curiosity as to whether I'd had a lovely day. When I got to the desk, they did everything but roll out a red carpet. There was great apology that I'd been given the wrong room and they hoped the new one to which my possessions had been transferred would be more to my liking. It was a magnificent suite for the same price as the other. When I opened my only message, I understood. It said, "Sir Laurence Olivier looks forward to your discussion tomorrow in his dressing room following the matinee performance." That was the highlight of the trip, the status inferred because of some small association with a revered acting great, with a creator infinitely larger than life.

Gisela and I had the same experience when, while staying at a far smaller and markedly more humble hotel in London, we wew scheduled to have a meeting with Glenda Jackson, who preferred to meet us where we were staying. Thank goodness the Durrants hotel had a very charming paneled library. The staff brought us tea on far better china than I'd seen there before. I talked her into letting us do an Oscar campaign for "Hedda," although she felt no one in Hollywood had seen the film. That probably was true, but many had seen her on stage when she did Ibsen's "Hedda Gabler" in Hollywood earlier that year, and she was on a run of three fairly consecutive nominations, including a best actress win for "A Touch Of Class," for which Guttman & Pam had done the campaign. Moreover, I had a secret weapon in having invented and secured for Guttman & Pam's private use the single way of showing movies to Academy members on cable TV. (More on this, my favorite coup, in a later chapter entitled Damage Control.) Only the films Guttman & Pam handled would enjoy that advantage. I was pretty sure our nomination campaign for her could be successful. She didn't believe it until her production partner, Bob Enders, called her to advise that she'd received her fourth best actress Oscar nomination. Gisela and I had already banked our reward for having attracted an acting immortal to the little Durrants Hotel. The next morning we all got double portions of marmalade at our breakfast table. As for Olivier, when I met him backstage on that prior trip, he was charming, kind, indulgent and intransigent. He listened politely and then politely declined. I pressed him for a reason, offering to have interviews no longer than twenty minutes. He said it wasn't the time of the chat, "It's the forever that the words they put in my mouth will exist." I offered to have each interview tape recorded and they could draw only from that. "No, no," he smiled gently, "that would be even worse. Then I would have only myself to blame." Go to America to promote "The Entertainer?" Not, he insisted, until he had first swum the English Channel.

It's hard to talk larger-than-lifers without mentioning Johnny Wooden… Coach. He lived his values. We had, during the magic UCLA basketball years of the 60s, the pleasure of some social contact with him and his wife Nell and some of his various teams, particularly with Mike Warren who was for a short period my intern, Mike Warren who later honed his considerable acting chops on "Hillstreet Blues" and whom Coach Wooden called his smartest guard ever, the best review any athlete ever received. At a party following a one-point win over USC, Gisela was talking with Mike and with Coach Wooden, and she started to celebrate the thrill of the final play in which Mike drove to the basket for a contested lay-up and then, at the height of his leap, made a last second no-look pass to Lucius Allen who had a clean eight-footer which went in at the buzzer. Throughout her enthusing, Mike was making no-no-no signals with his index fingers which were pointing up and quivering like uncertain compass needles. Coach, Mike explained, doesn't like anyone to go for a shot he isn't *certain* he can make. "Michael did something wrong, and then he did something right," the greatest coach of all time said. "It's better to know you're going to do it right the first time." If that isn't a guideline for life, I don't know what is. We all get by with something we did right after we did something wrong, but Coach's outlook can save you a lot of sweat and, sometimes, a lot of grief. You don't always know that that no-look pass is going to lead to points.

Back to Henrik Ibsen. His "The Wild Duck," which delves into the insanity of committing one's life to the whole truth, blunt and uncompromising, is a great salve to a press agent's conscience and elected professional set of values. That may be his appeal to me. One time in the market we bumped into the delightful actor, comedian and poet Henry Gibson who, along with the rest of the "Laugh In" cast, was in a period of intense currency. My daughter Monika was about eight then, and I introduced her to Mr. Henry Gibson. "My daddy loves to read your plays," she told him. "My plays?" he responded, "do you mean my poems?" "No, your plays. He keeps them in the bathroom. The one I want to read is 'The Doll's House.'" "My dear, he said to her, "I'm honored to be confused into such company." I met Henry in another market a few years ago. It was Oscar season, and I invited him to one of our screenings. He said he couldn't go because it would be the first anniversary of his wife's passing. It was the way he said it, and it was no surprise when, shortly thereafter, he left us, too.

The Ibsen/Gibson connection reminds me of another occasion when we had some contingent of our European star firmament over for dinner in our little valley house. The conversation was very sophisticated and we were having to be very cryptic in our discussion because it was quite anatomical with numerous references to the male genitals which we, by unspoken common consent, were referring to with the term "phallic symbol" because Moni was sitting at the table with us. Even though she was only six or seven, she was trying to structure what it was we were talking about. And it was phallic symbol this and phallic symbol that. Suddenly, Moni brought her spoon down on the table loudly enough to get our full attention. "OK, you guys," she said, "who's Felix Gimble?"

Long daily drives to and from work are the heavy price I pay for the bucolic pleasures of living in the far western reaches of Malibu. To retain sanity, I fell into the habit of listening to books on CD. Michael Redgrave took me through "Paradise Lost," Stacy Keach embodied Hemingway and each of his characters in every short story Papa ever wrote. That is a don't-miss as is author James Dickey's reading of his "Deliverance." In his soft Georgia speak?... better even than the great movie John Boorman made from it. One book that charmed me was George Burns' reading of his ode to Gracie Allen, "Amazing Gracie." In it we learn that Gracie was an expert Irish step dancer, and that when Fred Astaire expressed interest in having them in one of his films, a condition was that they be able to dance. Gracie asked George to show her his stuff, and he tried. "You can dance only with one leg," she concluded. He argued, but she insisted the other leg couldn't dance. She taught him some steps with which it might LOOK like he was dancing with both legs.

When they auditioned, Astaire watched him and then said, "Nice try, except you can dance with only one leg. I think we can work around that. "

One day in Burns' reinvigorated post-"Oh, God" career, I answered my office phone, and the caller identified himself as George Burns. Now anybody can do a George Burns, so of course I was suspicious. He said he'd met a young songwriter and how could he (George Burns or the fellow purporting to be him) find a contact to get one of his songs to Barbra Streisand . I knew who could help and who, in veneration of George Burns' comedy brilliance, might help. But how could I be sure this wasn't the old I'm-George-Burns scam? So I asked the fellow on the other end of the line if it was true that he could dance with only one leg. Suddenly he was very animated about the subject and gave me some further laughs about his one-leggedness. "Which leg was it" I asked. His answer corresponded to what was in the book. I put him on to the right guy, but nothing happened to it. Maybe the song was nothing you could dance to.

I had a similar call from somebody purporting to be Harpo Marx. Our paths had crossed (although we hadn't met) when he'd contributed one of his personal paintings to a big charity art auction I was assisting, a beautiful oil, a quiet, graceful, intricately detailed landscape. It caused him to have my name and number and he wanted help with arrangements for a trip he was making to Israel. The trouble was…. How can you recognize the sound of Harpo Marx' voice? I'd never heard him speak. Oscar Levant wrote about him copiously and lovingly in his various ingenious memoirs, so I had plenty of questions to throw at him in a kind of interrogation. He stood up to the test, and when I met him, those soft eyes reassured me I had the right guy.

BEL AIR CIRCUIT REDUX… I've already mentioned the function of this privileged means of putting films before industry "taste-makers" in the happy comforts of their own lavish homes. It was a valued privilege to be on the guest lists for film-viewing of such catered luxury. Of these pleasures I will now speak. Even the advent of DVDs and the advance availability of new films in that format has not materially reduced these coveted screenings, with projected DVD now the norm. But a half century back, being on Bel Air invitee lists was a social and even professional imperative. It was always good company, good food and a good chance to see upcoming releases just a little bit ahead of the others. Best of all, you met the most interesting people.

We had numerous charming exposures to Groucho Marx, mostly because he was a regular at the Saturday night screenings at famed agent Abby Greshler's home in, yes, Bel Air. Every time he saw Gisela, Groucho would say "Who IS this broad?" She always took it as a compliment, and it certainly seemed to be an expression of either admiration or lust, and in Hollywood they don't really distinguish between the two. Lust is considered a good review. On one occasion, much further into the famous mustachioed one's infirmities, we were at Sidney Sheldon's Beverly Hills home on a weekend morning, and Groucho, as was his habit or at least the habit of the attendant who walked him past the house each morning, came in for his customary bowl of cereal. When he saw Gisela, he said, "Who is this broad? Is she the same broad that I always say who's this broad?" Assured that she was, he demanded to know why she hadn't been served cereal, too. So she had to have cereal with him. But that was the end of the conversation.

One screening night at Abby's, Groucho came in a little late. Abby politely enquired if he could take Groucho's coat, to which Groucho snapped, "Why? Is there going to be a fight?" At which point, Ruthie, another regular, lamented, "If I knew it was going to be this kind of party, I'd have worn my best underwear." A night at Abby and Vi Greshler's palatial manse was like a night at a Friars Club roast. Even a bad film could be an entertaining experience at Abby's. One night it was an adventure flick with a distinguished cast but which was so preposterous that in any other projection circumstance it would have ground to a halt by popular demand at the end of the first reel. However, within minutes of its start, at the first warning clinker, Groucho came up with a crack that drowned the next two minutes of dialogue in laughter. Then it was Tony Randall's turn, and Don Knotts, and even the less famously comedic among us tried our comedic hands. Vince Edwards, who incarnated TV's first big hit doctor, Ben Casey, dished out amusing cutting comments with surgical precision. Soon it was a competition, with the sharpness of each crack rated on a scale ranging from cheers and hilarity to boos and hisses. Gisela and I agreed on the way home that the ridiculous action flick had been the most enjoyable comedy we'd ever seen. And not a thought for the poor people who had loaned out their film to spread word of its excellence throughout the film community.

Speaking of fame, which is one of the purposes of this exercise of recall, it is indeed, fleeting. Which perhaps is the *raison d'etre for* press agents or at least the reason some people hire us. Gisela, not averse to rubbing it in, likes to remind me that the commodity I sell... fame... is "passing, of the moment and evaporative." "So are flowers," I countered, "but that's no reason not to grow gardens." Fame is an unstable element, but it wasn't always that way. The Greeks and Romans carved their venerated contemporaries in stone. We have Mount Rushmore and the various memorials in D.C., but, no, immortality is not what it's cracked up to be and certainly not what it used to be. In these fickle times, even immortality is here today and gone tomorrow. A very talented soon-to-be star asked me who I thought was the greatest actor in films. "Well, I've handled so many of them, I can't differentiate," I parried. But he pinned me down, persisting, "Ok, then the greatest actor you've never represented." The greatest one I never represented? My mind flickered on Brando and Bogart, Olivier and March, Nicholson, DeNiro, Tracy, but I said, "Charles Laughton." And the dedicated young actor said, "Who's that?"

Chapter 3

Fame Isn't the Prize, It's the Price

I have an actor friend who gets through a crowd and through life with one overriding rule… don't make eye contact. It's a great and effective policy, especially for stars who inspire a dangerous sense of possession in fans when in the open public. Eye contact is a signed invitation. Having legions of fans attracted to the flame of your talent or acclaim can be a very mixed blessing. *Fame isn't the prize, it's the price.*

A BROAD DAYLIGHT KIDNAPPING AT CHICAGO'S O'HARE. Often stars are betrayed by their own good manners and wind up being held hostage by intrusive fans. Gene Hackman and I were on a flight to Buffalo for the "Superman II" press junket. One might think that "civilians" (Hollywood-speak… anyone not in the entertainment business) in first class might be a tad more considerate of a celebrity's privacy, but some of these privileged individuals presume. For the last hour before the Chicago stopover Gene was prisoner of a large and noisy man pitching his ownership of the film rights to the life of "the greatest baseball star of all time." "Well," Gene said, too polite to tune the guy out, "I'm too old, unless it's Satchel Paige." The wannabe producer didn't get the joke and didn't blink. He kept going on about how it was the role Gene was born to play, finally revealing that the player was Ernie Banks." "Are you aware that Ernie Banks is black?" Gene asked with greater civility than was called for. "So is Satchel Paige,"

the guy persisted, "Five minutes ago you were DYING to play HIM. The miracle of movies, Gene! The miracle of movies!" At which point the pilot mercifully set the plane down. "Chicago," Gene smiled, "I guess this is where you get off." "I'm gonna sell you on this," the guy said, "I'm not getting off." "Then I will," Gene mumbled, and we exited into the terminal.

Now here is where the story takes a turn that confirms that Fate is indeed gracious and where it bestowed upon us one of my favorite moments. Hackman and I had a particular affection for the late and lamented critic, Gene Siskel, whom we suddenly saw walking ahead of us, obviously on his way to join the plane that would take us all to Buffalo. When you really like someone and he really knows that you do, you are free to pull really mean jokes on him. I don't know how we decided it, there was no discussion, not even a nod. It was just something we simultaneously understood we would do. Gene and I came up behind Siskel and each of us clasped him firmly under an elbow, while Hackman held Siskel's neck from behind in a firm grip that defied the turning of the head. We lifted him a few inches off the floor and started scooting him across the terminal. Siskel, in a strained voice about an octave higher than his handsome Midwest baritone on Siskel & Ebert, began to explain to whoever we were that his paper had an absolutely ironclad rule against paying ransom, "actually to discourage situations exactly like this. And I don't have the kind of money you might think I have" and so on with a very convincing recitation of why this crime would not pay. At short length, we set him down at the check-in counter for the flight. A little dazed, Siskel turned around to see us. "I knew it was you guys," he said with a grandly stated nonchalance.

I had a personal opportunity to see how Gene Hackman always has a firm grip on things. It was the day of the Mohammed Ali/Ken Norton rematch at the Forum in Inglewood somewhere in the early 70s. Gene was working, as I recall, on Arthur Penn's "Night Moves." Considering the excellence of that script, I understood when Gene called that morning to say that he wanted to take the screenwriter, Alan Sharp, to the fight and did we know any good scalpers? Apparently we did, because Christy Cane, our Dashiell Hammett-esque Jane-of-all-trades whose mysterious contacts I never questioned but about which I often wondered, called him an hour later to say that she had two tickets in the 19th row, $1600 apiece. Gene was pleased. Christy, Effie Perrine with a 40 inch bustline, got things done. With her, Sam Spade wouldn't have needed a gun.

Shortly after noon, I got a call from Hugh O'Brian, TV's first great western series star… whose Wyatt Earp made TV safe for big hit western series just like the earlier Wyatt had madeTombstone safe for school marms and western dime novel authors. Hugh was a client who owned my affections because his Hugh O'Brian Youth Foundation helped and continues to help thousands of kids get a fair shake in life and he has generously availed each youngster of his personal help and considerable contacts for years. There long have been and still are always dozens of HOBY kids in extraordinarily high positions in Washington and always a few in the White House… kids without access until Hugh O'Brian came into their lives. "How would you like to see the fight?" he asked. "Hugh, thanks, but I'm not really a fan." It was and is true. I was a sports writer as a teenager and during my time in Europe, I would constantly visit the American embassies for the two things I missed most… malted milks and the chance to hear the college football games. In the half century since then, I haven't had more than a dozen malts or seen more than a dozen games live. But boxing was especially low on my need-to-see list. "Hugh, it's a great gesture, but don't waste something that special on me." "Second row." "Even so…" "Guy who's inviting?… interested in investing in films." "Second row, huh?" I said, suddenly engaged. "Soap guy from Fresno." We arranged for Hugh to pick me up at the gas station on La Cienega and Olympic and we were directed to a special parking spot at the Forum by a half dozen guys who greeted him with "Hey Wyatt." The soap guy proved an interesting conversationalist and after he hosted a very expensive meal in the Stadium Club, we proceeded with him to our second row seats.

I was enjoying the pre-fight experience immensely. Even representing Elizabeth Taylor's and Kathy Ireland's famous jewelry enterprises, Jane Seymour's new eminence in the gems trade and having exalted Harry Winston Jewels, Kazanzian Jewels and others for pay along the way, I can still honestly say that I have never in my life seen at the same time as many karats as glistened in those front rows. Well, I suppose in the Iranian treasury vault in Tehran, but it's a very close call, because on that fisticuffs evening, territory was being marked in diamonds and emeralds… and that was just the guys. Suddenly my reverie was interrupted by a vice-like grip from behind. "How did you get better tickets than I did?" a deep and familiar voice growled. "Because I have a better press agent?" I offered with unturned head. "Second fucking row?" Gene said. "Soap guy from Fresno. Interested in backing movies. Want to meet him?" I asked. "No," Gene said, "I'll just go back to my seats next to the hot dog stand and behind the steel beam. Know where I can rent some binoculars?" I told him that if anything happened in the fight, I'd send word back.

With all due respect to the people who buy the tickets, the word "fan" derives from the word "fanatic." From the start of Hollywood publicity, a key goal of studio press departments was to make stars the object of public fantasy. That can get amazingly and sometimes amusingly out of hand. A perfect example of the convoluted psychology of fan fanaticism was driven home to me once when Gisela and I were in New York with Christopher Reeve for a junket promoting one of his films. Junkets occur thirty of forty times a year, usually a weekend, during which a studio gathers a hundred print press and electronic press in a hotel shortly before a film's release. The stars and the film's other interview-worthies grind out the charming chitchat to gather free minutes and free inches of promotional exposure. Like most free things, it's expensive.

On this one, held at New York's Plaza Hotel, Colin Dangaard came to the hospitality room for the Sunday buffet breakfast during the junket for "Monsignor." Colin was a junket regular, a widely syndicated Australian journalist who (his nearly unintelligible Down Under accent aside) was almost a dead ringer for singer/song-writer John Denver. This incident transpired at the height of Denver's well-earned mega-popularity.

Colin had a bemused smile as he ladled bacon and eggs onto his plate I asked him what her name was. "I never found out," he answered. "For the first time in a long time, Colin, you have my rapt attention," I said. "Well, I came back to my room last night at about three… you know how it is. And I get in, and I realize that the lights had already been on and that there's this girl in my bed." "Talk about room service." "No, she was there on her own, sitting up reading. So I say 'Oh, excuse me, I must be in the wrong room,' but she says 'No, Mr. Denver, this is your room. And I'm your biggest fan, as you are about to find out'. And I come back with 'no no you don't understand.' But she says 'no it's YOU who doesn't understand. I want to thank you for all the pleasure you've given me and are about to give me.' At which point she drops the blanket and I can see it's quite a present she intends to extend. But this I can't do under the circumstances, and I insist I'm not Denver and she insists I am, getting a little testy in the process. So I say, 'ok, I'll prove it,' and I launch into 'Rocky Mountain High' and suddenly she's convinced and really pissed and leaps from the bed screaming at the top of her lungs 'You're not John Denver, you fat-head phony' at which point I realize how attractively naked she is and I start to give the whole thing a second consideration, but she's pulling on her clothes, screaming at me that I'm a lying sonovabitch who lured her there under false pretense, that she has a mind to call the cops, yelling that I'm a fake and a sex pervert and throwing everything loose at me. And then, just as the door is about to close behind her, she whirls back in and screams 'And I'll NEVER buy another one of your fucking records!!'"

You can discount that as garden variety schizophrenia, but actually it's very typical fan double-think... a common case of a fan's fantasy taking one step or more back from reality. Here are some other fan lunacies that almost any star can match. I arrived at the Guttman & Pam office one morning to find a headline about our client Jaclyn Smith slashed across the top of the Herald-Examiner, one of LA's two top morning papers at the time. "JACLYN SMITH SUED FOR DISRUPTING FAN'S SEXUALITY" or something very close to that. The gist of the story was that a law suit had been filed in an Orange County court by a man who wanted reimbursement for the fact that every time he saw Jaclyn on television, he was deprived of the ability to be sexual with any other woman for some stated period of time.

She was, the suit alleged, casting a spell on him to keep him from being unfaithful to her with any other female. I called Jackie's lawyer and learned that it is legitimate, or at least legal, for any publication to print a story about any duly filed civil suit. And as for the plaintiff, anybody can sue anybody for anything. The fact that it is a filing makes it, per se, not libel. Jackie could not even have countersued the man for malicious prosecution. A judge might easily rule that if the guy legitimately thought the charge to be true, that would make it not malicious. If you wish to spread some libelous thought about someone and still be libel-proof, apparently you just have to press a suit charging the other person with whatever deleterious behavior you wish to bring to public attention. Such inequities are, apparently, the necessary knocks and pings in the motor of a free-flowing legal system where no one's case is prejudiced in advance. Public figures are particularly at the mercy of such legal Catch-22s. If you pull that on Mack the barber, it doesn't make the news.

On another occasion, we started getting calls from a man in Utah who demanded to speak to Jacqueline Bisset because, he kept charging, she was the mother of his child. His pursuit of this became intense and was soon very worrisome. We had to put an end to it before it became dangerous to Jackie. The Beverly Hills Police Department, with so many stars in the public it protects, actually has a division to deal with this kind of unwanted pursuit. I invited one of its officers to visit our office to try to resolve it with me.

It is counterproductive for a publicist or lawyer or manager to call these delusional people, these "celebrity obsessives," because it just validates in their minds that they are establishing or continuing a relationship with the star in question. Contact with some official rep of the object of obsession becomes a tangible level of reality. It only confirms the fantasy. But getting someone to flash a badge. to interject a voice of somber authority, is different and can serve to challenge the delusion. We finally tracked down a phone number, and the officer conversed with the man, conveying great and reassuring calm. The man was insistent and exhibited a tenacity born of the fact that it was real to him, not a fantasy but a conviction.

"No, sir, Miss Bisset did not have your child…" the officer said firmly, repeating responses so we could get the gist of the conversation. "How do I know that it wasn't yours? Because Miss Bisset has never had anyone's child… no, sir, she is not a mother…. No… sir… sir… take my word for it… no child…yes, absolutely positive… What? No, wait… don't hang up." But apparently the man had done just that. The officer set the phone in its cradle with a look of extreme exasperation. "What happened?" I asked. "What happened?… what happened?" he muttered, still fuming… "Sonovabitch said, 'Well, maybe it was JOSIE Bisset."

These convictions are real to these people, triggering the stalker pursuit. The delusion of having fathered a child with the object of their obsession validates in the stalker's mind the concept that they had shared sexual congress. At its base, being annoying or threatening is a way to make the star aware that they occupy the same planet.

On the other hand, the reliable support of fan groups offers a terrific support system. Jackie was once invited to make a presentation at an important gathering of top members of Hollywood's gay community. Barry Krost, an important producer and artists manager, called me to request her presence. I said I wanted to be sure she would be well-received, and he said he could guarantee her a standing ovation upon her introduction. I suggested he couldn't possibly guarantee that. "Of course, I can," he insisted, "I will simply say… 'Will everybody… who would like to BE Jacqueline Bisset… please stand up.'"

Richard Simmons once, to my great discomfort, did an improvisational take-off on stalker fan excess, acting it out in the hallway connecting the dressing rooms at The Tonight Show, kissing my shoe because I worked with the superstar he most adulated. It was a sheer piece of Richard Simmons theatre, and I was the stooge, which didn't go unnoticed by the people in the hallway who witnessed it. I was sodden with embarrassment. Richard was doing a parody of a burdensome aspect of the fame game. At a certain point, devotion can become toxic.

Or it can become intoxicating. Jane Seymour's avid fandom has enthusiastically followed her into her current prominence as a painter and brand name in the world of jewelry design. Their devotion has made itself very evident in specific instances. The first was the motion picture "Somewhere in Time," the film in which Christopher Reeve's character, a writer, is transported back in time into a romance with a turn of the century actress incarnated by Jane. The bittersweet romance touched something so hopelessly and hopefully romantic in audiences that it drew together hundreds of thousands of people who were not so much fans as addicts. Tens of thousands gather to celebrate the film and the place it has in their hearts, joining at the site where the story transpired, the great hotel on Mackinac Island in Michigan. Romanticism is not dead. The celebrants come attired for the period, committing themselves together to a story about the immortality of love. It struck a nerve common in human wanting. Jane and Christopher were bound together in that vast longing for a simpler time and a simpler and more enduring concept of love. Later, Jane was of untiring assistance to Christopher and his wife Dana following his accident as they strove to support research and care for the kind of quadriplegic damage Christopher had suffered so tragically. The family of "Somewhere in Time" fans joined them in the effort to fund the search for a cure.

An equally devoted vast audience gathered about Jane's gritty but uplifting series, "Dr. Quinn-Medicine Woman. The essential element in such fan fixations is identification. "Somewhere in Time" touched their need to connect with something romantically hopeful. "Dr. Quinn" told human tales relating to medical practice in a time and place when the supporting science was pretty basic. What she brought to it was a passion and commitment that most people found missing in their relationships with HMOs and doctors who they felt were handling too many, charging too much and caring too little. They maintained the show's popularity for six years and two well-received two hour movie-of-the-week sequels. The fanbase builds to intensity when the performer carries out aspects of the same role in personal life… in this case, Jane's unrelenting work to protect children through such organizations as ChildHelp USA and City Hearts. Much of Jane's success has to do with caring and hearts, which is reflected in the wide sales of her jewelry and books, her burgeoning industry actually, relating to her primary theme of "open hearts," hearts open to love and to helping. Jane's fans are so in sync with her own wide open heart that they joined together to campaign for and then raise the money to pay for Jane Seymour's star on the Hollywood Walk of Fame. It was one of the rare instances of that honor being sought by and bought by the star's conjoined fan bases. Over 500 fans flew in from all over the world to see her unveil her nine square feet of fame on Hollywood Boulevard across from the (newly renamed) Grauman's Chinese Theatre. That little piece of real estate in front of the historic Hollywood Roosevelt Hotel, where the first Oscars were awarded, is a personal favorite of mine since I've had eight or nine of my clients enshrined there.

Fans make pilgrimages to see their favorite star's name inscribed in a bronze star on a sidewalk. Is it because they know that their favorite once stood there and knelt there and felt honored there? I think, rather, that it is a kind of incandescent symbolism with which an enterprising chamber of commerce has driven traffic to its streets and commerce to its stores. But in some ways it's pure of heart, a salute not only to people of achievement, but also to fans and to the phenomenon of fandom. There was a $15,000 fee (now $30,000) attendant to being honored with a coveted star on the Walk of Fame on Hollywood Boulevard. That covers the simple cost of the event. Hollywood, which is big in the minds of the world, is actually a small town which can't afford to absorb that cost so many times a year. Does an emplaced metal star have real weight as a recognition of distinction?… especially since there are nearly three thousand of them? The surprising answer is yes. Just ask the hundreds of fans who descend upon one with flowers and other expressions of devotion when the name on that star passes away. A star, even among that multitude, is a tangible evidence of having achieved a certain level of popularity, excellence or usefulness. When they say "attention must be paid," this is a very powerful way to pay it. First you have the huge press turnout for the unveiling and then the lasting place of eternal existance. The measure of that occurred at the time of the sad and exploited passing of The King Of Pop, Michael Jackson. Since his star was being "used" that evening… it was placed in a position of honor which just happened to be where the premiere of "Bruno" was transpiring and therefore roped off and tread over by hordes of red carpet media… the entertainer's desolated fans converged on the star of another Michael Jackson, the radio host, and piled a Kilimanjaro of flowers, toys and other remembrances upon it. It was a case of any star in a storm and an evidence of the tremendous magic and mojo these plaques carry.

I usually find a studio or distributor to fund a Walk of Fame star for promotional purposes, usually with a plush party afterwards. MGM underwrote Pierce Brosnan's to launch his first Bond film. For Loretta Swit, who will be seen as Hotlips in TV's "M.A.S.H." until someone passes a law against beloved reruns, the division of 20th Century Fox which syndicates that show's repeats gladly forked over the costs. Columbia coughed up for Jimmy Woods for the launch of "John Carpenter's Vampires." That occasion provided the funniest testimonial speech I think has ever graced a star unveiling. Usually before the plaque is uncovered, two personalities associated with the star of honor pay oratorical tribute. John Carpenter was one, giving his usual acerbic and grudging praise which, at the end, made you know that in his opinion Jimmy is a grand pro who had passed hard muster. Melanie Griffith had starred with Jimmy in a brilliant and violent crime flick called "Another Day In Paradise," and she readily agreed to offer the second testimony. She explained that she had just given birth and the thought struck her that making a film with Jimmy was a lot like having a baby. The act of inception is an experience of dizzying delight, ecstasy if you're lucky. Next comes the joy and excitement of the planning and anticipation. This is supplanted gradually by the discomfort of the gestation and eventually getting sick your stomach every day building to relentless pain culminating in a final experience of screaming agony. And then in its wake is this glorious baby that you're so thrilled has come into your life. I paraphrase, but she had the gathered large and savvy crowd on a building roll of laughter, particularly Jimmy who, master of the verbal arts, most appreciated its eloquence, structure and wit.

Of the thirty or so star emplacements I've generated and supervised, the two most interesting choices of location were Jay Leno and Randy Quaid. Randy has his star right in front of the Hollywood Roosevelt Hotel where the bus dropped him off when he first came to Hollywood from Texas. Jay Leno asked for his to be in a less exalted area in front of the Robert Ripley's Believe It Or Not museum. The reason?.... it was on that spot that he was picked up on charges of vagrancy when he first came to California. The cops drove him around in the back all night, and he kept them laughing. They were his first California audience. They gave him the best possible review, letting him off without booking him.

All of these placements are the same, and yet most have special twists and heart tugs, like two in which I was involved in recent years. Mickey Rooney was a long-time client, and I would take a special pleasure in helping him, on occasion and sans fee, maintain his fame as he moved into and through his octogenarian and nonagenarian decades. He was so powerfully one of the last remaining, sustaining and insistently active of the great stars of the Golden Age, ... even beyond the passing of his much younger "National Velvet" teammate and star of stars Elizabeth Taylor. How can one help but tend the garden of a friendship and an admiration based on such talent and spirit? His occasional irascibility and incomparable vigor came right out of his great well of talents whose depth never were sounded. One year, and this was an annual occurance, the Deauville Film Festival called in its yearly effort to get Gene Hackman to agree to be honored, Gene Hackman who is so allergic to honors. I directed the festival's genial American ambassadress Ruta Dauphin (widow of the remarkable character star Claude Dauphin) to the fact that it was Mickey Rooney's 80th birthday. The festival, as result, gave The Mick a lush retrospective of a great dramatic, comedic and tuneful selection of his storied films. Some years later I was helping out Mickey and my longtime friend and truly beloved Honorary Mayor of Hollywood, the regrettably late Johnny Grant, in the placing of Mickey's fourth star on that star-studded boulevard. This one was for Mickey and his last (of what?... seven or eight?) wife, Jan The star was to honor their successful international touring in his "One Man, One Wife" review. Mickey, always in the spirit of things, showed up in tux with Jan in sparkling gown, and they had a combo backing them for a set of songs for the gathered crowd. That's my point here... the gathered crowd. There were hundreds and hundreds on hand for the honoring of a guy whose reign as a top boxoffice star was in the 30s and 40s, with beautiful sparkles further on along the way, of course, but the great body of it long before most of them were born. Hollywood is a place and fans are a tribe where legend is honored. That is an extraordinarily large part of the charm of doing PR, of having been in a business which serves this miraculous and sustaining relationship of entertainers and the people they entertain.

One of the difficult aspects of undying fame is that the nature of it alters over an extended physical lifetime. Some, like Eastwood and Streisand, carry it at peak heat throughout. For others, there is often the challenge of adjusting to its different stages and the revised immediacy of their importance to public, to media and to industry even though they have never stopped being classic stars. Most wear these crowns lightly and well however grey the hair on which they rest. Some had suffered a fandom so intense during those years at the very top that the memory of it tricks the mind in time to feel that something is missing, Mickey Rooney had the stage to himself from the time he was a blazing little wunderkind in burlesque and the top box-office star in the world throughout adolescence and his sky's-the-limit pubescence. It created in him an impatience and belligerence with anything that couldn't be immediately accomplished.

One of my favorite experiences with Mickey Rooney came upon the heels of some news stories about Willie Nelson's tax problems, a rather awesome debt. Mickey called in a particular state of invigoration and excitement and concern. He noted that Willie had almost single-handedly powered Farm Aid, the great telethon fund-raisings for the embattled small farmers of our land. The nation, Mick said, owed this guy a debt of gratitude. He was certainly right on that account. Mickey's idea… nay, dedication… was to create a national fund-raising to pay off Willie's debt… "to get him… are you ready?… on the road again. Get it? On the ROAD again!" I told Mickey that it was a great idea, certainly merited, but I thought that he had to ascertain Willie's feeling on it… to get Willie's permission before he put it forward. "Why, for crying out loud?! We're doing it FOR him!" "Mickey, I know. But you have to see how he'd feel about it. Not hard for me, Mick. I'll get Kris Kristofferson's number for you. He'll be able to advise you or maybe put it to Willie." "What the hell for? I'm not asking Willie to sing. This is America showing up for Willie Nelson. Why ask?" Mickey demanded, suddenly very angry at me for shooting down such a great idea. "I don't know…," I said, "… maybe because it might embarrass him?" "EmBARRass him?!" Mickey roared at the very idea of such an ingratitude, "let him pay his OWN fucking taxes!" and slammed the phone down on me.

Can you wonder in any way at my affection for that pugnacious star? There has never been a more irrepressible… and uncontrollable… force of talent and passion and energy to hit Hollywood. In the time of the movie capital's most dazzling blitz of stars, his films, often with Judy Garland, were always among the top moneymakers. He could do it all except hold his temper. He was so beautifully and impetuously Irish. Catch him playing "Fascinating Rhythm" on the 88 with Tommy Dorsey's band in "Girl Crazy." Even Oscar Levant would leap to his feet and applaud… and probably did.

I saw him perform in Vegas with a six piece jazz group backing him, and at one point he sat down in the seat of each of the guys and took each instrument as far as it would go. One Sunday he insisted I join an "angels tryout" at his house for a stage musical he wanted to do with Kay Ballard, based on the longtime hit comic strip about Maggie and Jiggs. The music was by the guy who celebrated my home town with "The Trolley Song." I was part of an audience of eight who saw what might have been the only performance of that show. What a shame other audiences did not follow, and what wondrous blessings my silly job bestows!

One golden rule by which our industry should abide is "you always honor legend." There are so few people or things in our business or in our world that truly deserve the title "legend," and I represent and have represented more than my fair share. Barbra Streisand and Dame Elizabeth Taylor alone are more than anyone's fair share. It is always a thrill to work with each and every one. And Mickey Rooney, no question about it, WAS one. During the 30s and the 40s, they paid a lot of attention to such things as who was the number one box-office star. And Mickey was always duking it out for that honor with the Duke himself, John Wayne. As powerful as are the performances we remember… "National Velvet," "Black Stallion," "Boys Town," any of the Andy Hardy films… filmic Norman Rockwells with laughs… it was in anything having to do with music in which Mickey shined most brightly. Music is in the DNA of every cell of his body, and it took no more than a downbeat to spring it to vivid life. His dramatic fireworks portraying lyricist Lorenz Hart in "Words And Music" was trumped by the fact that it contained his final film teaming in song with Judy Garland in the Rogers and Hart classic, "I Wish I Were In Love Again." At a star-studded luncheon we held for Geoffrey Rush during the Oscar campaign for "The King's Speech," Rush alluded to that culminating Mickey-and-Judy moment as a favorite movie memory. He confessed that Mickey's presence was the over-riding thrill of an event jammed with Hollywood's biggest, brightest and most current stars. I've always liked that the meticulous Hart got the subjunctive case ("were") right in that song title, just as I've loved that Irving Berlin, born and honed in the poverty of the great Jewish immigration of the late 19th century, made his up-from-the-streets colloquialism part of his music, as in the yearning beauty of "What'll I Do?" This is commemorated in an apocryphal story one can only hope is true. When he married a true love who was from social status and pristine education, Berlin, it is lovingly reported, asked her which of his songs she particularly liked, and she responded without hesitation, "Oh, of course it's 'What Shall I Do?'"

I'm sorry Hart died so young but I'm grateful that he didn't live to see (and hear) the computer world and to have to hear "you've got mail" a dozen times a day. What group of computer geniuses programmed that one, the Bowery Boys?

I was, of course, on hand for a luncheon honoring Johnny Grant, the master and guiding spirit of the Hollywood Walk of Fame. It was an event of some major distinction further illuminated by the presence of the still arousing Mamie Van Doren who recalled, for those gathered, how upon her arrival as sexy ingenue wannabe in Hollywood she became a friend, a romantic friend one was compelled to assume, of Johnny, who it turns out was quite a roué in his earlier years. She said she couldn't recall if she was seventeen or eighteen, and Johnny yelled out, "You were EIGHTEEN!" I was happy for his and Mamie's fond memories. He was the only entertainer who could match Bob Hope in USO tours to entertain troops in war-torn lands. Angie Dickinson, who is a great sounding board and divining rod for the goodness in other people's hearts because you have to have it to know it, was a career-long friend of Johnny and of course was there at the lunch and then again at the funeral which sadly preceded Johnny's long-planned retirement as the Mayor of Hollywood and return to the other-kind-of beauties of his native North Carolina. But fittingly, he was still in residence in the penthouse of the historic Hollywood Roosevelt Hotel right smack on the street he loved and had made even more famous than it was when he came to it… which is pretty darn famous.

One Sunday I got Johnny to come all the way east to the Pomona Fairway and thoroughbred track for a fund-raiser I was assisting and to which I had drawn a bunch of my clients. They were there to compete in a horse race to raise money for training physically-challenged kids in equestrian skills and pleasures. Among the stars in the stirrups were Carl Weathers, Gil Gerard and Jenny Agutter. It got very competitive, and, in some close proximity passing, Carl was knocked to the track, miraculously spared passing hooves and then he chased down his mount, sprung up and finished the race. It might be hard to find a stuntman for that one. Even though this was a cold and early morning, Johnny was there to man the hosting duties, call the exciting race and generally lend his pizzazz. At the end as we were walking to the parking lot, I told him, with gratitude, that I had never asked his participation in any charity endeavor that he had turned me down. And he said, "Because I trust your heart." No one ever came up on the short end trusting Johnny's heart.

Another distinctive trip to Hollywood Boulevard was for the star-dedication for Erik Estrada. I'm deeply impressed by Erik's decades-long work with law enforcement to achieve the protection of children. He arrived with an escort of... I'm not exaggerating here... scores of motorcycle officers on siren-blaring, lights-flaring bikes, over a dozen fire trucks similarly in full sound and splay of circling red lights, a fly-by of police helicopters, hundreds of police and sheriffs officers and public servants of every stripe and uniform. All of this motorcade had assembled in the parking lot of the Hollywood Bowl just up Highland Avenue from Erik's waiting-for-the-moment star in front of the Graumans Chinese Theatre. I had to laugh at the thought of the guy driving the last car to pass before they hit the road. Imagine looking in your rear view mirror and seeing a few hundred lights flashing at you with the loudest choir of sirens you will ever hear. You would feel like OJ Simpson making a run for it. It was a dazzling spectacle of the sort that the French call "son et lumiere" (sound and light) at the highest decibles. It was, by far, the most bedecked and certainly the noisiest star unveiling to which I've ever lent my press-gathering abilities. We heard it arriving a long time before we saw it arriving.

Celebrities sometimes suffer the misfortunes of never being 'perfect strangers" to anyone. Most of us would never intrude on perfect strangers, nor would we have the nerve to thrust ourselves upon the most famous people in the world. But many people do not hesitate to do that in the case of a celebrity of any stature, with the most celebrated being the most vulnerable. The fans feel they know them and in some cases own them. This occurred to me on the occasion of the Golden Globes show when Barbra Streisand was to receive the Hollywood Foreign Press Association's Cecil B. DeMille Award, the lifetime achievement honor which was about the only award not previously bestowed upon her. Barbra and her husband, James Brolin, had accommodated a large number of the interviewers on the red carpet, and as result, we entered at the back of the International Ballroom after the show had commenced. The protocol and courtesy of that situation requires late arrivers to stand at the back and wait quietly for the first commercial break before they move to their tables. As we stood there, Jim's press agent, the terrific Susan Dubow (and I was about to find out how terrific) was situated on the other side of Barbra. Just beyond her was a woman who very rudely, considering that the show was in progress, was talking rather loudly on her cell phone. Her voice was carrying, and we could hear that she was telling a friend that she was standing next to Barbra Streisand. "No, I'm not kidding," she said, "here, I'll let you talk to her." At which point Susan reached over and closed the phone, cutting off the call. "No you won't," Susan said. I wanted to give her a Golden Globe.

The advent of the Internet has changed the nature and, even more, the impact of fan celebration of artists. Fan clubs existed when I was a kid, mostly among people in a geographically concentrated community. Now they span the world, especially since the advent of the Twitter and website realities. Streisand admirers have fashioned some very sophisticated fan sites, and they chronicle her new records, films or DVD releases or political or charitable activities on a daily basis. They certainly played a role in helping "Meet The Fockers," her teaming with Ben Stiller, Robert DeNiro and Dustin Hoffman, become the first live-action comedy to exceed a half-billion dollars in box-office gross or to sell three million copies of the DVD in 24 hours or to having her become the first and probably eternally the only recording artist to have a number one album in five consecutive decades and spanning 45 years.

Time does not stand still, and neither do legends. Five years later she raised that never-to-be-equalled-or-exceeded accomplishment to six consecutive decades, hitting the charts at number one with "Partners" at the age of 72 and raising the span of time between first and most recent Number One CDs to nearly 50 years.

So she gives her fansites plenty to celebrate. They monitor the thoughts she blogs on her own website and discuss and help disseminate her activities, new releases and points of view. Their knowledge about her is so meticulous that I often go to them to verify information and I rely on them to catch print coverage or television breaks I may have missed. As press agents and marketing people all over the entertainment industry are finding out, fansites can be an incredible sales force and great sounding boards for a celebrity's heartfelt causes and social activisms.

Knowing News Before It Happens

Prior knowledge of what will become news is a common and essential part of being a press agent. You develop sources that can alert you to upcoming events or currents of news. A common call a press agent receives will go like this: "Do you have anyone (or usually they specify a client) who wants to talk about (let's say) cheating politicians? So and so is going public about his whatever." We also know things in advance because we are brought in to make them happen with a bigger splash, a smaller splash, a designated spin or a built-in damage control. Very often, these consultations or event managements are pro bono because they have a charitable or public service aspect we support.

For me the most outrageous and dangerous look into a crystal ball came when we were nest-sitting a Time cover on Molly Ringwald. Molly was at the Miley Cyrus apogee of her career heat as America's screen queen of teen. In that period, Time always had a late spring movie cover, a look at what was reliably projected as the screen event of the summer movie-going. That year they had selected the Robert Redford-Debra Winger romantic-thriller, "Legal Eagles." Neither actor could have been hotter, and the film was foreseen as a hit… at least until it finally was seen. Racing up on the issue, Time concluded this was not the film on which to hang their movie issue. The only other compelling movie theme of that moment was the box-office dominance of the John Hughes teen angst films, "The Breakfast Club," "Pretty in Pink" etc., and Molly Ringwald was the primary star of the trend. So, Susan Geller who was Molly's account exec, was busily working all of the details of that most incredible of breaks, a Time cover.

On the Thursday before the weekend on which the issue was closing, we received a phone call from a Time editor asking if he could come to our offices right away for a meeting. Obviously, it was not something that could be handled on the phone. And when he arrived, that tension was evident in his demeanor.

Basically what he said was that they had to push back the movie issue a week and that they wanted us to hold off on any ancillary press we had scheduled for Molly. We were stunned, worried that this meant a key, career-shaping story was a scratch, that a trigger element in Susan's meticulous campaign for Molly was going to be ripped out from under us. The editor seemed to take our stunned silence as our refusal to cooperate. How could we not cooperate? It was their magazine, their call. Why he then laid his cards on the table I'll never know, but he asked us if we were aware of the Libyan plane that had just attacked a U.S. airbase in Italy. Of course we were. He confided to us that the US would bomb Libya on Saturday and that Time had to hold its cover for that. At that moment I was truly stunned. I was stunned even that Time knew it. We assured him of our understanding and cooperation, and when he left we agreed that that information would not go out of the room. I was so burdened with the responsibility of that knowledge, I never told my wife until we saw it on the evening news that Saturday.

On that occasion, we knew world news two days before it was out of the lock box. But on another occasion, I had a preview of things to come two decades before they hit this country right below the belt. In 1988 the Glass-Steagall Banking Act was on the chopping block in the House of Representatives. It was one of the cornerstones of Franklin Delano Roosevelt's strategy to put the United States on a road to recovery from the Depression. It was a New Deal legislation which instituted regulations on America's banking community, excluding it from investment banking, insurance and other financial activities FDR and Henry Morgenthau thought best placed in separate hands and under the microscope of federal regulators... For a half-century conservatives and free marketers chafed under that restriction, and in 1988 the act was facing repeal. Our most financially savvy client, Wayne Rogers... he of Trapper John fame on "M.A.S.H." and his own adventurous film producing... was a financier and a banker, among other things. And he worried that if Glass/Steagall bit the dust, so would the U.S. economy. How prescient he was.

He asked if I could get him invited to be an expert witness before the House Banking Committee, which was holding sessions on the repeal of Glass/Steagall. It was a Democratic congress, and Rep. Henry Gonzales of Texas was chair. He was impressed with the Wayne Rogers bona fides I put before him and Wayne's take on the legislation. So Wayne and I flew back to D.C. and he appeared together with a Nobel Prize economist. Once the committee members got their Trapper-John-doing-triage-on-the-economy jokes out of the way, Wayne, a banker, gave dazzling testimony about why bankers were not to be trusted. Committee members were worried that nine of the ten biggest banks in the world were Japanese, and Wayne explained why that ordained that those Japanese banks and the Japanese economy would soon be paddling down white water in a leaky boat because they were so bloated and unregulated. That was soon the case. Wayne then laid out why Glass/Steagall was an imperative gate-keeper for our economy, as well and why regulations imposed on banks by Franklin D. Roosevelt's administration were necessary. When a bunch of bankers and their lobbyists think they're smarter than FDR, look out, Wayne said. He returned four years later to help save Glass/Steagall again.

My opportunity to join Wayne Rogers for his testimony had been for me a living lesson in democracy, its strengths and particularly its weaknesses. Exactly two decades before Henry Paulson and George W. Bush informed the world that banks and brokerage firms and their AIG-type allies had gamed the deregulated system to the very brink of worldwide bankruptcy, Wayne explained to those saner Congresses how that would happen But he wasn't recalled to give witness in the late 90s. The last bill President William Jefferson Clinton signed was the repeal of Glass/Steagall orchestrated by Newt Gingrich and Phil Gramm. This then permitted Bush and Paulson and Congress and the SEC and the Fed to green-light the banking industry's bunco game with credit default swaps or whatever those creatures from the Black Lagoon are called.

I had witnessed Wayne Rogers and a Nobel scholar in economics giving congress proof positive that we can't give the foxes the keys to the henhouse, that regulation and pre-emptive caution were imperative, and that Glass/Steagall was the greatest legacy of a New Deal that had had to dig us out of the crater once before. So when Bush and Paulson threw in the towel, it didn't come as a surprise... nor should it have to anyone else... but it did come as a shock. The day with Wayne in the Capitol was memorable for that and for our lunch in the Senate commissary with George McGovern and a host of household name Senators of both parties hopping Wayne's table. Being a Hollywood press agent can have its unique rewards in terms of life experience. But the lesson Wayne laid out went for naught, and congress undid (and never redid) Roosevelt's bank supervision controls, and nearly bottomed-out our nation.

Feeding the Wolves

Which came first, fan hunger for every dire, tragic or private detail of the lives of their favorite stars, or the commercial desire of media to feed that appetite. My bet is on the media. It's the nature of all enterprise to cultivate and maximize the hunger for something they can sell. Movies started about when William Randolph Hearst was putting big money down on what came to be called "yellow journalism." My other bet is that the earliest film press agents and their successors worked damn hard to put the media on to this scandal news scam. The press agents just wanted to sell movies, and the media (as we used to say) just wanted to sell papers. In the process, the public got a taste for scandal that never wavered. In a way, this led to my incredible opportunity to appear before the Judiciary Committee of the United States House of Representatives.

When Paul McCartney's wife died suddenly and tragically, the media knew that they had a story they could ride for days. Why? Because it had a big question mark attached to it, An improbable set of circumstances had been set in motion. Since media is always looking for some unusual hook, even for a tragedy, a bizarre cyclone of interest was stirred up because it was reported that Lynda had expired near Santa Barbara, California, and there was this big brouhaha about why there was no hospital report issued there. Did she die there? Why won't the family give the facts? All of that nonsense. It was the top of the news, not because a noted photographer and wife of a music icon was gone, but because of where she was when it happened… the brutal news imperative of the unanswered question. The family, in a seclusion of grieving in Arizona, was beset with this need-to-know pressure from the media "on behalf of a breathless public" (or so the media pretended or maybe even believed.) We are talking here of the entertainment side of news, not the news side of news.

One morning in the midst of this sad and silly furor, the exploitation of the story on a morning news show really annoyed Gisela and me. Protecting celebrities from nonsense has been part of what she and I do. I could see immediately that the Santa Barbara rumor had been thrown out by a bright press agent to throw the dogs off the trail and to give the McCartney family a chance to come to terms with their pain. Gisela asked why I didn't have some client speak out about this press excess, but we agreed there was no point in that. It would be too gratuitous. When I got to the office, I got a call from CNN on that very subject, but I said I had no clients to speak out on it. No, the producer said, they wanted me to….

me, the same me who abhorred the idea of press agents blabbing off. But it was so strangely coincidental with the conversation Gisela and I had just had. I told them I had to consult my wife. I asked her if I should make an exception to the rule. She reminded me it was something I achingly wanted to complain about. She asked what I was wearing, and I told her. "Oh, hell," she said, "go ahead and do it anyway."

So an hour later, I was staring into a camera debating via satellite People Magazine editor Peter Castro, a key contact, about the presumption of the press. In the middle of the interview, they cut away to a press conference which the Santa Barbara sheriff was holding to announce… nothing. He had nothing to say because the whole story was just a dust-devil of… nothing. When they cut back to us, I pointed out that we had just witnessed millions of dollars of media resource being wasted on nothing. It was ok. I had my angry say. It didn't really accomplish anything, but it did send me to Washington. That afternoon I got a call from an official at the Screen Actors Guild asking if I would appear on behalf of SAG before the House Judiciary Committee considering a bill that would protect performers and other public personages from invasion of their privacy by intrusive and endangering paparazzi, who bear zero DNA resemblance to the good-guy event photographers who work our red carpet press lines.,

I had stage fright the second I said yes. Four minutes… did I have enough opinion and fact to fill four minutes… and how could I possibly squeeze all I wanted to say into it, and what the hell could I possibly say to keep talking for four minutes without making a fool or a pomposity out of myself… or to justify taking up two and a half hours of congressional time (four minutes times the number of committee members.) I told Gisela I thought I should consult Marty Landau for pointers on how to act it out, but she said his understanding of performance was so sophisticated I could never comprehend it. I consulted our lawyer son in law, Moni's husband Mark Robertson, a top hospitality industry legal exec. Luckily, both of our sons-in-law now are distinguished lawyers. I planned to refer to a Supreme Court decision which found that high tech surveillance by police requires a warrant. The legislation that SAG and its expert witnesses were addressing concerned the rampant ambush paparazzi (stalkerazzi is my preference) invasion of stars' *privacy*. The prior Supreme Court opinion I was citing was issued in a ruling relating to a Fourth Amendment (*due process*) case that might not pertain in this matter. In D.C. I discussed that at dinner the night before the hearing with a Harvard law professor who was also giving witness, and he advised against referring to that ruling because that case before the Supreme Court had concerned due process, not privacy. But I felt this specific Supreme Court ruling established that technologically-enhanced surveillance, both visual and audio, can constitute trespass. Well, I did use it, and it went over pretty well. The professor, who spoke after me, used it, too.

The main point I made, something relevant to a book about PR, is that these stalkerazzi employ dangerous and rude techniques in order to get their guerilla shots, the ruder and uglier and more intrusive the better, that they were not only invading but also shredding the privacy and dignity of their quarry. I told the committee how a photographer can hover in a helicopter for an intrusive shot, but that, by FAA regulation and common sense, the sun cannot be mirrored back at the craft to block the shot, as John F. Kennedy Jr. once pointed out to me. It would be a crime, he explained, to interfere with an aircraft and manslaughter if something were to happen. So I withdrew my hand from the make-up mirror for which I had been reaching. Saved from a life of crime and stupidity. It was a technique I've actually used in on-the-ground paparazzi/stalkerazzi situations. There was, I learned, a similar legal impediment which prevents celebrities from getting police protection when their car is being pursued by a car or cars of stalkerazzi as had been the case on the occasion of Princess Diana's death. This, as I put to the committee, actually happened to a major actress, famous and pursued for her fame and beauty by these long-lens poachers on privacy and sanity. When the trailing car started to bump her car from behind, she called the local police on her cell phone and asked what to do. The police officer said that in that case, the law required her to stop and exchange insurance information with the other participant in the collision, and, only if the damage was over 500 dollars should she call the police. His advice, get out of the car and become a sitting duck. In other words, let them memorialize and profit highly off of your anger. So, I pointed out to the committee, here are two cases where FAA and California Motor Vehicle Code regulations prevent a celebrity from taking effective defensive action. I actually saw some of the committee members making notes.

The memory most indelible from that day occurred before our appearance when I was with the other witnesses, Michael J. Fox and Paul Reiser among them, in the ante room, variously chatting or trying to memorize our comments or to calm jangled nerves. Rep. Henry Hyde, the committee chair and a legislator with whom

I almost never agreed, came over, introduced himself, thanked me for appearing and then asked if I was nervous. "Eight point one on the Richter scale," I answered. "Well, think about this," he said, "you're an expert, and we are all very interested in hearing your expertise and your opinion as it bears on this legislation." It was such a civilized and decent gesture that I was humbled and even slightly calmed.

On a later occasion, I told Marty Landau about it and that I had been tempted to seek his advice. He asked how I'd played it, and I explained that I'd read the body of my statement, but that I'd memorized the four passages where I really wanted to drive it home, and that enabled me to give it to them looking them in the eye. Marty smiled and said, "That's what I would have told you to do."

A most important rule of daily function as a PR guy or gal is that a press agent should not be seen and should not be heard. I was going to do a chapter on this, and then I realized that it's not a chapter, it's a paragraph or three. *Press agents know better than anyone, except those who have been mentally, morally or spiritually undone by fame, that public attention, however useful, comes at a high cost. Not only high cost of privacy but also of distorted self-perception.*

Teeny-bopper crazes can throw some young actors into delirious fan *attention* and confusing wealth much too early in their lives. Some of them used it to get invited to the Playboy mansion. Steve Guttenberg used the riches and prominence of the "Police Academy" and "Three Men and a Baby" films and sequels to create housing for young women thrown on the streets after abusive childhoods in the foster care system, hiring social workers to guide them through the desperate transition. Ian Zeiring used fan hysteria from the "Beverly Hills 90210" series to power his constant effort to get at-risk youngsters to commit to available educational programs. It's what you do with what you get that determines who you will be.

The celebrity faces this question… *am I the person out of whose eyes I see every day, the person whose foibles I know so well, or am I that selectively perceived person seen through the media eye, distorted, for better or for worse?* Most deal with it very well and remain integrated personalities, but it is stressful. We all face that duality to some extent, but one pays an exorbitant price to be a public figure. This is because the public perception is so insistent and so contrived to meet the needs of the media much more than the needs of the subject.

Chapter 4

Heart Tugs

I expected a lot of the Faberge Film Festival At Sun Valley, the biggest stunt of Guttman & Pam's early years, but I never expected it to touch my heart in a way I never would forget. It may have been the tallest I've ever seen a great star stand, and, not surprisingly, that star was Cary Grant. It was 1973, shortly after the launch of our filmtown PR firm, and it had grown very starry very quickly. I needed a big summer promotion for Sun Valley, one of our first big corporate accounts, and I sat down with Jerry one day to discuss an ambitious idea. We represented Faberge Perfumes and its film division. Its boss, George Barry, had energy, charm, charisma and an enthusiasm for vast and adventurous ideas. He also had a G-14 plane that could carry a lot of stars great distances in great comfort. He also had Cary Grant on his board. I wanted Cary to host our event, to have the invitations sent in his name. What could be more compelling? It was a big ask. We couldn't go to Cary with it, not an idea of such personal commitment as this, but Barry could.

I wanted to throw a summer film festival in Sun Valley, which was our client because my charismatic friend Chuck Dwight, ski entrepreneur extraordinaire, hauled us everywhere he took his ski resort-developing fast-moves and bright-accomplishment. He was now building the Cottonwood condo project with Paul Anka at the queen of American snow playgrounds and he had told Sun Valley owner Bill Janss that Guttman & Pam was the greatest thing to hit ski resorts since super-moguls. He had told Bill that Jerry Pam and I were the super moguls of publicity. We had to live up to it, and this idea was one it would take a super-agency of 30 or 40 publicity operatives to pull off, not a little boutique firm like ours. Except…. except that all the excepts fell into place very nicely. Sun Valley could handle the physical aspects of the event, however vast, with facility. And when the star acceptances raced in, it got extremely vast extremely fast. I wanted a festival that we controlled completely and that benefited only our clients, and when we shook this idea down, all the pieces were in place or fell into place with a few knowing nudges on our part. Nobody was saying no, and everybody who was saying "yes" was a somebody. We were only five in staff then and, with Gisela, six. Our daughters, Monika and Danielle, were fourteen and twelve and excellent and very cheap labor. They had their mom's verve and could wrangle stars and media with the best of them. We could do it. I didn't count on the fact that *every* major press outlet would want to attend, even though they would have to get themselves there. Well, I'd contemplated… or, at least, flirted with… that possibility. After all, how often does a journalist get an invitation from Cary Grant to spend a weekend at Sun Valley, Idaho with many of the top stars in Hollywood? But I didn't think it would wind up looking like a laid-back Hollywood premiere, with press to match, lifted from the forecourt of the Grauman's Chinese Theatre and set back down in the summery slopes of the Hood River Valley.

All the strings were already in our hands. Faberge had its first three films already in the can, "A Touch of Class," the Glenda Jackson/George Segal romantic comedy which would go on to win Golden Globes and a to score Oscar gold as well; "Night Watch" with Elizabeth Taylor and Laurence Harvey co-starring again as they did in her first Oscar winner, "Butterfield 8," and "Welcome to Arrow Beach," a thriller which Larry directed and in which he starred." They proved to be the final two films of Larry's career, which we fully feared at the time and which is part of this tale about a kind of breath-taking generosity that should be counted twice when they ask if Hollywood has a heart.

The engraved invitations from Cary Grant went out, and the positive RSVPs came zooming back. starting with many from our own client list… Gene Hackman, Jim Garner, Jim Brolin, Bob Stack, Hugh O'Brian among them… it was a starry bunch. We had lots of friends, and George Barry had more . When the eventual size of the press became apparent, we wondered how we could stage enough events to keep them busy, but Bill Janss had his staff cooking, and there were raft rides down the Hood River, ice-skating shows at the great rink behind the lodge where Olympic and Hollywood super skating star, Sonja Henie, had twirled her magic in "Sun Valley Serenade," swimming in the same steaming pool Gary Cooper and Marlene Dietrich dunked in after bracing runs down the white winter slopes, bowling contests and other diversions to keep everyone involved. Our main events were the three premieres, of course, presentation dinners, interviews with the cast members and creators of the films including George Barry who not only was a social and business leader of great status, executive producer of "A Touch of Class" but also, later, the Oscar-nominated composer of that film's song. All that and Sun Valley and the glory of the Sawtooth branch of the Rocky Mountains to boot. You couldn't lay a more delicious smorgasbord of delights before any group of junketing press and visiting stars.

But the piece de resistance, the crème de la crème, the icing on the cake for the press was the fact that Cary Grant had agreed to give a forty-five minute press conference which would be held in a tiered convention hall with theater seating for several hundred people, such was the audience of press who had signed on. This was scheduled for the final morning of the festival, so we had no early departures. I'm quite sure that was the main draw for such a tremendous turnout. All of the attending stars were there, as well. An in-depth look into the specialness of Cary Grant, whose charm, aplomb and courteous interest in and conversation with everyone illuminated the entire weekend.

Larry Harvey was a major star of the festival, of course, not only as a star of two of its films and director of one, not only because of tthe immortality of "The Manchurian Candidate" and "Room at the Top" and "Darling," the cult greatness of "Summer And Smoke," "Walk on the Wildside," "The Good Die Young," "The Alamo," "Butterfield 8," "The Long, The Short and The Tall," "The Outrage" and his blazing Shakespearean stage career, but also because he appeared before us on this final stage as an extraordinary incarnation of courage that amazed and inspired everyone there.

It was no secret. You could see it. Larry was dying. He was rail-thin, walking around in a burnt orange jump suit that was now a month or two of emaciation too large for him. No more erudite, more wickedly witty or charming... yes, a charm that matched even Cary's... a man or woman you would ever meet, and all of those qualities were generously shared with the festival goers. The only things missing were the glass of Pouilly Fuisee or the long stemmed cigarette holder, one or the other of which he always seemed to have held in one hand all our shared lifelong. You would never know that Larry was dying... except if you looked at him. Not in his eyes, for they were alive and vivid as they had been on all of the occasions of delight Gisela and I had shared with him. All weekend he kept us laughing, but Gisela would start to cry every time we left him. Was there ever a sharper or wiser tongue with a quip? Even Peter Ustinov, Michael Caine, Roger Moore, Carl Reiner, Billy Wilder, Merv Griffen, James Mason, Milton Berle and Tony Randall, some of the quip masters of my happy experience, stood in Larry's shadow. Well, Jay Leno of course, but that's his métier. If Larry ever got around to discussing the fine points of "Richard III" or Harry or "Hamlet" up there with Will Shakespeare, I would like to have heard that bandy of words. I'm quite sure now as I write this that I thought the whole Sun Valley festival event to life for Larry, to honor him as a stage for his final leg-bending bow and display of gallant gesture. And I'm equally sure that that is why George Barry had backed it so extravagantly. But I had no way of knowing how much it meant to Cary.

One of the media circus occasions of the weekend was when we took Laurence Harvey, Cary Grant and Gene Hackman down to the airfield in nearby Haley, which is one of the renowned capitals of soaring…. glider flight. None of them including Gene, a veteran of aerobatic flight even then, had ever experienced soaring. The photographers had a feast on the three climbing into their graceful, sensual crafts. A shot of Gene and Cary leaning on a glider was one of the few photographs I've ever had featured in both the People page of Time Magazine and the Newsmakers page of Newsweek. Each came down thrilled with the experience of soaring soundlessly along the reaching peaks and the green and river-striped valleys. Cary commented on the particular delight he'd experienced and was asked if he planned to take it up and do it forever. "At my age," he responded, "you don't plan to do anything forever, and a continued search for new experiences seems the best approach."

But for Larry, the experience of silent glide in a sleek and silvery craft at play among the updrafts and caprices of winds on nature's most glorious field of beauty was an absolute epiphany. When he alighted, Gisela and I… all of the gathered press and stars… could see how much had been lifted from his heroically wide but now thin shoulders. "How did it feel, Larry?" Gisela asked, putting an arm around him. "Free," he said.

It was stomach cancer, and it worked him hard. He never spoke of it or evidenced any of the pain, although you could see it boring into him. He couldn't have been on much medication for it, for his mind was sharply ready and bright. But you knew. And so it came to the promised mass interview with Cary Grant to which everyone had been looking forward. It was a medium sized amphitheatre, like a large university classroom, probably something used for conventions. However, this was an unconventional event... Cary Grant, open to all questions, his career, his thoughts, his memories. All of the storied stars who came up for the festival had chosen to skip the kayaking or parasailing or hiking or ice-skating which were available to them on the final morning. They chose instead to be there to experience the mind and spirit of one of the very greatest of all superstars. Larry Harvey came in last. You didn't ask yourself what circumstance of dealing with his reality might have delayed him. He chose to stand at the back, at the top of one of the aisles.

Cary was in great form. He was in Cary Grant form, and all of the pleasures of watching him in "Bringing Up Baby" or "The Philadelphia Story" or "North by Northwest" or "Notorious" or "An Affair to Remember" were so casually accessible and cheerfully and generously shared. And then there came a question... I'm embarrassed and frustrated to say that I can't remember exactly what it was, but what evolved from it was so powerful that I suppose the question itself was just washed out into the sea of memory... a question that gave Cary pause. As he searched for an answer, he looked up and saw Larry in his burnt orange jumpsuit at the top of the stairs, and that comfortable smile came across Cary's face. "You know what?" Cary said, "I think Larry Harvey can answer that one better than I. Larry, want to give it a try?" Larry, who had been caught up as we all had in the great Cary Grant-ness of this experience, was embarrassed. But answer it he did, and the huge room was filled with that most glorious and melodious of all voices, the rich resonance and softly precise enunciation that glided into your mind and filled it with astonishing colors. ... that cultured elocution and caress of sounds wrought so astonishingly from the raw brawl and snarl of the street languages of his rude childhood and from his determination to re-create himself into such a master of all the arts of spoken word. The unforced power of his communication belied the frail body from which it emerged.

Whatever he said... again, that irrelevant specific was lost for me in the great shared experience that followed so immediately... it absolutely riveted the audience. It had wisdom and grace and humor. When he finished, someone asked another question of him. Larry was embarrassed because this was, after all, a Cary Grant experience, but Cary nodded for him to go on, and all of the heads in the hall were turned, some of them painfully, toward Larry. Cary smiled and then, as Larry responded, Cary moved up the stairs and, at the completion of the answer, took Larry gently by the elbow and guided him down the stairs. He firmly sat Larry into the chair from which he had previously been responding. Cary gestured to the audience for the next question which, of course, was addressed to Larry. And then, as Larry answered question after question from a group of tough news people, pros unaccustomed to the emotional tug of what was transpiring, visibly involved, exploring Laurence Harvey and honoring him for what everyone knew would be the last time, Cary stood behind Larry and massaged his shoulders and neck. After a while when the questions and possibly Larry were exhausted, Cary said, "Thank you very much. I appreciate your having joined us for this festival and for this conversation." There was a silence for a brief period, everyone too caught up in the moment to know what was appropriate, but then there was applause, not wild but rather modulated and respectful and sincere. And all the while Cary continued to massage Larry's shoulders.

That was Laurence Harvey. And that was Cary Grant.

The one bump in the road on that weekend occurred one morning when I found the producer of one of the films, a dear friend and meticulous film-maker, in the Sun Valley movie house with some kind of meter. It seemed to suggest that the projector lamp was not quite strong enough. We were showing his film that evening, and he didn't want it poorly projected. I checked with the projectionist and he said that they replace the lamp every three years, and this one was only one year old. But the producer, a perfectionist, was adamant. We determined that the nearest lamp to be purchased was in Denver, and George Barry generously ordered it and a small plane to bring it to Haley, the nearest airfield. There were delays, and when 8PM arrived, , the scheduled start of the premiere, and the audience was seated, the plane was only then approaching Haley. It was now getting dark, and Haley wasn't equipped for instrument landing. Cary Grant had just come to me and said everyone was complaining that we were almost a half hour late. The pilot could land at Twin Falls, at best an hour and a half by car, or they could attempt the landing. I wasn't about to risk someone's life for a light bulb and I told them to have the pilot leave it in Twin Falls and then I went to the producer and told him the new bulb was installed and that I was starting. After the film I asked him how the projection was and he said, "much better." If he ever reads this… my trusting and longtime buddy, I'm sorry. Press agents under duress do desperate things, even to friends.

The mysterious ways of the human heart can add a poignancy even to so skeptical a trade as flacking for flicks . In London, on my very first and last as it turned out film as a full unit publicist, "The Man Inside," tough guy Jack Palance and I had circled our two wagons against some forces that had made it a rather tense shoot. We were filming a sequence at Victoria train station, and between scenes Jack and I were just walking around talking. A middle-aged lady kept following behind us… the kind of grey lady you saw so often in London in the mid-fifties when bomb craters still scattered about and bus drivers struck to raise their salaries from eleven pounds a week to fourteen. She was tailing and hovering, which can be very unnerving. Jack finally turned to her and said, "Yes, madam, what is it you want?" "Your autograph, please?" in a very timid voice. "Can't you see I'm talking to my friend?" "Yes, but my son so admires you…" "Well, thank you, but…" "…and I'm on my way to visit him at the sanitorium." Jack hung his head a moment as his considerable humanity suddenly engaged, and he wrote a kind and charming note of some length and bought her a large bouquet of flowers which he said were for her son. You have to play these little glimpses as though you weren't yourself moved and then go on with the conversation as though nothing had happened.

When the tension on the set came down too hard, sometimes I, rather than his driver, would drive Jack back to London because he wanted to talk. I had a little Porsche, and his legs were a tight fit. Gisela and I were just married. We were living in a seven-pounds-week basement apartment in a little hotel in Shepherd's Bush, and it always smelled of curry because we shared the cellar with the coal storage area and with the kitchen of an Indian restaurant. We had a Porsche, but we didn't have any money. Driving into London from Elstree, we saw a little pub ahead standing alone at a road crossing. Jack asked if I minded if he stopped there for one drink. New brides are not happy when new grooms show up late, however I said, "Sure, but one." As malevolent fate would have it, the pub was filled with Ukrainians… in England. My luck. It got very Ukrainian very fast. The Slavic banter got mushier, the singing louder and the time later. They were coal miners from the Ukraine, as Jack's father had been. When I finally got him to the car, it was dark and he was none too steady. I hadn't been able to call Gisela because cellar rooms don't have telephones. I dropped Jack at his place and headed to Shepherd's Bush to try my luck. I didn't have any. She wouldn't open the door. I tried to explain, but even I wouldn't have believed my tale. I drove back to Jack's apartment, forced him to get dressed and we went together to Shepherd's Bush. He explained and apologized through the closed door, and then she opened it, studied him a moment and said, "You need some coffee." I asked Jack if he wanted some Indian food, but he said coffee would be fine.

A few decades later I was in the backstage green room at the Academy Awards the evening Jack had won Best Supporting Actor for "City Slickers" and had memorably celebrated on stage with one-arm pushups. His daughter Holly dragged me over to him and said, "You have to direct Jack. They want him at the end–of- the-show curtain call to lead everyone on stage in pushups. Should he do it?" "Jack," I said, "paraphrasing Voltaire, once is exuberance, twice is egomania." "Thanks," he said, "I didn't want to be ungrateful, but I didn't want to look like a jerk."

To my knowledge, he never did.

When we handled Romy Schneider and Alain Delon, they were Europe's two biggest stars, they were the most adulated lovers in 90 percent of the world, they were the hot new stars of Hollywood and they were without any doubt the most beautiful of all the beautiful couples with whom I have ever worked… and those are legion. They had separately and *ensemble* become dear friends for my wife and me. Romy called one Saturday and asked if we could dine with her that evening. It wasn't easy but she seemed really to wish it. She and Alain had the same managers, partners in life as in business, and they called us to urge that we come. When we arrived, one of them, Georges Beaume, took us aside and said he was grateful we were there and showed us an envelope which Alain had asked him to give Romy. It was clear that it was a Dear John. The evening suddenly took on a dark undertone. After the salad, Georges handed Romy the envelope. She looked at him with anguish, and he nodded. Her hands didn't shake as she opened it. A lace handkerchief fell out… antique and of matchless design and detail. She looked at it and then read the letter, and then asked if we would excuse her. Grasping the letter, she got up to go to her room, but then came back to take the handkerchief with her. We sat in a silence which continued when she returned in about ten minutes and resumed her place at the head of the table.

We weren't struck dumb. We simply didn't know what to say. We longed to see that bright Romy Schneider smile which owned the heart of every movie fan in Europe, but we didn't. Just a brave little resolve to be a good hostess. She patted Gisela's hand and said in German, "I'm so glad you're here." Her hand stayed on Gisela's a few moments, and then she served the entrée.

A few decades later, shortly before she died tragically in the middle of a life that had become tragic.... why her of all people?.... Romy was at a party in London at which my partner Jerry Pam also was a guest. They happened to be leaving at the same time, and Jerry, knowing my affection for Romy, waved down a taxi and offered to drop her wherever she was going. As they rode off, Jerry told her that he was partnered with me, and he said that seemed to evoke happy memories for her. She asked him if he would deliver something to Gisela and me, and then she kissed him flat on the mouth. Jerry has always maintained that that was the only truly valuable benefit he derived from our partnership. When Romy died a short time later, I thought of it as her gesture of goodbye to us.

Robert Urich did some very good films, but it was on TV that he reigned as a true star. He went from series to series and starred in such mini-series as "Lonesome Dove." It was impossible not to have loved him in a guy kind of way or in a girl kind of way in "Vegas" and "Spencer For Hire." But it was Bob, not just the characters, that the people really loved. And, I can tell you, he was verifiably the caring and grounded guy he played. The affection was because you could see what a good guy he was. I saw it in the love between him and his wife, Heather Menzies (she sang "I Am Sixteen Going On Seventeen" in "Sound Of Music"). And I saw it again at one of the Revlon Run/Walks for Women's Cancer, the one we held shortly after Bob's first bout with cancer and during his courageous fighting it at least to a détente. It was a celebrity-studded event, as they all were and are, each drawing tens of thousands of survivors and their supporters. I take pride in these occasions because our daughter Danielle was so instrumental in developing them with charity promoter supreme Lili Tartikoff and, of course, the staff of the Entertainment Industry Foundation where Danielle joined with the industry charity's Chairman, Lisa Paulsen, in a partnership of initiating such annual events for various charities, raising hundreds of millions of dollars. The Run/Walks funded the UCLA women's cancer clinic where Gisela would be treated. They also helped establish the National Women's Cancer Alliance combining and coordinating the knowledge of great hospitals and research centers across the country.

This particular event held at UCLA was memorable to me because of Bob and Heather. It was a pretty dazzling show generally, with Candice Bergen the host and Oprah among the dozens of stars who ran or otherwise participated... Oprah was the first star across the 5K finish line. Doing the publicity on them, we were deeply involved. Because of Bob's high visibility as a cancer victim resisting his disease with all the fight and heart in the world, I had asked him to drive the pace car. Later, I suggested he join Candy and some of the other stars in the 1-800 Flowers booth where celebs were handing out a long stem rose to each of the thousands of women cancer survivors who were there to run and to share their pride of survivorship. Heather and I were standing together watching Bob lovingly involved in the encouragement and honoring of these ladies, and I mentioned to her how much I appreciated Bob's being there, that I had felt he was a symbol of courage even though it, obviously, was not a female cancer with which he struggled. "Yes," she said, "but I'm an ovarian survivor." That I had not known, and it knocked me back a bit. I took her hand and led her over to and slipped her into the line waiting to receive a rose from Bob. I explained to the other ladies what I was doing, and, with deep feeling, they welcomed her in, well invested in the moment that was about to come. Danielle and I stood together as Heather moved toward her husband. It was one of those earth-stands-still instants when he picked a rose and handed it forward to the next woman... and realized it was his wife. It was so powerful that you had to look away and give them a moment of privacy among the tens of thousands of people. All of the women behind Heather were sobbing, and you knew it was a moment they would remember when things got them down.

That long-stem rose was one of the inspirational moments in a PR career you might imagine has far fewer than is the case. We received a nominal fee for publicizing the EIF's good works, but a much higher recompense in the people we met and the courage we witnessed. Inspirational people and experiences do abound in this or any occupation. As tough as this wide world around us often seems, humanity is not in short supply. Robert Urich's generously shared soul is a shining example.

Freddie Fields, who headed MGM, involved Guttman & Pam thoroughly in "The Year Of Living Dangerously" right from the beginning. He had Jerry there the day that director Peter Weir gathered the MGM brass to show the actor he had selected to portray the key role of the strange, complex and dwarflike assistant to the journalist played by Mel Gibson and who ultimately becomes Gibson's alter ego and conscience in the story of political and romantic intrigue in Indonesia. The film literally hung on that casting, and the actor in Weir's test was a revelation. Only afterwards did the filmmaker tell Jerry and the others that it was New York stage *actress* Linda Hunt who, of course, went on to win the Oscar for her performance in the male role.

But the emotional tug for me in our experiences working on that memorable film came the night Weir showed his rough cut to an audience of ten or twelve of us in the huge Cary Grant Theatre on the historic MGM (and now Sony) lot in Culver City. I chose to sit next to Maurice Jarre, who would do the score. And what film student wouldn't take the chance to have a conversation before the screening with the genius whose prior scores included "Lawrence Of Arabia" and "Doctor Zhivago.?" We had worked with him on several John Huston films, "The Man Who Would Be King," among them. There was so much more I wanted to know about Jarre's work with David Lean that I boldly, maybe rudely, took the opportunity to sit beside him even though there were 400 empty seats in the Grant Theatre that night. The first cut of "Living Dangerously" unspooled and it was one of those rare first stabs ("Dirty Harry" comes to mind) where you can say "send it out as is." Obviously, the diamond would be polished and perfected and was even more superb upon release, much thanks for that owing to the skills of Maurice Jarre. As is the custom with such first cuts, Weir had given the film a "temp track," meaning that he had laid in existing music which gave a rough idea of what he thought the score might contribute at various parts.

So I was an uninvited witness when Peter Weir came over to Jarre after the screening to get his reaction. There is a particularly integral sequence in the film when Mel Gibson and Sigourney Weaver flee a boring embassy party and sail through a police blockade, a passionate reflection of the romantic and political turmoil into which they are impelling themselves and the film. "That sequence where Mel and Sigourney drive off?" Jarre noted. Weir nodded and said he'd laid in something by Vangelis (composer for "Chariots of Fire" and "Blade Runner") which he had found. "Keep it," Jarre said. Even Weir was startled at the idea, one of the greatest composers of film history suggesting that someone else' music be integrated with his own? I knew at that moment that I was listening to one of the most generous and impeccable gestures any great artist would ever make. "That music for that scene can't be improved upon," Jarre re-iterated. Weir went with Jarre's advice… and it cost Maurice Jarre at the very least a certain Oscar nomination and possible victory. A score cannot be considered for nomination if it includes prior composition by another composer. And Maurice Jarre knew that very well. Great music is one thing. Great integrity is even more impressive. It was a privilege and an education to have been there to hear those words.

Gestures of generosity come in all shapes and sizes, almost always surprising in their originality. Nobody lives so intently on the brink as knife throwers in the circus, construction guys atop the skeletons of eighty story buildings and ballet dancers. The intensity of all of these people is amazing. They are so in the moment they crackle. Ballet dancers must sustain perfection of murderous duration. I think that's why by and large the great ones have disdained publicity. Alexander Godunov gave early promise in his acting of being as important a film artist as he was on the ballet stage. I knew him through his relationship with Jacqueline Bisset, which made them definitely the reigning media focus couple for a long period. Magazines fought for the rare pictures of this couple which had the distinction of being not only very hot and very beautiful, but also super talented. Alexander defined his power and range as an actor from the start, from the dignity and controlled strength of his Amish suitor in "Witness" to the terrifying force of evil he transmitted in "Die Hard." In his first two or three films, he conveyed a range that few actors exhibit in a career. There was not only breadth of character but also depth of character there of which I had a few glimpses. One comes to me through a mist of delicious fragrance. On my way to a screening one evening, I dropped some papers off at Jackie's canyon home as Alexander was making English bangers and mash for her and her mom. I hadn't realized until I smelled the hot sausages that I probably didn't have time to stop at a restaurant before seeing the film… Alexander saw how voraciously I savored the fragrance , and he took me by the shoulders and planted me at the dining table for perhaps the finest simple meal I've ever had.

Another evening wound up with our taking steak dinners at the Pacific Dining Car downtown. The evening had started with abundant tension. A limousine was scheduled to take Jackie and Alexander to a sneak preview of her new movie "Class" at some mall on the suburban checkerboard of cities an hour and a half to the south and east of LA. My cousin Benjamin, who could actually make sense of the stupid directions they give you, was picking me up at my office, and we were just leaving when Jackie called. The limo had never arrived. I had them drive down to my office, and cousin Benjamin would deliver us all in good time. Benjamin's enthusiasms and unfailing positivity sapped the tension from even a no-show limo. Benjamin was simply the most enthusiastic and affectionate person I ever knew as well as one of the most cultured. After the screening, Jackie's agent, Ben Benjamin, invited us all to a very late dinner. Alexander and my cousin Benjamin (the evening was afloat with the cordiality, knowledge and wit of the multiple Benjamins) connected through their shared cultural enthusiasms. Knowing how avidly cousin Benjamin devoted himself to the arts, I was surprised that he was so sanguine and casual in the company of one of the most gifted ballet dancers of all time.

In the course of the meal, we were discussing Japan, and Alexander had occasion to say that something had happened when he was there for "Le Corsaire." Benjamin gasped… I mean gasped aloud… at the reference to the ballet. His voice erupted into a crescendo of awe ending in high soprano. "Oh, my GOD!" he shrieked, "You're Alexander GODUNOV!!! I've traveled the WORLD to see you!!" It was a thrall of such magnitude and charm and sincerity, it startled us (and the nearby tables) and then elicited warm smiles. Benjamin remained in a state of astonishment and barely spoke after that. About a half-hour later, we were going to our cars in the now almost emptied parking area. "Benjamin," Alexander said, "this is for you." And then he performed a *tour en jettand*, a linked chain of curling spins, twirling in the air like a top at a 45 degree attitude to earth and sky, seemingly frozen for elegant moments at the peak of each, leaps of once-in-a-lifetime height and grace around the darkened lot. A *tour*, as well, *de force* which lit up the night. Benjamin was wordless all the way back to my office. It was a highlight of what proved to be a tragically shortened life. Actually, it was the sole and revealing intersection of two tragically shortened lives, since Alexander passed from this world not long after. You never know that at the time. When Benjamin died a few years later of suffocation during an epileptic episode, his wife, Janeen, had him buried in his tuxedo, placing in his breast pocket the tickets for the opera they were to have seen that weekend.

Chapter 5

Justifying Publicity

It doesn't make anything you can eat. It doesn't propel your car or heat your home. It doesn't dispose of your trash but rather adds to it. It doesn't take science to the next stage or hold back new perils. But it impacts how you and more than half of the nine billion other people on this planet think about almost everything. It's called Public Relations

Publicists don't have to pass an exam or to obtain a license. They are not even certified… other than by reputation. But the large majority are skilled in how to shape awareness and how the careers or other interests entrusted to them are perceived. The pursuit can be particularly inventive in the Hollywood jungle. Stardom is a hard job and it exacts a heavy toll, but it is almost invariably the only road for talent. The degree of fame or recognition determines what roles and other opportunities a star is offered. *Fame, however, is not the prize…. it's the price.*

The crux of a whole life is sometimes confided to a press agent by a client in a single gesture or statement. Often it is entrusted as the element the artist wants or needs to be part of the telling of his story. Tony Perkins, a unique and complex acting talent and an infinitely kind person, had been with me at a book promotion on Hollywood Boulevard, after which I invited him to lunch at Musso and Frank. Over that bistro's signature tomato soup, he asked me about my children's names. Monika and Danielle. "MOHnika," he repeated, "with the long O? Not mah-nika? " "Yes, it's German." "But don't her friends standardize it?…. make it Mah-nica?" "All the time," I said, "but I always tell her that it's important to be a little different than other people and to stand up for it." He thought about that for a while and then said, "That's the story of my life." He wanted me and his public to see what it took for Anthony Perkins to bring so many memorable characters to the screen, characters that stand alone and have become reference-points... the deranged obsession of "Psycho," the gentle humanity of "Friendly Persuasion."

Truth was important to Tony, far beyond any consideration of wanting to appear a big shot movie star. During the promotion of "Friendly Persuasion," we'd booked him on The Tonight Show with Johnny Carson, which was originating in New York at the time. Tony wasn't completely comfortable on talk shows, and Johnny asked him if he'd enjoyed his previous visit to the show. Tony answered no, not really, and when Johnny asked why he said, "I had to walk home." "HAD to walk home?" Johnny prompted. Yes, Tony explained that during the last show someone stole the front wheel off his bicycle which he'd chained to a lamppost outside the studio... and he'd had to walk it home. He was just a guy who never hid the truth. It broke up Johnny Carson, and that and so many other truths paid off in a long and illustrious career and in the affectionate regard of a wide audience and the avid fascination of interviewers.

That should have taught me something about truth and New Yorkers, but apparently it didn't. Jerry Siegel who was heading Guttman & Pam's New York office... (full disclosure: he WAS our New York office)... and I were to have breakfast at a New York deli with Sam Waterston, seeking him as a client. Jerry was late, and he apologized saying that his bicycle had a flat and that he'd had to take the bus. It was a good meeting, but after Sam left I asked Jerry why he had to get into the bus thing. "You want him to think he's so insignificant to us that you didn't take a taxi to be on time?" "Oh, he'll understand," Jerry said. Apparently so. Shortly thereafter, Jerry went on his own, and Sam Waterston remained his client for decades.

So the point of all this is that in publicity, the truth is very important. The truth, actually, is the point, because what you're selling has to... well... *it has to live up to its publicity.* The point also is that... because of the demands and traditions of our craft and because the media are in the entertainment business as well as the news business... publicists sometimes have to take a circuitous route to get there... "there" being the truth. The truth is not always all that interesting all by itself. It needs to tell an arresting story to get itself heard. When I started, the publicity field was the wild west. The circuitous routes to the truth, the stuff we had to do and CHOSE to do to get a story in, were very colorful and imaginative. The bizarre fact is that now when the internet is redefining or at least bending the media… rarely for the better… and when economic factors have made media survival supremely competitive, even at the peril of hallowed traditions, *the news business is more in the entertainment business than ever.* However much they may distrust and deplore press agent device, they frequently welcome the bells and whistles of a well-constructed and entertaining news pitch or written item because of the inventive angle or twist it is given… as long as, in the end, it hews to the actual facts.

If a press agent doesn't cherish his or her memories, the rich parade of great and amusing and inspiring characters encountered in any PR career, that flack is eating the bones and leaving the meat. The work experience of every press agent I know is a cavalcade of the entertainment business through his or her unique perspective, enriched by the personalities of the people he or she represented. Whatever made them stars also made them indelible and original companions. Furthermore, many of the most astounding people of my experience were great characters who never made it to acting or to the headlines or even to public awareness, but who memorably amazed me. You may or may not believe that these experiences I unfold actually transpired, that the dialogues actually were conversed, but could any imagination possibly have conjured them all?

Putting It In Perspective

Even careful, cautious people do stupid things. And so I once found myself on a narrow open ledge at virtually the highest point that man had constructed on the face of the earth, no safety wire in event of a slip, no rail to hold on to. I was a quarter mile or so above the bustle of the Toronto traffic so far below that cars no larger than ants were crawling across roadways no wider than narrow strips of ribbon.

I was standing on a fifteen-inch wide concrete ledge, nothing protecting me from gravity or grave but an eight-inch high steel I-beam reaching barely to ankle height which formed merely a lip on this narrow, narrow circular rim atop the visitor viewing center crowning the CN Tower. The wind tore at me, flapping my clothes about me like shreds of flag, abrupt changes challenging every effort to stay balanced. The fear of imminent plunge to death scrambled my mind…

spasms of vertigo… I flirted with the idea that I might just as well step forward and get it over with.

A wall inclined behind me sloping back at a 75 degree angle up to the ultimate roof of the Tower about 20 feet above. The door through which I'd emerged onto this idiotic enterprise was 15 feet away and open, still in my sightline but about to disappear in the curvature of the inclined wall. The PR guy for the CN Tower who had escorted me at my request to this stupid predicament, leaned out his head and waved to me encouragingly. "Everything ok?" he called. No, everything was not ok . His face, the wind kept telling me, would very likely be the last I would ever see.

I intrude into my recollections this idiotically true incident not to expose my least rational self, but because it is a reasonable analogy for a life in high-stakes PR. A press agent's existence is vertiginous. Those who entrust their careers to you are venerated artists, the anointed people whose beauty defines beauty, national treasures, legends, and that raises the height from which you can fall. The view is great, but the missteps are costly. Unlike my precarious teeter on the world's highest ledge, at least in PR you meet some interesting people. The ones I dealt with in these first six decades of my occupation were the classic stars who will live forever. That is, sadly, no longer the life expectancy of newly-minted stars.

Chapter 6

The Guy Who Wrote the Rules

Warren Cowan came at PR with such a passion and with such glee, that by the early 1950s Rogers & Cowan had become the paradigm forever for high-powered, superstar, independent Hollywood publicity… "independent" as distinguished from the studio PR machines that had long dominated the star-making business and were, at that transition moment, dragging their heels against turning over the reins. There were grudgingly cordial relations between studio publicity chiefs and the rapidly rising stars of independent publicity. They did, after all, have one thing in common… they wanted the films of their newly shared stars to succeed. The stars now were paying part of the cost of publicizing films and were exacting greater control over their own exposure in return… or at least their PR reps were doing that for them. Territory was being redrawn, and soon studios would be hiring agencies to assist in promoting films. There were crazy and unforeseen curves in the road. Because their lawyers said so, studio PR machines, for instance, weren't allowed to announce castings until the contracts were signed. Contracts often weren't signed until the film was almost fully shot. So most star assignments, to everyone's relief, were leaked rather than announced… and then let the ballyhoo begin. One studio guy asked me once in annoyance, "When are you guys gonna leak this baby? We've got stuff backin' up."

In the process of pioneering these new realities in partnership with Henry Rogers, Warren Cowan established many of the basic rules and practices of agency PR. During one Rogers & Cowan morning staff meeting, someone suggested that we didn't have enough to go with on a story we were planning. To which Warren responded, *"It doesn't have to be a million dollars. It can be three dollars and ninety-eight cents in a big box."* If you could grasp the genius of that, you were a press agent.

The Cardinal Rule of PR

At the start of my career, I asked Warren Cowan to give me the cardinal rule of press agenting. *"Get the hell out of the shot,"* he said without a blink. Now, that has two meanings, and I have religiously subscribed to both.

One is get the hell out of the shot... meaning that a publicist's machinations should never be seen. That's primary, mandatory, immutable. Whatever good befalls or is reflected upon your client, it is and should appear to be, the natural consequence of the client's talent and importance. Of that neat disappearing act Warren was a master. The second interpretation, get the hell out of the shot meaning literally get the hell out of the SHOT... don't be part of a photo, don't get personal publicity... to that one he wasn't so dedicated. That could be because he was "indie" from the start, never having worked at a studio.

Henri Bollinger, who has headed the Publicist Guild for decades and is one of the town's most savvy indie PR men, tells me that this rule (staying behind the camera) derives not only from the good sense it makes but from the fact that in the iron-fist studio days every publicist understood that one could get bounced for sharing a shot with one of his or her (more his than her at that time) studio's stars. A half-century back, before he became the west coast office for Lee Solters' New York-based independent PR firm, Henri got his start at television station KTLA adjacent to and owned by Paramount... and staying out of the shot was a delineated job-dependent rule.

Warren Cowan, however, enjoyed and accepted awards and maintained visible celebrity throughout his career, which is to say his life. When Paul Newman passed away, almost every TV news shot of Paul at various events had Warren right behind him or guiding him through the clamor of press, selecting the most important interviews, guiding Paul at the elbow. Warren had preceded Paul through the Pearly Gates by four months, but there they were going out together. It was as poetic as justice can get.

Joined at the Hip

Paul Newman's acting skills never diminished, and his greatest role, his astonishing philanthropy, continued and grew until the end. It actually has continued after his death and very notably so under Joanne's compassionate oversight...

Paul's Newman's Own philanthropy last year contributed $21,000,000, the largest giving of any entertainment figure, living or dead. Warren Cowan died with his boots on, as well, notably sharp and integrated at 90. On what would be his death bed, on what would be his last day, with the final sweep of his white plume, as Cyrano de Bergerac described the grand eloquence of final gesture... "mon panache"... Warren assured a journalist quite close to him, someone for whom he truly and deeply cared, that Paul Newman was not in perilous health even though Paul was himself at that moment hospitalized in dire decline. Truth matters, but it can have consequences which a press agent is honor-bound to control. Warren knew that Paul's family wanted the last months to themselves. Obligation to client was not something Warren invented, but nobody played it better.

Fame Is a High Maintenance Sport... and a Costly Addiction... for Flacks

A most important rule of daily function as a PR guy or gal is that a press agent should not be seen and should not be heard. A publicist comes most easily undone if he or she courts celebrity. I've spent my whole career not being a celeb, and a happier man for it. When your name appears in print, it is not by dint of your accomplishment but rather your client's. Press agents are like bartenders in that they each can always pour themselves a shot of the poison they dispense. Publicists can always insert themselves into a story or into a shot. In fact, sometimes it is difficult to avoid it. The media always wants a mouth to put the facts into or to take them out of. The TV media demand talking heads. But a sip of fame here, a slug a recognition there... and pretty soon you're just another fame-aholic. I make it explicit to journalists that a condition of anything I say is anonymity. It doesn't always turn out that way.

Our clients require exposure in controlled bursts in order to conduct their career and to exercise their talents happily and successfully. Measured dabs of visibility and attention keep industry awareness of and interest in them successfully in orbit. A flack is best attired in a cloak of absence. A client once demanded why my name was in a story about him, a question I'd asked myself when I saw it. I explained that the journalist apparently felt he had to source some fact. Well then, the client pursued, why was my name was the same size as his. I explained that newspapers are printed in eight point type and that it would be bizarre to print a press agent's name in six point letters. It would serve only to call further undue attention to him or her. But that client was absolutely correct. A publicity story loses something when you see the puppeteer's hands, or discern his/her name, and that something is called credibility.

And yet here I am, pouring out exhibition while my life's theme has been invisibility. I've been a tranquil island of anonymity in a stormy sea of fame. When I started writing down these recollections, I thought the stories were going to be all about other people, but I found that it was actually only through some revelation of my own life that I could give these tales a coherent connection. Having now written down these disparate episodes, I can release myself from being forever and ever the oral historian of my own life.

Anticipation

Warren Cowan was often a blink ahead of the game, and that's all you need if you're smart. He quickly recognized when a concept or phrase or even a word would have that most short-lasting and useful of all things, currency. He then would find a way to use it to add a special sparkle of currency to some client's campaign. He had an instinct for what would have resonance, however momentary. The work of noted photographer Steve Shapiro always captured the perfect moment. I once asked Steve his secret, because I could see a shot in my camera, but could never catch THE moment. "You shoot it the second you see it?" Steve asked. "The exact second," I affirmed proudly. "That's too late," Steve said, "You have to anticipate it." That's what you have to do in publicity, too, anticipate.

No one in publicity had the anticipatory skills of Warren Cowan. One morning he arrived at the office, and his first word was "Compleat." "What?" "Compleat… c-o-m-p-l-e-a-t." "What happened to e-t-e?" "That just means having all its parts, while e-a-t means top of the world." "Quintessential?" I suggested. "Exactly." "Where did you come by this information?" "It's on a Jaguar billboard, the compleat driving experience or something." "Why not quintessential?" "Compleat is coming into heat. Use it today… a story… a catchphrase. It's a story-selling hook… but today. It'll be gone tomorrow." He was right in both assumptions. It was indeed a hook that made some campaign or other cook for us, and we used it in a half dozen letters I wrote for him. And in just a week it was totally passé, erased from memory, so much so that the inevitable one-usage-too-many brought a gruff note from an editor saying "check your spelling."

Another thing on which Warren had the lock was *"selling the sell,"* merchandising your work to the client or the client's reps. We were doing the pre-publicity for an American tour by Tom Jones. Weeks before its kick-off, it was a near sell-out, and we had a budget for a double-truck (two adjacent pages) ad in the trade papers using a photo of Tom Jones. In the composition of the shot, Tom's head was so far back that the photo was horizontal, without the fold-break disturbing the essence of the picture... Tom singing up into a handheld mic... leaving the left-hand page only suggesting his torso, basically an empty setting for a strong and concise ad-line at the top. But we didn't yet have a strong and concise ad-line. I came in one morning and gave Warren something I'd come up with in the car. He grabbed the phone and dialed. "Tom, the ad? We've got it... six letters... Of course I know your name alone is eight letters, but we don't need your name, we have your photo.... Ok... are you sitting down?... Well, do... Sitting? Tom... the photo, at the top of the left-hand page, six letters... ready?.... 'USA... SRO'... Yeah, it really is.... Tom, that's very gracious of you, thanks." And he hung up, smiling. "He loves it." "The idea or the sell?" I asked, amazed by his unfailing ability to sock it home. Warren looked at me as though my question made no sense. It was inconceivable to him that I didn't comprehend from birth that the *Idea and the Sell are the yin and the yang of publicity, one notion indivisible.*

An Inadvertant Life

I had never heard of public relations and was certainly not looking for a job in it, much less a life in it. But approaching the summer before my junior year in college, I needed a job. I'd spent the previous summer and most of my sophomore year as a ramp serviceman loading luggage on the graveyard shift at LA Airport. United Airlines didn't hire college kids. They wanted guys who wished to stuff suitcases into the bellies of planes unto their deaths. But I lied that I had quit school because I was engaged and I needed the buck sixty-eight an hour.

I had never required more than a few hours of sleep a night, so the 8PM to 4AM schedule was do-able for me. I could get a lot of homework done on the downtime between flights and still grab enough sleep before leaving for school in the morning. The other ramp servicemen were just guys trying to feed a family or get dates on that pay, decent guys, sports-page-reading guys, a surprising number of them former boxers. They weren't interested enough in books to look at what I was always reading. And nobody gave me any trouble. It was 1953 and the LA sports world was humming... Art Aragon was the Golden Boy of boxing... so they had plenty to keep their conversations interesting while waiting for the next flight to come in.

My only friendship was with a kid on summer break from BYU whose dad knew someone who got him the job. He was a very nice guy, intellectually curious, and we had studies in common. It came to a sad end at a midnight lunch break when he said, over a bowl of pea soup that cost only a nickel in the staff commissary, "You know, I'm impressed that you never smoke, drink or swear. You'd make a good woman." I thought it was a joke, so I said, "You never smoke, drink or swear either. You'd make a good woman, too." "I am one," he answered straight-out and exceedingly proud of the revelation. I certainly had friends who were gay, but trans-sexuality (it wasn't trans-gender yet) was complex, well beyond my psych studies to that point. It was a half-century before LGBT awareness liberated us, both gays and straights, from the tyranny of perception. At 19, I had no business setting up office inside the belly of a DC-4 to practice psychology without a license. I feared giving bad advice. I begged him not to tell that to any of the ex-boxers and muscle guys we worked with, which really offended him. I began to make sure that when work gangs were divvied up, I was always on a crew other than his. I was afflicted with the ignorance of the times.

What had been a friendship devolved into a resentful distance. Just as he was about to return to school, he caught up with me one wee small hour when we were heading for our cars. "Hang on a second," he said rather sadly, "I just want to know what happened to our friendship. You made your rejection quite obvious, and it was a pretty darn lonely summer. I'd really like to know why the change." "Are you kidding? I didn't know how to handle it when you told me you were a woman?" "After I what?.... told you I was a WOMAN?!" he exclaimed in outrage, and then, "I told you I was a MORMON!" That was the only memorable event in the numbing year of airport nights. And when a crew foreman finally thumbed through some of my books and saw they were psychology, anthropology and theatre history, I was summarily fired. A dollar and ninety cents an hour (I'd had a raise) down the drain. I needed a new job for the new summer.

On the bulletin board of the UCLA Bureau of Occupations were pinned notices of work availabilities, and there was a "wanted, mailroom boy" listing for a company called Rogers & Cowan. It was just a job... not a life direction... and a job was something I needed. It was a nice office in Beverly Hills, walls covered with Musee d'Art Modern posters. The company had something to do with art, I supposed, and that was ok with me. I was well-qualified... I had a car and they had deliveries. They asked what would happen when school started up again. I assured them I could work my schedule to give them five hours in the afternoon. That seemed fine, all systems go. But some client's nephew needed a job, so I had a great summer as counselor and director of theatre programming at a kids camp on the high slopes of Mount San Gorgonio, learning and then teaching canoeing and forestry lore, writing and directing plays for parent days and parent campfire nights. One evening, after I had led a group of 12 to 15 year olds on a climb up Grayback, Southern California's highest peak, I made camp for them alongside a creekbed, failing to notice the plentiful hoof-prints in the dust. That night a herd of wild burros galloped through our campsite. Only one kid got stepped on and that without injury. I would never entrust a child to me absent other supervision. But it did prove something that would stand me in good stead as a press agent. I was lucky. In publicity, on those occasions when you are not smart enough, it is absolutely imperative to be lucky enough.

In September, I got a call from this Rogers & Cowan company that the office boy job was open if I was still interested. I worked my classes so that I could start work at one each day, 46 dollars a week and a little extra to be made on deliveries at 10 cents a mile. There were these Henry Rogers and Warren Cowan guys, about eight other workers at whatever it was they did and a half dozen secretaries and accounting staff. There was a lot to do for a lone and part-time office boy, so one Friday I didn't get to distribute the new telephone books. I came in on Saturday morning to do it, but they were gone and in their stead a note saying "Since you were too busy to pass out the phone books, I did it. Henry C. Rogers." But, as I said, it wasn't a career, it was just a job.

Things changed for me at Rogers & Cowan one day when I had to make a delivery to a Beverly Hills mansion and Kirk Douglas opened the door. Hold on... what is it these guys were doing at that office? I was a film student, so maybe this was up my alley or at least a door opening onto other promising alleys. I started to read the memos before I distributed them, to read the newspaper and magazine clippings which I mailed to clients. I was assured it was a job of grave repsonsibilitys. A light bulb switched on. So the art posters were just pretentious décor. The people in this office were in some mysterious and slowly-to-be-deciphered way engaged in the grand scheme of Hollywood. I devised and dedicated myself to a crash course in what publicity is and how it threads into the very woof and warp of the entertainment world fabric. Up my alley?... it was the alley I had stalked from childhood. I'd been a journalist wannabe all my life; I'd written high school sports from age 15 for one of William Randolph Hearst's top papers, the Los Angeles Examiner, and I had a weekly column in it when I was seventeen. I'd thought long and hard about being a sports writer. Sports... apart from their visceral tensions and releases, their exultations and life-lesson disappointments... are where we play out our metaphors of victory and defeat, determination and skill. I grew up a Pulitzer (my grandmother was a cousin of Joseph Pulitzer from the poor side of the family) in St. Louis, a town dominated by the Cousin Joe's flagship, the Post-Dispatch. I was writing and editing school papers from fourth grade on. This publicity thing combined the only two things to which I'd ever aspired... journalism and movie-making. Sure, I'd toyed with the idea of becoming a therapist, but who wants to be depressed all your life? I'd dabbled in documentaries, but having, at Rogers & Cowan, fallen into this collateral aspect of movie-making, this publicity thing, the decision of what to do with my life seemed to have been handed to me right off the rack, pre-cut to size. Publicity tied the disparate aspects of my aspirations into a neat knot. I'm drawn to any confluence. I read them like tea leaves. Confluence is the closest I come to metaphysical speculation or conviction... confluence and Chinese fortune cookies. And PR was a confluence of my interests. I started to study how they did it.

It was the flip side of journalism. A journalist has to identify, research, interpret, organize and then economically, intelligibly and accurately convey news. He or she is expected to do this objectively, but it is almost impossible for some conclusion by the reporter not to color the facts. We all are subject to opinion and to response. A publicist, quite the contrary, has to evaluate what the operative news factor of a story is, and then must determine which elements of the story will benefit his or her client and the client's interests. The press agent has to structure news so as to get the media to use it in such a way as to retain your plug element. It helps if you know how to construct a story from the ground up and to do so in a way that bends reader conclusion in a client-friendly direction.

It's important to understand that you are not writing an ad. You must bring to your copy the well organized information, clear and comprehensible writing, structure and the sense of what makes this story relevant to the readership or viewership of the outlet or outlets to which you are submitting it. The reporters and editors who will consider it are people at the top of their craft. They know their stuff and they will judge your stuff with a sharp eye. Sloppy writing can kill a solid piece of news. Keep your purpose clearly in mind and find an angle that will both intrigue the media and that will project and accomplish your purpose. Find the element that locks your plug message inextricably into the story. One difference between the reporter and you, the press agent, is that the journalist has to BE objective, and that you, as a publicist, have to HAVE an objective.

Warren and Henry were too importantly occupied for me to reveal and explore my growing interest in the craft. Their top account executive, Ted Loeff, much beloved and respected by artists, studio heads, magazine editors and journalists alike, had an open mind and an open door. He taught me to learn the skills and to learn the clients, arguing that *you represent talents well only if you formulate common intellectual ground with them. You can't sell what you don't understand.* Ted was an integral element in one of Hollywood's main gatherings of liberal and activist *mensches* (worthwhile human beings)… among them such of his personal clients as Martin Ritt, Mark Robson, Robert Ryan and Charlton Heston… yes, Charlton Heston. I started writing sample copy for Ted, stories about Heston's deep quest for social justice. Ted delivered lesson one… "This stuff isn't going to stoke women's interest in Chuck. They don't love him because they think he has a huge heart." "Why do they love him?" "Because they think he has a huge dick."

Ted arranged for a subscription to Weekly Variety to be sent to my house. (My parents' house, to tell the truth… and, yes, I actually lived at home throughout college and substantially beyond… how cocooned can you get? I made Thomas The Innocent look like a gang-banger… a house where never was heard a discouraging word… well, maybe discouraging, but never expletive.) Ted's idea was for me to read the Weekly cover to cover and to mark stories that could be adapted… I think his word was "extrapolated"… to fit one of Rogers & Cowan's clients.

His reason for the Weekly Variety discipline was thus… "Each of those stories has passed the muster of a top and tough editor, which means it's fit to print. Most people in Hollywood read the Daily, not the Weekly, the editors of the Daily included. They'll never know it's a hand-me-down." Not only did it hone my sense of what made a story, but Ted would slip my extrapolations to the company "planter" who shuffled them into the mix of the items he was selling. Ted kept a copy of every story I wrote that broke to have in hand when he demanded that the company up me from office gofer to press agent. The fact that I still had two years of college to go and would have to be a part-time press agent made that a hard sell.

At a PR firm in those pre-digital decades, the "planter" was the guy who sold the stories to different outlets, the limited number of specific columns and other media who trafficked in entertainment news. To my good fortune, at Rogers and Cowan that designator hitter was Larry Laurie, the best planter since Johnny Appleseed. No one who ever walked the face of the earth could more adroitly squeeze some loser item into life. Larry was a handsome, glib and charming Irishman, smartly over-endowed with the gift of gab. He had the first little Porsche roadster convertible in town, in which he dated many of the top young starlets and had their hair and their dreams of stardom madly flying. Larry could get any story into orbit. In selling a story, he did not merely enthuse… he exuberated. Larry and I once were conjuring a what-if story that had David Niven trying to buy the film rights to the life of the English driver who had just set a world speed record on the salt flats in Utah, a story which would remind the industry, the media and the public of the adventuroso aspects of Niven's playbook, complimenting his evident way with romantic comedy. We couldn't, however, think of the driver's name. (This antedated the Internet by forty years.) I had Larry call the LA Examiner sports information desk to find out. Larry, in seeking the name, was describing the driver in such vivid flow of adjectives and adulation that the sports "morgue"(digging up dead stories) guy at the paper said, "Can't find his name, but I sure as hell wanna see the film."

Ted had armed me with a simple philosophy of PR success. One of the first and most sacred rules was *"never miss a shot," meaning never let an opportunity go by without at least taking a shot.* Part of my education was reading every memo I carried from office to office. Ted also imparted the corollary rule of a career in anything… *make your break. MAKE YOUR BREAK.* What does that mean? I asked. You'll know when it hits you, he answered. He was right. It did hit me and I did know. It hit me when I was of reading a memo from Warren Cowan that I was delivering to Henry Rogers. Jack Webb's obsession with "Pete Kelly's

Blues" (the second of four films he would direct) wasn't going away, the memo said quite urgently. The company needed a home run. Jack Webb, a very prestige client, had revolutionized television with that early TV sensation, "Dragnet." But R&C was coming up blank on creating a break-out piece of PR to fast-track Jack Webb's beloved new project, a period blues musical in which he had invested not only his talent and his clout, but also his soul.

There are some stars who leap into legend early on. Their art, stature and charisma is such that it quickly evolves into an eternal flame... Cary Grant, Barbra Streisand, Marilyn Monroe, Elizabeth Taylor, Judy Garland, Gary Cooper, the Hepburns, Audrey and Kate, Sinatra, Brando, Garbo, Eastwood, Bogart, Bette Davis, James Dean, Wayne, Newman, Welles, Beatty, McQueen, etc. There are always, by a very different measurement, a few stars who are the hottest thing in the business at any particular time. Some will ascend as legends, and some will fulfill their season as dominant stars or acting talents of a specific period. And that is an extraordinary thing, too. It's in a constant state of change and of being assessed and re-assessed. The reason for this scrutiny is that *while you have it, you damn well better use i*t. And the people around you, press agents among them, have an obligation to make these judgments often and accurately and to protect and build on any advantage they perceive. Tony Curtis was just slipping into high gear in his long and defined time of pre-eminence... the same kind of most-profoundly significant star as Tom Cruise or Julia Roberts or George Clooney or Angelina Jolie or Johnny Depp have been in their continuing time. Warren Cowan constantly took the pulse of fame, and knowing who was hotter than whom helped keep his clients and his company at their respective peaks... He and I went for a meeting with Tony Curtis, Dean Martin and the producers and studio execs for a film in which these two leading leading-men would co-star. I noticed Warren's eyes shifting back and forth between the two during the meeting (they were both clients) as though he were measuring. As we drove back to the office, Warren said, "You know, I think Dino's a bigger star now than Tony, and I think Tony knows it." It was a complex and subjective conclusion, but I realized Warren was absolutely right. A place in that wavering line had subtly changed and, as these things do, would change back. . It would shape for that moment what Warren had to devise and execute to best serve each. Rogers & Cowan probably handled forty to fifty percent of the truly top stars. How big was R&C? Do you recall that amazing shot of all the MGM stars of the '40s? I have it on a wall of my office to remind me what stardom is. A shot of the Rogers & Cowan client list at any one of twenty points in history would have been far more starry.

How Warren prioritized the relative fame and stardom of his own aggregated version of more-stars-than-there-are-in-the-heavens… and my office-boy perception of that… gave me the break I needed to get out of the mail-room about a half-year into my gofer stint there. I knew who was on his mind. With all of the Coopers and Crawfords and Sinatras and Douglases, Newmans and Berles, the Brynners and Rex Harrisons, Audrey Hepburn, Elizabeth Taylor, Heston, Curtis, Wyman, Kaye, Allyson, Grayson, Doris Day to Johnny Mathis, Judy Garland to Bobby Darin, Diana Ross and The Supremes and nearly ad infinitum, the biggest biggest star, the one whose pleasure and gratitude Warren most sought at that point in 1955 was… Jack Webb. "Dragnet" had created the curt neo-realism that would make police procedural series TV's go-to genre. He had become such a singular sensation that Webb was the one particular client at that moment upon whom Warren most doted.

Webb was aware that this was a moment when a job really had to be done on and for him. The task of the moment was to deliver an indelible campaign on the movie Webb had just produced, directed and starred in. "Pete Kelly's Blues" was more than a film for him. It was a passion. He was brilliantly learned in jazz and had gathered the top musicians of the genre, including Ella Fitzgerald and Peggy Lee, for the film, his tribute to the music he loved. R&C needed a home run badly, but it would have settled for a bunt. I was still a junior at UCLA, and I often ate my lunch in the six hundred seat auditorium of the Music Department where, as good fortune would have it, the Roger Wagner Chorale rehearsed every noon just when I had my lunch break. I had become friends with some of the top people in the department because, no dummies, they took their lunch then, too.

I went first to the music fraternity and proposed their sponsoring what I called "A Seminar On Blues featuring Jack Webb and the musical stars of his 'Pete Kelly's Blues.'" I let the words Ella Fitzgerald and Peggy Lee flutter in illusive possibility lightly coated with a sheen of promise. With the fraternity's slavering backing, I went to Music Department brass and was promised the auditorium at no cost, and I was pretty sure I could fill it. I threw in a special department award for Webb, which was enthusiastically embraced. I brought this back to Ted Loeff in a one page proposal and he took it to Warren. "Who did you say is putting this together?" Henry Rogers asked Warren Cowan incredulously after he read the note. "Dick," Warren said. "Let me get this straight," said Henry Rogers, "You're putting our biggest-clout client in the hands of the office boy?" "Give me a better idea," Warren said earnestly. I worked with the music fraternity in covering the campus with postings. I'd done special writing for the *UCLA Daily Bruin*, so the advance coverage in that school paper was heavy.

Warren was nervous the day of the night. He was hurtling toward the river and could only hope that the bridge wasn't out. When he arrived with Jack Webb and five of the greatest jazz and blues instrumentalists of the '50s, there were nearly 800 students and faculty jamming the 600 seat hall. Either the fire marshals had gone home, or they were as passionately devoted to Kansas City jazz and blues… not to mention to Jack Webb… as the rest of the crowd. It wasn't a seminar, it was a revival meeting. The yelling started when Webb and the musicians walked in at the back of the auditorium and the noise lasted through the musicians' setup. It took another five minutes for Webb's waving arms to bring them back to sanity. His brilliance at everything was immediately felt. He had prepared an extraordinary syllabus on the music he loved. The evening was a history of blues, one of the great and gloried instructions on a respected campus. He told the story in words, and the musicians told it in music. Even Ella and Peggy, had they shown, couldn't have taken that crowd higher. There was love flowing back and forth between artists and audience in great tides. When it was over, Webb didn't want to slip out the stage door. He gloried in the crushing enthusiasm, and it took us a half-hour to get him out. As Warren ushered him and the musicians into their bus, Webb said, "Warren, I never thought I'd say this to anyone but a woman, but you've given me the greatest night of my life." I had still been toying with the idea of becoming a shrink, but Jack Webb sealed my deal.

If I'd been a year further into publicity, I would have told them to take that act on the road and replicate it in five key cities before the film opened, doing it as a fund-raiser for some important music cause in each city. It seemed someone else could have come up with that, but I think they were happy just to be off the hook. The one rule it taught me when I knew enough to take a step back… *being off the hook is never enough. You take it as far as it will go.* It wasn't just a night… it was a whole campaign… or could have been. But it got me in the door.

In new client solicitation and in pitch meetings, most press agents have their own special stump pitch. But even good clothes-off-the-rack can rock if tailored to the buyer, a tuck here, a stitch there. And that was a Warren Cowan specialty. I remember very well being in on Warren's pitch meeting with Christopher Plummer when Chris was about to start filming his role as Captain Von Trapp in "The Sound of Music." Plummer, with well-earned pride in his acting chops, felt that engaging publicity to draw career momentum from this much sought-after role required him to stoop to conquer. His mindset that it was beneath him was clearly visible in his occasional reference to the project as "The Sound of Mucus." Warren, undeterred, pointed out to him, as he had to others, that *"each new role is the stepping stone to the rest of your career"* and that Chris had to be aware that his association with a such a huge hit could be every bit as important in getting him a continuity of major roles as is his unique and considerable talent. Warren stressed that stamping Plummer's name on that film's success, as only we could do, would encourage other significant roles to come his way, that he had to get great visibility to keep this film's clearly ordained box-office success from being Julie Andrews' stepping stone to the exclusion of all others. Warren's relentless don't-walk-away-from-the-biggest-opportunity-of-your-life sell finally broke down Chris' clearly valid my-work-speaks-for-itself resistance.

I tried to be patient with his anger about the film and, worse, his real distain for publicity. One of the great breaks in Hollywood publicity then was Louella Parsons' column which appeared in all of the Hearst newspapers, including the Los Angeles Examiner, the only serious competitor to the LA Times as the dominant morning rag. Especially important was her Sunday feature story, one of the most read exposures in the country. Louella's daughter Harriet was to do the interview for a Sunday piece, an exceedingly prime break, at a lunch with Chris at the Beverly Wilshire Hotel where "Captain Von Trapp" was staying in the penthouse. It was an accommodation I knew well because Warren Beatty usually lived there. Time passed as Harriet and I sat in the hotel restaurant, and Chris simply did not come down for this important interview. I finally went up to see what was delaying him. I found him on the phone describing to the concierge a shoe he had thrown not out the window but through the window in some dispute with his wife. He was more interested in pursuing that tension than coming down to do a career-assisting interview.

That attitude notwithstanding (I'm getting back to how this relates to Warren Cowan,) Chris and I had a respectful relationship, and the job he allowed me to do was pretty good. So I was surprised when I showed up on the set one day and Chris began the conversation with "Don't take this personally, but I'm dispensing with the services of Rogers & Cowan. Don't argue the point. I have damn good reason." "I am taking this very personally," I said, "because you've had a damn good job." "Excellent, but I bid you adieu." "Because?" "It doesn't matter." "Because what?" "Do you remember that powerful sales argument Warren gave me in his office? You were there." "Of course," "His insistence that the promotion I would obtain from the studio would be for the *film*, not for *me*? He stressed that I needed publicity which sold ME, me specifically, and not just somebody, what he described as the unique me who could bring to a film something nobody else could?" "He sold *me*," I said. "He sold me, too," Chris said, "and last night I was dining at La Scala and by chance I heard Warren in the booth behind me selling someone else with the exact same goddam speech." I said… "Well, maybe…." "Maybe nothing," Chris said heatedly, "the exact speech. So I turned around and who do you think he was saying it to?…. Eddie fucking Fisher!"

I did get Christopher Plummer back the next year, and with that re-association came one of the most cherished gifts my craft ever brought me. Chris went off to film a BBC production of "Hamlet" with the Royal Shakespeare Company shooting at Elsinore Castle itself. Rather than bringing him good luck, the BBC "Hamlet" network broadcast in America received reviews you don't send home to mom. Gisela and I could not have more disagreed with these pans… It was a powerful performance, and we said so with passion in a telegram, the old-fashioned Western Union telegram with pasted-on verbal brevities… pronouns and articles sacrificed to telegram-speak. Apparently it touched Chris because he sent a return telegram saying "Dear Gisela and Dick, Your message cheered me greatly. See you on my return. Love." It was lovely in itself and a collectible object of astonishing significance because of how Western Union garbled his name. They added a letter. It read in full… "Dear Gisela and Dick. Your message cheered me greatly. See you on my return. Love, Christ." See you on my return. Everybody… and we showed it to everybody… was impressed.

Actually, Plummer was dead wrong in his indignant despisal of Warren's having used the same sell on him and on Eddie Fisher. The same philosophy applied to each of them and applies to all sells. It simply has to be tailored to the specific product or talent being sold, which we had done for Chris and did for Fisher. Obviously, I had failed to make him see that our job for him had been differentiated to sell the idea of a great dramatic actor adapting his thespian powers and his skill in developing a compelling character, to a big and commercial musical project. For Christopher Plummer, we were working the proposition that this had become a recent tradition of the theatre and the screen… Rex Harrison and "My Fair Lady," Richard Burton and "Camelot," Yul Brynner and "The King and I"… three very apt superstars with whom to associate Chris. It had been paying off. It is one of the first concepts of flackery, *placing the star's work in a context of and association with success.* It's like selling the futures of a really promising commodity. That way, the artist's representatives can start reaping the next roles on the basis of the anticipation, not having to wait to sell the eventual success post facto when the potential buyer can say… and this is a line that I actually heard uttered… "yeah, but that was last week." *Anticipation can be more motivating than attainment.* This town buys futures. But there was no rationale which would remove the Eddie Fisher factor from Christopher's craw where it was securely stuck. Maybe that epiphany at La Scala Restaurant cost him the chance to have harvested more from being one of the two stars of one of the biggest commercial hits of all time. It did not, I must emphasize, deprive him of his talent, and he lived and prospered happily ever after. He may be at his peak now, winning the Oscar and a run of great roles in his 80s, more than four decades later.

The La Scala restaurant, where Beverly Hills' hip-crowd crushed in from twilight to midnight to do its eating and chatting, was Warren Cowan's night-time office. One night, during a Dodgers/Yankees World Series, he introduced Louella Parsons, the Hearst newspapers' queen of gossip, to the New York team's superstar, Moose Skowron, whom Louella kept calling Mouse. Warren surreptitiously wrote "Moose" on the tablecloth in front of Louella. She didn't notice, so he underlined the second O and then started tapping the tablecloth to direct her eye there. The only one who noticed was Skowron who, uninitiated into the customs of Hollywood, was a bit perplexed. There was a similar event at the office one time in a prospective client meeting with someone named Patrick. The guy who headed our personality department kept calling him Peter. Warren wrote "Patrick" large across a piece of paper and held it up, but the Peters rolled on to the irritation of

Patrick. Even though Patrick could plainly see that Warren already had his name in print, we didn't land him.

La Scala was sort of in-the-family because we handled the owner Jean Leon and his effort to start professional soccer in the USA, which everyone knew would never happen. When Gisela's parents visited us from Germany, Warren hosted us all at La Scala. It started on the wrong foot because when we told her parents in advance that Warren had invited them to La Scala, they thought we were going to the opera. Warren, as was his habit, was exceedingly gracious. With Gisela translating, they got along well and, of course, the food was delicious. Throughout the evening, Warren was introducing Gisela's parents to all the stars dining there who stopped by to say hello. That's the measure of a superstar press agent's fame… when he's the one who gets table-hopped. The trouble was that her parents spent their lives in the Black Forest in the elegantly distant world of Baden Baden, and their big stars were Beethoven, Maria Callas, Van Clyburn, Mozart and Bach. They had no idea of the importance of the top box-office draws with whom they were shaking hands. So when Warren brought Peter Lawford to the table, he introduced him as "the President's brother-in-law," and that was a winner.

Warren Cowan's conversation with Eddie Fisher on Christopher Plummer's night of disenchantment, actually, was to re-sign him. In our prior tour with Fisher, one memorable crisis on which the R&C staff had to weigh-in was the PR ramifications when his romance with and marriage to Elizabeth Taylor came to a madly publicized end. Whatever the other calamitous world events of the day, it was the termination of this famous relationship that ate up the front page headlines. Warren was due at a big emergency meeting with Eddie and his reps at the studio where Eddie was rehearsing his television show. We had an intense head-knocking session about publicity approaches that could be taken, how to mitigate the damage and the embarrassment. Warren wanted to be armed when he got there. We were satisfied with the list, and Warren drove off to the meeting. When he returned, several of us convened in his office to find out how the strategies went over. "We never got to them," Warren said. "All we talked about was what songs he was going to sing this week. 'Am I Blue?,' 'I'll Go My Way By Myself?' 'Don't Get Around Much Anymore?' 'On the Street Where You Live?' 'Our Love Is Here To Stay?' 'They Can't Take That Away From Me?' 'Bye Bye Blues?' 'It's The Talk of The Town?' ' 'I'll Never Smile Again?' or, going the other way "I'm

Sitting on Top of The World?' 'On The Sunny Side of The Street?' It was driving Eddie crazy. Every song will get a laugh," "What did they decide on?" someone asked. "When I left," Warren said, "I think the list was down to 'Oh, My Papa' and 'Happy Birthday to You.'"

One instructive day, Warren asked me to join him at a meeting. Russell Birdwell was coming in that afternoon to sell Warren on some idea, and Warren said I would learn something valuable. "What?" I asked. "We'll see," he answered. Russell Birdwell had preceded Henry and Warren in the super-flack business by about 20 years and 10 years respectively. Like Warren and Henry, he was a great self-promoter, too, even more dedicated to it than they were. He had pulled super-stunts for Goldwyn, Stanley Kubrick, Darryl Zanuck and Howard Hughes. Birdwell did the blow-away campaign introducing Jane Russell in Hughes' "The Outlaw." His name had been synonymous with big bang press agentry, but he was at that moment a bit more legend than player. He was coming in at 3PM, but at 11AM some guys showed up with two huge crates, each about the size of a hutch. They set them in Warren's office, unpacking two large pieces of furniture which ate up much of the office's space. This was when music was sold on 12 inch platters and just before the advent of hi-fi stereo. The big boxes were the first stereo equipment either Warren or I had seen or heard, sizable banks of tweeters and woofers. But we didn't know that. They were just big pieces of furniture.

At 3PM, Russell Birdwell came into the office exuding Big Sell. His was a different style than the primarily Jewish press agents who had followed the primarily Jewish studio chiefs to Hollywood. He was a Texas boy who brought his daddy's barnstorming evangelist preachering to the entertainment field. With great flourish, he opened the big box furniture and explained the new magic of stereo. We thought he was going to try to sell us the equipment, but no. With further flourish he removed from its opulent wrapping a 12 inch album which he placed on the turntable he had just revealed. Laying the needle in the groove, he sat back, smiled and gestured with one hand to the machine. Suddenly an enormous sound was bursting from the giant speakers, a woman singing. That first experience of the blasting stereo was mind-bending and eardrum-bursting. Russell Birdwell was beaming and Warren Cowan was giving him nods and eyebrow bounces to show he was impressed. The song ended and Birdwell said the singer's name with grave importance. "Warren, this girl's future may be too big even for me. I may want you in on it. Think about it and call me." He rewrapped the record, smiled to each of us and left.

His presence was so energized that a big empty space remained where he had been, and we stared at it for a few seconds. "Well," Warren said after a bit, "what did you think?" And his voice had a reverence that told me he expected a positive response. "Warren, I prefer singers who hit the notes," I said. He looked at me with amazement and raised his hands forward as though handing me a baby. "The presentation!" he exhorted, "the presenTATION!"

Warren was a great teacher, but I think he also was a great student. When he joined Henry right after the war, it's quite clear that no one had to teach Warren Cowan brash and dash. But PR, as simplistic as it must look to an outsider (dream up item, give journalist hard sell, send clip to client,) has its skills and its moves, and many of these had been authored by Henry C. Rogers for well over a decade before a knowing wind blew him and Warren J. Cowan together.

From no less an authority than Bob Thomas (already AP's dean of the wire service reporters when I started and who sadly just left us at 92, sharp, funny and human to the end) I received testimony that Henry had virtually invented the concept of "the Academy Award campaign" in 1945 when he meticulously planted and grew the idea that Joan Crawford was the ordained Best Actress Oscar winner for "Mildred Pierce." And so she proved to be, with Henry's work certainly a factor. Bob knew publicity as well as any journalist because his father, George A. Thomas, had headed that pursuit for David O. Selznick for whom Thomas pere contributed significantly to the earth-shaking success of "Gone with the Wind." One insight into the precarious plight of PR guys in the '30s came from Bob's observation to me recently that his father, as esteemed and pre-eminent as he was, moved from one studio or producer to the next, "and we didn't eat too well in between." In his highly regarded biography of Crawford, Bob acknowledged Henry's having invented the strategy which creates an industry mindset that can lead to what's inside that Oscar envelope. Invariably, all nominees in any category are qualified to pick up the prize. Publicity seeks to help voters see why one of them deserves it more.

Warren learned from Henry's master plan, and he added the idea that the positive effects of an Oscar push can begin before the film is even completed, that this is a strategy which has commercial value in-and-of-itself quite apart from any effect on Oscar voting. The initiating venture into this idea involved Joan Crawford again. In 1959, we were handling "The Best of Everything," a big hot romantic novel which producer Jerry Wald was bringing to the screen. Wald was savvy and hungry, a guy who, rumor had it, took pride in the prevailing legend that he was the model for Budd Schulberg's novel "What Makes Sammy Run?" about the quintessential Hollywood scrambler, Sammy Glick. Wald was a key mover in Hollywood and, therefore, a prime client for Warren. Warren always knew where the power was and gravitated to it. Working for Jerry Wald and doing it with excellence had great significance to Warren. "The Best of Everything" was expected from the word "go" to be a big box-office pot boiler, and Warren thought he could win Wald's heart and mind with the idea that it also could be projected as a serious critical success. One way he elected to start this was by starting Oscar buzz while the film was still shooting, reprising his partner's earlier device for the same actress. Her prior Oscar acknowledgement made it all the more credible. Wald's skepticism notwithstanding, Warren was pumping up the anticipation by labeling Jean Negulesco, director of the film, as a "great woman's director." Negulesco had guided Jane Wyman to the gold statue a decade before in "Johnny Belinda." *You bring to an effort all of the substantiating factors you can when you're trying to "float an expectation."*

Warren started planting the story that Jerry Wald was bringing studio execs in to see Crawford's rushes for "The Best of Everything" because her work "already had Oscar written all over it." I was in Warren's office when he received an angry call from the easily angered Mr. Wald. Warren took many of his calls standing up with the phone on speaker, and he would annotate the proceedings with meaningful nods to whoever was listening to it with him. Wald asked if Warren knew who was "doing this Oscar crap." Warren proudly owned up to it and pointed out that it was giving an expectation of class as well of box office to the film. "Yeah," Wald fussed, "but me bringing people in to see Oscar in the rushes?, it has PR hype written all over it. This is a Harold Robbin's kind of novel we're making. Who's gonna buy that Oscar crap?" "Jerry," Warren said, nodding to me, indicating he was establishing the set-up, "I haven't sent you any of the clips yet. How did you know about this?" "From Sam Goldwyn, that's who. He calls and says, 'Jerry… another Oscar for Crawford? You know what she'll be asking?' Goldwyn, and from the studio guys here, that's who. They want to know why I haven't brought THEM in to see it." "Well, Jerry," Warren said, looking at me and pantomiming a finger-slash across the throat and then pointing that fore-finger at the speaker, "seems like SOMEone's buying the Oscar crap."

When the film came out, it was respectfully treated by critics, even though it was, as Wald had pointed out, the same sex-and-scandal weeper the Rona Jaffe novel had been. But Warren socked home his angle that it was the first film to treat the new idea that professional success could supplant marriage as the natural goal for some women. And Crawford's work was honestly appreciated. I wasn't involved in the campaign. My baby that year was "Room At The Top," a labor of love for me because Larry Harvey was already a friend and Simone Signoret had become a dear friend for life. They and the film and director, Jack Clayton, and script were all nominated, and Simone won Best Actress, with the screenplay winning, too. Warren received a complaining call from Wald the morning the nominations were announced. Rogers & Cowan represented four of the five Best Actress nominees, Audrey Hepburn for "The Nun's Story," Elizabeth Taylor for "Suddenly Last Summer," Doris Day for "Pillow Talk" and Simone. Wald's total conversation, Warren told me, was, "I thought this was supposed to be Crawford's year."

However sincere that complaint, Wald happily continued his association with Warren. For a proud interval, the time between Warren's planting of the Crawford buzz and the morning of the nominations announcement, Wald had been the producer of a contender, and he had used that edge well as he used every edge. That little history always reminds me of my ex-partner Jerry Pam's sage observation… *"Every Film Is Fifty Million Dollars And Five Nominations Until It Comes Out."* And that was when fifty million bucks was MONEY. Which, in turn, reminds me of Jerry's comment the time someone asserted to him that Guttman & Pam was one of the best PR offices in the business, to which Jerry snapped, "That's like being the world's biggest midget. You still can't slam dunk." I try to remember that sober truth every time I start to feel too good about myself. It keeps your feet on the ground. Another quote, not from Jerry but from Signoret, stays in my mind as a reminder that sometimes the client knows better than you do. Shaping a campaign that could help win her the Oscar for "Room At The Top" wasn't merely an assignment for me. It was a devotion. I was 26, still uncertain of how balls would bounce, and I worried that the Oscar was out of reach not because of the power of Simone's performance but because of its size. Simone was on screen only for about a third of the film. I pointed that out to her, perhaps as an advance cop-out. She consoled me that "much more important than being on the screen is that when you're not, the other characters are talking about you."

Few Oscars have thrilled me more. Simone treated me like a little brother from the start, perhaps because Paris is where my life had started 23 years after my birth, perhaps because I fearlessly imposed my dreadful French on everyone. Most of all, we were attached because I had known her brother, who was an assistant director in Paris on "Love in the Afternoon" which was my first film overseas. Part of what developed into our friendship is that Alain and I dated the same girl, the vibrant continuity woman on the film. Asking Simone to give my love to Alain, I found out that he, as handsome and vivid as Simone was beautiful and vivid, had died when swept to sea in a swimming accident. Maybe that was the bond, but even after she abandoned thoughts of Hollywood, she would call me for years to ask, "Are you steel een that sheeety beezness?" When I was pushing "Room at the Top," we were doing an Associated Press interview and the reporter, Rick Dubrow, who was the same age as I (our mid-twenties,), asked if she minded that people knew she was 38. (Obviously, that fact was established before she fell into my age-sheltering hands.) I intercepted the question by saying "Oh no, in Europe there's no stigma attached to being middle-aged." Both Rick and I froze in the realization of what an arrested adolescent I had just revealed myself to be. But Simone came over to give me a hug and a kiss on the top of my head.

We last saw her decades later when Gisela and I were in Paris and were invited to coffee (black, French and in which a spoon could stand on its own) with her and Yves Montand at their storied apartment on Ile la Cite. We were sitting in the kitchen surrounded by dozens of hand-painted Picasso plates, each inscribed to them by their friend Pablo, sitting at the table where Sartre and de Beauvoir and Cocteau and, yes, Picasso had sat to nurse the same dark brew and the same wise and ironic musings. A lot of life had been shared between our conjunction on "Room at the Top," the international cause celebre of Yves' fling with Monroe not the least among them. But it was beautiful to see these two lovers and creative and political soulmates in their lair, still the spectacular mating of artistic legends and social rebels. We had been drawn into their epic leadership in challenging Charles de Gaulle and the French right wing on the matter of Algerian independence. It had cost each of them dearly both in France and in Hollywood. They were the very soul of what Gisela and I had experienced when we were kids in the artistic and philosophical ferment that was the Left Bank in the '50s. The Café de Flore and the Café Deux-Magots had been infused with the humane concerns and historic debates enjoined by Simone and Yves and their existential compatriots. For Gisela and me, they still are, and the cafes-crème of the Parisian bistros runs in our blood. We make our pilgrimage to St. Germain des Pres every time we return to Paris. The square is now called Place Jean Paul Sartre et Simone de Beauvoir.

A few years after Warren Cowan's launching the concept of promoting Oscar buzz *during*-production ("planting Oscar seeds while the film's still on the floor,") I borrowed it for something that worked out, but backfired. I had Rex Harrison on my list while Joseph Mankiewicz was filming "Cleopatra." The PR pouring out of the Rome set, as the world recalls, was all Richard Burton and Elizabeth Taylor, each of whom my own company would eventually and proudly represent. But at that time, Rex was my charge, and he was getting lost in all the Dick and Liz furor. I gave a columnist a story stating that the word from the 20th boys in Rome was that "'Cleopatra' is a Caesar salad." It's the kind of word play that sticks in the mind and gets pick-up," like a joke you heard last night on a talk show. Once you get a break like that, it works itself. *Everyone has the courage of someone else's conviction, right?* The someone else in this case was an unnamed (and, actually, non-existent) 20th exec in Italy, but quickly such things often become "everybody's saying." So the story showed up in various forms as did another line I floated, "render unto Caesar that which is Caesar's." Clearly, it's madness to infer that such bleeps of consciousness construct a nomination, but it's foolish to ignore that they do give things a nudge. What got rendered unto Caesar was a Best Actor nomination for Harrison. This actually came as an strange surprise to me. I had thought it would be for supporting and that Burton and Taylor would be nominated for Best Actor and Best Actress. Maybe romantic mojo overwhelmed deft performances when people put pen to ballot.

I had zero relationship with Rex Harrison, other than watching Carol Reed's "Night Train To Munich" and Preston Sturges'"Unfaithfully Yours" every time I had (or still do have) the chance. Even working on "Midnight Lace" and "Doctor Dolittle," I never sensed a moment to start an acquaintance. In truth, the Rogers & Cowan publicity campaign probably didn't have much to do with his Oscar win for "My Fair Lady," a thought which occurred to me as I led him through the winner's press gauntlet. Rex Harrison and Professor Henry Higgins were born to hold that statue from the moment they stepped together onto a New York stage. The other four nominees were as brilliant a vintage of Best Actor nominees as any year had or has since provided, Burton and Peter O'Toole for "Becket," Tony Quinn for "Zorba The Greek" and Peter Sellers for "Dr. Strangelove." What that year needed was a five-way tie. But the world had become accustomed to and enamored of Rex Harrison's face in that role, and Oscar-worthy it certainly was. That year was a traumatic strain for Rogers & Cowan, even though we had the two actor award winners in Harrison and Peter Ustinov for "Topkapi." It was more bitter than sweet because Audrey Hepburn wasn't nominated for her rapturous Eliza Doolittle while "My Fair Lady" was nominated in all other acting categories. And the stinger was that during the voting period there was circulated (by persons unknown) the question of whether Audrey deserved honor since she had lip-synced Marni Nixon's performance of the songs. In Academy Award positioning, the first and last rule is that *a campaign presents its artists' or film's qualifications and never challenges those of a competitor.* However much the Academy cautions members not to discuss their choices among themselves, that is often vigorously ignored. People have opinions and are inclined to voice them. But an Oscar campaigner doesn't disparage the competition.

There's a fact that is not often noted because George Bernard Shaw's play took on another incarnation and primacy and size in our minds when Lerner and Loewe added music. Forgotten by many is the wondrous 1938 film, "Pygmalion" in which Leslie Howard, both as actor and co-director (with Anthony Asquith), gave readings and inflections to Henry Higgins' delightful exasperations which echo in Rex Harrison's infinitely and duly awarded interpretation.

The distance at which Rex Harrison seemed to have held his minions at Rogers & Cowan is very much an anomaly. Most relationships with clients are reciprocally personal. I recall one visit to Warren Beatty's aerie atop the Beverly Wilshire during which his career-long (because she is smart, efficient, human and funny) right hand gal, Jane Payne, advised him that a producer (another malefactor we shall call Frank) had called him. "Are you doing a film with him?" I asked. "He's trying. Why?" "Well, we're submitting a project which Michael Caine and his agent

Dennis Selinger like, and Frank's office turned it down." Warren asked Jane to place a call to Frank. "Frank, question, do you think Michael Caine's a good actor?… no, you're right. He's a great actor. And do you think he's smart?…. Witty, right, and smart… uh huh. Smarter than the 22-year-old readers in your development department?……. Then why would you take the opinion of one of them over that of Michael Caine on that project that was just sent you?…. OK, fine, I think you *should* take a look at it…thanks. Gotta go. We'll talk." Whether or not Frank read it is immaterial. What *is* material is that Warren made the call.

RENDER UNTO CAESAR THAT WHICH IS CAESAR'S… Yes that phrase which I shamelessly put in play for Harrison's "Cleopatra" Oscar momentum, also captured a key to Warren Cowan's dominance of his field. Warren was not only a great press agent. He was a great emperor. He and Henry Rogers were the duumvirate which ran an empire… the first great empire in the entertainment world's independent publicity field and certainly its most sustaining. Rogers & Cowan, quite amazingly, didn't miss a beat when Warren and Henry were sent into the wilderness after they sold it, such was the inertial power of that company name and its history, and such was the skill of those who succeeded them. And for whatever tensions we sensed or speculated had sizzled between Henry's and Warren's adjoining offices, I don't feel it ever showed up in the job the company did for such a variety of clients. Each addressed his own bailiwick, with Henry concentrating on the TV and corporate accounts, and Warren the film and personal artist representations. The most important thing I ever learned from the two of them is that I never wanted to oversee an empire, and I've kept Guttman Associates at a manageable (for me) boutique size, although Guttman & Pam did verge on empire for a while, to my distaste. Also, empires tend to become things that people sell to larger empires. That became all the rage at a certain point when Guttman & Pam had become a bit too imperial for me. Jerry Pam had become infused with the selling-the-empire idea. There were buyers, and I couldn't go along with it. For one thing, when you sell an empire, you're actually selling the people who inhabit it, and for me that was too much like selling the old family plantation with all aboard. And, in a larger sense, there are just too many things that can go wrong in an empire.

Empires, for instance, need receptionists, a position to which bosses don't pay much attention, so wires can get crossed. The receptionists at Rogers & Cowan, having to keep 150 or more clients straight in their minds, were a source of worry.

Burt Lancaster came in once (we didn't handle him, but we worked with him on ACLU and other charity or "cause" accounts and on several films) and he said to the receptionist, "Will you please tell Mr. Cowan that I'm here?" and she dutifully pressed a button and said, "Mr. Cowan, Kirk Douglas is here to see you." On another occasion, Tony Randall came in and informed the young woman at the desk that he was arrived for a meeting with Mr. Guttman. The receptionist, with great savoir faire, said, "And *whom* can I say is calling?" Tony, a grammarian par excellence, was amused. "Just tell him, please, that it's the King Of Comedy." She nodded her thanks, plugged in to my intercom and said, "Dick, do you have a meeting with Jack Carter?." It is a tribute to the character of those gentlemen that neither stormed out. Tony, in fact, told the story with glee.

I must be the one person whom the attraction of being part of an empire has eluded. Gisela and I bumped into Paul Bloch at a Malibu store recently. Paul, long a prince of the publicity world and master of the PR fates of many of the top stars, informed us that he was approaching his 50th anniversary at Rogers & Cowan and he noted that the company now had over 150 publicists, more than 30 in New York alone. My mind snaps shut at such numbers. We rarely have had more than 50 or 60 clients, and anything beyond that defies my imagination and my ambition. I've always thought of myself as a publicist, not a captain of industry, but through Gisela's veins flows the blood of Hanseatic traders… as well as robber barons, although all larceny had been sifted from the genes in the intervening ten centuries… so she keeps the business part clockwork smooth. Paul, with his imperial persuasion, said that it's the empire part of it which he loves, averring that men have been drawn to empires for ten thousand years. That attraction may have worked for Alexander and Caesar, for Warren Cowan and Paul Bloch, but very early on I cast my lot with Henry David Thoreau, and Guttman Associates has remained my little Walden Pond.

Warren Cowan and I had a close relationship until I resigned and started my own company in partnership with Jerry Pam. Maybe I left because I was ready for a new challenge, or maybe I'd tired of life within an empire, or it may be that it really was because of a clash Warren and I had over an idea I'd proposed for a specific campaign. In a business which relies largely on flexibility and compromise, much of my life has been shaped by my obstinacy and resolve. And I'm ok with that. For a year after that, Warren Cowan had an impulse to be somewhere else every time he caught sight of me at some event. And, in Hollywood, events follow each other as the night the day. They are, in fact, night and day. Coincidental attendances happen constantly, so I started to position myself to avoid Warren's eye contact. The problem was, we each had to WORK these events. Neither of us could skip them or skip out on them. But where respect abides, friendship resumes. And so did ours in a year or two.

Twenty years later, Warren and Henry sold Rogers & Cowan to some mega-company which, strangely I thought, sent the business' two fountainheads into non-compete limbo. Warren's closest and most dearly-held clients went with a group of his staff disengaged from the mother company. I gave them an umbrella of office space and some oversight and honchoing of key accounts in their continued work for clients like Paul Newman, Aaron Spelling and Kirk Douglas, while Warren dutifully kept his hands off. Then, after a few years when Warren's proscribed banishment ended, he returned to the fray and the two companies continued under that umbrella and in the Guttman & Pam Beverly Hills offices. In one major way Warren's and my philosophies were diametrically opposed. I like a tight, small company with an elite, small clientele. Warren, long acclimated to empire, was always inclined to more staff, more clients.

One day, shortly after Gisela, the only financially and organizationally skilled part of my brain… had supervised the dissolution of my two decade partnership with Jerry, she came into the office of the co-functioning companies, the newly reconstituted Guttman Associates and Warren Cowan Public Relations, flowing side by side like two rivers of different colors and temperatures. She saw five members of the two staffs standing in line waiting to use the copying machine. She went into Warren's office and said "Warren, there are too many rats in the cage." "Meaning?" "Meaning that when there are two rats, they get along in a very accommodating fashion. But when there are ten, there's a lot of shoulder bumping and snarling. There are five rats out there waiting to get on the treadmill." "When do you want me out?" he asked. "That depends on how you define 'as soon as possible,'" she said. You have to understand that this was all amazingly amicable since they had really liked each other for thirty-five years." "Gisela," Warren said, "I've always thought Richard and I would go into partnership." "Warren, he's going to have one partner the rest of his life, and you're looking at her." Thus a very fine friendship was preserved and enjoyed by Warren and me until one of us took leave of mortal coils… and quite beyond that I discover as I write this remembrance.

Chapter 7

They Broke the Mold

When I was a kid, my heroes were the pathfinders, Kit Carson and Daniel Boone, Jim Bridger, Sacajawea and Lewis and Clarke. I lived as much of my childhood as I could in the still pristine woods of St. Louis' Forest Park, walking in the moccasin-prints of the great spirits, Indian and pioneer, who had tread these leafy, tree-darkened spaces in silent steps when the wilderness went on forever.

I never lost my awe of trail-blazers, and a life in PR is filled with them. I loved introducing our grand-daughter, Alyssa, at age three to Buzz Aldrin, watching her mind enchant with the thought that he had flown the first human craft to the moon , that he had walked its surface. She looked up at him as though he were out of a fairy-tale and then asked me to take her outside so she could stare at the clear winter sky above Canada to gaze at a moon providently full.

This section is a salute to pathfinders whose company a life in PR has afforded me, people who definitely did things their way, people who made an impression on me and not because of their mere fame. Fame was not always the common denominator.

They Broke the Mold — Buzz Aldrin

When Buzz Aldrin… Dr. Buzz Aldrin, scientist, key space technology inventor and space exploration visionary, Col. Buzz Aldrin, military hero, Astronaut Buzz Aldrin, one of the first two humans to tread upon the moon… published his first space travel novel, "Encounter With Tiber," I broke one of my prime rules… *"a client can become a friend, but a friend can't become a client."* I had instituted that rule to make sure my wife never would be able to accuse me of losing a friend for her by doing a less than dazzling job. I had lost her enough friends with inappropriate jokes. With rightful caution, I resisted Buzz' request that I promote his book, even though I thought it was terrific. Long before Jim Cameron's "Avatar," Buzz created a world of interstellar-system species encounter, a "Planet Of The Apes" in which the humans were the apes. I guess it will have to be turned into a comic book to be filmed. Hollywood development people don't seem to read much other than comic books these days. I gave in to representing it finally at Buzz' insistence and at that of his even more persuasive and persistent wife, Lois. It turned out quite well, but the rule stands.

Our most recent and current campaign with him, controlling the powerful PR forces attached to the 40th anniversary celebration of his and Neil Armstrong's placing their lunar landing module and their feet on the moon and Buzz's planting the American flag there, a flag that will truly wave forever. Well, not wave really, since there is no atmosphere to disturb it. His second memoir, this one dealing with his struggle for personal stability and meaning upon his return to earth, "Magnificent Desolation," was being published concurrently with the anniversary, and we had to make sure it went straight to the best-seller lists, including the New York Times. Which it did and where it stayed for an impressively long time.

To do that, we needed something that would generate wide coverage in focusing attention on Dr. Buzz Aldrin the man and not just on astronaut Buzz Aldrin the historic personage. The first thing you do is you clear away the moon dust and check what unexpected (a very important word in effective PR) opportunities lie hidden. One "unexpected" was that Buzz' daughter-in-law Lisa… a lawyer but also a former pop singer… had written a rap song for Buzz entitled ""Rocket Experience." She played it for me and my associate Danielle Owens who worked with me on Buzz' account, and it was pretty good. But you don't just crack the rap charts, even with the assist of an historic moment of celebration. Age is not venerated in the rap world.

We had previously had an invigorating success with a website called "Funny Or Die." It is sort of Saturday Night Live in internet broadcast, a brainchild of Wes Farrell, the continuing success of which is the product of the comic inspirations of the website's chief Mike Farah and his skilled and whacky writers and producers. Danielle induced them to take a meeting with Buzz, and it was at the start a pretty hard slog. Buzz is dedicated to leading America's youth and America's future into rational further venture into space, and it is serious purpose for him, not a laughing matter. Even when we started to kick around the ideas of what could be done with a rap song taping, it was not docking with Buzz (who invented docking technologies.) Buzz and I were listening, but we didn't hear the door unlock when Farah said, "Snoop Dog, Soljah Boy." But Danielle understood what that meant, and so the project surged forward.

The recording of "Rocket Experience" blasted off, and Farah did indeed deliver those rap stars and Quincy Jones to a hilarious capture of Buzz Aldrin's first and most assuredly only venture as a rap star. It immediately surged to one of the hottest comedy entries on the internet, with hits spiraling toward a million pouring in to watch it on "Funny Or Die." It ignited the publicity campaign, gave it a powerful second dimension and poured on the second spotlight we needed to draw America's youth to Buzz' vision of our nation's future in space. Within a brief period his Facebook and Twitter audience was approaching one million. This sent his book "Magnificent Desolation" into best-seller orbit, tuning in and turning on the generation which will have to accomplish Buzz' commandment, "next stop, Mars."

With that in mind, it was a short step… and a dance step at that… to place him on "Dancing With The Stars." My associate Susan Madore is close to the show because of her adroit representation of their top dancers, their longtime most beautiful judge and many of the most popular and winning celebrity stars who pranced upon that top-rated show's stage. I presented that idea to Lois and Buzz a month after his 80th birthday, and he was game to go from the start. This is a guy who shrinks from no challenge. We all know how extraordinary was his landing a craft on the moon. What most people don't know is how much more extraordinary was his taking off from the moon. As he and Neil Armstrong clambered back in their lunar landing module to prepare to take off for return to the orbiting mother craft and then back to earth, they noticed something broken loose and lying on the floor of the craft. It was a switch. It was the *starter* switch. The clock was ticking on their one shot at not staying on the moon forever. They couldn't use a screw driver to reinsert it because the metal would have short-circuited the LLM. Frisking himself, Buzz came upon a felt-tipped pen he'd stuck in a pocket after some notation aboard the mother ship. There was no manual on how to fix a LLM with a pen, but with not a lot of time to spare, he got it back together. Nice to have a rocket scientist aboard when you really need one.

They Broke the Mold — Paul Newman

I was driving to an interview once with Paul Newman and I ignored another primary rule, *"caution trumps curiosity."* I'm afraid I have a habit of breaking that rule, usually with disastrous consequence, but not in this case. "Paul," I ventured, "why do you do publicity? You get first offer on almost every great role anyway." There was a long pause, and then he explained, "Al*most*."

"Almost" is a powerful word with big magic. But, actually, that was only part of the reason for Paul's enduring relationship with Warren Cowan. As Paul understood very well, my question was rhetorical and not as stupid as it may read in print. He understood that press agents serve a lot of functions, even for a guy whose only limitation is "al*most*." A good press agent can contribute to his or her client's most rewarding career, to his or her widest range of artistic opportunities. The press agent is also a gate-keeper, warding off the unnecessary and irrelevant tasks studios, celebrity hitchhikers or friends shower upon anyone with fame. These needless tasks not only squander the artist's energies, but they diminish stardom. There is such a thing as being too available. Also, it waters-down a key tool in publicity strategizing… *the power of "exclusivity"*. The key break you need at some urgent moment often depends on its exclusivity and also how rare you and your client have kept his or her exposure.

The career-long association of Paul Newman and Warren Cowan is Exhibit A in validating the imperative contribution of public relations to a great artist. As an actor, Paul Newman was a truth-teller. And Warren Cowan and the people Warren hired to help him, including me, told the truth about Paul Newman, which is that *he was the guy*. Or, in Paul's case, one might say he was *The* Guy, the one who at any given point in time is the eminence whose picture should be in the dictionary next to the word "star."

Now, it's also true that at any given point in time, there are about five guys who are each *"the* guy." Paul was indeed a pre-eminence in the *"the* guy" group for decades and decades. Only a small number, like Paul, were and in some cases still are at the very top forever… Clint, Wayne, Cooper, Stewart , Tracy, Gable, Cagney, Grant, Beatty, Holden, Hanks, Hackman, Redford, Fonda, Douglas, Brando, Lancaster, Poitier, Nicholson, Peck, Washington, Harrison Ford, Mitchum, Pacino, DeNiro among them and others like Bogart and Dean and Clift whose death-shortened stardoms were only a decade or two long or, rather, a decade or two short. Tragically, merely a half decade in Dean's case. Bogart's reign at the peak lasted only from "The Petrified Forest" in 1936 to "The Harder They Fall" in 1955. How did he possibly pack in so much greatness and so many great films? The point is that these top dog male stars fearlessly took on all challengers and all challenges, and if the films were mostly but not all five-star classics, as can happen when you work with such intrepid incessancy, they... the actors themselves... still were always five-star to watch.

Paul Newman, with Warren Cowan still at the PR tiller, later told a further truth about himself when the grand charity effort of his Newman's Own products became the passion of his later years, the paradigm for celebrity philanthropy and, above all, the culmination that everyone had always expected of him.

The special point I was making about Paul Newman, about Paul and Warren Cowan, the one which explains the long and uninterrupted relationship of a great star with a great press agent for a half century is as follows: Paul Newman was a guy who was as bright as he was talented, bright from the gut. He was the kind of savvy guy who would never have stuck it out to the end of days with a particular press agent were it not win-win. It was not just friendship, it was mutual respect. He remained on salary with Warren even during the few years when Warren was contractually out of the game and I was overseeing and participating in his staff's work on Warren's clients for him, a kind of creative custodian. Paul Newman and Warren Cowan, each in his own way and jointly, validated the organic efficacy of publicity. You don't have to look any further. That's what it's about.

It was from Catherine Dent, TV's prettiest tough cop on the Fox series, "The Shield," that I got another angle on how Paul tested the truth of the people who swirl with personal objective around the top movie star in the world. At a penthouse-warming party on Malibu's Carbon Beach (where so much of Hollywood's behind-the-scenes producing takes place) I discovered that she and I have a Paul Newman experience in common. Catharine had worked with him early in her career, but well into his top star reign, in a film called "Nobody's Fool.". She, too, had observed that Paul, one of the best of actors and best of guys, told the dumbest jokes with the misguided conviction that they were funny... and that that made the experience funny.

She also cast a revisionist light on the time Paul had showed me an early cut of "WUSA." Over the end credits, he'd demanded my honest response, warding off my evasions until I admitted that I didn't think it worked. It must have been his own such conclusion which caused him to put me on that spot. And the film went out and proved us both right. At the start of the filming of "Nobody's Fool," Paul had given Catherine a tape of one of his first starring roles on TV. He'd asked her to watch it and to then tell him in detail what she thought of his performance. It was, she told me, that rarity of rarities, a vividly disappointing Paul Newman portrayal. She was just starting a film with one of the preeminent and most talented actors in the world, and now he was obliging her to put the knock on some of his work... or to lie. She had my full sympathy. So she told him her honest conclusion. He nodded, never again mentioned it, and then they had a terrific relationship of mutual trust.

What I concluded was that Paul Newman, catered to by all because his association was coveted by all, knew full well that people would tend to tell him what they thought he wanted to hear. So he had this little litmus test for truth-telling, checking which people would flatter him for a performance or a film which didn't deserve it. Paul Newman was about the exchange of truth. Except I doubt if anybody ever told him the truth about his joke-telling. It was that charming and insignificant imperfection which makes perfection bearable.

This brings to mind a comment Maximilian Schell made to me that in any drama, a character never should be perfect, that perfection is unbelievable because to be human is to be blemished in some way. Max' point was that perfection is boring. This was in his thoughts because he was directing a production of the Lawrence Durrell stage play, "Sappho," about the ancient Greek poetess. Durrell describes her as a creature of absolute perfection, a paragon, and so she is popularly regarded by classicists. To make her human, Durrell devised that she should stutter. Nothing terrible, just a point of human reference against which the perfection could be set in relief. Durrell himself, quite tragically, was no paragon.

Coincidentally, many actors stuttered or overcame stuttering, even such a master of speech as James Earl Jones. That may be why the ancient Greeks celebrated Demosthenes for having perfected his riveting powers of oration by going into the wilderness and practicing with pebbles in his mouth. The pebbles, very possibly, were simply a metaphor for stuttering. And his conquest of his fate, to my way of thinking, is the Greek acknowledgment of my favorite adage, a problem is a solution in disguise. Peter Ustinov passed to me a story about British author/

critic Kenneth Tynan, also a noted stutterer, who in the early 60s on a television panel discussion of evolving freedoms of speech, averred that, "Someday we will even hear someone on television utter the forbidden word f-f-f-f-f...." Everyone else was madly trying to wave him off, but to no avail. This was a story Peter Ustinov told me with great and reverential delight. Henry Rogers' carefully honed eloquence was, to my observation, the victory over his own stuttering, only mildly perceptible when I knew him.

They Broke the Mold — Peter Ustinov

My recollections of Peter are almost always about delight and frequently about eating. Why not? The food and the conversation were invariably first class. But one was sacrificed to the other on occasion. Gisela and I were in San Francisco with Peter as I'd arranged for him to host the opening of the San Francisco Film Festival. After he had delighted the first-nighters with his customary aplomb and wit, the grateful festival organizers led the three of us to a limo which would take us to a restaurant of their selection for a meal equally of their designation, a Japanese meal that will remain in grateful recall forever... shabu shabu with which none of us were acquainted, a circular pot of boiling water into which one chopsticks the selected morsels from an array of raw meats and vegetables, quickly brought to edibility in fifteen or twenty seconds and then lightly dipped into a sauce that defies description or comparison. At the end of the abundant boilables, the remainder of the sauce is poured into the broth and consumed, bowl to lip, which we did in a state of stunned delight. At no point, after the first taste of the first dipped morsel was a word uttered, only oohs and aahs and the occasional "oh-my-God" which sounded like a precursor of Meg Ryan's "Harry Met Sally" restaurant scene.

Another dinner with Peter Ustinov was at the long-beloved, deeply mourned Luau Restaurant in Beverly Hills. It's Polynesian décor of tables tucked into palmy nooks, the privacy of fern plantation, and aisles climbing over little bridges spanning South Pacific streams. On this occasion, it was the wonderful Asian and Tahitian cuisine which was absently consumed, barely tasted, scarcely marveled at, and it was the conversation which kept us enraptured. Peter had inquired if we had plans for the evening, and we told him we were dining with my client Dory Previn, Oscar nominated song-writer, fascinating singer and the former wife of conductor Andre Previn. She was riding a giant wave of attention and praise for her first album of painfully personal and richly inventive songs, including one detailing how her best friend, Mia Farrow, came to abide with and then marry Dory's music prodigy husband, Andre Previn. Another song delved into sexual abuse by an uncle and a third called "With My Daddy In The Attic," which appears to be the reclusive madness of her father. I have never worked on… or heard… a more personal or revelatory album, pain distilled to high art. It was a music milestone and a psychoanalytical one as well. Rex Reed did an ode to it for me, an interview in Newsweek as I recall (but why was Rex writing for Newsweek?,) and then the dam-burst of praise and adulation poured in. Peter begged to join us, which Dory considered perhaps her best review. "She may be the most courageous artist with whom I will ever have a chance to dine," he explained. Keep your dinners with Andre… any Andre. The table talk of Dory and Peter was spoken English and mental process as performance art. I don't believe Gisela or I said a word other than our dinner choices. It was a repast more for ear and mind than for palate.

For one moment about two decades back I thought I could return the Luau as the fun restaurant of Beverly Hills. The two people joined with me in its sacred memory included the town's most flamboyant entrepreneur of all trades… manager/producer/exuberant Alan Carr, his heart as vast as his waistline and who on his own popularized the muumuu. I put him together with Bob Morris whose high personality restaurants stretch from Malibu to Beverly Hills. We were on track to resurrect the Luau when Alan made his ill-timed exit before the end of his second act. I had already begun practicing my chopsticks chops. With Romanoff's and the Brown Derby and Chasen's also gone, restaurants just serve food now.

They Broke the Mold – Jimmy Woods

They definitely broke the mold when it came to Jimmy Woods. And given his penchant for the trenchant, speech especially, some people would like to have broken that mold over his head. Not I. One of the most vivid and certainly informed talents with whom I've worked is Jimmy Woods. When he was working on "Ghosts Of Mississippi" portraying one of the most loathsome of civil rights assassins and thoroughly enjoying pinning that ugly moth to the wall, he called to ask if I thought we should get together again. "Well, Jimmy," I responded, "I do miss you. One can never have too many acquaintances of equivalent intellect, and…" At which insinuation he exploded and yelled into the phone, "Equivalent intellect?!!! When I'm fucking ASLEEP!!!" Which, of course, reminded me why I enjoyed working with him, and we resumed our association and enjoyed a really fun campaign taking his portrayal of that degenerate to the big ball, his nomination once more for the Oscar. The relationship has had a spirited and vivifying intermittency spanning decades. You can put any two of his performances, let's say "Promise" and "Citizen Cohn," side by side to see the range and exhausting intensity of his characterizations

He could be exhilarating or exasperating, but he always kept you wide awake. Jimmy has a great sense of the moment and his mind seizes an opportunity with both hands, occasionally around the throat. One of my proudest moments of client representation was when I placed him, before dawn one Sunday morning, on CBS's Face The Nation. The entirety of the show was a debate between Jimmy and right wing ideologue William Bennett who was in the full flush of his campaign to get the National Endowment ForThe Arts flushed down the funding toilet. Bennett was for me, certainly at that time but almost invariably, one of those guys I love to hate. He has potent language skills, so it was no easy battle. Match point came as the show was racing toward a commercial break, and Jimmy had just delivered a very lucid argument on the futility of maintaining other aspects of a nation's greatness at the sacrifice of its culture. Bennett's response was something like "Ah, I knew we'd hear that word" but I believe it was more directly dismissive of "culture." Before they could cut to an ad, Jimmy quickly slipped in, "That reminds me of a quote from Hermann Goering, 'When I hear the word Kultur, I reach for my Luger." Bang!… go to commercial. . The sacred insertion of commercial message left Mr. Bennett choking on some unexpressed retort that I'm sure would have been effective. But one of the many things of which Jimmy is master is… timing.

The entire show went that well, and afterwards Jimmy and I stopped at the Polo Lounge for a celebratory breakfast. Jimmy's crack was definitely a better mousetrap, because a distinguished portion of the whole world beat a path to our table in congratulations. The Beverly Hills Hotel must have been hosting a convention of the town's liberal intelligentsia that morning. The strange thing is that Jimmy, by his own insistence, holds most of my liberal kneejerk-isms in abject contempt. And he often expresses that to me most colorfully. But my convictions can stand on their own two feet.

One place Jimmy and I connect is our sense of what's funny, perhaps because we each like it with a dash of audacity and even insult and borderline suffering.

Jimmy was guesting with Jay on the Tonight Show and we were watching Jay's monologue together in Jimmy's dressing room. Making sure the guests you book on a talk show view the monologue, quite apart from the pleasure and courtesy factors, gets them into the flow of the game, the flow of the audience and gives a laugh or two to refer back to in their own time upon the boards. It provides a point of reference for a laugh during the interview when the joys of the monologue are still very fresh in the audience mind. One of Jay's key subjects for assault-by-laughter that evening was the fact that NBC had instituted a policy of drug testing for all employees. Jay was outraged that each member of his staff had been forced to make a trip to the john with a plastic cup, and he drew plenty of laughs from this. Jimmy and I looked at each other. It's always valuable for a guest to make a funny entrance to turn the *de riguer* audience applause to laughter. I went into the Green Room, the waiting/viewing place for those visitors without tickets and without dressing rooms. I knew I would find there the transparent plastic cup and the can of ginger ale that I needed. When Jimmy walked out to his introduction carrying a plastic container half full of piss-amber liquid, it was a roar and even broke up Jay. We had Jimmy work the laugh with angry protest. "Jay, I know your *staff* has to do this, but…" We had considered his tripping and spilling the stuff toward the front rows but not onto the audience, but you would never do that without the prior knowledge, contribution and permission of the host and the producer. Also, someone in the audience could sue you for the trauma of *thinking* that a top star's urine was about to be spilled on him or her.

And then there was the great potted palm adventure. Jimmy arrived at another Leno guesting with a spirit-crushing headache. When executive producer Debbie Vickers looked in brightly to say hello and to ask if he needed anything, Jimmy suggested "about three bottles of headache tablets?" She assured him that help was on its way. When she left, I asked why he wanted to put that poison in his system when it wouldn't kick in until after the closing credits, he said… "… anguish. Why? You have a better idea?" And I answered, "Yeah. Hypnosis. Let me take it away for you." Why I slip into a hypnosis mode at that show I have never figured out. Always courting disaster. But the higher the subject's intellect, the easier the induction, so I was pretty sure it would work with Jimmy. He was really in pain, so he gave it real focus, and focus is what hypnosis takes to the bank. He went right out. All that Jimmy Woods intensity slipped away, and we walked his wolf of a headache out the door. Then we did the counting backwards thing, and when he opened his eyes, the headache was history. That kind of guy would rather have it back than admit that it happened, and he demanded to know if it always works like that, and I admitted that one time, calamitously, it had not.

It was one of those worst nightmare stories, and why I told it to Jimmy is another thing I don't know, other than that he asked. Gisela was in the last hour of preparation for an important exhibit she was presenting of oils and watercolors of the noted Irish painter, Patrick Morrison. Patrick is famous for the intensity of his paintings and the intensity of his panic attacks during a show. His panics tended to take Gisela along with them into the land of frazzled nerves. So, in self-defense, I caught Patrick in a quiet moment and asked how he would like actually to enjoy one of his shows. "No real danger of that," he responded, but I asked him to let me do a little focus exercise with him, and to my amazement he was very quickly quite and quietly hypnoidal and I started to speak of the many pleasures he would enjoy during this show… So into this gentle interlude walks Gisela, who has no patience with my hypnosis voodoo. She sees Patrick in this dangerously uncustomary tranquility and she recognizes this was that long-anticipated moment when I would screw everything up for her. "You've hypnotized Patrick?" she passionately intones…. "You'll NEVER get him OUT !!!" Well, that's the worst thing you can say in the presence of someone in hypnosis. The whole process is one of bringing the subject to a state of absolute suggestibility. He or she will believe even to the marrow of his or her bones, what is said. I looked at Patrick and saw him slipping down… down… like a great flat stone making soft, sinking swoops… down, down toward the mud of… a …very… deep… pond. He did just what she said. He sat there, head collapsed forward, drooping like an old potted palm. It took me over a half hour to get him out, sweating myself through as I did. And then I went home to shower while he and Gisela stayed to enjoy the show as he had never enjoyed a show.

Jimmy absorbs this story, and then he's called to make his entrance. Jay tells him how great he looks? "Really?" Jimmy demands, affecting a seething outrage over what had just befallen him… "Five minutes ago I was a potted palm in my dressing room… thanks to my publicist, Dick Guttman… *my publicist SLASH HYPNOTIST* Dick Guttman. You were THIS close to doing this interview with a potted palm." And suddenly the Patrick Morrison story becomes the Jimmy Woods story… the "you'll never get him out of it," the flat stone swooping slowly to the bottom," the half hour effort to restore him to consciousness. Doing business with Jimmy Woods, it should be required that the press agent be read his Miranda rights… "anything you say may be held against you."

They Broke the Mold — Kathy Ireland

Kathy Ireland has a better sense of news value than I do, and I'm not bad. She has the courage to deal with painful subjects which come churning up from the gut. When she was the kickoff speaker for the YWCA Greater Los Angeles' symposium on human trafficking… dozens of top attorneys general, DAs, leading legislators and social activists gathered to address one of the nation's most horrific crime sprees…. she made it personal. She revealed the trafficking which afflicts the elite world of modeling and the very personal experience that has long compelled her to help others similarly helpless to defend themselves from exploitation. In the halls of the Museum of Tolerance, marking the depredation of human dignity, Kathy upped the ante on that summit meeting's sense of purpose. Atrocity is always personal.

Courage is defined in many surprising ways, and a life in PR bonds you with people of invincible courage, people who accomplish with shimmering self-belief, determination and creative gift what no one would have conceived possible. Kathy Ireland's parents had given her the genetic wherewithal to become one of the top supermodels of Sports Illustrated history, and that modeling success had deprived her of the opportunity to pursue formal education past high school. Her beauty and timid sweetness had bought her a series of limiting acting roles. She claims she was never an actress and offers that she has the films to prove it, although when she performed Edward Albee's "Three Tall Women" on stage, it was a performance commended by Albee himself. Venturing into TV production, she starred in two holiday films which for several years reigned as the PAX network's highest ratings-getters.

But her belief in constructive life purpose insisted that there was a great deal more to be accomplished. Among these was providing answers to facilitate people's lives… especially busy mom people. That, she elected, would be her destiny. She began from the ground up, as she says, manufacturing socks, talking a bank into loaning her $50,000 to do so. She ignored what others might have seen as the discouraging difficulty and even impossibility of what she was about to venture.

Ten years later, she sold her hundred millionth pair of socks, and along the way she became the most successful and varied lifestyle designer in the world, sought out for partnership by people like Warren Buffet and top companies in their respective fields , building her empire to over $2 Billion (by the assessment of Forbes Magazine) in retail sales a year. We were lucky enough to come along for the ride early on, giving us front row seats to observe her skills, never exercised at the expense of her humanity. It was an education, one of the many benefits of doing PR on which you don't have to pay taxes. A Forbes cover story we engaged called Kathy Supermodel-turned-Supermogul. It was a term we campaigned to become the default mini-bio of her… Kathy Ireland, supermodel turned super-mogul. Like Michael Jackson, the king of pop. Those things don't take unless they nail it. I saw her as a top-of-the-line pathfinder. You'd think she wouldn't have the time for her and her children to call you on your birthday to serenade you with "Happy Birthday."

It took courage, too, for her to undertake "Dancing With The Stars." Terpsi-chore is a tough gig for tall ladies, and Kathy had never worn high heels, partly because of the comfort and agility demands of being one of the nation's top female business leaders and partly because of the towering impertinence of going high heels when you are already five ten. But the money and the promotion for her dancing efforts were going to good charities at a time when charities needed (as they still do) every buck they can get. When our office arranged for Kathy's design accomplishments to be celebrated by her tossing out the ball for the game which the Dodgers hoped would bring them the National League West pennant, it was suddenly discovered that Kathy had never thrown a ball. That was accommodated when we got a former pitching coach named Tommy Lasorda to go out to the mound with her and teach her how to throw… to a sold-out crowd's delight. That's also called, in publicity, throwing a puff ball to the photographers.

The night of Kathy's pitching debut, the Dodgers clinched the pennant. The day we had her ring the closing bell at the New York Stock exchange, the Dow closed above 8000 for the first time in the dark and dour months since the reces-sion sucked Wall Street down the drain (and vice versa.) She has been a good-luck charm for a lot of people.

Three magazines played seminal roles in confirming in the media's mind Kathy Ireland's unlikely and hard-earned recognition not as a captain of enterprise, but as a four-star general thereof. Her Sports Illustrated swimsuit issue covers got their attention, and why not. One of the three remains the highest selling such issue. On the recent occasion of the 50th anniversary of swimsuit issues, it was voted the best ever. But at the start of her efforts as an entrepreneur, her modeling accomplishment invited the business world's skepticism. Her presumption to think she could overcome that stereotype to conquer the world of product design and marketing evoked a you-can't-get-there-from-here response which made all the more astonishing her unerring rise to international brand prominence. License Global Magazine's annual verification of the 125 most powerful brands in the world was soon giving witness to her mastery, most recently acknowledging her number thirty-one position, ahead of such super brands as Pepsi Cola, Ford and NBC, far ahead of such other individual brands as those of Martha Stewart and Donald Trump, with only Ralph Lauren's individual-based brand ahead of her on the golden list. But it was the Forbes Magazine cover, accorded only the masters of the universe, which proved the coronation. Writer Dorothy Pomerantz's meticulous presentation of Ireland's accomplishment brought belief which was finally undeniable. She was asked to be keynote speaker of Dubai International CEOs convention and was similarly honored even by the business wizards of China, winning the cover on that corporatoccracy's Forbes as well. A very long way to have come in only two decades from the confining definition of bikini-ed fame. People believe it when they read it. They all quickly assumed the courage of Forbes' conviction and License Global Magazines number-crunching. A two-billion dollar annual gross goes a long way in making believers of skeptics. Not bad for a girl with only a high school diploma… and, oh yes, a couple of honorary doctorates.

Speaking of educations, riding with Buzz Aldrin in the sun-filled glass dome of a luxury train racing through the outrageous beauty of Alaskan glaciers while this doctor of space sciences explains the "Big Bang" theory, is a matriculation you wouldn't want to miss. One of the banes of being one of the first two men on the moon is that there is a small group of people who dedicate their lives to asserting that that moon-landing never happened. One guy was particularly fixated on this, and Buzz was tricked into a confrontation with him when this antagonist and his camera crew trapped my moon-dusted friend in the small entranceway of a building to which Buzz had been lured as part of the set up. When this guy, half Buzz' age or younger and bigger and heavier than he by far, pinned Buzz into a corner, pressing his inquisition, Buzz fought his way out with a left to the chin that dropped the guy like a sack of moon rocks… This made the news since Buzz' ko'd pursuer released his footage of it to media. The LA District Attorney made plans to arraign Buzz for assault. I figured this would show up in Jay Leno's monologue, one of the most powerful perception-shapers in the country. I would never suggest anything for inclusion in Jay's monologue, but on the assumption that this might be referred to, I mentioned to Jay before the show that the district attorney was readying to arraign Buzz on this. Jay confirmed it was among the jokes, and he simply said, "Don't worry, you'll be happy with it." At a certain point in the monologue, Jay set up the story, telling how Buzz Aldrin, a national hero, had been cornered by this guy twice his size and half his age, and then he showed the footage,… When the punch came, it was punctuated with the explosive noise of a Rocky Marciano roundhouse… after which Jay exclaimed with enthusiasm and a swing of his arm, "It makes you PROUD to be an American!" Coincidentally… perhaps… the DA dropped the case the next day.

They Broke the Mold – Prince

Prince, radiating charisma, is unlike anyone else you've ever met. He seems isolated by his own talent, surrounded by very bright people who fully understand that his imagination and talent are hitting notes of inspiration both audible and inaudible to our perception. Part of it is the cocoon he wove about himself, at least when I so indirectly worked for him on the release of "Purple Rain." In my limited direct involvement with him, it seemed to me he deliberately avoided eye contact… not just with me but with everybody who filled the conference room at the Goldwyn Studios lot (or perhaps it had become Warners Hollywood Studios by then) for the one boundary-setting, target-identifying meeting determining how he would be employed for the "Purple Rain" promotion. The impression I drew was that he didn't want his space invaded but he didn't want you to take that personally. He was remote but polite. He poured so much into a performance that possibly he felt that he didn't have to bring anything to a promo meeting but his presence.

His management team, Robert Cavallo, Joseph Ruffalo and Steven Fargnoli, had contacted me just at the start of production (on what basis of reputation I don't know) to explore my interest in representing "Purple Rain." From all of the top film-makers and film-sellers with whom I worked, I knew that the campaign is not imposed on a film but grows out of it. And this film was Prince. It moved in sync with Prince's sense of movement and visual as well as music, and it was charged with his kind of moody electricity. His management wanted a campaign done in a manner consistent with how they were positioning Prince. Working to style I understand. When we started on "Thank God It's Friday" for Neal Bogart and Casablanca, I wasn't really aware of disco, but I learn fast. That film had a diverse and effective publicity history, too. Cavallo, Ruffalo and Fargnoli were supremely aware of Prince's unique gift and style and the kind of space he needed to function creatively.

That's what great managers do… they protect their client's talent and his or her need to function with independence. They assure conditions which allow the talent to express his or her art without being told by record label or studio execs how to be a better him or her. Fired by their understanding and awe of the talent, these uber-managers make sure creative instincts are unfettered. And, that accomplished, they make sure the talent enjoys the highest equitable rewards for his or her accomplishments. I've watched Marty Erlichman function in that manner for Barbra Streisand, and it is a thing of beauty when talent and management are so harmoniously in tune.

Two who leap to mind for most inventively and most devotedly accomplishing the fulfillment of their clients' talents and potential are Marty Erlichman and Elvis Presley's most significant "significant other," Col Tom Parker. They expertly and effectively and creatively wielded the great power of their respective legend's supremacy. I had up-close-and-personal with Col. Parker only on the occasion of Rogers & Cowan's engagement to do the promo on an Elvis Presley TV special. I was preparing a national press mailing to 200 or so newspaper TV editors, and we needed the right photo for it. The right photo meant the photo Col. Tom Parker felt was right, so I called him, and he said, "I'm looking at it." "That's great," I replied, "may I send a messenger for it?" "Hold on," he cautioned, "that'll be five bucks." "Five bucks? For the negative?" "NEGATIVE?" he exclaimed, deeply offended. "You don't get any *negative*! Five bucks… A PIECE!" So, at a time when eight by ten reproductions of a black and white photo cost about 35 cents, Rogers & Cowan paid five bucks A PIECE for two hundred photos to promote Col. Parker's and Elvis Presley's own damn TV special. That, my friends, is management. When I reported the situation to Warren Cowan, he just laughed and said, "Well, that's a new one on me." And he was right. It was worth the price of admission.

But great management always starts with devotion to and amazement by client. And that's certainly what Prince was getting from his guys. I looked forward to a sneak of "Purple Rain" near San Diego to get an idea of how it played to its intended audience. Our daughter Danielle, who was attending the University of

California at San Diego, picked me up at the airport and came with me because I needed a viewpoint contemporary with that of the audience I would have to reach. Looking at it through very different eyes, we were each similarly astounded by what Prince had accomplished. It wasn't music to which you merely listened. The vi*suality* and the verve and the beat of the music had that audience dancing in its seats. *My job would be to convey to the media the hunger of the audience for Prince and his first film venture.*

A few weeks later we had our one and only planning meeting. So there, finally, we all sat… Prince, Mssrs. Ruffalo, Cavallo and Fargnoli and all of the other essential people who pertained to Prince's life, career and product. … something, thanks to TV, we now all know as entourage. It was the first time I'd met Prince, and I didn't really meet him. He came in shortly after the rest of us and sat at a chair that was positioned right near the door, pretty much in the middle of the long conference table. I was introduced and there was a cordial exchange of nods. It was immediately apparent that Prince was there as an auditor of the meeting which would help shape how his film would be sold. Various pertinent matters were discussed by the others, all skilled operatives in the facilitation of Prince's great talent. Prince sat looking at the wall opposite him. This was a meeting on the Goldwyn Studios lot in Hollywood, the place where my company Guttman & Pam had started in an office not a hundred yards from where we all sat. I mention that because in short order it became a possibility that the Goldwyn Studios was the same spot where my company could come to a crashing stop… or at least to a bumpy part of the road.

Joe Ruffalo, the prior business completed, threw the ball to me to explain what I planned to do for that film. I started to lay it out and just as I was swinging into some specifics of what I would be asking Prince to do, Prince simply stood up and headed out the door behind him. I felt he should have at least given me the chance to prove myself worthy of his disdain, and as the door was about to close behind him, I called out, "I look forward to not working with you." It was one of those things that just comes out. The door closed, hermetically sealing the horror of everyone else in the room, all of whom were life-committed to this extraordinary artist. I have to admit I was fairly horrified myself and fully understood how badly this would portray me when the word went out. At the end of this brief but suffocating silence, the door opened again, and Prince looked in and said, "OK, you've got one." With which he sort of smiled and then he left for good.

To their great credit and to my great gratitude, everyone left sitting weakly in the room understood that this meant I had carte blanche to make a demand of him, one demand, and he would do it. More gracious you cannot possibly get. It was a very heavy challenge of opportunity. I would have to use that one shot wisely. I didn't really hear as much feel the great sigh of relief in the room and then a little release of tension through a mild spurt of laughter.

I knew fairly quickly how to use that one free pass. The kids would *be* there, but the adult audience hadn't yet caught Prince fever. Job One was to let the entertainment industry establishment and the media know that this train was coming and that it was coming for everyone, not just the kid audience. There was a six minute sampler of the film, and I merely asked that some more of the stylized dancing be added and emphasized. It was hard for anyone of any generation not to see and hear that this was the beat of that era. The timing of that film's release was summer of 1984, a fact I remember because I used the coincident LA Olympics to help impel our key promotional objective for "Purple Rain." My one free shot would be used to reach out not to the natural youth audience, but to the older public and media who ritually watched Johnny Carson on "The Tonight Show." Surprise that Carson audience, raise its awareness and curiosity and, voila, cross over. I'm telling you that you could not watch that six minutes without bouncing in your shoes.

I sent the six minutes to Jim McCauley, one of the top talent coordinators for "The Tonight Show with Johnny Carson," and asked him to show it to the powers that be. It was not the kind of talent that the show presented often back in the '80s, but I wanted them to know that Prince was, all by himself, a significant "movement" in the music scene, a great change-of-pace, a keeping-up-with-the-times booking for the show. Jim called back in sad amazement. He thought the clip and the booking were great. The six minute clip had been shown to someone significant in the network production of the show, and the response had been, "Get me the Ink Spots." I mean... literally... that was the response. I don't believe for a second that that was a racial remark. It was simply an evidence of the time- disconnect between the generations at that point. Significantly, in Jay Leno's long reign as the beating heart of the Tonight Show and unrivaled king of late-night TV ratings in that time, Prince was one of Jay's favorite and most prized guests on the show and even did a two-night participation in the especially admired final week of the

Late Night domination by Jay Leno when Leno had acceded to Conan O'Brien's demanding his own early succession to the best desk in TV thus precipitating Jay's early (but, as it turned out, temporary) departure. But the recognition of the genius of Prince had not been the case on that show a quarter century before.

After the Tonight Show door-slam, the big emphasis was concentrated on a lavish premiere at the historic Grauman's (it was never anything else to me) Chinese Theatre on Hollywood Boulevard which was melded with an all-night celebration on MTV, already establishing itself as the heart-beat of teen/twenties music entertainment tastes. The cable network, as part of it, covered as a highly promoted TV special the spectacular party and concert by Prince and Sheilah E, which, following the premiere screening, was wildly presented at the old Hollywood Palace, scene of more staid Hollywood entertainments of the past like "Ken Murray's Blackouts." The party and the live performance were initiated and produced by the studio and Prince and his associates, not by me. I was just there to add to the importance and the impact of the evening, of the opening, in the media's mind. And here's how the 1984 Olympics played into my hand on that one.

Gisela and I had, a few years before that, come into the affectionate acquaintance of Benjamin Baron, a cousin of mine by no direct blood connection but an exceedingly kindred soul. He was a vastly educated and sophisticated young dabbler in various arts, mostly writing, whose enthusiasm for and great humor about everything was a vital tonic for my whole family of which he was quickly a beloved member. We had met him only once before, and that was when he was one year old. Bringing Gisela to America for the first time, I had stopped in St. Louis to introduce my mother's extended family to my wife. My mother had not yet met her mystery daughter-in-law, and I could hear my Aunt Blanche on the phone trying to convince her worried sister that they all really did love Gisela. When he came back into our lives, Benjamin, having been a sickly child, did not have great health but he did have considerable wealth since his nonagenarian father was perhaps the leading corporate lawyer in the mid-west. Benjamin had contacts to get anything he or you wanted. So in the time of deadly competition for the best tickets for the best events of the Olympics, Benjamin was a gold medalist ticket acquirer. My birthday present to me that year was watching Michael Jordan and his buddies cop the Olympic gold in basketball. Benjamin not long enough at all thereafter died very suddenly and very young, but he had lived a life of enthusiasms of culture, friendship and cultural tastes fully explored and delighted-in and he had finally enjoyed a very rewarding marriage. But in 1984 he was in the full vitality of life and he was king of the Olympic tickets. One of the hottest of these was the grand finale, the closing ceremonies. I told him I wished to endanger his possession of these, but that if my hunch proved correct, he would be able to keep them after a flurry of notoriety and press coverage.

My problem with the "Purple Rain" opening was that while the prospect of the premiere had the galvanized attention and anticipation of the pop and youth culture across the nation, in Hollywood we really weren't getting a big response from the traditional red carpet decoration types, the super-structure taste-makers and mainline stars to whom we had sent invitations. We didn't want coverage of the premiere to affirm that this was a niche occurrence. We needed the regular famous faces there to convince the media that Prince-fever was raging across the board. "Purple Rain" had to have the appearance of wide cultural anointment. That is where Benjamin came in. I had him take ads in the trades, the Hollywood Reporter and Daily Variety, that he had a pair of prime tickets for the closing ceremonies of the Olympics...... a get-of-all- gets for the Olympics-crazed in our event-loving entertainment industry. In the ad I designed, Benjamin stated that he would happily trade these two tickets for two tickets to the premiere and after-party for "Purple Rain." I then arranged for his strange and startling ad to get wide pick-up in the media... a guy willing to give up the golden tickets of the Olympics. Who knew he was my cousin? Suddenly the premiere RSVPs from the town's elite started to pour in. Benjamin dejectedly reasoned that they just wanted them to trade out for his Olympic finale seats, but I made a side-bet with him that he would get no takers. I felt his ad was the ultimate expression of the old *courage-of-someone-else'-convictions* rationale. How valuable were tickets to "Purple Rain?" More valuable than tickets for the Olympics closing ceremony. You couldn't get a point across more compellingly than that. I won my bet, and I rewarded Benjamin with "Purple Rain" premiere tickets which I would have given him anyway.

While working at Rogers & Cowan in the 60s, I touched base with many of the leading acts of that first hard-rock decade. Most of them still sang songs that I, a *devote'* of the American song book style of music, could revere. But the second world of hard rock and heavy metal was making music in a language I didn't understand, even though I tried. For me... perhaps for me alone in the whole world… the same thing applies to rap. Poetry?… certainly. Poetry whose rhythms and meter are cleverly abetted by percussion? Yes, of course. But I was brought up on gospel and blues and pop and jazz and country and bluegrass, opera, operetta, ragtime, barbershop, non-metallic rock and even voted for "It's Tough Out There For A Pimp" to receive the Oscar….but I just always thought singers were supposed to sing. One night recently I was talking to a top-of-the-charts rap artist and told him that, while I didn't really understand rap, as he might imagine from the grey of my beard, I thought that his music was very melodious, and he said, "What's that?"

They Broke the Mold — Maurice Chevalier

Maurice Chevalier was to Paris of the' 20s and '30s what Elvis and Michael are to rock America. In the '50s on the set of "Love In The Afternoon," because of the '40s, Chevalier would sit between takes wrapped in his own thoughts, like a computer that turns itself into a default "off" when not in use. For ten years he had lived with the fact that he was considered a *colaborateur* because he had performed for German troops during the Occupation. He wore his off-camera withdrawal like a protective armor. When Chevalier returned to public performance in 1956 at the newly renamed Alhambra Maurice Chevalier Theatre, France swept aside any resentments to welcome him back.

I could see him in the wings before his introduction, the same withdrawn and drowsy recluse, separating himself from all about him. But the moment they said, "Mesdames, Messieurs, Mau-rice Che-vah- LIER, it might just as well have been "SHAZAM!" because he exploded to life, burst out onto the stage with Captain Marvel energy, erupted into song and the French charm he, best of all Gauls, could turn to music. The cocooned old man on the film set unleashed a musical dynamism and charisma on that evening that justified the legend. I concluded that such performance clearly demands energy expenditure impossible if you leave the lights on all the time.

It was quite an honor that M. Chevalier presented me with two prime tickets for his opening. Perhaps we had made more of a connection than I'd thought. He did seem to spark to promotional ideas I suggested. Since he was portraying a sleuth, I posed him in one of those double-billed Sherlock Holmes hats while he held a magnifying glass which enlarged one of his famous sparkling eyes. The photo had remarkable humor and verve, and the shot got wide breaks in the States as well as prominent and very respectful exposure in France. After his having been in semi-reclusion, that response to publicity of his teaming with three icons of the American film world seemed to brace him.

I had just met this incredibly vivacious German girl from some fairy-tale back-water called the Black Forest. Was she going to be impressed! I was not aware that Tolstoy and Chekov, Dostoyevsky and Tchaikovsky, royalty and aristocracy had repaired to Baden Baden for their sophisticated pleasures for centuries. She *was* impressed, however, because Chevalier was amazing, living up to his legend. And his pianist was no less than a youthful Michel Legrand. As piece de resistance, I had told Gisela that afterwards we would go back to M. Chevalier's dressing room and she would meet all of these adulated and important people. Which we did, and there gathered were Gary Cooper and Audrey Hepburn and Billy Wilder and the elite of the French entertainment world, to all of whom I proudly introduced the first and, as it turned out, only object of my romantic obsession. I could well imagine how caught up in my distinguished contacts she must be. As we left the dressing room, she turned to me cheerily and said, "Now are we going to meet the important people?" She wasn't kidding. "There wasn't anyone in that room," I protested, " who hasn't won an Oscar or the Legion D'Honneur." "I know," she said, " but the way you were talking, I was expecting Albert Einstein and Albert Schweitzer." She was right. I didn't have a single Albert up my sleeve. It occurred to me how much I would need her sane cynicism and perspective.

They Broke the Mold — Doris Day

Doris Day's first film was Warner's "It's Magic" in 1948. In her second film, "Romance On The High Seas," she rose to stardom when she sang a song called "It's Magic." I was present at a much later moment which proved that it really WAS magic that brought her so powerfully to our affections

Sometimes it is incident more than dialogue which memorably defines these remarkable people. Film stars can amaze you with gesture. I think particularly of an insight into what made Doris Day so uniquely Doris Day. I was part of a team that worked her at Rogers & Cowan, and that was substantially through the filter of her husband/manager, Marty Melcher. It gave me a close up look at her dominant stardom, the adulation she inspired and the media's skepticism about that. When someone at Time magazine defined her sexuality as "boyish," you knew this was a guy who had some real gender recognition problems. How could they argue with how both her acting and her singing connected with the public? One thing was certain, their reservations were not shared by that public.

Ticket-buyers fully understood that the comedies with Rock Hudson, Cary Grant and Jim Garner and others were soufflés. Don't sell the public short. It loved the true pitch of her dramatic work, as well. Doris had it both ways, hitting all the right notes in the dramas, too… "Love Me Or Leave Me," "Midnight Lace," "Young Man With A Horn," "The Man Who Knew Too Much," expertly drawn characterizations all and yet indelibly Doris Day…, an acting skill which helped her dominate the grandest flood of great singers in American pop musical history. The Big Band Era was an Ivy League school for singers.

My second go-round with Doris was when Linda Dozoretz, Doris' longtime press agent after Rogers & Cowan, had brought her impressive stable to Guttman & Pam. Doris was set to receive the Hollywood Foreign Press Association lifetime achievement award, which was to be Doris' return to Hollywood after many years of seclusion in Carmel. That occasion had to be celebrated with major press, and Linda had arranged for Charles Champlin, the true dean of the film critics and commentators, to interview her at Doris' small inn in Carmel. This would be for a major Sunday story in the Los Angeles Times. Since Gisela and I were going to be up near Carmel at the time (we were handling the Monterey Film Festival,) I would babysit the interview. Doris, absent of pretense, stopped in at the hotel at the end of a run with five or six dogs, and she had her hair pulled back simply and was wearing a muted pink running suit, sweat pants and jacket. Chuck understood Doris' unique significance in film, and the absence of artifice simply sharpened his delight in the conversation. It wasn't until the end of it that Chuck, with deep apology, dropped the bomb.

Doris was scheduled to shoot the portrait photo for the story the next day, Chuck acknowledged, but the Times' esteemed photographer, Mary Frampton, had to race back to Los Angeles because her father had just passed away. Could Doris possibly accommodate that tragic problem and do the photograph right now? Mary could set up in the lobby of the hotel. Doris felt her pinned-back hair and gave a quick look at her non-designer sweat togs nicely dampened and clinging from her run, wiped a still insistent rivulet of sweat from her brow and said…. "Sure." Chuck said, "she doesn't know you guys know," and we went out to the lobby. Mary thanked her and showed Doris where she wanted to shoot with natural light. She wanted to climb up on a table and shoot down with Doris looking up at her. Doris said, "Can I have five minutes to freshen up." Of course, and she disappeared and Mary said, "What a champ."

Mary set her position, and when Doris returned she did look somehow freshened, but it was far from a glamour presentation. This was for her big return bow in the film capital. It just looked fresh, which was what Doris Day was all about. Doris sat down, Mary climbed the table. Mary said, "Ready?" And Doris said, "just let me find my light." Just let her find her light? Doris looked around at the natural light sources in the room and then said "Ok." She smiled and looked up at a certain spot, and her eyes started to... Sparkle. I kid you not. There was light dancing out of her eyes. Mary and Gisela and I were awed. Mary said "wow" and then clicked off a couple of shots. Doris carried her own special effects with her. It was called knowing the camera. Of course the voice was great and her comedy and drama right on, but she carried her stardom inside. The photo in the Sunday Times was, naturally, terrific. Now I ask you, is anyone ever going to forget that experience? Any word or gesture of it?

PATTERNS OF SPEECH ARE LIKE THE PATTERNS OF FINGER-PRINTS ... no two exactly alike. Here's to the wondrous coloration and imagination of human speech. My life has been filled with so many original voices and story-telling skills. It is amazing how often and with what ease the bright people of our star ranks tie their conversational bits up with true punchlines, or word constructions of almost musical charm. I'm thankful always for that signature good fortune of my life, the universally acknowledged wits with whom I have worked... Peter Ustinov, Larry Harvey, Tony Randall, James Mason, the acerbic Jimmy Woods, Greer Garson, Michael Caine , David Janssen, Roger Moore... for having experienced first-hand the generous wit, even for an audience of one, of such masters as Jay Leno, Milton Berle and Carl Reiner. Merv Griffin's soft-sell humor was unbounded by ego. We were doing a series of promotional interviews by satellite with morning TV talk shows around the country to promote Merv's White House interview with his friends Ronald and Nancy Reagan. He had set up an ad hoc syndication for that "at home with the First Couple" and he wanted to sell it big. For these "satellite tours," there is always a few minutes of down time in between. It had been mentioned that we were doing it from the CNN facilities in Hollywood, and we received a phone call there from a viewer in Portland who asked us to tell Mr. Griffin that he and other people who tuned in to watch the various satellite conversations could view not only all the interviews but also what was happening during the down time. He said that they appreciated how polite Mr. Griffin was when he was just being himself, "but please tell him we can see him picking his nose." Merv got a big laugh out of that and an even bigger laugh when he mentioned it on his own show. One of the smartest, richest guys in the business, and not afraid to let it be known that he was human.

Many of the most interesting and idiosyncratic people a press agent collects are not stars in the Hollywood sense of the word. On a film amalgamating the personalities of Audrey Hepburn, Gary Cooper, Billy Wilder and Maurice Chevalier, it may seem strange to relate that the most fascinating and dazzling personality in our "Love In The Afternoon" complex at the Studios de Boulogne was a guy you never heard of named Gerard Lang. He and our cat Claude were actually the only creatures who, with absolute certainty, saved my life. Oh, and a black gentleman who said "Look out" when I stepped into Wilshire Boulevard just as a van was running the red light in the curb lane at 50 miles an hour. What if he had taken one more call before heading out for lunch? And, oh yes, Dr. Carlson who carved out that cancer just as it was about to go viral. I suppose there is a lot of credit or blame for my still being, but Gerard, at least, was the first and therefore saved more of my life than the others.

Gerard Lang was the French press agent on that film, so he had to share an office with the kid who was the assistant American publicist. Gerard, in his mid-forties I supposed, was the most contained man I'd ever met. He had disrespect for and suspicion of practically everything, because that had been his job in the French Maquis or underground during the Nazi occupation in World War II. He had nerves of ice, since his job during the Occupation had been test piloting the fake IDs that were created to get downed American and British flyers out of France. He had to get arrested by the Gestapo over and over again. When he didn't want to get arrested, he would wear flamboyant clothes, neon blue or bright green suits and ties, cavorting at race tracks gaudy as a pimp or the tourjours gai niteries that were filled with swastikas. Nobody looks for someone that easy to find. When he had some papers to acid test, he dressed and conducted himself as though he were trying to fade into the wallpaper. It never failed, fifteen minutes and he was being grilled at Gestapo headquarters.

Gerard had lived while most of his compatriots had been killed, lived because of the skill of his unerring nose. When the Maquis put up barricades on the Left Bank opposite the Place de la Concorde to trap and kill the Nazi troops trying to beat it back to Deutschland, the game suddenly shifted when Panzer tanks came into play for the Germans. His friends all hightailed it back into the Left Bank, and the tank cannons mowed them down... Gerry (pronounced jeh-ree, each syllable equally accented, the rule which makes French sound so sexy) took off straight at the Germans who were so startled by the one man charge that he ran through them and five minutes later was quietly having a double expresso at the Café de L'Opera. Another time during the occupation, he came home and started up the stairs to his room. Everything was perfectly normal, too normal. When he came to the first landing he flung himself through the stained glass window, and a dozen guns opened up on him as he cleared the back fence. He could smell trouble just as he could smell if a woman wanted to be had and how to have her. He was a coldblooded womanizer, but hot blood was one of his tools. His weapon of choice was a flashlight. He would darken the room as soon as his quarry's nakedness was achieved, place a flashlight against his fingers so that the red and vermillion that seeped through their translucence was the sole illumination and he would move his glowing hand above various parts of her body without touching, and her job was to watch. I know hypnosis when I see it, and I also know when I've almost gone too far. I'll leave the rest to your assumption. This is not a how-to book. I had all of this sexual protocol confirmed by two of his very satisfied victims, each of them a bit unworldly, even mindless, which seemed to be the only kind of women to whom misogynists are drawn . He had grown up without a mother and was certain he had no real need for women except as prey. But many of them found him charming and even gallant.

Gerard was not really a press agent. He was a gangster. Here's how his racket went. He had been one of the top race track handicappers, but it was all part of a mob scam to turn horse races into sure bets. You could in those days place bets a month ahead of a race, and if you knew which top horses would be scratched for injury at race time, it cut the odds. His handicap column in a top newspaper was a great tool for the mob, and he was a highly paid functionary. Somehow, someone had pulled a fast one, gaming the scam and leaving the mob holding an empty bag. He was assumed to have been the culprit because nobody trusts a guy who gets laid that often.

So he was on the lam but reluctant to leave Paris, Therefore he became the most nondescript and singularly insignificant and inconspicuous thing a man can be… a motion picture publicist. In this guise, he felt perfectly anonymous. He was also, he said, a sometimes ghost writer for a top French thriller author, the mention of whose name would only get me sued by his estate. This I believed because he sometimes talked and thought like a French Raymond Chandler… or Phillip Marlow. Why he trusted me with all this I don't know, but he seemed to like me. I was so his opposite,, a prankish college kid, as wide-eyed and innocent as I appeared. There was almost one prank too many. As he was coming into our office once, I… the oldest, dumbest prank of all… pulled against the wall and said "boo." What made me duck at the same moment is anybody's guess, but his hatchet-formed hand swept back, passing just above my head, and cracked the door jam in two, the thick ancient boards sticking out like half of an x. So when he later told me he would break both of my legs, I had reason to believe that he would and the absolute certainty that he could. I'd seen that his levat kick could go through a wall.

The broken leg thing came up because this was October of 1956, and suddenly a couple of hundred miles to the east of us, Hungarians had risen up against the Russian occupiers. 1956 was a seminal year in the Cold War which stirred emotions and patriotism and demagoguery and confusion that disturbed and bewildered all of us. I had come politically of age in the early '50s amidst the protests against Joe McCarthy and the House Un-American Activities Committee's oppression of anyone with an open mind. The Hollywood black-listing was just one aspect of right wing assault on our freedoms from within, only one reason for the great resistance and fear in which so many of us were conjoined. On the other hand, the Cold War was real, the depredations by the Soviets and the puppet regimes they had established in Eastern Europe were horrors we despised. The turmoil of this new revolt, the jolts of hope and the shifting news reports of who was prevailing filled my mind.

At night I would have to go home through machine gun nests, showing my papers, because the Russian embassy was around the corner from the modest little Hotel du Bac where I had my small and barren room. Dinners in the corner restaurant were eaten to the tramp, tramp, tramping of French police patrols marching the streets. Every 23 year old wants to do something to protect his country, and now Hungarians, my father's people, were being killed in the streets little more than a day or two drive from where I was. Billy Wilder's driver, Ivan, was Hungarian. He had contacts with the Hungarian resistance and was raising a group to go there for the struggle. Gerry came into the office with a grim face, closed the door which by now had been fixed and said, "Ivan tells me you're going to Hungary with him. Do you speak any Hungarian?" "Hodjvod and egeshegera." "Meaning?" "Meaning hello and here's to your health." "Well, that will certainly get you through an insurrection. Have you ever shot a gun?" "No, but…" "Do you know anything about underground organizations?" "No." "Well, I do. Their first job is to distrust everyone. You will be one of two things to them, a stupid American do-gooder who can't speak the language and who can get other people killed, or a Russian spy pretending to be a stupid American do-gooder. So the first thing they do is give you a mission… a suicide mission, only you won't know that. If you take one step forward, the Russians kill you. If you take one step back, the Hungarians kill you. In any case they have you out from under their feet." "Well, Ivan thinks he can arrange for me to do press liaison for the rebels with the international press there." "Not dead you can't." Gerry offered me a deal. If I relinquished my intention, he would let me walk out of the office. If I didn't, he would break both of my legs so I would have to be carried out. The revolt collapsed three days later, but Gerard assured me I would have had more than enough time to get killed.

Gerard was always trying to save me from things, one of them being Gisela. When I met her shortly after the 1956 American elections, Gerard would see us together on Boulemiche or in the down-and-dirty jazz "caves" on Rue La Huchette. He finally met her the time I arranged for her to be an extra in a night scene shot at Maxim's. I could afford to take her to dinner only once a week, and she preferred to spend her scant money on philosophy books, Gitanne cigarettes and black coffee with brandy rather than food. So Maxim's was a good chance to feed her well, with Allied Artists picking up the tab. The next day Gerard told me to leave her because she would never be mine. "'Pourquoi?" I demanded. "Par-ce-qu'elle est une pyrotechnique. (Because she's a fireworks display.)" He didn't trust a 19 year old girl, barely enough money to scrape by on, but so buoyantly on top of every moment. He couldn't tolerate women who were indomitable. Decades later when she faced her fight against cancer and had rejected her doctor's demand that she submit to chemo, there was a moment when she wondered if she could pull it off. I asked her if she knew what had first attracted me to her. "What do you mean?"

she asked. "Well," I said, "there's always something you fall in love with first, the smile, a look in the eyes, the bounce of the hair, the figure." "So what was it for you?" "Your indomitability."

I bet Gerry one hundred francs that I would marry her. When she finally dumped me, just after 1956 stepped aside for 1957, I saw him on Boulemiche and gave him a hundred francs. When I finally got her back, months after "Love In The Afternoon" had wrapped and I'd returned from my escape to Mallorca, he saw me with her at San Germaine des Pres, read the body language, came over with a look of absolute astonishment and, saying nothing, handed me two hundred francs. I saw him one more time, and he told me Paris was getting too hot for him, and he was taking off for Canada to translate American movies into French. He'd been in South America, and they'd tracked him there, but, he figured, who would want to go to Canada, even to kill him?

Some press agents miss the point. They so fixate on the remarkableness of the stars they serve that they miss the wonder of the other special personalities who swirl about a Hollywood press agent's life, people like Gerard Lang. A lot of them are journalists who can be remarkable characters. I liked Jim Harwood of Variety, a guy who took great joy in his bachelorhood and the various devices one who eschewed committed relationship might employ to enjoy an evening's company with a beautiful woman… or just a woman. Since he worked out of San Francisco, he sometimes haunted lesbian bars on the supposition that some sweet young thing who had just had a falling out with her partner might be open to a freaky night of heterosexuality just to make a statement. He enjoyed a lot of such statements. There was Joe McBride, also of Variety, who did an interview for me with Michelle Phillips and fashioned a good story from it, even though Variety rarely ran interviews with stars. I asked him after the interview why he had done it, and he said he just wanted to meet a woman who could infatuate so many powerful and creative men. She had swirled through the lives of Jack Nicholson, John Phillips, Warren Beatty and others and they through hers. She never surrendered her own compelling originality nor did she become an apostrophe to any of them.

During our representation of her, I arranged for her to meet Ken Russell, one of the most iconoclastic of film-makers who painted with an eye vastly more erotic than Hollywood was venturing even in the sudden freedoms of the early

1970s. Russell, white hot off of the successes of "Women in Love" and "The Music Lovers," fearless purveyor of exposed emotions and exposed anatomy, was readying a film about Janis Joplin, the film that eventually became, under Mark Rydell's direction, "The Rose." We worked on that because we handled Mark... As different as were their musical styles, Michelle could have rolled into that Janis Joplin challenge like sliding into the warm part of the bed. Guttman & Pam was able to bring Michelle and Russell together because we represented that director's close collaborator, Glenda Jackson. In publicity, everything connects to everything else. Michelle was being urged by others to skip the Russell meeting because it was rumored Russell wouldn't be able to get the Joplin project, then called "The Pearl," off the ground. I argued that Russell would certainly get SOMEthing off the ground, and who knows where this would lead. And who better to recognize Michelle's incredible sexuality than he? There was/is just something in the way Michelle looks you straight in the eyes and finds you and everything else funny that cranks up the sexual ambience her presence stirs. Russell never did Joplin, but a few years later, he handed Michelle the lead in "Valentino" opposite Rudolf Nureyev. If Joe McBride still had any questions as to why so many extraordinary male artists, powerful personalities and stars all, were mesmerized by her, he need only have bought a ticket to that film. It wasn't the stripping away of clothes. It was the stripping away of pretense. She was presence over pretense. It was Russell's camera catching the take-it-or-leave-it power of her knowing who she was. You can't buy that at Escada or at a nip/tuck-torium. The Mommas and the Poppas wasn't just the voices, it was the four fearless personalities taking joy in their own feeling for the music and for their times.

During the time Michelle was attending LA's John Marshall High, her close friend and fellow rebel was John Paul DeJoria whose natural reluctance to do it the way he was supposed to would lead him to homelessness and then to a classic rags-to-riches success unimagined even by Horatio Alger. And whose Paul Mitchell Haircase System empire I would represent. They spent so much time passing notes in class, that a teacher stopped his instruction one day to appoint them John Marshall High's Least Likely to Succeed. One wound up in the Rock And Roll Hall of Fame and the other a billionaire mogul and philanthropist. On JP's 50th birthday, we had a surprise lunch party for him at a Mexican restaurant where he had, decades before, celebrated his first solvency about a half year after his launch of Paul Mitchell. On hand were Michelle and a high school teacher delighted that his predictions had proven so inaccurate. This was set up for me by another Marshall High grad, Tom LaBonge, Mayor Bradley's right hand then and currently a powerful councilman on his way to some other high public service. Marshall, for all of the challenged minorities in its tough area, did all right. The point is that no matter how modest their prospects of survival, charismatics fashion their own keys to open the doors of success.

When Mark Rydell first showed me "The Rose," I remarked on the honed skill of Bette Midler's performance. He had refused to do the film until producer Marvin Worth finally got the studio to OK Bette Midler, who had never acted before. Mark insisted he didn't "direct" her in the sense of telling her what to do, but rather pointed her in the direction of what he wanted from a scene and then turned her loose. When the Academy recently honored the film, him and her on the film's 30th anniversary, we used the occasion to launch a campaign to achieve a DVD release of the re-mastered print which was debuted that evening. Significantly, Bette's two Oscar nominations were both under Mark's direction. The scene which most intrigued me directorially, however involved a screaming argument between a cop and a chauffeur who have no pertinence to the story and who are seen only in the background of a scene in which two of the main characters are having a comparatively placid dialogue exchange in foreground. The intensity of the background action was the energy of the scene, a contrast to the civility of the main action. I asked Mark how he got those performances from two guys in very subsidiary roles, and he explained that he had taken each aside before the scene and had given each the same story... that there was another good scene in it for the actor who won the argument. They went at it tooth and nail. Neither won but not for the want of trying... and each got another scene. Directors, it turns out, can be as insidious as press agents. I had written that tale into this book before I saw the film again at that Academy screening, at which I discovered that there WAS no such scene. So I went home and deleted the above passage. At lunch today, I told him this sequence of events and confided that I was worried that I could recall so vividly something that didn't happen. "It happened," he reassured me, and then he held up his hands and clicked forefingers and middle fingers against each other... it had been cut. What a relief... what a shame. "I loved that scene, too," he consoled me, "sometimes it just doesn't work for the film."

For "On Golden Pond," Mark extracted career-topping performances (and what spectacular careers to top) from Henry and Jane Fonda. by "letting them explore and resolve a lifetime of misunderstandings through the scenes of the film," he told me. "I felt that's what Jane hoped would happen when she bought the rights to the stage play. It was very brave of each of them, but what else would you expect of a Fonda? Or, even more, a pair of them." And you thought directing involved just saying "action" and "cut." Mark, Sidney Pollack and Martin Landau long headed the Actors Studio West, and I would guess that just living out a film with any one of them would be the equivalent of a masters degree in acting. Not coincidentally, Pollack and Rydell, along with Huston, Preminger and Von Stroheim, were sensational character actors in other directors' films. I'm excluding directors who started primarily as actors. Martin Ritt held his own in front of the camera with Jon Voigt, Robert Shaw and Jacqueline Bisset in Maximilian Schell's film "End of the Game." It was a shame that it came toward the end of his life in films and couldn't have launched a a second career in acting. He was a rumpled bear awakened from the torpor of hibernation. He would have been one of the great character actors

Any reference to Rudolf Nureyev reminds me always of writer/director James Toback. Jimmy is an inveterate gambler. He sought out dangerous bets and won some and onetime even wore one. His characters were compellingly improbable, and he was one of them. We first worked for him on a noir film called "Fingers" which was sort of an American "Shoot The Piano Player," connected in tone, humor and the profession of the protagonists. It was exciting because top critics picked up on the film, and suddenly I, as its press agent, had a movie that was doing its own publicity. Like a jockey giving a win-hungry mount its head, you just hang on, trying not to fall off and working to keep it going in the right direction. Years later, Jimmy came into my office wearing a large overcoat in the middle of an October heat-wave. He looked like a street person. He told me of a film called "Exposed" he was preparing to shoot in France, and in this one, the hero was a violinist played by Nureyev. He said it would cost two million dollars, and I asked if he had the money. He stood up and spread his coat open like a bat cape. Inside there were twenty pockets, each with a hundred thousand dollars stuck in it. "Jimmy," I yelled, "you can't walk around like that. What if someone steals the coat?" He waved me off… "Who's going to steal an overcoat in the middle of a heatwave?" I guess he was right… he made the film.

I find generally that directors are more idiosyncratic than actors or, for that matter, writers. Directors make weighty decisions while one hundred people await their pleasure. That's pressure. I once was writing a project which dealt with satyriasis… male nymphomania… compulsive and constant sexual adventuring. I was researching a script that I eventually optioned several times for a film that never got made and then redid as a novel which never got published. I discussed this condition of extreme sexual compulsiion with a famous acquaintance who legendarily knew a lot about sex, and I asked if he knew of any true satyrs to whom I could speak. "Only one," he said… and then mentioned a director of my acquaintance. Somehow, I knew it would be a director. Compulsive sex has more to do with power than pleasure. But, it's difficult to go up to someone and say, "Tell me about your incessant fornication," so I did the research the old-fashioned way…. reading books, talking to experts. It wasn't hard. Everyone knows what it feels like to be desirous. You just have to extrapolate that into what it must be like to feel it *all* the time. And, yes, I did finally ease into a conversation about it with my director friend… not a direct interrogation. I was just dipping a toe in to see if there might be any ripples, but there weren't. If anyone brags that he is satyr, he isn't. Finally he did say (I chose to assume admit) to me, "Being constantly over-sexed probably isn't sexy. I would think that it's…" He stopped and, after a painful introspection, he said, "I would think that It's a kind of… burden."

Lee Strasberg and the Method acting approach he imparted via The Actor's Studio honed the realism of American film acting post World War II. His American refinement of the Stanislavski acting approach illuminated screen acting both through his own vigorous and rigorous teaching and via the bright example of the work of such of his acolytes as Brando, Newman, Dean, Landau, McQueen, Pacino and Steiger in their stage and film work. I got an exposure to it during our early '50s UCLA film school matriculation (we actually were Theatre Arts students with dedicated studies in film) exactly during the years when Brando's performances in "The Men, " "Viva Zapata," "Streetcar Named Desire" and "On The Waterfront" were blazing that acting discipline upon our consciousness. One of our fellow students was Strasberg's daughter Susan and another was the extraordinary character actor and teacher, Jeff Corey, who was sitting out his black-listed years in our company, although considerably our senior. He was a gentle, compelling and knowing man. But I learned as much in one night about the bohemian mindset of the Method community (how absolutely cut loose it was from the small-minded constraints which had been passed on to the rest of us) as I did in those four years of study. It's a story I was prepared not to include because I didn't want to embarrass anyone else in my telling of tales. There was too much else to talk about. But I'm including this at the insistence of Marty Landau who was and is as much a part of the Actors Studio tradition as anyone. Marty very kindly and correctly pointed out to me that the only embarrassment in this story is my own. It is an anecdotal glimpse of how that mystic group was set apart from my *petit bourgeois* life-view.

The evening began with a very private but very starry screening of director Jack Garfein's tense, moving and studio-buried film "Something Wild" starring his wife, Carroll Baker and Ralph Meeker, all of whom had strong Actors Studio background and training. The film is now, forty years later, is being disinterred, rediscovered and celebrated by Turner Classic Movies and festivals and schools around the world. But in the 1960s it was so emotionally rigorous and demanding of the audience that it was barely released. Jack was a major product of and force in the Studio, a Boy Wonder director on Broadway merely a decade after his liberation from the death camps of the Nazis. The evening was set up by Franchot Tone who had told Garfein that he hoped Jack lived another forty years to be there when they finally realized what they'd missed, which is now precisely the case. Landau assured me that Strasberg, the guru of that whole Method group, did not like failure. He considered "Something Wild" a failure and had refused to see it. Tone pulled the night together in order to sit Strasberg through Jack's film so that Strasberg would see the marvels of Jack's and Carroll's and Meeker's achievement. The night took on Joy when Strasberg admitted the film was great. By 3AM we were hours into food and conversation and pool (both billiards and water) and more impassioned philosophical discussion at the home of Ben Gazzara and Janice Rule, both of whom were engaged with several other distinguished Method practitioners in a competition at the pool table, all smoking large cigars, including Miss Rule.

A heated discussion was being conducted in the garden near the pool, the two participants of which who most stick in my mind were Strasberg and Tone, one of the great stage-trained stars of the '30s and '40s and a Method veteran, whom Hollywood trapped in light comedy and "the other guy" roles. Two fine directors gave him a chance to show his acting chops, Frank Lloyd in "Mutiny On

The Bounty" and Billy Wilder in "Five Graves To Cairo. They show why he was an honored hero among the Method group. The esoteric subject of this debate of which I was merely an avid and fortunate witness has faded from my mind for the following reason. Susan was swimming nude in the pool and, at a certain point came out and, drying herself, joined the discussion among the half dozen men. The thing was, she was drying herself, as one often does in the privacy of one's bathroom, with the towel behind her, that diagonal buffing of shoulders, spine and haunches, standing there with her father and his close male associates. What impressed me was that I, at the insistence of my middle-class Midwest morality with all of its rigidities, was the only one who actively averted his gaze. It's not that anyone else availed themselves of her nudity and her beauty. They didn't look, but they were not, as I was, actively *not* looking. It was simply a case of the situation's being of no consequence to them. I was too bourgeois to process such attitude. On the way home, I mentioned it to Gisela, and she said, "It's because they're artists." She, a sculptor, was accustomed to live models. I, a plebian press agent and not much more than an aspiring writer, needed a cultural passport to cross that border where sexuality became merely conceptual.

Art Murphy

The first thing you have to understand about publicity is that disaster always and forever sits in the corner waiting to pounce. Disaster comes in many forms, and one of the most feared was Daily Variety's top business reporter, Art Murphy. Art was the master of the numbers. It was he with his unerring business sense who could read the numbers and tell the future like a mystic can read tea leaves. He would juggle the hidden meanings of the box office results and anything else numerical, shaping them into accurate reading of the only fate the business understood, profit and loss. He was superb at the task and his findings were like court judgments on who would rise and who would tumble. He also passionately enjoyed holding press agents to their highest calling of accuracy, factuality and succinct and organized semantic expression. He could and would quite brutally deride in print a faulty release or a silly publicist error or, the not-always-merciful heavens forbid, an outright lie. This public castigation was often right up there on the front page. It was a reverently regarded Variety tradition. His derisions could send an offending or careless press agent into hiding for weeks. The word humiliation would not be overstating it. You checked and double-checked and then had someone else check before you sent a story to Art. That notwithstanding,

I had always enjoyed his intelligence, ethics and acerbic wit, maybe because my number had never come up. And then, one not-so-fine day, it did.

This occurred as we were readying Warren Beatty's and Hal Ashby's "Shampoo" for a late-in-the-year run at Oscar nominations. The film had been released earlier in the year, too early for automatic Oscar consideration, so we had to take some special shots. One of these would be a November or perhaps it was early December re-release predicated on the fact that the film was included in nearly every Best Ten list by reviewers all over the country. The master of this plan was Columbia's massively respected head of distribution, Norman Levy. Because of his respect for Warren Beatty's intelligence and instincts and the high skill-sets of the people with whom Warren surrounded himself, Mr. Levy gave close consideration to my suggestions which he knew had already been vetted by the x-ray intelligence of Warren Beatty. For this re-release, I felt a key element would be the anticipated box-office regeneration. Nothing backs up great reviews like great business. Tracking was showing that it would have some strong numbers as it came out of the gate again, and I really wanted to hammer that home on the Monday following the weekend.

To facilitate and expedite this key planting, which Norman Levy and I had agreed would be an exclusive to Art Murphy… the town's most credible and respected journalistic numbers-cruncher… I pre-wrote the story laying in phrases that I thought would be substantiated by Monday morning when we would want to whip this over to Art. I wrote it out to be sent by messenger (no functioning email or even fax then, not by several years) to Norman Levy. We could adjust it the next day over the phone, insert the eventual numbers early Monday and have it hand-planted with Art Murphy. I even typed in the Exclusive to Art Murphy, but it clearly stated "draft" and there were empty spaces for the numbers. I assumed that was apparent. Press agent rule: ASSUME IS DOOM. Or, as Jerry Pam often said, "A-S-S-U-M-E… assume makes an ass of you and me."

I handed it to our new secretary/receptionist (something we still had then) to retype. Then I came back to oversee its being messengered to Norman Levy. I asked the secretary to call a messenger. "Oh," she said, "I've already sent it off." I was surprised and said, "But I didn't give you Mr. Levy's address. " "Oh, I didn't need it," she said, "I just sent it to *Variety*." I knew that I was done in… or maybe it was "undone." A press agent draws up a glowing story on a weekend's gross before the weekend. And to whom is it sent? Art blooming Murphy. The next day I would be the laughing stock of every conversation at The Palm, The Grill or The Polo Lounge. On Friday I skipped breakfast for which I had no stomach and raced to the office, grabbing Variety the moment I got there. I didn't look at it until I was safely seated. I steeled myself and only then reluctantly cast my dreading eyes upon the front page. Nothing. Nothing inside either. I was bewildered. A messenger arrived from Variety with an envelope addressed to me. Inside was my draft story and a note saying, "I look forward to getting this on Monday. Have a good weekend. Art."

Jerry Pam aptly described it as "a bloody miracle."

Art, it is true, gave Jerry no chance to see that kinder, gentler side so generously reflected in that envelope to me from Variety. Jerry was sure that Art disliked him, and I said that was nonsense and I called Art and asked him to have lunch with Jerry because he's actually an amusing lunch partner and, additionally, there seemed to be some misunderstanding and I was sure it could be worked out. Mind you, this was about 1975 or '76. When they sat down, Jerry said, "Art, if there's something I've done to offend you, Dick was hoping that maybe…" Art looked at him and then nodded. "Well," he said, "in 1954…" Art Murphy always had his numbers straight.

Chapter 8

Starpower

Bringing stars together is a mathematical exercise not in addition but in multiplication. One is one , and one plus one is ten, and so the power of star gatherings increases logarithmically until it reaches saturation… the Oscars or the Golden Globes, the point at which the addition or subtraction or one or two stars, ten or twelve, doesn't alter the perception of how star-powered the event is. It doesn't take a lot of stars for an event, for a cast, or for a client list to seem "star-studded." Such is the "wow factor" of stardom. It takes only a few to seem like a lot. And stars feel comfortable in the company of other stars because they are fans, too. Some can be exasperating under the tectonic pressures of career or of a moment, of lives as subject to disappointment as they are to gratification, each of which must be played out in the limelight. Stardom is privilege and advantage, but it exacts its dues. Public and press want to feel happy for you, but they feel happy feeling sad for you, too.

When Julia Roberts was just starting to suggest the superstardom to come, Premiere Magazine wanted to proclaim it with a cover of her and the film world's top male stars. I said I thought I could bring together Warren Beatty, Clint Eastwood and Gene Hackman, three of the most evident power players and reigning superstars of that moment and of many decades of moments to follow. Guttman & Pam was working with all of them, and I was given a very bright green light to try. It was an intriguing idea to put the different magics of those three guys together in one Big Bang shot, a riff on stardom. It would be three guys who had come at it from such different angles, each nailing it solidly in his distinctively own way, a movie equivalent of the Yalta photo… the Roosevelt, Churchill and Stalin riff on the stardom of power and the power of stardom. It was a good idea, a Vanity Fair kind of idea, a photo which would have been about Julia Roberts' coming and inevitable stardom, yes, but which also would be about the complex variety of ways in which great talents/personalities become superstars. But good ideas have a high mortality rate and so do the magazines which don't have the resolve to take them all the way, and of course it didn't happen.

Another magazine cover that did happen proved once and for all that William Shatner was not a Vulcan. Guttman & Pam was representing the duumvirate of the Starship Enterprise, Bill Shatner and Leonard Nimoy, and I had set a rare cover of the two for Omni Magazine, befitting its slant to the future. The moment came. The lighting completed, the photographer laid the theme of the shot on them… the two looking into camera and each giving the Vulcan salute… the V with the index and middle finger on one side and the ring and little finger on the other. "Ready?" Each of the actors smiled and nodded. Each raised his hand… Nimoy, whose hand was an old hand at this, flashed his perfect V. Bill, quite sure he can do anything because he usually can, assumed he had, but he wasn't even close, not on the third try, not on the eighth… just a succession of grotesquely clawed digits. It had never occurred to him that he couldn't do the V because the scripts had never put that to the test. Who among us has never flashed the old Nimoy V? After thirty years at the helm of the Enterprise, William Shatner was devastated to discover that his lone Achilles heel was the space between his middle and ring fingers. His middle finger had never failed him before. We sent out for transparent violin string with which to tie the appropriate fingers together.

On the occasion of some ski event I was staging at the Sun Valley ski resort, I went up a day or so early to check that arrangements were coming along. Four actor friends flew up with me for a practice day of skiing… Janet Leigh, Jim Brolin, Lloyd Bridges and Peter Graves. Jim's "Marcus Welby" series was the reigning number one show on TV, Janet was shining in the glory of "Psycho," "The Manchurian Candidate," Orson Welles' "Touch Of Evil" and other recent films, and Peter Graves with "Mission Impossible" and Lloyd with "Seahunt" were iconic stars in every home in the land. A limo had been sent to whisk us up to the resort. There was still an hour of whisk left when we decided we were hungry, and we stopped in a small Idaho town to raid its single small-town-sized super market. Each of us had an assigned food stuff to pull... white bread, mayonnaise, sliced ham, sliced cheese, lettuce, paper plates, cups and milk. In every store there is musak slightly drowned out by people noises, the chatter and the clatter. As we moved about the store, we sensed a change. We actually could *hear* the musak, no people noises. The other customers were standing, mouths slightly agape, bewilderment, eyes moving from one famous face stepped out of their TV screens to another. It was as if Martians had made this store the first stop in their conquest of the planet. As we stacked our picnic on the checkout counter, the population of the store had gathered in a semi-circle, soundlessly staring. The famous intergalactic visitors smiled at them. There was nothing to say. When we got back in the limo, no one laughed. It hadn't been funny. It had been strange.

That ski event honored Frank Welles, then the president of Disney, who in his previous existence as superlawyer to the superstars shared a number of clients with me, Clint Eastwood and Larry Harvey among them. Of all the people I've met in Hollywood, I felt Frank was the one who most surely could have been and should have been President of the country. I'd met Ronald Reagan only a few times, but I still think Frank was the guy... just something about him. That fate and all others ended in a helicopter crash on one of his ascents of Mt. Everest. But that weekend, the future was blissfully unknown to us, and Brolin won the tournament over a list of stars MGM would envy. Jim and I were discussing that weekend a few days ago and the Martian invasion of the Idaho grocery store, and he said that nothing had changed. He and his wife, Barbra Streisand, love to do driving trips, particularly in the vast openness of the west, and he said they frequently make country grocery store visits so Barbra can do up picnics while he drives. He says the startled looks and respectful distances are the same they were on that movable feast four decades back.

I witnessed a similar mutual consternation on one elevator stop in Las Vegas. How many times in your life has an elevator door opened and closed and left not a spot on your memory? Vegas is a place where one expects to see stars, but not in over-whelming congregation. Columbia had gathered a press junket there one weekend to promote two of the studio's films, the adaptation of Carrie Fisher's "Postcards From The Edge" directed by Mike Nichols and "Narrow Margin," a thriller with Gene Hackman and Anne Archer. Gene was in both films. He was never a fan of interview, certainly not forty in a row as a junket entails, so I'd arranged for him to dispatch all in a single press conference. But there was some other occasion that entailed the presence of all of the stars of each film, and I was helping gather them together and hustling them down in the elevator to the event. And we descended, all of the famous participants standing in line-up configuration. I was pulled suitably off to the side. The others splayed in their single line across the width of the elevator like wax figures being moved at Madame Tussaud's. There was no conversation. Even stars can be struck dumb in a linear constellation of so many of their number. At the second floor, the elevator stopped at the behest of some waiting button-pushers. The doors opened, and we saw five civilians prepared to enter the elevator. The five civilians saw Meryl Streep, Richard Dreyfuss, Gene Hackman, Shirley MacLaine, Mike Nichols, Carrie Fisher, Dennis Quaid and Anne Archer. The people on the outside stared in with bewilderment. It was contagious, a two-way sizing up. Time froze, and then the elevator doors closed and, in lonely isolation from the rest of the world, the star line-up continued the additional floor of descent. Again, nobody laughed. It was an interlude at the opposite edges of a great no-man's land, a DMZ dividing stardom and those who adulate it.

It said something about the mystery of fame. As I know all too well, a single celebrity is very vulnerable to approach by his or her admirers or perhaps by people who simply admire and speculate about fame and long to touch it. If a star breaks the don't-make-eye-contact rule, it ignites a fan's compulsion to establish lifelong friendship, share the amazing news (as was the amused experience of Tony Randall) that in the fan's home town "there actually is a fella the name of Gary Cooper, 'xact same name… that actually is the case," or give advice or even scold. It verges on a sense of ownership. And when a star is in the possession of one requited customer, it can quickly become a feeding frenzy that can be quite dangerous. On the other hand, suddenly confronted by a who's-who of celebrated people as those would-be elevator passengers were in Las Vegas, it becomes fame in the abstract, a wall that cannot be breached. There was eye contact aplenty in that confrontation and mystification on both sides. Nobody ever really has written the rules of such engagement.

When a superstar is campaign chair of a charity, it creates very positive thrust. A succession of superstars is even better. This occurred to me one time when the Entertainment Industry Foundation, the show biz charity arm, was having a luncheon we'd arranged at which Gene Hackman was handing over the campaign chairmanship to Clint Eastwood. How did we follow that? The stars-stars-stars factor took care of that. Our daughter Danielle was one of the EIF leaders, and I was happy to help my daughter's and my industry's cause. They went in a short time from one and a half million dollars a year in fund-raising to thirty or forty million, and this was materially assisted by laying on a parade of the top entertainment stars to be successive campaign chairs. We started with Gene who ceded the post to Clint who helped me get Quincy Jones to succeed him whom I followed with Warren Beatty and then Jay Leno after whom Pierce Brosnan in all of his resplendent Bondhood. Yes, I was doing most of that within my own little circle, but with the fundraising expanding so remarkably, who cared? Each served several years, by the end of which EIF had upped its ante for key charities by a factor of twenty, one of the most spectacular charity organization growths ever. It reflected the organization's leadership and the industry support, but that killers-row lineup of major campaign chairs did not hurt.

Guttman & Pam worked with Arnold Schwarzenegger at the time of the release of "Conan The Barbarian," because we handled the film and after that because his press agent, Charlotte Parker, came into our employ. I first met him when he still had as his primary identification his position as the top-of-the-list body builder. He had turned that achievement, knowledge and fame and his enormous charisma and enterprise into a direct-sale empire of numerous related products. We met at his Venice (California) offices near Gold's Gym, where he had a very small staff efficiently moving all of the Schwarzenegger goods out into the world. You knew he was destined to seek and to suffer higher management challenges. This was when John Milius was in a long pre-production period getting "Conan The Barbarian" off the ground.

Milius and I first spoke because one of our star clients was planning a celebrity hunting party… no, I'm not kidding… at his Colorado ranch. A celebrity hunting party! It disgusted me, but the actor was (quite briefly) a client of my office, and

I was obliged to solicit celebrities who I thought were involved with hunting. I called Milius... not a client, just a guy I knew to be a noted gun enthusiast. I extended the invitation. He declined, and I said I thought he was very much into guns. "I am," he said, "but when I was a kid, we had to hunt in order to eat. And I've never seen a kill without agony." That formed an interesting bond, and Guttman & Pam worked with him on such films as "Conan" and "Farewell To The King," and I obtained festival honor for his prior films including his powerful "Dillinger," that bank robbing all-star's most gripping trip to the big screen. In the process, I met Arnold. At about that time, before "Conan" came out and before we came to represent him, somewhat before Arnold burst into top-of-the-heap stardom, we were thrown together in Washington, D.C. at a Georgetown party. We were the only two relatively unknown (Arnold) and completely unknown (I) people at a brunch at the home of Eunice Shriver, mother of Maria to whom Arnold was already committed if not betrothed. Arnold had already appeared in "Pumping Iron" and some other smaller films, and he was the noted body-builder which didn't quite register on the stardom scale at such a gathering of film-world and political super celebrity. He wasn't yet brightly on the radar of this gathered group. It's the Hollywood rule of "no star before his time."

The point of this is that stars, by and large and like the rest of us, are the fans of stars after they ARE stars. With exceptions. Larry Harvey, after his first scene with Julie Christie in "Darling," called me to pronounce her queen of the coming untold decades, as Gene Hackman one time was touting Vince Vaughn's coming stardom at first contact, ditto Warren Beatty about Gene Hackman during early scenes of "Lillith." During the filming of "Judgment At Nuremberg," Maximilian Schell told me that a young actor playing one of the courtroom's officer rank guards would be a star before long and for a long time. His name was William Shatner. Talent recognizes talent.

Arnold was simply not yet on their radar. The gathering was part of the premiere events for "Superman 2," and I was there for and with both Gene Hackman and Christopher Reeve and some other members of the cast whom we represented including Margot Kidder and Sarah Douglas who were, respectively, the deliciously sexy heroine and the deliciously sexy villainess of the piece. Everybody else at the brunch (in celebration of the premiere's raising funds for the Kennedy clan's beloved Special Olympics) was super famous. I wasn't and never would be, and

Arnold simply had not yet made his claim to celebrity-beyond-celebrity. Two years later he would be "Conan, The Barbarian" and shortly after that he would be The Terminator and then he would be in very capital (and capitol) letters, ARNOLD SCHWARZENEGGER. This was still a relatively anonymous trip to D.C., but he would be back.

The post-premiere party was a carnival on the grounds of the National Naval Observatory which doubles as the home of the Vice President of the United States. At a certain part of the proceedings, all of the stars and big wigs of the film were to go inside the Vice Presidential mansion for a more exclusive reception, but somebody forgot to take the director, Dick Lester, in with the group. I saw him and asked what he was doing on the outside. We had come to know each other in Iran when Guttman & Pam had overseen the publicity for the final Tehran Film Festival. The Shah's reign was coming apart at the seams at that moment, and Americans and Europeans felt a bit endangered on the streets, especially since some of our countrymen had been attacked and dare I say killed. It was that shared awareness and vague sense of peril that made for quick friendships, and Gisela and I had found Lester and his wife to be brilliantly funny companions. I took him up to the front door of the vice-presidential residence and knocked, and amazingly George H.W. Bush opened the door. "This is only for the important people," he said. I responded, "Mr. Vice-President, Mr. Lester's the president of the movie. He's the director." He nodded Dick in, a bit annoyed. Another damn president pulling rank. Well, he would have his chance. Had I not turned back to the fun part of the party, hundreds of kids exuberantly romping in the carnival set up on the VP's lawn, the door would have shut in my face. Hey, I'd been kicked out of better towns than that.

Stars enjoy the company of equivalent stars. But one star species to which they are particularly drawn is royalty. Put a royal into a situation and many Hollywood type stars are all suddenly monarchists. This came to mind when the 1984 Olympics were coming to Los Angeles, and the world's most illustrious personages were jamming into town. Guttman & Pam was overseeing the publicity and much of the organization for a fund-raiser for the British Olympic team at the Beverly Wilshire Hotel with the attendance and participation of Prince Andrew.

We were involved because of the substantial Brit element of our client list. Jerry had supplied Michael Caine and Roger Moore as the hosts and emcees for the evening, with fellow Brits Dudley Moore and Julie Andrews performing. Thanks to the royal star presence, we had star clusters of every national extraction on hand and bidding up the auction items which Michael and Roger were hawking so amusingly from the stage.

Our company's minor and sporadic tie to the royals (all through Jerry's happy devotion to his native land) continued when we were representing Beverly Hills Rolls Royce, and Princess Margaret made a visit, the reception party of which transpired rather astonishingly at a huge Rolls Royce garage and repair facility. All royalty geeks were on hand with their best curtsies and bows, but the star with whom the princess spent most of the evening talking was David Janssen who bowed to no man or woman. Well, at least it showed she had great taste. His sense of humor was second to none and like a fine drink had just the right touch of bitters.

Pat Kingsley and I, in our tandem client-sharings at Rogers & Cowan, represented Queen Saroya following her divorce from the Shah of Iran for the crime of having failed to produce a line of male succession. Succession to what? He and his CIA buddies and underwriters were whisked off the Persian plains a little over a decade later, and he cooled his royal ass in Panama and other lonely paradises while his repressions spawned the new repressions of the Ayatollah regimes. But back to Saroya, whose exceeding beauty and charm and newfound freedom and fame held promise of a very starry movie career. My portion of the Rogers & Cowan client list also included the two actors with whom Saroya became, in succession, romantically involved, Maximilian Schell and Omar Sharif. Each of this pair of award-winning stars won the hearts of quite a number of the most beautiful women over a number of decades. (All of this intimate chatter was long ago chewed over as the stuff of headlines which I note because this just isn't a revealing-secrets-you-didn't-already-know kind of book. I'm dealing established facts, not confidences.)

Max and Nancy Kwan were, during their twainship, certainly "the handsomest couple in town," which in Hollywood is a soubriquet usually shared by three or four couples simultaneously at any given time. Nancy rose very naturally to the most beautiful woman throne after she popularized the skin-tight chong sam thigh-slit silk dress as the eponymous star of "The World Of Susy Wong" in which her sexiness was celebrated in the fascinated admiration of Bill Holden, one of the most real-guy guys ever to fill that silver and rainbowed screen. If a female star in the full flame of her screen persona captured Bill Holden in a film, she captured the audience, too. Bill was somehow a barometer of beauty. Nancy and Max borrowed our year old Danielle for a day of baby-sitting to see if that shared experience would be part of their future. I'm not sure diapering is conducive to romance, unless it's your own personally-spawned little butts you are buttering.

But at another given time, his *romance de l'anee* was the former Shahbanou, the Empress Saroya. My mom loved our taking clients out to dinner since she was the baby-sitter of choice, and joyously so on her part. "And what royal personage is it tonight?" she asked as we headed out the door, and Gisela answered, "Mom, you wouldn't believe it if we told you." We all suffer amazing coincidences in our lives, but when you consort with vividly famous people, they simply occur more often... and more vividly. Nutty things happen in PR, and the laughter serves to take the edge off the pressures of the job, perhaps a reflection of some brilliantly forgiving Darwinian evolutionary process which allows press agents to survive and procreate.

My mother was incapable of pointed irony. Her world was so simply honest and accepting that a little joke was just a little joke. If she uttered a *double entendre*, it was not in the intention but rather in the coincidence. My father, on the other hand, was a master wordsmith of daily spoken communication. Of punsters or word-players, there were no better. That he didn't become a writer, even of letters, I attribute to the fact that he had to support his family from the time he was eight. That each came from families of abject immigrant poverty with more mouths to feed than could be fed and then graduated from acknowledged universities was unusual in the nineteen teens and twenties, especially since my mother came out of high school only a few years after American women acquired suffrage, almost a century and a half after our national proclamation that "all men are created equal." I suppose it took that long to realize that by referring to "man" in its pluralization in the Declaration of Independence, Tom Jefferson and the other founding fathers alluded not to gender but to species.

I so envied her uncomplicated view of the world. As a young press agent, before one incautious act tore the cartilages of my sanity, disintegrated my bovine sense of security and commanded me to another continent and another life, I and some of the other junior press agents at Rogers & Cowan would sneak into Academy of Motion Picture Arts & Sciences screenings by mingling with the crowd outside for a smoke (they were smoking, not we) after the first film and then we just floated in with them for the second. I occasionally took my mother with me, and the criminality of it filled her with wonder and fear, but I think it secretly intensified her enjoyment of the films. During one such entre-film mingling we came into conversation with a good friend of mine, a young movie reviewer who prevailed over the years to become a lion of that demanding craft. Hold it, ambiguity be damned… I was going to mask this, but let's be explicit here. It was Kevin Thomas. This is a story of courage and pride, the forthright manner in which Kevin lived his life at a time of don't-ask-don't-tell even in Hollywood. Maybe especially in Hollywood. The time was the mid-'50s when many people were protectively mum about their homosexuality. It was a time of many kinds of black-listings. Kevin was courageous and forthright. That gave a particularly dramatic flair to his brave and almost balletic body language and spoken language. He could communicate as eloquently with a grand gesticulation, a graceful wing-flapping of arms and hands as he could with the sweeping enthusiasms and almost musical intonations of his well-chosen phrases. My mother was deeply impressed. When he left to get back to his paper, my mother watched him all the way down the street. Then she turned to me and confided soto voce that no one else might hear, "I think someone should advise that young man that he may be a latent homosexual."

Kevin starred in another of my treasured bons mots memories. He had written a review of a war movie in which a hot-with-the-teeny-boppers music star, male, had a role. Kevin did not water down his disdain for the performance and for the blatant casting choice to lure the bobby-soxers. About six months later, the guy showed up at the LATimes and popped Kevin in the jaw. When Kevin was ushered back to consciousness, someone wondered what had taken the guy so long to express his displeasure, and Kevin offered, "Maybe he's a slow-reader."

During my first Christmas break in college, I took a job with the Postal Service handling the vast flow of holiday mail. Afraid of dogs, as I was at that time, I didn't want to deliver mail, so over-night I memorized the entire scheme of the streets each mailman covered in the 90036 zip code area so I could do my time sorting mail rather than delivering it. Sorting was so dizzyingly boring, that I begged to be put onto the streets with a bag. Let the dogs do their worst…. which

I quickly found out did not, in practice, inspire fear in me. I also found that if I could whiz through the deliveries, I could still make it to UCLA for some of the afternoon lectures. My mom was at home when I was racing out to a Humanities 101 lecture by the inspired Professor Gian Maria Passinetti (I may be off on the first name,) and I begged my mother to come with me. The subject was "Anthony And Cleopatra," and my mother sat enraptured. Thereafter for about a month, there was no subject of discussion that she couldn't turn with all innocence and sincerity, her signature traits, to Shakespeare's take on Roman/Egyptian history and passion. "Well, you know, in 'Anthony And Cleopatra' Shakespeare did seem to suggest that…"

The stars-love-royalty equation, which actually trumps stars-love-stars, was in major evidence the night Kurt Frings hosted his party for Queen Saroya at his Beverly Hills home. All of the superstars-who-show showed. But the astonishment was the turnout of such never-ever-shows as Danny Kaye, Fred Astaire and Marlon Brando. Even the amazing other attendees of the occasion were amazed. This night was in orbit around the moon for its few and wondrous hours. It wasn't just Saroya's royalty that impelled the night. It was her sad story… one of the world's glorified beauties kicked out of her wife job because her royal spouse couldn't come up with the chromosomal goods which was his own damn royal obligation in the first place. Another accelerating factor was the reality that Kurt Frings' home wasn't a spacious Hollywood mansion but rather one of the intimate and lovely homes that straggle up the little hill-climbing streets off of Benedict Canyon north of the Beverly Hills Hotel. The consolidation into a few adjoining entertainment spaces compacted not only the guests but also the sense of being part of an event… as sardines must feel in a can when among their number are a handful of big-fish-on-campus… wow, they're here and we're part of it.

The pick-up band that gathered around to jam included Anthony Newley at the piano, Bobby Darin making magic with a guitar, Sammy Davis and Dean Martin joining them in batting around the words, Sal Mineo doing percussion on something… the body of the piano I think… and Marlon Brando giving a set of bongos a workout and then giving Gisela a lesson in their use. The true nature of Hollywood parties is reflected in the fact that there was not, for this starry musical performance, a hushed and riveted audience. Stars of stars were banging it out, yet the party yakked on. I was in conversation with Omar Sharif, on whom I was account exec through "Dr. Zhivago" and "Night Of The Generals," and we were joined by an actress who most definitely didn't like me and who said to Omar, "Certainly Dick Guttman isn't your press agent," to which Omar responded, "And my friend." The transitory nature of friendship in our town and the casual employment of that most significant of all F words was demonstrated three decades later when Max Schell starred in Larry Schiller's mini-series of "Peter The Great" and Larry threw a grand party at Spago's in Max' honor. Omar, having a key supporting role in the project, was there. I introduced myself to him, noting that I had done his publicity in the sixties, and he said, "No, that was Henry Rogers." Sic transit amicus, but I completely understood. When there was crisis during the filming of "Funny Girl" because of an uproar in some Muslim nations over Omar's imminent love scene which included his kissing the world's most famous and adulated Jewish artist, Barbra Streisand, it was Henry who took the meeting with Columbia. Henry was a lord of the craft he invented, and remains so with good reason long after his passing. Those founding father PR guys earned their lasting stardom. There was every reason for Mr. Sharif to remember Henry Rogers as his press agent. Therein lay status, and also Henry's accumulated knowledge and power, which met a major crisis in Omar's life, gave him that most necessary of star-accoutrements, the sense of being safe. Press agents realize they are only among the many people who pass through the lives and needs of stars. In some circumstances this matures into lasting association and awareness, and in some cases, in the great snowstorm of a career, we are only one of the flakes.

There was a memorable summit of stardom at one point in the late '70s when Guttman & Pam had helped our client Mike Douglas (talk show host Mike Douglas, not actor/producer Michael Douglas who was also on our client list at the time) gather in round table for one show a power lineup of Francis Ford Coppola, Clint Eastwood, Marlon Brando and Gene Hackman. The eminence of such talk shows is defined in large part by the voltage of the stardoms they can attract. At the start of our relationship with Mike, he and his wife Gen had wanted to throw a Chasen's party for the top stars who had gone all the way to Philadelphia to do his show, but we talked him into doing a big fete honoring not the stars but the press agents. It would flatter the entire PR community that he should honor its contribution. And each publicist would feel in a competition with all of the other press agents and would each wish and labor to achieve the validation of bringing a top client with him/her. Which they did, gathering together a group of stars which validated, as well, Mike Douglas' star access.

But the night of the power guys... the conjoining of titans... made everyone sit up and take notice. Coppola and Brando signed on first, and Clint followed... why not?... and Gene, uncustomarily, was happy to be part of it because of his awe of Brando. That royal flush materially changed the manner in which Douglas' show was regarded in Hollywood and it stepped up his incidence of A bookings.

On another occasion, I was deliberate catalyst for a friendship between Mike and Sidney Sheldon, since Mike's show was a big deal for a best-selling author, even for THE best-selling author as Sidney Sheldon most definitely was. At that time when authors firmly enjoyed superstar accord, l arranged for Mike to write the review of Sidney's new book for one of the Hollywood trade papers, another good exposure for a talk host, and Mike assured Sidney he would have him on the show. At that point, a new producer came onto his show, and one of this newbie's provisos was that they would not interview authors. I explained that the Sheldon booking had been at Mike's invitation, but provisos are somehow holy. I then explained as an absolute that the next client on my list who would guest on that show would be Sidney Sheldon. The standoff went on for three months, with Mike not wanting to over-ride his new producer. Finally, the producer called and asked when Sidney could do the show. The miraculous thing was that we weren't fired during that period or even afterwards. I asked Mike about that remarkable fact at some later time, and he responded, "I knew you would have done the same thing for me." He was absolutely right, but actually I was doing it for me, too.

Malibu is a town that can roll out the star power. At one point in the late '70s we faced the failing funding of the Malibu Emergency Room which was our only go-to spot in crises including those of the half million people who pour onto local beaches every summer weekend day. The town's talent... gigantic for a village of 13,000 people... put on a star-studded show, over 20 acts from Linda Ronstadt and Olivia Newton John to Fleetwood Mac and Cheech and Chong, for which Guttman & Pam did the pro-bono promo. The ignition key to its sold-out success of several thousand high-priced ticket purchasers was getting Johnny Carson to kick it off with a monologue. He showed up on a burning hot Sunday afternoon in full tuxedo. As he got rolling, he seemed to really feel the heat and slowly began to strip off his clothes, item by item but never missing a comedy beat. When he got down to his tennis whites, someone handed him his racquet and he bid us adieu. It was a tough act to follow, even for the hall of fame roster of stardom we had waiting.

In accordance with the thesis of this chapter... that stars turn out for stars, I offer the Silver Cloud party which attracted one of the most glittery of star-spangled guest lists of my experience and which Sidney Sheldon hosted at our request. Sidney, because of his great success, his great wealth and his great wife, delighted in presenting events of royal (Hollywood royalty) dazzle, style and ebullience. The Sheldons lived in a sequence of extraordinary homes because Jorja was simply one of the most educated, elegant and creative home environment and landscaping designers the town has ever seen. (I'm sure you've remarked with some annoyance by now that press agents live by the adjective and die by the adjective. You must excuse the recurrence of the word "great." It is an indispensible tool for a press agent... expansive and elevating but somehow more discreetly modest than "spectacular.") Her crowning glory was the palatial Holmby Hills estate in which they lived to the ends of their respective lives, Jorja having passed from the scene far too soon. She had a passion for hand-painted ceilings and other perfections. It looked like what the little place William Randolph Hearst called home, the Hearst Castle, could have looked like if WRH had had her taste rather than merely Sidney's wealth squared.

When Rolls Royce handed Guttman & Pam the challenge of introducing the first new model Silver Cloud in 38 years, Jerry and I pondered what could possibly do justice to and bestow elaboration upon such an event. Strange circumstance is a common occurrence in our business, so by not so strange circumstance did Sidney Sheldon call at that moment to find out if we could help him purchase one of the first of the new line of cars. Light bulbs usually go off over your head by spontaneous combustion rather than by dint of your own personal genius. So that one exploded, and I said, "Sidney, you can have not only one of the first. You can have THE first." Their home was perfect for the party. It was, in fact, the Rolls Royce Silver Cloud of Hollywood homes. In that toniest of Los Angeles neighborhoods, Holmby Hills which lorded it over even nearby Bel Air, Sidney and Jorja's mansion was supreme. It rose up from Sunset Boulevard in a curving grace of sweeping driveway, landscaped as only the Tuileries is landscaped, arriving at a vast circular motorcourt, impeccably bricked in classic spiral design and in the center of which the glorious new Rolls styling would sit under a velvet cover until the moment of revelation. It had been flat-bedded there under cover of press agent device, the wrapped and thus undivulged car moving through the streets of LA, its secrecy the subject of news photos.

The car was a superstar even by Hollywood standards, and superstars arrived to wonder at what beauty was so velvetly unrevealed. Sidney and Jorja's special quality as hosts was their mixing superstars past with superstars present. Where else could you meet Norma Shearer or Gloria Swanson? For the evening's piece de resistance, the invited greats drew in a circle on the motorcourt as the velvet was pulled away in a shimmering sweep of showmanship to the gasps and applause of its celebrated gathering of honorary witnesses and the television crews which they... and the dramatic build of the event... had drawn. When it all came together, publicity was a fun and fulfilling calling. Stars were the name and stars were the game.

First Among the Stars

Something true of almost all essential aspects of our lives is that our first experience of anything is a revelation that never loses its powerful precedence. So it was for me, and she was the seductress into my first warming glow of being captivated by stars. The first star whose acquaintanceship I ever really made and whose friendship I ever really gained was.... Billie Burke. Of all of the spectacular novas who fill the cast of my memories, she remains for me one of the most important. She made me comprehend that once you saw past the glow of their stardom, these imaginary beings could be enjoyed as human beings

Billie Burke had well earned her way into the pantheon of Hollywood greats even before she became my star of stars. As you may have perceived, my most dearly held category of stars is the grand reservoir of Hollywood supporting players who were the foundation strength of the memorable films of the '30s, '40 and '50s and their next generations who still make films real and wonderful. These were the people who filled my childhood Saturdays with delight at the Hi-Point Theatre or the Esquire and then, when my family moved from St. Louis to the holy-of-holies... Hollywood... at the Fairfax. And Billie Burke was brightest among them, not just in her glowing bubble as Glinda the Good Witch Of The North in "The Wizard of Oz" (in which she was, in special salute to her supporting-superstardom, fifth billed after Judy Garland, Ray Bolger, Bert Lahr and Jack Haley, ahead of wicked witch Margaret Hamilton and even Wizard Frank Morgan.) Her addled frivolity was a staple of three dozen films between "Bill Of Divorcement" in 1932 and "The Young Philadelphians" and "Sergeant Rutledge" in 1960. She wasn't just whacky and whimsical. She was gorgeous, the Ziegfield Girl that Ziegfield made his Missus. She made the "Topper" film series tick because you understood that, however pixilated and peevish and flibberty-jibbet she was, she could hold the affections of her husband, the sorely abused Cosmo Topper (Roland Young,) even against the powerful magnetism of Constance Bennett's diabolical beauty and sexuality and ghostly (literally) devil-may-care. There was no one... NO one... in America who didn't know AND love Billie Burke.

Here's how she came into my life and I, if not into her life, at least into her constant audience. As soon as we got to Hollywood, I became an instant radio audience-oholic. My family wound up in Hollywood not because I had dreamed of it all my life but because Jewish families felt relatively safe there. The Ku Klux Klan was still an active force in Southern California in 1945, so Jews gathered in their own comfortable palm-studded, stucco-covered "districts," once known in Cossack Russia and the other pogrom places of middle and eastern Europe as schtetlas. The three most prominent of these areas were Boyle Heights to the east of downtown LA which was within the decade stirred in with the fast-growing Latino population triggering a bracing element of clash, Beverly Hills where who could afford to live there because the houses even south of Olympic were an extravagant $14,000 each, and then there was Fairfax which had become the district of choice for Jewish families still reeling a bit from the Depression.

Los Angeles was not an easy place in which to find abode in 1945. The aircraft factories and other defense industries had drawn vast populations of Kansans and Iowans and Tennesseans, of Okies and Arkies, Missouri mules such as we and West Virginians and all the others to the promise of well-paying employment. There was nothing to rent and even less to buy. My father had sold his drugstore in St. Louis because he couldn't find anyone to work it with him anymore. They were all in the shipyards of Moline or Brooklyn or were riveting wings and ratcheting on propellers in California. At first we couldn't find even a room to rent and we did time in a rundown boarding house where our family of five lived in the part of a garage blanketed off from our neighbors, about a half dozen hard-drinking southern-fried war-plane assembly line workers. So when my parents found a thousand square foot bungalow in a safely Jewish area, there was celebration. Yes, it was over-priced at $7500, and everyone *knew* that home costs would tumble after the war, but I was jubilant because we were within hitch-hiking distance to the great radio networks around Sunset and Vine where transpired the dozens of beloved nationally-broadcast radio series which had held me captive every night of my childhood... the Jack Benny and Lux Radio Theatre and Eddie Cantor and Baby Snooks and Our Miss Brooks delights of our entertainment universe... the shows which knitted America together by the radio every evening and even on weekends. And there I met Billie Burke.

I, of course, had wanted to be a journalist all my eleven years of life... well, maybe not starting until age four... but hidden secretly in my heart was that my fate might also include writing for radio or the movies. And the sudden serendipity of our new geography raised this expectation. I felt I could better study radio writing, comedy and drama, watching it enacted rather than merely listening to it. I hitched to the network studios to case the possibilities... and they were bleak. Minimum age for attendance was fourteen. I was eleven and small. I would be hard-pressed to pass for ten. But I was a nascent journalist, and I knew how to research. I soon discovered that all of the shows which I lusted to attend not only were *sponsored* by ad agencies for their clients, but they are also *produced* by those agencies. The Batten, Barton, Durstyn & Osbornes of the ad world, the five or six ad houses which made all of the shows I coveted, were clustered in the Taft Building just up the street at Hollywood and Vine or in other edifices close by. Watching people in lines ushered into those shows, I noticed that some were not any more fourteen than I. This, I discovered, was because they had what were called "agency tickets," tickets on the backs of which were stamped the designated blessing of the producing agency. You could get into a show with an agency ticket if you were still in diapers. Each and all of these agencies had something in common. Enter their doors and you were greeted by attractive women called receptionists. Even though some of them were elderly, perhaps 23, I did at that distant time have curly hair and an ability to charm older women. Placed in the company of girls my own age, I was reduced to mute terror and never knew what to say nor would I have had the courage to say it if an intelligible sentence had formed in my brain. But these older women were easy pickings. And every day when I showed up they smiled at me, listened to my jokes and handed over a ticket or two (sometimes I took a bedazzled friend) for every show they had. Mostly, I was a lone wolf. I made up schedules and could attend four, five even six shows a day because I was already pretty fast and could make it from Vine to

Gower in just over a minute. Some of the shows were the musical performance broadcasts of Perry Como and Tony Martin and other great voices of the time. I liked Perry Como's fifteen minute show best because I could get home in time to hear its later taped transmission on the west coast, and I could always hear my special laugh. What a little jerk.

I even became a regular at the Queen For A Day show, where we sat at tables in the famous Earl Carroll's Theatre and luxuriously were served a Coca Cola. On three occasions (because I was fairly glib the first time) I was brought up on stage to be a contestant and I gave answers interesting enough to win prizes. When I came home with a woman's hat worth an extravagant sixty-four dollars and a Wilson tennis racquet, my mother was sure that I had stolen them until one of her friends told her that she'd heard me on Queen For A Day. For a while she thought I had put her friend up to saying that. She had reason to be suspicious because when I was six she found in my possession a five-cent wax pan pipe and, under the third degree, I confessed to having swiped it at a five and dime. She marched me to the office of the manager of the dime store... walking up some steps to get there which heightened the sense of imminent hanging... and he explained that they could send me to prison if I hadn't had such an honest mother. Talk about scared straight. Missouri built character the hard way.

Not content with my agency-ticket scam, following many of the performances I, having seated myself well toward the front because I was a fast scooter, would run up on stage and ask the stars if I could have their script, and they often signed them for me. Lux Radio Theatre was best because it was different stars each week. After watching Ginger Rogers and Ray Milland reading "The Major And The Minor," I scrambled onto stage with a breathless, "Miss Rogers, may I have your script please?" and then was so gluttonous that I turned and said, "Mr. Milland, may I have YOURS?" Some of these people even got to know me. About the third time that I had jumped on stage after a broadcast of "Mayor Of The Town," Mr. Lionel Barrymore greeted me with a cordial, "Oh, it's YOU again." He was such a good actor, but I perceived beneath his affected grumpiness a spark of kind feelings for me.

I had become addicted to reading and re-reading these scripts, studying them. Radio was my hobby. Then I discovered a magical place behind the studio buildings where the trash was thrown out. Here were deposited the early versions of scripts for shows such as "The Adventures Of Ozzie And Harriet," "A Date With

Judy" and "Our Miss Brooks," some of which shows I had graced with my presence in their audiences. I was Hollywood's first dumpster diver, sneaking in and rescuing gems. I even found a script for one of the first television shows starring a band leader named Ted Fiorito. Then on Sunday afternoons, when my family was picnicking in the park, I would go to the car radio to listen to the broadcasts, carefully annotating the scripts where there were changes, then figuring out why the change had been made. It was a great early lesson in how to structure and dialogue comedy and drama.

I got to know some of the radio luminaries through my hitch-hiking. I would stand at the corner of Sunset and Gardner and, at each red light, would run out and greet drivers of the stopped cars with, "Hey, Mister… are you going down to Vine?" One of these was that hall-of-famer wordsmith Johnnie Mercer. He was amazed at how well I knew the territory, and he invited me to watch his show from the booth where the producers and directors and engineers sat. Incredibly, neither of us realized at the time that he would be the author of one of my three holy commandments of PR, you gotta ak-cent-chu-ate the positive. Another time it was Herb Vigran, the title star of the show adapted from the "Sad Sack" comic strip. I could quote his dialogue back to him and even suggested some specific panels of the comic strip that might make good shows.

But Billie Burke was my first and abiding star. She had a lovely half hour show which illuminated Saturday mornings across the country. It was performed and recorded at 8AM Los Angeles time in order to be heard live at 11AM on the east coast. One Friday when I was making my ticket collections at one agency, the receptionist said, "I don't know if you can do it so early, most people can't, but Billie Burke does her show at…." Wow, Billie Burke… Glinda, Mrs. Topper… I love Billie Burke. I was out of the house before seven Saturday morning and was in plenty of time to join about a dozen people lined up to go into a small studio which didn't even have permanent chairs, just folding card chairs, and then Miss Burke came in a made us feel like we'd stopped by at her home. The show was as cheery as she was, and then afterwards she personally poured coffee, hot chocolate for me, and served donuts and such to the people who had laughed and clapped their way through her half hour. She garnished the goodies with her conversation reflecting her real interest in who each person was.

My mother had become mystified and disturbed that I was out of the house every Saturday morning before everyone else arose for breakfast. She finally confronted me on this, and I explained that I was helping my friend, Miss Billie Burke. "Oh," my mother complained, impatient of my exaggerations, "*you* don't know Billie Burke. She's very famous." "No, mom, I…" "She starred in 'Becky Sharpe' and 'The Man Who Came Dinner.'" "Yes, mom, but…" "She was married to Florenz Ziegfeld." "Mom, I'm very important to them. I have a special kind of laugh they really like."

I convinced my mother to join me one Saturday morning, and, since I couldn't have her walk the mile up to Sunset Boulevard with me or hitch-hike with me to CBS, my father dropped us off on his way to work. And at a quarter to eight, we joined a few others, filed into the little studio, about half the size of a classroom, and seated ourselves on the folding chairs. When Miss Burke came out to greet the audience and to explain the procedure, she seemed happy to see my mother with me and she smiled and waved. My mother turned to see whom this famous star had acknowledged, but there was no one behind us. This was very strange. Could I actually have been telling the truth for once?

After the show, during which I whispered insider information to my mother (particularly directing her attention to the sound effects guy, everybody loved the sound effects guys) Miss Burke was passing out coffee and hot chocolate and loading plates with cakes and cookies, she reached across the little table warmly to grasp my mother's hand in both of hers. "So you're Dickie's mommy. How sweet of you to get up so early." "I'm a great admirer, Miss Burke… 'The Man Who Came To Dinner?'" "Oh, yes, Monty Wooley," Miss Burke smiled and then, in lowered and confidential voice, very *entre nous*, "he was every bit the scoundrel he seemed." They both had a laugh about that, and my mother later informed practically everyone she knew of how I had taken her to meet my friend and of how Monty Wooley was every bit the scoundrel he seemed.

What a way to launch a lifetime dedication to stars.

Chapter 9

Touching Great Films

Beloved films have significance far beyond their two hours of diversion. They stand for something. They bind us together and reaffirm our common humanity. If they did not exist, our shared consciousness would be poorer. When I mention the motion picture, "It's A Wonderful Life," you know what I mean… that unselfish love and kindness makes us worthy of this blessing of existence. Each great film is shorthand for human qualities we're happy to share or for their lessons in how far we can fall. When Gary Cooper as Lou Gehrig, standing tall beside his fast-approaching death, addresses a Yankee Stadium crowd and pronounces himself the luckiest man on the face of the earth, we understand the message… that courage times gratitude is grace. Just remembering the film makes us want to strive for that state of calm resolve. "Hoosiers" means more than basketball. It means that there can be a last second shot in everyone's life. It is a torch of redemption and belief. Great films hold our torches high for us. I'm always impressed that when you discuss Gene Hackman's unsurpassed filmography, "Hoosiers" is always up there at the top of our remembrance. It confirmed something we all want to believe in.

For those actually associated with such films, even in the small way a publicist is, it's a little like having knocked in some rivets on the Eiffel Tower or the Brooklyn Bridge. There is that sense of having participated in something that is forever. Workers on the set of "It's A Wonderful Life" may not have known they were touching history, but they carried that pride later on. Frank Capra's Christmas card to the world was first received as just a heart-warming comedy, and over the years it reconfigured itself in the public consciousness as a touchstone of what so many of us hold true and important. It became finally the film that Christmas comes wrapped in, just as "The Wizard of Oz" is the film that childhood comes wrapped in. "Citizen Kane" describes for us all the fatal audacity of power.

All of Warren Beatty's productions have been departures in one way or another. As soon as the critics saw it, they knew that "Shampoo" was more than a movie. It was a mile marker in how we had come to think about sexuality. It became the popular paradigm of the "sexual revolution." At the first public screening, a sneak preview in Santa Barbara following the 7PM showing of the smash hit "The Towering Inferno," you could tell immediately that the audience that elected to stay to see the second film was moved… right out of their seats. The audience was halved by the end of the first reel. Each walkout took with him/her a little chunk of the high hope Columbia's execs had placed in this film. They had trusted Warren Beatty and Hal Ashby to redefine sexuality in films in the same smash hit way that Warren Beatty and Arthur Penn had redefined action thrillers with "Bonnie And Clyde," adding the heretofore missing amalgam of mercurial madcap and unforgiving fate.

By the time David Begelman and his Columbia guys and Warren and his creative guys gathered in the theatre manager's office it had a sad sense of wake about it. We'd seen the film in the studio screening rooms, and it had been moving and hilarious… no, make that moving and uproarious. The best policy in this kind of tense, looking-for-someone-to-blame situation is to shut up. But here we were at a wake with no potato salad, and it was the only time in an association of well over forty years that I ever saw Warren Beatty mystified, so I finally said, "I'll tell you what's wrong with 'Shampoo.' 'Towering Inferno' is what's wrong with 'Shampoo.'" I'd seen "Towering Inferno" play before because Guttman & Pam worked with Bill Holden and Bob Vaughn. "Inferno" was such a by-the-books studio crowd-pleaser that it was made by two studios from two books, and it had a star-studded cast big enough for at least two films. But it was popcorn, and it was pop and it was corn. That family audience was not there to see a sexual revolution… and that revolution in "Shampoo" started over the opening credits. With no foreplay.

Even though this meeting, this crisis forum, in the manager's office was a scene in which I arguably had no lines, I suggested they put their gloom on ice for a week and then screen it at a theatre playing "Lenny," the Lenny Bruce biopic which was also a hard-hitting and no-punches-pulled kind of film and was bringing in that whole different audience for which "Shampoo" was perfect. Anyone else there could have and soon would have reached that same conclusion, but at that moment they were too busy being frantic. A week later, they *knew* "Shampoo" would be a hit. Then they went out and worked to build "Shampoo" the huge audience it deserved.

Having a studio sales team know in advance that they have a hit is not always a positive thing. Gene Hackman as Popeye Doyle and "The French Connection" were as winning a combination as Hollywood can present. No one thought Billy Friedkin's delivery on that film could be topped, but 20th made "French Connection II" anyway. John Frankenheimer came back from France with a helluva movie. With his tear-your-guts-out cold turkey recovery-from-drug-addiction sequence, Gene Hackman gave a performance that went toe-to-toe with his Oscar-winning go on the first film. The culminating chase scene in FC2 with Gene as Popeye tracking down Frog One through the streets and harbor of Marseilles had the tension of his mad car chase under the elevated train tracks in the first film, and this time the machine Gene was red-lining at 8000 RPM was his own body. Most of it was on foot chasing trolley cars and boats. You felt the pain in your own lungs and your own muscles. When 20th sales chief Jonas Rosenfeld (one of the very best) showed it to his national staff and me at the studio, they were all revving, too. "This film," he said, "is thirty-two million dollars (a spectacular gross at that moment in 1975) right now, and it's our job to build on that." Well, thirty-two million sounded pretty good to those guys... and that's what it did.

When I finally was allowed to read the "Shampoo" script... well after shooting started... I felt It spoke most hopefully of love in a time and place where sex had become most cynically trivialized. In a way which I'm sure will elude everyone else, it reminded me during my reading of it of the theme of Josh Logan's screen version of the William Inge Pulitzer Prize play, "Picnic," in which Bill Holden and Kim Novak, like Warren and Julie Christie, transcend a specific society's expectations of their astonishing beauty and sexuality to find love. "Shampoo" approached that conflict much more explicitly. Inge set his "Picnic" in small town Kansas I suppose it was, the capital of the constraining standards of the

'50s. Warren and Hal Ashby explored how such a theme played out against the wealth and dissolution of Hollywood and Beverly Hills in the full flood of the sexual revolution.

Making Them Come to You

Publicity always functions better when the press are working you rather than when you're working the press. When media outlets are making the asks, not you, you have much better control of the direction and the volume of the media exposure. But they don't always line up when you think they will. "Shampoo" was one of the first films we handled after I went into partnership with Jerry Pam. Warren Beatty, Julie Christie, Goldie Hawn, sexy subject and giant media stars combined with the super-sensual milieu of Hollywood hairdressers who were at that early '70s moment a hot celebrity sub-species. And when the word was finally out on the film, almost every name hair-dresser in town was claiming that it was based on his life and sexual escapades. Apart from that, It was a script that made an important social statement. However, when it started filming, the town didn't know that yet because... no one had seen the script other than the few whose work on the film required them to have read it. And not even many of those.

We came aboard just before "Shampoo" went to the floor (began shooting) and Warren, as was his custom, had held his cards very close to his vest. The press had not yet lined up. It didn't know. It needed a nudge to ignite the anticipation and give it the sense of, to use an expression of that moment, its being a "happening." I called Joyce Haber, who wrote the Los Angeles Times' only entertainment column, one of the film industry's best-read news flows. I confided to her that the magazines were ready to write big checks for the first shots of Warren with Goldie and Julie. They were but they just didn't know it yet. I revealed that the then-most-famous paparazzo, Ron Gallela (famous the hard way... Marlon Brando had popped him outside some nightclub,) had called us to see how he could get on the set and that I had told him the ONLY way was to hire a helicopter. Only an hour or two into the morning of the break of that story which I had made up, our assistant, Christy Cane (as cutting-through-the-crap and funny a Girl Friday as Hollywood has ever imagined), tells me, "Pick up line five and fasten your seatbelt." "Mr. Guttman, this is Ron Gallela." "What can I do for you, Mr. Gallela?" "Did you..." he started. "...read Joyce Haber's column today?" I finished. "Yeah," he said, a bit thrown that I was playing his lines, and then, climbing back on the horse, "So, ok… I can find out from the cops where they're shooting. Now, where do I hire a helicopter?" "Well, I think you should ask that of Joyce Haber. Here's her number." After the resulting and very much read second break on the story, the town was finally on my doorstep, and we could pretty much play pick-and-choose for the publicity campaign which turned out to be an 800 pound gorilla… as did the film.

The chronology of certain experiences in a publicity career (which should actually be a jumble because so many things of import are happening at the same time) can be fairly accurately time-set as result of how some of those adventures overlap. For instance, I can remember when "Shampoo" was filming because I can remember very precisely when the Goldwyn Studios in Hollywood, Guttman & Pam's first office site, burned down. Not really burned down, but a substantial portion of it did. Jerry, Christie and I were working in our offices in the lot's main building fronting on Formosa Avenue. From our windows, we could see out over the sound stages, especially Sound Stage 1, I believe it was, which faced us. It was one of those afternoons when you hear fire engines in the distance and wait until they get a lot louder before you know they're coming for you. It's when the siren scream winds down to that ominous purr that you realize you're part of the game. Rising outside our windows were plumes of black smoke, and revolving red lights were patterning themselves on the east wall of Sound Stage 1. We, along with people from neighboring offices, moved out onto the metal staircase on the west side of the building to assess the immediacy of our danger. "Doesn't seem to be coming here," someone said, at which point the east wall of Sound Stage 1 collapsed, and we could see the charred and flaming blacks and reds within.

Jerry, Christie and I went back to our office, looked about, and I said, rather ungrammatically, "I think the only things worth saving here is us." We poured into the hallway, leaving the doors unlocked and made a break for our cars. As I carefully stepped over the lines of fire hoses and around the fire trucks and out of the way of the firemen, I did not have any of the sense of dread and breathless excitement I would have twenty years later when our home in Malibu burned down around me along with about 270 others on our street. With the Goldwyn fire, I just had the feeling that I had to subtract myself from the scene, but how the hell to get out through the studio's blocked streets and gates. I made it to my car which was parked facing the tall chain-link fence that bordered Formosa. It was late Friday, and I had the sense that I would be camping in my car for the weekend, roasting marshmallows over the remains of the sound department, but what if the other cars started blowing up around me? At that moment, a fireman appeared directly in front of my car with a long chain saw and carved out a high and wide exit right there, a new access to the lot for his trucks. He came to my window and very kindly commented, "Move your ass, buddy. We're comin' in." A more felicitous direction I've never heard, so I drove over the shreds of chain link and eastward into the fire-free world. I kept going east for the few blocks to the Hollywood Center studios where "Shampoo" was filming. When I got to the sound stage, everyone was gathered around television sets watching the coverage of the fire. Goldwyn was a landmark. Goldwyn was Hollywood. As I joined them, someone said, "Goldwyn's burning down." "You're kidding," I responded. Friday was a bad day for it to burn down, because I had a whole weekend to wonder if our offices and their poor contents were still not among the missing. On Monday, I found that we had been saved by the guys in the yellow rubber coveralls.

But the studio needed to find space for the production company offices that had been obliterated, and shortly thereafter we were asked to cease being the only indy PR firm on a Hollywood lot. George Barry, head of our client Faberge, graciously turned over to us his sumptuous offices in Beverly Hills, where the remaining traces of his residence were the colorful wall-paper and our next door neighbor, Polly Bergen who oversaw her Oil Of The Turtle part of the Faberge empire from that location. And thus I returned to offices in Beverly Hills following my only brief attempt to go Hollywood. Fate toasted me back to Beverly Hills. In over 50 years of work doing Hollywood indie PR, all but three have transpired within a half mile diameter in Beverly Hills. Maybe I'm not a Hollywood press agent. Maybe I'm a Beverly Hills press agent.

"Brazil" was an amazing film on which to work, an obstacle course unlike any other film. Start with the fact that the salient aspect that we had to work with was that the studio hated the film. And, if not the film, the director. That's not actually true, but it was the perception which prevailed when Guttman & Pam had been brought on by Terry Gilliam's people at the recommendation of person or persons unknown… although I always suspected it was Warren Beatty. Terry was the kind of brilliant contrarian one would expect from a primary creative and revolutionary force of the Monty Python brigade of comedy grenade-throwers.

What was known about the film in advance was a fascinating nothing, other than that it was unlike anything you might possibly guess. "Orwellian" or "Wellesian" were the prevailing adjectives of assumption, and that was pretty close. ... probably referring simultaneously to Orson and H.G. along with George Orwell. Critics and film commentators had their antennae up because the word was that there was a non-meeting of the minds between Gilliam and the studio brass, a very volatile and exclamatory and dystopian divergence at that. It was rumored to be very personal and that a negative studio attitude to the project had evolved. That's what we were handed. The prevailing assumption was that the tension was over the fact that the film was as far from standard Hollywood studio fare as Monty Python was from, let's say, "The Mary Tyler Moore Show." We were given to understand that we were not there to play the tension down but rather to play it up. And that was the strategy we had brought to the first meeting based on the rumors we, too, had heard. That was Terry's instinct, because he is such an instinctive artist, but it was our strategy based on Jerry's and my acquired knowledge that *tension builds attention.* The idea was to enlist the sympathy and support of the media for the creative artist, and we assumed that could be achieved because we are pragmatic realists. The film, as history attests, would bear out our expectation and the critics' expectation that it was very brilliant but in ways that could un-nerve any front office (the old term for the studio executive suite.)

We saw the film, and it bore out that assumption in spades. It was plowing new ground on every level. I knew our campaign was working, because other great filmmakers were calling us to see how the effort was working. Warren Beatty, perhaps the least conventional and most adventurous of the town's cinema hit-makers, called about once a week to keep up, but as always I knew that Warren's sources on it were better than my own. I always feel with him that it's more a pop quiz than a phone call, just checking if I'm doing my homework. The other part of our strategy was to not antagonize the studio to the extent that it would try to undermine the film's public appeal. If you rub two sticks together long enough, you can burn down a film. I had seen that one time before on Francis Coppola's "The Conversation." As you will read shortly, we struggled to mitigate the damage on that one and I'd had to come up with probably my most inventive and effective publicity device ever to make possible for the film to get the Oscar penetration it deserved. But with "Brazil," Universal kept very clearly in mind that the ultimate bottom line was dollars, and they marketed it quite adeptly, even bringing the controversy into play as a box-office lure. I'm sure resentments remained intact on both sides, but I think there was a consensus joy in its being received as a hit.

I didn't read Terry Gilliam's book on the making of and selling of "Brazil," because publicity is a killer business and in the building swirl of your career you don't have time to look back. That changes when you decide to do "your book." You regard each film as a mine-field of opportunity to prove what you can do. You can't get through the next one if you're looking back at the last one. So I don't know if Terry's take on this wild ride is the same as mine. I was told that his only mention of me... and I don't mean to imply that I felt I deserved any mentions at all... was "Dick Guttman, good press agent, bad toupee." Well, I guess that's better than the other way around.

If I am to be remembered for anything, I would like it to be for the nice things I have done. But since these are in such embarrassingly short supply, let it be for the Academy Consideration Screenings idea I invented for "The Conversation." That one hummed, and for two years it gave Guttman & Pam a twenty-five yard head start on everyone else in the annual fall and winter race for Academy Award nomination.

This strategy, which I sort of fell into and which I convinced the town's primary (maybe only) Cable TV movie channel to undertake for me, I dubbed and officially presented as the "For Your Consideration Screenings." I couldn't use the copyrighted word "Oscar," but For Your Consideration was and remains the phrase used in most Oscar campaign ads in the trade papers and other publications substantially impacting the awareness of Academy Award voters. I will elaborate a bit later in this chapter on this unholy advantage, a device I used to achieve justice for "The Conversation" and which Jerry Pam and I owned exclusively and employed fruitfully for at least two wonderful Oscar campaign years.

But first I wish to explain the strange plight of one of the finest and most artful films ever made:

Saving "The Conversation"

Few if any films exceeded "The Conversation" in originality, danger of concept or the sheer daring of execution by one and all. It was a chilling insight into human nature and human fear. Gene Hackman had described it to me shortly after he had received the script and the offer from Francis. We were sitting in the Colorado State Prison outside Canon City where he and Al Pacino were filming "Scarecrow" with director Jerry Schatzberg. It's amazing how you can shut out the claustrophobia and anxiety of a prison ambience when you know you can walk out any time you want. I gathered that Gene was excited about "The Conversation" precisely because it had ten reasons to fail for every one prospect of success,, and he loved that challenge and had faith in Francis' grace under that kind of pressure. Gene seemed enormously excited about Francis' energy and appetite to deliver what he had placed on the page with this new script, "The Conversation." Francis Ford Coppola at his best is like Harry Houdini, a stunning escape artist from the most insoluble perils of his own construction. These guys rev their talents well past the red line when they feel most endangered. To illustrate: I was informed at the time by one of Coppola's closest associates that he had undertaken his now celebrated and adulated winery and vineyards as a way *to make himself do* "Apocalypse Now." He had put himself into such financial peril that he had to plunge into his major opus to keep the cash coming.

Francis Ford Coppola pours so much into each film that it apparently requires a monumental incentive of imminent peril to start the cameras rolling. Obviously, he fully understood the herculean effort the filming of "Apocalypse Now" would demand of him? No one knew that better than he. And to deliver himself to the starting line, he pumped all of his personal fortune into the wine business that had so long called to his Italian blood, an enterprise with higher rate of failure-to-fortune than jumping 40 feet into a damp sponge, or even making a film as costly and perilous as "Apocalypse Now." He was then in a state of financial imperative which compelled him, according to plan, to get this demon masterpiece made, this astounding statement he felt compelled to make about war's madness.

So what was the desperation that drove Coppola into the making of "The Conversation?" Perhaps because he knew that this was the greatest script he'd ever written and might ever write. Maybe he thrust himself into it because he saw the production of "Godfather II" coming on like an avalanche and he worried when he would find another window to make this amazing script. Whatever the need, thank goodness it existed and prevailed. I made one trip to San Francisco to get a sense of how it was progressing. It was a scene in the cold stripped-of-humanity warehouse where Harry Caul (Hackman's character) carried on his stripped-of-humanity work of high-tech spying into other people's lives. I stood around for twenty minutes as Francis set up a shot, waiting for Gene to show up. Finally, I turned to some big guy who had been standing next to me and asked if he knew where Mr. Hackman's dressing room was. "Schmuck," Gene said.

Gene disappeared off camera as well as on into that contained character so the opposite of himself. Only the gruff-voiced, derisive "schmuck" reassured me that it was really Gene. This forceful guy, in one of his greatest performances, dissolved into the guarded, cautious Harry Caul, drawing invisibility around him lest someone invade his life as he had invaded the lives of so many others. When Gene and I saw the film the first time, it was already haunting, even though the scene on the bus, a dreamlike fantasy in the finished film, was a narrative scene. Francis and his editors Walter Murch and Richard Chew miraculously altered that by weaving the sound and visuals into a mysterious fabric of realism and surrealism, Harry Caul's and ours. Francis and our mutual friend Fred Roos (we were all part of the early 50s UCLA film school where Francis was a Brown alum doing grad work. By the time "The Conversation" post-production was finished, Francis and the rest of his company were in Italy filming "Godfather ll." They weren't getting expressions of excitement from Paramount about "The Conversation," and I saw a golden opportunity about to be missed. This was a film that was made for festival discovery. I insisted that Fred use Francis' "Godfather" clout to get "Conversation" into Cannes. We had to let the festival world communicate excitement back to the studio. "The Conversation," apart from its excellence, was the perfect film for festival cineastes yearning for product so distanced from studio film-making. Little was it suspected how distanced its home studio was from this finished film. It won the grand prize at Cannes, the Palme D'Or, but that didn't change the studio stance. It was when the film was NOT released that alerted me that the disdain was real. It was long ready for national release that October, which was the traditional release time for small, arty films with real award pedigree and prospect. Any casual student of indy or arty film distribution, not to mention Oscar strategy, could have seen that this film was, by devine contrivance, created to be released in October of the year in which it had earned the Cannes Festival Palme D'Or.

But that didn't happen. It was when the film finally DID come to release date that I understood how deeply Parmount's antipathy went. It seemed that not only was Paramount was not behind "The Conversation" full throttle., but that somebody seemed to be riding a very heavy foot on the brake. Here are the facts. You decide. It was a film that would depend on critical response rather than being a powerhouse action entertainment that could build its own first weekend. It was, in effect, an art film which had won Europe's most coveted prize but which had been held for release for nearly a year and then scheduled to hit the theatres in March, *two days after the Academy Awards*. Why is that a sign of disregard? The Oscars then were held on Mondays, and movies then were released on Wednesdays. That means that on the day of its release, every film that won any Oscar… for Best Song, Best Cinematography… would be rushing back into the theatres with full-page ads. An editing or costume Oscar merited a big "Oscar winner" ad. "The Conversation," would be swamped by films coming off the momentum and racing back into theatres with ads of Oscar wins.

We knew that Charles Champlin, the Los Angeles Times reviewer and arguably the most important review voice in town and for whom we had arranged an early screening , was going to lavish loving praise on "The Conversation" and, beyond that, would be an advocate for it. However laudatory, that review was would be drowned out in the blast of huzzahs for the Oscar awardees from two nights before. The strange opening date meant that Francis' little masterpiece would jump into the boxoffice race and the awareness race with its shoestrings tied together. The prior Sunday papers would be swept up in Oscar-related stories. I urged Fred that Francis' "Godfather" capital be spent at Paramount by demanding that the film be pushed back a week so that Champlin could precede that opening with a powerful story on its excellence on the Sunday after, not before, the Oscars. There was one other rather glaring evidence of indifference.

This was a tight little art film that needed to go into small theatres and build word of mouth . It was scheduled to go into the Pantages in Hollywood and the Plitt in Century City… two of the biggest barns in town. A small word-of-mouth film couldn't possibly fill them. A nice even terrific turnout opening night would look lost in the sea of empty seats. The booking was misleading as to the kind of film it was. Big bravado films opened there, not personal and interior films of excellence like "The Conversation." The Plitt and Pantages constituted the film's worst release scenario. Lastly, a release exactly one year before the next Oscars was a suicide pill for a film with honorable claim to Oscar contention. Tell me, if you can, that this was not, in aggregate, an orphan being turned out into the wintry streets. Films with Oscar potential sometimes come out in early fall, possible very late summer, but usually October, November and December. Even adulation has a short memory. Voters actually forget that a first-months-of-the-year release is on the table for their votes. They think of it as a terrific film that didn't get its due the previous year.

The push-back from its natural release in the fall of the previous year now put it in the further (and even much greater) peril of having to compete against Francis' own masterpiece (*other* masterpiece, I should say,) "Godfather Part 2." So when fall crept up and "Godfather Part 2" was quite rightly the dominant Oscar favorite, everything conspired to make Francis' other release in the qualification year of 1974, "The Conversation," dead in the water. With Paramount actively ignoring "The Conversation," Francis and Roos dropped the full responsibility for exploring its Oscar chances into the laps of Mssrs. Guttman and Pam. And it seemed impossible. So, how did it turn out?

Francis was nominated for Best Director for both "Godfather 2" and "The Conversation," and each film was nominated for Best Film. A self-destructive conflict ? you ask, a prescription for failure? Paramount certainly thought so. But that wasn't the case at all. Competing against himself, Francis won both Best Film and Best Director for his second "Godfather" film. For the first "Godfather," with his having "only" one film among the nominated five, he had won Best Film but was defeated for Best Director by Bob Fosse with "Cabaret."

Francis had employed us for "The Conversation" since our campaign for another "little film" of his involvement, "American Grafitti," had contributed to a sensational success its distributor (Universal) had not expected, creating an awareness which resulted in its being nominated for best film against a slew of well-reviewed biggies.

But Paramount was making it evident that they thought the nomination for "The Conversation" put a nail in the tire of the vehicle carrying "Godfather Part 2" to an Oscar win. I felt that having two nominations in the same year can impart a special aura that enhances the chance for the "big film" to win. Hollywood is a town where such things are usually ascribed to "luck."

As anybody in publicity can tell you, and as most artists will affirm, LUCK TAKES A LOT OF HARD, SMART WORK.

I witnessed a similar such contradiction recently when I was consulting on the Weinstein Company's campaign for "The Reader." The film's nominations included Best Director, Best Film and Best Actress for Kate Winslet which, very deservedly, she won. It was an astonishing performance, creating understanding and empathy for a character whose actions are revealed to have been reprehensible and, except for the subtle wisdom of the script, direction and performance, incomprehensible... Why was that a contradiction? Because the "Reader" campaign very intentionally and specifically had been aimed at a Best *Supporting* nomination for her. She was being submitted for Best Actress for her performance opposite Leonardo DiCaprio in "Revolutionary Road," a film directed by her then husband. She had asked Weinstein to go for Supporting for "Reader" to avoid compromising the Oscar prospects of her husband's film. The category specified in the ads notwithstanding, the Academy's actors branch members, the ones who vote the acting nominations, had disregarded the "Reader" Oscar ad campaign's stipulation and voted the performance into the category of their own perception. Harvey Weinstein had envisioned that outcome, but he'd been obliged to respect Ms. Winslet's request. Harvey and I had a conversation in which we concurred that, once she was nominated as Actress, she would win. The Academy members had cared enough for the performance that they had imposed the category. And the ones who loved her in "Revolutionary Road" would be influenced by that and could easily transfer allegiance to her other great performance. So in a very direct way, her husband really did play a key role in securing an Oscar for his then wife.

I understand the psychology of carry-over-of-affections from one performance to another. I had voted for Diane Keaton when she won the Oscar for "Annie Hall." But a key factor in my vote, although I thought she was terrific and fully deserving to win for the Woody Allen film, was my feeling that truly the best performance by an actress in that year was Diane Keaton in "Looking For Mr. Goodbar," for which she was not nominated. Academy voters are only human. VERY human, I've discovered. They put a lot of heart and conscience into their votes.

"Bonnie And Clyde," like "The Conversation" was a prodigal child. It was not beloved by its studio (Warner Bros.)... at least not until it started to explode as a boxoffice bonanza as result of the critical ebullience with which it was received. Word of mouth took it from there. I would put "American Graffiti" in that group, too. "Bonnie And Clyde," barely escaped Jack Warner's determination to lock it in a closet and throw away the key. It just wasn't Jack Warner's kind of film...

Warner Bros? "Little Ceasar?" "Public Enemy?" "The Roaring 20s?" "Scarface?" Well, apparently for Mr. Warner, the '30s gangster films were of-their-time, and "Bonnie And Clyde" wasn't. And only when Warren Beatty personally dedicated himself to kickstarting its national release and turning it into a seat-filler did it become a NOW film for Jack Warner, but not one he personally endorsed. "Bonnie And Clyde" and "The Graduate" were two of the most "now" films ever to come out in the same year. They captured the twin zeitgeists of the decade of the 60s… "Bonnie & Clyde" was rebellion and "The Graduate" was what the rebellion was against… suburban platitudes, self-satisfaction, and ennui-driven dirty little secrets.

"Bonnie And Clyde" had done nothing in the prior test market release in Indiana. And for Jack Warner, that was *plenty* of nothing. He had the film out of his system. I wasn't party to that initial trial release, but I know it was a lethargic launch… just rolling it into the street and hoping a truck doesn't run over it, which in that instance it did. Or maybe Mr. Warner was hoping it would. Gisela and I spent a very long and interesting weekend in Bloomington once when she was brought in by the Kinsey Institute to review its vast collection of erotic art, second largest in the world, The Kinsey people asked her to consult on a possible touring museum exhibition. Of course we made the trip over to Nash, Indiana to visit John Dillinger's birthplace. That state had a personal pride in '30s bank-robbing, and it was just aching for a big PR launch of the film that would revive the most colorful, or perhaps I should say fabled, chapter in our criminal past. So someone at the studio must not have tried very hard, considering how thoroughly it was buried there.

How Warren turned that defeat into victory I'll never know. Of all the people in Hollywood, Jack Warner was absolutely the least likely to be swayed by Warren Beatty's considerable charm and intellect. How Beatty badgered (battered was out of the question with a tough guy like Warner)… how he badgered Warner into the Toronto Film Festival exposure that lighted up the sky for the film is shrouded in wonder. In Toronto, Jack Warner's dismissive attitude toward the film was shared by one person only, probably the most important person there… Bosley Crowther, the New York Times' influential film critic. He hated the film, hated it so much that in the course of "Bonnie And Clyde's" clean getaway to twelve Oscar nominations, Crowther wrote seven-count-'em-seven scathing attacks on the film but was never able to shoot out its tires. I always contended he was a crucial factor in its success. In the Catholic Church, for someone to get canonized, a devil's advocate has to be part of the deal. On the occasion of a nomination for sainthood, the *advocatus diaboli* is the guy appointed to dispute before the papal court the claims for the candidate's canonization. Bosley Crowther was Warren's devil's advocate and he kept putting the film's great critical reception into sharp and attention-building relief. The success of a great film is never a sprint. It is the 400 meters hurdles. You have to get over some high pieces of wood they stick in your way to win. If there aren't any hurdles already on the track, someone will put them there. In this case, it was Jack Warner and Bosley Crowther. In a way, it was like our campaign for "Brazil" in which its studio, Universal, hated the film or the director, Terry Gilliam, or, more likely, both.

Mr. Crowther's vehement disdain... nay, dispisal... drew a sharp interest to the campaign, because we layed so heavily on the adulation heaped upon the film by such great critics as Pauline Kael and Judith Christ. Crowther's carpings were in such strong contrast that it made the degree of support in the great body of reviewers stand out all the more vividly. It made the great reviews not merely reviews but also news, rebukes of Crowther's having taken arms at the end of his career against a lauded and industry-changing film. It was definitely a film that opened doors and imaginations and impacted the way movies would be made. And Bosley Crowther helped it do that.

Heading publicity for Jack Warner was a very clever and somewhat feared guy named Max Bercutt. Max was a brilliant marketer of films, and even more than that he was the marketer of Jack Warner. He was the guy who actuated whatever Jack Warner wanted to achieve. In this Warner case, it was the residual resentments stemming from "Bonnie And Clyde's" not having proven to be the dog Mr. Warner had expected it to be. For its having proven to be a historic success. Loyal to his stockholders, including the brothers Warners and their heirs and assigns, Mr. Warner at last saw the light shining on the film and wanted it to bring in all it could. In a strange way he and Max, while not washing their hands of the film, gave Warren and, by extension, me, a lot of latitude. On top of which, two of the most brilliant guys ever to apply their sales talents to the selling of films, Joe Sugar and Dick Lederer, were the sales honchos for Warner Bros., and they loved that movie and affectionately believed in Warren. With Max stepping slightly aside, they were able to launch a great campaign, and I was along for the ride and allowed to speak up when reason occurred. Warren loved them back, and one time he commented to me, "If Joe Sugar and Dick Lederer weren't under contract, I'd start a studio with them." He was serious, and he wasn't even 30 at the time.

Max Bercutt actually liked what he saw, which was a good thing because not only was he a publicity genius, but he was an enforcer who spake with the voice of a Burbank God and could twist arms with the strength thereof. He saw we had a handle on it, and he allowed me, with his supervision, to dream up the trade ad campaign for the Oscar chase. That was an amazing latitude, one which I enjoyed otherwise only on "Room At The Top" in 1959 and with producer Robert Radnitz' and director Martin Ritt's "Sounder" in 1972.

Guttman & Pam later had a similar challenge of a film which had been released too early for the good of its Oscar prospects. Producer Ed Feldman hired us to obtain Oscar awareness for Peter Weir's sensational "Witness." It, too, was a natural contender. This was definitely *not* a case of studio abandonment. "Witness" had been lovingly issued by Paramount to a successful run. Huge profits had ensued, and now was an opportunity to gain nominations and awards which could increase the profit. The other reason for a studio or distributor to push good work for Oscar consideration is to show talents… actors and filmmakers… that the distributor is artist-friendly and talent-appreciative. "Witness" had been released in May as a prospective summer boxoffice smash. Action thrillers often benefit from that kind of release. And this one did big time. However, in Oscar terms, May is not October. A half year throw is often beyond Oscar-think's statute of limitations. How could it compete in the Fall/Winter Oscar consideration period with the release currency of other films of excellence. This was 1985, before the the employment of "screeners," the video-tape and now DVD copies of all the contention-worthy films which are sent annually to Academy members.

The Paramount marketing guys had run a powerful release ad campaign and had a strong strategy of ads and screenings laid out for the Oscar run for "Witness." Then why did Feldman bring us in?

Even though it wasn't the case with "The Conversation" and a few other films, our Oscar work is almost always supplemental. In the case of "Witness," it was specifically to remind the Academy membership that "Witness," released so far back, was a 1985 film and strongly in contention *this year, not last*. I had, as reflected elsewhere in these pages, a kind of exclusive relationship with the management of the Malibu Theatre because I had initiated the idea of special Academy membership screenings there. It wasn't easy talking the Malibu Theatre owners into letting us *re*-release "Witness" there because the prospective Oscar films were starting to back up in the key early fall period. The management owed me something, My playing the Malibu card for Warren's films had bought the theatre a front page story in the Wall Street Journal about the unusual and effective impact of our strategy. I decided to collect on that chit by having them run "Witness" instead of the holiday films waiting in line for a place on that crucial theatre's marquee.

The return of "Witness to the theatre for a few weeks gave voters a chance to see it again and contemporized it, establishing an industry awareness that "Witness" was that year's release. It had worked for "Shampoo" more than a decade before. In both cases, it was a time when you had to get them into a movie house to see your contender, and the competitors of "Witness" were just opening or soon would be with the hot enticements of current reviews and ads and the fervor and PR spin that attends such first release. "Witness" did fairly well in the voting, as it certainly deserved, getting one of the five nominations for Best Film (and other key categories) along with such late-in-the-year releases as "Out Of Africa," "Pritzi's Honor," "The Color Purple" and "Kiss Of The Spider Woman." It was a very competitive year. Well, they all are.

It's fine to practice the same arts and devices everyone else does. It's more than fine, it's imperative. But to have any kind of momentary edge, you have to keep coming up with new modes of advantage.

There are in Oscar politicking ways in which momentary advantage can be derived. In the 1990s when DVD had not yet supplanted video, I was at a client's house one evening as they were installing a new widescreen TV. They wanted to take it for a test-ride, and my client's husband asked which video she wanted to see. "What do we have on DVD?" she asked, and luckily it was "Blade Runner." What I took away from that moment is that DVD was not an alternative… it was a *preference*. This was in a day when only video copies of contending films were sent to Academy members to view for Oscar voting consideration. I called Harvey

Weinstein the next morning and mentioned that experience, and that year on the postcard mailers the various studios send to Academy members prior to each voting season to verify address for mailings of the "screeners," the Miramax (Harvey and Bob were still Miramax) card inquired as to preference of VHS or DVD. Why not give them one more reason to put your film in ahead of the others? Not all of the films sent out get popped in for a look. If your contending film is among those left in the cabinet, that's a vote you don't get, even if it's the best film that voter will never see. The overwhelming rationale of promoting Oscar contention is that they won't vote for what they haven't seen. The let's-be-the-first-ones-sending-DVDs idea addressed that directly. For "Unforgiven" I pushed, to the point of irritation and then effect, to have the screeners in Academy members' mailboxes before the "which films have we already received?" holiday of Thanksgiving. After Miramax' video-or-DVD innovation, all studios made that request and soon all sent only DVDs... not because of us but because it was obvious and because that's how technology and its acceptance advances. It was a one season advantage, but, hey, you take what you can get.

All of these things morph over the years. What I gathered from the 2013 race was that all of the major awards were locked into cement by the end of September, with the possible exception of the screenplay award for "Her." The previous year, "Argo" had pretty much made its case solid by that time. Just as I was wondering if this constituted a new combination to the safe, if August may not be the new October, in 2014 we reached November with no real certainties. *You fall into a rut only at your own peril.*

WARREN BEATTY'S MEMORY is one of the most amazing storage units I've encountered in my long history with supple, accurate and probing minds. He retains experience and information in razor sharp detail and pertinent emotional context with the essential meanings to be drawn from the events unconfused. He can access these files with "click here" immediacy. This all is particularly remarkable because Warren's life is so crammed with event and accomplishment and honor.

Now here's the paradox: Warren Beatty can't recall the night he walked off the Tonight Show With Johnny Carson with possibly the greatest ad lib of all TV talk-show time. It occurred in March of 1975 just before the release of "Shampoo." The film was created for and was seeking a very sexually sophisticated audience, and Johnny Carson's "The Tonight Show" definitely reached that crowd. So I encouraged Warren to make his first late-night guesting. He agreed as long as Johnny had seen the film. The producer of The Tonight Show quickly agreed to that, and several times before the night of the booking, he assured me that Johnny had seen it… "seen it and loved it" And this assurance he provided to Warren again when he visited Warren's dressing room before the show. "Saw it and loved it." "He doesn't have to love it. I just want to be sure he saw it," Warren responded. "Saw it and loved it." So there was a certain sense of surprise, not to say betrayal, when Johnny's first words to Warren after his entry were "I hear you have a helluva movie." A long pause and then Warren pointed out that the producer had assured him that Johnny had seen "Shampoo." This devolved into explanations as to why the producer might have thought that. But "getting off on the wrong foot" does not adequately describe the dislocations of this situation, and finally Warren looked at his watch and said, "I'd better be going. I have to be on a set in October." Any candidates for a more candid and inspired exit line?

This unique history, to which I was such personal witness, long seemed to be remembered by me and by me alone. That is a testament to the fact that memory can be very selective and protective when the actual occurance does not fit our expectations or is better left to gather dust. I mentioned it once to Warren, and it simply was not in his active memory… one of the most active active memories I've ever encountered. He had dealt with a strange situation and then gone on with his life, most immediately the very successful selling of "Shampoo," a film massively honored by the critics and by the audiences who lined up around the block to see it. Moreover, none of the people at The Tonight Show in 1975 have ever remembered this event when I brought it up over the years. This suppression illustrates an important escape hatch of memory. It relieves you of having to chew every untasty cud over and over again. In the face of all of this negation, I actually started to question my own memory, and I put that to the test when Warren asked me to be interviewed for a documentary which was to accompany the blue-ray release of a restoration of "Bonnie And Clyde." The documentarian, Laurent Bouzereau, as avid a student and admirer as I of Warren's seminal contributions to film, enthusiastically confirmed the occurrence as "one of the most audaciously honest moments" ever interjected into the bland pleasantries of talk-show guestings. Of course today that abrupt departure would go viral. But before social media turned the world into one big gabfest, such things faded into the wallpaper.

Guttman & Pam's Unholy Advantage

You don't *create* really effective ideas. You *recognize* them. The institution of the Z Channel "For Your Consideration" screenings is my only claim to fame. Much more claim than fame. It was a device of intravenously feeding our Oscar contender films to the great majority of Academy voters through a viewing procedure on cable TV, a procedure which for an excellent period of time only I could manipulate, my one moment of significant originality. It is a matter long since blanched from the uncaring pages of history, but it was very significant to Guttman & Pam and to our client films and artists during the few years it glittered in Jerry's and my hands and even after we had to share it with those who finally caught onto what we were doing.

To resurrect "The Conversation" from its release hell, I knew we had to come up with something radically more powerful to get it the viewership it simply hadn't received in its release. "Witness," early release or not, still had been one of the year's fantastic box-office success stories and widely beloved films and, presumably, was substantially "seen" by people in the Academy. "The Conversation" was a secret.

It appeared to be almost inexhumable that fall when its Oscar prospects fell so exclusively into our laps. An orphan film which had done poorly in release, it's glowing reviews hardly in memory three quarters of a year later, it's proud victory at Cannes over a year and a half past, the heat on Francis focused on his triumph with "Godfather ll," which went on to win Best Film and Best Director among others. In October when Oscar-thinking starts, "The Conversation" was the film that wasn't there. I took the challenge very seriously, my devotion to it and to Gene's great performance being quite personal. We were in competition with such current and exhalted films as "Chinatown," "Lenny," "Alice Doesn't Live Here Anymore," "The Towering Inferno," "Young Frankenstein," "Murder On The Orient Express," "Day For Night," "Harry And Tonto," "A Woman Under The Influence," "Thunderbolt And Lightfoot," "Blazing Saddles" and, oh yes, a little film called "Godfather II"... well, you get the idea. And the tough thing was that I really cared... and I really thought that anyone who saw "The Conversation" would vote for "The Conversation." Only trouble? Nobody had seen it. This was before video cassettes of Oscar-worthy movies. Yes, some old movies were starting to show on cable channels, but they were old movies. If you didn't see a contending film in the theatres or studio screening, you didn't see it.

And then it dropped in my lap, a gift that gave Guttman & Pam an almost immoral advantage in Oscar campaigning over the next two or three years.

One day I sat at my desk thinking "Conversation," trying to make a bright thought pop into my head… trying to conjure a way to drag Oscar voters to this movie which I truly loved. It turned out that what I really had to do was to find a way to drag that movie to the Oscar voters. Face up on my desk, atop a pile of unopened mail, was a sales promotional piece from a cable television station called Z Channel. This was 1974. The networks still ruled the TV roost. Cable was just coming in, and Z was pretty much the only movie channel available to viewers. It was a lone precursor of the blessings of TCM. Industry folks who lived in Malibu and other glittery boondocks far from the studio screening rooms had to catch contending films in their theatre runs or not at all. And Z was our lifeline to movie excellence, showing all of the golden oldies.

On the front page of the promotional brochure was a map of all of the areas that were served by Z Channel. It was, I suddenly realized, an almost exact overlay of all of the areas where card-carrying Academy of Motion Picture Arts & Sciences members resided… Beverly Hills, the canyons, Sherman Oaks and Encino and Woodland Hills and all of the other film industry residential sites… the Valley, Holmby Hills, Brentwood, Bel Air, Santa Monica, Malibu…. Hold on, pilgrim! This is a diagram for intravenous injection of movie-viewing directly into the body of the Academy's human component, the crucial few thousand who decided Oscar nominations and winners.

I called the head of Z Channel and told him I could get him Francis Coppola's acclaimed and award-winning "The Conversation" for exclusive TV viewing. No film previously had been seen on cable in the year of its release. He wasn't with me… he was ahead of me. I didn't need to throw in an interview with Gene Hackman to seal the deal. I needed it to alert Z's Academy viewers that for the very first time they were going to be able to see an Oscar contender in the comfort of their own home. Gene loved the film and understood that this was the only chance I had to get Academy viewership for "The Conversation." He agreed to do the interview and otherwise helped me buy a Z ticket to put it in front of the voters."

The other wild card in this was a guy named Jerry Harvey, a film buff extraordinaire who was the programming director for Z. His understanding of and enthusiasm for film excellence was such that you could turn on Z any hour of the day and know that you would love what was playing. Jerry Pam and I decided we would describe the multiple showings of "The Conversation" as "For Your Consideration" screenings, and Jerry Harvey threw himself into them. It was a godsend not just the screening-challenged Malibuans but for everyone with an Academy card. "The Conversation," the award quality film least seen by Academy members that year, even though it had won the top award at Cannes, was going to get put in front of the eyeballs.

I depended on Fred Roos to sell this radical idea to Francis, and Fred came back with the sad fact that some other cable operators had heard about it and were trying to unsell Francis on the Z Channel screenings. Fred told us Francis' associates had given it a no-go because the cable operator in Fresno had said he would cancel any licensing of "The Conversation" if Z got that edge. When Fred checked, it turned out that we were talking only a $6000 loss. I told him to tell Francis that that was (at that time) only two trade ads, and that I thought the Z idea could get us a nomination for a film Francis loved. Francis gave us a go.

I was getting great feedback, one hundred percent of the people to whom I spoke having made a point of tuning it on and one hundred percent of them loving it. A first run movie on the home TV screens, it simply hadn't been done before. It was big news and getting the heat and word of mouth that come of being something new. Of course I was being hammered with the inarguable fact that seeing a film on a small screen is not equivalent to the theatre experience, and I would respond that it was a helluva lot superior to having it not seen it at all, which was our other alternative.

When the nominations came out, we were all over them... Best Film and four others. I was devastated that Gene wasn't nominated for Best Actor, but he consoled me with the argument that his character "didn't have a scene," meaning that one explosive scene that hammers into the memory. I countered that the entire *film* was his scene. I had a real sense of failure, that validation of my strategy notwithstanding. Francis wound up with two best film nominees in the same year... and two Best Director nominations, a real rarity. There was a general air of consternation in town that "The Conversation" had been nominated for Best Film over so many fine films that had enjoyed lines at the movie houses. They couldn't figure out how a film so hidden had come out of the pack. I knew why.... the voters had SEEN it.

Some people at Paramount were telling Francis we had cost him the Oscar because it would split his vote for Best Film and Best Director. We knew that wasn't true. The people who wrote "The Conversation" on their ballot... I'll put my hand in the fire on this one... had written "Godfather II" as well. In nominating, you mark five films in order of preference. They came to those ballots in awe of the cosmic range of a great director. Everyone knew that if Francis were to win, it would be for "Godfather II." For "The Conversation," its Oscar was the nomination, the little film coming from nowhere. But it *did* come from somewhere... the voters' TV screens. And there it was, standing up there with such fellow nominees as "Chinatown," "Lenny" and "The Towering Inferno" and "Godfather 2."

Here was the funny twist on that. During the process of that Academy Award season, we had reason to believe that Paramount really hated Guttman & Pam because we had brought "The Conversation" in as a wild card in their very important and monocular pursuit of Oscar for "Godfather II." But they apparently gathered from the surprise "Conversation" nominations that Guttman & Pam was on to something, although nobody knew quite what. The following year, they enjoyed the great prestige, if not the great boxoffice, of releasing Ingmar Bergman's extraordinary "Scenes From A Marriage." Paramount chief David Picker very nobly wanted to give the film, Bergman and its star, Liv Ullmann every possible shot at Academy consideration. But how? It was a six hour movie... and in Swedish with subtitles. Actually, it had been not a film but an epic television presentation in Sweden. It featured, among its other Bergmanesque glories, a luminous performance by Ms. Ullmann. The six hours was the catch 22, but we put it on Z Channel with a For Your Consideration screening schedule just to give it a chance. Before we did, Mr. Picker said I had to get permission from the town's great exhibitor of foreign art films, Max Laemmle, a personal friend of all of the significant European film auteurs. He was playing "Scenes From A Marriage" at one of his key theatres which was right in the middle of Z Channel country. The TV runnings could hurt his business, but he felt he owed it to Liv Ullmann and to Bergman who had put so many lines in front of his theatre. What happened is that a six-hour film with sub-titles at the bottom of the screen not always completely visible was tough TV viewing. But Z aficionados saw enough to want to see it all... and the business the film was doing at the theatre kicked up substantially.

Z was still working its magic, and the next year or years we pushed two films Guttman & Pam represented, "The Man In The Glass Booth" and "Hedda," with Z

Channel "For Your Consideration" screenings, facilitating Oscar voters' viewing from their couches the films entrusted to us and which they simply hadn't summoned the energy to go see in the theatres. Two of our clients, Maximilian Schell and Glenda Jackson were Oscar nominated for Best Actor and Best Actress for those films seen primarily on TV screens. Jerry and I kept Z a kind of open secret and our private advantage for several years, positioning our films (PR guy possessive meaning films on which you work) for Oscar consideration. Z Channel, naturally, hired Guttman & Pam to represent the channel on the basis of the unprecedented attention we had brought them. The amazing thing was that although it was vividly apparent to the industry at large, since they were the beneficiaries, that these films had been made available for them to see at home, it was a long while before anyone else made the connection that this was an invaluable means of bringing deserved votes to their own fine films. Jerry and I were thrilled that we'd been allowed to hold the dice for so long. We'd had the magic wand all to ourselves for two or three prestidigitory years. The Z Channel edge was the best gift I've ever given myself, a gift that kept on giving.

In 1977, Lloyd Leipzig, who ran some of the town's great Oscar campaigns for United Artists, caught on. He demanded to have Woody Allen's "Annie Hall" presented in that year's For Your Consideration screenings, and we were delighted because it brought our client Z Channel into a bright, bright spotlight. A year later, Warren Beatty bought into the advantage those screenings represented, given the fact that private videos of film were not yet going out in the mail for Academy members. He not only green-lighted our putting "Heaven Can Wait" in the For Your Consideration schedule, but he personally selected the scheduled times. They don't come any brighter.

Perhaps the greatest opportunity deriving from our unique discovery and use of and service to Z Channel was that Guttman & Pam went into production of a heralded Z Channel series of interviews with great filmmakers and top stars hosted by Chuck Champlin and entitled "On The Film Scene". It was one of the premium exposures in the industry. This we interspersed with regular programming throughout the year, putting us in on-going business with Jerry Harvey, the programmer for the channel and respected by all as The Man Who Loved Films. I don't think anyone ever exceeded his knowledge of and his passion for the presentation and preservation of classic films. Over about seven years and well over

100 shows, directors like Spielberg and Coppola guested with Champlin many times, and you could see them growing in years and enthusiasms before your eyes. It was a constant flow of exposure... directly to the industry, to the people who made and cast films... one that we put to the advantage of the full contingent of Guttman & Pam clients as well as most of the other significant stars, each of whom was thrilled to sit down for a chat with Charles Champlin, that most loving and sophisticated of commentators on film.

Some time after Jerry Pam and I ended our partnership, CD Roms were becoming the progenitors of what DVDs are now and CD Roms had come to be a promising educational tool. I had several requests to transfer the historic sweep of industry observation which "On The Scene" most certainly was and to make it available to film schools or the collection of film aficionados. I assume Guttman Associates owns them, together with the last of the chain of hands into which Z Channel eventually passed. Unfortunately these tapes have disappeared. Jerry Harvey had, so tragically, perished at his own hands. If anybody ever finds them, I'll consign permission to release them with profits going to the Entertainment Industry Foundation, the town's charity arm. I hope someone does. They document a decade of important transition and delve serially into the hearts and minds of some of our greatest film creators.

Michael Douglas inherited a lot more from his dad than that cleft chin. They had a family tradition of making great films on controversial subjects and then working their tails off to achieve both the success and the acknowledgement the films deserved and to make sure that what they had to say "took." Michael, having brought Guttman & Pam aboard for the glory ride that was "One Flew Over The Cuckoo's Nest," signed us on for "China Syndrome" which was meaningful and challenging even before Three Mile Island, the radiation spill at an American nuclear power plant. That tragedy underlined the sizzling urgency of the film's theme... the possibility of radiation catastrophes at nuclear plants. No sooner was the film out than evidence of its relevance and prescience dominated the news. Three Mile Island took the film right into the headlines which is not always a comfortable place for a press agent. *You must make sure that the issue is not exploited*. With real-life issues at stake, you're out there dancing with all the lights on. Michael, with a heady understanding of publicity, knew this, and the trick was to let the film illustrate the issues being discussed, not simply ride the

crest of interest and fear the news had generated. Kirk would have handled it
in exactly the same way. That dedication to what they believed in boiled in the
Douglas blood. And it didn't make any difference how much money they had at
stake. They always had their belief at stake above all.

However much of himself Kirk had poured into "Spartacus," he floored the
accelerator even more for "Lonely are The Brave," a brave and lonely little film
he loved and which he felt needed his devotion. It was the second film for which
Kirk invited blacklisted writer Dalton Trumbo to explore the oppressions of the
black list period in exciting narrative metaphor. Kirk literally WAS the cowboy
from an earlier time, the free spirit whom our modern technological society had
to track down and stomp out. It was Dalton Trumbo's story as well. And while
it was a tenth of the budget for "Spartacus," Kirk sold it as if it had cost the same
$50 million, a staggering fortune at that time...

The real life dangers on which Michael Douglas and his creative collaborators
had predicated "The China Syndrome", the possibility of nuclear plant disaster,
became a reality in its most awful form with Chernoble, and by then China Syndrome had become the catch-phrase for the environmental and human disaster
inherent in careless custodianship of nuclear power... Michael was as great a
promoter of what he believed in as his dad. He was dedicated to using the success
of "China Syndrome" to convey what it had to say about the care and regulation
missing in the nation's and the world's rush to nuclear power.

The nominations for "China Syndrome" included Best Actor for Jack Lemmon
and Best Actress for Jane Fonda, as well as a Best Screenplay call. The Best Film
nods went to "Kramer Vs. Kramer," "Apocalypse Now," "Norma Rae," "Breaking
Away" and "All That Jazz." But "China Syndrome" had lent itself to history. It was
one of those rare films that changed the world, underscoring that nuclear power
was not something that could be as loosely regulated as it had been. That was a
major reason Michael had made the film and had signed so many other top-line
talents to join him. As terrific a cinematic narrative as it was, the reinforced public
awareness was its greatest legacy.

Michael Douglas had been a client during his early starring work with Karl Malden
on "The Streets Of San Francisco," and he enlisted our help on his first history-making
film production, "One Flew Over The Cuckoo's Nest," which achieved the remarkable
acknowledgment of winning what many consider the "big five" Oscars, Best Film,

Best Director, Best Script, Best Actor and Actress… although the Academy goes to lengths to establish the equivalence of all awards. I actually had been involved with that project at its earliest development when Kirk had purchased the book in the '60s and translated it to a Broadway production in which he starred. Even my mom was involved in the launch of the property, as detailed in the first chapter of this recollection. A personal reward of working on the film version was the brief acquaintance with Ken Kesey and conversations which helped me bounce my own personal experiences off someone who could comprehend them. Kesey, as I, had been subjects of the CIA LSD testing. Our discussions were sometimes argumentative, since the tearing of order and safe harbor from my mind had been an experience of torture and chaos, while he felt enlightened by his own explorations with LSD and some of her mind-bending sisters. It certainly didn't keep him from becoming one of the most brilliant and important writers of that time… a significant literary and social force of the '60s and '70s and still reverberating.

It was terrific being account exec on Rogers & Cowan's Mirisch Company work. Warren and Henry did the heavy-lifting, interfacing with Harold and Walter Mirisch, and I got to play with the public relations opportunities and the exciting problems that attended the Mirisches' reign as kings of the hill. One of the publics to which they had to relate were the great directors who constituted that film company's unique claim to fame and success. They had created a protective and facilitating habitat in which such gods might work freely, but like any proud parents they had to make each kid feel like the favorite. This came to a head one year when in November, at the start of Oscar positioning season, they arrived at the happy realization that they had five great films jockeying for the five Best Film nominations. Happy, yes, but not without its problems.

Not even a miracle could deliver all fiveBest Film nominations unto one company. How do you make Billy Wilder and William Wyler and three other cornerstones of your business all feel comfortable with the equality and non-favoritism of the campaigns? Talk about an embarrassment of riches. It was a problem which needed an answer. I recommended that they embrace the problem, harvest the positive industry awareness of their dominance of the year and then celebrate it in all of their ads.

I suggested the phrase "see them all, judge for yourself" be featured in all ads. I've never had another idea so readily received, possibly because it could keep all of their famous kids happy. Everyone agreed that even Pontius Pilate or Solomon couldn't have dodged the bullet more subtly. That catch-line ran at the bottom of every ad for every film, right next to the Mirisch Company logo. As the device took on notice, it brought some good comment in print, so we expanded it and used it separately from the ads for individual films, taking a front page banner ad, two inches of space across the bottom of the front page of each trade paper. It said simply "See them all, judge for yourself. The Mirisch Company." It actually had impact because this was decades before Academy voters could see films at home. So the ad campaign was taken as a reminder to see all films, not just the Mirisch's Fab Five. It wasn't quantum physics, just an idea that solved a problem, and in publicity that's good enough.

An embarrassment of riches does compel studio heads to do some real soul-searching during the promotional period building toward Academy Awards nominations consideration and also during the final jockeying after the nominations are announced. It is the only downside of making a lot of films deserving of Oscar consideration. The Weinstein bothers often find themselves, as the Mirishes did, in the unique, enviable and troublesome position of backing competing films. This came to a crisis for them a few years ago when they were presenting both Anthony Mingella's "Cold Mountain" and the Brazilian masterwork "City Of God" in the same year. Foreign language films are rarely nominated in the Best Film (as opposed to Best Foreign Language Film) category, nor has any non-English language film ever won what most industry observers consider "the big award," not even "Life Is Beautiful," on which we also were among the Weinsteins' consulting PR firms and which, a very big exception to the rule, actually had a fighting chance.

One Sunday, in the middle of the pre-nomination campaigning , I received a phone call from Harvey. He asked quite earnestly, "Am I backing the wrong film?" The answer was "no" because, although he was pouring it on for "Cold Mountain," which wasn't (for someone with a sensitive finger on the pulse) a truly top contender for Best Film, he was not short-changing "City Of God." Film people usually can tell you which two films are battling it out. What Harvey really was asking was if he was doing enough for "City Of God. " He was backing both films to the hilt and then some, which simply is his nature. He was giving "Cold Mountain" everything he had because he and his brother Bob, like the Mirisches, ran a 'great directors" company, and "Cold Mountain" director Anthony Minghella had brought home a Best Film Oscar with "The English Patient" a few years before. On the other hand, "City of God" was flat-out probably the best film of the year and maybe the previous decade. But there was simply no way that enough voters would have watched a subtitled film of such violent dystopia to give it the shot it deserves for Best Film, however indisputable its superiority to the rest of the field. Subtitled films like "The Emigrants" and the Weinsteins' own "Il Postino" and "Life Is Beautiful" have found their way to Best Film nominations, with Roberto Begnini's "Life Is Beautiful" bringing him Oscars for Best Actor and Best Foreign Film.

The Academy fully understands the how-do-you-get-them-to-see-it? impediment which stands in the way of Best Film nomination of non-English films. That's why the nomination process for Best Foreign Film is by a huge committee, each member of which is obligated to see all of the submitted films. It's a very loving and time-consuming task for which they volunteer. Up until 2013, one hundred percent viewership by voters was guaranteed in the foreign and documentary final voting because you couldn't vote unless you had seen all the nominees. The power and emotion of "Life Is Beautiful" was far more "embraceable" than the punch-in-the-face brilliance of "City Of God." Even when he had the accelerator floored on the "City Of God" campaign, Harvey felt he wasn't doing enough because he knew it wasn't going to get the film what it deserved, which was everything. The call simply showed why he's so good at the game... why ANYone who's passionate is good at their game. If they feel an obligation, the word "enough" simply isn't in their dictionary.

Harvey is a true believer. When he was presenting Denzel Washington's "The Great Debaters," a late release in the Oscar year, it was obvious that several films had already locked-in for nomination, enough of them that a film would have to come in with massive steam to dislodge one, there being only five films nominated at that time (something I would love to see resumed.) Harvey is unrelenting in covering the bases for any film in which he believes, basing his determination on two certainties. The first is that there ARE no certainties in the Oscar nomination process and the second is that there are always surprises. To the outside world, it may seem that an Oscar voter's chores during the voting period is another name for paradise… get a DVD of every top film of the year and feast out on them. In fact, for anyone who has an Academy card AND a job, it is almost impossible to see them all. Harvey set high bars, and now virtually every studio exec goes to weinsteinian lengths to make sure that every move that is within the rules will be undertaken to assure that the town sees that company's films before ballots are filled out and, if humanly possible, that it will be seen on a big screen. Big films, to repeat the obvious, look bigger on the big screen. Much of the campaign press agent's job is to make sure that the screening availabilities are duly hammered home.

My philosophy has always been that *ads are designed to do one of three things… 1. to remind you why and how much you loved the film when you saw it, 2. to establish that you owe it to yourself and your Academy membership to see this film before you vote or 3. best of all, to get you to see it again and talk it up.* Quotes and pithy ad lines and key art elements that grab you and blow-away designs are all pressed into the service of those three objectives. Since the start of the practice of mailing Academy members "screeners" (DVDs of each worthy film,) it is harder to get voters to see films on the big screen. I repeat, every big film looks bigger on a big screen, but you take what you can get.

Chapter 10

Perception of Power

The term "powerful press agent", occasionally evoked in news stories, is misleading. PR people are not great ships carrying valuable cargo. They are simply the tug boats which nudge those floating cities to safe harbor. But just try to slip a tanker or container vessel softly into dock without their tugs. Of "powerful" indy firms, however, there are many. That adjective applies to star-studded talent agencies as well as PR agencies or management firms. Each of these "controls" (a word agencies use, but "represents" is much more descriptive) a swath of talent useful to the industry. This confers power to the respective agencies, and many artists gravitate to these firms in the solemn belief that this power will be used in their interests… that their reps will say "you won't get Superstar X if you don't use Not-Yet-Superstar Y in that film." Alas, it doesn't work that way. Established Superstar X is the one whose interests prevail. When you are yourself finally Superstar Y and of bargainable or clout-conveying value to the agency, you'll like it that way. In the '50s and '60s Henry Rogers and Warren Cowan, Lee Solters, Arthur Jacobs and John Springer who grew and rooted himself in New York were defining the business of independent press agentry and becoming its first war lords. Russell Birdwell and George Thomas had set the pattern in the '30s and '40s, usually hiring out to great producers f'or specific films or campaigns rather than, as Henry Rogers and his 30s indy peers did, wrangling stables of actors just starting to wrest the control of their publicity from studio chiefs holding their contracts and rights to their first born… including the right to accord them no publicity whatsoever.

I think of publicity as a field in which people can grow old. Warren Cowan and Lee Solters a few years back took their careers all the way to their graves, the name going directly from door to headstone at the very brink of their nineties. There were also impressive dominions carved out with the feminine touch in those early years... New York based Lois Smith and Marion Reese among them with Rene Leff the go-to gal for art films or European film festivals. Peggy Siegel came later, and no one was a better straight-ahead runner than she, finally using that energy and persuasion to become the absolute "potentate of events" to whom all of the important invitings were entrusted. RSVP is not only her email address, it's her middle name.

They were queens, but Pat Kingsley became the first empress. When I returned from my youthful years in Europe and re-upped at Rogers & Cowan, Pat was Pat Ratchford, and shortly after I rejoined the company she became Warren Cowan's secretary. That is now a sexist word, but that is what, female or male, such valued assistants were called in that Wonder Bread era. At a certain point, Pat became my assistant and, almost instantaneously, my partner in accounts, such was her force of energy and her dedication to the visibility of the clients. It was a close relationship and friendship, and I was sad when Pat moved to New York and shortly thereafter joined and soon became a partner in Pickwick Publicity, a very aggressive and talent-laden matriarchy teaming her with such giants as Lois Smith and Pat Newcomb... a matriumverate, one might say.

It's not easy to be a whole and transparent human being in a firefight world like press agenting, but Pat Newcomb certainly was one who proved it is possible. In our time together at Rogers & Cowan, working under Pat Newcomb's heading the R&C "personality" department, I had first-hand witness why the town's female superstar royalty depended on her for protection, projection, counsel and friendship. Elizabeth Taylor, Audrey Hepburn, Marilyn Monroe and others all knew their secrets were and remain to this day safe with her. All three of those Pickwick ladies (two Pats and a Lois) were superstars themselves. Pickwick became the P in PMK which became, alongside Rogers & Cowan, a touchstone of press agently powe. From that firm Leslie Dart then grew and inevitably headed her own empire, 42 West, definitely and deservedly the largest independently-owned entertainment PR firm with Guttman Associates on the other end of the size spectrum.

Dan Klores and Howard Rubinstein and Ken Sunshine certainly cut the same kind of wide and powerful swath as the current Rogers & Cowan and BWR or PMKHGB (Pickwick's eventual transmogrification) and the strong companies which seem to have fractured out of these. To my dyslexic eyes, any string of consonants just looks like a bad scrabble hand or a license plate that doesn't give your memory anything to hang on to. At any rate, the P and the M and the K are all gone from or transformed within the imperial tickings of PR, just as are now the Rogers and the Cowan. And others carry on under (if not "in") their name or their initials. Mark Pogochevsky and Rachel McAllister have a strong firm called MPRP which my mind orders as Mr. PR. I can't think of it otherwise. Other matriarchies are headed by Kelly Bush (her extremely heavy-hitter IDPR even branches into management) and Lisa Kasteller and Annette Wolf. Where once there were east coast agencies and west coast agencies and then east-and-west coast agencies, now the enveloping technologies have made the guy or gal sitting alone at a PC in a single office a national operation if he/she so aspires and so conspires. That's a good thing. PR is a land of opportunity.

The Often Touching Bonds Between Flacks and Clients

Client loyalty in those first decades of indy PR… more so than now, I think… had an element of emotional dependency. When I decided to leave R&C for a partnership with Jerry Pam, Raquel Welch called. "First Pat (Kingsley) goes off and now you. What am I supposed to do?" She had been a faithful and appreciative client for both Pat and me. But, quite understandably, what she did was stay at R&C because it was the acknowledged power, and *the perception of power makes people feel safe.* That's the reason power is self-perpetuating. Many times when Jerry and I were starting we were referred a potential account with Rogers & Cowan the competing bidder. We usually lost to R&C. Once, it was for an Italian promotional event called the Valentino Awards, I knew what the R&C pitch was because they were still using some of the 30 page pitch presentations I'd written for prior account solicitations. So I knew we had some more compelling and novel elements in ours. But it went to them. The guy who had been navigating the PR selection for the Valentino family, called to say he was sorry. I said, "Sorry? Why? Because we didn't get it or because our pitch was better?" He answered, "Both. But you have to understand… I look bad if the eventual campaign fails. But if I go with R&C which has the aura of being the most powerful PR firm in the world, even if they fail I can't get fired. I got them the one generally conceded to be most powerful…" Nothing untrue in anything he said.

Jerry and I were a small boutique firm... and I've pretty much tried to keep it that way for the past four decades... because it made me comfortable. But in very short order we became a pretty big little company. At first it was just the two of us and an assistant, Christie Cane, who was as brash and as fun as her name. Then a secretary, a series of secretaries... and finally a good long-time studio press agent, Joel Rose, who could handle the writing all of which I could no longer do myself, although Jerry could put pen to paper very well. However, our little client list became rather prestigious fairly quickly. Jerry already had long and close relationships with Michael Caine, Roger Moore, Robert Aldrich, Robert Stack, Ernie Borgnine and others. Directly after we started, Warren Beatty recommended Gene Hackman to us to handle his "French Connection" opportunity, then Warren also brought us aboard for "Shampoo." Some of my former clients like Clint Eastwood and Robert Radnitz (that iconic producer of great children's films) brought Guttman & Pam in to handle "Play Misty For Me" and "Sounder," respectively. United Artists, located just down the hall from our offices at the old Goldwyn Studios in Hollywood, put us on such films as "Last Tango In Paris" and "Sunday Bloody Sunday." In fact, under its publicity steward-ship of Buddy Young and Arthur Krim, UA put us on the release publicity of all of its key films. Oscar winning screenwriter Sidney Sheldon hired us to handle his first novel, "The Naked Face." When Sidney wrote "The Other Side Of Midnight," our company's rising visibility was accelerated by the red carpet we rolled out to celebrate Sidney's arrival as THE superstar best-seller scribbler.

As did Peter Falk's quick establishment as king of TV with "Columbo." His agent, the excellent and true-believing Bill Robinson, brought us along for that rocket-ride and then did the same with James Garner. When the start of "Columbo's" second season was challenged by having to face off against the first TV presentation of the huge James Bond smash, "Thunderball," which promised to be a major television event, there was concern for poor, little, merely-a-tv-show "Columbo. In any sport, when number one starts the season with a loss, suddenly it's vulnerable." I told Peter we should take a trade ad saying "It's the same old 'Thunderball,' It's a brand new 'Columbo',," and Peter protested that the Bond film was such a blazing success that saying "Thunderball" was like saying "Gone With The Wind.," so how could we say "same old?" I insisted that's what made it funny. The ad created comment within the trade and among media who read the trades, so that when Columbo won that battle of spy vs. sleuth, it was actually alluded to in some of the news reports as an "upset" victory. It was because in part the event had been framed as a contest between a superhot movie attraction and superhot made-for-TV fare. As such, the "upset victory" subtly reaffirmed Peter's unchallenged reign on the small screen. And it seemed to add to the star glitter of our new little company. Some prospective clients told us the ad had induced their interest. Audacity makes its own waves.

PR firms, like the clients they serve, languish or prosper on the perception of their power. Sometimes it boils down not to the press that you *know* but to the press that know *you*.

Chapter 11

Being 22

*F*reud said, "In our subconscious mind, we are always 23." Good thing for me.

We had a staff lunch at our office recently to celebrate the 23rd birthday of one of our group. The rest of the staff agreed that 23 had been the worst year of each of their lives. 23 was the best year of mine. 22 had been a train-wreck, but an interesting and consequential one. It led to everything else. When you have, as I now have, enjoyed six decades in the same profession and almost that in the same marriage, you weigh how much of it was choice and how much fate. I made some terrific choices and some fortuitous terrible choices, but fate really mapped out the trip. Fate has an audacity you could never remotely match.

I step back from anecdote here for a moment to offer for your consideration the idea that memoir and auto-biography are not the same thing, but they overlap and intertwine in some essential aspects. One of the things I want to convey in this examination of entertainment publicity is the fact that publicists... flacks, even... are people. And I've found many to be very vibrant and interesting individuals. To autopsy a career and its profession and to access the extraordinary people along its way, it's informative for the reader, I'm told, to know what kind of person lived that career and interfaced with those people. So this is a road sign that this chapter and the next are much more personal than professional and they can be skipped without dislodging your understanding of what publicity is. Personally, I would not have missed them for anything. I'm sure you've remarked of your own life that the personal and the professional are as linked as your body and your mind.

One of the first clients Jerry Pam and I acquired was the noted therapist, psychologist and author Dr. Irene Kassorla. She recently had business in the 1930s streamline-moderne Beverly Hills building where I've long had my offices. I don't mean to glamorize it. It's period creakiness is part of its charm. The two story high streamline-moderne window at the midway landing of the front staircase is of translucent Hollywood glass bricks. It's a masterpiece of period design. It gets me into my day every morning as I climb to my office. And there Irene and I bumped into each other, and she asked, "And how is Gisela? Are you and she still together?" "Of course," I answered, and she responded, "Ah, divorce. Well, two such intense personalities... it was meant to be." I'd never thought of myself as intense or even as a personality, but about one thing she was very right. A lasting marriage... to a profession, to a beloved partner... always "was meant to be." Trace it back and you see fate calling the shots at every turn. All of the smart moves you made and all of the stupid, they were each and every one the right step for fulfilling what was written.

In the UCLA film department, we had been trained pretty much to be documentarians or film teachers. Some friends and I had to form the Delta Kappa Alpha Film Fraternity there to invite Hollywood creators to come meet and lecture us. But our training was such that when representatives of the Pakistani Film Commission came through to interview trained filmmakers to document the start of their new nation, I was intrigued. Capturing a nation-building on film and teaching its first crop of young filmmakers might have led to an interesting life. However, publicity put in a counter offer. Its prospect of adventuring in the Hollywood forest of tall tree personalities and talents seemed natural selection, and it turned out all right.

Then came graduation and then came 22, and publicity did another very compelling thing to me and for me. It became boring. Without the other-life of college and after the excitement of my first discovery of PR subsided, publicity seemed not monotonous so much as repetitious. I became filled with a sense of missed adventure and thwarted fate. I had to fill it up with some distraction.

Stu Roe, hotshot photographer and cartoonist on our high school paper, was the guy who had dragged me into film school after I'd exhausted my interest in six other majors in two months of college. It was, as Bogie put it, the beginning of a beautiful friendship, struggling together to accumulate knowledge about film-making that we weren't getting from a film school that was largely the disregarded stepchild of the Theatre Arts Department. We buffered each other's frustrations for four years. He buoyed my spirits by telling me he'd heard our animation professor bragging to another teacher that my animation work was really prosaic. Well, at least it taught us each a new word. After graduation, when the real world was getting boring for both of us, we gathered together six hundred dollars to make a series of documentaries in Mexico over a two week visit. Publicity even directed me in that, because one of my accounts at Rogers & Cowan was Jose Cuervo Tequila, and I arranged for us to shoot the lifestyle which attended the making of tequila and existed because of it. We rented a Bell & Howell 16 mm camera, a tripod and reflector, sound equipment, bought lots of film, took the bus to Tijuana and caught a cheap plane to Guadalajara where we were picked up by Jose Freytag Gallardo, a great gentleman in the finest tradition of Mexican patrons, owner of Cuervo and director or president or something of the Bank of Mexico. He'd decided to invest his own time in these two kids who had come down to tell the story of the native life style associated with the agriculture and fabrication on of tequila. When we shot in little villages in wooded areas skirting the cactus fields, the village chief would always want to carry the tripod, apparently a sign of authority, but Senor Freytag Gallardo did those honors. He drove us from the airport to the town of Tequila and put us up grandly in his in great home there which was in and part of the main fabrica or brewery where the mescal cactus hearts were cleaned, chopped, steamed, crushed and then fermented into the Mexican drink that was sweeping America.

Driving with Senor Freitag Gallardo in the bed of a pickup truck that moved us on bumpy dirt roads from mescal fields to villages, I felt obliged to tell him that I had seen a pistola stuffed into the back of a trabajador's pants in the fabrica the day before. He pulled out a Luger and showed it to me. "Everyone who can afford it has one, even some who can't." He fired at some cactus. The truck swerved madly as Stu and the driver ducked. Stu looked back to make sure I hadn't just been executed. He always felt I would make one dumb joke too many some day and he must have assumed that the third richest man in Mexico could kill anyone he damn pleased. "Doesn't that have consequences?.... all those guns?" I asked the third richest man in Mexico as he stuffed the Luger back in his pants. "Every few weeks, yes. If it was tequila they were drinking, I pay for the funeral." He smiled, but I wasn't sure it was a joke.

Stu and I had determined to do three short films called "The Village Made Of Cactus," "The Village Made Of Net" and "The Village Made Of Copper." "Net" was set and would be shot on and off the shores of the island of Janitizio in Lake Patzcuaro in the state of Michoacan, famous because of the romantic photos of butterfly net fishermen, their twin six foot nets extending like gossamer wings from their little boats. The third film would be shot in the nearby Santa Clara de Cobre, a mountain town where every extended family was a little factory pounding out the most beautiful folk art copper plates and pots in the world. It was amazing how much film we shot and adventure we squeezed into two weeks.

It was on our first shoot in Tequila that I discovered my knack of getting into trouble in foreign countries. I wish I'd been paid for every time someone has pointed a gun or a knife at me or jabbed them into my ribs. It's like some people always get buzzed by mosquitos? With me it's knives and pistols. Stu and I were walking about the little town of Tequila capturing "color," ambience. As we were shooting B-roll of the beautiful cemetery, a small funeral procession entered, a family carrying a child's coffin. Stu was filming near the entrance, and I was further in, observing grave stone inscriptions, making notes. The little funeral proceded to an open grave near which I was standing. I remained in what I thought was respectful attitude. A bottle of Tequila was passing from mouth to mouth around the grave. After the brief ceremony, one of the mourners, a young worker in white cotton, now visibly "boracho" and carrying the bottle which had gotten him there, approached me and held the bottle out. I don't drink . That has carried me into as much trouble in my life as the consumption of alcohol has caused others. This was a prime example. When I politely declined the viscous liquid and said "gracias pero yo no bebo" (thanks, but I don't drink,) he pointed to the grave, said "mi hermano" (my brother) and then crashed the bottle against a nearby gravestone. I was relieved when he dropped the dangerous shard of it. He put his arm around my shoulder and pulled our heads together in sudden and close friendship and started walking me out of the cemetery. I waved at Stu and he waved back and disappeared. I realized why. My new friend kept jabbing my ribs with his hard finger, and when I looked down, I saw it was, instead, the muzzle of a revolver. We progressed in this manner through the little town, and I held on to him to keep him from stumbling, afraid a fall could cause a pulled trigger with great resultant trauma to my lungs or intestines. At one point I saw Stu ahead, and he waved to me. I didn't know if he was waving encouragement to me or waving goodbye. But he motioned me to follow him and turned down the street to the Cuervo fabrica which was what I had in mind. One good thing about drunks is that they let you navigate. My own private pistolero kept talking to me and jabbing me, and the town's women paused to look at us as they hung clothes from second story windows on lines extending between opposite structures. Catching the action, they stopped their chatter and quickly closed wooden shutters to deflect any shot that might carom off of my backbone. And so we finally reached the open door of the fabrica and stepped in together, and the gun went off and I felt myself blown to the side. Except that, through Stu's good offices, there actually had been men waiting there, those on one side grabbing my friend and some pulling his arm up so that the bullet merely rippled the warm air, the others ripping me away. Thanks to Stu's arranging my salvation, it brought happy conclusion to my first preview of death.

I don't know what there is about me, but I do seem always to have wound up at gunpoint or knifepoint... Tequila... the town, not the drink... was, I think, the second occasion, but it has happened in Bethlehem, Nairobi, Istanbul and twice in the vicinity of Uruapan, Mexico... once in a village just west of the town and one just east. I'm sure there have been others. I was at meat cleaver-point in Alexandropoulos, Greece. Some of it stemmed from my youthful zeal for getting just the right photo. In a muddy little town in Michoacán where I had dragged my wife and daughters to look at some shrine or other but where we saw only pigs lying in murky street puddles, I got separated from them and the taxi. As I waited on a corner to be found, a gentleman came up and began an unintelligible conversation. Suddenly, something annoyed him, and he pressed a knife just under my ribs, drawing a tiny spot of red into the surrounding shirt. The cab in which Gi and the kids were looking for me drove by and honked, distracting my friend's attention, and I made a run for the open cab door. As we drove off, Gisela dabbed idly at the stain, suggesting it would come out in cold water. Then she asked, "What did you say to provoke that?" "I asked him what time's the next oxcart to Uruapan." "Maybe it was the way you said it," she reflected. They were already sort of used to all that.

It all started in Ensenada. While we were still in school, Stu and I and another film student/friend, Mike Barrier, went down to Baja to camp. We were directed to a mountain canyon about 20 miles south where there were, we were assured by the guy who was selling bottled water, "fewer rattlers, mountain lions and banditos than anywhere in the area." That advice convinced me that I would sleep in the car. The other two bravely curled up by the fire, But then came unfamiliar night noises which easily could have been one of the perils previously described to us. It was really hard with three of us sleeping in the same car, but luckily my two door sedan didn't have a back seat. The next night we opted for the luxury of a two buck Ensenada motel, going into a cantina to hear some great mariachi. A drunk was given the bum's rush out of the place, and as the bouncers returned, he followed them back in and sat at our table. We smiled him a cordial welcome, and he raised his hand and brought it down, driving a large knife into the table, neatly bisecting the space between my thumb and my forefinger, which were not too widely spread. It soon became apparent that it had not been his plan to miss. As he pulled on the knife to take another stab at it, Stu and Mike grabbed him and threw him out. When they came back in, the management, sizing us up quickly as trouble-makers, threw us all out.

Gisela is actually better at these things than I am. When she was a 17 year old au pair girl in London, some jerk would often follow her late at night when she got off the Underground (subway) after her college classes. One foggy night he actually accosted her as she crossed the center garden in a residential square in the gentrified district of Chiswick. He was still on the ground when the bobbies got there. She had applied the one-two attack of a knee to the groin plus strategic jabs into the afflicted area with the high-heels of the red pumps she favored.

What impressed me about Stu Roe during our location filmings in Jalisco and Michoacán, quite apart from his knowledge of the camera and how he could make it sing, was his courage and his easy character, his quiet response to any challenge. The bravery impressed itself upon me in Santa Clara de Cobre where each family was a gathering of adobe huts to form a little foundry for the tooling of their beautiful copper crafts. They started with a large, thick pancake of copper which had to be flattened out. It was heated by furnace and bellows and then flung onto a large stone. One man squatted near it, turning it with two tongs as six men circled it and with huge metal sledge hammers, pounding it in succession. Their timing was cued to the music of the blows...... *da-DA-da-DA-da-DEET*

and a two beat pause, which sounded to me like the opening guitar vamp for "Malaguena." But a missed blow could be deadly. How do you shoot that tight, dangerous process after doing the wide angle master? Stu lay down on his back beside the hot copper target and shot up at the descending blows and the laboring faces, the hammers crushing into the copper only inches from his head and his lens. He never flinched, but I was really frightened because we didn't have any insurance on the camera. The intercutting of what he captured, together with our sound recording of the singing hammers made a remarkable scene.

The only time I saw fear in Stu was months later when we were spending nights at the moviola cutting that sequence. In the course of the editing, I accidentally knocked over the bottle of splicing mucilage, and it began to pour off the moviola and the table onto Stu's leg. But we were creating art, and we just charged ahead, focused on the cutting for hours until the scene was perfect. It was only at that moment that Stu got up from the chair... or tried to... and let out a terrible scream. "My leg!" he cried... "It's paralyzed.... paralyzed." He was right. He couldn't unbend it and was standing like a stork. He tried to move and crashed to the floor as might a felled tree. Only then did we realize that the liquid cement had dried and turned his pants leg into a plaster cast.

After we finished our three locations shoots, Stu and I hopped an overnight train to Mexico City because I had a PR task there for Cuervo Tequila. The president of the U.S. distributor was flying in to sign a contract extension, and I'd offered Senor Freytag Gallardo to stage an airport arrival press conference with him and the head of Youngs Market Company. This was all a little alien to his PR people, but, then, so was I. The Cuervo ad agency helped me and obtained, at my request, a three foot diameter globe of the Earth that I wanted for the occasion. Another first rule of getting PR coverage... .*create a good visual to tell your story*. There were several TV crews and I staged Senor Freytag and the American executive doing a hands-across-the-border shake concluding the new contract while each pointed to the other's country on the globe. I noticed the crews shooting me setting it up and I waved them off until I felt it was ready. Then I let them go ahead... handshakes, smiles, pointing to the two countries, a bottle of Cuervo situated in front. That evening I went to the restaurant/bar where I was now in the habit of taking dinner and asked them to turn on the news. There was I on the tv screen, setting up the shot, then turning to wave off the crews and then putting it all together. Everyone in the restaurant thought it was great, considered me their star and wouldn't let me pay. I realized that it was more fun doing PR on the other side of our borders. What I also learned was that the pro-active publicity approaches I'd gathered in my work at Rogers & Cowan, clicked very well in a foreign country where publicity was done less aggressively.

By the time I got back from Mexico to Beverly Hills and to the domestic practice of publicity, I thought I had adventured out of my system and went back to trying to find ways to make PR a worthwhile total involvement. Stu and I were cutting the films, and that seemed to fill up the vacuum I'd been experiencing, and a big vacuum it was because I'd always carried 20 units even while working. But little adventures, like other things that come up from across that border, can be addictive. There had been so many experiences in my first escape-valve adventure out of my own country. For two weeks I had felt like I was IN "The Treasure Of The Sierra Madre." That poor guy mourning his brother and drunkenly massaging me with the point of his pistola was an indelible memory. I'd lived just a little more intensively in those ten or fifteen minutes than in the equivalent time it takes to write the news release for a film deal. When the gun had gone off and I thought I was being blown to kingdom come, what I'd felt was excitement. Maybe discovering I was still alive had something to do with that, but it had been as invigorating as hell. What had filled me up was now what was starting to make me feel emptied out. I knew something else big was brewing and I just didn't recognize it or the price to be paid when it arrived on my doorstep.

Stu's uncle worked at a nearby federally run neuropsychiatric hospital for veterans. Stu's sister Carol taught art to the patients in various stages of psychosis there. Stu knew about some experiments which were transpiring there and he knew my fascination with psychology had never gone away. I was always volunteering for psychological studies. And Stu had heard of a doozy. I wasn't just enticed. I jumped in with both feet. It sounded like a great adventure and something that would give me an edge… or at least an experience… as a writer. It was called pseudo psychosis, the chance to experience insanity without being insane… for no longer than that brief and proscribed period, seven or eight hours at most. If I ever decided really to pursue psycho-therapy as a profession, I could truthfully tell my patients that I knew how they feel.

I went to the hospital/asylum one night after work for an introductory discussion with the noted neuro-psychiatric specialist who was running the program at the hospital. I was familiar with his work through various courses, and he explained the origin and history of a new hallucinatory substance called lysergic acid, noted that it was being used "recreationally" by some people and was being administered by some doctors therapeutically. But given in extraordinarily strong dosages which was the protocol of these tests, he said, it was determined that the subjects experienced very specific psychotic perceptions and behaviors. He told me that it had no residual effect, providing that the subject was basically sane and balanced to begin with . He assured me that they could bring me out at will with another drug. Bear in mind that I'd never even sampled cigarettes, not to mention marijuana, never drank anything stronger than coca-cola and was addicted to nothing beyond really bad practical jokes. They would, the doctor explained to me, put me through the complete bank of Minnesota Multi-Phasic exams, which I'd done in various testings before. The MMP runs the gamut from Rorschach Tests measuring your projective interpretations of ink blots to determine emotional and intellectual functioning and integration, Thematic Apperception Tests in which you're shown picture images and you're required to describe the story they suggest. Of course there's the old and ever-green true-of-false puzzlers, "my mother is poisoning my food" and "people talk to me in my brain," which seem pretty funny when you're sane and quite an accurate capture of the horror inside your head when you're not. The structure of the experiment is that while I was under the influence of the drug, I would take the same test again. I've experienced it both ways. After a few weeks of such testing to make sure I was a lot saner than I sometimes seemed, the date was set. I hadn't even read Huxley's "Doors Of Perception," his adventures into the Mexican hallucinogens like mescaline and mushrooms. Intoxicants held no lure for me, didn't even tease my curiosity. My whole philosophy was based on staying in control. If others around me had a few drinks and got a little crazy, slightly south of coherent, I could get just as crazy but stay in reasonable command of my senses. Substance abuse seemed stupid and pointless to me, still does. But this pseudo psychosis thing, that was interesting. I could BE the lab rat and the scientist at the same time, experiencing things from which most people don't come back. Sure, I'd read "Dr. Jekyll And Mr. Hyde," but I kept telling myself that this was science… lightly marbled with curiosity and the sense that something was afoot.

I fully realized I could wind up with some seriously crossed circuits at the end of the day of the testing. Another young press agent had mentioned that his parents were going to be away, So I asked if I could spend the night at his place. I didn't want my parents or sisters to pick up on the strange vibes I knew I would be emitting. Like eyes wide as saucers or bouncing around like unleashed neurons? I needed a halfway house. The night before the test, Dave told me the halfway house was closed. He had a chance to get laid. Priorities were clear. Somehow, I was not really surprised when, years later, he became one of the town's top producers.

Publicity did not have any real hand in my self-elected and ill-fated trip into the now-infamous lysergic acid testing. I would like to add "unknowing" or "unintentional," but I'm not sure that would be exactly true. I just crashed the wrong party. Chalk that one up one hundred percent to my curiosity and stupidity and my (by then) autonomic habit of volunteering for psychological experiments. I can't blame it on my youth, because when you're 22, you should be capable of better decisions than that. But it was certainly that misadventure which sealed the deal that I would leave my job-for-life at Rogers & Cowan and traipse off to Europe. All of my certainties were washed away in the sudden confusion of pain and fear for my sanity which followed the experiment. If I was going to lose my mind for real, I didn't want to further distress my parents with front row seats. And there's no better diversion from madness… or at least companion for it… than a few good adventures on your own and without a net. Fate was just pulling strings to get me to Paris to meet Gisela. But first I'd had to take a side trip to Mexcio to make those documentaries.

The bus dropped me off in front of the neuro-psychiatric institute at 7:30 that morning and I was directed to the appointed padded cell… at least that's how I conjure the plain little room in the facility's maximum security section… bed, couple of chairs, little table. "Oh, that's in the snake pit," one orderly cheerily embellished his directions. And then I sat down at the little table on which sat a glass of water and a pill. I was attended by the doctor and two huge orderlies who would have to use their muscle a lot that day as I struggled from one stupid impulse to another. As loonies go, I was a pain in the ass. Also there was one of the world's great action and combat photographers, Jack Hamilton. Here is where I eradicate any illusion of heroism from this escapade. I fully intended to do an article entitled "For Eight Hours (it was closer to ten) I Was Insane." I'd spoken to the editors of Coronet and Pageant, the two top pocket-sized monthlies, neither of whom believed I was doing it but if it wasn't bullshit, they'd be happy to take a look at it… providing I was still sufficiently integrated afterwards to write it. Dick DeNeut headed the major photo agency Globe Photos, and he assigned Hamilton to cover it. I'd neglected to inform the doctor or the hospital about that, and there was some consternation, but they really wanted to get that pill down my throat, so they said ok. Jack told me afterwards that it was as intimidating as any battle he'd covered, watching a guy pour that horror down his throat as well as the manic struggles that came after that.

Strangely enough, I remember most of the confusion and fear pretty clearly… to this day… although the nightmares and the rolling high surf of fears for my sanity lasted only about two years. And even more strangely, as the doctor struggled to get me to do the Minnesota Multi-Phasic and other psychological tests, I was nuts and sane at the same time. I was able to remember exactly how I had responded before, but something else was in control of my mind. The thematic apperception tests came just as I went into catatonia, and while I could remember every word of the story I'd previously perceived, I… didn't… have… the… strength… or… desire… to… say… a… word. It… hurt… too… much. Every… word… weighed… too… much to lift up into my vocal chords. I just wanted it all and them all to go away. I wanted the pain to go away. On the other hand, the dervish-spinning top curve of my manic-depression was exhausting… I was manic and maniac in every sense, I couldn't shut up. The doctor asked if I could keep quiet for sixty seconds. Hey, I could do anything. The sonovabitch kept it quiet for five minutes, and I started to scream my just fury at that. It had been twelve seconds. During some schizophrenic phase, I arrived at the questions about my being persecuted and conspired against… yes! yes! a thousand times yes… how could I ever have denied it? The world was awful and it wanted to eat me up. Every so often I caught a glimpse of Jack Hamilton, snapping away, and he seemed more horrified than I was. The only rest I had was in the blanking out period. When they tried to

walk some of it down a notch, I tried to throw myself down an elevator shaft...
except that the elevator was there to receive my falling body... next time I'll try
the windows. They felt they'd better get food into me. The cafeteria was in little
blurts of awareness... the beginning of the line... halfway down... a toasted cheese
sandwich on the table... half of it gone... Jack's face holding back what?... tears?
revulsion? The disorientation of that period hurt almost more than the rest of it,
because I had sharp awareness of how muddled and desperate my brain was.

About when the light started to go... this was in March... they gave me a shot,
and sanity started to return, or at least something I vaguely recalled sanity used to
feel like. But certainty was gone. I knew what madness lay inside my brain, waiting
to come back for me some time when I let my guard down. My friend Al Litrov
picked me up at the front door of the institute. He took one look at me and decided
not to talk or ask any questions. I didn't sleep for the next seventy-two hours. I
was too afraid, afraid to let go of an iron grip on my consciousness, afraid of what
dreams might bring, afraid the dreams would become me and I would just be the
tattered bag in which they carried themselves around. I spent the nights writing the
story of what had happened, experience for experience. I must have slept... nobody
can stay awake that long... but it could have been only when I wasn't looking. All I
remember is the fear of falling asleep. And then I forgot about magazines because
I didn't want anybody to know. That would make it more real. For over two years,
nobody ever read it... except my mother. She, exercising the God-given right of any
Jewish mother, discovered that text while going through my room. I came home one
night to find my parents waiting for me at the door. She'd read it, and it had made
her crazy, too. All she drew from it was that I was an active drug addict. She doted
on me but always figured I would eventually do something to chill the happiness
of her days, and now I had. She kept referring to the LSD as "my reefers," the only
word for an addictive substance that she knew.

My dad alleviated it a bit by reminding her of Vat 59. When I was taking an
art course at UCLA, we had to do a still-life using unusual forms. I can't draw
a stick-man now, but in those days I could do a pencil study that looked like a
photo. To gather suitable shapes for this assignment, I went through my parents'
liquor cabinet and found an interesting bottle, but the label said "Vat 69." Not
being a drinker, I knew nothing about booze, and I didn't know that this was a
brand about which most people were aware, and so, not wanting to put something
in the drawing that might be seen as sexually inappropriate, I'd changed it to Vat

59. The professor was furious about my turning art into a dirty joke. But my dad brought this up and reasoned with my mother that anybody who could be that ignorant of the commonplaces of alcoholic consumption could not possibly be an addictive personality.

As far as I know, only one other person ever read the record of my psychological agonies. I never read it after having written it. But over the years, I did mention it to some friends, including Warren Beatty. One day, a decade or two later, he asked if he could borrow it. He wanted to show it to a friend who was entertaining the idea of doing LSD "recreationally." I don't know if it had any deterring effect. I would hope that some good came out of it.

In a very large sense, it did. It completely altered my life. I was, in its wake, a kind of emotional cripple, living in fear and knowledge of insanity, knowing as a good psych student the high incidence of the crossed wires of psychosis, the theft of lives and personalities. I was in terror of being subjected to that horror once more… There was, as well, my vivid new awareness of the pain and confusion of those afflicted. For years when I saw photos of patients in asylums, staring blankly or pulled into tight fetal knots, I could, quite literally, feel their pain and I would become dizzy and short of breath because of it.

In the months after the LSD experiment, I came to understand that I needed a drastic change of scenery and life, so I got a passport. I had no direction in mind or destination… just somewhere else. At first I thought it would be the Tahiti location of John Huston's filming of Herman Melville's "Typee" (he'd just done Melville's "Moby Dick,") and if it was good enough for Paul Gaugin, it was good enough for me. But that film didn't materialize . There were some films coming up in Europe, and I just needed to be somewhere else. And with that I will resume the peculiar tale of the great personalities who amused and amazed my life and of how publicity fashioned my life by a sequence of fates. But first I wish to recount what was to me an interesting and amazingly somber journey I took in researching after well over fifty years the impetuous and incautious act that shaped everything that followed. The doctor who supervised my test was, I think, legitimately concerned about the toll it had taken on me. He invited me to lunch every Wednesday for six weeks to talk me through it.

For years I assumed it had been an exploration of pseudo psychosis just as I'd been told. A few years after the tests, when Gisela and I were married and remaking our lives in Los Angeles and I'd returned to Rogers & Cowan and to independent publicity, I was contacted by a young man who said he was part of a follow-up survey of people who had taken the LSD tests. LSD was surfacing as a dangerously addictive plaything, and a top LA TV journalist, Paul Coates, had asked me to recount my experiences in order to make the dangers and consequences of it evident to his viewers. That is how this pollster had found me. He was checking into aftermaths, and I learned more from him than he from me. I got the feeling that he, who had been in the LSD program too, was seeking to conclude that the experience had ushered its subjects into drugs, which I gathered was his personal cross. It was my first indication that I might have been part of a larger program of a government agency, although CIA was never mentioned. And I also gathered from him that some, possibly many, of the subjects had committed suicide over the four year period of time. He said he was hired by the government, and I assumed it was the hospital which was part of the VA. A few years later, he stopped coming and, afraid he'd been a suicide, I called the hospital for information, but they had no record of his ever having been employed.

Over the years there were rumors of CIA involvement in such tests, and in the early seventies news about that started to blossom, and I had reason to believe I'd been subjected to that. Most of my fears had faded with the years, but an occasional rage would spring up in which I could exert great strength and irrationality, and Gisela, probably rightly, thought the jolt had burned out some pathways in my brain. The rage part materially shaped my partnership with Jerry Pam. At the very beginning of our association, we went to the Westwood sneak preview of a film starring a new client, and Gisela joined us for that. In those days, one parked in gas stations closed for the night. Knowing that we would want to leave this particular film early, I paid the guy extra to make sure I wasn't blocked in. When we left the theatre an hour later, I was thoroughly blocked, and the attendant and all associated with this station were gone. I picked up an oil drum and flung it at the building, and then lifted one wheel of my car… all right, it was a VW bug… up onto the curb that blocked us, which made it possible for us to leave. Jerry, standing with Gisela and watching this, asked her very apprehensively, "Does he do this often?" It is true that after that he never said no to me in over 20 years, but I assumed that was because we agreed on so many things and that I respected his publicity judgments. Similarly, when our house burned down, I made my way up the burning street in time to see the front of the house ignite. I could climb up to the back of it by scaling a very unstable nine foot fence from the street below, the house being on a steep hill. There was another fence, a staked wooden fence, at the top of the garden, and it was locked from the other side, too. And in my growing rage I just pulled the fence down. I wasn't going to mention that because it fractures the credibility of this story. But it happened, and there it is. When I got to the back of the house, I realized I had a key only for the front door, now fully aflame, and none for the thick glass sliding doors down by the pool. So I picked up a very big potted cactus, the kind it takes me and someone else to lift a few inches off the ground to move, and threw it through a giant picture window to my room. The thing I feared was getting sliced up by shards. Maximilian Schell came with us a few days later to pick among the ruins and the ashes for anything that had made it. He was astounded that the convulsions of the fire had moved the giant plant inside. I looked at it with disbelief, too. The point is, quite apart from the terror that lingered so long, the LSD experience did leave its mark on me. I have no recall of any rage before that time, nor does anyone who knew me. I understand how the others were sufficiently disturbed to have taken their lives.

When we read of a class action suit against the CIA by survivors, Gisela suggested I join it. I declined because, other than a couple of fear-burdened years, for what damage could I seek re-imbursement? Everything good in my life had been impelled by that experience and by my resulting psychic need to re-do my life. Without it, I never would have met Gisela . Secondly, I still wasn't really sure I'd been part of the CIA experiments in mind-control drugs. I had long made the blithe assumption that I was, as in my discussions with Ken Kesey, and yes it was a very mysterious business with the young pollster and his possible tragic fate. So when it came to the writing of this section, I felt I really had to reassure myself that I'd been a CIA stooge… or not. I couldn't write this portion without finally knowing for sure. So the internet and I went at it for a day, and the evidence piled up. I used the name of the doctor involved as my hunting dog, and the facts revealed themselves and an article unfolded in which the doctor acknowledged that the CIA was fully involved… that there was, as he put it, "not one element of the experiments and its conclusions that the CIA did not know." I read of terminal cancer patients who were tested upon without their knowledge. I read of the complicity of great institutions I knew were involved in my own test. I don't want to use the doctor's name or the institutions' names as I'm sure most of those people have passed on by now and they very possibly had paid a high price in reputation or conscience for what had happened. Not as high as the people who committed suicide, if the allegations that such happened are true. The strange fact is that after that research brought me to the undeniable and inevitable conclusion that I had been a pawn, a dupe. After I finally understood what had happened to me, I suddenly felt very ill and very betrayed and I finally could feel a very different kind of rage… helpless and sapped of strength…. for all the people who may have suffered. I knew what they had felt. I don't ignore my own culpability. I'd leaped into it willingly and with partial if not full knowledge of what it involved. Maybe more aware than I'd acknowledged to myself. Twenty-two is too old to say you were too young. But, still, I was sorry I'd finally become so certain, so confirmed. So I'd been used as little more than a human litmus paper. They wanted to see what color lavender or purple or pink I would turn. What happened to the litmus strip afterwards was the litmus strip's problem. It's much easier to live with suspicion and fanciful imaginings than with incontrovertible fact.

Chapter 12

Our Girl, Our Guy

The girl in our story is born in Germany in the mid 1930s to an upper-class, somewhat aristocratic family. Germany is already in the crushing vice of the Nazi regimentation. She is born two years before Kristalnacht, but the nightmare to come is already on the table and in the streets. When the Allied bombing reduces her home town of Cologne to a cathedral surrounded by miles and miles of rubble, she is one of the few in her first grade class to survive. She spends the next five or six years as a nomad whose family dwindles from bombings or from the travails of their being homeless itinerants. Before she is eight, she has learned each dialect and each local scheme of customs wherever the family wanders. She has become adept at stealing coal from machine gun-guarded trains in order to be allowed to go to school where a chunk of coal is the mandatory price of a day's learning, adept at pretending not to see the bodies hanging from lampposts, getting an extra bowl of pea soup by being the perfectly Aryan blue-eyed blonde tot sitting on some *Wermacht* soldier's knee for the happy homeland publicity shot, surviving because a strafing Brtish fighter pilot sees at the last moment that it is a mother and a little girl huddled in frozen fear on the country dirt road watching the bullets pump toward them She has looked out windows on flame-flickered nights watching as the bodies are thrown on horse-drawn carts after a bombing. She has played the game of fitting in to each locality while her parents remain the displaced and mistrusted intruders despised for their perfect German and good manners and urbanity, surviving only by working harder than the jealous country folk upon whose lands and exploitations they are thrown.

The war comes to its desolate end of shattered towns and people, with even little girls clearing the rubble of the old buildings and the old lives. She is sent off to convents to fashion a structured life from which safe haven she is constantly slipping out of windows at night to escape and causing problems in class in order to endure intellectually. But she is compelled to acquire an education in business because her father is rebuilding his factory and she is to be part of it. She determines to have a life in art. At 17, with no money and no other language, she leaves Germany because after all the years of slaughter and coercion and starvation and rigid horror and public death, she sees that the Holocaust is being swept under the national rug. She is too much the rebel in church and school and family to go along. London, ten years after the relentless Luftwaffe Blitz and the V-1 and V-2 rockets, is still pocked with bombsites and hatred of Germans, but she is beautiful and sparkling and again fits in as an au pair. She winds up a few years later in Paris studying at the Sorbonne and at the Alliance Francaise and earning her meager way by ironing and baby-sitting for some communists with whom nobody else will traffic Teachers take her under wings, but she is still just gloriously scraping by. She picks up money from German tourists, showing them underground Paris, decorating her perfect German with a French accent so they think she's part of the city, the real thing. And the real thing is exactly what she is. By this time, still in her teens, she's so vigorously and extravagantly herself that it's almost impossible to cast her… a rabid existentialist smoking Gitannes and sipping her brandy coffee in the same cafes and brasseries as Sartre and de Beauvoir, wearing the costume… tight black jeans, black turtleneck and blue duffle coat, but with high-heeled red pumps instead of the tennis shoes of all the others. The only luxury she affords herself, flashy shoes. Even impoverished, she's already a shoe fetishist.

Our guy… well, you already know his story. …a mainline and placid go-along-get-along guy.…buys charcoal grey jackets and mint green shirts just as others are moving on the next mild fashion compliance… grew up in St. Louis, as a regular kid in that most regular of Midwest towns… finding Tom Sawyer adventures in the preserved wilderness and museums and zoo and other cultural opportunities of the nearby Forest Park while his parents struggle to survive and escape the Depression… living at home all the way through college and even after… 22 and already set in a sort of run-of-the-mill career that he fell into and could 9-to-5 (plus evenings and weekends, actually) the rest of his life without working up a sweat. Dabbles in this and that to cut the boredom... a dibble of documentary filming, an occasional dabble of his leftover college psych habit of volunteering for psychological-tests. Takes the wrong one and finds himself in mid-life crisis thirty years ahead of schedule with all the wheels pulled out from under everything he had held certain. He needs a change of pace, a change of continents, a change of expectations, basically a change of self.

It is at this point that publicity takes over and walks him into the only fate that could fulfill his life. That, obviously, is very melodramatically stated, but "melodrama" isn't given its due. "Drama," of course is "drama" which itself derived from the word for "feat." "Melo" comes from the Greek word for "song." So... a word that conveys the idea of a drama heightened by music... or any experience being *heightened*. Our girl in this melodrama is already in Paris filling her life up with art and philosophy. Coming from the most exquisitely furthest ends of existence and experience, there is no chance in the world that they will ever meet, that they will ever talk, that they will ever discover what if anything they might so improbably have in common. She is the person least likely to share any sensibility with him because she has dangerously dared everything which he thoughtlessly had been handed. She has lived three lives compared to his none. She, on the knife-edge of poverty without a concern in the world, would be the most sure of herself person he would ever meet, and he is no longer even sure of his sanity.

Even his big adventure is well-stocked with security blankets. The job he has come to Paris to look for is looking for *him*. Publicity sets his course. Paris it is, but he finds a lodging in the town's stodgiest arrondissement. The French publicity staff on the film kidnap him and place him in a dingy little hotel room on the Left Bank where Paris truly breathes. It is all suddenly heart-poundingly alive. Now he is within a half mile of her, spending a lot of time at the Cinematheque Francaise, around the corner from the little student hotel, the Moliere, where she lives. It's easy to meet girls in Paris, but not girls like her. End of story? No, publicity steps in again. One of the big competitor firms of Rogers & Cowan is Arthur P. Jacobs Publicity, and Arthur P. Jacobs himself visits the set of "Love In The Afternoon" and contacts our guy because he has another film in Spain starting a few months after the Billy Wilder film winds. He offers our guy a job. And he has a favor to ask. His main client is David O. Selznick, and Selznick's son Jeff is in Paris and he doesn't know how to go about meeting girls there. Jeff Selznick is, if it is possible, even more unworldly than our guy. But the favor is do-able, and young Selznick is directed to meet our guy on Boulevard Saint Michel… Boulemiche … at 8PM that night, just when the young women who are open to life and open to new acquaintance, open to being sat down beside, are just starting to gather at the bistros and bars.

8 PM comes, 8PM goes. Jeff shows up at 10. There are no longer empty chairs next to the girls who might invite you to sit down. Our guy suggests to Jeff that they try it the next night, but Jeff doesn't know if he'll still be in Paris. And, yes, Paris has already taught our guy that you always pursue your tomorrows today or, in this case, tonight. They begin to trek up and down Boulemiche, from the Jardins De Luxembourg to the Rue La Huchette across the Seine from Notre Dame, again and again and again. No empty chairs, but Jeff remains convinced that the night holds promise. At midnight, miraculously, two beautiful blondes, apparently in their late teens, books piled in front of them are sitting at a table at Le Biarritz. Jeff urges an approach, but our guy knows that these aren't the type. At one AM they are still there, and Jeff may be right. They do seem nervous, expectant. Our guy agrees to take a stab at it, knowing that it's pointless. He tries his best French, "*Excusez-moi, Mademoiselle, mais est-ce-que je peux m'assoir ici?*" (Excuse me, miss, but may I sit down here?) And our girl sizes him up, looks over to a table where four men sit, looks back to him and says, "That's ok. You can speak English." The two Americans sit down. Before he can try an opening line about the book on Freud in her pile, she says, "Do you see those four men over there?" Yes, the four men at the other table staring at them through black sunglasses at 1AM. "They're trying to kidnap us." "Kidnap?" He'd heard the rumors or glimpsed news stories about beautiful students, mostly German and Swedish girls, suddenly disappearing from time to time. But human trafficking had not yet struck a chord with media. There was too much other news to fill their pages, news which had convenient beginnings and middles and ends. Disappearances were too vague and didn't resolve. The four guys in such attentive audience are evidence *per se*. Black shades don't blink, and the eyeless gaze is unsettling. The two German students had been studying together, and a car began following them as our girl walked her friend, Doris, halfway home, to the well-lit but only slightly greater safety of Boulemiche. The girls had ducked into the bistro, the four men following immediately thereafter. The standoff is now in its second hour, with

little recourse for the girls. French bistro owners don't poke their noses in other people's business. France's effort to keep Algeria a *department* (federal state) is starting to make things jittery. It is a time when cafes are known to blow up before the morning. Our guy turns to Jeff who is built like a third string defensive tackle, out of shape but big, and with the sweetness which often attends that. "Jeff," our guy says, "when we get up, stand real straight." Our girl rises from her chair, glares at the four men, hooks her arm in that of our guy, and they walk out followed by Jeff and Doris. Outside, cloaked in the relative darkness of the closing-down-for-the-night boulevard, our girl stops to watch what the four men in the black shades will do. They argue among themselves and then stay glumly seated. One of them kicks a chair. Walking the girls to their respective lodgings, a date is arranged for the four to see "Sunset Boulevard" the next night at the *Cinematheque*.

The next evening Jeff has had to return to London and our guy winds up double dating two gloriously beautiful frauleins. Amazingly, Gloria Swanson is at the screening, but he is so captivated by his two new friends that he neglects to ask the great diva to visit Billy Wilder on the "Love In The Afternoon" set. Or maybe it's her silent film grandeur and glamour, very much like that at the end of "Sunset Boulevard," as cineastes crowd around her. And his mind is on something else. Our girl is so outrageously outside his ambition, so beautiful but more than that so concluded and resolved and certain... and also, in her high-heeled pumps, so much taller than he... that he arranges a date with Doris. She reveals during its gentle course that she is studying to be a dentist and then spends the rest of the date responding to unapologetic interrogation about our girl... There's an antique uniform shop next to our girl's hotel, and our guy becomes very interested in antique uniforms and spends much time staring into its windows. Days into this, after the girls with whom she shares her apartment, resenting this bumbling stalker, complain to her of his constant hovering, she surprises him as he is looking in the *objets militaire* window. "I think you're making the man who owns this shop nervous. Why don't you just ask me to dinner? I'm free on Friday." She becomes the most interesting person... not just girl, but person... he's ever met or ever will, and they do seem to have attitudes in common if certainly not histories. He spends his time at the used book stalls along the Seine buying her inexpensive books of poetry which he annotates with reams of observation of how the verses apply to him and her. Every morning her mailbox in the hotel is filled with letters, poems and annotated poetry books from him. D.H. Lawrence is his biggest ally, and soon Lawrence's poems "The End"...

> "And, oh, that you had never, never been
>
> Some of your selves, my love ; that some
>
> Of your several faces I had never seen!
>
> And still they come before me, and they go ;
>
> And I cry aloud in the moments that intervene."
>
> and "Trust"...
>
> "Oh be, oh be a sun to me, Not a weary, insistent personality."

become the themes of his devotion, a gesture not lost on her. The half dozen French guys, doctors, lawyers, who are pursuing her furiously, often several of them dining her together like a club of devotees, become very discouraged. They couldn't read much less write the volumes of communication that spill out of her mail box. They can take her to restaurants our guy can't afford, but he does get her a job as an extra on the scene shot at Maxims where Billy Wilder, being Billy Wilder, wants his extras to sample the cuisine of that supreme eatery. One evening our guy brings her papers to apply for American citizenship, but she is merely and politely bemused. The problem is, he can afford to take her to dinner only once a week. Still sometimes there are chance meetings, and then more often the evenings' conversations which follow take them to Les Halles at 1 AM, where a dollar bowl of onion soup *gratinee* is better than any dinner even in this uttermost city of cuisine. And on one foggy wee small hour when they exist separate from the world on their way back to the *Rive Gauche*, halted on the *Pont Neuf* to listen to the silent song of the Seine below and the nighttime murmur of Paris, it all assumes its romantic destiny. There are things more romantic than sex, unquenchable longing for one and the desperate strivings to express it... to become it. And that romanticism absorbs him totally in the month of glowing new existence which flows from *Pont Neuf* like the river itself.

And then "Love In The Afternoon" is over and the holidays invade their lives. She returns to Germany for a rare visit with her parents, and he goes to London to buy an English-keyboard portable typewriter. He's ready to begin his career as a writer. He, at last, sees the world in all of its infinite dimension. While he's there, he visits the Piccadilly offices of publicist extraordinaire and all-around good guy and wild man, Jerry Juroe, who is overseeing the press on "The Prince And The Showgirl" then filming with Marilyn Monroe and Laurence Olivier. It seems a task bursting with tension, and at the end of a frustrating phone conversation, the excitable Juroe slams the phone back on its cradle so hard that it disintegrates in his hand. He regards with some perplexity the shard he still holds. It is right out of a Preston Sturges film. Our guy decides he would like to work with Juroe.

When he gets back to Paris, he moves into a hotel closer to that of our girl and begins to parade the street in front of her hotel night and day to kill time until she gets back. And then one morning in early January she is miraculously back, and he races up the flights of steps to her room, and when she opens the door it is with an expression he hasn't seen, a different and reserved expression, rather cool and tenuous, and she suggests they go down into the Jardins de Luxembourg to talk. Wasting no words… she never would… saying it straight… she always would… she tells him that there's something she has neglected to tell him. She's been engaged to someone else for a half year. The air, he discovers, has somehow become so heavy that it just won't suck in. It was someone she'd met in London, an engineer, solid and purposeful unlike our guy (she doesn't say it, he intuits it,) and he'd come over the holidays to the Black Forest to meet her parents. They'd liked him, and her father had felt this was someone who could take over his steel strapping factory.

Paris suddenly becomes very pointless and painful. Sure, he can still see her, glimpse her, watch her, but why? He is excluded from her life. He immerses himself in movie houses running Marx Brothers films around the clock. The Left Bank and other *arrondisements* are full of them. He buys books like "Auntie Mame" to amuse away his dark and pursuing thoughts, but the books always wind up at some chapter where nephew Patrick loses the girl of his dreams and succumbs to the madness of despair. It is his depressing discovery that every funny and distracting book seems to have such a chapter. What next? Well, there is the film in Spain in March, and Paris is almost too cold to walk about brooding, which every once-shared corner or bridge invites him to do.

So he buys a train ticket for Barcelona. They change trains at the border city of Perpignon because Generalissimo Franco has made his country's rails all narrow gauge so that enemy armies on their wide gauge trains cannot just roll in past your defenses and destroy you… very much like a vibrant and dazzling girl engaged to another man. A distraught lover's problem is that he doesn't come with built-in narrow gauge rails. Then an overnight ship to the island of Mallorca. Arriving in Palma, he has a tourist office book a room in a remote farm where he can concentrate on becoming a great screen writer. That will definitely show her. The designated stone farm is so remote that the electric bulb isn't bright enough to type by until everyone else goes to sleep, and then the clatter of his little portable causes a revolution among the would-be sleepers. It is colder inside than outside, and the menu is cauliflower mush for breakfast, cauliflower soup for lunch and fried cauliflower for dinner… day after day. No one tells you that cauliflower is the staple food of Mallorca. You have to make that delightful discovery for yourself. The next little town, Valdemosa, is too expensive because that's where Chopin and Georges Sand had lived, and visiting music lovers pay a premium for such proximity. So our guy hitches a ride to the little railroad terminal town of Soller, where a room in the Hotel Guia next to the station is only $1.64 a night including three meals. The hotel owner proves to be the greatest cook our guy will ever encounter, and many of the world's greatest and most lauded chefs will be his friends.

And there he finds people to fill up his life and give the illusion of forgetting. This cut-rate paradise is sprinkled with European and American expatriates, each with his or her own sad and funny story and reason for being there in soft and desperate retreat. There is, for instance, the fiftyish English woman whose life has dribbled down to nothing and who has come to Soller because it is an inexpensive nowhere and who had responded to Spanish immigration officials when they filled out her papers that she had no profession and so they had written "without" which in Spanish is "*sin*" ("seen" in Spanish but "sin" in English) and "profession: *sin*" is the first distinction her life has accorded and she feels like someone here. There is the American screenwriter, 60, who had drunk away her career and who is in Soller because the gin is only 40 percent alcohol instead of 80 proof so she can drink twice as much, ignoring the fact that 80 proof *is* forty percent. The expats wile away mornings at café tables over coffee, jointly solving the word puzzle in the Herald Tribune which is now up to nine hundred dollars which, even divided, would be a way out. But some arcane word always eludes them, postponing their salvation. The small Mediterranean fishing port of Puerto Soller is a short trolley car ride to the west, and a Dutch lesbian couple, who never utter anything more than the obligatory Mallorquin greeting of "*dia*," arrive from there on their motor scooter each morning at eleven. The locals call *them Las virgenes de la Vespa*… The Vespa Virgins. There are the Germans and Swiss and Italians and Danes for whom this is the last place to flee, penniless painters and former painted women, concentration camp survivors and other survivors of life and love playing out their days and scraping by where the scraping is easy, although the prices have a worrisome habit of going up each year, all wondrous personalities of breathless fragility and sadness and eventual doom. He tucks it all away for a book to be called "The Other Side Of The Island" that he will never write because there are too many people whose hearts, already broken, could be broken again. He knows and respects the broken heart.

Two post cards arrive (at the Palma American Express office) from our girl, and he gloomily observes that the pictures are London landmarks. He forces himself to read them, and they are merely kind and cheery, how depressing since he knows she had gone to be with her fiancé, and they tell how Jeff Selznick has offered her roles in films (she does look like the Ingrid Bergman of "For Whom The Bell Tolls" only younger) or film production jobs. His copy of "Auntie Mame" becomes the rage of the expat community, and he gives them all of his books. He's busy writing. Our girl's pleasant notes only confirm that she is in his past, and nothing will really distract him from that reality until he starts the new film in Madrid. And then one day a British mother and her twenty year old daughter, newly arrived visitors to Soller, are on the little train to Palma where he goes once a week to collect any mail and to buy the latest edition of the International Herald Tribune. The crises he has worried about the whole week since his last newspaper are always forgotten in pages filled with furor over something new about which to worry. He never learns how anything turns out. Well, if they can forget, maybe so can he. As the train begins departure, he offers to help the two British women close their sticking window which extends behind their seat where a man in the seat behind them has placed his hand half inside and half outside the window while conversing with a friend who is walking along the quai as the train slowly lurches away. The window unsticks with crashing suddenness, and our guy and the women immediately realize they have smashed their fellow passenger's hand. The man is less quick to the discovery. His conversation pleasantly concludes with words called back to his friend, and he turns and sees his fingers in their distressed situation, and he screams out in somewhat tardy pain. Our guy and the two women are joined in a conspiracy of suppressed laughter subverted as first one and then another of them bursts into frantically withheld giggles. This daisy chain of guilty spasms continues several miles toward Palma, following which a conversation proceeds in which he realizes that the girl is as beautiful a porcelain-skinned English rose, blonde of course, as he has ever seen.

In short order, she becomes the potential distraction for which he has longed for lo these many (six) weeks. She has great sweetness and the attraction of being as uncertain of her life as our girl is certain of hers. Compounding his necessary address of the English girl's insecurities is the fact that he is still struggling in the losing cause of putting the horrors of the pseudo-psychosis experiment behind him. Forget post-traumatic. He's still in mid trauma. Unsure of his own sanity, he fears all the more the complexities and pitfalls of someone else's doubts. She is a communist and yet when they visit cathedrals, she prostrates herself on the floor. On the other compelling hand, Our Girl, a Catholic, had merely lighted candles. But there's nothing to make you remember/forget romance like romance, so he and his English friend both try, and he feels she's in the process of forgetting something, too. He hopes he helps her as much as he hopes she helps him. There is, he discovers, a great caring for people in her compassionate dedication to saving the world from capitalism.

There are, in the little Mallorquin town of Soller, no bookstalls on the Seine for him to explore in search of pertinent and annotatable books of poetry. But he has a pretty good memory, and he can recite many poetic thoughts verbatim for her delight and her sense of being valued. Of course the one closest to his heart and best remembered is D.H. Lawrence's "The End." So much for the integrity of love, but he is in pursuit of important purpose, replacing love with love, and all's fair in love and war, especially when they are one and the same. So "The End" becomes an anthem in his new relationship, too, and Madrid looms not far ahead in case things get too serious. Which seems to be her point of view, too. A fling has its own rules and rationale and its own defined boundaries.

This is where publicity comes in to guide his steps and his fate once more. On one Palma visit, there is a note from Arthur P. Jacobs informing him that the film in Madrid has been cancelled. With no mandatory and immediate destination, or prospect of income for that matter, where does he take his broken heart now? He cannot return to America in this tattered and unresolved state of heart. And what about a fling that is suddenly without a defined curtain call? He is lost in limbo. However, not to worry because publicity is still looking out for him and commanding his fate. The next visit to Palma brings a letter from Jerry Juroe who has signed to do the unit publicity on a Bob Hope film entitled "Paris Holiday," and Juroe wants our guy to be his back-up. The title alone raises a jumble of emotions. Paris instead of Madrid. Juroe insists it will be fun. With the March deadline now back on, there is once more a fixed final scene or next to final scene of his happy distraction in the garden of English beauty. As a remembrance, she gives him a silver bracelet engraved with the Spanish word "*fin*"… pronounced "feen" and meaning "The End," a nod to Lawrence, a nod to the reality of a friendship now diverting onto separate paths. But he knows he will wear it forever.

Upon his return to Paris, again residing a block or so from Boulemiche at the tacky and inexpensive Luxembourg Hotel, the fifth floor garret from which he can see the Tour Eiffel if he leans a bit too far out the window. The downside and the upside is that he is risking seeing our girl in case she ever gets back from all of her opportunities, romantic and professional, in London. Risking that heart-wrenching and maybe seeking it, he discovers that she is, in fact, not returned. That is in a way a relief, since his English friend is visiting him in Paris on her way back to London. He is, above all, a coward. That goes well and sweetly, the bracelet glistening on his wrist, and then is over. And soon Paris suddenly explodes once again into Paris when he spies the clear brow of our girl as she is buying a baguette at a local boulangerie. He watches her from across the street. On the next chance sighting, it is she who sees him. She comes over and smiles, "Maybe we'll have a chance to talk." It is so pointedly, politely and excruciatingly casual. Casual is the death nell of hope. The proximities of Left Bank life provide that the encounters are more frequent, but always her glowing friendliness is painfully kind, never any allusion to or reflection of any of the romance that had once passed between them. It is nothing more than the extension of an acquaintanceship. The Left Bank is somehow a place where you always see people you are fated to see. Perhaps he should move.

He strikes up a friendship with an actress on the set of the Hope film and, *mon dieu*, another blonde. What is it with him? But it makes the now-more-extensive conversations with our girl almost bearable. He can try to delude himself that he actually has a life of his own. Our girl finds him easy to talk to and, in painful irony, she chooses him as her confidante. The long (for someone still just 20) and amazing story of her life and experiences is utterly fascinating and fills him again with the wonder of which love is compounded. Life is full of rash decisions, and hers, perhaps because of chaotic dangers of her childhood, is particularly impetuous and yet strangely rational and informed. She is the most stable person he's ever known. One evening she discusses the jobs she had been offered in London, with good pay and opportunities. That she had returned to the poverty of her studies is so rash that it simply defies our guy, especially since her fiancé is in London. He asks her if she did it for this reason, and she says no, for that reason and no again, and again on the third and the fourth. He is out of possible reasons. "Well, then," he says, "I guess it's an enigma." "What does enigma mean?" she asks. "A puzzle without an answer." She suddenly smiles and says, "Yes, *that's* why I did it... my enigmania." All of his good resolve not to love her is shredded by that true and over-riding factor. She's an enigmaniac. What could be more compelling, more unrelenting in its grasp?

He plays the dispassionate friend role well, but it takes a toll. Her vivacity and originality tattoo her upon his longing. He shares his feelings, too, but he never mentions the English girl. Soon they are seeing each other for long conversations in the little lobby of his hotel or over chocolate (for him) and jet black coffee (for her) at cafes or bars several times a week, the mutual revelations and philosophizing going well into the night. The world is a whirlpool of might-have-beens for him. The confidences are so evident of "best friend" status, trusted friend, as to rob him of any residual hope that it might again be more, but he is addicted to the sad compensation and excitement of her company.

One night when they are visiting other parts of Paris, they are on a metro train that goes over the Seine at one point and the window is open to savor the suddenly fresh air. And, out of the deep blue of the Paris night, she says, "Throw the bracelet in the river." F-I-N in Spanish is pronounced feen and it means "The End", and F-I-N in French is pronounced faan (with the merely-hinted French N).... and it means "The End." He knows that his response will determine the rest of his life, and he takes off the silver bracelet he'd vowed never to remove and throws it into the Seine.

Chapter 13

Deciding to Write It Down

Over the years I'd toyed with the idea of jotting down some of the memories. I'd pulled selected ones out of a hat in campaign meetings from time to time as they related to or illustrated some point of discussion. I'd been privileged to work with many of the great talents and personalities of our business/art over a tumultuous half century and much beyond and continue to do so. Why quit when you're ahead? Ahead is terrific. I'd had the opportunity in ways that others hadn't to observe what made these renowned people extraordinary and what made them human. Some incidents could teach others in the same way they had instructed me, a hard-earned lesson here, someone's surprising observation there. We all haul out and share our experiences throughout our lives. It's one of the luxuries of communication. But at a certain point it starts to define you as an old codger, an expression which probably comes from the obsolete "cadger" which meant peddler. If I had become in my work and in my life an old codger, a peddler of tales, why not write it down and be done with it? But between Gisela's raising our family and my building a career and then a business and our growing up and burning down and writing scripts few of which would get made, who had the time?

One night, my dreams were full of Warren Cowan and our shared bits of life. I awoke and for a few hours wrote down those anecdotes which had for some reason insisted themselves back into mind's focus for those vivid hours or however long dreams take. I was surprised to find the dialogue as bright and clear for me as when we lived it. I've always told my memories in their dialogue because that's what they came wrapped in. I arrived at the office a bit anaesthetized from lack of sleep, which proved to be a good thing. The first tidings of the day were crushing. Warren had passed away that very night. One of the things to which I've looked forward over the winters of Oscar season strategy meetings was that he was on so many of the same films and that I could refresh my own pilot light with his untiring invention and enthusiasm.

His funeral had a Hollywood premiere cast and a Greek chorus of all the great press agents who had passed through Warren's brain. Paul Bloch was the most faithful and enduring of Warren's mentees/collaborators, and he and Pat Kingsley were the most successful. Paul and I were exchanging memories after the service, and I told him of the strange nocturnal visitation I'd experienced, the fly-by of remembrance the night of his passing. I confessed it was moving me to put between covers the bizarre experiences of a life in PR, always in proximity and service to the talent and fame of great artists of our time. Now, however, I felt I wanted to write it as a way of documenting Warren's verve and his messianic invention of our business. "Then do it now," Paul said sternly. "Now?" I asked, surprised that it seemed such an urgent point to him. Warren's widow... the second Barbara in his eclectic sequence of wives, third, actually if you count his having married Barbara Rush twice (and who wouldn't have? Either Barbara)... had given Paul Warren's notes and dictations for his autobiography, almost complete. Paul had been taking them to publishers to memorialize what had made Warren special. "You know how they always say 'dead men tell no tales?'" Paul said. "Yeah," I nodded, "I think it was Al Capone who said it first." "Well," Paul noted sadly, "it's publishers who say it now. They won't touch an autobiography or memoir unless the author is able to tour and do the book signings. Can't do that after they bury you." "I plan to be cremated," I told him. "Well," he said, "that proves my point."

I have a memory for what delights me. And in a business of so many clever people, you develop a knack for hanging on to deserving *bons mots* and originalities of conversation. I collect them like other people collect stamps. The cast of characters of a life in PR is diverse and memorable. Their ways with a word or a phrase are well worth the effort of remembrance, the gestures and thought processes of each so very much his or her own. I will be relatively truthful about my lies, so why would I bother to lie about the truth? Sure, there are places in stories where I could embellish them, pump them up, construct a funny line. I know how to do that. But if you don't stick absolutely to what you remember, you lose your place. This is all how I remember it having happened. And my memory is reliable. Yes, I will camouflage anything I think might embarrass someone. An important part of a publicist's credo is *"not at someone else' expense."* The little protective gauze in which I cocoon a few of these tales doesn't alter the point or the other-people's wit which made the stories memorable.

About the idea of relating anecdotes in dialogue: We live our lives out in dialogues. Scrupulously verbatim? They were pretty indelible. They stuck to the mind's walls, tucked away to draw upon… maybe to steal for a scene in a script or maybe for the sheer delight of the something-learned aspect of the memory. Almost every good line I've written for a woman in a script was something I'd heard Gisela say or was uttered by one of the other originals to whom my life has exposed me, the extraordinary women and men I've touched. *Sometimes it would be incident or gesture more than dialogue…* Michael Crawford's going in to see his wife Gabrielle in the hospital after delivery of their first child. The sign on the door (this was in England) read "engaged," and he scratched it out and wrote "married." Conversations which I don't find compelling are gone from recall the moment the cochlea of my inner ear stop quivering, but other expressions and thoughts and gestures have stayed the decades.

I retained even the character-revealing experiences of others. Once when Pat Kingsley and I shared an office and client responsibilities at Rogers & Cowan, Pat made a run to 20th to go over contact sheets of production and set photos with Doris Day. I believe it was when she was shooting "Move Over, Darling" with Jim Garner. Pat came back with the report of her and Doris' having discovered several shots of Doris, clad for the scene in a negligee, bending over to pick up something at which moment her gown, surrendering to gravity, revealed her bosom in its rather splendid totality. It was a moment of startlement for Doris and Pat, the kind of moment which could have occasioned outrage, embarrassment or frustration., Doris however, according to Pat's report, laughed and commented, "Well, that ought to put to rest the myth of the boyish breasts."

While I try to avoid tried-and-true lines that can get you out of specific situations, Warren Cowan was a master of them. And they always worked because he delivered them with such enthusiasm and spontaneity that they seemed to have sprung from the moment. If a meeting was going too long and getting repetitive, Warren's impatience would catapult him from his chair and he would shout, "Let's make it happen!!" in a manner that made everyone else in the room leap up, too, to celebrate that sealed dedication. They would then charge happily from the room like a Notre Dame team after a Knute Rokne halftime exhortation. And very often he did make it happen.

Any press agent's life swarms with so many remarkable characters that the press agent may seem the least relevant persona in his own existence, drowned out by all the great voices who roar through his life. The press agent is sometimes not even an animate object in the scenes of his professional pursuits. Using hydration as a metaphor for how a press agent functions in the serving of client needs, if an artist's career requires a slug of hard-earned respect, a sip of accurate reportage or a gulp of deserved awareness, washing it down with an ounce or two of due fame, the press agent is the cup by which essential bodily fluid is rendered. With that functional invisibility as a career device, if you're good at observing and listening and remembering, you can soak up remarkable and antic life without ever having to be remarkable or antic yourself. We publicists are absorbent and vicarious ciphers.

Is total recall possible? Exhibit A… actress/author and long-time client Marilu Henner. She's a textbook example of hyperthymesia, instant access to almost everything stored in her brain. She can give you the day of the week for any date of any millennium, recount, for instance, the date of Princess Diana's death because she can recall in detail the circumstance and conversation during which she learned of that tragedy. During our decades representing her… actress, musical star, talk-show host, best-selling author… I've never stumped her precise recollection of any event or fact.

The rest of us hang memories on hooks. Places make very good hooks. Gisela and I stayed only once at the esteemed Elysees Hotel in Manhattan, but I left with several fond memories in my bag. I was just coming into the lobby on a rainy day when I saw one of New York's top film journalists waiting at the bank of house phones, one pressed to his ear, his overcoat dripping from a long walk without umbrella. I went over to say hello and quickly I saw it was the wrong time. He was pissed. A Bergman film was opening and the writer was there to interview Erland Josephson, who must have answered the phone just as I arrived. "Mr. Josephson," the journalist said, "there are no taxis to be had on a rainy day in New York, so repeat after me. The Elysees Hotel is at 64 Fifty-fourth Street and NOT at 54 SIXTY-fourth Street."

I went up to relate this to Gisela, but she was in a state of unhappiness with the blatant colors of the wall-paper. She's an artist and dueling colors clash in her brain. "It's a terrific hotel," I said, "lots of artists stay here. Marlon Brando." The phone rang and it was a New York friend who reiterated that the Elysees is a great hotel." "Not according to Gisela," I said. "Really," he wondered, "what room are you in?" Three sixteen (or something.) "Oh my God," he said, "Tennessee Williams DIED in that room." "Darling," I called to Gisela, "Tennessee Williams died in this room." "He must have choked on the wallpaper," she reasoned. How many of our memories reside in hotels. And I found out years later that he actually had choked.

The Way Press Agents Are Perceived

If you venture to write a book about having been and still being a press agent, you have to share with your reader what press agenting actually is. You have to convey what, if anything, it means in the grand scheme of things and, in the Darwinian sense, how and why it evolved.

It is widely held that P.T. Barnum invented the concept of entertainment promotion in the 19th century, but he was a master of an ancient craft. Itinerant minstrels, story tellers, religious advocates, town criers, drummers (think 'drumming up interest') and trumpeters (think 'trumpeting his glories,') pamphleteers and muralists or graffiti artists... they all served the purpose of what for the past century and a half have been called "advance men." Travelling players, commedia dell arte troops, performers of feats of wonder of all kinds... they all required advance men... even in Biblical times. In its most humble and heart-breaking illustration, Giulietta Masina as Gelsomina, Anthony Quinn's "drummer" in "La Strada." Hamlet served as the advance PR guy for the stage company that visited Elsinore. Every "opry" troupe or snake oil salesman, the distinguished artists like Lily Langtry or Edwin Booth playing the towns of our western frontier had a "front man," someone preceding them, posting ads and spreading the word.

Enter Warren Cowan

So Warren Cowan wasn't the first press agent by far, but when he started, the idea of hiring a *personal publicist* was just becoming an indispensible entourage adjunct for actors who were suddenly and perilously cutting loose from the studio star-building systems in the late '40s, early '50s. That is when Warren started, shortly after completing his Air Force service in WWII. It was a perfect time for a night-and-day hunter of new clients like Warren. The vast percentage of stars were still unrepresented. Everyone was up for grabs. Even when I entered the trade in 1954/55, the studio contract system still prevailed in the film business. Most stars were under contract to a studio, and the studios not only PROVIDED each and every actor's publicity, they DEMANDED that control, control that was all-inclusive, all-intrusive...

They gave actors names, insisted that some gay performers take spouses of the opposite sex, dressed them not only for their roles and their photos but for their private lives (since the studios didn't really believe in private lives.) They concocted the stars, determined many of the stars' favorite activities and favorite friends, dictated dating, created new names and fabricated their prior lives through the simple fiat of diddling with factuality of biographies, sent them on USO and war bond sales tours to effect how the public viewed them and how the public viewed Hollywood. The studios, after all, HAD created them with the assign-ment of roles and the focus of attention, reshaped them with diction lessons and fencing lessons and athletic training for the specific niche of each actor in the studios' larger plans. It was a dictatorship not only of contractual strangleholds ("morals clauses,") but also of opportunity, the sluice gates of which the studio bosses opened or closed at their will (of which they were never lacking) or their discretion (not a common denominator.)

The studios could make or break an actor or actress, young or old, by assigning career-helpful or career-hurtful roles at the studios or in loan-out deals to other studios. The actor either went along or was sent on his merry way. The studio publicity bosses truly and comprehensively made and kept the stars who they were, and the stars had better not forget it. But some of them didn't want to be manufactured and wrapped in cellophane. Increasingly, the strong-willed and the talented and those empowered by the very degree of their stardom balked at the control and fabrication. Some were sufficiently armed with fame and self-respect to do something about it. Bette Davis and Jimmy Cagney famously confronted the super-feared Jack Warner and even won some battles. By the late '40s, the hiring of independent press agents became a symbol of their assuming control of that part of their lives. Especially after the federal government's anti-trust separation of studios from ownership of theatre chains, independent films started to noodle their way into the supply line, and actors started to have alternatives to studio domination. The entertainment media, which in some ways had been as much under the studio thumb as the actors were, liked the idea of a market-based flow of news and access to stars, and they formed friendships with the new "indie shops" that were gaining prominence.

Warren Cowan's partner, Henry Rogers, had made a living of indie PR from the mid-'30s, prevailing against all odds and planting the roots of the craft deep and strong. Warren then came in and imposed his giant concepts and his indefatigable energies on the new industry, so much so that in the span of a few years, he was Henry's partner in a very successful yin and yang. When I stumbled into their company, Rogers & Cowan was the undisputed master-house of the trade. I literally never had entertained the thought that publicity could be a field of gainful employment because I never knew it existed. It was all new to me, even though I'd been training for it all my life.

Seeing it first through Warren's and Henry's eyes was like learning to fly from Wilbur and Orville Wright. They didn't impede my developing my own perspective that would eventually send me off on my own. It took me over fifteen years (spread over an 18 year span) to make that move. Maybe I was a slow learner, or maybe there was, quite simply, a lot to learn.

Once you're your own boss, it's hard to go back to servitude to anyone or anything other than your clients' needs. 'Most of the major publicity firms were being bought up by larger media companies starting in the early '80s, it was something Jerry Pam wanted to explore as a next and logical step for Guttman & Pam. He referred several attractive offers to me, selling them hard. Gisela opposed it, questioning why I would want to buy myself a boss. "They'll just pay you what you would have paid yourself, and load you up with stock options that will never pay off. And, above all, they'll never understand or go along with any of your instincts and quirks." It was a philosophical disagreement that brought her to sever my partnership with Jerry,

With the corporatization and subsidiary incorporation that has recently been the fate of many… and, indeed, the aspiration of most… independent PR firms, the unaffiliated indie is becoming a dying breed. I always wanted to be part of a dying breed. It's somehow a little romantic or, at least, idiosyncratic. The big companies, in the process of conforming to the corporate cultures of the companies that had purchased them, had become themselves compartmentalized, bristling with specialized units. That would make me crazy. At one point, I learned that my alma mater, Rogers & Cowan, the firm that helped give birth to indie PR's flamboyant and guiltlessly imaginative past, now had a "faith-based division." I struggled with the congruity of that until I realized that Guttman Associates had pioneered faith-based PR in the mid-'90s.

That occurred when CBS had hired us to convince CBS (I kid you not) to greenlight "Touched By An Angel" as a series. Andy Hill, who headed CBS Productions, engineered that one because he intuited what a hit the series could be. It was a bet that paid off in the hundreds of millions. The surprising details of our test flight with the Angels are described in a chapter entitled, appropriately "Damage Control." Who better to sell anything faith-based than Hollywood PR guys and gals? Every crazy idea we wing out is an act of faith.

Warren Cowan preached and lived by the gospel *of persistence, persistence, persistence.* I had the delightful occasion a dozen or so years ago to see Warren get masterfully worked over by the strategy himself. It occurred at the Screen Actors Guild Awards at which Kirk Douglas, once again securely a Warren Cowan client, was getting a special honor. Our daughter Danielle, then one of the heads of the Entertainment Industry Foundation, the show biz charity arm, had made a tie-up with the start-up new internet search engine, Excite, a tie-up which would bring a cool million dollars to her wide charities. Crucial to the deal was that right after receiving his award, Kirk would do a live exclusive interview on Excite. A transmission area had been set up just off the press areas. Danielle had obtained Warren's commitment that Kirk would do the interview after he finished the press. I was honcho-ing it for Danielle, but when he got to the end of the press, Kirk told Warren to take him back to his table. I angrily reminded Warren of his commitment, but he wasn't going to buck Kirk. Danielle saw Kirk sailing back to his table in the auditorium and went face to face with Warren with heated charge that he was costing her charities a million dollars. But Warren said he didn't have a gun big enough to make Kirk do it. "Well, I do," she said, and slipped away through the tables to kneel down beside Kirk's chair. There are three things our kids inherited from their mom... charm, brains and persistence, which Gisela ladled out in gobs to both of her daughters, with Monika applying hers to investigative journalism and activism. "A hundred to one she doesn't," Warren said as Danielle sought to persuade the notably intractable Hollywood legend... Spartacus, The Champion, the guy with the steel jaw and the steel resolve. It took Kirk about three minutes to melt. As Warren and I followed Danielle and Kirk into the elevator and up to the Excite room, Kirk, evidently amused at his own capitulation, said to Warren, "The kid's a helluva scheister." To which Warren replied, "You're telling me." "Persistence, persistence, persistence," I said to Warren. "Yeah, but you loaded the dice. It's like dealing with Gisela. Who do I make the check out to?" "The Entertainment Industry Foundation," Danielle instructed. He made it out for *two* hundred. You don't turn out kids with a cookie cutter, but both of our girls turned out to be tough cookies.

Warren well knew the futility of going up against Gisela. When our house burned down, Guttman Associates and Warren Cowan Publicity were operating together. It was one of his periodic interludes of bachelorhood, and he graciously offered us use of a small pied a terre apartment he had in Beverly Hills which we occupied for the two weeks it took Gi to find the right house to rent. She was so protective of the few items she had saved and of all the new replacement possessions we were compelled to buy night after night, that she wouldn't even let his cleaning lady in. She brought in her own maid... tried, trusted and trained to Germanic order. During that period, Gisela was in the office one day and I overheard Warren advise her that he hoped she wouldn't be at the apartment on a specific afternoon because there was a meeting that he needed to have there. "Warren," she said, "just get that out of your mind. You're not having any meetings in a bed I'm sleeping in."

I had only one face to face with Danielle in all of the years that we represented (at a very below-market price, by my choice) the Entertainment Industry Foundation for her and the EIF president, Lisa Paulsen. It was a crucial Earth Day back when the environmentalists were just trying to crank up a very lagging public concern about our deteriorating planet. It was a fund-raising walk starting on the Universal back lot, wending through the streets of Burbank, through the NBC and Warner Bros. lots, per Danielle's arrangements, and then back to the start. We had about 20,000 walkers, remarkable since that day the city was on trouble alert because there had just been a ruling in the Rodney King trials. Jay

Leno and Leonard Nimoy were hosting it for me, and we had several dozen top celebrities… Chevy Chase, Jane Seymour, Olivia Newton John, Woody Harrelson, Jack Palance etc. on hand for the pre-walk ceremonies. The tensions of the day had us running late, and Danielle wanted the walk to start, to skip the ceremony and just have Jay send the walkers off. She was afraid of losing her traffic hold on the streets. I said that the people wanted to see the stars and the stars had hit their marks at 7:30 AM and deserved to be seen. I streamlined it, proposing that each star go up to the mic, introduce himself/herself and say one great sentence about environmentalism. Danielle said, "Well, I'm pulling rank. I'm your boss." And I replied, "Well, I'M pulling rank. I'm your father." Paternity trumped client privilege. The stars breezed through their green greetings quickly and everyone was pumped up with shared passion and ready to hit the streets.

The coverage, camera crews and photographers, was quite remarkable because the truth was that this was the only action in town. Fear about what might erupt in the streets… the court had taken a pass on disciplining the accused officers in the Rodney King incident… seemed to give everybody in every part of town a great reason to stay home and catch the action on TV. The last such situation had triggered rioting and violence. Except there wasn't any action or reaction this time. The wonderful news was that the city had kept its head, and the streets were relatively empty… except in Universal City and Burbank where Danielle had filled them with environmental activists. The news for that morning wasn't self-destruction but self-preservation. The cameras focused on the starting line, and Leonard Nimoy, flanked by the usual Charlie Chaplin, Elvis and Groucho Marx lookalikes strode the first steps of the five kilometer march, and thousands surged forward in sequence behind him.

Danielle got the preparations underway for the big party of music and food and sponsor goodies that would greet the walkers on their return, and finally I told her to get in the car with me because I wanted to show her something. She had arranged for the route to be the first studios (plural) tour in Hollywood history, looping NBC, Warner Bros and back to Universal for the activities promoting a clean and salvaged planet. There were officers and barricades protecting the walkers from traffic at each cross street, but we were the only traffic. We drove along the route, thousands of people jubilantly forming a river of life in a town which had for that day decided to play it safe. The sense of having stood up for normalcy and hope pervaded the group. "Look at that, darling," I said, "you put them there." "Their concern for a livable planet put them there," she said, and she looked at all the happy and involved faces and I saw a little smile of pride. "Let'a go back and get the word out," she said, covering it up.

Our daughter Monika solved the problem which for a very long time made me doubt I could move all these recollections to publication. Moni is a tough-minded journalist, cutting through to the hard, cold facts of any story, tempering it as do so many gritty journalists with a heart of soft, malleable, even molten gold. During the early formulation of this writing, I showed a few chapters to Warren Beatty who understood that this was a grateful and loving recall of and tribute to the exorbitant mass of talents for whom, with whom, I'd been privileged to work. The title he suggested was right on the nose and totally impossible. "Call it 'The Way They Were.'" Obviously, I couldn't borrow into a specific fame of one of my clients. But he was pointing me in a direction. Title-wise, I stood like a deer in the headlights for about two years, stumbling over variations of Warren's precisely appropriate theme…things like "The Stars Were So Much Brighter" or "A Time Of Legends" or "In The Gardens of Fame." They were all mawkish, having nothing to do with the pragmatic and even unsacred practice of PR, the wonderfully guerilla-type warfare I'd learned to wage in the Hollywood jungle. It all sounded too awed and distant for something that had been that much fun.

Moni was back in Malibu for a few days, and over our family Greek salad at Taverna Tony, she asked where I was on the title for the book. "Superstars and Legends?" I offered without much conviction." "That's nuts, dad. The anecdotes and witticisms may be theirs, but the book is about a very strange profession that defies all expectations or even credulity and about a guy who fell into it and had a very interesting life. You know what I always said when people asked me what my dad did?" "I'm afraid to ask." "I said that you're a starflacker" My women have always saved me.

When I was at Rogers & Cowan, I hated the getting-the-client-to-sign-the-contract part. One of the reasons I've never had contracts with clients in my own companies was that I always wanted the client to know that he or she was with me by choice, not by contractual obligation. Fortunately, we always received a flow of new clients through recommendations unsolicited by me, on the strength apparently of what seems to have been our reputation… or through the pursuit and contacts of my associates. I've always been much more a gatherer than a hunter. My predatory skills I reserve for the doing of publicity. That's the part that's fun. Christopher Reeve, one of my longest and dearest friends among my clients, was the only one who insisted I have a contract with him. Then one day when the "Superman" series had run into a little box-office kryptonite and the town was still too mesmerized by the blue tights and red cape to keep Chris' Juliard-honed acting chops in the equation or to give him parts that would show them off, Chris had a time of doubt and decided to clean house. He called to tell me he was discharging Mike Ovitz (as dominant an agenting force as the town had seen,) Barry Hirsch (the omnipotent and trusted shining knight of the business' legal contingent) and me, a mere press agent but with some good ideas. I told Chris that I had never been placed in such distinguished company and that we would remain pals, which we certainly did. Performers remarry a former spouse more often than they return to an agent, manager, lawyer, business manager or publicist they had previously dispatched… maybe because they sometimes later regret the hasty action as a misguided and costly judgment, and who wants to admit to poor judgment, or maybe because they celebrate it as the best thing they ever did. In either case, that kind of return of the prodigal usually entails scaling a wall of embarrassments that is simply too high. But friendships are undeterred by walls. Friendships can leap towering embarrassments in a single bound.

The best part of being a press agent is that a publicist is always one great idea away from having a happy client. The plugging away is imperative, no doubt, to avoid the errors of omission, but it's always an inspired idea, the double pump slam dunk, which carries the day.

Every press agent has ways to convey to a media outlet his or her special need for a story to get in. If the story has merit, that need will usually be accommodated. However, it's exceedingly poor business ever to say the words "I really need this one" or even to convey it in body language. In the first place, you're selling your own story short. *You don't ask favors, you deliver opportunities and sell points.* A favor compromises both you and the journalist. But the pressure of having to produce some "action" (some publicity result of demonstrable benefit to the client's career) can, in extremis, be brutal. *The press agent equivalent of the shine on a salesman's shoes remains the conviction in his or her sell. If you don't believe it, you can't sell it.* If you beg it, you've made it perfectly clear that you don't believe it. It's a great way to unsell a perfectly good story and even undo a key press relationship, since you effectively made sure that the next one you "really" need falls on deaf ears.

What Makes Publicity Special?

It was while lecturing a class at UCLA that I discovered what really makes publicity special. A question from one of the students reminded me of Peter Ustinov's comment that he enjoyed interviews because they gave him a chance to find out what he thought about things. If you're never asked about something, you may never come to an interesting conclusion that's just waiting to be born. A student challenged me with the question, "What makes you so special?" "Me? Me personally?" "No, guys who do publicity" I hadn't thought of us as special, but then, in the face of his curiosity, I realized we are... that it has to do with what it is we sell. What makes PR people different, not special but really different, is that what we sell is something that most people dream of but never will have. Fame. Unless you were a star quarterback in high school or the best singer or won a lottery, what's the one thing you probably will never have? Fame. It's what makes all those people do idiotic and humiliating things on reality shows. Think of it. If some guy has a Rolls Royce and you have a VW, there's no big difference. Each has a motor, an accelerator, four tires, a steering wheel. And it gets you places. But the one thing you can't even imagine... you can dream of it, but you really can't imagine what it feels like... is fame. You can't even imagine the special problems and anxieties that come with it.

One of the artists Gisela curated and exhibited at her Windward Gallery in Venice was Richard Bernstein, the Andy Warhol protégé who created all of the celebrated covers of Interview Magazine during the Warhol period. Many of those were on her walls and for sale. A key artwork was the original of his representation of Marilyn Monroe with a wash of the word "fame" running diagonally across the image. It had been reproduced four stories high in Times Square. Gisela bought it for me and hung it in the entranceway of the Guttman Associates office so that every day we are first reminded of what it is we sell. Even in this internet age when anyone can create exposure on Facebook, Twitter or You Tube or the next content delivery service of the year, press agents are still a reliable and uniquely trained source of publicity that moves products or solves problems. We sell or maintain or direct fame. Fame (or its demure sister, Awareness) is the yin and Talent is the yang. *Fame without talent is merely notoriety. Talent without fame is frustration.* Fame has useful function only if it facilitates your clients' careers and lives, only if it gets them jobs or gets them the contacts and access to make real and tangible progress towards accomplishing their goals. Or helps them do other things with their lives like supporting the charities or causes in which they believe... or it can be the edge which first attracts that seemingly unobtainable only person they will ever love.

The Ethics of PR... There *is*... oh, yes, there is... such a thing as an ethical code in public relations. Your first point of reference is ethical commitment to the client's interests, creating awareness which impels the career. A press agent must assume the same professional confidentiality to which a doctor or lawyer is obliged. You have an ethical commitment to the media to give them a good story that won't boomerang. You have an obligation to keep it lively or newsy enough to merit a break. You let it be as revelatory as your client's interests require and permit, and no more. You may dress a story up, but you don't distort it. *Above all, you don't want to embarrass either the client or the journalist.* A story must be win-win... for your client, for the media source. How you handle a story is predicated always on your professional obligation to the client. This requires constant vigilance because much media today is content to treat rumor as fact, and each and every flack daily fields calls about some client's health or the health of another's marriage or an essential project that someone would like to see go sour. *Rumors, by their very nature, are almost invariably negative.* You don't let a media guy on a fishing trip drag you into the quicksand of rumor. *Rumor is rarely fact and often the antithesis of fact.*

Publicity is pragmatic. Publicity is a science of shortcuts. You have to recognize or construct the one story that will get you from here to there in one easy bound? That's the shortcut you want. The trouble is, most people don't know where "there" is... the place they want to go. When I get a new client, the first thing I ask is "what do you want publicity to DO for you?" Many of them don't have the slightest idea. The first thing we do is decide on what they want. That's the first step to getting "there." Most people think they want only "more." when what they really want is something they haven't even had the courage to conceive. I collect shortcuts in publicity work and in life… shortcuts driving, shortcuts getting what I want, shortcuts getting what my clients need.

There is one drawback to the shortcut. Some people feel short-changed if… bingo… you just pull the rabbit out of the hat. They feel you didn't work hard enough. If it appears too facile, then why are they paying you so exorbitantly to do it? There's a joke which describes this whacky aspect of doing publicity. A guy comes to the office of a top entertainment power broker. He sings a sad song about how nobody can get him a meeting with (let's say) Mike. Mike can change this guy's *life. "I'd pay, I don't know… anything… for ten minutes with Mike… hock my house.* He can make it all happen for me. A guy (who) can get me to him?… sky's the limit." The power broker, nods picks up the phone, dials. "Mike there?… tell him it's Roger…. Mike… great, buddy, and you?…. great, great. Mike, you have an opening this afternoon? Friend of mine… has a great idea and needs, oh, fifteen minutes of your time… Four o'clock?… you got it." The power broker hands the guy the address he'd scribbled out during the call. "Fifteen minutes. Good hunting." The guy is in ecstasy, his dreams fulfilled. "I can't believe it, all because of you. How can I ever repay you?" "Write a check for ten thousand dollars." "Ten thousand dollars?!" the guy screams… "for one fucking phone call?!!!!"

I tried to write that one making it "with one *lousy* phone call?!!" but that just doesn't have the Hollywood resonance of the line's original and imperative adjective.

The Expletive Nature of Show Biz

Show business is colorful, which means that it's not always polite or delicate. This is as good a time as any to deal with something you probably already find disturbing, maybe even repulsive, a verbal aspect of film-town … the fact that its vocabulary often veers towards the vile. But this is something which needs be accurately incorporated in any precise capture of the town and if reported conversations are to have any degree of fidelity to how they actually are spoken. It was first articulated to me this week by one of my female associates in publicity, Susan Madore, a very grounded young woman shaped in the reserved but tough-minded traditions of her native Maine. What people don't understand, she told me, is that in Hollywood, the F word and its past and present participles, are not swear words. She is absolutely right. This choice family of expletives is so common a tension-releasing resort in its wide and accepted Hollywood usage that it has become merely part of the *patois*. I was brought up not to swear, nor did I do so even well past college. Three things acted to change that. A. I was working in Hollywood where these F icons are merely the tools of expressing sincerity or disdain. B. My children were bringing it home from second and third grade where it was at that tender moment of maturing and immaturing a delightful verbal shocker and then, a few grades later, a common denominator. But most of all…. C. My wife, for whom American profanity was defanged as merely sounds because it wasn't HER profanity. It wasn't German profanity, and she soon realized that she could yank my chain any time she wanted by using swear words as a resort of emphasis or shock, and Gi is very big on both. I needed desensitizing and I needed it fast. Two of my clients obliged. This very famous and, at that time, romantically-involved couple, together or individually, would ply me with dirty phone calls, long arias of the most disdained of four letter words and even some polysyllabic. OK, all right, it was Warren Beatty and Leslie Caron, guardian angels conducting me into the new mundanity of speech, wrenching me from the' 50s into the bold, if not brave, new world.

The point of this matter is that if I am to capture the dialogue of my life in PR and the vivid spirit of the entertainment world, you're just going to have to get used to it. This is how the language is most commonly… in both senses of that word… spoken in the once-upon-a-time land of Hollywood. It is not meant to be offensive. It is meant to be authentic. And sincere… oh yes. Sorry, but you're not in Louisa May Alcott country any more.

Beware of Perfect Lines…

We all suffer the great "I wish I'd said"or "I wish I *hadn't* said" moments of our lives, those inspirations that come to us in the slow-burn frustration period after we had failed to rise to an occasion or those regrettable moments of hasty pique… that perfect line which was perfectly inappropriate. Occasionally they cost you an account, but invariably they leave you feeling like a jerk for having been so witlessly smart-ass. Those lines stay with you as lessons hard learned.

One that stands out for me was what should have been the joyous morning of a client's having achieved an Oscar nomination that was well deserved but by no means a sure thing. It was for the screenplay for a spectacularly successful film, a great feel-good romantic success. The script's reviews had been very good, and our campaign had been particularly effective, but we were all sweating out the announcements. In those days, before instant internet access to all of the information, the reveal of nominations had been moved up to 5;35 AM west coast time to accommodate the opportunity to have the nominations revealed simultaneously on the national morning talk shows. So every press agent in town who had something to gain or lose… personal or studio… gathered at the Academy at 5AM for coffee, lox and bagels, and nervous joking to relieve the tension. It was even before cell phones, so the really early-comers hovered protectively over the few available telephones at the back of the Samuel Goldwyn Theatre so that they could be the first to inform their honored clients or to bring the bad news if they had been directed at gunpoint to do so. The others ran for whatever phones were in the vicinity. My partner Jerry was on the phone he'd been baby-sitting, having almost completed his notification of most of our nominated clients. When he was finished, the phone was passed to me, and I awoke our writer client with the good news.

I was surprised when, a few hours into the rest of the morning, he arrived at the office. I supposed it was to bring candy for the secretaries or perhaps just to savor the excitement with us. But when he came into my office and shut the door behind him, I smelled trouble. Shutting the door behind you is always trouble. I feinted with a casual, "So, congratulations." To which he jabbed, "I don't know if you're aware of it, but I was nominated this morning." "Yes," I acknowledged, readying for something unpleasant, "I called you at 5:43 to tell you." "So then you know." "Yes, I do. That's why I said congratulations." "Well, I came over to make sure that we're both on the same page." "Which page is that?" "That we both agree that I am the greatest writer in Hollywood." "The greatest writer in Hollywood?" "Yes. If we're not agreed, there's no point in continuing our association."

It was at that point that I took leave of reason and my own megalomania came into play. "Are you telling me…" I started in a controlled tone that I always recognize in myself as incipient rage and insanity, "that there has been a terrible automobile accident and that Bo Goldman and Robert Town and Alvin Sargent and Michael Crichton were killed? And that John Sayles was driving the other car?" There was a long silence in which I could hear him gulp… or maybe it was I. "So," he responded, "you don't agree that I am the greatest writer in Hollywood?" "Frankly," I said in an on-rushing ego maximus and in monumental distortion of the facts, "right now I don't think you're the best writer in this room." This to a guy who had just been, quite justly (with maybe a little assist from our campaign,) nominated for an Oscar. As the door slammed behind him again, I realized how stupid it had been, how stupid I had been, but I couldn't think of any other way I could have handled it. The strange epilogue is that it was the end of an account, but not the eternal termination of a friendship. Years later circumstance brought us back together. Either he had forgotten or else we were both burying it and moving on. In honest retrospect, I'd felt exceedingly small and stupid... and inaccurate... for having said it. I think the years allowed us to look at it as the messy handling of a morning over-wrought with good news.

I've always maintained that THE ONLY THING TOUGHER TO HANDLE THAN FAILURE IS SUCCESS. If you're considering a life in PR, tattoo that one on your wrist, and you will be able to muster consideration and empathy when they seem most out of reach. We help navigate great talents through the equally dangerous shoals of success, failure and the horrific waiting for one or the other. But we have to navigate our own little rowboat well, too, and don't always.

You have to be crazy to write a memoir, and you don't find that out until you're halfway through. By then, you don't want to waste everything you've done. So you find something to motivate you after you hit the wall. For me, it was the words. Not my words, but the words I've heard. I've collected words all my life. And I've associated with people who used them well. My life is remembered in conversations as well as situations

There were very few from the exalted age of legends who didn't have wit and a personal style of expression. That made them... that greatest of all gifts of friendship... invigorating. In Hollywood... Hollywood Then much more than Now... that verbal dexterity seemed the price of admission, or maybe it's just that the boring ones defy memory. You can get spoiled. Two other people who could always make me laugh with their originality or or sheer word-play were my father and my wife. We've never had an argument that she didn't end by making me laugh. Invigorating? She is tinglingly so. They don't put that in the marriage vows, but it should be given serious consideration. My father never had a caution, a command or an exasperation for me that didn't come wrapped in a play on words. Our first granddaughter's baptism occurred on his 95th birthday. At 91, having locked himself out on his balcony waiting for my sister, he climbed in one of those five-feet-off-the-ground kitchen windows, braced his foot inside on a chair which turned out to be a paper basket, and the fall resulted in a brain hematoma which turned him into a vegetable in a week. Brain surgery restored, it seemed, only his wit, clouding reality but not philosophy. So he had only a vague idea of where we were going when I picked him up to go to the lavish baptism party which Alyssa's godparents, director Joe Sargent and his wife Carolyn, held on their ranch. When Carolyn asked my father if he was enjoying the elegant occasion, he told her "I will remember your hospitality for the rest of my life." When she asked if he would like to kiss her llama, he replied, "My dear, I will kiss you wherever you wish." He was barely compis mentis, but he never passed up an opening for wit. When I introduced him to Gene Hackman at a talk show, Gene was impressed with his vigor and repartee and said, "So Mr. Guttman, what are you, about 72?" And my father, confirming that, said, "Yes, we had Dick when I was nine."

Oh, and on that "rest of my life" stuff, when I was driving him back to the nursing home, I said, "So, Dad, did you enjoy the party?" And he answered, "What party?"

Picking Up the Pieces

A life examined in retrospect is a ten thousand piece jig-saw puzzle dumped on the floor with only the barest clues as to how to hang them together in comprehensible mosaic, especially minus the pieces which slipped under the couch. Recognizing that the author is himself the through-line, there is the challenge of how to weave that in without seeming self-possessed in the worst sense of the word "possessed?"

As for the design of the thing… the merely chronological approach doesn't do it. The parts connect more in their affinities. I have a day job, so it is years since Warren Cowan's passing impelled me on what has been a long and dizzy picking through bits and pieces and shards which defy chronological order. When I was pouring out screenplays in my forties and fifties, the prospect of long periods, months of two hour or three hour nights of sleep was a lot easier. Since the start of this search party sent out to find the past before night falls, about four years of challenging campaigns and Oscar seasons and sheer life have intervened and interrupted. I feel now like the pharaoh must have felt when the pyramid was only ten thousand slaves' lives shy of completion. Except in this case, I'm the slaves.

It is a journey of discovery… or maybe recovery. I stumbled upon all of these conversations neatly intact within my head, the easily memorable and surprisingly accessible words of the people with whom I was swept up, the ways in which each was clever and unique, all of that still brightly, sharply shining. They were just waiting for me to come looking. Perhaps I'm simply trying to draw what we all seek from the chaos of experience… order, closure, some comprehensible meaning, some sense that it was not in vain and also that it was not *merely* vain. It's a process which demands of the writer a full complement of contrition and embarrassment and remorse but which compensates him with an ordered recall of how much he treasured the people along the way and, in loving detail, the extravagant rewards of wife and daughters and grandchildren and friendships.

Chapter 14

Locations, Locations, Locations

The Brash Freedoms of Poverty and Youth

Doing film publicity on a foreign location is the PR equivalent of Spring Break. Unit work as I practiced it in Europe during my years 22 to 24, the penultimate segment of my adolescence, was the exhilaration of being free to do pretty much what you want as long as it gets your film in the papers. It seems that from the time I landed my first job in Paris, I always had a free hand. On "Love In The Afternoon" my great good fortune was that the unit publicist, a respected veteran, one of only a dozen big name unit guys working the sudden glut of overseas productions with big name stars, was a fine writer, had great press contacts… but he absolutely hated the rough and tumble of working with the giant talents on a film like one with Billy Wilder, Gary Cooper and Maurice Chevalier, legends all, and Audrey Hepburn, on her way at 26 to being one of the biggest of them all. The full weight of these contacts fell to me. It was great.

A mandatory rule for anyone in the start-up years of a career in any field is that you must resist seeing yourself as you think others see you. You have to make them see you as you see your own best self. It's a rule I almost never practiced. I always thought of myself as a kid, and in many ways I still do. I know that I now have a more mature judgment, a modicum of reputation which opens doors, loads of experience both positive and negative, the latter being by far the more instructive. But you should never mature out of your adolescent enthusiasm.

One thing about great pros… they think you can do your job until you prove you can't. Billy Wilder was too busy making his movie to notice what I did, and the real unit man was fine with what I dreamed up as long as it was my neck that was sticking out. I came to our director's and our cast's attention only when I saved all of the penises from being circumcised back to their scrotums. Yes, that was I. Everyone seemed to take a personal interest in that. Mr. Wilder, being Billy Wilder… being "Five Graves To Cairo," "Double Indemnity," "The Lost Weekend," "Foreign Affair," "Sunset Boulevard," "The Seven Year Itch," "Ace In The Hole," "Stalag 17," "Sabrina Fair" Billy Wilder (and that was only up to that point with all the joyous triumphs to come)… was not subject to a lot of home office interference as long as he was on schedule and on budget. By 1956, even studios had learned to trust his film-making instincts. They did, however, take a look at drawings or photos of actual Paris sites which would be re-created on Studios de Boulogne sound stages by Billy's resident art directing genius Alexandre Trauner.

One site that was already being reconstructed onto a Boulogne soundstage was the historic Paris music conservatory where Audrey Hepburn's character Arianne studies cello. The studio had just seen recognizance photos of the actual ancient building Trauner was replicating right down to the anatomically correct statues of naked men lining the entrance against which Audrey would play some of her key dialogue. Cable messages of consternation and horror sailed back to Mr. Wilder from the front office. What kind of movie was he making?!! All of those male parts were not going to play in Peoria, and what would the world think of having Audrey Hepburn, it's most beloved virginal princess, playing a narrative conversation in front of all that explicit genitalia. Get another Ecole de Musique.

Unfortunately, the one with the penises was already pretty much finished at the studio with all requisite male parts where they had appended on the actual statues for centuries. Another batch of cables… cut the penises OFF! That was an order… each penis had to be sliced to the base reproductive glands. The gonads could stay, but they had to have maple leaf covers of a size sufficient for modesty. Billy Wilder's adamant refusal roared across the set in hilarious outrage. Without telling my boss who, being a studio guy, surely would have nixed it, I gave our angry leader an idea, and he gave me a green light. I had Gerard Lang, our French publicist, call the photo editor at France Soir, the country's leading daily and the

French nation's most subscribed-to awareness. When the photographer arrived, and with the whole company gathered about, we staged a shot of one of Trauner's workers on a ladder, one hand firmly grasping the statue's doomed penis and the other sawing it off at the testicles. This appeared on the front page of France Soir the next day with an acerbic story about American studio maturity. It was not a shot that could ring out around the world since there were no American papers or magazines in 1956 which would touch it with a six inch pole nor was there an internet where it would go viral and get a billion hits. But the clip in the French paper certainly made the rounds of the home office, driving home the realization that they were about to become laughing stocks. Billy Wilder received a wire granting commutation for the penises on the condition that he would be mindful of prevailing mores in his shot selection. No angles of genital specificity.

France in 1956 was pretty hypocritical about its own moral failings. The title of the film had to be changed in that country to "Arianne," the name of Audrey Hepburn's character. It seems that "Love in the Afternoon" evokes the French phrase "cinq a sept," which means... harmlessly enough one might assume... "five to seven," Those late afternoon hours are a sacred part of the day in France, the time when, traditionally, French bosses had affairs with their secretaries or girlfriends or best buddies' wives. And it was when their own wives were similarly disporting themselves. Hotels rooms could be rented at reduced rates as sites for these splendidly forbidden and generally practiced two hour afternoon romps, trysts or hijinks. And these brief room rentals were called cinq a septs. Love In The Afternoon hit too close to home. Au revoir "Love In The Afternoon," Bonjour, "Arianne."

Since "Love In The Afternoon" (je m'excuse:, "Arianne") was a love story, everyone was pleased when I, with the help of a new friend at the embassy, was able to bring 1956's biggest real life love story to the studio for a visit. At the 1956 summer Olympics in Sydney, the American men's shot-put champ, had fallen in love with the Czech women's discus champ and, while the whole world of romance held its breath, it had taken them a quarter year to get permission from the Czech communist regime to marry. When Harold and Olga Connelly made their first stop out of Czechoslovakia in Paris, I arranged for them to be celebrated on the Billy Wilder set, the conjunction of two stories of unlikely love. Billy and Gary and Audrey excitedly ringed around the newlyweds in the photos I set up. Everyone goes gooey over the triumph of romance.

"Love In The Afternoon" wasn't a film… the penises apart… which you could "stunt" for publicity. It required, rather, simply creating awareness of the gathering of such respected and elegant talents. Casting is always a chemistry experiment, and it was quite remarkable how great directors chose to pair Audrey Hepburn, only in her mid-twenties in those first astounding years of her stardom, with actors very much her senior. For her first five films as a true star, William Wyler had her opposite Gregory Peck in "Roman Holiday," Billy Wilder placed her opposite Humphrey Bogart and Bill Holden in "Sabrina " and then Cooper in "Love In The Afternoon," Stanley Donen paired her with Fred Astaire at an advanced stage of career in "Funny Face"" while King Vidor romantically teamed her with Henry Fonda and Mel Ferrer for "War And Peace." I never figured out that common denominator. Was she too elegant for youthful on-screen love? Our reigning princess rarely had a leading man who did not very much exceed or even double her age. Shortly after, although not romantic pairings, Fred Zinnemann had her opposite Peter Finch in "The Nun's Story," with just a frisson of forbidden attraction, and John Huston put her with Burt Lancaster in "The Unforgiven." Then Donen brought her Cary Grant for "Charade" and Cukor gave her Rex Harrison for "My Fair Lady." Wyler again gave her an elder-than-she Peter O'Toole for "How To Steal A Million." The closest she came to the boy next door was Albert Finney in Donen's "Two For The Road" (an age spread of maybe just a deade) and George Peppard in Blake Edwards' "Breakfast At Tiffany's, and in that one she was actually married to Buddy Ebsen who was already ripe enough to play an elderly pater familias in "The Beverly Hillbillies." None of this held her back from stardom. She would have been desirable opposite Lionel Barrymore. A press agent sees these eminences very much up close, and I never saw a blink of petulance in her. She deserved the love we lavished.

The objective of publicity on such a film of gentle graces as "Love In The Afternoon" was to build a public anticipation of wit , class and charm, and one gathered plenty of breakable items (little stories that would make it into print) just staying on set with eyes and ears open. What a dream assignment for a kid in love with classy movies. The filming abounded with subtle comic invention. The "Lubitsch touch," that most rare and exquisite of Hollywood comedy traditions, was notably carried on by Billy Wilder, Preston Sturges, Howard Hawks and a few others. Privileged to be on set of a Wilder classic, I felt obliged to absorb everything like a sponge. One "Love In The Afternoon" Lubitsch/Wilder touch

(Billy was one of the writers on Ernst Lubitsch' most classic classic, "Ninotchka") comes lovingly to mind. It is the screen moment I most treasure having seen being born . It came when Gary Cooper's character has brought a gypsy musical group to his room to relieve him of the lovely misery of having fallen madly for Audrey Hepburn's character, a man who has never made that mistake with any lover before. Coop leads this ensemble, continuing to play, out of the room to a Turkish bath to sweat out this sudden entrapment of love. In rehearsal, the musicians simply followed Coop out of the room in rhythmic sway to the music, the zither player the last to exit. Billy knew the scene needed a touch. He took the zither player aside and demonstrated his idea. He mimed exiting the room with an imaginary zither, cheating it so that the zither is seemingly too wide, and he bumps into the door jam and then, without missing a beat, dances a few steps backward and then glides sideways forward out the door, still playing, still dancing. The actual zither was clearly narrow enough to have made it through, but if Billy Wilder wants this little grace note, who are we to quibble? On my many viewings of this film, the audience has always rewarded that little flourish of a scene-capper with a big laugh. You can see how Billy dances the audience through a film. No wonder he survived as a dancing partner for partner-less women in that same city in the '30s during his flight from Nazi Germany. It's but one of the charming touches of a lovely and beloved film.

Billy cherished Cooper for his many graces. Sure, everyone in the world (including Mel Brooks' Frankenstein monster) wanted to be "looking like Gary Cooper, super dooper." On the set during a shot, you often watched Billy's face reflecting his breathless wonder with what his actors were giving him. I recall that best in the shooting of the steam room scene, Wilder's utter enchantment with the guy as Coop sits languidly conducting the softly basting Gypsy musicians. The movement of Coop's long and sculpted fingers is an art form in itself, which Billy skillfully captured. The close-up on Gary and those elegant hand movements was one single, perfect take, which Billy allowed to go on well past its completion, like allowing a master singer to sustain a perfect note. And then he didn't say "Cut." He said *Merci, Gary. Merci bien.*

I had an opportunity to succeed Billy Wilder in the dancing-partner-in-Paris trade, a little known part of Billy's resume that his editor, Doane Harrison shared with me. My office mate, the French press agent Gerard Lang... he of the incessant and compulsive pursuit and conquest of innumerable women... sometimes amused himself and facilitated this hobby by working the *"the' dansants "* or tea-dances where older women could meet younger men with whom to dance, just as they had in the '30s when Billy Wilder had to, between writing assignments, sustain himself as an immigrant passing through the frenzy of pre-war Paris on his road to glory. These dances were, perhaps still are, held in respectable ballrooms from four to six PM, *quatre a six* rather than *cinq a sept.* Gerard didn't do it to make money, the tips sometimes being generous, but rather because it was an amusing change of mode for his feral sexual dabbling. Gerry knew that my salary was meager (from the French *maigre* meaning thin,) but he also suggested that it would be an interesting experience for an aspiring writer. Because of my CIA calamity, I'd gotten some of that "interesting experience for an aspiring writer" stuff out of my system. I hadn't even met Gisela, but I somehow knew I didn't want to trivialize or deceive some poor women... or myself.

I recently received a very welcome phone call from journalist and film producer Peer Oppenheimer who, in the '50s and '60s did the major personality profiles, often covers, of top actors for Family Weekly, one of the most widely distributed Sunday supplement magazines. So many of the people who shared my adventures with me had passed on by the time of his call, dozens leaving us during the extended writing of this book, but Peer was still there.

Peer had joined us in Paris during the filming of "Love In The Afternoon" to do a cover story on Cooper, and the interview was set for 8 o'clock in Cooper's Hotel George V suite. We arrived at the appointed hour to the apparent consternation of Cooper's valet. After a half hour, the door to Cooper's bedroom opened and Coop appeared, immaculately attired... super? of course... dooper? you bet. He was preceded by two tall and gloriously beautiful women fashionably coutured as though they were about to step onto the Balmain runway. "Gentlemen," he said, 'I apologize. I recall having set the interview for tonight, ignoring that I had prior commitment. Peer, if you'll pardon the inconvenience, I'd love you and Dick to be my guests for a wonderful dinner tomorrow night, and I promise to make up something that will give you a good story." You always felt flattered in the glow of his smile. Tomorrow night sounded great, and at that epicurean dinner at Cavaldos he regaled Peer with the delights of making "Love In The Afternoon" which is what Peer had come six thousand miles to get. We went away with absolute certainty that this film, now a cult classic, would engage audiences forever, quite as Gary Cooper engaged us.

Fifty-five years later, during our lunch of renewed friendship, that evening was still a very warm memory for Peer. 'I was very flattered that Gary knew that I would never reflect in my story the circumstances of the night before," Peer said. "He never mentioned it. He trusted me."

Peer's remark reminded me that in a time before Facebook and Twitter, a very legit media understood its function as one of the three co-dependant sides of the basic triangle of stardom... *A. the stars, B. the media and C. the public's image of the stars*. That period's intense esteem and affection for movie stars was influenced to some degree by PR and media. But to a greater degree, it was constructed of the qualities and traits the public recognized in each of these stars, and of the dreams they invested in them. The stars did their part with great performances and by living up to the images and charm quite accurately ascribed to them.

That's one reason such indestructible, imperishable stardoms can never come again. The stars and their stardoms were, for that long and now squandered "once," the hallowed dreams of their audience. Today the public doesn't have to dream. It has the instant gratifications of digital babble and at-your-fingertips porn. Every worst thing you want to know about anyone?... yours for the digital asking. The objective now is to feel equal-to or better-than. Now, when a star's misjudgment or ill-placed trust falls into the hands of the internet, it is eagerly devoured, becoming a news story, viewing content for which ads are sold. Media and public pretend to be scandalized, but cyber voyeurism and its social media exploitation have taken us far past a capacity for scandal. The subject stars are not humanized by these gaffes. They are dehumanized. Back in the day, nobody chortled over Judy Garland's struggles. They loved her.

I was discussing "Love In The Afternoon" at lunch with Elizabeth Guider who was then editor of the Hollywood Reporter. She told of having once rented it to show to a group of women friends. The video tape broke in the middle, and they drove all over the Valley to find another copy so they could finish the film. "On Golden Pond" director Mark Rydell was our other lunch partner, and he recalled seeing Wilder's film as a young director and sobbing as Audrey seemingly slips from Cooper's arms and from his life in the train departure scene. Preparing to see "Love In The Afternoon" again decades later, after having exacted tears in many of his own films, Mark knew he would now be weep-proof. He found himself crying twice as hard. Wilder shot that train station scene over two days at the grey and forbidding Gare Austerlitz in Paris, days described by crew members as the two coldest Paris had ever suffered, dry cold that went through you like skewers, and it is one of the warmest moments of love in movie history.

Even without the tabloids and TMZ, in the mid-fifties the newspaper columns did traffic rumors of sexual behavior.

Antics, as they usually were called then, did abound in the columns, but always with a little wink. Columnists hinted them, usually wrapping them in cotton-candy phrases like "a certain star" and with a gentle and genteel air of reproving "tssk-tssking." Confidential Magazine and a few scandal rags were the only publications that printed the tales. But these escapades found their own course and discourse to public awareness.

The '30s, '40s and '50s were not so completely white bread that a little bad couldn't sometimes be good for a career. The divorce trial of Mary Astor did bring to wide public attention her diary with very detailed documentation of adulterous behavior. You may, however, recall her as Judy Garland's adorably proper mother in "Meet Me In St. Louis," filmed less than a decade later. So, obviously, such things were not completely stigmatizing then. On the other hand, film buffs most treasure her as Bogey's leading lady of easy virtue and deadly terpitude in "The Maltese Falcon," a mere five years after her sensationalized divorce. Who knows? It might even have won her the role.

It is less gossip than history to note that the town and the world pretty much knew Gary Cooper to be a ladies man. Such were his acting and comedy talents, however, that in "Ball Of Fire" he could convincingly play a 40 year old virgin. In "Love In The Afternoon," it was quite the opposite. His character was a noted and adulated "roué" or "playboy," which were the common and celebratory catchphrases then. The corresponding labels for a woman were much less forgiving. "Loose" was a prevailing adjective. Or, if she was loose and really beautiful, "harlot." So much for gender equality.

Cooper's character, Frank Flannagan, in "Love In The Afternoon" was a playboy, yes, a Don Juan, of course… but Wilder's and Diamond's script didn't indulge that powder-puff tradition. It established that Flannagan was a serial adulterer. That was strong stuff in 1956, and even some serial adulterer studios bosses didn't want that in their movies. Billy and Cooper had a lot of fun during the production photo shoots of Frank Flannagan as the stalkerazzi of that day might have caught him in wild escapades with various individual women or groups of women. These photos are seen in the film in scandalous newspaper articles describing the flamboyant Flannagan. Initiating the plot, Audrey's Arriane discovers these in the files gathered by her private eye father (Chevalier) who is investigating this cad on behalf of a gentleman currently being cuckolded by him. Beautiful young women in various states of dishabille (this was the '50s when bikinis were hot stuff) stood about awaiting their photo op romping with Coop or, rather, Flannagan. It was amazing how many French crew members could slip unnoticed into a relatively small photo studio and remain in undiscovered silence. I was allowed to slip some of these photos out to key press to stir an advance curiosity.

On the night we were shooting at Maxim's and just as the company was breaking for the midnight "lunch," a glorious Rolls Royce pulled up on the other side of the square where were located the dozens of vehicles which so mysteriously and expensively are part of any location shoot. A chauffeur came over, found Mr. Cooper and then led him back to the Rolls. The chauffeur was invited to join the company's midnight meal. It was in this fashion that the crew learned that his passenger was Rita Hayworth. It was the night that I'd arranged for Gisela to be among the extras. After a brief repast, we went off to walk the dark nearby streets and talk. We returned to discover that a partisan debate was in process among the crew. Cooper had been in the Rolls 24 minutes… they'd timed it… and half believed that coitus had transpired and the others rejected that idea. The French are romantics, and those on the *"oui"* side held passionately to their belief and felt themselves to have been present at the mating of titans. This discussion brightened everyone's spirit in a long and cold night. It was as though they had just attended a historic soccer match. For the rest of the night, as the *oui* side gained concensus, everyone who had direct involvement with Cooper… the make-up artists, the costumer making infinitesimal correction of a tie… would complete the task and then give Coop a nod and a knowing and conspiratorial smile of encouragement. They would find in any general proximity to him a reason to smile and say, *"Ah… Monseur Coop"* or *"Tout va bien, Monsieur Coop?"* And Cooper would smile back at them, that whimsical and innocent, bemused smile of his that is part Gary Cooper and part Stan Laurel. My guess was that he knew what was up, and it amused him. It was that same goofy smile he had in "Along Came Jones" or "Ball Of Fire" and early sequences of "Mr. Deeds Goes To Town."

What a film on which to have grown up!

I think that that film had a very special significance for Gary Cooper, too. I was working with him back in the U.S. three years later when he was doing "Man of the West" and was a Rogers & Cowan client. He had no reason to remember me specifically. In our first interaction on the set, he nodded and said, "How're things?" which could be either recall or common courtesy. But then he brought up "Love in the Afternoon" and Billy Wilder, and it was an important common ground. He loved the experience of both the film and the man. Billy would keep the energy up between scenes with funny tales, usually told at his own expense. He came to the set one day in full bloom of a roaring cold and spoke of the terrible night before in which he kept sweating through shirt after successive shirt. Finally he was down to a tuxedo shirt, and he had everyone painful with laughter as he lamented the horror of having to put in dress shirt studs in the dark, dripping with sweat and blowing each near installation with what he called "Billy Gilbert sneezes." Billy Gilbert was a brilliant comic character actor of the '30s and '40s who was very famous for his volcanic sneeze bits. Wilder, invariably, would start to tell a story to one person, often Coop but sometimes to his writing partner IAL Diamond or his editor, Doane Harrison, with whom he verbally cut the film as he approached each scene. He knew the cuts before he shot. And, as people closed in, he would raise his voice little by little, finally treating it as the full comedy routine for cast and crew that it was intended to be, generous of comic gesture, razor- sharp observation and delicious word selections and positionings. His high, reed-thin, comedy-perfect voice and German accent, a voice honed for cynicisms and ironies and self-deprecations, accentuated the bite and exasperations which were the comic art of his story-telling.

When you're with the people who *made* the history of film, it's permissible to ask them about the holy moments in which they were participant. We're in agreement on that, aren't we? So In one conversation with Cooper, I had to ask him about the scene in "Meet John Doe" in which he on the harmonica and Walter Brennan on an ocarina dueled a duet of the most famous passage of the William Tell Overture, the one on which "The Lone Ranger" galloped into our radios once a week in my pre-adolescence years. Only the dueling strings of "Deliverance" matched their exuberant combat. They each tore into it with such glee that I had to know if they had actually performed it or if it was just a lip-sync. So I asked. "Why do you think we didn't?" he asked. "Because it was so damn good." "And why do you think we might have?" "Because of how gleeful you both were that it was so damn good." Gary Cooper gave me a long and wounded look which I realized in retrospect was a master-of-timing drawing from a silence the kind of emotional tension he evoked in "High Noon." Then, his eyes never leaving mine, he slowly removed from his coat pocket a little blues harp and, still holding my gaze, blew me the first twelve bars of Wagner's immortal musical romp. I was stunned with envy and finally managed a "wow." He gave me a little nod of which I'm always reminded by Robert Redford's punctuation of his confession to Paul Newman that Sundance can't swim, prompting Butch's incredulous, "Are you crazy? The fall alone will probably kill you." In PR, there are a lot of leaps that will probably *kill* you, but somehow you always make it down river.

You don't argue politics a lot with superstars whose views disagree with yours. That Gary Cooper's politics were conservative was established fact. But he had great affection for the crew on "Love In The Afternoon," even though every time there was a communist demonstration in Paris which the police had to break up, half the crew would come to work the next day with black eyes and cuts and bruises. The French police carry lethal weapons... their capes. These are (or at least then were) loaded with heavy strips of lead sewn into the bottom seams, so when a French cop waded through a mob swinging his cape like a crazed torero, he would take out a half dozen protestors with a single graceful swirl. The grips and gaffers told me that you always go into a riot smoking cigarettes and carrying Bic lighters because fire counters the effect of the tear gas. Gisela, whose studies delved deeply into politics, went to one rally for ex-Prime Minister Pierre Mendes-France who was on a downslide of popularity... certainly not because he was Jewish but because he had said French kids should be given milk rather than wine. When the rioting started and then the tear gas, Gisela shinnied up a lamp-post, happy to be wearing the Existentialists' mandatory black jeans, pitying her poor friends who, skirt-clad, had to stumble down the street with sweaters over their faces.

Coop... in fact all of us... respected the crew because each one was a real and rounded person of surprisingly classical education. This came to our attention because Audrey Hepburn had just finished filming "War And Peace" with Henry Fonda and her husband Mel Ferrer. And so "War And Peace"... the Tolstoy novel, that is… was a grand and frequent subject of discussion and argument on the set. Not one of these guys hadn't read that (what?) 900 page book and not one faltered at arguing its sweeping philosophical premises. They were widely and intellectually aware, and Coop knew each one by name. You had to observe the protocols. When you came to the set each morning, you shook each hand, one per person. I had a great relationship with the prop guy who got me all the crazy things I needed for my publicity photos. And then suddenly, one day he was snubbing me, and things I asked for failed to appear. When I asked his friend, I learned that on the previous day I had failed to greet him with a handshake and my morning joke in my lousy French. I had to make it up to him. When I shook hands with him the next day, I said I'd thought his handshake was too strong and that I'd given my hand a one day rest. Everybody watched, listened and nodded approval.

"War And Peace" held a warm place in my heart. It was part of the vast reading requirements of Humanities 1A at UCLA, but the assigned chapters were 1 through 11 and then the final chapter 19. I was too overwhelmed with the power and beauty of Tolstoy's novel to ruin the rest of the read by skipping to the last chapter, and what chance that out of 12 chapters the main "War And Peace" thesis question on the final exam would be on chapter 19? Of course it was. "Platon has what significance in 'War And Peace?'" Since it began a sentence and was therefore capitalized, I couldn't tell if it was a proper noun… a person or place rather than a thing. I made the rash and yet reasonable assumption that the question would relate somehow to the overall theme of the classic novel. I wrote a thesis that this word (which I used only to start a sentence so I didn't have to worry about capitalization) was a metaphor for bread, for the Russian people, for the will to survive as a people and as a country, the essence of what fueled their opposition to invasion and subjugation. My prose was pretty vague and passionate. Unfortunately, the word was the name of a specific character, but he actually represented the same values I had ascribed to the word, a Russian peasant prisoner whose philosophy sustains the hero, Henri, on Napoleon's death march retreat. When I got the paper back, scrawled on it was "Thank *God* I read the book or else you would have *had* me. Enjoy reading the rest of it this summer. A."

I had one opportunity to tell Ms. Hepburn that I had worked on the publicity for "War And Peace" in Los Angeles. Rogers & Cowan was handling the US PR for it, and we were hampered because we weren't getting much copy from the set… PR stories, the sending back of which is one of the most important things a unit publicist (or assistant unit publicist in my case) does. At Audrey Hepburn's request, I had occasion to explain this engine room aspect of film promotion to her, and I told her that I was compelled to write stories to supplement the little we were getting from the unit. She was actually amused by my description of one I had written about an elderly Russian immigrant in Rome (where that film was shot) who supported himself with the one treasure he had taken with him when he fled the Bolshevik revolution, a fabulously intricate antique Russian samovar or urn which he would not sell but rather would rent out for films like this, and he always insisted on being an extra in the scene so that he could stand near his samovar and protect it. The last line of the story was "and that's how he *urns* his living". It was a human interest story that actually got picked up and added to the general awareness of that film. Audrey Hepburn smiled and said she'd never met him. "Because I made him up," I said, and then she laughed. She'd never imagined that tawdry and silly and yet useful side of the movie process. Why should she? She was born to be a princess, but a princess who came to the set each morning and smilingly shook each hand.

Photography on a film is much more about the female star than anything else. Every magazine in the world wanted Audrey Hepburn on its cover, but we were selective... only the top magazines, only the top photographers. Phillipe Halsman joined us, and we set up one of his famous jumping shots... each a shot of a star leaping up, and you could really determine individual characteristics and personality in the way they jump. Phillipe became a close contact of mine and then of Gisela's as well. He said Audrey was born to make photographers happy, and he was right. Her charm invigorated every photo... and every role, but each role was essentially different in the way she incarnated it.

I may have worn Gary Cooper out with my curiosity about the film history of which he was such a spectacular part, but he was kind and sharing. Most of our conversations were my gathering stories for the "press book." And the longer exposures were interview situations with visiting press. A big part of our job was luring to Paris top journalists from the US and England and setting up set visits and interviews for them and for those media people stationed in Paris. Even with Audrey's instantaneous glamour and importance, most of the press requests were for Gary Cooper because those ten letters were how you spelled "stardom" at that point in movie history... and for ever more, for that matter. From Capra to Von

Sternberg to Hawkes to Zinnemann to DeMille to Wilder to Wyler to Mann to Vidor to Wood to Milestone, every great director wanted a piece of him, and it always panned out to be a piece of solid gold. How did Ford miss him? That's a film I would love to have seen.

Where There's Hope, There's Belly-Laughs

But if you want to know freedom-to-go-wild as a PR guy, you can't do better than working on a Bob Hope film in Paris. Flacking Bob's "Paris Holiday" was a free pass to try anything, especially since my boss on that film, Jerry Juroe, was a guy who drove without touching the brakes, too. Bob's teaming with Fernandel, the most revered comic presence in France and all Europe, was the focus of press interest from the start. Our very first job was to immortalize this two man summit meeting of the gods of laughter with the official announcement and the first photo of the two together. So during pre-production Jerry and I were summoned to Bob's suite at the Georges Cinq Hotel with our photographers, the remarkable Jim and Julie Swarbrick of whom I will remark elsewhere, and with my typewriter readied so that I could create an announcement to which the great Fernandel with that remarkable face-and-a-half long visage of his could agree.

It was an intense day, the entire French capital drenched in red, white and blue… rouge, blanc et bleu… colors of both the "Tricolor" and of the "Union Jack," the flags of France and of England whose queen was visiting Paris for the very first time that evening. France, the country which popularized the guillotine-ing of monarchy, a birthplace of anti-monarchial sentiment… the Bastille, the Reign Of Terror. And when Queen Elizabeth's light-drenched bateau-mouche sailed her up the Seine that evening, half of Paris' population of *Vive La France* patriots crowded along the quais of the Seine, and the whispered wonder of "*la Reine…. la Reine*," amplified hundreds of thousands of whispers over, was like a hushed roar, drowning out one hundred seventy-five years of distrust of crowns. You heard it preceding the flotilla up the river, like a towering wave slow in coming.

In Bob Hope's suite, the red, white and blue we had set up for the immortal shots of the two greatest comedians meeting for the first time, shaking hands on comic partnership, were the Tricolor and Old Glory. And Fernandel, the beloved and raucous star of the Don Camillo films and their international popularity, suddenly appeared out of the excitement that swirled through the city. Bob and the rest of us were all smiles for the happy occasion. Bob greeted him with open arms and an all-encompassing "Fernie." But Fernandel stopped at the door, and his famously dour face was at its most dour, and suddenly joy, levity and celebration were on hold. Bob forced a smile and said again, "Fernie," but it was more like a question, and there was no smile in return. The French funnyman was anything but amused at this moment. He held up an imaginary copy of the script and said, rather sternly, "*Bobe.... le screept*." He measured its imaginary presence with thumb and forefinger at a width of about two inches. Then he held those two digits about an inch and three quarters apart. "*Vous*," he said, the French word for "you,"now holding his thumb and forefinger about an inch and a half apart. Then, as his fingers tightened to a quarter inch of space, "*Moi*." The French word for "me" was followed by a windshield wiper swipe of the forefinger, a single gesture dismissing the whole concept, orchestrated with a firm, "*Non!*" Following which, he turned and left.

When the script was hastily corrected, extending by two weeks our prep period in Paris, filming began. Anita Ekberg had arrived to take her part in the film, and I met her first for a photo shoot to establish to the world that she was in Paris to do this film. The women in Bob's films were always an important element, the great beauties... most notably Dorothy Lamour, Hedy Lamarr, Paulette Goddard, Lucille Ball, Jane Russell, Madeleine Carroll... so Anita's casting was a key promotional hook. She was three years shy of becoming the world icon of sexuality in Fellini's "La Dolce Vita," but John Wayne had just given her major presence with key work in "Blood Alley," and she'd already traded laughs with Abbott and Costello and Martin and Lewis. So I needed a very Anita-in-Paris image that could splash its way around the world. Rather than stand her in front of the Arc de Triomphe, which was only a half block up from the Raphael Hotel where she was staying, I took her up on the roof of the hotel to a spot where the *Tour Eiffel*... the Eiffel Tower... could be seen in the background. I positioned her so that if she held her hands about a foot and a half apart, it seemed that she was holding the Eiffel Tower between them, and that shot rather amply established that she was in Paris. And it got ample breaks. "Ample" is a word which springs trippingly to the tongue when speaking of Anita Ekberg. (I borrow that literary allusion not from Shakespeare but from Greer Garson. I was at her home one day when a new plumber arrived. She asked his name, and he said Frank Zanuck. "Ah," she said with a bright smile, "that's a name which springs trippingly to the tongue," and he said "Thank you.")

Youth Is No Excuse, a Brash Overstepping of Taste

I had reason to regret Anita's residence at the Raphael because that is where Ingrid Bergman was residing when she won the Oscar for "Anastasia" and this circumstance gave birth to one of the worst PR stunts I ever had the poor taste to pull off. I learned from media contacts that Mademoiselle Bergman would have a press conference in the Raphael lobby the morning after the Oscars which she had not personally attended. I took Anita down to stand in the hall outside the huge press gathering, and, in the middle of the press questions, I had this one Swedish actress rush forward to congratulate the other enthusiastically on behalf of their countrymen. It was, I freely admit, an atrocious case of guerrilla press agentry. I was twenty-three years old. The cameras, of course, had a joy ride. The breaks were substantial, all conveying that Anita was in Paris for the film with Bob Hope and Fernandel. No one on the set questioned my taste or ethics in inciting this invasion of a great actress' space and of her moment, but then they hadn't seen, as I had, the look of confusion and even alarm on Ms. Bergman's face when the beautiful but formidable blonde came running at her. It was then that I realized that I needed to give more thought to the ethical bases of my publicity stunts.

Years later, Guttman & Pam was handling the Oscar campaign for "Murder On The Orient Express." A great deal of attention was given to Albert Finney in the role of Hercule Poirot, but for the Oscar campaign we had the problem that he'd adopted a make-up so deft and complete that audiences and even voting Academy members would see the film and still not recognize which role Mr. Finney had played. Jerry Pam and I had the idea of doing up and distributing to Academy membership our own newspaper with a front page story showing the difficulty and intricacy of the make-up and what he had had to endure to achieve such a physically demanding and selfless portrayal. It served that purpose and also to promote Ingrid Bergman's transformation from her still evident and distinctive beauty to the timid and fade-into-the-wallpaper grey lady character she played in the film. For someone who did no interviews, she got a good campaign. And both she and Finney were nominated. When she won the Oscar for Supporting Actress, she handed Jerry the card from which her name was announced. It was framed and then always smartly presented on our office walls. For me it represented expiation. I had done a small thing to right a terrible wrong.

Vivre La Difference

Speaking of springing a beautiful woman on people, it was just such a stunt which truly introduced us all to the wicked… oh, let's not beat around the bush…

the vicious and deliciously so nature of Fernandel's sense of humor and taste in practical jokes. There was no lack of beauty on the set of "Paris Holiday." In addition to Anita, there was as the more direct love interest for Bob's character, the elegant Martha Hyer... also known as Mrs. Hal Wallis. And the set, being that of a Bob Hope film, abounded with glamorous women in other roles, small and smaller. But one day after lunch, Fernandel, a smile of lascivious pleasure a yard wide across his yard high face, introduced to the company, but actually to Bob, one of the most luscious creatures any of us had ever seen. Her tight red dress gave explicit evidence validating Fernandel's claim that this celebrated beauty, Cocinelle, was the queen of France's nightclub entertainers. She was very touchy-feely and seemed to love and purr up to everyone, especially Bob. All of the men on the set were very flattered and otherwise enthused by her interest. Warm feelings did abound. Gisela was with me on the set that day, and she seemed to be the only one who had an idea of what was going on. During the shooting of the group photos, Gisela alone noticed and pointed out to me that France's number one female nightclub star's tight red dress revealed that she had an erection. And it was not the only one in the shot. Only shortly after that did Fernandel reveal that Cocinelle was actually Europe's most famous female impersonator. Fernandel had definitely gotten back for his vous-moi-non resentments at the start of the film. Needless to say, again, all of the photos from that day were destroyed, although Gisela kept one as a memento for a few years and then finally destroyed that one, too, because she loved Bob. Who didn't?

Persona Non Grata

There were two occasions when I was banned from the set of "Paris Holiday" because of publicity activities. One was by fiat of Fernandel, and it involved his little two-seat bright red Alpha Romeo convertible. He loved that car more than life itself... even more than comedy and vicious practical jokes. It was a practical joke kind of set, a place where, if you sat down for a moment in one of those conventional set chairs... the folding wood kind that have a piece of canvas as the backrest and another piece of canvas slung between the wood frame sides as a seat... someone would sneak up from behind and hold a lighted match under your butt. The prevailing rule was that you could never do this during a take because it invariably elicited a loud "Yeowww!"

Most of Fernandel's practical jokes had that kind of subtlety, so a lot of people were not averse to his getting some kind of payback. I, being a card-carrying practical jokester myself, rather admired his style and delight, so it was strange irony that I was the author of his payback. This occurred on the occasion of a transit strike in Paris. It was big news, and the company had to make transportation available to get some of the crew to the set. I sold France Soir again on a news-related photo opportunity. I explained how everyone, including Bob and Fernandel, was participating in this. I persuaded them to shoot Fernandel driving his beloved Alpha Romeo convertible with Bob in the passenger seat and a few of the burly crew members piled on to get to the studio. When the photographer arrived, we set up a traffic jam in front of the studio, and the director, Gerd Oswald, called a break so that everyone could go outside to watch the staging of the shot. We had it set up with Bob and Fernandel to have three other men squeezed and balanced into and onto the car in what would appear an acceptably practicable mode of transportation. Suddenly and all at once, about eight other crew members got the idea of getting into the shot. They began climbing on as the France Soir photographer snapped away. And then there was a great squealing of tortured metal and a terrible crash as the shock absorbers of Fernandel's fetishistically-cherished car gave way. The body of the car, almost disappeared beneath the ton of humanity, suddenly dropped about eight inches until the red metal of the bottom rims were almost on the street. Fernandel's face fell even further and even faster. He was shocked, furious, outraged. Jerry Juroe, the publicity field superstar who was my boss on the film, as any good boss would do, turned to me and said "You better get the hell out of here!" I couldn't wait to get a ride, so I had to walk back to the Left Bank, a sad trudge of about three hours. Jerry called my hotel that night to say he thought it best if I found somewhere else to be the next day. Fernandel had been raging about the disaster and my part in it.

The next morning I went out to catch the papers at the newsstand at the corner of Boulevard Raspail and Boulevard St. Germain. And there on the front page of France Soir... the entire top half of the front page... was the shot of the traffic jam in front of Studios de Boulogne with Bob Hope and Fenandel smiling brightly (this was before the shocks gave way) and about six guys hanging on... obviously a gag, but a great visual commentary on the transportation strike that was paralyzing Paris. It was a totally affable and positive shot and story, with renewed celebration of the great collaboration between the world's two greatest comics. A lot of good that does me, I thought as I contemplated the possibility of my being fired. When I got back to the hotel, the concierge said I'd had a frantic phone call from a Monsieur Jair- roh. That was it. I was bounced. Reluctantly, I called Jerry to take the bad news standing up. "Yeah?" I said, preparing myself." "Get your ass back to the studio... I'm sending a car," he said. "Can't you just fire me over the phone?" "No," Jerry said, "I'm telling you... all is forgiven. Fernandel loves you. He's never been on the front page of France Soir before in his whole life."

The other time I was banned from the set was much more serious and of longer duration... and it involved the President of France! The biggest summer social/charity event in Paris is called *La Nuit de la Chancellerie*. It takes place at the glorious Palais de Chaillot at the Trocadero across the Seine from the Eiffel Tower. It is the grandest of gathering places, and the great theatre on this night holds several thousand of the most venerated and financially powerful people in France. It is THE *crème de la crème* event, with snazzy people paying fortunes to see and to be seen. All of the great entertainers of France perform, although my mind sort of stops at the ballet *pas de deux* of Zizi Jeanmaire and Roland Petit, the goddess and god of French culture at that moment. It was, and this is a laborious part of the story, something like a four hour show, with an intermission in the middle with all of the great artists and writers and philosophers and government and social elite in attendance to be lined up and presented formally to the President of France, Rene Coty, with every TV camera and news photographer catching it all and a selection of the glorious introductions broadcast live on national television. That, it turned out, would be the biggest part of the problem.

The performing talent was a who's-who of French arts, and Bob was to do about five minutes which was among the most anticipated star turns of the evening. *Bub Up*, as his name is pronounced in France, was as super a star there as he was in America. My job was just to help out. The company rented a tuxedo for me for the night, a splendiferous twelve dollar rental. I could have gotten a more elegant fit by hitting the *Marche Puce*... the flea market. I really wanted to share this night with Gisela, and I convinced the company that I needed her there with me to help since we not only had to pick up Anita Ekberg and her mother, but also I would be in charge of getting our whole cast, the director and the producers into the line to meet the French president at intermission. Gisela's wardrobe was largely her existentialist jeans and turtlenecks, some inexpensive blouses and slacks which, their modest cost notwithstanding, all flowed on her like a dream. There was nothing she could do to look less than beautiful. I still mourn having lost in our fire an issue of Freundin Magazine about German girls in Paris in which she is walking along the quai of the Seine in slacks and blouse looking like that other Germanic girl in Paris, Marie Antoinette, wishes she had looked. But of fancy gowns Gisela had none, not even any dresses actually. She was a student. And this night was do-it-up-with-dazzle. Every fancy couturier was clearing its shelves of the most expensive fashions. I had exactly thirty-eight dollars to buy her something with which to meet the night. We found a little floral dress, bare arms and lightly strapped, cut in a jaunty flare at the knees. It was slight, but Paris was a hundred degrees and it was right however wrong it was. She looked like thirty-eight million dollars. And she was twenty as no girl had ever been twenty before, and she would steal the evening. And that, too, was a very big part of the problem. The biggest part of the problem.

The limo picked us up at Gisela's dollar twenty a night hotel in the student section near the Sorbonne, and we picked up Anita Ekberg and her mother at the Raphael. Gisela conversed with them in something between German and Swedish and it was pleasant. The event was bright and gay and we were having a great time as the poorest church mice there, the *only* church mice there. The first act of the show was long but astonishing. Then came the intermission, and our passes got us into the huge reception room where the line would form for President Coty to meet the great stars assembled. Gisela and I got Bob and Fernandel, the director Gerd Oswald, Martha Hyer, the fabled song-writers for the film Sammy Cahn and Jimmy Van Heusen and some others appropriately situated in the line. But by the time we finished, President Coty was entering the room. Gisela and I hastened to get behind the cameras, but the President was starting down the line, and the officials wouldn't let us get the hell out of the shot… as Warren Cowan had always warned me to do. I can't remember any moment when I more wanted to get out of the shot, but the government handlers kept shoving Gisela and me back into the line. Finally resistance was futile. The President was only a few celebrities down the line, and the chief of protocol preceding France's head of state was asking each person who they were, what they did and their nationality. Gisela, in her thirty-eight dollar frock, was positioned right after Anita Ekberg. I was at Gisela's other side, and right after me was the director of "Paris Holiday," Gerd Oswald. The TV cameras were pushing in on us, and that was adding to everyone's tension. I'm sure Gerd was wondering what the hell the assistant publicist on the film, lowest man on the totem pole, was doing being introduced to the President of France. So was I. In spades. Anita was beaming and swathed in all of her astonishing beauty and Viking queen physicality, which I'm sure quite engaged the President's attention. She was duly introduced as *"Anita Ekbairg, la vedette Suedoise"*... Anita Ekberg, the Swedish star. Gisela had been asked her identification, and she had said simply, "Gisela Angenendt, *Allemande.*" Gisela Angenendt, German. No indication of her profession. The gentleman presented her to the President by saying, *"Gisela Awnjenawn, la grande vedette Allemande,"* Gisela Angenendt, the great German star. Gisela and Anita and I were all startled by that one, and the President had a brief and interested conversation with her. All we could figure out is that they thought she was Romy Schneider. I was still focused on that when the guy asked me who I was. I barely knew what to say but idiotically mumbled, "Dick Guttman, assistant publicity director of 'Paris Holiday.'" You can't get any more humble than that, but I elected to try it in French. Unfortunately, the French word for "director" I selected was "realisateur" which does mean "director" but only in the sense of "director of a film." So I was introduced as *"Deek Gutemawn, realisateur de 'Paris Holiday.'"* He introduced this pimple-faced kid in a twelve buck tuxedo with the cuffs rolled under and pinned so as not to cover my knuckles as the director of the Bob Hope/Fernandel film. Things got worse. Now it was Gerd Oswald's turn, and he understandably (imperatively, actually) told the guy in no uncertain terms that he was the *"metteur en scene* (another phrase for film director) *du film 'Paris Holiday.'"* But here was the introducer's problem. He had just introduced ME as the director of the film. How could he introduce Gerd as the director, too? He didn't. Gerd was presented to the President of France as the assistant director of a film he was directing... assistant to this pint-sized piss-ant in a black tie clown suit. All I could manage was a wide-eyed what-can-I-do? grimace, which I'm sure he read as a gloat.

We sensed a lot of hostility around us, so Gisela and I became quite scarce after the horrifically bungled presentations. For the second half, we found seats away from the others and thoroughly enjoyed ourselves, particularly since we had washed some of the tension down with the abundantly flowing champagne which I, particularly, had no constitutional ability to handle. Everything for the rest of the evening seemed very funny. After the event, we didn't choose to join Anita in the limo for reasons of exceeding cowardice. We stayed at the after party until about three, but the problem was that the only thing to drink was champagne, and with the wee small hour heat still in the nineties, we were very thirsty. Champagne doesn't cut thirst. On the contrary. So with Paris finally almost asleep, we started walking back to the Left Bank, looking for some place to get water. Other than the Seine, Paris was fresh out of water. At about six AM we found a café opening up and we had coffee (Gisela) and hot chocolate (I) and *beaucoup de l'eau…* lots of water. Then, still in the splendor of our big event costumes, we walked up Boulemiche to her hotel and kissed goodnight, each on the verge of collapse. I got back to my hotel at about eight, and I was told by an angry concierge that Jerry Juroe had already called. "I started getting calls at three AM," Jerry said over the phone, "I wouldn't merely not come to the studio. I'd get out of town. *Regisseur* of 'Paris Holiday'"?!!" he said, not angry but just sort of wondrous at the enormity of the gaffe. "How did you know about that?" I asked. "Because I was watching it on TV," he answered, "You and *la grande vedette Alemande* were the only two people from the film who were shown meeting the President on national TV." I stayed away several days and when I came back, it seemed to be forgotten. Anita Ekberg, who must have a great sense of humor, was particularly nice to me and continued to be so when we worked together again the next year on the filming of "The Man Inside."

Shortly after the *Nuit de la Chancellerie*, Bob Hope was interviewed at some event, and Bob, being Bob, always had a snappy joke. On this occasion it was "We lost a day's shooting recently. Nobody could find the bottle-opener." That one broke big, and the entire crew refused to show up the next day. Since I was the only one who spoke a little French… very little. I went to the various newspaper and TV offices to explain personally that Bob was merely congratulating France on the excellence of its fine vintages, that how could one begin a day of artistic creation without first toasting this beautiful country with one of its great wines? Or at least that's what I thought I had said. My -French is awful. In France when you make an apology, you don't phone it in, and my drop-ins seemed to convey sincerity. At any rate, the crew came back the next day and I was given some of the credit, so our little *contretemps* over introductions to the country's leader was soon well in the past. It also helped that everyone on the company, all of the cast, creative talent, director, producers were terrific people and enjoyed life. And why shouldn't we? We were all in Paris making a movie with Bob Hope and Fernandel. However the film turned out, the shoot would be treasured as sheer delight forever.

When Gisela and I first were committing ourselves to a life together... those glorious going-to-be-married, just-married days when it's all about having fun together, when we were in the middle of a muddle of three weddings (London, the Black Forest, sunny California) which were probably the reason we've stuck it out together for over a half century. During that great period of being not-quite-grown-up together, we thought we would spend our life on locations. We met on "Love In The Afternoon" (Paris,) became engaged on "Paris Holiday" (Paris again) and got married on "The Key" (London.) We were set to spend our first year on "A Nun's Story" (The Congo,) but pregnancy (Los Angeles) got in the way. Our second, following a miscarriage (Spain.)

Working on foreign locations is fun... it's a kind of vacation where you really drop roots into some exciting new soil. And you don't feel guilty because you're working, and you don't feel money-pressured because you're getting paid and sometimes even per-diemed. Even "The Man Inside," the film I did with Jack Palance and Anita Ekberg and on which both Jack and I had severe problems with the producer, had its signature experiences. We filmed at Elstree Studios in London, but there was a two week location in Madrid where I set a photo layout with Anita getting bull-fight instruction from one of Spain's top matadors. We shot it on the sand of the most famous bullfight arena in the world, the Plaza de Ventas. I had witnessed a corrida from those stands from which the ring seems tight and the barreras... great wooden structures behind which a torero might slip for safety... accessible. What seemed a sprint from the stands seemed a marathon from the hot blaze of the killing ground. I never visited a bullring again.

I spent only two years of my life doing film PR on foreign locations, but they fill up an incredibly spacious and treasured part of my memory and seem a constant source of reference points. Growing up is always going to be the worst thing that happened to you or the best, and usually both. As Freud observed, In your subconscious mind, you are always 23. He sure nailed it in my case. The highest high and lowest low are always waiting just around the corner. 23 had so many of each, it was pure jazz.

Chapter 15
My Reckless Youth

"Oh what a tangled web we weave when first we practice to deceive."
—Sir Walter Scott

Movies are largely responsible for the immutable public image of press agents as desperate, sweaty hustlers with "sold" signs on their souls ... Eddie O'Brien in "The Barefoot Contessa," Tony Curtis in "The Sweet Smell of Success," Tony Franciosa as the press agent/manager in Kazan's "A Face In The Crowd. Jack Carson's portrayal of the studio flack in the 1954 "A Star Is Born" and Lionel Stander's go at that role in the 1937 version, Wendell Corey's portrayal of a vicious studio PR boss in "The Big Knife," a guy for whom even murder was in the playbook. It also tells you what writers and directors like Clifford Odets, Ernest Lehman, William Wellman, Joseph R. Mankiewicz, George Cukor, Moss Hart, Dorothy Parker, Elia Kazan, Robert Aldrich and Budd Schulberg, creators of those works, thought of their PR reps. That's a lot of high-powered distain. Odets double-dipped on that odium, opprobrium and contempt, having written both the screenplay of "Sweet Smell" and the play from which "The Big Knife" was adapted. But at least they all gave the pr characters some of the funniest lines of dialogue, and they did establish flacks as cut-through-the-bull realists... guys and gals, lest we forget that babe with the long-drink-of-water legs and the bulls-eye tongue, Eve Arden, who took a couple of shots at PR type roles. What they shared were resourcefulness, pragmatism and the determination to prevail, which are pretty much the common denominators of successful press agents.

Director Michael Curtiz did give press agentry a better shake with "Four's A Crowd," not among his many great films, in which he had Erroll Flynn give his PR guy character a charming edge. But he was still a quintessentially scamming scamp. What Curtiz did get right with Flynn's flack was the reflection that a lot of charities have raised a lot of money with the help of a lot of PR pros. But it was less about publicity and more about whether Flynn would wind up with Olivia De Havilland or Rosalind Russell.

Billy Crystal's portrayal of a Hollywood press agent in "America's Sweethearts" and a few other flack incarnations may have gone lighter on the scam and sleeze, but it was the venomous ones that took root and tainted the brand. Even though the bevy of studio flacks in Preston Sturges' immortal "Sullivan's Travels" were neither duplicitous or venal, at best they painted the same face for PR that the Keystone Cops did for law enforcement... ineffectual chaos.

PUBLICITY IS THE ART OF THE POSSIBLE. A press agent can dream, but he/she can't waste time on jerky no-go schemes. Publicity is also the art of the glib. In films and in life, flacks have to have a way with words and a way with people in order to pull it off. There were other films that dismissed press agents as suave or unctuous counterfeiters of the truth with thousand dollar threads, five hundred dollar vocabularies, hundred buck manners and buck-and-a-half ethics. I don't want to sound like I'm fixated on this disrepute. The most cutting and paradigmatic of all those slick and slippery flack portrayals is, of course, Tony Curtis' hustling, groveling maggot of a Broadway press rep, Sidney Falco in "The Sweet Smell of Success." It holds up the same mirror of darkest shadows to PR that Gordon Gekko in "Wall Street" held up to big bonus financial world hustlers and that Sammy Glick of Shulberg's "What Makes Sammy Run?" held up to let's-make-a-deal Hollywood producers.

And here is the factor which sharpens the knife with which Sidney Falco inflicted his thousand cuts on everyone who has ever hustled a story... it was a flack who conceived him and bore the conniving Sidney Falco into slithering life. Yes, Ernest Lehman (who later wrote the screenplays for "Who's Afraid Of Virginia Woolf?," "North By Northwest" and many other distinguished films) was a disaffected PR guy with obvious revulsion for the mandated courting of imperious press like Walter Winchell. Like his protagonist, Mr. Lehman was a night-hunting Manhattan item planter who tracked the top columnists to the nighteries and eateries and beaneries where they hung out and where they hung out their nets. He vented it all in a 1950 short story for a glossy monthly magazine, shortly thereafter expanding it into his first novel. In this fashion did he introduce Falco as his worst-case PR guy, possibly exorcising some dread alter ego. When it evolved into the 1957 film "The Sweet Smell of Success" with Clifford Odets adding his own acerbic take to that of the novelist, it was still as real and timely a reflection of the prevailing dark side as it was at the time that Lehman had so reluctantly flacked.

The '50s were pretty much the '40s. Publicity did not change in those conjoined decades, nor would it until the tabloids shouldered their way into the game during the '70s and began infecting journalism, after which the internet broke the news trade into dot.com nano-particles over the ten years book-ending the millennium. In the intervening half century, Sidney Falco has cast his shadow over the perception of all press agentry. Watching "Sweet Smell" yet again on TCM recently, I had to wonder that the whole tribe of entertainment flacks didn't go into witness protection for a year after that film came out.

I touched the Oscar campaign of "My Week With Marilyn," a fine film but with a regrettable and unfair portrayal of her then publicist, Arthur P Jacobs, in the stereotypic slime-ball mode. This Arthur Jacobs guy whom they so discounted went on to produce, in the best hands-on and loving sense, "Dr. Doolittle" and "Planet Of The Apes," so his humanity was not without testimony. Yes, he was a rough, tough master PR guy, and he cut corners, the same corners we all do in pursuit of the profession's guiding commandment... *prevail*. If it weren't for Arthur P. Jacobs, I would never have met my wife, yes. However, I defend him not out of gratitude but rather out of truth. Sidney Falco was a fictitious character, and his shadow should not fall on everyone who ever worked a red carpet. Arthur Jacobs was too smart a guy to have been the obnoxious cliché he was painted on film.

Steve Shagan was another press agent who went on to glory as a screenwriter and then novelist. When Jerry Pam and I were starting up Guttman & Pam in 1973, Steve approached us to run an Oscar campaign for his film, "Save The Tiger." It's a kind of honor when another press agent believes in you enough to hire you. He felt that Jack Lemmon had a chance and deserved to be honored for his performance as a desperate and failing garment manufacturer, and he knew the studio wasn't putting up much of a fight. We set up a series of screenings which Steve personally underwrote, and then we fashioned a campaign on the angle that a writer believed in the work of his star to the extent of funding the key impact campaign. Naturally, we tied this initiative in with Shagan's PR background, a slant which cultivated a stream of positive coverage. Lemmon, of course, won Best Actor and Steve was nominated in the original story and screenplay category. How this ties into Ernest Lehman and Sidney Falco is my certainty that the pressures driving Lemmon's character most definitely mirrored the grueling and sometimes demeaning urgencies with which every press agent lives. It's a trade in which the red light is always flashing.

AN ODE TO THE PHONEY (please note: I will spell this practice/device with the "e," a dictionary variation, to differentiate between the adjective and the noun. A press agent can deal phoneys without being phony.)

The long dominion of the "phoney" as a characterizing element in the publicity trade is not gone, but it is diminished. As one of the grateful ghosts of its joyous moment, I plead Guilty as charged. A parade of harmlessly deceptive untruths simply no longer fits in our rigorously de-romanticized world. The phoney was that made-up story which moved your chess piece from here to there. The phoney was a significant piece of Hollywood history, in a way a symbol… maybe THE symbol… for the place and the state of mind in which Hollywood grew. It was the key to wonderland, to the exciting and terrifying place where you could in a flash grow too big or grow too small, where party chatter made no sense apart from its whacky diversion and where mysterious cats would manifest themselves only in insincere smiles. It was the music on the carousel. Those little flights of fantasy, charming in their reading and exhilarating in their creation, were very effective practice of salesmanship in the wild and wooly days when Hollywood was still a game. This is not to imply that public and industry perceptions of a talent or of a project are no longer manipulated. But as Hollywood PR firms became intertwined with big "respectable" business, businesses which bought and sold them, where a respectable PR firm could become a "derivative," the practice of the phoney became impracticable. It morphed.

One reason might be that the media which tolerated and celebrated these fabrications died off or came under greater scrutiny or realized the extent to which it was selling not only news but also entertainment. So it may be that significant parts of the new media are perfectly happy to do their own fictional-izing. I haven't been aware of the common practice of the out-and-out phoncy for about 20 years. That doesn't mean, however, that we don't still enjoy "creating" news or stunts in homage to the fluid realities of our past. Imagination still has its pertinence.

Let's get the matter of veracity out of the way right now because PR guys are so famous for being incapable of it. And yet, for the most part, press agents are as honest as any people I've ever met. Shortly into the 20th century and for the first sixty or seventy years of the selling of movies, the dispersion of publicity owed no particular loyalty to the truth. Rather, it was led by the all-consuming dedication to the desire of studio bosses to sell their movies and to sell the people they put in those movies. A lot of the tripe that was fed to the media was like that protection-against-lawsuit line which used to run at the end of movies... any similarity to persons living or dead is purely coincidental.

Deliver Us From Evil, Lead Us Not Into Respectability

Today the practitioners of my craft seem to think of themselves as "public relations executives," business people. Up until a quarter century ago, reality could be molded, and the dark and cheerful arts of shaping and reshaping it were valued and were accorded moral dispensation. Those were much simpler and more defined times, just as the media which we served and which served us was so much simpler and more defined than it is now. It was a time in which PR and journalism both were more fun, more rambunctious and more adventurous. You couldn't go by the book because there wasn't any book, certainly not on the PR side of the ledger. You were free to cook up crazy ideas, and the people for whom those ideas worked, your clients, were more open to your adventurism. I mentioned this to the distinguished director Joe Sargent, and he said, "Oh my God, it was like being on a wild stage coach ride, but somehow they always got you to the next town. I'd been trying to reach a certain studio about a project, but calls just weren't returned. My press agent was always stirring up dust, except he almost never called me to see what actually was happening." "Maybe ," I defended my unknown peer, "because usually nothing IS what's actually happening." "Sure," Joe said, "but one morning I open the trades and there's a story about Joseph L. Sargent Productions opening an office in Tokyo. An office in Tokyo? I was humiliated by the desperation of that story. The first call comes at 9:30… AM… the head of the studio I'd been trying to reach. 'Joe,' he says, 'Tokyo? You're opening an office in Tokyo? I know their banks are hot, but our money's good, too.'" Maybe if Joe hadn't done that film, he wouldn't have had the chance to make "The Taking of Pelham One Two Three," one of the greatest thrillers of all time, or direct more Emmy-winning movies then the next two guys together. Chalk one up for some gutsy PR guy.

Part of it has to do with the strange disparity of how much more easily a colorful and neatly structured fabrication can get into print. Winston Churchill seems to have paid heed to this when he said, " In the time that it takes a lie to get halfway around the world, the truth is still getting its pants on,"

As I was, at 20, setting out to develop press contacts, a terrific young reporter at Variety, Eddie Kafafian, called to say he liked the angle on a story I'd submitted and that he wanted to buy me lunch. A journalist buying a press agent lunch… that doesn't happen often. In my experience, it was very likely both the first and the last time. The essence of the lunch was that if we were to become key contacts, reliable sources and reliable outlets for each other, we had to establish rules of engagement. "The times will come, times plural, that you have to lay phoneys on me," Eddie said. "No, never," I assured him. "Grow up," he snapped, "it's part of the game. There are dream-ups in every paper every day. You'll need the space and we have space to fill. The ones that are plausible can get in. You'll give me some great leads on some terrific legit stories and what I'll give you is the benefit of the doubt when you slip me one that's marginal. But this I tell you loud and clear… never let one bounce on me." "Bounce?" "Blow up in my face. I don't go down alone." It was a warning that became the basis of a beautiful friendship… and it proved a career navigational device that kept me off most of the reefs until the time when fabricated (or at least lubricated) news so sadly ran its course.

I had lost my virginity as a press agent. It was, in sad fact, the only virginity I had lost. But PR was like free love… no limiting consequences. Free your inner rapscallion. Not all the news that glitters in print, in broadcast or in digital incarnation can be expected to be 18 karat. Even today… even in the sober and pretentious and yet mendacious today. But glorious liberty was the case in the great and golden Then far more than it is in the low-glitter Now. In point of fact, much legit news that breaks even today eventually doesn't happen… not lies, just things that fell through. Man proposes, fate disposes. Only a limited portion of announced projects actually make it to the starting gate. Once, during my formative years, I had a discussion about this fluctuation factor with Abe Weiler. Abe covered production news for the New York Times. I was reasoning with him about a column he'd written detailing all of the film projects studios had announced in his column over the prior year but which never made it to a sound stage. His point was that he was sick of the phoneys and of the phonies who sold them. Among the lies he included a film called "Bogart Slept Here," big studio, big director, big stars. "Abe," I argued, "everyone mentioned in your story thought they'd be sitting in a studio projection room right now looking at the first cut. It simply didn't work out." Abe remained dedicated to the proposition that all press agents are created equal… lying bums.

HAND-PLANTING… The Flack As A Door-To-Door Salesman:

Back before email and even fax, there was an essential practice of PR called the "hand-plant. To show what hand-planting wasn't, I give you Gene Hackman's tale of how he and Robert Duvall and Dustin Hoffman as young actors tried to get agents in New York. They made up 8x10 photos, glued some jacked-up resume on the back, then went to agents' offices, slipped their life's hope under the door, knocked on the door and then ran like hell. That's exactly what hand-planting wasn't.

Part of my office boy job at Rogers&Cowan was "the trade run"… dropping hoped-for stories off at Variety and the Hollywood Reporter. The press agents, to up their chances of getting stories in, taught me not to drop that crucial news on an editor's desk, but boldly to utter some key value of the plug story *as I put it into the editor's hands.* You learned to talk fast and hit the key points with precision and belief. I liked to do my own hand-planting even when I became a press agent. I had an occasional scam of making up believable groups to vote my clients this honor or that. Once, and this was after I was married, I got some starlets to form an imaginary group called Starlets United, and I was pushing a story of their selection of Hollywood's ten sexiest male stars, five of whom were mine. I printed the news release on lavender paper to infuse some extra note of attention and verification, but my first exclusive plant didn't draw blood. As I was leaving our mid-city low-rent apartment the next morning to try it on another paper, the lavender sheets in hand, I explained the gambit to Gisela and told her that it had bombed. She spread the sheets on a table, got a bottle of perfume and sprayed them with what a group of starlets might consider a charming idea. It was a quick sell.

The creative press agent knows which truths to give out and which truths are nobody's business but the client's. *The press agent is as obligated to confidentiality as is a doctor or a lawyer.* The press agent surveys the facts and decides which should be shared and which should be emphasized and which should be put in a lockbox. You decide the story you wish to tell and present the facts which support it. You may have latitude in these decisions of presentation, but in the end you make sure that not only are your facts true, but that the story you're telling is true. There are, of course, exceptions, and some of those are fun. But, basically, it does no good to promulgate lies about who your artist is, since they always catch up with you. However, there are many roads to the essential truth about anyone, and a good press agent is a wise navigator. In the old days, the route chosen got a bit scenic, and that, I happily admit, was a big part of the fun.

Not infrequently in this day of the "new media," a journalist will call pursuing a tip or a wild guess on a story that not only invades a client's privacy and best interests but also strains credulity. *The very nature of celebrity puts privacy at risk.* Most media, those who are wise and journalistically trained, understand that a press agent does not work for the media. They understand that the press agent's first obligation is to his or her clients' interests. They understand that a press agent is an intermediary, an access, an organizer and a distributor of news, but not an adjunct *of* the news outlet. Because *media have to entertain their own public* and to meet its appetites for vivid and colorful information, the journalists back in the days of Oz didn't protest the occasional joy ride on which the truth, rolling off the publicity assembly line, was sometimes taken… as long as it bore the semblance of truth and didn't bounce and provided that it entertained.

It is not for nothing that Hollywood during the '30s and '40s and '50s and even' 60s was regarded as the world capital of fantasy. That's what the films were and that's what the publicity was. Truth is a fragile and fungible commodity when hundreds of millions of dollars and those even dearer treasures, careers, are at stake. You can make love to the truth. In those times, everything about Hollywood conspired to have truth become, shall we say, relative.

The geography of film production shifted as far west as it could go in 1909 when film companies wanted to put a continent between themselves and the bully boys whom Thomas Alva Edison had hired to discourage competitive use of his invention (although there are other putative inventors,) the camera that captures continuous motion. It was, he thought, *his* damn machine, and he wanted to control *content*. The first immigrant to arrive on Southern California's shores, or rather its hill-skirted plain, was the William Selig Company which set up shop and studio in what was then called Edendale… a rather appropriate site for establishing a creative paradise. Biograph followed shortly thereafter and then the New York Motion Picture Company deserted its eponymous city. The new film Eden was underway, with, it would turn out, a serpent in every tree.

As for the malleable role that truth would serve in this industry, consider that it was an industry grounded in fantasy and launched by people skilled in the unbridled practices of huckstering. For the first half of that century, the Studio Contract System was in place. The artists "belonged" to their contracted studios. Almost every star was "signed to" a studio. In the Middle Ages, the noblemen (one of history's great oxymorons) enjoyed the Droite de Seigneur, complete command of their subjects, even unto sexual privilege. Well, the new lordships and serfdoms of Hollywood continued that tradition in all of its flavorful and despicable aspects. One of the first great film stars, Clara Kimball Young, acquainted me with this part of Hollywood history when I interviewed her on tape in 1954 for the UCLA film archives. She was, by 1914, the top boxoffice star and very shortly among the first to form her own production company. Two of the first moguls, Lewis Selznick and Adolph Zukor were in the heated mix of those competing to put her box-office draw under contract. By her own account, the attendant dramas, romances, loveless bed-tumblings and lawsuits were often sexier than the films they made. Their dresses may have been buttoned up to the neck, but that didn't mean they were never unbuttoned. Even Clara Kimball Young's reputation and popularity never quite insulated her from Hollywood's noblemen and their exaggerated proprietary sense and grasping hands, she confided to my recorder.

One has to understand studio rationale during the contract star era. After all, the big companies, to their minds, had sculpted these star personas, carved them from base anonymity as Geppetto had carved Pinocchio from wood. Proprietarily, the contract era studios felt they had singularly accomplished this with the assignment of roles and the focus of attention, reshaped them with the athletic training and artistic training of each actor for a specific niche in the studios' larger plans. It was a dictatorship of contractual strangleholds. There were in these contracts morally ambiguous "morals clauses" which could be invoked any time they wanted to show someone the exit. They could make you or break you by assigning career-helpful or career-damaging roles at the home studio or in loan-out to other studios... or keep you on the shelf. But above all, *they could control the publicity that shaped public perception of this exotic new species called stars, and this was the heart and soul* (two very dubious metaphors as applied to those czars) of the studio bosses' outright ownerships.

Hollywood's independent PR business as it first twinkled in the mid-'30s willingly carried on the studio penchant for tweaking the truth. The career-affirming positives continued to be accentuated and the deglamorizing negatives eliminated. Without the studios' resources, however, it was not possible, certainly not advisable, to re-invent the facts of an artist's life. Never-the-less, new private press agents were adept at taking a nip out of the truth here and tucking away something unpleasant there long before the all-consuming age of plastic surgery. And all of these facts have great relevance in this, my confession of the joyous sins of my (and Hollywood's) reckless youth.

Henry Rogers Invents a Business For Me

I acquired some knowledge of early independent PR practice, in all of its vivacity and invention, from its primary practitioner, Henry C. Rogers. He was charming to be sure, the very Cary Grant of the public relations world... handsome, witty, perfect in attire and manner... and, very definitely, creative and skilled, a supreme ladies' man one would assume. I often felt he was his own greatest invention. Like my friend, Laurence Harvey, Henry was in all respects the antithesis of his background. Some of this I got from his father, Mr. Rogesin, whom I, the lowly office boy, drove home quite often after he paid visits to the office. HCR was rarely convivial with or revelatory to his staff in the office, and he had a way of letting chit chat seem vaguely judgmental, which I used as a tool to run some horrific practical jokes on my co-workers. Three of them and I had just unloaded among ourselves over lunch our complaints about Henry and his, from our underling point of view, imperious style. An hour later, I found the others still at it in their shared office, and their idleness with so much to be done annoyed me. I entered the room and dropped in a chair as though wrung out. They took immediate alarm. "What?" one inquired nervously. "Henry… you know how when you go by his office and he says, 'Dick, come in for a chat?" Faces had already turned white. "And?" "And he said, 'Did you have a nice lunch?'" The room was humid with anxiety. "Very nice, thanks." "And where'd you eat?" "He didn't," one said hopelessly. "The next table," I confirmed Two of them, Larry Cohen and Mike Zagor became big writers, and Jim Flood became Jerry Lewis' manager. I like to think I hurried them on their very successful ways. Distant as Henry might have been, he did let his hair down at office parties.

The entertainment media, which in some ways had been as much under the studio thumb as the actors were, liked the idea of a market-based flow of news and access to stars, and in a very hush-hush way they formed friendships with the new "indie shops" which were plowing first ground. Henry Rogers, had made a living of it from the mid-'30s, and in his new confederacy with Warren Cowan right after WWII they imposed their giant concepts and indefatigable creative energies on the field. Henry, which I learned at holiday season office parties when everyone but I was getting drunk and loose-lipped, had exhibited as rowdy a hand in his pre-Warren days as anyone. I looked forward to those occasions of slightly inebriate intimacy as great learning opportunities. Henry's profound dignity and reserve dissolved into revelations of some of the down-and-dirty PR of his earlier days.

In the mid-'30s, Henry was representing the handsome and dashing actor Patric Knowles, always the hero's best friend. That is probably why Knowles had taken the then-daring decision to hire his own press agent. In the flow of Christmas spirits, Henry confided a break-through adventure from which Knowles was elevated from hero's best friend to competitor for the girl. Knowles was an aviator, which not that many people knew about nor did media care because he was, sadly, merely a "best friend." Well, they found out rather emphatically one day after he took off on a solo flight to Fresno. The duly-logged estimated time of arrival came and went, and no Knowles. His very concerned press agent, one Henry C. Rogers, called the authorities and then tipped the media. That was key to Henry's finesse even then in his one-man operation… he *tipped* the story rather than announcing it. No tell-tale fingerprints. No skepticism about press agent skullduggery to drag down the story's credibility.

Hours went by, and media curiosity quickly grew to avid interest and then top-of-the-news alarm. A movie-star had crashed. There is no star story more enticing or welcome on a slow news day than violent demise. Radio, the only media with real immediacy at the time, rang with the hold-your-breath, cross-your-fingers story. Henry had timed it so that it was early enough in the day that it caught the headlines in the bull-dog editions of the morning papers... the ones that in those days hit the streets at sunset of the day-before. Knowles was growing more important and more handsome by the moment. It was not until the middle of the day after the feared crash that a farmer some place between Santa Monica airport and Fresno, called authorities to report having found a crashed plane and its injured pilot somewhere on his back forty. Henry excitedly called the very incomplete news to the media. That was the key... incomplete. Had it been complete, the story would have been resolved, which is not what a good press agent wants. He had to stoke a slavering press need-to-get. Only the uncertainties fanned the flames, and Henry and the media raced up to the designated farm on which the calamity had taken place.

They found that Knowles, still dazed from the near-death adventure, was somewhat recovered from the state of incoherency in which the farmer had found him, amply illustrated by discreet bruises to the head. The plane hadn't crashed, but rather Knowles had, for some unexplained reason, been forced to make an emergency landing on a dangerously rolling field and had managed, thank God, to bring it to a stop just before crashing into a large tree. Henry and the media were massively relieved. Well, in truth, the news guys were a little disappointed that it wasn't a real crash with a more calamitous conclusion, cheated of a movie star body dangling from the branches, but it still had some unresolved questions like what had forced his "crash" landing. Questions keep a story alive. They continue the mystery.

The mystery paid off big time for everybody, especially the local authorities who were very happy to pose in all of their evident pomp and efficiency for the flashing bulbs of a press contingent that had never before made it this far into the hinterlands. What strange circumstance had so disrupted Knowles' flight? They all scrambled around the downed plane, while Henry steadied the bruised but undaunted movie star. Suddenly, the sheriff made an astonishing discovery... a bullet hole in the wing close to the cockpit, so close that it had grazed the fuselage only inches from pilot and cockpit. Stop the presses! Patric Knowles had been shot down! The story rang out around the world, sort of, but more importantly it rang out around the studios more than sort of. And the mystery, the mind-boggling mystery of why this handsome and adventurous movie star had been shot down and by whom, would continue the story into tomorrow and tomorrow and tomorrow. No one in Hollywood had realized how importantly the public and the media regarded this under-used star who certainly deserved to get the girl now. And a good aviator role! Shortly thereafter, Patric Knowles was allowed to (spoiler alert) win the heart and the hand of Olivia De Havilland in "Four's A Crowd," while Erroll Flynn wound up with Rosalind Russell. Amazing what a little near-death can accomplish. Within a half decade, the downed pilot went on to soar with brilliant performance in John Ford's classic "How Green Was My Valley," holding his own with one of the greatest ensembles of character actors ever ensembled.

I was truly impressed with Henry's stunt, but I commented that he and Knowles were lucky the country cop had found the bullet hole. "I paid him to find it," Henry smiled. "How did you know it was there?" I demanded in a sudden gush of wonder and respect... "Because I shot it through the plane myself before Patric took off at Santa Monica airport, waiting until a plane was landing to cover the gunshot." Now that's press agentry! The guy who had the creativity and gumption to do that was absolutely doomed to head the first and still most important independent public relations agency in the world. It wasn't just the gumption and the gall, it was the brilliance in which he had played all of the elements of disaster and mystery... and, most importantly, the suspense of the inconclusive twist. He had pulled off the perfect publicity stunt. I never even got close to that one. Well, maybe close.

It was also on an occasion of Christmas cheer that Henry shared with me the evolution of his supreme philosophy of business success... Keep The Client Happy. I don't recall if it was Gabby Hayes or Smiley Burnette... I have a hunch it was Smiley because I had the impression that Henry was dredging this tale up from the '30s, and Smiley started his sidekick-ship with Roy Rogers in 1938 with "Billy The Kid Returns." Gene Autry and Gabby Hayes didn't get going until 1941. At any rate, it was a contrivance Henry dreamed up for one of the bearded western super-costars... the ones who were always some cowboy king's best friend but never made it to the center ring of stardom like Walter Brennan did. But Brennan cheated... he was a brilliant actor. It was in those days before the evolving system allowed Henry to dream of, much less achieve, empire, and every client then and forever more was a client, part of the list, part of the gross and therefore exceedingly important. Keep the client happy.

I suppose Henry had done everything a good PR guy could do to keep Smiley or Gabby in the industry eye, probably had him at the right events, associated him with key charities where what had not yet been dubbed "networking" could take place. Henry may even have taken columnists Louella Parsons and Hedda Hopper to the point where they could spell his name, whichever one of them he was. Perhaps there were a few breaks in fan magazines, a place where cowboy movie sidekicks had never drifted like a tumbleweed before. But Smiley or Gabby was unhappy and he let it be known. What more the dissatisfied sidekick could wish Henry could not figure out. So he asked him. In response, Smiley or Gabby uttered the name of a small town in Oklahoma or Texas... his hometown. "The folks back there don't know if I'm alive or not, not unless one o' my films happens 'a show up at the movie house." Henry checked out the one weekly newspaper town and started snowballing the local newssheet with stories about Gabby or Smiley. He and the editor, who also ran the printshop, were on a first name basis, and this heartland journalist finally threw up his hands and said there was only so much about Gabby or Smiley that he could print. Henry suggested a deal. He would send the guy one story a week, along with a check for ten bucks. In return, the newspaper guy would print one copy of the issue in which that story would replace another which had actually run. He would send that proof off to Henry who then sent it off to Gabby or Smiley. It went on for years. The client wasn't getting the same good job he'd received before, but now he was content. Keep the client happy. I loved looking into Henry C. Roger's true press agent soul un-camouflaged by Brooks Brothers suit and striped silk tie with matching breast pocket silk handkerchief.

I so deeply regret that Henry didn't get drunk more often. It's clear that the most colorful and flamboyant period of independent Hollywood publicity was during that first decade and a half of sound movies when flacks were fleet-footed outsiders, guerilla fighters hustling a system which held artists in tight grasp, teaching and expanding the benefits of personal control of one's publicity and reputation. For all of his dignity, sagacity and stature when I knew him, I have good reason to suspect that the earlier Henry was one helluva delightful, creative and daring scamp. I would prefer to have said "rogue," because its connotations better capture his lithe sophistication and grace, but it has a tinge of "outlaw," and his son Ron and daughter Marcia remain friends of mine. They might not understand how I honor the youthful Robin Hood in anyone.

There's a great irony in this new era in which the suppositions and blind items of blogs and websites can become the well-springs of new "news." *It is no longer the press agents who are creating whoppers.* The proliferation of gossip blogs have nothing to lose in their flailing for attention. And if they actually get a story right... or even wrong in the right attention-getting way, they can go viral. This can impose pressure on mainline media who feel compelled to follow up on the wild stories.

The legit gossip media do it using real and not imaginary sources. Matt Drudge, an irrepressible innovator and provocateur of this frantic website-driven news age, maintained a kind of credibility and fear factor by acquiring a coterie of tipsters, as did entertainment trade bomb tosser Nikki Fink who set herself apart with her access to insiders with reasons to help her beat some hot industry news to the street. That is the oldest and most legitimate tool of journalism.

Harvey Levin was a long-respected "conventional media" journalist, who brought the traditional disciplines of news-digging and verification to the "agent provocateur" reporting for which his TMZ set the pattern and reigns supreme. The jokey group rap format in which TMZ's news unfolds on TV catches the irreverent spirit young viewers bring to their lust for celeb news. Not my taste, but it is the taste of the times. He and TMZ, on television and on line, have become driving discoverers and initiators of significant news which dominates the rest of the media for days or weeks. How did TMZ uncover and shoot out of a cannon the footage of Baltimore Ravens running back Ray Rice's pounding his fiancée in an elevator when the exorbitant resources of the NFL had seemingly failed to do. That failure became a big part of the unfolding story. Conventional media had merely dipped their toes in the water of this outrage until TMZ brought the smoking gun... or smoking fist... to indisputable attention. What did they suppose happened in the elevator before Rice dragged an unconscious woman out by her hair? Isn't that the living image of how we always depicted Neanderthal sexism? What more apt evidence of this NFL mentality than when one league spokesperson told TMZ that the person they would never let get back in the game was Janet Jackson? Wife beaters, child beaters and dog torturers? Sure, everybody deserves a second chance. The elevator camera scoop didn't merely uncover the news… it *made* more news happen. Often the most compelling news-streams are the cover-ups which succeed juicy news occurrences. Look no further than Watergate, that most history-making of scandals.

I first dialed into the transition to tabloid in the mid-seventies when one of Jerry Pam's Brit journalist friends, a former London Daily Mail gossip reporter named Robin Leach, hired us to help throw an introduction-to-Hollywood party (which some memory tells me we held at the old DGA theatre and office building) for an Australian publisher who was starting a super-market paper in the US called the Star. He had set Robin as his show biz editor, and his name was… let me think… oh, yes, Rupert Murdoch. This was well before Robin's champagne wishes and caviar dreams days… And don't mock that much-mocked tag line. Robin built it into one of the first big winners of a then-new phenomenon which we know as… branding. *It's very possible for something to annoy you into awareness.* It took Robin viral before anyone knew what viral was. And before there was an internet to send things coursing through our digital veins.

It all tied together nicely. Fanciful smoking-gun gossip news-hawking had long driven English journalism which is called Fleet Street in the same way that American financial scrambling is called Wall Street. Mr. Murdoch was planting the seed deep by bringing Fleet Street's top gun to our shores. A year or so later I knew that the game was over when I received a call from a TV Guide reporter, and he had a British accent. Too late for Paul Revere… the British had landed and dug in.

I intended this section to be confession, not accusation. Back to my own reckless youth and the reckless and colorful youth of Hollywood promotion. Movie publicity early on glamorized its stars with fabricated lives and backgrounds, well earning the low esteem in which the craft became held. This continued as independent publicists grew to relevance in Hollywood, and it was in full flower when I injected myself into the game in the mid-'50s. It was all very fast and loose, and had been since they first started charging money to see flickering images on stretched sheets. The guys the nickelodeon moguls brought in to talk up the new amusement were not going to be shackled by mere truth. The faces on those sheets got names and adventurous back-stories to go with them. With no one to fact-check them, they could bring unlimited imagination to the publicity game, and when the baton was passed to us, we liked that it really was a game.

Less-than-accurate "yellow journalism" was one hallmark branch of newspapering in the late 19th and early 20th centuries, and the nickelodeon film press agents happily plowed this fertile field of fable, perfecting the art of credible wild stories… Publicists since have gentrified their secret weapon with many names. "Spinning," "dressing up the truth," "a likely scenario", "making it sexy," "stretching the truth," "selective truth," "presenting it to advantage," "putting rose-colored glasses on it," "emphasizing the positive," "doctoring," "bending the facts," "getting creative," "massaging it," "putting a little make-up on it," "dream-ups"… It has been euphemized and qualified, excused, justified, purified and rationalized in one hundred self-forgiving catch phrases… the age-old dynamic tension between utility and conscience. Press agents thus created permission to select, edit, interpret or adjoin the facts a touch to make a story fly and to give it the most positive impact.

Bill Feeder was one of the great pros I worked with at Rogers & Cowan, a former trade paper reporter and editor who, when he came over to our side (the dark side, many journalists would argue) became the most accomplished trade paper planter of all time. If a story didn't break with a front page banner headline, he had a sense of failure. Bill made one of the most profound analyses when a bunch of us were discussing "phoneys.". "There's no such thing as a phony," he said. "There are only plausible realities." This from a great journalist who knew both sides of the coin. By the desperate justifications of press agent logic… what a brilliant construction! It preceded the political concept of "plausible denials" by several decades. Speaking of which, when it comes to inventing the truth and sticking to it, Hollywood has nothing on Washington, D.C. Inside the Loop, the claims and dissemblings are even… yes… loopier.

As improbable as it seems, press agents have conscience and a strong sense of self-preservation, each of which argues strongly for adherence to essential truth. *PR is a vehicle of propulsion, and in any locomotion, the most important element is the capacity to brake,* to be able to slow down and stop before you go over the cliff. Every story has to be credible and to be able to stand up to the strong forensic challenge to which it just might be subjected. To accomplish that, it has to have a strong frame of truth. You can't wander far from the truth without losing credibility. I was at a studio meeting once, each press agent at the table representing some element of a film. One of them had had a story bounce sky-high that morning... the refutation by a college that it was presenting an honorary degree to a top personality as had been recklessly announced. The afflicted star's press agent had to leave early. He had sensed throughout the meeting the sizzle of nobody's knowing what to say, and that silence became particularly oppressive as he got up to leave. "Helluva break we got this morning on (whoever,) huh? Tomorrow they'll all think he got it." Maybe a few would, maybe most, but the client certainly would not. Do not send to know for whom the bell tolls. If a non-factual "plant" is so rife with incaution that it bounces, it tolls for thee.

It can work the other way... a story that's plausible but not true can be flown so often that it infects the minds of those concerned. While I was at Rogers & Cowan, the company was representing Queen Saroya, whose marriage to the Shah of Iran had ended for reasons of son-lessness. She hadn't given birth to a male heir. The separation was super news, Mohammad Reza Shah Pahlavi and the Shabanoo (or Shawano) Queen Saroya, joined in what would prove to be the last reign of the Pahlavi Dynasty. This great and dignified beauty, made more glamorous by the sadness of her story, was agented in her new acting career by Kurt Frings who had a "stable" of prominent actresses of the time... Elizabeth Taylor, Audrey Hepburn, Caroll Baker, Elke Sommer among them... and most of these Rogers & Cowan represented because of Henry and Warren's close relationship with our next-door neighbor, Kurt Frings. At one point Queen Saroya was added to the list. Dino de Laurentiis, at Kurt's persuasion, signed her for a film and announced his intention of starring the former empress in "Stories Of A Woman," with three top male stars to appear opposite her, each in a separate episode. Two were quickly cast, but the third role remained open. Pat Kingsley and I were on the Saroya account, and I thought that I could use that remaining male casting to benefit a prominent young actor, a client or ours, who was in the desperate midst of a dry spell. I started planting stories that Dino de Laurentiis was thinking about him for the role. I rationalized that... why WOULDN'T Mr. de Laurentiis at least have THOUGHT about him? And media seemed to be buying it. For some reason, I was able to get that story picked up (printed) over and over again in different guises. One afternoon, I saw Frings as he and I were each parking our cars behind our adjacent buildings. Kurt called out, "I just had lunch with Dino de Laurentiis." My first thought was "oh, oh, that story is about to blow up in my face" but what I said was, "And?" "And I asked him who he has lined up for the third role opposite Saroya." Ignoring a sudden queasiness, I bravely said, "And?" "And he said that who he wants is (the name of my client,) but he hasn't heard back from him." Kurt knew I was behind the stories, and he laughed uproariously, not a common behavior for him. Even a mega-mogul like de Laurentiis had been spun by a story about himself. Dino had read it so many times, he'd come to believe that he'd actually made the offer. I quickly called my client's agent and he called de Laurentiis the next morning, but the producer had already heard back from somebody else's agent.

I continue to have the honor of serving quite a few of our great, national treasure legends, but I grew up in an age when a very high percentage of what we call stars really were legendary in that substantial way. Who today represents charmingly cynical manliness as Clark Gable, Humphrey Bogart, Gary Cooper, Bill Holden and Paul Newman did or such sweeping elegance and charm as Cary Grant and Greer Garson, Katherine Hepburn, William Powell or Gregory Peck had? Nor is there a Clint Eastwood, John Wayne, Burt Lancaster in the ranks of the boxoffice dominating comic book films which have supplanted crisp and clever noir thrillers. A Fonda, a Stewart, a Mitchum? Nowhere. A Stanwyck or Bergman to bedazzle and not merely entice. A Jean Arthur or Veronica Lake to do sexy riffs on beguiling innocence with delicious comedy timing? Every so often a Jennifer Lawrence comes along, and you hope, but then who will supply her with the roles and directors that Davis and Streep enjoyed? And who will do the hard work of scrabbling up funding for those kind of films? The love stories on the screen then made you breathlessly participant and the comedies in which you shed your daily concerns drew upon wit and personality and not vulgarity. The media, for its part, awarded awareness to what they considered the true accomplishment of these people and not the mindless excess as is now so often the case. I'm not suggesting that the unbridled imagination of the publicity then heightened the magic, but it did paint the industry and its people in the vivid colors they deserved. Publicity then was in Technicolor even when the films were in gorgeous black and white…

A reputation for veracity matters big time if one seeks longevity in the PR trade. They do still cut you some slack for a dream-up that makes a good story, one which is a harmless elaboration (rather than a manipulative fabrication,) a story that does at least tip its hat to the facts… The rule, very definitely, is that a press agent has to have… to have and to have EARNED… a track record of accountability, reliability and a true grasp of what is news, or else you don't stay in the business for 60 years or even 60 months. Another imperative is that you never feed any member of the media a story which can prove to be untrue… unless the journalist indulges or invites that kind of adventurism, as was the case with one major columnist of whom I shall shortly speak.

A press agent is best attired in a cloak of invisibility, the one I'm shedding to write this thing. Anonymity serves a publicist well, but who more than a press agent is impelled to determine what is on that stone they place at our head?… that final spin of your own story. Press agents do it for others, but everybody should be able to take a stab at it for themselves. Obviously, the stone is where the grieving family pays their respects, so maybe there should be a website where each person could have a place to suggest their own death-long summation.

The truth in our business… maybe in all businesses, maybe in life… is fungible, and I found out a dozen or so years back that a reputation for honesty is not totally dependent upon unvarying truth-speak. On that occasion, I was contacted by magazine writer Ted Casablanca who was doing a piece about a half dozen of the top entertainment publicists for Premiere Magazine, at that point a very premiere show biz publication. He already had some real superstars lined up… Paul Bloch, Pat Kingsley, Leslie Dart among them. My general reluctance to have visibility is vividly real. I mean it is viscerally real, bordering on dread. This collection of flashbacks is different, time to get things off my chest and onto paper for my grandchildren to read when they're old enough. But it was readily apparent that Ted's story was one in which you are either notably in or notably out. You were either on the list or you were not, with "not" the greater of two evils. Declining wasn't an option.

I asked Ted to meet me in my office at 7AM, , because I didn't want my staff to know I was doing it. And I had to offer him instant coffee because I don't know how to brew it fresh. It was one of those everybody-answers-the-same-questions articles… if you were a car, what would you be?… that kind of thing. I blew the one about what star you've never repped you would most like to have had as a client? I answered Marlon Brando, who would be in anybody's top three, but wouldn't Bogie have been fun? Anyway, I knew the one that was most definitely show-time was when he asked, "Do you ever lie?" My answer was "yeah. Y-e-a-h." Everyone else felt that absolute veracity was mandatory or that it was appropriate to fib only in the case of white-lies-to-protect-the-fragile-construct-of-someone-else'-very-being. I... I myself... simply didn't know how to say I don't lie without lying... and without very visibly inscribing that across my face. When the story came out, I got a call from a magazine editor who said he would like to work more with me. "The Premiere story?" I asked. "Yes, you were so honest." "Actually," I explained, "the answer was honest but it proved that I'm not." He wouldn't hear of that, and a nice contact was made.

The dream-up is an undeniable element of the craft, and its application from time to time even now cannot be refuted. Except that now it would have to be dream-up-lite, because the internet is such a jealous watchdog. What also cannot be refuted is that once upon a time and for a long time the wildly imaginative stories were fifty percent of the job and ninety percent of the fun. And if you're not having fun, PR can be a rough and tough way to make a living. I can't imagine how young people new to the game can ever come to love it the way we did. Even if you indulge the rationalization that we didn't lie as much as create new and more interesting truths, that's kind of a lie in itself. Press agents were and still are story-tellers, even as they employ only actual facts in their conveyance of news. They have always been "spinners" of tales. Telling the facts selectively, which of course is what we do, is not the same thing as telling the empirical truth. We are hired to persuade... just as are lawyers and bond salesmen and ad guys and a long and comprehensive list of other people who influence our lives and our purchases. Even doctors, rewarded by pharmaceutical companies for pushing their wares, are hired to persuade. The ads you read massage you and sometimes insult your intelligence. Wake up. Do you believe every word your insurance guy or stock-broker says? The guy who shows how, at $40 K a year, you can afford to buy that home of your dreams? Your life is aswirl in the insincerity of others.

Do press agents tell the truth, the whole truth and nothing but the truth. Of course not. And the spin on that answer?… who does? Ok, you're right… that's immaterial. We're talking the existential and categorical reality of press agenting. For many decades, the made-up stories… indeed, the lies… were an elusive and effusive (but certainly not exclusive) joy of the job. A lot of that fun went out of the game when we became, more's the pity, sanitized professionals. I still mourn that they ever closed down Dodge City. Press agents became solid citizens, but occasionally a made-up story still tells the truth more directly and more effectively than a boring set of misleading facts. And old habits die hard. Many of the talents my company has served and serves are so vividly and legendarily established and their doings past and present are of such import that the-facts-and-just-the-facts works just fine. On the other hand, in the noisy and fractured Now, with the cacophony of internet media running nonsense with wild abandon, media-generated stories are hastily gathered and spit out just because these outlets are by their digital nature instantaneous. A part of the media creates a tangled web of untruth… one we often have to correct. They have to bleat their news beats out ten seconds before the competition, and fact-checking much less journalistic triple-checking-the-facts be damned. Press agents are now often merely traffic cops trying to keep the news from racing the wrong way up a one-way street. Rumors are now, in the digital rush, co-equal with facts.

PR clients don't pay their pros to have fun. For the clients, it's the results that count… results and results alone. It's not just getting space which is evaluated. No, it's the RESULTS of that space which matter. It boils down to reflecting a sense of your clients' activity. It's all predicated on the fact that everybody puts money down when some guy is rolling sevens. The immediate specific result… the newspaper article or the great break on ET… that is transitory. The second they put an article down, they forget the specifics. The real value is the cumulative effect of these puffs of awareness which conveys a sense of a star's or a director's or a production company's or studio's or network's momentum. Momentum is self-perpetuating.

To be effective, those dream-ups, those made up stories which were for so long a primary instrument of PR, had to relate the basic truth of what you were selling, had to convey the basic truth of your sales message. They had to have a steel rod of truth at their core, some essential truth about the client. A publicity story, fact or fiction, has to convey in some way the true essence of the client.

There was no point in selling a story that Marilyn Monroe had delivered a treatise on James Joyce to the Oxonian Society. It wouldn't sell what she sells. It wouldn't convey her heat as a superstar, the deep public affection for her in her troubles, her comic skills, the world's sexiest lost puppy. Most important of all, it simply wouldn't be believable. Very often an absolutely true story is not believable, but you accomplish nothing but your own disaster and your client's embarrassment if you try to sell a story that is neither true nor believable. You have to be selling what is unique about them and what is valid about them. Once again, *that which is publicized has to be able to live up to its publicity.*

Starting Out on the Left Foot

For the half century before I came on the scene, Hollywood studio publicity had always played fast and loose with the truth. Biographies were dictated by what the studio chiefs and their publicity henchmen thought would sell their contracted performers. Backgrounds were always colorful, and some of Hollywood's most riveting fictions came out of the typewriters of publicity department copywriters, not those of screenwriters. I was ushered into a "great tradition." So when I became a publicity pro somewhere in the middle of my junior year at UCLA, and when they realized I could write, nothing was off the table. Any wild story that could get printed made everybody happy. Well, not always. My Rogers & Cowan bosses needed some ink on how successful Johnny Weissmuller was, so I dreamed one up that the guy who swims like a fish was investing part of his film fortune in fish… that he was negotiating to buy a sardine cannery in Bangor, Maine. There were over 20 top syndicated columnists, and far more key locals. Los Angeles had six major papers and 16, count 'em 16, columnists, and an item in any of them could make an account very happy. It wasn't as cut-throat or desperate as "The Sweet Smell Of Success," but it was in that ballpark. Erskine Johnson was one of the most sought after syndicated columnists, and he was the one who printed the Weissmuller blurb as a lead story (at the start of the column.) And, as result, his column got yanked permanently from his paper in Bangor, Maine… where they didn't have any sardine canneries. What made people think these things worked? Perhaps the fact that they did. If people were talking about a star, it meant that he or she was hot. My bosses thought the Weismuller backfire was funny, even though we were banned from Skinny Johnson's column for a month. Warren Cowan told me that "Skinny will forget it in a couple weeks, and Johnny loved the story. He even has his people looking into investing in a cannery. People will never stop eating sardines." Well, at least I wasn't canned. The message to me was "keep writing."

In the interest of my own company's reputation and the reputation of my peers, I point out emphatically and somewhat nostalgically that the roller-coaster ride of "imagined reality" rolled to a stop somewhere in the early '80s. Like all good rides, we hated to see it end. It had been fun for everyone while it lasted... and effective PR for the clients. What brought it to a halt was that damned determination by the independent publicity pros to go "corporate," the new word for respectable... I would estimate that the golden age of imagination died at about age seventy-five, since the promoters of the early movies had played fast and loose with the truth since before the 20th century reached its teens. The pranks of the old free-and-easy days hadn't been merely fun. They got the job done. But the rules changed. We are no longer fly boys.

Henry Rogers, who had been an impelling force in the anything-goes day, was also a large part of that sad transformation to dignity. From the time I'd joined Rogers & Cowan, Henry was moving the business... certainly moving himself... toward respectability, shedding the Hollywood hustler perception that still colors our craft. He was the right guy for the job, tall and of impressive bearing. He had the manners and Bond Street presentation to accomplish that difficult morphing of the socio-economic status of flacks. Henry personally delivered press agentry unto social stature in the mid-'60s when Prince Phillip, royal consort of the Queen of England, made a tour of America, and Henry Rogers was appointed and anointed his press attaché for the historic visit. It shed a great aura on Rogers & Cowan and, in fact, on the entire clan of Hollywood publicists. Henry, who had almost completely triumphed over stuttering with impressive precision of speech... his occasional hesitancy, as he struggled to suppress some consonant repetition, conveyed thoughtfulness. He comported himself impeccably. The only slight setback was when Henry accompanied Prince Phillip on a tour of the 20th Century Fox studios. Afterwards, Henry was asked in an impromptu press conference how the Prince had reacted to the experience. Henry smiled and shared the amusing fact that "Prince Phillip referred to the studio as 19th Century Fox." Rogers & Cowan was immediately fired off of two films for 20th, including "How To Steal A Million" with R&C client Audrey Hepburn. It was a worthwhile trade-off. Press agents no longer had to come in the back door. Henry had taken one for the team. More than anything else, it was that one gaffe that really drove home the fact that Henry C. Rogers, a Hollywood press agent of some Jewish orthodoxy, was a friend and trusted associate of British royalty.

The sad legacy of our once-wild antics, the conviction that will not fade, is that we still are bundled with D.C. lobbyists as people who would do anything to make a sale. Let me make this perfectly clear... a press agent cannot sell something that isn't true or that the public doesn't want... can't sell it. Can't fly it. We are in the silk purse business, not the sow's ear business... except when there is a market (as there now is in some aspects of reality TV) for sows' ears. We might get there via an artful exaggeration or clever elaboration, but .when it comes down to it, we can sell only the truth. The selective truth which accentuates the positive. Most people live lives of selective truth. In my own case and as with most top Hollywood press agents, the kind of talent we represent makes that easy. But a truth must be re-iterated many times before it is part of public record and public consciousness, and that is where the art and validity of press-agenting comes in. Writing it and getting it in the first time is easy. The fifth time takes creativity.

The Abstract Metaphor

The practice of whatever-sticks-to-the-wall flackery had its own ethics, its own stringent rules. First, it had to be a good story. Second, it had to be a credible story. Third, it had to be a story that benefited the client's career. (No evidence of ethics yet, only pragmatism.) But fourth, it had to in some way capture the essence of the client, be consistent with who the client actually is. It shouldn't mislead the reader as to what it is that makes the client unique. It's that fragile factor which determines if you make it as a press agent.

It was an observation offered by my then five year old grandson Dashiell at the Christmas dinner table which put into perspective for me what it is exactly that I do as a professional. He explained how a publicity story is, in fact, a metaphor. At a lull in the Christmas table conversation, I asked, "Do you know what part of the turkey I like best?" No one cared to fashion a guess. "The gravy," I said as though that were obvious. Dashie and his year older cousin Alyssa said in unison, "I don't get it." "Ok," I said, "I'll explain. Do you know what my favorite part of an apple is?" Again, no guesses. "The sauce," I said. There was a pause and then Dashie said, "OK, I get it. You're using 'gravy' in the abstract to signify the experience of eating turkey at a holiday meal, the taste and the happiness of it and all of us together." It took my breath away, because that is exactly what I was doing, but I could never ever have articulated it. *A publicity story is an abstraction, a metaphor for all of the positive values you want to convey about a client.*

There had once been dignity in imagination… and respect. For the pros, reading someone else' clever puff piece was an experience of wonder, like watching a Cirque de Soleil artist defying gravity and instincts of self-preservation in some impossible feat. You'd see the other guy's dream-up in print and admire its grace and execution. It wasn't as though the media wasn't in on the gag. One of the classic movie press agents was the late and sadly-subtracted Bob Yeager. The trade papers would always give front page breaks to Bob's signature device,. slinging stories about fictional film people with ironic names… a comedy writer named R.U. Kidding or a sound guy name A. Lyttle-Lowder or a stunt guy named Bjorn Fearless. I just made those up… Bob was much better. Bob would work them into stories that let the world know that the film he was working on was in production. It was the trade paper equivalent of the comics section, and every producer or star loved it when Bob put a knuckle-ball across the plate for them. Crew workers on the set chuckled over it all morning. Bob Yeager was a treasured performance artist within the industry. The trade papers were in on it, happy to swish the spotlight over to Bob's trademark gags, most often in a small box on the front page. In the morning three people would say to you, "Did you see the Bob Yeager in Variety today?" The Bob Yeager. The Publicists Guild chose to give me an award once, and though I don't accept awards (or wouldn't if someone were so misguided to offer,) I did show up for this one because it was, after all, called the Bob Yeager Award. I also made a point in my little speech of establishing that I was accepting it not for myself but on behalf of the people behind the charities at the Entertainment Industry Foundation. But nobody seemed to hear that, and I was another guy getting another award as if he felt he deserved it.

My kinship with Yeager was in his delight in doing it his way and making the industry like it. Guttman & Pam hired him to unit several films we handled, not only because he helped you make your client film visible, but also because he was so enjoyable. He lived up to his legend, the acerbic sense of humor and the somehow completely compatible and amusing dour demeanor, the innate understanding of what made a good and breakable (able to break into print) story, the de rigueur cigar he always chomped at the corner of his mouth. He was a deservedly famous PR guy and personality. How Preston Sturges or Howard Hawkes neglected to slam him in front of the camera as one of their stock company of comedic supporting stars I will never understand.

Another high visibility PR joker with a gimmick was David Epstein… not a unit man but a kind of one-man band indie PR firm. You have to understand that Bob and David and the rest of their comic ilk were good PR pros who happened to have a calling card gimmick. As such, they reflected how happily the industry press played straight man to… or at least played along with… these flacks' satiric flare with a phoney. David's specialty, the double-headed quarter with which he could always win a PR toss, was the famous producer J. Farrington Howard (I'm approximating that name but it had that kind of patrician flare to it… a name connoting great power and wealth.) Every time David needed a break on a couple of his clients just to keep the dish of his representation twirling on the stick, he pulled J. Farrington Howard out of his bag. A publicist is like that vaudeville act Ed Sullivan had on his show so often, the guy who lines up the tall, flexible sticks and then sets one, two, three dishes spinning on them having to rush back to one and two to rev them up again before he could race on to four and five. So each time Dave had to keep a couple of clients spinning, he would hit the trade papers with a story that producer J. Farrington Howard had purchased such and such a script from Epstein writer client so-and-so and had hired Epstein director client what's-his-name to "meg" the film (directors once called out orders through a megaphone) with Epstein actor clients who's-that and him-again to star. J. Farrington Howard got out his check book several times a month. The part of the town that was in on the joke loved it, and the other part told their casting directors to look into who's-that and him-again because they seemed to be working a lot. That's the real point of this. David kept his clients' careers alive. *Awareness, awareness, awareness. People don't remember where they heard something or even precisely what they heard. They just remember that they heard something.*

That third half of the town, the media who chronicled and facilitated the industry's toilings, gladly passed these eye-winks along. As my Variety reporter friend had revealed to me, the papers had to fill space and they had to entertain. You can't fill up a daily dose of laughs just with clever headlines. So we all followed J. Farrington Howard and the merry ménage of David Epstein's pied piper parade through the list of films that never got made. And then one morning… one shocking morning… we all woke up to read on the front page of the Hollywood Reporter that J. Farrington Howard had passed away… probably of over-work. The story went on to list all of J. Farrington Howard's films, citing the titles Epstein had dreamed up. The pall-bearers enumerated were all of those Epstein clients who had written, directed and starred in J. Farrington Howard's impressive filmography. Announcing the tragic death, of course, was well-known independent press agent David Epstein at whose home the memorial would be held. No one was more surprised and saddened to read the front page of the Hollywood Reporter that morning than well-known independent publicist David Epstein.

So now we acknowledge that other group of specific players who joyously made the Golden Age of the Imaginative Dream-up possible…. the wise journalists and editors who knew this gagging was good for the system. Don Gillette was a long-time editor of the Hollywood Reporter. He was a scrappy little guy who knew how to keep his pages alive with real news. He spoke with a raspy kind of whisper voice because he had been mustard-gassed in the trenches of World War I. He didn't have a chip on his shoulder because of that bad draw of the cards, but he also didn't have time for Hollywood sharpies to screw him or his pages over, guys who would deceive his staff to try to sell an unfounded news story. He drove his staff to get the news before it was ready to be gotten and to check the facts and then check again. But he had a soft spot in his kind heart for a vintage gagster like David Epstein and was glad to participate in the charade… up to a point. On the day before that morning of J. Farrington Howard's passing, he pulled a gag out of his sleeve, too. Who knew Don had that good a sense of humor. Editors all over town wept that they hadn't got the beat on Farrington's sudden demise, and they tossed Gillette a tip of the hat. David Epstein was not left sobbing at the grave. He and his stable, former pall-bearers all, continued as functioning pros in the industry for many years thereafter.

The fact that the legitimate media were all aware of the strong current of invented stories that were part of press agent planting, reflects that they knowingly tolerated it with amusement and conspiracy. They did not merely tolerate it, they welcomed it. It helped them accomplish that other major aspect of their task…. entertaining their readers or viewers. Wouldn't you draw that conclusion from the following passage from a major article Time Magazine ran in 1958? Time

Magazine, the very fountain of journalistic veracity, featured a substantial piece eulogizing the still-living-and-kicking Russell Birdwell, that early practitioner of the fine art of fabricated news planting, referring to him in the story as "the bird," "Hollywood's busiest huckster" and, again, as film town's "flashiest flack." In the piece, Time related with clear admiration:

"Not long ago, Birdwell sold gullible movie columnists the phony yarn that Greta Garbo had expressed an interest in the movie version of 'Lolita.' Director Stanley Kubrick, who is Birdwell's client, is supposed to have ruled Garbo out of "Lolita" but offered her the part of Marlon Brando's mother (there's no such part) in Brando's new picture, 'One-Eyed Jacks.'" This must be taken as witness from Olympus that media understood that the flow of show biz news is inherently boring and therefore the enrichment of press agent imagination was to be cherished rather than condemned. We seem to have been admitted to the media modus operandi as both town crier and court jester. As long as it didn't bounce and embarrass the reporter or the media outlet, the laugh wasn't on anybody. The bolder the con, the more bi-lateral the joy in it.

A tangential point I include only because I just mentioned Marlon Brando's "One Eyed Jacks" (or, at least, Time Magazine did) and because this following story has always made me laugh… It's an item which appeared in Belle Greenberg's nightclub-hopping column in the old Hollywood Citizen News during the production of that film… "One Eyed Jacks." Belle had bumped into Pina Pellicer, the Mexican actress who told Belle through a heavy accent that she was here making her American debut in the Brando western (as Belle heard it through Pillicer's accent) "One Night At Jack's." For the record, Brando, not Kubrick, directed "One Night At Jack's"… just kidding, "One Eyed Jacks." But that story, recalled a half century later, shows that a silly item can implant awareness of a film in one's mind for a lot longer than its run at the corner movie house or that modern transplantation, the mall multiplex.

The amazing thing is that these fabricated press agent puffs earned a lot of credulity. And still more incredibly, many of the people who had pioneered and deftly exploited the art of plausible puffery were absolute suckers for other people's cons. As I've noted, Warren Cowan habitually took the fame pulse of his clients, assessing which was riding the highest crest of fame that day… determining his favorites among the favorites on the fame-ometer of his client list. For Warren

Cowan, Danny Kaye was always right up there at the apex of the pyramid of fame which was the Rogers & Cowan talent representation, many of whom were not merely stars but galaxies. Danny Kaye was that for all of us. When, as kids, my friends and I saw him in his debut film, "Up In Arms," we thought he was comedy incarnate. We didn't merely want to see him, we wanted to ingest him, assume him as an alter ego. I remember still the ad line which Samuel Goldwyn had splashed across the newspapers for that film… "From now on, you'll spell clowning with a Kaye." If the product doesn't live up to a line like that, you don't remember it for over seventy years. I told Danny once that my wife had learned English by watching him in "The Court Jester" six times. She still can do the "chalice from the palace, flagon with the dragon" routine.

Danny Kaye was always and forever in Warren Cowan's heart as his client of clients, and why not? A stand-alone talent if ever there was one. I'm addressing here obvious PR stories tailored of whole cloth, and a perfect fast ball of that decorated Variety's front page one morning. The story in the paper on that particular day was that Red Skelton had signed a deal with Toho Studios to make a film completely in mime and that he would co-star with the members of the Imperial Kabuki Theatre. I couldn't wait to hand it to Warren to brighten his morning. Its sheer transparency had the daring of a perfectly planned highway robbery. It was a great dream-up that any PR guy would surely salute. Warren read the story and then his face started to turn dark shades of unhappiness. "Oh my God," he lamented in loud agony, missing the point, "why couldn't we have gotten that deal for DANNY?!"

You may justly ask what was the difference between those created stories spiced with plug elements, and the nasty fabrications of today's tabloid papers? The difference lies in that word "nasty." The press agent contrived beaux jests were written to be positive, while the object of tabloid fictions is anguish, punishment and humiliation. But you're right. If those sins-against-truth are truly gathered in St. Peter's pages, we'll be lucky to make it to Purgatory.

It's important to note that gag stories… that's what they were called, gags… almost always strove for some element of credibility as well as the essential element of plug. They had to make a point. They had to achieve some positive spin reflecting the clients' legitimate accomplishment, esteem and heat within the industry. It all had to add up to the basic premise of the game… what are you trying to convey and to whom? The point was always to help a career, to help sell the client's projects, make the sales bigger, make the success resonate in the minds of industry people who decide castings. Yes, we were reaching out to the public, building fan base. But in fact, a campaign is actually directed to about 600 people… the industry people who can cast your client. So if a story didn't work toward that end, it wasn't worth the effort of dreaming up and planting it. Why lament the passing of gags and gimmicks? They served to take the edge off the inescapable fact that PR is a pressure-laden business. Blowing off a little steam was so restorative.

James Mason and Tony Curtis were clients who sufficiently enjoyed planted mis-information as to have demanded that of me. And others were not inured to its fun and effect. This was confirmed to me recently when my friend and longtime client, actor/director/renaissance figure Maximilian Schell (now so regrettably the late Maximilian Schell) called from his farm in the Austrian Alps for holiday greetings, during which he told Gisela that one of his favorite adventures in publicity had been those relating to "the countess." He had always punished me for that one, but he apparently had enjoyed the hell out of it, even though it had such a tragic ending.

Max, often derided me for creating stories designed to keep the film industry acquainted with all of the great projects his talents and his Oscar and other awards had earned him. "When I get a new film," he would say, "just put it in the paper." That would suffice, perhaps, if one hundred percent of the people who can cast him were to read and to retain the first story announcing his work continuity. That assumption borders on absurdity. *Repetition is the very soul of awareness… repetition, repetition, repetition.* And the press agent has to find different and effective ways to achieve that repetition. To do so, you have to find new angles to work it into the print or electronic media which reach the attention and awareness of decision makers.

So Max Schell wins the Oscar for Best Actor over one of the greatest fields ever to grace that category. He is rakishly handsome, beloved by women and a legendary lover of many of the most famous of them. All of these things were constructive elements of stardom. So there he was, at 27, of impeccable sophistication and a newly crowned prince of Hollywood. So what does he do? Bury himself. He goes off to film a "Hamlet" in GERMAN for German TV then takes off to Vienna to star in some obscure stage play that isn't going to get reviewed in our town's single German language paper read by no one in Hollywood anyway. Four months after a historic Oscar win he is for all Hollywood intents and purposes retired. His Oscar follow-up is such an invisibly foreign event that even the Hollywood Foreign Press don't know and don't care. AND he's my best friend. What am I going to do?... let him wander off into the desert? So how to make a play in Vienna resonate here and drum up some heat re-attaching the Oscar association. I begin a series of stories about a mysterious beauty who has taken the Royal Box at the Viennese theatre for the run of the production. Vienna is agog with the wonder and rumors of her identity. She is never seen behind the curtains of the box. A few stories later, it evolves that she is a Countess (with no indication of whether there is a Count getting dis-Counted in this unfolding romance.) The dozen red roses continue to appear on the stage for Max at the end of each performance. Is this tale going to bounce? Who in Vienna other than Max is going to hear of it? This German play in an Austrian city (yes, I fully comprehend Vienna's artistic supremacy, but what's an Oscar winner doing there? Can't he get a real job?) is getting more ink than the top SRO production on Broadway. After Max starts to get a slightly more career-enhancing project, "The Condemned Of Altona" with fellow Oscar winners Sophia Loren and Frederic March, directed by Vittorio deSica, the Jean-Paul Sartre play adapted by Abby Mann who wrote Max's Oscar vehicle, "Judgement At Nuremberg." Ok, now we're back in the groove. I can ease up on the Countess romance. But it doesn't ease up on itself. It keeps showing up in press speculation, and I'm telling people that Max doesn't tell me anything about the Countess, which is the only aspect of this escapade that is true. And that I've never met her... also true. Her specter and the media hunger for her is weaving its own magic. Max goes off to Indonesia to film a huge volcanic spectacle adventure film, "Krakatoa, East of Java" (VERY far east of Java because it is directly to the west of Java,) and media speculate why she doesn't join him and wonder if sheer distance will cool that blazing and possibly adulterous romance.

Max comes back to do the press junket for "Krakatoa," and during the foreign press portion, a mass Q&A at a Tahitian restaurant (well, at least Tahiti is east of Java,) the question of marriage plans for him and the Countess comes up and it cannot be shrugged off. Max becomes very grave, appears trapped, and he says, "This is going to come as a terrible shock to all of you and particularly to my friend Dick Guttman (my God, he's going to out me in front of all these people who work with me and trust me) Particularly to Dick who was closer to her than anybody. The Countess (I hold my breath) recently shed her mortal coils. (They are still waiting breathlessly) She passed away," he clarifies. "Dick, I'm sorry to tell you, but she is no more." It casts a terrible pall on the evening, but his bereavement is respected and she is not mentioned again.

So it was a pleasant surprise when Max made his holiday phone call from his Austrian farm (an annual entreaty that we visit him there) and revealed that, of all the adventures we'd had together, his favorite was the countess. "I think I should have let her live a little longer," he told Gisela. "She always made me smile."

Max once drew me into a press-boggling publicity skit of his own, although I had to be careful to walk a fine line between helping a friend out on a great hoax, and my obligation never to tell an outright lie to media, especially not one like this. This was such a whopper, I didn't want my fingerprints on it. Max had had it up to here on stories both false and mean which had been printed on him by a certain German language newspaper. His annoyance reached the point that he contrived to let this gossip paper conclude that he had committed suicide. He placed a call to one of its writers from a New York phone booth to inform him in a most distracted manner that he had been driven to thoughts of suicide by a rash of denigrating stories they had written about him. Remember, we're talking about one of the greatest actors of our time. He said he had instructed the one person he trusted, the one person he turned to in his troubles (obviously, but not identified directly by him as such, his psychiatrist,) to spread word to the media about who was to blame in the event that he went ahead with some desperate act to which their stories had driven him. I could imagine them practically salivating on the other end of the line. Wow, driving a big name to the big S, something to which even they had never aspired. Max gave them the number of his confidante on the guarantee that they would print her words exactly. Of all the great pieces of theatre he has produced, directed, written and starred in, even those which were Oscar/Emmy/Golden Globe honored, I actually think this was his favorite production.

The German paper, of course, called the person they were convinced was his psychiatrist, played brilliantly by his wife Natasha Andrechenko, one of Russia's greatest actresses. Her vague responses, not saying anything specific, being agitated but very covert, led them to believe that they were on to a hot-selling tragedy. What could be better? They were letting worst-case possibilities gestate in their hungry imaginations. Visions of black-draped sugarplums danced in their wee little tabloid heads. When they called next, she could hardly speak, so distracted was she. Mein Gott! Es ist schon passiert! It must have happened! The story leaked beyond that paper's editorial desk, because soon Natasha, or rather Max' shrink, was fielding calls from everywhere. It was about at that moment in the game that Max called me to say it was imperative that I not squelch the story, but he wanted me to know he was ok. He wanted the story to simmer long enough to get the paper very pregnant, so could I please shepherd it a little when I received calls? I told him I couldn't outright lie on such a gigantic deception, but I could tell the truth very intensely, in such a manner that they would think I was covering up some more awful truth. Which is how it proceeded. When one of the great papers of Europe called, quite delighted and excited to be on top of a juicy celeb suicide, I forced them to admit that they had obtained this story on a tip from the other less accredited paper. Wouldn't it, I argued, make more sense for the other paper to be tipped to a true story of this dimension by THEM? It could not possibly be true, I frantically reasoned with them. My emotionalism was fueling rather than dampening their conviction that a towering giant of German arts had taken his own life. I was distraught and adamant beyond any possibility that I was telling the truth. Press agents are all wannabe actors, and I was having fun. I advised them that they would be very sorry if they printed it, that I was absolutely positive these rumors were false. Everything I said was absolutely true. Max could not possibly commit suicide. If you hear a rumor to that effect, run in the opposite direction. He loved life. Well, what could they expect from some mendacious Hollywood press agent? A blatant cover-up. The story broke. By the time Max chose to put out the truth by calling other papers in outraged amazement that these two papers had made such a gross and offensive error, Max' bête noir paper had printed a bald-face lie, a horrific false story which Natasha and I had very truthfully denied up and down the line.

Chief among the unrepentant confessions of any film town flack, certainly the most joyously unrepentable ones of our shared reckless youths would have to involve the columnist Harrison Carroll who plied the readers of Hearst's The Herald-Express and then The Herald-Examiner with daily tales of the dangers with which movie stardom is fraught... except that I would be surprised if more than a sixth of these stories were the dictionary definition of "true". I don't really regret any lie I dreamed up for Harrison, because he relished every tale, and they sure were fun in the fabrication. Checking the unlikely possibility that I might be overstating that, I called Stan Rosenfield, a knight of the publicity round table, to double-check the truth about those lies. "Of course," Stan confirmed, "the highlight of the day was making up a whopper for Harrison. Don't you remember? We called them The Five Ds." "We did?" "Sure, a story with any of the five Ds was a lead. Danger, Death, Disaster, Divorce and Desperation." It was an automatic headline break. It was just Harrison's calling card, and we all played it. For instance, when Maximilian Schell was starring in the title role of "Bolivar," a South American production about that continent's beloved liberator, who cared? Most studio heads didn't know who Bolivar was. It wasn't, in the United States and particularly Hollywood, like playing Abe Lincoln. It was a Jay Walking question everyone would miss. But attention was paid when they read that during the filming of a scene of Bolivar's attacking an ancient fortress, one of the parapets crumbled under the weight of a heavy cannon, and huge chunks rained down on Max and other actors at the base of the castle walls. They cleared out fast, but one stumbled and Max, not one to leave a man behind, pulled him to safety. Ten seconds after the reading, the specifics would be forgotten, but there would be a vague awareness that this Oscar winner was gainfully employed in a big production. Every press agent vied to be the Harrison lead each day.

A Near-Death Experience

I personally was the victim of another Harrison Carroll near-miss calamity, one that was terrifyingly real. While I was at Rogers & Cowan, one of our top European stars was filming on location about thirty freeway miles west of the San Fernando Valley, and I arranged to pick him up and drive him back to his home in order to have some concerted time to go over our plans for him. Warren Cowan insisted I take his Cadillac convertible rather than my VW bug. His car had one of the first car phone units, as was Warren's determination to be the first to employ any new advantage. It was the early kind in which you contacted an operator to place your call with the incoming voice broadcast over the radio loudspeaker. On the way back, we had a blowout at about 85 mph, and the car was really fighting me. Our client was an experienced competitive driver, and he quietly directed me to a safe stop by demanding forcefully that I not hit the brake. We got to the side, and he wanted to change the tire himself, caving in the side of Warren's car in the process. It suddenly hit me that here was a perfect Harrison Carroll near-tragedy story, and I had a car phone on which I could actually put the star hero of the event (I was placing him at the wheel) on the phone with Harrison to recount the adventure. As we drove back, I kept urging the operator to put the call through for me, and she kept responding that she couldn't get through, which our client could plainly hear. This went on for the rest of the half hour drive, and, in frustration, I asked the operator to try again as I drove up the star's driveway. Again no contact. It was maddening. The star went into his house, and as I drove down the hill, the operator announced she could put through the call. Ten seconds after the hero of my story had exited the car, drat the luck . A perfect opportunity missed. Harrison's voice came on with his customary kindly "Hcy, kiddie, what's up?" I proceeded with the pitch. "Hey, Harrison... you know,," and I gave the name of the star, at which point Harrison's voice over the radio speaker phone said, "Oh, yeah. I hear his wife's screwing everyone in town." My blood drained to my feet. My client had been sitting in that seat in that car fifteen seconds before. What would I have done? What could I have said? I was gasping for air, literally, but I croaked, "Harrison, I'm on a car phone." "Sorry, kiddie," he said, "what's the story?" I composed myself sufficiently to give it to him, and then pulled the car to the curb and sat there with my hands on the wheel for about ten minutes, still listening to the bullet skim past my ear. Cutting it close is a little like taking it at the base of the skull. The next day, Harrision, who was a very sweet man, went with that story as a lead and decorated the story with a lot of nice comments about my client. It's great to be lucky, but too lucky can really spook the hell out of you.

Harrison Carroll's Last Lead

My Reckless Youth came to an end the sad day that Harrison posted his final column. Wally Beene and I sat in the Guttman & Pam offices the day before and vowed that Harrison should be saluted for his valued service with a Harrison Carroll special, a story of stories, one that could never ever again be planted with a straight face and crooked intentions. Guttman & Pam was at the time, representing a film in production entitled "Viva Max," its star, Peter Ustinov, and its director, Jerry Paris. It was a comic tale of a contemporary Mexican general leading a motley band in a planned retaking of the Alamo. It was shot for no logical reason, as were many films then, mostly in Cinecitta Studios in Rome. But that would defy any credulity for the phantasmagoric story we felt was the only one which could do honor to what that column had meant to press agents for decades.

So we shifted the production for the time and purpose of this story to a Texas location along the Rio Grande. In our story, the company had selected a location for a night shoot, but the light spill from a nearby small town would disturb the lonely nowhere the scene in question required. So they, according to our commemorative item, moved the company's cast, equipment and trucks a mile or so up the Rio Grande. And as Peter and John Astin and Jonathon Winters were in mid-scene, there was a great light which flashed like a streak of diagonal lightning in the clear sky and then they heard a huge rumble of impact back towards where they had originally intended to shoot. I actually had stolen the gist of this from a short story by the great American humorist and tall tale teller, O. Henry. I thought that appropriate because Harrison and O. Henry did have a whacky adventurism in common. In the morning the company discovered that a small meteor had landed exactly where they would have been filming. Never before was there and never again would there be the story of stars who almost were demolished by a shooting star.

That was Harrison's final lead. You can look it up, if such things are look-up-able. He went out with a bang and not a whimper. It wouldn't bounce… we knew that. Harrison's stories never did. I truly believe they were read like Aesop's Fables, and maybe Harrison was purposeful in that. I choose to believe that. No one disputed this report, no one said that there was no record of a meteor impact in Texas. No one even at the studio pointed out or even gave considersation to the fact that the company was having a pasta breakfast in Rome at the given time that this meteor had torn into the Texas landscape. The story left no footprint or fingerprint, no outcry or murmur. It was for all but a curious reflection in the morning's perusal of the printed news. Not an "oh my God," but an "imagine that." A blink. It was simply an awareness that such a film was being shot, and yet it was the perfect outrageous plug story to mark the end of the magnificent Hollywood tradition of phoney plants… a tradition known until your reading of this only to the brotherhood and sisterhood of flacks. I don't know if other press agents in town read it for what it was and understood. I would think so, and I would hope so. We were doing it for the fraternity and sorority of press agents who would have this hallowed outlet no more. The greatest Hollywood tradition of devil-may-care phoney plants was laid to rest with just the right tombstone,

one that had traveled the universe to land just where Ustinov et al had been. And the rest was silence…. sort of.

Rationalized Truth

There is, I learned from Warren Cowan, such a thing as "rationalized truth," my phrase, not his. I observed this when that most humane of directors, William Wyler, invited Warren to come to Columbia Studios to see a first cut of his film, "The Collector" starring Terrence Stamp and Samantha Eggar, both of whom I represented at R&C. When the titles started to roll, Mr. Wyler went out… and so did Warren. He was asleep before the writer's name came on. I watched the film alone, and it was not my favorite Wyler film by far. As the end titles started, I awoke Warren and started to give him some coaching on the film, but Mr. Wyler came in before I could communicate very much. "Warren," Mr. Wyler said, "what did you think of the film?" I was really interested to hear that answer. Warren didn't even know if the film was in black and white or color. "Willie," Warren said with grave sincerity, "you know what is really wrong with Hollywood? It's the fact that people throw around the words 'sensational,' 'moving,' 'brilliant,' 'historic' for everything they see. So what do you say when you really believe that a film deserves all of that and so very much more?" William Wyler was visibly moved. "Warren, that is one of the most beautiful compliments I've ever received. It's a film that's very demanding of an audience, I know, so I really appreciate your open mind and enthusiasm." Open mind, perhaps, but not open eyes. Warren had us beat a hasty retreat. On the way to the car, I told him that the devils were building a special bonfire for him. "Why?" Warren responded with unblemished innocence, "I didn't lie to him. I didn't say the film was any one of those things. I just asked what one could say if they really DID love a film that much." That, my friends, is rationalized truth. No lie was told, but no truth was told either. There was only inference from which all could be drawn.

Warren's sage commentary on what I call "Hollywood adjectives," was brilliantly punctuated years later when Jerry Pam and I chanced to meet at Ma Maison restaurant the producer of the film adaptation of our client Sidney Sheldon's "Bloodline." It was in post-production. Jerry said, "How's 'Bloodline' shaping up?" "Sensational," the producer said, "fantastic, terrific and unbelievable." "Really?" Jerry said in that British way in which "really?" expresses admiration, sort of a limey "wow." "Yes," the producer responded, "And I think we know how to fix it." But they never did.

The once-wild antics of the publicity tribe left and still leaves the pall of suspicion of duplicity, the cloud under which we flacks all still toil. Our inescapable tinge of original sin, no matter how long abandoned. In my own case and as with most top Hollywood press agents, the kind of talent we represent makes adherence to the truth easy. But a truth must be re-iterated many times before it is part of public record and public consciousness, and that is where the creative art and validity of press-agenting still comes in.

We come to the evaluation of relative evils. I think that good old-fashioned press agent prestidigitation…harmless, amusing and effective… has it all over today's corporate-think which is what got us into the recent worldwide depression. Suddenly we found out that all of those corporate truths on which investments and life savings and pension plans were bet were spurious and cynical beyond our darkest imaginations. I've always felt that press agents have the same Hippocratic Oath as doctors… "first, do no harm." If only that were true of the financial sector.

Here's another dirty little secret of publicity… press agents give media tips on news items. Doesn't sound very dirty, but let me add… some tip stories concern news items that are really none of the dispensing press agent's business. And that is not really a secret because every press agent and every media source is aware of the commerce in information in exchange for good will. Press agents, almost religiously, avoid pulling the rug on someone else' story and will quite often call the peer to say, "Are you planning a release on such and such? Well, you should know that it's about to leak." People have done that for me, and I've done it for others. The good press agent will never traffic in negative or scandal news because at least one person other than you yourself will know that you're that kind of low-down, conniving good-for-nothing… the journalist to whom you confide it and whose confidence in you and reliance upon you is your intended purpose. Secondly, there is no such thing as totally covering trails in this business, especially when it comes to negative news. Anyone who has a good reputation has certainly abided by this taboo. And, if he or she is wise, has also adhered to the good old mantra of *First Do No Harm. Nothing good comes from something bad.*

There is no ethical justification for "the tip." It's just a common practice between media and publicists, a favor done a friend, one small aspect of a smooth relationship of mutual assistance. It is not even a distant cousin of the noble and courageous Deep Throat-type "whistle-blowing" salvation of a nation's honor or the beans-spillings of the tobacco industry's nicotine cover-ups. It is simply a way each helps the other do his or her job most efficiently. It's not a quid pro quo kind of thing, simply a consideration between two people with occasional chance to assist each other.

But it does on occasion leave the press agent who is saying "why don't you look into this?" hanging on the hook of his own tawdry morals. A very famous press agent. got caught with his "plants" down one time when he tipped an equally famous columnist that a significant male Hollywood figure had become involved with the wife of a very famous man in a very different area of commerce. Am I being sufficiently obtuse? Good. That's my intention. Anyway, my good buddy press agent gave this up as a tip. By the very nature of tip-giving, the act challenges the journalist to do his or her own research to determine the story's veracity. Instead, the journalist just ran with it, not even identifying it as an apocryphal tip but rather putting it forward as probable fact. This is a cautionary tale that sheds a lot of light on the nature and dangers of "the tip," giving a hint of just how disastrous consequences can get. That the tip turned out to be a completely false lead, alluding to something that never happened, made it exceedingly more disastrous. In the dissemination of a tip, a press agent does not represent that it is a one hundred percent valid story. A tip is simply a suggestion of where the journalist with solid investigative technique might find a story that could be corroborated and, after the writer's and his publication's confirmation, printed.

The whole adventure turned out to be ill-advised, quite apart from the utter falsity of the tipped lead. The journalist printed the tip without checking it, and the paper printed it apparently without asking the columnist if the story was verified. A lot of people missed their cue, and a very big volcano of lawsuits and umbrage erupted. Journalists are not merely pretty good about not revealing a source, they hold it as an immutable obligation. They go to jail to protect it. But under the tectonic pressures from his or her publication and in threat of legal ramifications, this journalist gave up his or her source. So the press agent wound up facing a lawsuit for which his E&O insurance (Errors and Omissions) would cover only a small portion of the possible liabilities. He turned to me for assistance, not even knowing that I had once represented the gentleman involved in his tip. I called Mac St. Johns, who headed the Publicists Guild at that time, and we discussed that a tipped news story was not uncommon practice in our trade but that it has First Amendment aspects of some importance. That pertained even though this was a particularly misguided tip. Mac agreed to have the Publicists Guild send an "amicus curiae" brief to the court which was in another state, a place not likely to find empathy in its heart for a Hollywood hotshot who doesn't mind "making up lies" about one of that area's favorite daughters. The legal costs alone, even should he have won it, could have impoverished this press agent. I then called the subject of the tip, the person about whom the press agent had suggested the journalist might find some hot news. The star of the tip had by then moved on to assume some responsibilities within the federal government.

I appealed not to his forgiveness but to his devotion to the Constitution of the United States. We discussed the First Amendment ramifications even of a lie when it is put forward in a speculative manner and not as a truth, as despicable as even that was. We discussed the fact that a free press does depend on tips and speculations to enter into sometimes meaningful investigations to the benefit of the democratic process. None of that pertained here, of course, but we were talking principle. We discussed that, however harmful that story may have been, there is a fine line between tip and assertion, the blurring of which could do harm to First Amendment protections. An incredibly honorable and intellectual guy, he intervened to have the case dropped, but not his resentment of what had happened. This little anecdote does illustrate my prior assertion that there is no hiding the trail on the dissemination of negative news. I refer you again to that distinguished philosopher and close-confidant of Bambi, Thumper The Rabbit. and to his recitation of his father's advice that "if you can't say something good about someone, don't say nuthin' at all." Here's one where an incautious PR guy got burned, and the world's decided distrust of his peers got perpetuated

Some press agents go on to higher accomplishment. Jay Bernstein was a guy you had to love on the sheer basis of his audacity. He was another of my impressive list of former office sharers at Rogers & Cowan. Jay was justly a hall of famer among the interesting and successful people who survived occupying an office with me. He went on to run a publicity empire, a management empire and to produce such worthy projects as Stacy Keach's iconic Mike Hammer TV series.

During our office sharing, he often talked over his romantic life with me. Even in my twenties and thirties I was a kind of father figure. Press agents' dating or marrying of stars is an edgy business, a lot of them ending up punctuated by the letter ex. Steve Jaffe and Susan Blakely are one shining exception, and there are others. Undismayed, Jay had a number of notable liaisons, most prominently with the adorable singer, Joanie Somers. One day in the office, he motioned me to his desk, opened a drawer and took out a ring box, opening to flash a lot of ice on an engagement ring. "I'm popping the question to Joanie tonight," he said. I was mesmerized by the carats and I said I was sure she would be bowled over. "No," he said, "she'll be kind, but she'll turn me down flat. But I have it all planned out." It would be, he confided, a night of grand gesture, an impression she would never erase. He was so sure of being rebuffed that he had measured off the distance to a storm drain from the point where he would pop the big stone and the big question. Turned down in his romantic pursuit, he would say "If you won't wear this ring, no woman ever will," and, with that, he would fling the jewelry down the drain and on its way to the ocean. I begged him not to, appealed to the sane part of his broken heart. "Are you crazy? Save it for someone who returns your love." "This piece of crap?" he responded… "Zircon… forty-five bucks." The next day he said that it had gone well and that the ring now slept with the fishes. And his lost love would think long and hard of a gesture of love that no one else would ever match for her.

Years later, that sometimes publicist and longtime super wire service writer and syndicated columnist, Jim Bacon, had a story about Jay Bernstein in his fifteen inches in the LA Herald-Examiner. Jay had broken a leg while skiing, but he had contrived to turn that into the cast-of-thousands… in this case a cast of thousands of dollars. Around the fireplace during après-ski hours, Jay had had the who's-who of movie and music stars sharing Aspen with him sign the cast which would then be auctioned off for charity. I called Jim, and we shared our common delights in Jay's irrepressible gift of creativity and con. I told him the Joanie Sommers ring story. I don't know why I thought it would be off the record… nothing ever is. It was, of course, the lead story in his column the following day. The phone rang and it was unmistakably Jay's soft Oklahoma accent. He asked if I had read the Joanie Somers ring story in Jim's column that morning. I did my best "In Jim's column?… I… er…l um… Jim's column?" stutter of wordlessness, as though my authorship could be swept under a rug. "Now, don't lie to me, Dick," Jay said, "you're the only living person I ever shared that with. I *know* it was you. You're the only one I ever shared that with." Thus trapped, I grudgingly 'fessed up." There was a long pause… I assumed rather guiltily that he was trying to fathom the faithlessness of a trusted friend who would…. at which point Jay said, "Dick…… I don't know how to thank you for such a lovely and thoughtful favor. If there's anything you ever need…." I did, over the years, represent at least a dozen of his management clients. We could talk PR in short hand, Jay and I. On one occasion, one of our mutual clients (he manager, I PR) was being profiled by 20/20, and Jay asked if I would let them interview me. So I did it, and was rather relieved when he told me they wouldn't use any of my stuff. I thanked the director of the segment and asked if he knew why. "Well, the producers thought you were reading from a script… all those florid metaphors." "That's how I talk," I protested… but I was still relieved.

There are times when the truth… the cold, hard facts of a matter… seem to matter not at all, however startling or exculpatory or incriminating. One rash act of truth-telling could have made me appear a person of interest in a murder case. A new manager in town introduced himself, proposing to bring his one key client, a top TV star, to our client list. This manager had a problem in this past which I resolved for him. He had been indicted for soliciting college sports stars for representation while they were still undergraduates subject to NCAA restrictions. I wrote a letter to the sport's page of the LA Times in his defense, and it took the pressure off him. I introduced him to stars looking for management, and he gave each and every one of them the same thing…. the runaround, promising five different ladies the femme lead in his star client's upcoming film. Sometime later another agent/manager friend of mine called me to say that he was going into business partnership with the other fellow and what did I think about it. I thought it was a lousy idea and told him so. "Why?" my friend asked. "Why? Because Frank is the most untrustworthy guy I've ever met." A week or so later, Frank called me early one morning and asked, "Dick, did you tell Eddie that I'm the most untrustworthy person you've ever met?" So caught in a malicious act was I that I could hardly breathe, and I asked him to call me back in fifteen minutes. When he did, I said, "Yes, Frank, I did. I told him that." "Why would you do such a thing?" "Because, Frank, it's true. I've never known you to tell me a straight sentence." "Well, then," he said, "I have to earn back your trust. Let's have lunch. I have some people for you to rep." I protested that it wasn't necessary, but he persisted. The last thing I wanted was to work with him, but I was trapped by the awful true words I had uttered. A date was set. The day before that appointment, he called in the morning to say he might have to cancel. Then he called back… it was on. Then off, then on. There were probably six calls of correction. The next morning I came into the office and was advised that Frank had been murdered during the night… yes, murdered…at a beach house not far from our home. I called Gisela and told her I was going to get grilled by the cops. "Why?" "Because," I answered, "they'll discover that a guy called me six times in the 18 hours before he was murdered. What was he calling me about? What did I know? What did I not want them to know? I'm going to be looking into a white lamp because somebody didn't merely kill him. They killed him and then killed him again, emptied six chambers into him. It was just down the beach from us, and I don't have anything that even looks or smells like an alibi." The call from the police didn't come the next day or the next or ever. A repeatedly murdered man was in constant contact with me before he was turned into the toxic dump for a load of lead. He was murdered, and nobody was curious. Nor, to my knowledge, was his murder ever resolved. That's when they really don't care.

Trapped In My Own Phoney… Bing Crosby's Other Son

For a long time as a child, it was my guilty conviction that I was the worst liar in the world. Or, even worse, the best liar in the world. From age five to about ten, what people perceived to be my life was about thirty percent fabrication. I must have thought I was making myself interesting… like my school "what I did over the summer" report about my having worked aboard a whaling ship during the break between first and second grades. My teacher and class mates would certainly comprehend that what every whaler needs hauling in a ten ton whale is a 45 pound seven year old pulling on the ropes. But people pretended to believe me in these imagined adventures. And finally the realization struck that I told so many lies that I couldn't remember which lies I had told to which people. I was caught in them, recaught and caught again. I elected to tell only what I believed to be the truth. At least I would be consistent, which is a most compelling reason for scrupulous honesty. Not *the* most, but *a* most.

One regression at about age thirteen really scared me straight. In the mid-forties, the Freedom Train was sent as a traveling exhibit across the country, all of the great documents of our history… the Constitution, the Declaration of Independence, the Emancipation Proclamation, everything, hundreds of the true building blocks of our freedom, each displayed behind bombproof glass. As editor of the Bancroft Junior High school paper, La Cronica, I had received a press pass, and on the Saturday morning of its arrival on the tracks just north of the Coliseum, I was in line at 6:30. My dad had dropped me off on his way to opening the drug store. I was among the first in the media line. About fifteen minutes before someone cried "All Aboard for Freedom," our line parted as Bing Crosby came through with his four sons and they were taken onto the train with a newsreel crew following. A quarter hour later, I was among the first to have the privilege to read the amazing documents in relative quiet. When I left the train and headed for the street car home, I saw a really cute girl from school, Bobbie Fox I still recall, and she was amazed that I had already seen the exhibit. A life of crime dies hard, and this lily was crying out to be gilded. I took her amazement one step further, telling her about Bing Crosby and his sons, but adding that I had followed them aboard, telling the guard I was Bing Crosby's fifth son. That's something that, a few years later, I might actually have done, but on that morning I hadn't. (Gisela sure as hell would have... she out-audacities me five to one.)

The Freedom Train was there behind me, bearing all the documents of our nation's truth. And there I was selling this vainglorious whopper. And, sure, I had a twinge of guilt, but Bobbie seemed so impressed, maybe she would smile at me in the hallway and one of my friends would see that. I went home and wrote an awed and detailed report on what I'd seen, but leaving out the fifth son bit. That was between me and Bobbie. Our little secret. On Monday, I turned the story in to my journalism teacher for that week's edition, but she told me she wanted the rest of it... the good part. Bobbie had told someone who had told everyone. A LIE IS A TERRIBLE PRISON. How do you lie your way out of a lie? With great trepidation, I wrote the story of Bing Crosby's fifth son. It was almost the entire front page. It was one of the few lies I had ever told at gunpoint. The next week I was called into the principal's office, and the two words I didn't want to hear her say were Bing and Crosby. "Bing Crosby's lawyer," she said... the *three* words I didn't want to hear... "is a friend of mine, and I gave him a copy of your story. (only a principal knows the Chinese water torture of a well-timed pause) ... and he told me that Mr. Crosby... (another torturous pause)...was very amused by your adventure, but that you're still not in his will." I managed a weak "heh heh," too exhausted by relief to do much more. I probably would have been better served if I had done time for that desperate fib, but then I would have been scared really straight, and I might have missed the fun of those brief and lamented decades when imagination ruled in PR.

Chapter 16

Foreign Affairs

Gisela and I had set out to see the world, to be footloose and even housel-
oose. It had a good start in that direction with the first months evolving as an
extended honeymoon in the frugal and mellow delights of the south of Spain,
soft little fishing villages in Andalusia, forty dollars-a-month bungalow atop a
Mediterranean coastal cliff, and, before that, wandering on third class busses
and trains in Morocco or penniless on the streets of Gibraltar until a little bit of
our little bit of money caught up with us. It was a period designed to sustain our
very limited funds until the next film assignment. But the world imposes its own
realities. We conceived and then lost in miscarriage a baby in Spain. But back in
America which we visited for my parents to meet Gisela, children came to stay.
We had hoped it wouldn't alter our plans for a vagabond life of exciting foreign
film locations. A visit to the Congo for Fred Zinnemann's "The Nun's Story" was
next in prospect and then Italy to chronicle Clark Gable and Sophia Loren in "It
Started In Naples." Nice itinerary, but babies come with their own realities, and
you can't pack an infant or eventually two into the two suitcases out of which
we had hoped to live our married life. But two charming little people trump two
suitcases and the Congo every time.

Life became strung out on the axis between our first little home in "the Valley"
and my work in Beverly Hills. Diapers and then PTA meetings replaced the jazz
caves of Paris' Left Bank as the stuff of our evening habit. And then Malibu… mild
and nurturing nature with its flipside of natural tribulations and disasters. Our
occasional travels, now *en famille*, became more and more treasured because they

were occasional, usually work-related, Gisela's or mine. We took our daughters as often as possible to visit Gi's parents in Germany where the Black Forest filled them with fairytale wonder.

Some Americans already were experiencing too early demise or dangerous adventure in Iran In 1976 when Guttman & Pam, at the start of the Shah of Iran's tumble from oppressive power, agreed to honcho what turned out to be the final Tehran Film Festival. The tensions, glaring hatreds and bureaucratic madness packed a year's worth of memorable characters and startling adventures into a few weeks. The "incessant" excitements of the film business are actually intermittent, but the travel and the vivid, brash and unforgettable characters are major compensation for its exasperations.

Danielle, at fifteen, accompanied us to Iran. Moni, seventeen then, was already tromping the world on her own, polishing her journalistic independence, flying her own flag at about the same age her mom had. Marilyn Beck, Shirley Eder and Dick Kleiner were part of a little cluster of syndicated columnists who hung with us in Tehran as Gisela ignored warnings and led us through a city seething with anger and violent change. The Shah's reign was coming apart at the seams, and it became evident to me at a certain point that we and our stars and press had been brought in by the Ministry of Culture to plaster over the cracks. Among our bold recruits were Lauren Bacall, actor/director Otto Preminger and the Arthurs, Hiller and Hill, as well as Paul Mazurski and "A Hard Day's Night" creator Richard Lester and such Oscar nominees as Rita Tushingham, Sally Kellerman and Brenda Vacarro and Academy Award winner Rita Moreno, hardy souls all since the intimidating circumstance was no secret. The Ayatollahs had hijacked the hatred directed toward the Shah's regime and were about to give the USA the heave-ho. Through common sense and fear, most of our celebs hung out in the Tehran Hilton or Intercontinental when we weren't being bussed to the rainy gala opening night in 1940s school busses whose windows wouldn't close. With police cars, sirens blaring, leading and following us, we sped at about three miles an hour through the jammed wet streets. There was a pervasive sense of vulnerability. Those possibilities were only in our minds... but vividly so. American Ambassador Richard Helms, former CIA chief and a newsworthy Watergate figure, was at the opera house, and I set the press corps, hungry for new meat, upon him. At one party at some princess' palace which I'd arranged to crack the cabin fever, Ms. Moreno, duly furious with the virtual captivity, stormed up to me and demanded if I was Dick Guttman, and I explained that he was a tall red-headed guy.

Gisela led our columnist cluster bravely from bazaars to streets of antique dealers, all of us shoe-horned into the same taxi. At a certain hour, Marilyn and Shirley had other business. For Shirley, the local General Motors execs were picking her up to take her gold shopping… she was, after all, the media queen of Detroit. Marilyn, whose column appeared in the Tehran Daily American, had a lunch appointment at the paper. I begged her to let me put her in a taxi, largely because she was wearing a tight white pants suit that she filled out very nicely, dangerously so for those streets where feminine display was most often harshly received. She's a rugged news gal, so she walked. Shirley made out better, returning to the hotel with chains of bargain price gold. Marilyn returned with pants strategically decorated with dozens of dark hand prints, but no apparent post traumatic damage. Most columnists are pretty tough cookies.

In a crumbling dictatorship where the reigns of terror are about to be ripped from one bloody hand to another, the misinterpretation of a word can freeze the mind. And so it came to pass that, on the morning after our arrival in the Persian capital, half of the distinguished artists we had gathered for the festival jury, my nearly-name-alike friends Arthur Hiller and Arthur Hill among them, called me about a disturbing communication each had received in his or her welcome packet. It began with warm greetings and gratitude that they would honor the event and the country with their jury participation. It described the manner in which they would see the films, vote and then be presented at the concluding ceremonies, finally noting: "following which you will be shot." Yes, yes, they all assured me, they knew that meant "photographed," but they just wanted to check.

All of our festival attendees had that sense of reasonable-caution concern in a place where a revolution was brewing and America was on the wrong side of where the new political power would flow. Gisela seemed impervious to it, having grown up in political turmoil, and she insisted we experience the wonders of the great Persian culture while we had the opportunity. Our daughters and grand children all seem to have inherited this penchant from her, and I sometimes think they were all cut not from the same bolt of cloth as much as from the same bolt of lightning. Apparently when you've looked down gun barrels, as Gisela had done as a child and as our daughter Monika often did as a journalist, you grow more fearless rather than more fearful as one might assume. Shortly after the vestigial resumption of relations between the US and Vietnam, Moni trecked by herself to what had been South Vietnam in search of the little girl we had helped through the Foster Care Program during the war. But the communist bureaucracy was too good at burying the past.

One of the mind-blowing things about Iran is that its national treasury is a tourist attraction. If you enjoy jewels or jewelry, this is your paradise on earth. Instead of boring bars of gold endlessly and lovelessly piled, your sight is filled with jewels whose beauty and value are beyond imagination. Billons, trillions. A visit there would have to wait, because gathering that impressive star group in a city restive and perilous held major security challenges that the Persian government declined to handle. I had to walk everything through and had gone into town to check out safety factors before I would let our people attend screenings. I attempted to go out one of the theatre's side doors… the fire doors… and found them locked from the outside. I went to the management and told them I couldn't let American festival guests go into buildings whose fire doors were locked, and "why would you do that in the first place?" "To keep people from sneaking in." A year later 400 people died in a fire there. I pulled all of our people from attending screenings. Gisela and Danielle and I put the resulting free time to great use visiting the must-see sights, first of which was the Treasury, which made London's Crown jewels look like Macy's notions counter. It was literally the world's largest, richest vault. You entered through an opened steel vault door which seemed two meters thick. At any moment of alert… like someone plucking one of the golf ball sized pearls from displays of thousands of them (what's one more or less?) or someone's snatching Texas (an emerald or something similarly priceless and about the size of a pancake) from the huge, bejeweled globe of the earth, a massive mosaic of supremely precious stones… the vault door would slam shut making pancakes of anyone who happened to be in the process of ingress or egress. You went through that aperture quickly.

Gisela's philosophy that the stupid always win has pulled me through more than one bad scrape. There was a time when I was sitting on the curb of a street in Tehran with about twelve young Persian men literally huddled in a circle around me, arms over each other's shoulders, staring down at me, drawn to this chummy gathering by their shared hatred of America and of me in particular.

In this case, I didn't have to *play* stupid. I was the real thing. Gisela, Danielle and I had visited the Golestan Palace, home of the Peacock Throne, which I had photographed to the exhaustion of the film in my camera. I needed to put in a new roll, something my ten thumbs have never accomplished with facility and to do which I had to sit down. And there was this curb. I had barely unwrapped the film when I realized I'd drawn my angry audience. Gisela and Danielle were outside the circle, looking none too happy, and I told them to go to the nearby rug bazaar and I would join them. If this was the rugby scrimmage it resembled, I was the ball. The good thing about playing stupid is that you really get involved in a play and in a character. You are not you, the idiot who got you into this in the first place. There's no time to be frightened. Also, angry crowds don't quite know what to do with a clown... it's like punching a pillow. I came up with the scenario that they, like I, could never thread a new film into a camera and that they were gathered to see how I did it. So I was the smiling fool... look, I try this... it doesn't work, holding the camera up in a good-natured, beseeching fashion to whichever one could do it for me. Amused at my own idiocy, I was making a big show of my incompetence and my gratitude that they were trying so hard to help me, the grinning ninny. I finally gave up on the film insertion, closed the unthreaded camera, thanked them profusely, patting my new friends and advisors gratefully on the back, yakking gregariously all the way and slipped through, keeping up the stupid prattle and lots of waves of camaraderie reluctantly surrendered until I disappeared into the rug bazaar.

We needed a little respite after that, and there was this beautiful park across the street to which we repaired to commune with nature. We were enjoying the soft breeze, and then I realized that all of the people passing down the paths a few yards away were clerics. We had wandered, we discovered, into the gardens of the main mosque of Tehran. Two of the black-cloaked men noted the guy in the European suit with the two blondes and they wandered over to check it out. One said, "Salaam." One of the few words of Hebrew I knew was "shalom." It means peace. I responded "Salaam alechem." It seemed a good guess. It was. They smiled and started a conversation in Farsi which we gratefully recognized as friendly. We needed that.

To relieve some of our celeb festival attendees from the growing sense of being under house arrest in Tehran hotels, Gisela and I arranged with the culture ministry to fly part of our collection of top stars, creators and journalists to the storied Shah Abbas Hotel in Ishfahan. Since this fell on what, in America, was Thanksgiving Day, we were trying to convince the people in the hotel's restaurant how great a turkey meal would be. Our guide was not familiar with the word or the bird, but a helpful Iranian businessman gave the Farsi word for turkey. We expressed our great love of turkey, and our fond desire to eat if it on this day of our traditional consumption of it. That, for some reason was a real hackle-raiser. It turned out the gentleman had given us the word not for turkey, but for Turkey, not the most popular of near neighbors. Our partiality to and apparent affection for that country was badly received. Sally Kellerman calmed frazzled nerves by getting up to improv a torch song and sensual dance to the Persian drums, flutes and strings. We were once again welcome guests, even though we were Turkish.

Gisela and I once were visiting a Moslem cemetery in Spanish Morocco, watching mourners paying scribes to write little prayers from the Koran which they would place on the graves. I noticed a street of fascinating architecture behind us, and I asked our guide to take us down it. "No," he said, "it is very dangerous. It's the Jewish quarter." Hatred starts with fear.

Staying Sane in a Big Corporation...

Readjusting to corporate life after several years of location migration, was tough. I had first joined Rogers & Cowan while still in college. Even though it controlled 40 percent of the town's superstar roster, it was still small enough and tight enough in staff to contain my fear and loathing of mass bureaucracy. I can't operate in institutions that exceed human dimensions. When I came back from Europe, Rogers & Cowan had expanded into real corporate grandiosity... I missed the quick and short-lived intimacies of friendships and work on film units abroad. I missed the kind of instant families a film location breeds, with all of the exciting affections and disputations of a real family... I returned to the big company's bosom, my boyhood home, for what I thought would be a short stay, but the prospect of parenthood soon resumed. The realization set in. I would be doing time in a corporation, but it was a gathering place of talented individuals herded by Warren's mad drive for evident publicity results and Henry's equally insistent drive for company significance. Henry and Warren commanded the PR field because they were not content to COURT the power elite. They wanted to be counted IN the power elite, and that they uniquely were. They pulled the whole publicity sector up by their own bootstraps, a rare feat of strength, both of character and of will. Henry was the Bill Gates of the emerging, evolving and still ebullient world of publicity… or "public relations" as Henry insisted. That better reflected the status he and Warren were conferring on the business. Henry was the quintessential and possibly the first real non-studio "public relations executive" and, eventually, "mogul." He brought dignity and respect to a field that I've always felt is delightfully at its best when it is undignified and disrespectful. Suddenly Gisela and I had a baby and we had bills, and we were part of Henry's empire-building. And gone were the dreams of spending our youth on exotic locations publicizing film productions which were suddenly popping up everywhere on the globe, places we longed to go.

Never-the-less, the succeeding nearly sixty years, 14 at Rogers & Cowan and particularly four decades in our own firms, involved a lot of business-related globe-hopping. Guttman & Pam's brief involvement with Haiti, so poor and abused under the Duvalier dictatorships, father and then son, was a riveting lowlight. What we thought was a tourism account to bring travel to a small country so rich in the beauty, color and "pas problem" spirit of its oppressed and struggling people, came to a thudding halt when we made the unhappy discovery that we were, in fact, representing the country's strange dictator, Baby Doc. That awful realization came at the end of a memorable trip there. Gisela and I agreed we were off the account the moment we were delivered to his mountain-top aerie and introduced to the reality of what was expected of us. A *ton ton macoute* guard, eyeless, souless behind black glasses, let us in. With what casual assurance such terrifying rule sustains itself was an awful thing to observe. Baby Doc and his gang felt safe behind the terrible wall of terror they had built. We had to feign cordiality during a bizarre few hours of his "hospitality," holding us captive audience even when it was long past the time of our plane's departure. It then became our lot to endure a speeding ride-from-hell down long miles of mountain curves with him at the wheel, his driving quite as mad and heedless as his driving his tortured people into misery. In any horrifying circumstance, this deluded ogre did not know how to apply the brakes.

A year or so thereafter, Gisela and I were in Hong Kong at the end of a kaleidoscopic trip through the Orient. I realize that word "orient" has fallen out of favor, but it carries for me still the exotic and mysterious sense of a many-splendored part of the world. How impoverished we are now that "the East" just means New Jersey. The word "orient" in jewelry means "most exquisite," "highest grade," and that's what the word remains for us. Gisela and I were in that special jewel, Hong Kong, when I received a telegram from Jerry back at the Guttman & Pam office directing us to alter our return to make one more stop which could produce a new client and an extended experience of another special part of that world, the Philippines. Our fairly adroit handling of the dangerous complications of the final Tehran Film Festival had gained a lot of special and positive publicity for Guttman & Pam. John Simon, the critic who criticizes everything, had given our work a special plug in the New Yorker, and that had resonated. Its latest reflection, Jerry's telegram advised us, was that we had been requested to meet Ferdinand and Imelda Marcos who wanted us to handle the Manila Film Festival. I adjusted my mind to that and handed the telegram to Gisela, saying, "Looks like we're going to Manila." Gisela studied the yellow sheet of paper and said, "I think not." With which she tore the telegram into tiny shreds and dropped it in a wastebasket. I was astounded, and she looked up and said firmly, as only Gisela can be firm, "The Shah of Iran? Baby Doc? You've handled your last dictator."

HAITI was varied and exciting by any standard of judgment. It was, even before the earthquake tragedies, a sad place but vibrant with the spirit of its people who are so beautiful and colorful, industrious and kind, so captured in the simplicities of the rich folk art, a people oppressed but whose national mantra seemed to be "pas problem" (no problem.) Very few countries were so sorely exploited, both by oppressive regimes and oppressive economic interests. So it was a particular irony that most of the visit was hilarious, largely because we did it in the company of Elke Sommer, as funny and unconstrained as she is alluring, and her husband, journalist/author/iconoclast Joe Hyams. Joe was a close friend and official biographer of Humphrey Bogart because they were each, at heart, intellectual tough guys with the same dry amusement at how nutty normal is, with the same wry and imperturbable humor. Joe was skilled in martial arts while still remaining a patsy for what makes life funny and bearable. Gisela and I had first met him in 1958 when we, only recently married, had stayed on in London to work the world premiere of "The Key" for Carl Foreman. It was as gala as a gala premiere can get. Joe was already in the most heady group of elite journalists covering the entertainment world, and we wound up the evening in early morning with Joe and the beauteous actress Gia Scala, tramping the empty area surrounding Covent Gardens (think scene one of "My Fair Lady") looking for Eliza Doolittle. Everyone but I had indulged the ample spirits of the evening, but I can at will become as free and spirited and witless as my most inebriate fellow celebrant. Gia had succumbed first to the numbing effects of the wine, and we last saw them as Joe ambled off with Gia slung over his shoulder. That's a sense of who this raucous knight of by-line journalism was.

All of these commendable qualities of Elke's, Joe's and Gisela's own delightful madness came hysterically into focus on our first night at one of Port Au Prince's luxury hotels, a tropical paradise walled in from the insistent poverty outside. It was one of those balmy evenings that occur only in 1940s Warner Bros. Technicolor musical comedies... Betty Grable, John Payne and Carmen Miranda. Other than the fact that it exists on an island called Hispanola, Haiti is not in any way Spanish but thoroughly African and French.

We were dining in the luxuriously tropical outdoor restaurant, all clad in our tropical whites... light dresses, shirts and slacks,...melded in the soft evening amidst other pampered tourists similarly clad in whites and pastels, similarly luxuriating. And then IT suddenly came into the scene. I can't refer to it as anything other than it, because its presence was so sudden and so awful. It was a jungle bug of some terrible appearance and dimension, about the size of a swallow, but all huge evil eyes and spikey black armored appearance, claws and pterodactyl-like wings and pincer mouth, maybe even mouths, everywhere. It swooped several nearby tables, eliciting screams, made a dash for ours and then disappeared into Joe's opened shirt. There was a moment of disbelief, and then Joe... Joe who could lick any opponent, martial or intellectual... leaped up, swatting viciously at every part of his body and started to scream... "Get it off of me! Get it off of me!" Elke and Gisela, screaming in high sopranos of horror, threw themselves at Joe and started ripping off his clothes. People at neighboring tables rose, pushing their chairs back as though watching a dismemberment, women whimpering or moaning... "oh Gods" and "mon dieus" "heilege Vaters" sounding everywhere. The horror of it... the horror of it. As each shred of clothing was torn from him, Joe and Elke and Gisela searched for signs of the invading monster or whatever mutilation it had left in its wake. Very quickly, Joe was down to his underpants and shoes, with Elke and Gisela and helpful people from nearby tables peering in to make sure it wasn't in there. Not a sign of it, just Joe shivering with revulsion in the hot summer night. There were intermittent screams from around the room as a husband would caringly touch his wife's shoulder in reassurance that the dreadful experience was past, but she would spring up with gasps of dread, slapping at where something had befouled her. The thing was still very much present in everyone's mind. The whole place was exceedingly unnerved, degrees of post-traumatic stress everywhere. A lot of animosity was directed at me since I alone among this empathetic gathering had laughed through the whole thing and still had the uncontrollable giggles, especially when Gisela ripped the cloth from the table to wrap around Joe. Unlike that scene in so many movies where the tablecloth is extracted with a snap and everything else remains as it was, everything on the tablecloth went clattering across the room. That started my laughter up again, and I had tears in my eyes. People, no longer interested in their meals, filed past me fuming in a half dozen languages their disapproval of my disgusting behavior. When we got to our room, Gisela said firmly, "I'm not talking to you," but that didn't keep her from giving me a piece of her mind.

That might explain Gisela's, Joe's and Elke's deep satisfaction a few nights later when, at a black voodoo ceremony, I came down with a creeping crud which contaminated my body and spirit and induced the conviction that I had swallowed a dead and decomposing rat which was stuck in some passage near my thorax. Actually it had been only a piece of ritually slaughtered and then barbequed pork which was passed around by a woman so deeply into trance that white fluids dripped down from the corners of her mouth and her eyes had rolled back into her head so that only blood-veined white was showing. That should have been the tip-off for me, but it wasn't. Gisela, Elke and Joe took some, too, but dropped the vile and cursed pig under their seats where a dog came over to sniff it and then ran off with a whimper. Actually it tasted quite good.... going down. It was all very dramatic, being a rare evil or "black voodoo" ritual held in a strange open pavilion near the coast as lightning flashes danced about the ocean horizon. It had all of the theatrics... walking on fire, eating glass, wringing a chicken's head, the voodoo priest or houngan inducing trance by spitting a spray of wine over his subjects. We were given effigies blessed in the ritual, which occasioned terrible tragedies when we distributed them to friends back at home before we had them all destroyed. The next morning I lay in bed desiring death, but we had a nude layout to shoot with Elke on a gorgeous beach up toward Cap Haitienne. I rode with the window open... just in case... holding a large orange into which I dug fingernails to release citrus smells inadequate to battle the taint of dead rat from within me. At a certain point, the car filled with terrible sulfuric odors and I asked if we were going through a volcanic area, which we were, and I said "Thank God, I thought it was me."

One of the purposes of the trip was to do some artful nude studies of Elke for high art photo magazines around the world, great publicity for Haiti (I was, at that point, still under the impression that we'd been hired to do tourist promotion for that beautiful, suffering land) and sophisticated promotion for Elke as well. Not to mention a great trip for all. Gisela, who had come there partly to connect with Haiti's most internationally acclaimed painter, Bernard de Sejourner, didn't like the blatancy of the photos and arranged with de Sejourner that he would paint Elke's body so that she could be photographed as an integral element in one one of his paintings, a visual adjunct to and participant in his highly collected work. At a certain point when the fuschia gouache on her pubic hair, part of a jungle sunrise, had dried, she insisted that we feel how her pubis had turned to barbed wire. I demurely declined, but Gisela said "go ahead. If you're into barbed wire, we'd better find it out right now." Gisela was right. Barbed wire wasn't my thing, and the photos were glorious. A few years later, de Sejourner was selected to join Picasso, Leger and Miro in painting one of the labels of Chateau Lafitte Rothschild, another of our clients. I don't mean to infer that that was of my doing. Unfortunately, one of his great works was destroyed years later when we lost our home in one of the Malibu fires. It was packed to send to send to its purchaser, Germany's Barbara Walters, Margaret Dunser, but she had died before it could be sent off, and so it stuck around long enough to expire shortly after she did.

It was only at the end of the stay that I learned the nefarious purpose of our visit to Haiti. Our Air France flight to Miami departed at 1 PM, and our luggage had been taken to the airport for early placement on the flight. A car arrived for us and we were taken not to the airport, but up a long and perilously curving mountain road to the giant estate where the dictator Baby Doc Duvalier (son of the unlamentedly deceased dictator for eternity, Papa Doc) resided. I was surprised that the security seemed so lax, just the four sleepy soldiers shooting craps on the hood of a jeep, hardly rigid readiness. Nowhere did I see troops of the dreaded TonTon Macoute bully boys, terrifying in their black sunglasses which kept their eyes from ever being seen… just the one zombie who ushered us in. We'd seen the people in town cringing in their presence, each with his or her own perfectly good reason to do so, I'm sure. They materialized later when Baby Doc decided to drive us to the airport. If he hadn't been dictator, he would never have qualified for a license. The first thing I learned about him was the intolerable news that we had actually been hired to civilize and humanize him in the world's eyes. I'm not a creative enough press agent to accomplish that, nor did I have the stomach for that. We just wanted out, something we couldn't establish until we were safely out of the country. And that was going to take longer than we' reckoned. As his mother smiled benignly, he had to show Gisela and Elke each of his possessions. Dictators have a lot of possessions, and I observed my watch creeping towards one PM at which time our luggage, already on the plane, would depart for Miami and then, surely, parts unknown. I mentioned that our plane was leaving in fifteen minutes and that we were a dangerous 45 minute drive away from the airport. "Don't worry," Baby Doc said, "your plane will not leave without you." I realized that he probably distributed landing right at his whim, and that Air France would be open to his suggestion as to when a particular flight would depart. He had to play part of his Dixieland collection, and Gisela mentioned that we'd stopped in New Orleans to go to Preservation Hall and had bought a Muddy Waters album. "If we get to the airport before our luggage disappears, I'll send it to you," she said in subtle hint. He decided to get it right then and piled all of us into his BMW and sped with an awesome screeching of tires down the mountain road with his Ton Ton Macoute trying to keep up from behind When we got to the plane, it still sat on the tarmac, an hour past departure. As angered passengers stared in dismay from their windows, the plane was unloaded until Gisela found her large bag, rummaged through it to find the album and handed it to Baby Doc. The passengers were watching the dictator of the land having their luggage pulled out so he could get a record. Obvious to one and all was the fact that we were his very best friends. It was also obvious that we were the reasons for their long delay. Once the plane took off and all the rest of the trip to Miami, people took turns walking up and down the aisle accidently tripping and spilling their orange juices and coffee all over us... We had a sickeningly sweet smell and clothes as hard as cardboard all the way back to LA. Who could blame them?

All we ever have seen of Miami is the airport on the way to or from some Caribbean destination. I include this in a chapter on foreign affairs because that airport always seems to me to have the cacophony, static electricity, vivid bustle and simmering indifference of some of the exotic third world air terminals through which we've traveled. Places where you're very much on your own, alone among the interweaving and self-focused throng. These places are invigorating habitats for Gisela, who does not avoid confrontation and whose guerilla combat instincts are quickly engaged. This experience was on a trip separate from our escape from Haiti. We were killing time between flights shopping, an occupation at which Gisela is very avid, very skilled and intensely concentrated. The multi-lingual noise of the airport boiled around us, and suddenly Gisela shoved her purse at me, commanded "hold this," and then took off on the run. I'm used to such things, but my curiosity was engaged. I managed to hold in view her dash through the crowd, thousands of neurons on their own courses, undisturbed or surely undeterred by another's forceful passage. A woman ahead of her seemed to become aware of the pursuit. She hit the gas pedal. Gisela got close enough to grab the woman by the hair and pull her to the floor. It is the nature of that airport that no one seemed to notice the encounter or, at least, to respond to it. Gisela, not a hair out of place, returned with a bag of our purchases the woman apparently had stolen from us. Saying once more "hold this" and then "and hold it tight," she handed it to me, retrieved her purse and resumed shopping.

Sex, Persia and a Renaissance Ball...

As any time-pressured press agent knows, you never let an opportunity accomplish only one thing when it could, with some creative effort on your part, accomplish three. Or, in this case, five. So our engagement by Iran to oversee publicity for its final (but who knew then?) film festival fling allowed us to stop in several other countries to touch bases with Guttman & Pam clients or films. The trip to Tehran first set down in England where Jerry always had the Guttman & Pam thumb in a lot of pies... you are always married to your past., and Jerry was Brit to the bone. Then on to Rome where the Roman spectacle, or perhaps one should say "sexspectacle," "Caligula" was filming with Malcolm MacDowell in the title role and Peter O'Toole, Sir John Gielgud and Helen Mirren backing him up. Sounds good, but the film bore the sexual focus of Penthouse Magazine which was producing it. Until we got to the set with our 15 year old daughter Danielle and a number of American syndicated journalists in tow to discover that the scenes included nude female slaves bound spread-eagled to huge wheels, I had not realized until that moment that this was a film I could sell better over the phone. Shirley Eder clapped her hand over Danielle's eyes and we proceeded through the studio with our daughter thus defended from the rude world.

I was able to bring a junket of U.S. press to the film, at no cost to the producers because I'd made Rome the catch-your-breath stay-over point for certain media whom the government of Iran was transporting to the Persian capital for me. It was win-win-win-win just like publicity is supposed to be. Sidney Sheldon, the top selling novelist in the world by anyone's measurement, and his supremely remarkable wife Jorja, had set up shop in a modest 16th century palace in Oligiata outside Rome where he was writing the Italy-set novel, "Bloodline." The Sheldons had graciously agreed to put up not only the Guttmans but also the contingent of American press I had to deliver to Tehran a few days later. It was generous hospitality, yes, but it was also great PR for his books and his brand. It was, most of all, hospitality beyond any other we have ever been accorded or even envisioned. When Jorja, a southern belle- of grand style and taste, went all out for someone, she went ALL the way out. First, we each had a bathrobe on our bed with our name beautifully stitched on it, and the gift of a book for every night we would be there. A world-class chef did the culinary honors, and on the last night of our stay, Jorja and Sidney hosted a black tie banquet for us and our visiting press corps beneath the great dining hall's ceiling of Renaissance murals. Gisela's and Danielle's dinner partner was Great Britain's ambassador to the Vatican, and they said he was a great sit-down comedian. Mine was Alida Valli... no, I kid you not... Alida Valli whom Orson Welles' Harry Lime so sorely used and abused in "The Third Man" without losing her love and for whom Joseph Cotton's Holly Martins so sorely and futilely longed. Director Carol Reed had seen in her the woman a man will risk all to save, as had Hitchcock in "The Paradine Case." And now, thirty years later I had a chance to savor that beauty of inherent sadness to which those two master directors were drawn. I was impressed once again with how women, as they mature, not only retain but refine what was remarkable during the distractions of youth's unqualified beauty.

One night, the film company sent a car to bring me to the ruins of the spectacular Baths of Caracalla where the director of "Caligula," Tinto Brass, was shooting a scene of the red light district of ancient Rome, whores and lust and sexual excess all about. I asked Sidney to come with me, and when Brass discovered who my guest was, he excitedly announced it to the crew and cast of hundreds, and there was a roar of cheering and applause for Sidney. He was the author who more than any other had defined sexuality for our times. And this was a film literally celebrating sexual depravity... or at least celebrating a time when sexual depravity was public policy. Brass invited Sidney into a photo with him and about twenty women portraying prostitutes in the scene. At the moment of the shot they all raised their skirts to reveal... themselves. They had nothing underneath. It was, as one photographer of the seamier side of life had once advised me, referred to in the trade as a meat market shot. Sidney was a bit perturbed and asked me to get the negative of the shot for him because it could ruin his reputation. I said, "Sidney, you're Sidney Sheldon... 'The Other Side Of Midnight,' 'Master Of The *Game'* Sidney Sheldon... you're the gold standard expression of sensuality for the age." He said, "You know what? You're right." And he went back and took another shot.

Walking back to the car, we absorbed the throbbing and depressing ambience of peddled sex... the actresses playing whores all were gathered around large pits of fire, as the scene described but, they were also warming themselves against the cold November night. As we drove from the ruins of the great baths and into the surrounding park, we noticed the prostitutes of the modern Rome night, warming themselves around fires raging in metal trashcans... nineteen hundred years, and nothing had changed.

Apart from writing "Bloodline" at that time, Sidney was also outlining a later book the working title of which was "Rape Of Angels." That was a pretty good title for a Sidney Sheldon novel, but the publisher refused to use the concepts of rape and of angels in the same title. We all put our minds to a new title for months, but nothing very good was found. Jorja solved it by changing one letter. It was, of course, "Rage Of Angels."

One morning at the castle, surveying the bounty and pleasures his work had brought him, I asked Sidney if there was anything that still eluded his desires, and he said, "Yes... matzah brie." Matzah (or matzoh) brie is more commonly and more descriptively known as *matzah* (the traditional Jewish unleavened bread) *fried in eggs.* Here in this castle, in his glamorous exile in Rome while he wrote "Bloodline," he longed for that taste from his childhood. On that day, Sidney and Jorja insisted that we take their town car and their driver and visit what we wished to show Danielle of Rome. As evening approached, I asked the driver to take us to the Teatro Marcellus section, which was in ancient Rome and now in the modern city, the Jewish quarter. Something was calling me there. We worked our way through a market, looking for things we could buy to thank our hosts... roses galore, ancient books. And then I suddenly realized why we were there. "Matzah brie," I said. The surrounding streets, this being the Jewish area, was mostly "shmatas"... dresses, bolts of cloth. No delicatessen. We went in one store and I asked the Jewish owners, "Matzahs?" No comprehension. I broke an imaginary piece of matzah in half with attendant crackling sound and chewed the imaginary cracker noisily. "MaZOtay!" the man cried with delighted realization. He grabbed my hand and started running me out the door, him in the lead pulling me, Gisela behind me, holding my hand and Danielle behind holding hers. We wound up in a little half-cellar shop, and, yes, it was a delicatessen. At our new friend's instruction, the owner brought out boxes of matzahs, then eggs, milk... and... what else? And then I recalled the smell of it... chicken fat in which to fry it. "Chicken fat," I said and then in my best chicken impersonation... "bluck, bluck, bluck" and finally shaking the skin under my chin as though it were fat ... chicken fat... nobody got it. I turned to Gisela, discouraged, perplexed. "How the hell would you say schmaltz in Italian?" I wondered aloud. Suddenly, the man behind the counter erupted in joy. "Schmaltz!!!" he said, and then set several jars of the stuff in my pile." I've never seen anyone enjoy anything as much as Sidney Sheldon... the man who truly had everything... the next morning enjoyed his matzah brie.

Most of our travels seem to have had a PR spin to them, largely because it is a trade that will make itself 24/7/52 if you allow it to. If your travels are not specifically for work, you somehow manage to work work into it. When our daughters were young, we tried to spend several weeks each summer in the Black Forest with Gisela's parents who had a "landhaus," a country home, among centuries-old farmhouses at the foot of the vineyards which marched in rows up the foothills to the forests at the top which often looked very black indeed. The children were well aware that this was a land of fairy tales. When Monika was about four, she and I were working our way through the woods that ambled off from the back of Gisela's parents' home. I heard a snap and saw that she had just broken a twig extending from some ground brush. "What are you doing, darling." "Are you kidding?" she replied, "I'm marking our way back. This is where Hansel and Gretel bought it." I told her to guide us back, and she did. Both of the girls loved the sense of fable, and Moni was frustrated that she could never get up early enough to see the girarfs. My mother-in-law had a deal with the farm women to purchase a basket of newly plucked strawberries which they would place on the back fence every morning, like the milkman used to bring my childhood family bottles of milk. Moni was sure that a small tribe of enchanted forest people called girarfs... apparently a blend of dwarfs and giraffes for God only knows what reason... left the goodies. She was practicing her German to find out all she needed to know from them. Already she was the journalist.

Our summer trips hop-scotched Europe because Rogers & Cowan handled so many top European stars in the late' 50s, the '60s and early '70s, and I had bases to touch in most major capitols and on many remote locations. Or we would leave the kids with their oma and opa and race over to Paris where two or three clients lived or drop down to Arles where director Richard Fleischer was directing a film for Darryl F. Zanuck. You saw these places on the run sometimes, but at least you saw these places. During the time of the Berlin Wall, I had to make an overnighter there for the screening and next morning press conference of a client's film and to catch Alan Arkin on the set of "The Magician of Lublin." The only time I had to see East Berlin was before the early morning press conference, so at 5:30 AM, while it was still dark, I arrived at Check Point Charlie, was given a hard time clearing through... 5:30 AM was pretty conclusive evidence that I was a spy... and strolled around the sullen dawn as the early risers, all looking grey and hard-pressed, went about their before-work shopping. The sense of scraping-by was all about. I'd been advised that the things I should buy for my parents-in-law in East Berlin were Beluga caviar and Havana cigars. The only establishments open, however, were working class stores where people, to fit meager budgets, bought two ounces of butter or three eggs. When I inquired as to my purchases, it was announced to the store that "der Herr moecht Beluga caviar oder Havanen cigaren zu kauffen." The gentleman wants to buy... and then those items so incomprehensible in a workers' paradise. The looks were simply stupefied. I bought some chocolate and ran out. There was one souvenir store where the door was open but the shop wasn't . An elderly woman was mopping the floor. In those days, we collected dolls from different nations for our children, and there was a little Captain von Koepenech doll on the counter and I asked if I could pay her for it. She handed me her mop and ran out. I had to get back to the press conference, but

I couldn't leave the store open. Ten minutes later she ran back, breathing heavily, followed by a heavyset man who was stuffing his pajama tops into the trousers he'd pulled on. I felt obliged to buy whatever I could actually give to somebody. I hurried on to see the Bertold Brecht Theatre and was back on the other side of the wall at 7:30. But I had breathed communist air, and it smelled very different and sad indeed. Gisela had very different feelings about the Soviet satellite, having toured East Germany on a motor scooter and having seen a very different place, but she was sixteen and even East Germany tried its very best not to be grey or sullen to youth and beauty.

Generally, when we were in Germany, her parents were very possessive of our time there, which being ourselves grandparents with far-flung kids, we now completely understand. However on one trip we had promised Horst Buchholz and his wife that we would visit their home in the mountain village of Lenzerheide in easternmost Switzerland near the Lichtenstein border. They had planned to host us for three days, but we had to be back in Germany the next evening. Myriam had prepared three haute cuisine meals for the anticipated 76 hour visit, so we had them for that evening's dinner and for breakfast and lunch the next day. But a great trip it was and produced a most remarkable coincidence right out of he Twilight Zone. Two weeks before, Gisela and I had enjoyed a dinner with France's leading world star and Rogers & Cowan's client, Alain Delon. It was at The Bistro which was next door to the R&C offices, so after dinner I had Alain and Gisela come up to the offices because I needed to give him some papers. As I walked into my office and switched on the light, I had a slight jolt because an eight by ten portrait of Horst Buchholz was lying in the middle of my desk. Horst and Alain were two of the leading leading men of Europe, and I'd always had a feeling there might be a sense of competition. Before I could slip something over the photo, Alain said, "Deekee, you represent Horst?" I nodded. He picked up the photo and studied it. "Eef I had that man's talent!" he said as if to himself and in a manner quite deeply felt. It was rather touching, and Gisela and I exchanged a look. Thank goodness she was witness to this confluence of events or even I wouldn't believe it happened. So two weeks later we are in Horst's beautiful home with the Alps reaching up all about us. We had just finished Myriam's extraordinary breakfast of salade endive et marrons (endive and chestnut salad,) chicken cordon bleu, asperges aux abricots (asparagus and apricots) and soufflé aux Grand Marnier.

The béarnaise sauce of the artichokes appetizer was still tangy upon the tongue. What a breakfast! Sitting by their great fireplace trying to work up an appetite for the next royal feast soon to come, Gisela and I noticed that face-up on the marble coffee table was the latest edition of Paris Match magazine, beautifully portrayed upon the cover of which was the face of Alain Delon. Horst caught our exchanged look. "Do you handle Alain?" he asked, and I nodded. He turned the magazine toward himself and studied it, and then in the same contemplative voice I'd heard but two weeks before, he said, "If I had that man's looks!"

Several decades later, a friend of mine, Ron Samuels (whose prior wife, Lynda Carter, I had represented for him) called to see if I could get Maximilian Schell to star with Louis Gossett Jr. and Ron's current wife, Rachel McLish in "Aces: Iron Eagles III." Max wasn't available, but Horst was, and acting gigs with that kind of payday were a bit slow in Europe at that moment in the 80s. I pointed out that Horst had starred with Steve McQueen and Yul Brynner in "The Magnificent Seven," and that the new film was basically "Magnificent Seven" in fighter planes instead of on horseback. Horst got the gig. As it sometimes happens, even with friendship, in a busy work load, you lose touch with people for years, and we heard from Horst and Miriam only on occasion after that. Then during the Oscar campaign for 1997 I was, along with some other PR companies, working on the Weinsteins' Academy Awards effort for Roberto Begnini's "Life Is Beautiful." Living as I do in Malibu, I usually see films at home on DVD, and so I was, with rapture and tears, watching Begnini's masterpiece in our family room one night. Gisela doesn't see all of the films, and it is very difficult for her to watch films about World War II, the traumas fresh and deep even after a half century. I was taken by the powerful performance of the German doctor with whom Begnini's character exchanges riddles early in the film. It was only later during the concentration camp scenes that I realized that this powerful actor was Horst. I called Gisela urgently into the room and ran one dazzling scene back to show her, "Gisela, you have to see this... it's Horst... a miraculous performance." She came in reluctantly. Her childhood was a blaze of swastikas and horror. Although she was Catholic and certainly not in the camps, she was a nomad and a traumatic survivor of death and regimentation and terror aplenty. That she later had the strength to make a film about the Holocaust amazed me. She watched the scene with me, and we were both in tears, and then SS guards appeared for the next scene, and Gisela turned and was gone. I tried to get Miramax to bring Horst over for the awards campaign, but they were focusing, quite reasonably on the little boy for supporting nomination. Horst died not long after that, and the Academy was so kind as to include him at my request in the In Memoriam for that Oscarcast even though they had already completed and locked that segment. Horst's own war experiences had been harrowing. He was on a train on which kids were being shipped around Germany when the war ended. They all escaped and found their own ways home across the paralyzed, devastated land.

In deference to Gisela's pain upon seeing things which bring back experiences of her childhood in Nazi Germany, I had not seen "Schindler's List," but one night ABC was telecasting it without commercial interruption. I asked if she minded if I taped it to watch one night when she wasn't home. I was doing that, watching the beginning and then getting caught up in it and held captive as one so often does. Gisela came in about 15 minutes into it to ask how it was, and I answered "remarkable." She crossed her arms in front of her defensively and stood watching the next scene, ready to race from the room. She stood there with her arms crossed through the whole three hours and then turned and went into her room without saying a word. I have no idea how much that cost her.

The incredible thing was that both Gisela and Horst, their childhoods notwithstanding, loved laughter and never surrendered their ability to savor what is truly funny. Nothing makes me happier than to watch her laugh, which we often did around Horst. No one could tell a story better than Horst. My two favorites were true and classic tales of the theatre. One concerned Horst's run on Broadway in "Cheri," a performance that required him to be nude in one later scene. Horst had requested that two shirts be created for him for the demands of each act. In the first act he was required to be bare-chested and then put on a shirt which he had to shove into his pants, so he had that shirt cut very short so that it could be pushed in quickly without disrupting the scene. In the second act, he was nude in bed, then, pulling on his shirt as he emerged from beneath the covers, would play out the scene standing, clad only in that shirt. Understandably, Horst had that shirt cut very long so that his nudity would only be briefly glimpsed if at all. A night came when Horst was simply too ill to go on. Just before curtain, he felt compelled to bundle up, drag himself out and visit the back of the theatre to see how his understudy was doing. He was doing fine, but it arrived that when he got to the stuffing-the-shirt-into-the-pants scene, the wrong shirt was on the chair, the long one, and it took forever as he struggled to get the hanging sheets of it into his trousers while delivering the lines. It was so painful a labor that the audience was in stitches. Horst winced for him and ran out, hailed a taxi and sailed back to his hotel. He settled into bed with hot water bottle and scarf around his neck, closed his eyes and then opened them wide in horrific realization. Horst leapt from the bed, pulled on clothes and coat, missed several taxis and raced into the back of the seated and deeply involved audience just as the understudy was to grab the shirt off the chair, pull it on and climb to his feet. Only Horst's laryngitic voice… or absence thereof… kept him from screaming out "NO!" Up stood the understudy, and the under part of his body was indeed a study. He was clad, of course, in the especially short shirt, and he was nude from the belly-button down. With the shirt-stuffing fiasco still freshly in mind, that audience became hysterical. Horst shook his head with a sense of treason and fled back his hotwater bottle.

The second story, not apocryphal but true, was about a famous German actor who had arrived at the station in his career that he toured his most celebrated plays in less than major cities. His arrival was always a big event, and the cities would host a party for him after the opening. His most famous part, it turns out, was his private parts of reputed dimension, and he famously found occasion to expose himself at each party. It was a kind of expected ritual. But in one regional town, he was warned… begged is more like it… to remove that gesture from the evening's entertainment since the mayor's wife was a renowned campaigner against obscenity. He agreed, but the company manager was by no means assured. Things were going fine at the party when, at one late moment, he unzipped his pants and laid a phallus of awesome size on the table. The mayor's wife screamed. "If that offends you, *meine genadige Frau*," he said, and then picked up a huge knife and cut the thing in half. She fainted, as did a number of other women… and men, including the mayor. At which point, the great thespian pulled the rest of the bull's penis from his pants, dropped it beside its better half on the table and continued his recitation to that portion of his audience still conscious.

I had great affection for Horst. He was dashing and talented and funny as hell and sad for not quite attaining the super stardom to which all of the afore-mentioned attributes and his accomplishments so richly entitled him. At one point, I looked at his remarkable record of starring roles in great, even classic, films… his first five English language films were extraordinary, J. Lee Thompson's "Tiger Bay," John Sturges' "Magnificent Seven," Josh Logan's "Fanny," Billy Wilder's "One, Two,

Three," Mark Robson's "Nine Hours To Rama".... and I realized that he simply hadn't accomplished the star connection with the American public which one would think would follow such a run of lauded motion pictures. To my tortured mind, it seemed that his name, so Germanic... Horst Buchholz... might be the problem. He could speak English with the most clipped American accent... although none of his major films, with their specific nationalities of character, reflected that. We were still in the capture of World War II prejudices, and what name could be more resolutely Germanic? I thought perhaps... one thinks sometimes too intently when the client is also such a close friend... that it was the doubled H in the middle of his last name. We had no equivalent for that in Americanized or Anglicized surnames. So I convinced him to let me remove one H. When I sent out the first release with the new spelling, Daily Variety ran a front page story headlined "Horst Gets The H Out." It didn't help. Maybe I should have changed "Horst" to "Harry." Or maybe I just missed the point and failed to invent some personal device that more closely married Horst to American tastes. One problem was that he loved his wife and never courted celebrity romances which truly do imbed actors as romantic stars. Another was that his and Miriam's life was so firmly rooted in Europe, that they were here only for film functions and that none of his major films were actually shot here. I think of Horst whenever I'm tempted to think that I know it all or even that I know most of it. And then I remember that there are times when I don't know anything at all.

One discovers certain people to be especially entertaining travel companions, and we had that experience with Arthur Hill and his wife Peggy. We handled him during his hit series "Owen Marshall, Counselor At Law." When the series finally came to an end, he asked to have lunch with Jerry and me, and we assumed that it was to suggest that he go on hiatus as a client. He speculated that if must be twice as hard to do publicity for an actor when there was no current series, and I said "five times as hard." "Well, let's just say twice," Arthur responded, "so I'm going to double your salary." We killed ourselves to deserve that faith and to work miracles for him. There was one television film that meant a tremendous amount to him, "Death Be Not Proud," a true story about dignity and courage in the face of death. The only specific break he ever requested was that the Los Angeles Times do a major story on that show. I asked the Times' TV editor... and former drama reviewer... Cecil Smith for that coverage. He said he couldn't because the film would be opposite another major TV movie, "All Things Bright And Beautiful," the filming of which Cecil had personally covered in Ireland. The Los Angeles Times, he told me, has a policy of never covering and, in effect, recommending two programs directly opposite each other. He couldn't accede to Arthur's request. I reported this to Arthur in a phone call one Sunday morning shortly before the broadcast of the two films. He listened and then said, "Then what do you recommend?" "What I recommend, Arthur," I said, "is that you write down the home number I'm about to give you and that you call Cecil Smith and tell him why you feel it is so important that your film be advance promoted in his paper." A long pause. "That's it?" he said rather coldly, "You recommend that I, I the client, make that call? Not you?" "Yes, that's what I recommend. I think it's the only chance we have to get it done." A long pause, then, "OK," Arthur said.

The next day I got a call from Cecil Smith asking me and Arthur Hill to join him for lunch in the Los Angeles Times executive dining room. It was the only time I ever dined in that sanctum sanctorum, and I don't know many press agents who have. Cecil began the lunch by asking Arthur what was the greatest stage performance Arthur had ever seen. "I have no idea," Arthur said, "probably something by Alec Guinness." "Well, for me," Cecil said, "it was you in the original Broadway production of "Who's Afraid Of Virginia Woolf?" Cecil's article began with the fact that he'd never known an actor of such distinction to call to personally seek support of a project in which he believed so strongly. It was a great article.

Our first experience enjoying fascinating foreign climes with Arthur and Peggy was in 1979 when he was in Venice, Italy filming "A Little Romance" with Laurence Olivier and a preteen or barely teen Diane Lane in her first big role. Another client, Roger Moore, was there filming one of the Bond films, I believe "Moonraker," and producer John Daly (Oscar winner for "The Last Emperor") had paid my way over in order to present to Roger the treatment of a jewel heist film which Daly had hired me to write. The trip was memorable upon arrival because the room we thought was reserved at one of the great hotels wasn't. We quite improbably found a great little room at a great little hotel overlooking St. Marks Square, so we were prepared to enjoy the stay thoroughly. The Hills were superb companions, and their location took us out to the island of Torcello which I would be loathe to have missed. Tchaikovsky's "Capriccio Italienne" began to play in your head the moment you stepped off the boat.

So when the Guatemalan government asked Gisela to allow them to fly us to that country for her to advise them on some art, I asked the Guatemalan contact if they would like a celebrity… I suggested Arthur Hill… to join us. They immediately said yes. The Guatemalan government was planning an art exhibit at their embassy in Washington, D.C., and they wanted Gisela to comment upon and approve the art that they had chosen. As it turned out, she didn't, but that's the story of some rather hurt Fascist feelings. Amazingly, when we arrived in Guatemala City, there was vast media at the airport, and Gisela and Arthur were all over the news. We had secret police tailing us the whole time we were there and touring the country, and we never found out if it was for our protection or, more likely to keep us from doing something "subversive." Gisela had asked to meet with Mrs. Moshe Dian who was there for UNESCO to review indigenous art. Our personal escort showed up an hour late one morning, white-faced because the internal security guys had grilled him on why Mrs. Guttman wanted to meet Mrs. Dian. Under no circumstances was that to happen. It turned out that they met later in an elevator and had a good exchange. Gisela was trying to force the government to exhibit some great native art she'd found instead of the visibly Fascist tripe by some bigwig's lover they wanted her to ok. The secret police escort/spies, your pick, continued to observe us perhaps more obtrusively than they thought, as Arthur, Peggy, Gisela and I and some other visiting firemen were taken on a great trip to the country's extraordinary sites including the colonial capitol of Antigua, Lake Atitlan and the high mountain Mayan village of Chichicastenango. It was here that we learned by fortuitous chance that Arthur's "Owen Marshall" series, re-titled "El Abogado" (the lawyer) was the number one show in Guatemala. And a good thing that turned out to be. Chichi is one of the few places in the world where Catholicism is practiced in conjunction with celebration of pagan rites. We had an official guide as we moved through the fascinating market and then were taken to the ancient cathedral. There, we were shown how the priest gave official blessing to the pagan rites which were then practiced by one of the Mayan priests or witch doctors. One did not enter the cathedral through the front because there was a corncob fire at the top of the stairs, a fire which was stoked and protected by a group of Mayan priests who moved ritualistically about the it. No one… but NO one… other than these priests could come up the front steps. For someone else to do so was sacrilege, and we couldn't find out what would happen to the transgressor, but good news it wasn't. The fire burned all but five days of the year, and on those five days, the days of black luck, the absence of luck, everyone stayed locked in their homes because evil spirits were about.

Standing in the cathedral looking out, we suddenly saw a tall form rising up the steps through the smoke. It was Arthur who had not learned the dire consequences of such cardinal sin. As he moved up, the smoke swirling about him like the demon warning of Hell itself, the tiny but fervent forms of the witch doctors rushed at the intruder, and we, too far away to do anything other than Peggy's cry of "Arthur! No!" It seemed like the start of the cannibal scene from "Suddenly Last Summer." Just as something bad seemed imminent, the fire attendants lowered their heads and moved backwards, muttering something. And then we heard what it was, a ritualistic chant of two words... and the two words were,,, "El Abogado." "El Abogado." The name of Arthur's show. El Abogado had mysteriously appeared out of the sacred smoke. It was the only time I have ever seen publicity or fame actually save a celebrity's life or well-being.

My one incident of incurring Arthur's great scorn... well, not really scorn but more like indignation... occurred as we were preparing to go to lunch at a beautiful and atmospheric hotel in Chichi after the morning's adventures. It was another of my unwise resorts to one-jest-too-many. First, as we were headed for the men's room for pre-lunch formalities, Arthur was accosted by 20 Australians who went nuts because "Owen Marshall" was number one Down Under, too. So our mood was buoyant as we entered the men's room. Arthur went to relieve himself and I went to wash my hands. "You wash your hands *before* you pee?" he called out. "Before and after." "Why?" "Arthur, do you wash your hands before you touch something you're going to put in your body?" "Of course." "Well then, why wouldn't you wash your hands before you touch something you're going to put in Peggy's body?" Wrong guy, wrong joke. You could almost hear the roar of thunder on that cloudless Guatemalan midday as dark Canadian clouds gathered about Arthur and furrowed his brow in an angry scowl of outrage. There was very little charming chit chat for the rest of that day, but by the morning the weather had cleared.

The depths of the Hills' thoughtfulness was manifest when one night in a dinner at their home, Arthur asked who of all people in the world we would like to be. Gisela and I answered simultaneously, "Hal and Hadje Linker." They had the first great travel show on TV, visiting with their son David the most remote and fascinating places in the world, the one thing to which we had aspired. We were invited back a few weeks later, and the other guests were, as a surprise for us, Hal and Hadje Linker. Gisela and I had the same major question for them… how they avoided stomach problems. The answer was one we never forgot. They put nothing in their mouths that wasn't burning hot. Gisela is ritualistic in her care of what we eat traveling abroad. One time in Mexico she ordered fruit salad after assuring herself that all of the fruit would be skinned. And so it arrived, but with a bunch of grapes on the top… washed, not skinned. She waved the waiter over and said she wanted it "sin uvas" (without grapes.) "Sin uvas, senora?" he acknowledged and reached to pluck them off, but she whisked the plate out of his reach. "Una nueva," she insisted… a new one. "Si, senora," and he reached again to take them with him, at which point Gisela held them further away. He left. She wasn't going to bet her stomach that he wouldn't have brought back the same plate "sin uvas."

Her audacity is always funny, always sexy. One evening in Paris at a super-crowded outdoor restaurant in Montmartre, we and all of the neighboring tables had waited over an hour for ordered food. Finally, a small casserole of baked scalloped potatoes au gratin was placed in front of me, and I offered Gisela its initiation. Just as the potato-ed spoon was poised in front of her open mouth, a haughty-going-on-disdainful waiter commanded imperiously, "Madame, c'est pour une *autre* table" (it's for another table.) Looking up, holding him firmly in the grasp of her eyes, she slowly closed her lips around the spoon and even more slowly removed the spoon and ceremoniously handed it to him absent of its recent contents. It drew a round a applause from our neighbors. It cost us another hour's wait, but we had the joyous company of all our newfound friends whom Gisela's *beau geste* had engaged in happy community

We have argued our way across five continents, but even in the most dire circumstance she has always made me laugh. At the end of our money-challenged honeymoon in the south of Spain, we arrived in Madrid late one night after a harrowing experience in Granada escaping a gypsy mob working a scam to rip the luggage from atop our car. Gisela was feeling ill, and the next morning she would suffer the miscarriage of the baby we'd been gestating in Andalusia. We found accommodations in a pension in a once-beautiful 19th century apartment building. I went out to get her an omelet. The buildings in that section had huge wooden front doors, and there was a *llavellero* (a uniformed keeper of the keys) who walked the streets and when you clapped your hands, he would arrive at your door in time to open it, and you would tip him two pesetas. To let you, or any other clapper, know he was coming, he would with each step clunk on the sidewalk with a long wooden club he carried. When I brought her dinner up to Gisela, she asked if I'd tipped the *llavellero*, and I said yes, the required two pesetas. "You cheap skater," she screamed, "didn't you even notice that he has a wooden leg?!"

Our later Guatemalan experience ended with a big dinner at which, suddenly, fascist finery turned out in abundance and style. There were black uniforms and clusters of self-aggrandizing shiny medals on every chest and the even shinier black brims of officer's caps everywhere. One felt obliged to look for the SS insignias, but they must have left those at home. Gisela was treated with a fawning respect and attention that bordered on the sickening. She was the Brunehilde blonde of their Nazi fantasies. They had, however, rejected her rejection of the insipid, pretentious art they were dead-set on sending for the D.C. exhibit as planned. One cabinet minister, his self-satisfaction as shiny as his cap brim, asked her with an insinuating smile if it bothered her that he was a fascist. "Not at all," she responded, " I grew up with the real thing. Of course you're despicable, of course you're sub-human, but you're just *junior* grade garbage compared to the scum that ran my country." He smiled, said he hoped she'd enjoyed her visit and slithered away.

Quite a number of our most interesting trips related to Gisela's art business and not my PR or screenwriting. One trip throwing us into the super-monde of Tokyo's high fashion community came with her representation of Richard Bernstein, the brilliant originator of the covers of Andy Warhol's "Interview" magazine during its classic period under Warhol's direct hand. The director of the La Floret Museum in Tokyo's very stylish student section, Harijuku, had seen Gisela's comprehensive Bernstein show at her Windward Gallery in the arty Venice section of LA. He was there for the debut night when virtually everyone Bernstein had ever transformed into an Interview cover graphic showed up… probably the biggest celeb turnout for an art opening in the history of Hollywood's art connoisseurship, sycophancy and pop idol worship. He was impressed big time and signed on the spot for Gisela to bring the show to his fashion-setting museum in Tokyo's trendiest quarter. He staged it as a combination art exhibit and entertainment experience called "A Breeze From New York," with fans paying a hefty price to stare at the famous images with New York music blaring in an insistently kinetic New York ambience. Bernstein hit Tokyo like a matinee idol, interviews breaking everywhere, and by the end of the trip, Gisela had top bedding companies and clothing firms ready to go with the Bernstein designs. But (according to Richard's report to us when he called Gisela to pass on the deals,) Andy Warhol talked Richard out of it. One rich experience was a walk we took after Gisela had a business meeting in the bar of the Akasaka Prince Hotel. It ended early so we went out and headed nowhere in particular, and it led us past the gardens of the Imperial Palace. People were pouring through the gates. One thing no press agent can resist is a crowd, and we followed them in to where tens of thousands stood in silence in a large open space facing a wide, low building with what appeared to be a long glass-enclosed veranda stretching the width of the building. Spotted through this soundless mob were policemen standing on raised platforms, facing away from the building and watching the crowd. There was a kind of gasp from the crowd, its only noise, when several people in formal attire appeared within the glass-encased porch and one began to speak. It was Emperor Hirohito. It was his birthday. Then we left as silently as we had stood.

A similarly fascinating trip, for very different reasons, occurred when Gisela received a call from the University of Indiana in Bloomington… ground zero of true heartland America. Thornton Wilder America. Norman Rockwell America, Grant Wood "American Gothic" without the pitchfork. Solid values only and warm goodwill, and less than 50 miles from the birthplace of the Ku Klux Klan. Gisela was being invited by the Kinsey Institute to assess and possibly set up a national exhibition tour for the second largest collection of erotic art in the world… that belonging to the Institute which abides in the honorably hallowed halls of that highly respected center of learning. Yes, the second largest collection of erotic art, and no one chose to identify the first. That we learned from one of our most erudite and charming clients, Australian novelist Morris West, author of the longtime number one novel "Shoes Of The Fisherman" and director then of the Australian National Museum. His thorough research of and in the Papal State, in which his most famous book was set, revealed what he claimed was one of the Vatican's best-kept secrets, the vast collection of erotic art by some of the greatest artists of all eras.

I can tell you that during our own three day super-saturation with the Kinsey Institute's remarkable capture of human sexuality in every conceivable art medium or bodily contortion, it definitely did not *seem* second biggest or second best. Paintings, drawings, statuary exploring every perversity of human sexual desire are gathered there in mind-numbing abundance. A George Grosz vision of Hell depicts a man being devoured by vaginas. Gaugin is there in a form beyond any lustiness you may have imagined, his ladies doing a great deal more than lying on the grass. Great painters of great eras, anonymous artists pleasing their kings and masters, the unmatched sexual device of the Orient, of Japan, China and India.... perhaps India most of all. The authors of the Kama Sutra would have blushed to discover how much more their painters and etchers knew of sex than they did... rooms and rooms and rooms. Rooms of fetishistic photos... shoe fetishists and hair fetishists, artistic imagination and lust run wild in the fields of genitalia. It seemed some of the greatest artists had reserved their greatest genius for their libidos. It was hard not to be excited about the art and not to be excited by it.

To make matters worse or, to Gisela's devious mind, funnier, we were put up at the Union Hotel which was also the dormitories for that educational institution's most attractive female students. The building fairly throbbed with nubility. It was a challenging circumstance in which it was hard to put your mind on a short leash, but I thought I came through magnificently. I imaged a mind scalded beyond feeling or interest. It damn near worked. In the files and files and rooms and rooms and corridors and corridors of the Kinsey collection, we were not merely exposed to but absolutely submerged in man's ... and woman's in some cases I suppose... most prurient desire in its most crafted evocation. There even was an astonishing virtual reality device 150 years before its re-invention by our computers. It was called a "Stanhope," a crystal bead an inch or an inch and a half long, three-eighths inch in diameter, shaped like a zeppelin, the Hindenburg, but flattened at each end with a round and polished surface about a quarter inch wide. These were invented for communications purposes during the Franco-Prussian war. Artists who could write the bible on the head of a pin were employed to scratch detailed messages, even drawings of military emplacements, on one flat end... micro images of astonishing detail. To the naked eye, it simply appeared that one end was smooth and the other end minutely scratched. But put the smooth end to the pupil of one eye and hold it to the light. The complex information bursts upon the screen of your occipital lobe. It turns your mind into a Cinerama screen. It consumes your awareness. These were tied to pigeons' legs and files of information were flown back and forth across the battle lines and duly noted. They later became the medium of erotic excitation for the absurdly wealthy unable to visualize obscenity sufficiently on their own.

Imagine turning this medium over to inscribers able to evoke Michelangelo talents in miniature directed by imaginations of sexual obsession exceeding that of Rabelais-times- Boccaccio-times-Larry-Flynt. Your mind simply exploded with sexuality. It was created for the royalty and the aristocracy alone in all lands, people of wealth and power who could afford and obviously craved this stimulation. And considering how infinitesimal a part of the population was being served, it was remarkable that this eroticism... ok, pornography... was in such magnanimous supply. Gisela and I discovered that pornography... presently regarded as the diversion of the vulgate, of common folk..., was exclusively the prerogative of the powerful until the first decade of the 20th century. It was put to us that the first instance of this stuff being peddled at a reasonable price to the general public was the presentation of newspaper cartoon figures in little books of narrative and drawings of them in grind-it-out sex. What child of my generation was not deprived of innocent illusion by Popeye and Olive Oil? Now, instead of spinach we have Viagra.

Because of my film background, the heads of the Kinsey Institute felt it appropriate to unspool for us some extremely delicate cellulose nitrate copies of extremely indelicate movies made in the first decade of the 20th century. Some unknown filmmaker in Argentina was doing things that his counterparts in Hollywood and New Jersey had never even thought of. I'm not talking just about sexual things, but also filmic devices... pan shots (swinging the camera from one subject to the another... pan, embracing a panorama) or trucking shots (moving the camera closer to the subject) that American cinema didn't come upon for years afterwards. How devoted a film student must you be to notice pans and dolly shots when the filmmaker was doing his best to reach your baser awareness? I plead guilty.

The upshot was that Gisela did feel that an exhibition of premiere museum quality could be put together. But, more than a decade after the social revolution of the 60s had famously freed America of its puritan mindset, nothing was very much different after all. Those "if you have an erection lasting longer than four hours" ads were not even imaginable nor was the possibility that "erectile" and "disfunction" would be the two most uttered words on television and radio. Viagra and Cialis were a quarter century from turning American television into one long advertisement for non-procreative sex. Had they been around then, the matter of financing or "sponsoring" such a tour would have been simplified. Gisela reeled off potential sponsors at that comparatively discreet moment at the start of the '80s, mostly things you then had to ask the pharmacist for. It was condoms and Playboy who might kick in for the tour sponsorship they required, and that was pretty much it. And they responded, "But this is the University of Indiana."

One thing PR teaches you is the art of the bluff. I'm pretty good at it and I derive great creative gratification when it works. One might think that this predilection might drive me with the rest of the herd to poker. But poker is the classic *zero sum equation*, which means that you win only when some other guy loses. That's a little too Bernie Madoff for me. In poker, it's the stakes that charge the adrenaline, the thrill of eradicating some other guy's finances and self-confidence. I've just never been into competitive greed, That's what I like about publicity. It's predicated on the proposition of win-win. Nobody gets hurt.

One time *en route* to visit Gisela's parents in the Black Forest, we got off our plane from London at Stuttgart, but our luggage didn't. Gisela and the girls stood a bit apart as I blustered the airline officials for answers. It seems our luggage had been placed on another flight from London which was just about to land at Frankfurt on a plane bound for Istanbul. I asserted that I wanted our suitcases off that plane and on the next plane from Frankfurt to Stuttgart. They responded that that would be impossible, but that the bags would arrive from Istanbul the next day. Gisela doesn't like my employing certain skills of arrogant assertion except for cases in which she demands it. And she was in her country playing by local rules. She wanted me to calm down and be *gemutlich*. "What happens" I asked, "if our luggage gets to Istanbul and decides that it likes it there?" (Warning: this is not my prettier self, but it is revelatory of a certain gall that plays well in PR.) When the official came back, I told him in no uncertain terms that it would be to the advantage of each of us if he were to call the Lufthansa office in Los Angeles right now, right NOW, and find out just exactly WHO Richard A. Guttman was. He went away, had a fairly long conversation on the phone and then came back to tell us that our luggage was being loaded onto another flight and it would be delivered to us in Stuttgart in an hour. As Gisela and I waited while our girls played, Gisela said, "Nice PR bluff, but what if he'd called Lufthansa in Los Angeles? He would have found out that Richard A.Guttman is nobody." "True, " I admitted, " but in L.A., it's about three in the morning, so who's he going to call?"

Our mis-adventuring in disparate places and desperate circumstances commenced in the first month of our marriage with a little spate of impoverishment in Morocco and Gibraltar. We had a Porsche, yes it's true, but a bank account of not many hundreds of dollars, enough to get us to the next film job if we hurried some place still warm in the European dead winter and cheap enough to get us through. That would be Andalusia, the south tip of Spain. Not many people, it seems, know that Andalusia was the Moorish name for the entire landmass of Spain, and when it became the Moors' last holding on the continent under the assault of the forces of Issabela and Ferdinand, it became the final inheritor of the name that had once described the entire country. One of the excitements of that easy, sleepy geography was its proximity to the Africa which had long owned it. You could see that storied continent just across the narrow water-mass of the Straits of Gibraltar.

We had to stop first to pass Christmas with Gisela's parents in the Black Forest since she hadn't informed them of our marriage and they only vaguely knew of my existence. They may even have been under the impression that she was still engaged to someone else, since he had visited the Baden area the previous Christmas and her father had shown him his factory because this previous son-in-law-to-be also was an engineer. There had been the happy prospect that he could take it over at the proper time. On Christmas eve morning, Gisela asked if I minded staying in Karlsruhe while she took the train ahead of me. It was a lot to drop on them just as they were lighting the candles on the tree. To describe it as a period of cordial tension and consternation is fairly accurate. Her parents, having survived a half decade of war on the constant move, were quite resilient. But to spring our sudden union upon that small and rather staid community would have been to advertise that it had been a shotgun marriage, which it most definitely was not. So when I finally got there, I had to stay at a local hotel and I was introduced to one and all as Gisela's fiancé. Our connubial life, our conjugal visitations, were confined to the backseat of a Porsche on back country roads. Even prisoners have it better. When we started to suspect that Gisela was pregnant, we, quite obviously, couldn't go to a doctor, so we did the next best thing and went to the pregnancy section of a big bookstore in Baden Baden. At which moment some of her parents' friends came in, and we had to flatten ourselves on the floor so that they wouldn't see us in that particular and incriminating section.

Our trip down to our saving-our-money destination in Spain had its own adventures. Driving down France's Doub River Valley a sudden and furious blizzard stranded us with the possibility of a freezing night in a blackened white wilderness. Suddenly, right out of a horror film, an ancient structure, a former Napoleonic post stop or stage coach way-station, appeared in the darkness. A hulking mute giant appeared and took our luggage. Our host at this far-out-of-the-way English inn was a strange death-obsessed Brit… a former African colonial with evidences of all the animals he'd murdered and the weapons used decorating the timbered interior. He greeted us with the smile of a Bela Lugosi character, a leer bestowed only upon prey. We were the only guests. His good nature was tinged with ominous intention, as though he already could taste our blood. And as the blizzard roared about this haunted place, I pushed a large armoire against our bedroom door since it oh-so-conveniently did not have a lock. In our state of exhaustion from barely making it through the blizzard, we knew we would not make it through the night. I slept (after promising Gisela I wouldn't) through the night with a heavy zinc pitcher in my hand. We awoke in the morning alive and restored to our senses.

Spared of ghoulish murder, we then headed through Spain to Gibraltar because we had directed Bank Of America in London to transfer a few hundred dollars to Barclays Bank there. The money, for some reason, hadn't arrived. Spanish immigration rules, deriving from their hatred of the fact that England maintained its little Guantanamo type perch on otherwise Spanish soil, directed that Gisela's German passport would get her into and back out of Gibraltar into Spain only once. If we were to set foot on the continent of Africa, this was it. In 1957/58 this whole area was not much-visited by Americans, so no consulates, just a travel agency, Viajes Marsan, which was a far-flung speck of American Express where mail could be delivered and picked up. Waiting for our money to arrive, we decided to make a day trip to Tangiers, a couple hours ferry ride away, picking the least expensive hotel which of course was in the medina, the most resolutely indigenous quarter of what was then an international city, its own little country. The medina didn't play host to a lot of Europeans. It was Pepe Le Moko territory. We loved it and decided to stay as long as our thirty dollars would hold out. Ah, youth! We were equally nuts which is a dangerous combination for a start-up marriage. We wandered first with a visit to the arts city of Tetuan (or, variously, Tetuah) which was in Spanish Morocco, meaning a border to cross. The eighth class bus, apart from us, was filled with farmers bearing chickens and little sacks of grain that they didn't want confiscated at the border. So at one point the bus stopped in the middle of a hilly nowhere and everybody but we and our guide Achmed, got off and started to file up over a rise. The driver smoked a number of cigarettes and then started the bus up again. We made the border crossing, drove on and then stopped at another nowhere. A few cigarettes into our stop, the file of our fellow passengers appeared over a hill and then joined us for the rest of the trip to Tetuan. I had worn Achmed out with my questions. At an arts center there, I was impressed with some furniture I deduced to be embossed and gilded leather, and I remarked to Gisela, "Is this leather, honey?" And Achmed confirmed, "Yes, the finest leatherhoney in all Morocco." We didn't subscribe to the complete accuracy of his information thereafter. When we lunched, Achmed said that if I gave him our passports he could get us tickets back on the more commodious tourist bus. Ah, youth. Three hours later, neither Achmed nor our passports had returned. It was little over a decade after World War II, and North Africa was filled with ex-Nazis wanting to get somewhere. An American and a West German passport had value. But, then, so did Achmed. After a worrisome length of time, a restorative siesta's length of time after so many questions, he and the passports returned.

We hopped a third class train to Casablanca, and the honeymoon came perilously close to being over when the train crossed an invisible line between Spanish Morocco and French Morocco in the middle of a desert and some sort of distant war. We sat in our citrus fragranced compartment waiting for the passport inspection. The only other occupant was a veiled Arab woman who had held an orange all the way from Tangiers. We had made bets whether she would feed it to herself under the veil, but all she did was dig her fingernails into its skin, releasing sharp odors to counter the acrid smell of decades of overheated passengers. The French Moroccan immigration officers went over our passports on the train and then escorted Gisela and me to a mud hut among a little scattering of mud buildings, one of which was our detention room with Moroccan solders defending the nation my from subversive influence. When a French army captain came in, it was clear he was in charge. I was invited to fill out a series of papers, my registration for free accommodations in the mud hut a short distance away that was the French Moroccan pokey. Gisela's papers were in order, but, thinking no one would know what a publicist was, I had listed my occupation on the passport as journalist. They sure understood what journalist meant... trouble. They were having a war somewhere. The captain remarked with some interest that I was gauche' ...left-handed... and it turned out his daughter was as well. Gisela knew from wartime what I knew from PR, any spark can be coaxed into a fire. She gushed with admiration at Mon Capitain's modernity and liberated thought in not imposing the shackles of the past on his daughter. Flattery will get you anywhere, and when he suggested to us that our train was leaving, we ran for it. Our lone suitcase and the lady with the orange were waiting for us. Her eyes sort of smiled at our return as though she had been worried for us "Well," Gisela said after we caught our breath, "that was invigorating." She seemed to be enjoying the crash tests to which we were subjecting our new marriage. There is something about the smell of orange that lingers not only in the air but in the memory. The year before, almost exactly a year before, I had gone to the backwaters of Mallorca to recover from Gisela's having just dumped me and to start writing scripts in earnest. Every morning I would walk up the steep mountain road from Palma, trying to figure out how to fashion plot. One morning a bicyclist was coasting down the road while peeling an orange. The sharp, sweet citrus tang tailed behind him like a veil for nearly a mile as I walked up the road.

We spent our Casablanca days wandering and discovering, subsisting on bananas and dates purchased in native markets, staying in least expensive hotels, Humphrey Bogart and Ingrid Bergman on a shoe-string, but wide-eyed and hopeful and careless as our youth required. By the time we had squeezed our meager funds as far as they would go, a third class train was way too expensive for our return to Tangiers, so it was gloriously atmospheric eighth-class busses all the way. We returned to Gibraltar on a Monday, and our money still had not arrived, the teller going through the cable book each morning and afternoon with increasing disdain and finally loathing for our desperation. I spent our last three cents on a stamp to write an angry demand of Bank Of America London as to why our money hadn't been transferred. There were no American or German consulates or even naval attaches to contact. We were not about to contact her parents a month into our marriage to report that we were busted. The situation was as close to desperate as you might wish for your honeymoon. I had paid and tipped well enough in our previous stay in the Gibraltar Hotel, so we were tolerated without demand for payment for days. The hotel supplied breakfast, and we surreptitiously stole enough breadsticks from other tables to get us through the rest of the days. Friday morning, realizing that everyone's patience was wearing out along with ours, we went to the bank, asked for the cable book to be searched, and by now they weren't even looking. I was starting to look a bit dissolute because I shaved by electric razor then, and that instrument was in our Porsche in a garage from which we could not afford to rescue it. Late afternoon, with no other recourse, we went to our little American Express way-station to see if Bank of America had answered my letter. Yes. Yes! They had, and with proof of what the cable they had sent had said and when it was sent. It had been there all along. We ran to Barclays. It was one minute to three. The guard was closing and locking the door. I crashed into it, sending him hurtling back into the bank. Waving my proof, my letter from Bank of America, like a scimitar, I ran to the bank president's glass cubicle, slamming its door behind me in a fashion that caused the glass window to fall out, which really got his attention, and I began my reasoned complaint by reaching across his desk, grabbing him by the lapels and throttling him, raving about injustice and torture. Gisela still considers it the first evidence of the occasional rages of which the torching of my brain with LSD had rendered me capable. The bank president waved me toward the lady who had never found our cable, and she, a little wide-eyed as were all the other witnesses to this violence, began her same indolent search through the book. I pulled it from her and started through it myself, tearing out the pages and tossing them behind me. And then…. then!…. there it was and there it had been all along. I turned and waved it into the air with a triumphant "AHA!!!!" People stood about dumbly as I was paid our money. No one called the police, no one demanded payment for the damages. They just wanted me gone.

I was in no mood to be hassled by the hassle-compulsive Spanish immigration people as we gratefully fled Gibraltar. One guy was sure we were smuggling something and demanded that I open the trunk which revealed, this being a Porsche, the motor. Then he commanded the hood be opened. At the back of that space was a metal container with a wide screwed-on lid. It was the gas tank. He was sure it was the smuggling place and he reached his arm in. It came out with sleeve soaked with gasoline. Unnerved, he chose to prove he wasn't and, to show his undismayed and ever-casual aplomb, he started with shaking hand to light a cigarette. He was gang-tackled by his friends. Now they really wanted to grill me. I fell back on Gisela's ever-effective motto, "The stupid always win."

"Cuanto tiempo quieren ustedes quedar?" they challenged. (How long do you plan stay?) "Dos," I said… (two), holding up four fingers "Dos casas." (two houses.) They waved us through. And thus began our soft and lovely pregnancy period on Andalusia with the enchanting acquaintance of the kind fisherfolk and farmers. The big event for the whole area came in March when a Christmas card from Bob Hope and his family, having followed me from one American Express address to the next, finally showed up at Viajes Marsan in Gibraltar where I occasionally went for mail and supplies. which, yes, I smuggled back into Spain, usually placing them in the one place they wouldn't look, on the passenger seat next to me. The card showed Bob and his family gleefully celebrating on a Santa's sleigh in flight. I showed it to Gisela and dropped it on a table. Anita, the local girl whom we had to get as maid because we couldn't figure out how to use the charcoal-fired stove, saw the card while cleaning, looked at it and suddenly screamed, "Bobe Ohpay! BOBE OHPAY!!!," and, indeed, it clearly bore his signature. She ran into town to show it about, and we were asked to contribute it to the Los Boliches and Fuengirola alcalde's office or city hall where it was placed on prominent display and where it may still reside.

Singapore Sling

Travel with Gisela is always invigorating. One time we were in Singapore when director Joe Sargent was filming my script "Passion Flower" at the renowned Raffles Hotel. I'd set one scene in the Writers Bar, home of the Singapore Sling, and where the walls are decorated with signed photos of Kipling, Conrad, Hemingway. Maugham, Michener and other literary greats who guested there and no doubt personally decorated that famous drinking hole of many a smartly conversational evening. Joe wanted the set photographer to take a head shot of me that Joe would frame and put up there with the writing icons… for the scene only, of course. Gisela politely advised him that if he actually pursued this flim-flammery and if I actually participated in it, she would break all four of our legs and other unrelated bones in our bodies. The bartender was impressed with her zeal, and what she did get for her fury was the very secret recipe for a Singapore Sling written on a Writers Bar coaster. When we shortly thereafter went to Indonesia and the custom guys tore apart both of her suitcases looking for drugs (a hanging offense,) nothing was missing except for the Singapore Sling coaster. Luckily, they could not for some reason get my suitcase open…. luckily, I note, because at that time I was still subject to kidney stones and I had a bottle of Percodan among my toiletries. That recalcitrant lock or zipper saved Gisela the trouble of shipping home my crooked-necked body. The Writers Bar scene was, with great reluctance on Joe's part, removed in the final cut despite great comic performances by Joe's wife, Carolyn, and the renowned Australian actor, John Waters. The writer's lot is that you pour out these dialogues you love and terrific people say them, and then they just disappear. No wonder writers drink.

Just as the film was about to start, Joe had called me from Singapore to fill me in on his first lunch with the powerful British actor Nicol Williamson, who would brilliantly ignite a difficult and explosive role I'd written for my old English acquaintance, Trevor Howard, who passed away before we got the film green-lighted. This was just as Gisela and I were leaving for Singapore for last minute script changes, five days before the start of production. "Nicol sits down," Joe reports, "and he says 'The first thing, Joseph, is that the entire film has to be rewritten.'" "The whole script has to be rewritten?! In five days? ! Did he give you any specifics?" I panicked. "Yes," Joe says, "He asks if I'm familiar with the scene near the beginning where the banker describes how Nicol's character became the greatest white corporate oligarch of the Orient and I assured him I am. He then points out that the dialogue indicates that his character had sprung from the coal fields of Leeds in Northern England." "Right, the depths of poverty," I defended. "'Joe,' he begins, gripping my arm powerfully, 'that man would never have come from Leeds. He would have come from the Midlands where I'm from. We were far poorer than Leeds.'" "And?" I begged. "And I say to him, "Nicol, you've got it. The line now reads he came from the Midlands. What else do you want us to change? 'Well' Nicol says, looking at me intensely, 'That's it."

That project had moved toward production from the first treatment of the story, and, as usual, I was faced with a very fast draft. Luckily I had an acquaintance who had been an American ex-patriot banker working the Singapore financial scene and the ex-pat social scene. From the Singapore tourist office I had obtained a bag of tourist brochures from which I derived colorful locations and around which I quickly wove my characters and plot. So I arrived there with a sort of tourist brochure knowledge of one of the great and exciting and ever-so-clean capitals of Asia. And on our last night there, when the whole company was taking Gisela and me to dinner, I requested one of the fabled "banana leaf" restaurants in the Indian section about which I read, written and salivated. Some of the world's most stunning Indian food, but no plates or utensils. They put a banana leaf in front of you and someone plops a pile of succulent rice on it, and another guy comes with three former tin lard cans strapped to him, chicken, meat or fish curry, a generous pile of your choice deposited next to your rice. That was all of the formalities. You dig in with your fingers... and with ravenous appetite to judge from the way we all attacked our banana leaves. More tasty curry or fingers you will never enjoy. All, that is, except Joe. Curry, for him, is not finger food. He motions the restaurateur to his side and inquires if they have a spoon. "Yes," the man smiles broadly. "Well, may I have one?" Joe asks politely. "I'm sorry," the man says, pained to disappoint him, "it's reserved for tonight." Joe, disgruntled, picks at the food, his addiction to curry in serious jeopardy. Finally, he rises like a zombie in some kind of trance of self-revulsion. Holding his hands away from his body like abominations, he goes into the kitchen in search of sanitation. Suddenly the restaurateur comes running to us urgently. "Sir... please... your friend... he is washing his hands in our soup."

There's a reason that we are not all replications of each other, that we do not all go orgiastic over the exact same food, wear to the button the same clothes, fall in love with the same person. We all, according to our experience and predilection, develop priorities, an order of the qualities we look for in life or in others. It is not always something we ourselves possess, and maybe that's why we seek it out... as a complement to ourselves. I'm quite convinced that anyone married to or partnered with an intensely interesting person must some day conclude that he or she has bought a bottle of tri-nitro-toluene (TNT) and is not quite sure that his or her hand is steady enough for the job. Sometimes when Gisela becomes particularly agitated about something, I suggest she not slosh the liquid to the point of detonation. I am, for my part, incredibly attracted to courage. Not pugnacity... the looking-for-a-fight kind of courage. I'm drawn to a courage that is respectful of others and laced and braced with a calm, sure embrace of the unexpected.

Our daughter Moni inherited Gisela's love of reckless travel and fearless self-expression. A few years after the Vietnam War stuttered to a stop, she took off for that new People's Republic to try to find the little girl we had helped support through Foster Care. Even though Moni turned over all of the stones in the pertinent villages, it proved not possible, so we were left to hope for the best. Moni and her husband Mark Robertson have waded their way through the jungles of Malaysia and

Belize on native busses and in dugouts or tramping sucking-mud paths, depending on instincts rather than guides. When we hauled her around the world as a child, she would never sit with us on the plane, but ventured out to explore new people for the next four to twelve hours of life. Later, moving from the bucolic tranquilities of Stanford to the less patient manners and ruder streets of New York, even those abutting Columbia's and Barnard's hallowed halls, it might have been that she was bored with Stanford's polite expectabilities. To prepare for the change, she took a course in karate and self-defense during her last semester "on the farm." The wisdom of that was immediately established one evening early in her transfer when she went with friends to a bar. Some guy became more than friendly, placing his hand flat upon her chest. She slapped her own hand over his, which he probably first interpreted as an encouragement, but then she slammed her torso forward, bending over to break all of his fingers. For him, it was the quick and disappointing end of a beautiful friendship. For me, it was evidence that she definitely was her mom's kid. I don't mean to imply that either of our daughters was a carbon copy of Gi… Life is more interesting than that, but it would take a pretty big bear to back any of them down. Moni made things hot for some noted medics, for her school and, in a larger sense, for herself when, writing for the Stanford Daily, she tracked down a very resentfully-received expose of the errant disposal of radio-active materials at the Stanford Medical Center. It was a scandal with awful implications, and she didn't back down. Nor, to its credit, did the paper.

After her graduation at Stanford (which she found more competitive,) she migrated to D.C. to join her future husband (whom she'd met at Columbia where he was the John Jay scholar, who was studying for his work in the foreign service, having volunteered for the hot spots of the Middle East and having learned Arabic in the process. Moni quickly got an internship at NPR, but she had to support herself and she'd heard of an opening for an assistant in a plastic surgeon's practice. She had to establish some medical background to get it, so she resorted to something Warren Cowan would have admired as a true-lie, stating that she had worked at the Stanford Medical Center. She kept a Grey's Anatomy at her side to clarify any mysterious medical terms from doctors or patients, and they were thrilled to have such a thoroughly trained not to mention resourceful assistant.

This was at the time of the early discovery of the HIV/AIDS epidemic, a time when the Right Wing was selling the catastrophe as the scourge of God upon those of homosexual orientation… or, as they averred, choice. The demagogues of the religious right were making these ludicrous allusions, but the Big Guys amongst them were ducking any interviews which would expose their bigoted ignorance. So, driving to a meeting, I was listening as was my custom, to NPR, and it was proudly proclaimed to national ears that one of public broadcasting's interns had scored the first interview on the subject with Reverend Jerry Falwell. Suddenly, there was Monika who had somehow trapped this great blusterer into conversation by subtly hitting the stop button in an elevator they were (by chance?) sharing. She meticulously worked his self-righteousness and dragged him out onto the quicksand of his convictions and bigotries, recording his slowly sinking into its ooze. Such are the little life surprises which brighten a day more than any sun.

Chapter 17

Legends

How can you cultivate public enthusiasm for a talent, a film, a product, an idea or a cause if you don't first cultivate your own enthusiasm? When you're associated with legends, that's not a problem. Your first constructive action is to surrender to your own awe. Explore it, understand it. Realize the full dimensions of why that person occupies his or her own mountaintop... or why a cause galvanizes the hope of millions. You will be reinforced in this by the constant evidence of how he or she or it has illuminated the lives of others. This does not apply only to your own clients. You must be madly in love with all great acting, writing, directing. You must celebrate legend wherever you touch it.

A press agent's attention is always distracted and directed by the events of the day. You start out to do this, and then the day demands that. Today was a conjunction of startling events for two clients, the two women who individually have defined stardom and star power and star talents for the past half century more richly than any other two female artists of that incredible period. Not hard to guess: Barbra Streisand and Elizabeth Taylor. Their lives are, as a matter of fact, beyond legendary. They are epic.

The two events happened within a single half hour. It was in "National Velvet" that Elizabeth Taylor, barely into her teens, first fluttered the heart of every boy of the 40s, including mine, of course. After that, It was never questioned that her beauty and natural acting gift would make her a star as a teen-ager ("Father Of The Bride" and all the others) and then a star-of-stars as a young and maturing woman ("A Place In The Sun" and "Suddenly Last Summer" and "Giant" and "Cat On A Hot Tin Roof" and "Cleopatra," "Who's Afraid of Virginia Woolf" and "Raintree County. Nearly sixty films glowed with her beauty and her delicate and differentiated characterizations. Through a life of pendulum swings, victorious and tragic, always tempestuously alive and engaged with life, she sustained courage, glamour, and finally the enormous relevance of her leadership of the fight against HIV/AIDS, living an epic narrative to match that of any film she ever made. Afflictions were not strangers, but she maintained spirit and body by addressing the afflictions of others, not only heading but also driving Hollywood's and then the world's effort to treat and cure HIV/AIDS and, at the same time, bring forth one of the great fragrance lines.

The state of her health during the last five or so years of her life was of recurrent issue for all celebrity-oriented media, not just the tabloids. The tabloids' obsession with the matter, however phantasmagoric the headlines, heated up the general press' compulsion to follow and report the rumors. In her mid-seventies she determined to adopt a policy of conveying herself via social media the exact facts that might be otherwise speculated by others completely ignorant of such facts. She was, thus, putting the lie in advance to what she wished to not have falsely speculated. It was a simple but enormous innovation and adjustment to meet the venal idiosyncrasy of the times. She did this so adroitly today that I was humbled to see how far ahead of me she was. She had become her own media and would henceforth always have the scoop on the media. At mid-afternoon she tweeted about her going into the hospital for a fairly serious heart procedure, but not open heart surgery. She said what she wanted to say and said it in her own words with a signature eloquence and wit. Henceforth, I could simply direct press inquiries to her twitter site. The intelligent media, of which there are many, came to understand that if it wasn't there on her site, it wasn't true, and that what was true would be there.

Another day, forty-nine hours after she dropped her polite little bomb, she is back on twitter to say all went well, a little clip was applied and she feels like she has a new heart. We eblast to all media to access this first-hand report. She had perceived and perfected the precise way to beat the digital age at its own game. She injected her controlled news directly into the public awareness. I learned from her… the way to inform the madding crowd was to do it yourself, controlling and constricting the fuss. What could have been forty-three incoming calls, journalists wanting proof, wanting to talk to her is now the push of an eblast button. *They don't have to talk to her. She's talking to them.*

Within the half hour of Dame Elizabeth's off-to-the-hospital tweet, we received confirmation of extraordinary news about that other dominant female star of the past half century, Barbra Streisand. It's news which historically (as in something that may never again be achieved) reflects how overwhelming is her pre-eminence in the field of musical performance and production.

You might ask what else she still had to achieve In addition to her similarly documented accomplishment as director, actor, writer, producer, composer, activist, philanthropist and, most recently, author/photographer, she had during the last four decades of the 20th century and the first decade of the 21st received virtually all the awards there are to collect. Oscars, Emmys, Grammys, Tony, the DGA award, Golden Globes, Kennedy Center Honors (the only female director to do so,) Legion d'Honneur, National Medal of Arts, Peabody and AFI Lifetime Honoree, ten-time Grammy awardee including Grammy Legend and Recording Academy Lifetime Achievement Award recipient. She is by many millions and by measurement of the RIAA (the Recording Industry of America Association) the leading album seller among women artists. Most remarkably, she and she alone had until the day of which I speak *released number one albums in four consecutive decades...* FOUR consecutive decades. Few careers sustain that long, much less occupy art's highest rung throughout. It was and is something hard to imagine would ever again be accomplished, much less extended. And this fifth decade was getting down to its last ticks.

The suspense of the day was that, as the RIAA accounting of the previous week's record sales was conducted, there was a chance that she *could* extend that to a miraculous five consecutive decades with her new album, "Love Is The Answer." Mariah Carey had moved her own new release back to the same week, and there was a load of other superstars, including Madonna coming out the same week and being counted on this day. It was a nice dream, written off by most pundits, and then suddenly a phone call and it was confirmed that she had indeed achieved Number One albums in five straight decades. FIVE STRAIGHT DECADES. When Babe Ruth hit his 714th home run and then laid down his bat, it seemed inevitable that somehow a Hank Aaron would come along to hit 715 or more. It took decades, but it happened.

And now that Barbra's duets album, "Partners," five years later has added still another decade to her collection, her residence at the top of the charts spans SIX STRAIGHT DECADES, stretching the time between initial #1 record and the most recent to nearly 50 years. Probably only Queen Victoria and the current occupant of Buckingham Palace have spent a longer time at the top. Sure, records are made to be broken, but maybe not this one.

Such history-writing events are never left to, nor are they the product of, chance. Barbra's manager of well over a half century, Marty Erlichman, had meticulously strategized the making of, timing of and presentation of the album. Columbia Music and Ken Sunshine executed a vigorous and impactful promotion campaign, including the Big Event appearance of Barbra on The Tonight Show with Jimmy Fallon, whose musicianship provided the perfect matrix for her return after more than four decades to late night talk-show guesting. And, of course, producers Kenny "Babyface" Edmonds and Walter Afanasieff and executive producers Barbra Streisand and Jay Landers had delivered a superb album.

The historic six decades of Number Ones illustrated the continuity of talent and popularity, of course, but most miraculously it underlined the continuity of relevance. Six decades of supreme *relevance…* how often does that pertain in almost any field?

The public didn't know the stakes of the game, they just loved Barbra as much ever and, now as passages of the new album were played out on the internet and on radio, her enthralling duets with 14 of the greatest male voices ever, they ordered the CD as they did with her first number one, "People." That one had been discovery and this one was reaffirmation of a continuing and evolving talent and of their devotion. When we first listened to her "Love Me Tender" with Elvis, my associate, Rona Menashe, said "this will be played at every wedding in the south or maybe everywhere for the next forty years."

The publicity rule *applied* here was *"spin your primary news element BEFORE the news happens and before it breaks, but only if it can be done safely."* When "Love Is The Answer" went Number One in 2009, we had purposely left it to the media to realize that the miracle of five-straight-decades had just happened, but they didn't. It's hard to write advance spin when you have all of your fingers crossed. But far more importantly, while that album's going Number One was a possibility, it distinctly was not a sure thing. Had we floated the prospect of a fifth decade beforehand and Mariah had won, part of the reportage could have reflected that

Barbra Streisand had missed an opportunity. So we had to do a post-facto shuffle to position her fifth decade achievement into media play.

In the case of "Partners," during the lead time to its release I had a conversation with Keith Caulfield, Billboard's very savvy writer whose beat includes chart results and their significance. He, managing editor Frank DiGiacomo and editor Paul Grein fully understood that history might be in the making. We discussed the ramifications of a win for Barbra's new duets album. The prospects were favorable, and, unlike "Love Is The Answer," had "Partners" fallen short, it would not have ended of the hope of keeping the recording industry's most remarkable hitting streak alive. She would still have five years to do it. Keith saw in the first few day's sales evidence that "Partners" should prevail and that a record was about to be set which very likely could never be equaled. Four days before the fact, he put that exceedingly educated speculation on record in an article. On the weekend before the chart announcements and again on the day before, I sent Keith's story (and other background of Barbra's prospective rewriting of chart records) to the media. It resulted in making the six-straight-decades coup the salient aspect of virtually all reportage with primacy in leads and headlines.

Elizabeth and Barbra were each skilled masters of words. It is amazing how many artists express themselves in ways which bear grace, intelligence, imaginative metaphors, rhythm, surprise and distinctive style. That's something I hungrily look for in people and so often find in the people with whom I've been privileged to work. It makes communication fun. Barbra had, quite early in the digital communication age, created the Truth Alert section of her website to deflate the more troublesome falsehoods about her in the media... a reasonable way to refute media distortions, a way a number of other celebrities have since adopted. There were plenty of press assertions and public harangues to be defanged with Truth Alerts, particularly since her uncompromising opposition to the war in Iraq from its very start drew the fire of every journalist and demagogue of the right. It was, for a long and agonizing moment, heresy to imply that George W. Bush and Dick Cheney had contrived a pointless quagmire, so finely spun were the weapons-of-mass-destruction and other false reasons for the Bush administration's tragic blunder . But she stood up for the American principles and the American kids being squandered on the plains of Iraq, in the mountains of Afghanistan.

In a memorable speech before the Kennedy School of Government at Harvard during the 90s , she had laid out the right and the obligation of celebrities to exercise their freedom of speech and thought… a freedom equal to that of any other citizen… to engage in the public forum. That speech was prominent in a distinguished anthology of important speeches of our times. In line with that, her essays on her website and in such other respected outlets as Politico.com and the Huffington Post, lay out her observations articulately and clearly, leaving no room for strangers or people with other agendas to tell the world what she thinks. Unmistakably, what she thinks and writes is in her own words and her own spirit. When I first scanned the text for her first book, "My Passion For Design," I commented that I loved that it was so clearly written in her own voice. "That's because I wrote it myself," she responded. Yes, that's true, but a lot of authors are led to write in a literary voice lacking the spontaneity and individuality which makes them exciting personalities, afraid to reveal idiosyncrasies and contradictions which shape them as the compelling and creative people they are. When she sings or composes or directs or acts, she puts everything she is into it, never disguising herself, and that's how she writes and converses.

I heard that power recently in the words she gathered for the memorial for a particularly dear friend of hers. studio executive Gareth Wigan. I'd never heard anyone address so precisely what she called "the heavy labor of loving," how it is a construction, a monument, which withstands any tremor, even death, a miracle which over-rides the lives of all of us. If this book has a driving theme, it is celebration of the special way each of so many amazing people I've known have expressed themselves. It facilitated holding so much of it in precise memory…

An example of Barbra's insistence on the truth occurred when she returned to Greenwich Village for a promotion relating to her "Love Is The Answer" CD which shortly thereafter opened at the top of the chart. The occasion reflected her having begun her career as a teenager singing in some of the small yet famous Village boites. In this case, she was going back to her roots to perform a concert for 100 fans selected by lottery. One prominent publication, in its advance story, put forward that she had sung at the Village Vanguard, site of the intimate concert, only one time before as an opening act for Miles Davis. She quickly pointed out in an interview that she had merely *auditioned* there for that honor… and that someone else got the gig.

Before I leave the subject of extraordinary women who know what they want to say and always say it themselves without the aid of flack or ghost writer, let me establish that Kathy Ireland and Kathy Ireland alone puts down every word attributed to her. You'd think that running the $2 billion a year lifestyle design empire she created with her bare hands might rule that out, but it's all pure Kathy. Even as keynote speaker at international CEO conferences, she does not speak from a teleprompter but from her heart. Interesting, too, is the fact that all three of these glass ceiling breakers had no formal education beyond high school and all were recipients of multiple honorary degrees from distinguished universities.

It's another day, a rainy day. It has taught me lessons about how simply people recognize the personalities they want to love and about how fervently and graciously such love is evidenced. It is a day which we had put forward to the press that Dame Elizabeth would officially dedicate the opening of the first House of Taylor jewelry store, an establishment uniquely purple and lavender, a colorful addition to one of Beverly Hills' main glamour streets, Beverly Drive, less than a block down the street from our offices. The opportunity to photograph this star of stars going in, coming out, cutting a ceremonial ribbon had drawn about thirty of the town's best and most welcomed photographers and the crews of such leading shows as "Entertainment Tonight," "Access Hollywood" and "Extra" with their starriest interview talent on hand. And there they all were in the pouring rain of a sodden Saturday, compacted into a tent we had erected on the sidewalk facing the House Of Taylor's entrance, as violet as its namesake's eyes. So many press arrived that a dozen or so others were stranded outside the tent, relying only upon umbrellas which they somehow kept in play even while snapping away.

In the waiting period, they flashed enthusiastically as we had such beauties as Marilu Henner, Maria Conchita Alonso, Teresa Randall, Frances Fisher and others modeling millions of dollars of diamond and emerald earrings, necklaces, bracelets and other creations of Elizabeth Taylor's design. Standing to the side of this, I was amazed how the constant flashes created a stroboscopic backlightng of the falling rain, turning the space between the cameras and the star models into a dazzling curtain of thousands and thousands of diamond-like sparkles falling to the ground. Those jewelry fashion shots were, unfortunately, all these brave and, in some cases, drenched souls got for their trouble. Elizabeth had a cold, and at the last moment, her doctor refused to let her take it out into the daunting rain. That left it to me to go out and tell them, most of them quite affectionately-held friends after all these years and mutual occasions, that it wasn't going to happen. I'm quite aware that the expected photo op meant money to them in not the best of times. And I was withdrawing it. What impressed me was the absolute grace with which they took the news... kindness, actually. Elizabeth Taylor was more than a salable photo subject for them. Their response was the kind and, indeed, concerned acceptance of the pros who had waited and who had understood. They even thanked us as they left and offered to be back on another day. But, sadly, this would have been her last photo op.

It's often suggested that an important aspect of the legend part of Elizabeth Taylor's command of our affections was her skill with words. As the pain of her back problems limited her public appearances, the media vied furiously for any voice-capture interview. We had arranged a backstage "Entertainment Tonight" exclusive few minutes with her upon one of Dame Elizabeth's annual appearances at the Macy's Passport events which raise so much money to fight HIV/AIDS. Any Elizabeth Taylor sighting is a big event. The huge public discussion about her at that instant was her deep friendship for Jason Winters, one of her business partners and her frequent escort at public appearance. Given her much-married history, that question was front and center for the rumoring press. And after this interview explored her continuing passion to alleviate the suffering and obtain the cure of HIV/AIDS, the interviewer asked if she might be contemplating once more getting married. She said "no," and then her eyes twinkled and her dramatic/comedic instinct surged in, and she, aware the camera was running, said, "Would you please ask me that question again?" Which the savvy interviewer most happily did... and to which the entertainment world's most famous serial bride rose up strong, those violet eyes flashing with joyous horror, and literally screeched... "MAAAAried?!!!"

This is a town where the biggest legends never made it into the fan magazines. The ultimate power was wielded by behind-the-scenes legends, the moguls who shaped the film industry's beginnings and dominated its first half century. Two agency heads, MCA boss Lew Wasserman and William Morris Agency's longtime leader, Abe Lastfogel, had earned that status, too. I never met Mr. Lastfogel, but he influenced my life as much as any of the legends with whom and for whom I worked. When Guttman & Pam had its offices on El Camino Drive, across the street from the Beverly Wilshire Hotel and down the street from William Morris' imposing offices, I would watch Mr. Lastfogel walk from meetings at one to meetings at the other, invariably by himself... There was nothing diminutive about Mr. Lastfogel other than his height, not much more than five feet. Every day, even hundred degree summer and fall days, he made that trip in impeccable style, exquisitely tailored suit and faultlessly knotted tie. He was as erect as a marine at dress attention. He was the incarnation of well-earned pride and power, dignity and discipline. I always returned to my work with renewed vigor.

The reasons that public and media bestow love, fascination and mania on entertainment personalities are as varied as are the talents on whom it is bestowed. Two cases in point, Henry Winkler and the Fonziemania with which he infected the nation's youth and media, and David Janssen and the kind of gritty hold he had on our affections in "The Fugitive" and as a person.

Looking for the Missing Piece...

David was one of the singularly most attractive guys with whom I've worked, a reflection shared by all who knew him, yet it didn't seem to make him feel better about himself. My partner Jerry Pam startled a number of David's vast list of friends as they gathered to mourn David's passing. Jerry, a car lover, had purchased David's distinctive gold Rolls Royce convertible shortly before David so abruptly left us. Since those were now Jerry's wheels, he drove the Rolls to the funeral. Quite a few of the deeply saddened mourners reported having driven up in profound funk and having brightened quickly seeing the gold Rolls and thinking in a bright moment of subtraction from dour reality, "Oh, great... David's here. We'll have a laugh."

David was such a compelling personality that it was impossible not to feel good in his presence even when so often the kind of underlying sadness he carried showed through. He merits a salute in a chapter about legends, and not merely because the conclusion of his long number one series, "The Fugitive," displaced the Beatles' legendary debut on the Ed Sullivan show as TV's highest-rated event.

That series somehow reflected David's own mystery and gave his life a kind of legendary caste that he could not shake. As handsome and talented and loved as he was, I actually felt that "The Fugitive" was an appropriate star vehicle and metaphor for him. You sensed that David was always looking for some missing piece even though he sure seemed to everyone else to be the whole package. It wasn't just the drinking. It was more like the reason for the drinking.

Strangely, I had the same feeling about Bill Holden, another guy who so evidently had it all but who was the one person who couldn't appreciate it. He had so many of the qualities and accomplishments which qualify one for legend and which defined him, even in the early and sadly wasteful catastrophe of his death. Legend was a distinction he well deserved. The things that made Bill the most ruggedly masculine guy you knew, his species preservation work at Mount Kenya for instance, his adventuring and compulsive world-hopping, seemed part of the search for something missing by a guy who everyone was compelled to believe had it all. After we finished filming "Breezy," a romantic comedy under Clint Eastwood's direction, Bill leapt off on a one-man trek through Burma, not the least dangerous place on earth. He and David Janssen each had a kind of restlessness. Working with Bill Holden first in England on "The Key," I had a glimpse into what made his performance in every role so believable. Whatever the role... the gallant hero of his "bridges" films... "The Bridge On The River Kwai" and "The Bridges Of Toko-Ri"... or his many westerns, or the anti-heroes, most particularly the in-it-only-for-himself Sefton in "Stalag 17" (a film in which everyone had only one name... first, last or nick) in which his character masked his patriotism even from himself, or the cynical, opportunistic but ultimately romantic Joe Gillis of "Sunset Boulevard." The comedies, the aching romances... there was always some element, some aspect, of Bill that slipped right into the character. His comedy characterizations ran from worldly roué of "Sabrina Fair" to the innocent-of-worldly-ruse academic of "Born Yesterday," and there was always something charmingly Bill Holden in each. Look at "Born Yesterday" and "Ball Of Fire" and you'll see how Holden and Gary Cooper were somehow joined at the funny bone.

For "The Key," on which I worked in England, Bill portrayed a character resigned to doomed fate, somewhat in the manner of Jeremy Renner's accommodation in "The Hurt Locker" to the probable death his war had dictated. "The Key" gave

Holden a role whose gloom was relieved by a somewhat somber romance with Sophia Loren, following a group of men who passed along in succession the key, the apartment and the woman who went with it and then the command of a North Atlantic WW II ocean-going tug and the death that went with that. Much of the film was at sea… at churning, angry sea… aboard that giant tug, with many hours devoted to positioning the ship in turbulent ocean confluences of tides where the storms were always perfect. Most of the crew spent those hours below deck, and there was a continuous hot poker game of high stakes with Carl Foreman, Trevor Howard and most of the above the line talent. Bill chose to spend much of that time leaning on a deck railing watching the ocean in its constant change. I was up there not because I enjoyed the freezing winds, but because I wanted proximity to railings for a stomach constantly at battle with the rise and fall of the ship. At least I was until Bill shared with me the secret of the seagull bait. For many shots, they needed the roil of seagulls circling the stern, and there was a huge pile of stale biscuits or crackers to be tossed out to cue the seagulls. Stealing a cracker from that store every ten minutes as Bill had directed, I achieved a kind of gastronomic equilibrium, enjoying Holden's company and his stories in the process.

It was such a gloomy and arduous shoot that there weren't a lot of laughs, but that changed for the shoot of a scene in which a German U-boat surfaces off the stern with intention of taking down the tug with its deck cannon. There was some positioning of actors at the stern, but the shot was primarily toward the U-boat as it fired directly at the tug, directly at camera. It was smoke and noise but no actual discharge, of course. It was an interesting and diverting event, and each of us took a comfortable position behind the camera to watch it. Some of the crew set their bottoms on the top guy wire of the lateral railings near the aft, with their feet secured in the middle wire beneath that. What none of us was prepared for was the concussion the blast would transmit, even in the absence of hurtling shrapnel and explosives. The submarine was far enough back that there was a brief intermission between sight and sound, as there is if you're standing at the finish line of a hundred yard dash and you see the smoke of the starter's gun before you hear the shot. But in the case of the cannon attack scene, it wasn't merely a sound… it was also a pound. It was a Rocky Marciano punch to the chest. And a dozen members of the film crew blew back off their perches on the railing wire to curl awkward, tumbling dives into the freezing waters twenty or thirty feet below. They got high marks for degree-of-difficulty but none for style. However, had they been judged for the surprised looks on their faces, there would have been a lot of tens. There was much clamor and activity as life boats were hastily lowered for the rescues. All hands were, after a lot of ingested sea water, safe. Even while safe recovery was still in doubt, none of us could stop laughing. We would look guiltily at each other and then would burst out in laughter again.

Once we got back to shooting the film at the studio in Elstree, Bill told funnier stories between takes, and it was quickly apparent why he was so extraordinarily charming to both men and women. Yes, there were recollections of rolls in the hay with famous co-stars, one quite literally a matter of nocturnal meetings in a barn. He was the kind of guys' guy who makes the most devastating gals' guy. His death was such a shocking surprise because he had lived so intensively. A guy who courted danger and adventure so passionately and then is lost in a fall in his home? I was glad I was spared the pain of doing his obituary. The obits of legends are always pre-written. I wouldn't have known where to start… or finish.

David Janssen died with hard-to-accept suddenness. Death is always a surprise, but some really come out of nowhere. Contrary to some press speculation in David's case, the autopsy revealed that he had not been drinking. It was a heart attack. We are all mortal and we don't need to find death. Although some of us try. It will find us.

Writing obituaries is always a sad task for me, and some are tougher than others. The degree of David Janssens impact meant that his life was long since in obit files should the sad day arrive. But I put myself to getting my version out, because I wanted to have a hand in its spin, exactly as I did for Tony Franciosa, a great actor and a volatile spirit, and I wanted to make sure the emphasis was on the acting. David's was tough, and maybe the hardest work he required of us was after his death. You didn't want to lay too heavily on the roots of the sadness that was always hot on his heels. Much of his early life was spent in orphanages. His widow, Dani Janssen, and he met when they were each part of the Universal Studios star-development program along with Clint Eastwood who remained a friend of both. David finally, in the wake of other marriage, found his way back to Dani because she was and is such a brightly attractive light for everyone who knows her. Dani recently told me that they never planned anything big on Sundays. He was always sad on Sundays because that was the day his mother would take him back to the orphanage. The perplexing thing upon his death was that much media focus became concentrated on whether or not he was Clark Gable's son. That had been a recurring speculation during his life and it became a fixation for the media after his death. The fact was that David was born in Nebraska and that his mother didn't move them to Los Angeles, to Hollywood, until he was seven. But the similarities in the beautiful and edgy voices of Clark Gable and David Janssen had always commanded curiosity, It wasn't that they looked like each other, but that each had such highly individualistic and rugged handsomeness. Each had a self deprecating humorous edge, Gable's delivered perhaps with more glee. David's dry wit could always draw laughter. When he got back from shooting "Inchon" in Korea, my associate Wally Beene, a hands-on witness to most war zones, asked him if he'd experienced some Korean word. "Yeah, sure," David grumbled, "I either went there or I ate it." Janssen and Gable were each handsome enough to be beautiful, but the sum total was rugged masculinity. I never saw anyone command the interest of women as David did. When Guttman & Pam threw a reception for Princess Margret for Rolls Royce, her air of light and polite conversation with each of the gathered stars somewhat skidded to a halt when she arrived at David. When the remaining waiting line grew restive, she moved on and then gravitated back to David. You can't fault her taste.

Gable and Janssen each had "smolder." Barbara Stanwyck came up with that word for David, not I. After high school, he and I first bumped into each other again on the set of an episode of Four Star Productions' western anthology series, Zane Grey Theatre, for which I was doing the publicity. David, several decades Miss Stanwyck's junior, had been cast both as her antagonist and her love interest. The climax was a fight between the two of them in a mudhole, the combat finally turning romantically antic. When the director called "cut," Miss Stanwyck said, "Wow." Overhearing her elaboration on that in an exchange with the director, I went over to David who was toweling off. "Miss Stanwyck told the director 'that kid's got smolder,'" I reported to the guy I'd looked up to in high school. "She said that? Barbara Stanwyck said that about me?" David asked with wonder. "Is that a good thing?" "The way she said it? Yeah!"

I think David would have been happy to know he'd missed the intense speculation on the possible Gable connection, that last flurry of attention and invasion which attended his death but which couldn't obscure the fact he had well-earned, particularly in television, the highest stardom and that he delivered deep and moving performance when the scripts permitted.

When I began at Fairfax High in the primarily Jewish district which straddled Hollywood and West Los Angeles, David was the established Big Man on Campus, among the best pole vaulters in the city and an all-league guard in basketball. And he looked like… well, he looked like David Janssen. We met when track season started, and I was an inconsequential 110 pound sprinter on the C team. The first meet was against sworn enemy rival LA High, and I was nauseous with tension. The hundred is merciless, a blink of the eye to do what you can, a one-punch fight. There were no team busses to the away meets, just a gathering where guys who had cars selected which teammates could ride with them. I was the last guy left and starting to feel like the world's greatest wallflower, a loser even before I got to the starting blocks. David, seeing this, came up and said "Hey, kid, whoever you're riding with, why don't ya come with me? I need the ballast." During the meet, he stopped in to check on me, to clap me on the back after the hundred and he made sure I had my ride home.

You should never try to gauge where you stand in any line, as I found out when I sat down with David Janssen at Morton's restaurant one evening to go over some business before his dinner date arrived. When we finished, Stan Herman, Beverly Hills' leading and wealthiest realtor, arrived at the table to join David. "You guys must have known each other at Fairfax," David said, but neither Stan nor I recalled that. I suddenly realized how low on the Fairfax totem pole I stood. David and Stan were vast success stories. Herb Alpert had been part of my class, and another guy who did pretty well with music was Jerry Lieber, Alan Pappe was one of the top photographers with whom I would later deal, Dodger stars Norm and Larry Sherry. Jack Kemp… top pro quarterback, senator, cabinet secretary… was just behind us. The list of successes towered above me and I ventured that I was the class failure. Casting about for someone who might not have done as well, I focused on a guy who was kind of rowdy and who I felt was less dedicated to his studies than to being a tackle on the football team and an all-around fun guy. "Bob Zacky," I said, "I may have done better than he." David and Stan looked at each other, and then, with pity, at me. "Have you ever heard of Zacky Farms chickens?" David asked. "He probably pulls down a couple of million a day." I suddenly remembered our graduating class' name… the Vagabonds. They must have come up with that in consideration of my prospects of success.

That dinner made me a little less unsuccessful. Stan decided to hire Guttman & Pam to represent his ex-wife, Linda Evans, during her stardom on "Dynasty" and on the occasion of her starring with Steve McQueen in the film "Tom Horn." His ex-wife had an opportunity, and he was backing her. It said a lot about Stan and about the kind of people David chose as friends.

When the Public Is Ahead of the Media — Henry Winkler

It's very helpful for a press agent to have kids around as divining rods as to what already is hot and what is not. They know before the media and even before the industry. Now, with heat being measured instantaneously in metrics of internet hits and "trendings," the catch-up time is much shorter, but it was once and for a long time an arduous chore for press agents to clue the media and industry into what the public had already discovered and bounced into stardom. Fonziemania was a perfect example. It's not as if we built that juggernaut, but we were a bit more than merely conductors on the train. When Henry Winkler's agent, Joan Scott, called us to represent her client, "Happy Days" was already a surprise hit. Industry and media could see that in the overnight ratings, but the specific elements that drove that popularity were not immediately perceived. There was no immediate digital readout. Henry Winkler, soft-spoken and a Yale Drama School-educated young gentleman in the truest sense of the word, had donned leather jacket and the coolest of cool attitudes and had won immediate national stardom… among the kids. Nobody knew but the kids, which was the reason his agent had called us. The fan mail for him vastly exceeded that of any of the show's young stars-to-be. It did, in fact, exceed all of them together. The mailroom at Paramount was the first to know. And then Miller/Milkus Productions took note, and the Fonz' storylines started to get better. But of Winkler's success the entertainment industry was still ignorant.

When we arrived in Henry's life and he in ours a few months into the show's ratings rocket ride, the guy who would shortly adorn every pop culture cover and whose alter ego on the show would be a media by-word. If you didn't have acne, he was still a best-kept secret, a model of polite behavior in contrast to the Fonz' brash and endearing swagger. I'd first noticed him in the low-budget film "The Lords of Flatbush," which introduced him and some kids like Sylvester Stallone, Perry King and Susan Blakely. When I met him at Joan's behest, he was a well-read, well-mannered, a well and quietly-spoken young man who called everybody Sir or Ma'am to the point of madness. But how to wake up the world to it? When he arrived in some eastern city for a charity, 15,000 kids showed up at the train station in old fashioned fan-worship, traffic jam style. I called entertainment media icon Army Archerd with that popularity-revealing story. Army found it worthy of appearing in his column in Variety. But he asked me the correct spelling of Winkler.

Now part of that inquiry was the fact that Army Archerd was the most meticulously and compulsively accurate journalist I've ever known... ever, anywhere... each detail fully vetted before granted admission to those eight hundred words which entertained every eye and informed every casting evaluation in Hollywood Monday through Friday. Space in his column was intravenous injection into the industry mind since for over 50 years the town knew that he got it right and he got it early. How many ways are there to spell Winkler? It's just that Army left nothing to assumption. Army's question also was the perfect measurement of the secrecy of Henry Winkler's national adulation. Only the kids knew. It reminds me of how far ahead of this town our eight year old grand-daughter was about Brittany Spears who my wife insisted was named Wrigley Spears, Gisela having arrived in America just at the end of its chewing gum addiction. We realized with Henry that we had to use the kids for some grand evidencing to Hollywood of the dimensions of the craze he already enjoyed among teen fans of "Happy Days," which is to say the entire U.S. teeny-bopper population.

The Candy-Stripers are public-spirited teen-aged girls in starched red and white striped pinafores who voluntarily assist patients in hospitals. When their organization needed a morale-boosting celeb for an honors ceremony, they politely requested if Henry Winkler would show up, adding that they fully understood that that was probably an impossible dream. Henry, being Henry, was thrilled at the opportunity to thank these great kids. And we, being press agents, saw a door open... wide. I had finally obtained a national talk-show booking for Henry on the Dinah Shore Show... Henry, humbly aware that his acclaim was still hermetically sealed in the minds of his millions of fans, asked me to tell him truthfully if I had had to pull any special strings to get him the Dinah booking. I confessed that it was a trade-out for a Jackie Bisset appearance on the show. He was distressed about that until I explained that Jackie's first booking was a trade-out for Roger Moore. It's how the game was played.

Ok, an opportunity, but how to derive instant national discovery from it. I spoke to the Shore show's producers about the Candy Stripers and described with passion their inspiring devotion, and it was received with such sympathy that they granted me forty seats so that Henry's red-and-white striped admirers could be there for his first show. He was, I believe, third guest which is fairly humble, and when Dinah introduced him and he walked out, the studio erupted in screaming…. screaming that never stopped. Henry came over to shake Dinah's hand. You couldn't hear, but I'm sure he said "Miss Shore"… and waved to the audience, and the screaming heated up a hundred decibels. Dinah Shore, the living embodiment of cool aplomb, was astonished. Nothing, she realized, could be heard over the roar. She could express her amazement only in open-mouthed wonder and gestures of bemusement to the other guests. Nothing like this had happened before, and soon she and the other stars and Henry were all just laughing and swimming in the noise. It sustained through the entire segment. He never really had a chance to talk, and when Dinah concluded the show she commented that they would have to have Henry back some time when she could actually talk to him.

By the next day, the impact of that had spread to every booker at every show, and the requests for Henry Winker were pouring in. Fonziemania was launched. Henry handled his success with great class, taking it on to success as a producer and director as well as actor. But the measuring rod was that he remained open to lending the Fonz's considerable clout and promotional power to other organizations like the Candy Stripers whose task and whose reward was doing good. When letters came in from teachers that he could help kids who suffered jeers because they wear glasses, he and producers Ed Miller and Tom Milkus worked out story lines about Fonzarella having to wear glasses and establishing it as a new cool. Teachers wrote in that it had stopped the jeers dead in their tracks. Now that's wearing your legend well.

Chapter 18

Damage Control

There are, in a press agent's life, many real manifestations of damage to be dealt with, and each requires a unique strategy of control. I regret leading off this reflection with consideration of tabloids because most often they are not damage but rather irritation. Ignored, their mean nonsense devolves and dissipates shortly after their sad reading public enjoys the momentary titillation of pretending to believe the folderol. I sometimes wonder that these people are actually literate. Unfortunately, the tabs' having gotten it right with John Edwards upped the what-if factor which sends legitimate media into spasms of checking out ridiculous allegations from "a source close to the couple" or "a close friend."

The tabloids do have ambulance chasers… hospital orderlies or others who actually know if some celeb is hospitalized or rehab-alized. But that spark of truth is rarely needed to ignite some sensationalized and dire dream-up. What has tabloid value is not the specificity of the fact, because even a mindlessly gossip-hungry readership finally gets it that the "facts" are largely dubious, but rather the speculation they invite. Speculation is by its nature wild and damaging, especially the way it's played in the scandal game.

For this specific media, rumor sells better than facts, because it asks questions. Facts merely tell you what happened or what purportedly happened, but rumor introduces the question of what *could* be happening… in which case the terrible news could be infinite. The enticement of Rumor is that introduces the is-it-possibly-true? response.

Celebrities show up on the media radar most readily when there is some misfortune the headlines can exploit. We can't blame it all on the tabloids. There has always been the old adage that "Good news is no news, bad news is good news and terrible news is great news." A few celebrities achieve an extreme degree of fame in the thrall of which the tabloid media MUST have something to run on them, even if they have to make it up. And once they do, their more distinguished media cousins are compelled to run around trying to verify, and their very quest becomes perpetuation of the rumor. Elizabeth Taylor certainly was a prime illustration. Her beauty has long been, by consensus, the gold standard and will continue to be the operative comparative. She was the brave survivor of triumphs and tragedies which dizzy the imagination. In over six decades of superstar longevity, she lived a life, both artistic and personal, of astonishing dimensions. The media felt compelled to keep her in their headlines. She was and is forever timely and relevant by dint of her extraordinary lifetime of achievements, her unequaled movie stardom , her courageous endurance of personal travails and her crucial leadership of over a quarter century in the fight to treat and eliminate HIV/AIDS. Add to this her dominant posture as a designer of the most elegant and popular perfumes, her eminence in the glittery field of jewelry design and of jewelry collection and the other elements of glamour, and you had a media world intent on keeping a news flow on her, even after her passing.

Tabloid media found or fabricated reasons to worry about her health. At one point a few years back, it just boiled itself up into a frenzy of media trying to outdo each other in the size and immediacy of her perils. Such rampant rumors had a negative pull on her work overseeing her HIV/AIDS programs and were a bother and distraction from her other pursuits. I recommended an appearance on Larry King's show to give good and convincing evidence of her continuing humor and vitality, and to do it in "real time."

When I called Larry, his response was expectably excited, and he said, "We can make it easy on her. I can come to the house and we'll tape it there." I thanked him and explained that the whole point was that we wanted it live with her taking spontaneous calls at his desk so that the world could see how vivid and vivacious she is in "real time." He enthusiastically agreed.

It was one of his most intensively advance-promoted guest bookings.

As we expected, scores of film crews, reporters and photographers called about arrangements for coverage of her arrival at the CNN studios in Hollywood. We told everyone in advance that we couldn't promise that she would do microphone-in-face sound bites on the way in or out, nor did we worry that that would lower the coverage which we expected to be... and which proved to be... of event stature.

At a certain point before the arrival, that became the problem. The press was crushing into vantage positions for her arrival... celeb-getting-out-of-car is a key "get" for red carpet press... and then her moving to the front entrance between walls of media in her wheelchair to which the ravages of her life-long scoliosis compel her. But then during the waiting, a red light started to flash... I mean a literal red light, several of them, literally started to flash. It was a paramedic ambulance directly across the street (Sunset Blvd.) and which would be in the direct background of all of the arrival coverage... looking to anyone's surmise as if it were there just in case she might need critical care or rushing to a hospital. One of her close associates in her fragrance and jewelry empires sent a security guy across the street to remove the problem. He came back, and the ambulance was still parked with flashing lights. He said the paramedics were eating their lunch there and declined to move. I asked her associate the use of a one hundred dollar bill and crossed the street for a conversation. I asked them to think of a charity to which they could contribute this C note if they found another place to lunch. "Are you kidding?" one of them gasped. "Does Ben Franklin look like he's laughing?" They pulled out about five minutes before her car arrived.

The show rather famously was a dazzling display of Elizabeth Taylor energy and humor and candid honesty and dedication to important projects. It flashed her personality every bit as brightly as the extraordinary gems... white diamonds I should guess... with which she was bedecked as is her habit. If anything could put the lie to the deadly reports and mournings in the tabloid papers, this was it. Knowing that she wasn't going to stop for interviews on the way out... the massive media having stayed, of course, for a second crack at her, I asked Larry King to follow us down and to pick up the interviews after the press had ushered her to the car. It gave them extended coverage on the story. My associate Beverly Magid, who was working the assignment with me, and I watched as the ultimate movie star sailed down the corridor of clamoring press, flashing cameras and fast-catch TV crews who, unable to contain themselves or the peers shoving in from behind, crushed in on her so that some of the some of the coverage was in extreme close-up.

And then the car pulled away, and the cameras and the attention turned to Larry King who, better than anyone else, could testify to her evident health and good spirit and, above all, courage. It was all going well, but Beverly and I knew that, however much we had predicted it to them in advance, some of the media would be pissed that they didn't get sound bites. We left Larry in the chaos of the importuning press and insatiable cameras and we made our fast escape to our cars in the garage behind the CNN headquarters. To our dismay, we saw the Entertainment Tonight producer heading for his car, having left the pick-up stuff to his knowledgeable camera crew. We thought we were stuck with making apologies that what we'd said wouldn't happen didn't happen, but instead of complaint, he flashed a bright smile and thanked us for a great event. Apparently the crews were thrilled with having captured not only a rare Elizabeth Taylor sighting, but also "an old fashioned press mob scene" which he thanked us for staging. It had been not only a story about the most adulated of adulated stars, but about the press celebration of such adulation.

And just in case you might be tempted to conclude that one successful publicity exercise sets the record straight for everyone… on the Friday morning of the week of the Larry King guesting, I received a call from a CNN reporter who asked if I could provide her with a contact phone number for me over the weekend. I knew full well why, but I wanted to hear her say it. "Why?" "Well, you know," she said, "…just in case something happens." "Are you aware that she just spent a live hour on your network with Larry King?… a vital and spunky hour?… " I asked. "Yes, of course," she responded, "but just in case something happens…"

Sometimes you can do damage control up front. One time during the filming of a Bond film in England, Pierce Brosnan sustained a knee injury which literally knocked him into a wheelchair. He had to fly back to have it addressed by a specialist in Los Angeles. What nobody, particularly the production company, wanted was a photo bouncing around of James Bond in a wheelchair in the middle of a Bond shoot with all of its X Games-type physical demands. It would burden the shoot with speculation of watered-down Bond. The photographers in LA were already feeling out the story when Pierce flew in, and the airline helped us by ushering him out a side exit of the international terminal to avoid waiting stalkerazzi. We'd arranged for the procedure to transpire shortly after dawn the next morning at the doctor's office, with a private investigator coordinating the alley entrance arrival. Pierce walked out a few hours later. The stalkerazzi had been shaken, but not stirred.

The rules pertaining to damage control include A. don't over-react, B. accentuate the positive and eliminate the negative, and … very importantly when the occasion demands… C. *play the other guy's trump card.* This involves recognizing the negative factor that you will have to confront down the line and putting it on the table yourself. If you don't play the card, the other guy will, heightening the negative impact. But if you expose it first… perhaps something on the order of… "I want you to know up front that I was once charged with embezzlement, one of the best things that ever happened to me because it turned my life around" plays a lot better than allowing your competitor to say "you can't name him treasurer, Don't you know that…?" Be in control of any element of actuality.

You always meet damage head-on. You don't just let it bite you in the ass. I learned that lesson from my father-in-law and two British mastiffs. Our daughters were quite young when we took Gisela's parents to Palm Springs. On a hot Spring morning we were walking in an exclusive residential area, each house hidden behind high leafy walls fronting the street, the homes visible only through the bars of the high gates. Her father, in suit and tie, the heat notwithstanding, strode strongly ahead of us, heedless that he was in his late seventies and the temperature in the high nineties. He was ever the dignified German inventor/businessman, elegant down to his pearl and diamond tie-pin and silver-headed walking stick.

From behind the circular driveway gate of one mansion was heard an angry duet of furious mastiffs. I thanked the walking-with-your-parents-in-law gods that the gates were closed and locked. What I didn't know was that only one of them was. The two huge, angry and ravenous dogs raced out of the irresponsibly open second gate and charged at us, their territorial din preceding them. Without a moment's hesitation, my father-in-law charged straight at them, his cane raised in fury, roaring in a voice from a time primeval, *"Du renfi hundt"* (you miserable dog.) Make that DOOO RENNNFEEE HOOONT!! One thing dogs recognize is the voice of doom. The two huge beasts made eight skid marks in the asphalt street… nine, actually since one was using his butt for extra braking power. They then raced back into the driveway, doing everything but pushing the great gate closed behind them.

THAT's how you control damage, meeting it head-on, turning it back on itself. Or, even better, turning it to your and your client's advantage. It also reaffirmed my belief that no language is as indisputable as German. It is simply not a configuration of sounds with which one can argue. It is the very language of command.

Crisis Control in Persia

The persuasive power of Germanic speech, the sure, commanding punch of its consonants, came propitiously to my attention once again at the start of our action-packed supervision of the last Tehran Film Festival. It started with our arrival at the chaotic Tehran Airport. We arrived on a flight from Rome with 30 significant stars, directors and press in tow… all of them *Uber-Mensch*, people accustomed to bump-removed roads, none more *uber* than Otto Preminger whom (do not doubt our sanity) we came to love. Normally it takes a half hour to surmount the obstacles of arrival in Iran. Each of us was given a personal official Iranian facilitator, and we were rushed through in something just under three times that long. Nerves were exhausted and the night was no longer young (and neither were we) when we arrived to check in at the hotel. Check into what? According to the desk staff, no rooms were waiting. The helpful folks of the Persian ministry of culture were all hiding beneath rocks in some barricade. Each celeb was handed reading material for their wait, an introduction to the festival including the fact that each would be able to order up to 14 dollars at each meal. Actually, that turned out to be more than enough, but the apparent austerity was rubbing dampened spirits the wrong way. To restore order, I directed that vodka and caviar be served all around and then confronted the concierge with the fact that these people were the guests of his Shah. Did he want to talk to the Shah about the rooms? I pulled out my list, and his eyes started to glisten with concern. Lists… lists seem to instill fear. I pulled Gisela over to lay out her lists. The guys on the other side of the desk started to unravel and couldn't speak. She started to batter them with aristocratic German demand, something she does when she's angry (at which times she also tends to address people by their last name only, no Mr., no first name, very intimidating.) Their backs snapped straight like quivering sticks. I suddenly got it. They had all been *gast arbeiters* in Germany, guest workers. So lists and German were to them fear incarnate. I ran over and got the greatly feared critic John Simon… whose fluencies extended to every language family on earth… to add to the blitzkrieg of German now crackling like lightning bolts about the sullen guardians of the assigned rooms. I could have pulled Mr.

Preminger into the fray, but I didn't want to cause an international incident. After five minutes of German outrage, they suddenly started to find rooms that a bevy of stewardesses were about to surrender.

The Mysterious Case of Buster Keaton. Here was the problem that still pertained. I wasn't going to put Otto Preminger or Lauren Bacall in stewardess rooms. I calmly asked in my most polite German what kind of suites they had. There were three, but they were being held for Buster Keaton who was being honored at the festival. "*Ja*," I agreed, "*aber er kompt nicht.* (But he's not coming.) *Er ist zehn Jahre TODT!!!* (He's been dead for ten YEARS!!!)" They were still worried Buster might show since he was, after all, on a list. It took another five minutes to wrench those suites from the clenched hands of the dead.

Nothing got easier during the serial ordeals of that festival, but my father-in-law's rushing at those mastiffs with a raised stick got me through everything.

Particularly in medical crisis is it important to meet potential damage head-on. When Stacy Keach and the critically hailed national tour of "Frost/Nixon" were coming to Los Angeles for a two week run at the Ahmanson Theatre, we bumped up against the Los Angeles Times rule prohibiting major articles on local engagements of such short duration. We needed the break to maximize industry awareness of his acclaimed Nixon and his upcoming resumption of the role of Lear at The Shakespeare Theatre in D.C., to drive home his regard as America's greatest Lear. Suddenly there was a bigger problem. Stacy started experiencing a dizziness and speech impairment which rushed him to a hospital. The diagnosis was that there had been a minor stroke, and the word stroke is a bad one to let float without scrupulous control. There is an immediate instinct among family and medical advisors... and in this case the producers of the tour and directors of the Ahmanson had crucial interests as well... to try to hush such things up. I know that that buys you time and costs you credibility when the truth leaks out, which it does because such information has a price on its head. I had to fight my way past everyone's most well-intentioned instincts to insist that we get the word out projecting the actual fact before some hospital orderly got fifty bucks for slipping it to some media source. The media who have networks of such informants are usually of the exploitation variety, and there was absolute certainty that that outlet would put the most sensational and dangerous spin on it. After all, they had paid for that privilege.

The prognosis was very good. The words "mild" and "minor" thankfully could be applied with absolute veracity, and I arranged for the LA Times to get a prominent exclusive on it which informed all of the other media breaks which had suddenly focused on the situation. It added to the triumphant tone of Stacy's return to the physically demanding role of Richard Nixon only a week or so later, and that served to emphasize news, important to his career, that his recovery was quick and complete. It also brought us three major stories in the Times about this powerful period of culmination of his position as one of the great actors of the American stage and arguably it's leading interpreter of Shakespeare. Footnote: Stacy won the Helen Hayes Award for both his Nixon and his Lear.

Tackling damage control head-on is tough medicine, and a lot of people don't like the taste of it. An agent friend of mine mentioned a client who was very hurt by the fact the first thing that pops up when you Google her is the mug-shot from a long-time-ago alcohol bust, a problem she long-since put behind her but which Google keeps putting at the front of its reference on her. I explained the zero likelihood of successfully imploring relief. No harm in trying, but a surer rectification was called for. I offered a device by which the problem could be turned into a solution. The celebrity could do interviews calling it to public attention, not to complain but to explain how she uses that out-of-date and unfair depiction as a motivating force in her life, clicking it on once a day to remind herself how positive have been the changes she's wrought in her life. It would initiate a lot of visibility, all positive and would effectively defang the unfortunate circumstance. Also, and probably most importantly, it would offer other people struggling to maintain recovery from a debilitating weakness or addiction a very useful tool in seizing control of their own lives. It takes courage to take that approach, but courage is an exhausting exercise. Unfortunately, she didn't buy it. And the photo is still there… without the positive spin I'd suggested.

There are as many ways to control damage as there are damages to control. "Is San Diego Sexy" is the one I best remember. It validated so many of my cherished rules and worked so dramatically, it seemed a golden PR equivalent of alchemy.

From the very first, "Simon & Simon" vs. San Diego seemed a damage situation that could be turned around, especially because I was handed it on that most

velvet of cushions, the word that always gives a publicity campaign an edge…
"sexy." The TV series "Simon & Simon" was set in a California beach community
clearly identified as part of greater San Diego… and San Diego is pretty great. That
metropolis had embraced, one might even say "adopted," the brother detectives
and the two stars, Gerald McRaney and Jameson Parker, for their easy California
mojo. Gerald was a client as well, so we were doubly motivated to seek the show's
perpetuation and ratings prosperity. "Simon & Simon did prosper from 1981 to
1989, largely because of this campaign. Its vital signs chart swung from "going
down" to "how high the moon?" right after the campaign kicked in. Not too far
into its run (which eventually turned into a reign) it faced the imminent possibility of one- and-done or two-and-through fate and evaded it only because of
the following circumstances.

The fly in the ointment was that the show hovered unobtrusively in the
number 48 spot in the Nielsen Ratings. Because the network bought both "S &
S" and television's top show, "Magnum P.I." from Universal, CBS wanted to do
something nice for them, and it placed the Simon boys into TV's most coveted
spot, right behind the number one show, "Magnum PI." That should have sent the
Simon frères into some kind of top ten position, but the move had accomplished
only a ten point jump to 38th. That started CBS into wondering if the show was
good enough even to see another season, but the first penalty would be a cut in
production budget. It's budget was coming down. I was summoned to The Black
Tower at Universal City, the brain power of decision-making at the studio.

The producer, Phil DeGuere (one of the town's good guys, smart and
adventurous and funny… they do exist,) asked me how big a market San Diego
was. Eighth biggest in the country then. "Well, we're about to lose it, and I'd
like you to mitigate the damage," he said. The $50,000 the front office had
subtracted from the budget could be accomplished by moving the production
back to the studio. "It's a fait accompli," Phil said, "so I need you to go down
there and make nice and not let them kick up too much dust." "Why do you
have to move?" I asked. Press agents like to see not only the road but all the
land around it. You make better decisions. "Because," he said, "San Diego isn't
sexy." "Magnum P.I," I argued, "Vegas, Streets of San Francisco. Hawaii, Vegas
and the Bay Area are sexy," he explained. "And San Diego isn't?" I persisted.
"Not when I'm getting cut back fifty Gs. No. Now will you please go down
there and put out any fires?"

The head of the San Diego Film Commission, Wally Schlotter, was a wise and trustworthy guy and proved an extraordinary co-conspirator, so I asked him to set up a meeting for me with his group and with the Chamber Of Commerce. Every city needs a Wally Schlotter. They gathered, took the bad news badly and asked why. I told them the story... the whole story *including "San Diego isn't sexy,"* adding, "So what are you going to do about it?" "Do?" a few of them screamed. "We'll sue." "We'll boycott." I let them get it out and then Wally and I laid out the plan for Is San Diego Sexy? They would organize the city to prove to the nation that San Diego IS sexy. It would start with the city's DJs who would break the news of the show's departure to the populace, give the folks the allegation that San Diego wasn't sexy, and then organize a mass campaign for the citizens to prove just the opposite. "What are we talking here? Sex in the streets?" one Chamber guy murmured in horror. "Parading prostitutes?" another worried. "No," I said, "postcards. Wally can (and did he ever!) get all of the DJs to host one big party. You'll have tens of thousands of long postcards with McRaney and Parker... Simon and Simon... on the cover against the city's port and skyline. Across it will be written 'Is San Diego Sexy?'"

"Why can't it say 'San Diego IS Sexy?'" one proud city father asked. "Declarative sentences are disposable," l said, "You can disagree with them or you can kiss them off with a "says who?" But you can't disagree with a question. It makes you want to find out the answer... or disprove it." They agreed to the question mark. *It would never have worked without it.* Wally and I explained that admission to the Is-San-Diego-Sexy? party would be agreeing to fill out twelve of those cards with hand-written reasons why each person thinks San Diego is sexy. Each of the attendees would get a copy of the list of twelve top journalists whose names and addresses I would supply. After the campaign gained traction, the San Diego DJs would do phone-in chats on air with other DJs all over the country.

The list of journalists covered the Wall Street Journal, the Washington Post, the LA and New York papers, key columnists across the country, the wire services and the Hollywood trade papers. None of them could resist a story about sex, or could deal rationally with the flood of up to a thousand letters some received. Marilyn Beck, whose column appeared in hundreds of papers, called to ask if I was behind it. I told her honestly that it was organized and executed by the San Diego city fathers... and mothers. She stressed that, while she rarely got more than three letters a day (remember that it was before the internet,) she had received

600 cards in one day. It actually wasn't a complaint, just a cry of amazement. To my memory, no journalist who was targeted was immune, and the coverage was amazing. And from that point the ball accelerated by itself, and it was assuming gigantic dimension. I knew that a key test would be when someone called CBS to see if the network really feared that San Diego wasn't sexy. The network didn't know I was running the scam because it seemed so spontaneous. I'd confided the facts only to De Guere who'd given it his very amused support, not mentioning it to the studio or the network until we saw how it played out. I was sure that whichever network exec they spoke to would say something corroborative. And he did. He gave the media the campaign-clinching "well, the show IS set in a nondescript beach town" which I was sure he would because that was the mantra in-house. "Nondescript" in network-speak actually meant "unspecified," but it sounds pretty desexualized out of that context. And he did admit that Vegas and Honolulu and Frisco were sexier. That did it. The story had real traction.

And the voice of the people was heard. Allow me to restate that... AND THE VOICE OF THE PEOPLE WAS HEARD. The network figured that any city that could make that much noise and set off that kind of publicity fireworks was sexy enough to stay in the series... and for the series to stay in IT. The move order was rescinded. Each week of the campaign's blossoming, you could see the ratings going up. People were tuning in to see what all the noise was about and perhaps to take a look at all that sexuality. I'm not sure exactly how long it took. The ratings shift became sharp and didn't stop until they got "Simon And Simon" to Number Two, right after its lead-in show, "Magnum P.I." And finally it climbed over even that hurdle and achieved Number One. Finally, Phil DeGuere and I did let Universal Television in on what the strategy had been and how successfully it had played out. And The Black Tower handed Guttman & Pam another series.

A further positive repercussion was the way it ignited an interest in publicity for the two stars. They had known the details and intent of the Is San Diego Sexy? strategy all along. I had to tell them not only because I was using their pictures on the post cards, but because I knew they would be enthusiastic contributors and co-conspirators. The two actors discovered in the process that they really enjoyed the good natured scam aspect of publicity, especially when it could so sustain their show. Gerald liked the gamesmanship of these "gags" (that's what this kind of publicity adventuring is called in the trade... gags,) so much that when I came to him with another idea I thought would get a good play-out, he got Jameson to go along on it. He had mentioned to me their annoyance that the network had cut... or, rather, cut in closer on... a shower scene with the beautiful guest actress Camilla Sparv, who was also our client and whose lovely back deserved to be enjoyed in more than a shoulder close-up. We viewed a previous broadcast of the show in which, I recalled, there had been a soap ad featuring a young woman in the shower. We counted her vertebrae and discovered that eleven or so of them were visible, whereas they had held Camilla to only three. Thus began the Great Vertebrae Protest. The two actors jointly complained... live on ABC's "Good Morning America," with the ad and the Sparv shower scene shown in comparison. They were demanding vertebrae equality and freedom for actresses everywhere, but they were actually stepping in to free up restrictive network standards which held shows to a more Victorian regulation than it held advertising. It was a story that got pick-up. It had the magic word... sexy. I don't think CBS was thrilled to be dissed by its stars on another network, but when you're number one and a piece of publicity exposure keeps it rolling, who's complaining?

I apologize in advance for the immodesty of this, but it illustrates how effective a campaign can be when it's fun and sexy. "Is San Diego Sexy?" the campaign got a lot of publicity in its own right. One of the business weeklies... I think it was Business Week... gave the gag a three page spread. Wall Street Journal did a story on it and its impact, and years later I was advised that it was in a college textbook on PR.

It's supposed to be bad luck or bad manners to steal from yourself, but it's stupidity not to. So Is San Diego Sexy? got another workout when client Robert Urich's critically acclaimed and widely loved "Spenser For Hire" series based on the Robert Parker books, was marked for removal from the ABC line-up. It was particularly urgent because we were also handling the Massachusetts Film Board which had great interest in sustaining a show that brought I-believe-it-was $50,000,000 to the state. I didn't have the catch phrase "sexy" going for me, but Bob, with his affable and boyish good looks, supplied all the sex factor the campaign needed. The key element I reclaimed was that of involving the state's DJs (an idea Wally Schlotter had come up with for ISDS?, not I, and it was arranged for me in the Massachusetts case by the state's Film Board.) Not just Bean Town's platter-spinners, but DJs all over the state reached out with calls to DJs around the country to rally all the "Spenser" fans to stand up for their guy. This time I targeted the network bosses as the recipients of the protest letters, and the numbers worked for me far better than I expected. At one national TV guesting I was doing with Urich talking up the write-in campaign, Bob told me that one of the network brass had told him flat-out to keep it up because it seemed to be working, that they had received over 500 letters in the past week. Five hundred sounded pretty paltry to me, but Bob said the executive had confided that networks figured every letter represents five hundred other people who would have liked to write but didn't. This, again, was in the stone age before the internet. That kind of multiplication saved the show for one more year.

Urich, with his considerable talent for understated humor, was a great promoter of everything he touched, an especially welcome guest on almost every talk show or with every interviewer, a proven superstar of television over many years and many series. One instance, in particular, showed his light comedy touch to perfection. He was guesting with Johnny Carson on a key promotion for something, and was none too happy about it. He had a roaring cold and was in generally diminished humor. It's hard to be charming when, bleary of eye and of spirit, your nose is gushing like Niagara. His business partner and similarly good guy, John Wall, and I were in Robert's dressing room as he waited to be first guest. Robert went into the bathroom for a slab of toilet paper into which he might blow his nose. He emerged with a roll of toilet paper in his hand and started to roll up a wad. "Very elegant," John said, and then I told Bob to put the roll of toilet paper in his coat pocket.

At the commercial break, we got a message to Johnny. Bob came out looking under-the-weather but game, swiping at a runny nostril with the back of a finger, nodding an apology to the audience. Johnny used the moment to open the conversation commenting on what a classy guy Urich was to show up when he was that sick, and then doing an admiring riff about having always thought Bob Urich was just one of the classiest guys in town. Big applause from the audience, at which point Bob pulled the role of toilet paper out of his coat pocket, ripped off a wad and busied himself with some good loud and explicitly disgusting nose blows, as *déclassé* as he could make it and drawing a huge applause and laughter. It was the audience that was now in his pocket, and he hadn't even uttered a word. After that, every time he touched the toilet paper they roared . We had, of course, alerted Johnny at the commercial break about the gag, and he had set it up like the magician he was. The basic rule which had applied… a problem is a solution… works every time… especially if you have Robert Urich's light comic grace to pull it off. Carson certainly had it right… there have been few more charming or graceful guys than Robert Urich. He has been greatly missed.

Our injection into the "Touched By An Angel" saga (mentioned earlier) was in a sense damage control, but I think the folks at CBS Productions considered our hiring a Hail Mary to keep from losing a series in which they really believed but just couldn't get the viewer numbers on any of its test airings to justify a green light for it to go to a full year. *The network hired us to convince them … to convince the network itself… not to drop the show.* There were only fifteen ticks on the game clock, and they wanted us to help their angels complete a pass in the end zone. They had played episodes of the show two times before in test scheduling against very tough competition to try to convince themselves that the show had the legs to put on the schedule. Why were they so intent on finding a reason to say yes? It was the same reason that excited my associate Beverly Magid and me when we ran all three episodes at the office to figure out an emergency strategy. It was because tears feel so uplifting when a show sends them gushing down your cheeks. It reminds you are still a member in good standing in the human race.

But there aren't enough feel-good tears to float an expensive series which simply hadn't drawn viewers. The network felt the audience would discover "Touched By An Angel" if only we could lead them to it. We were sent in as the designated Pied Pipers. We had to come up with something within very few weeks that could grab the attention and the tune-in which this final do-or-die broadcast needed for the Angels to earn their wings and flap them for an hour each week.

I decided that the only related aspect big enough to work this miracle for us and for CBS was God, Him or Herself, We concluded that we could pull this off if we could raise the prospect on a national level and entice deep concern within the religious community that only THEY the viewers could keep faith-related programming on network TV. We had to call attention to the fact that drama concerned with religious principles and dedications would disappear completely from scripted television network programming if America's believers and church-goers didn't step up to the plate on this one night. Many of them had charged that television was Godless. Were they willing to give an hour of their time to keep that from being literally true?

Andy Hill who headed CBS Productions and who hired me for the campaign, told me flat out that I would have to "come up with a miracle." That word did it. I took him literally, and it gave us the concept I thought was the only way to make this pay off for the network, the show and, eventually, the TV audience. The idea either would work a miracle through Divine Intervention or else would fail miserably resulting in God's actually leaving the television building.

The show would be running in a dead zone called Saturday night. We had already played a small hand in opening up that evening to viewers, helping Jane Seymour and producer Gail Sullivan turn the "Dr. Quinn, Medicine Woman" series into a winner on that arid night, running up numbers considered miraculous for that least ratings night of the week. We'd represented the most noted "queen of the mini-series," Jane Seymour, for decades, even then, and we were constantly amazed how she brought super-human energies to both performance and promotion. And still does. Jane's incarnation of a wild west female medical pioneer, liberating women while she reclaimed broken bodies and afflicted lives, is what drove that series to well over a half decade of prominence and dominance. That and her indefatigable publicity energies which we spread thick upon the media.

Andy Hill had headed Columbia Pictures' movies-of-the-week division when I as a screenwriter had a run of films on CBS, mostly done under Andy. I had made an impression on him, not necessarily a good one, because I was the only writer who always showed up late for network meetings, I had a day job, but those MOWs put my kids through college. Andy had played basketball for UCLA under John Wooden, was deeply influenced by Coach's calm and wisdom and determination, and he also knew that you always show up on time for practice. Andy co-authored with the Wizard of Westwood the continuing best-seller "Be Fast But Don't Hurry" which captured John Wooden's philosophy. "Touched By An Angel" was a CBS production developed and produced and substantially written by Martha Williamson whose belief in angels and in the hidden good in people was contagious. It was impossible to be around her and not catch it.

As for publicity hooks for this show, there was only one, but it was a big one… God. The show was a believer which spoke to other believers. It also had some very lovely actors, top TV star names, who had guested on the first three episodes, and they all loved the idea of helping this become a series of hopefulness.

I asked Martha if her wealthy believer friends could gather together about $100,000 so I could place ads in USA Today, The LA Times and the New York Times I had an ad in mind that I felt could kick up some dust…… some angel dust. It started out with "God Is Not Dead on Network TV, But She Soon Might Be." I knew that the "she" would ruffle some feathers, but the headline had to be bold and provocative enough to make sure people would read the ad. The main thrust of the text was that the ratings for this broadcast constituted the last chance to reserve a pew for faith-based and inspirational scripted drama in the great church of television. It challenged the ad's readers to watch and to get their friends to watch this show. The ad ended with "If Anne Rice can take an ad for the vampires (which she just had,) we can take one for the Angels." Then I convinced all of the show's name guest stars to date to sign the ad. That part wasn't hard.

What was hard was getting the money for the ads. Martha couldn't raise it, and I couldn't go to CBS for it, because they were paying me to prove to them that the show was a winner, and I couldn't ask them to buy me that win. Finally, I asked Martha to find me the money to place my ad in at least one of the Hollywood trade papers. I wanted to reach the industry, yes, but I needed to reach the nation. The one ad in a Hollywood trade paper had to reach out to hundreds of millions who had never even heard of that paper. I thought this ad could buy me that reach. To do so, I didn't take the ad the day before the show, as is the custom. I took it twelve days before . Then Beverly and I sent every religious media outlet in the country… syndicates, papers, television and radio commentators and shows, church group publications…. copies of the ad together with a passionate pitch that Martha and CBS were offering the millions who mourned the absence of precisely this kind of show on series TV a last, best chance to restore God to a meaningful place in the nation's entertainment viewing habits. That was my pitch… *the pitch being the angle to which you think the media and then the public will respond.* My story… *a story being an interesting narrative that an editor might think will interest his/her readers, one that carries the pitch over the plate…* my story was that these twelve very caring famous actors believed in the need for inspirational TV content so passionately that they had taken an ad to alert America to this crucial last chance for believers to be counted, to turn the tide of what kind of stories their kids could watch.

The Saturday arrived, and we held our breath until the Monday morning when Andy called me to say that the numbers had been terrific. Months later, I had a chance conversation with a man of the cloth, and I told him that story. He nodded and then said "God Is Not Dead On Network TV, But She Soon May Be or some variation was the subject of sermons in a great many houses of worship on the Sunday before the show played," and even on the Friday before because it was, he said, picked up on in temples and synagogues as well. "And more importantly…" and he finished the thought by pointing up above. What he communicated was that we had gotten the word through to religious leaders and, through them, to people of faith. Martha kept us on to keep the faith for quite a few years, so it worked out pretty well all around. With "Touched By An Angel"and "Dr. Quinn" back-to-back, Saturday nights on CBS became an important ratings block.

All publicity is basically the same… what do you want to say? to whom do you want to say it? how are you going to do it? "Touched By An Angel" had two big things going for it that facilitated our work. First, people want to believe. Second, Martha Williamson, her eyes closed, can reach out unerringly and tug at our heartstrings. She could always elicit tears. *Faith-based PR may be the easiest PR of all for a very simple reason…. You're literally preaching to the choir.*

When the time finally came that the network concluded that Dr. Quinn had run out of medicine, it was announced that it had arrived at its final season. We couldn't go back to the Is San Diego Sexy or the Isn't Boston Sexy playbook, largely because the strategy for each of those shows worked off a contained geographical base. But we had Jane Seymour's sensational fan base, international in scope, and they turned out picket lines around CBS and mass mailing outreaches that brought tens of thousands of supporters into the fray. Guttman and Pam drew the diagram and her army marched forth. CBS didn't return the show to series, but the fans did spur the green-lighting of two Dr. Quinn television movie specials, which gave Jane and her husband James Keach, who directed both of them, a chance to wind up the story of Dr. Quinn in very high style, high numbers and good reviews. This was an important act of closure for the fans and provided two movie-length Dr. Quinn MOWs of feature film quality.

Thanks to the belief which the two leading sitcom firms, Carsey/Werner and Miller/Milkis, had in us, the 80s were sort of Guttman & Pam's Decade of TV series. we were contributing to the publicity and public relations of such shows as "Rosanne," "A Different World," "Amazing Grace," "Bill Cosby's You Bet Your Life," "Happy Days," "Laverne And Shirley," and shows like that can make a publicity firm look very good. To underline and extend the power of "Roseanne," I came up with the concept of Roseanne Country, researching the remarkable ratings success of the shows which over the years had "Roseanne" as their lead-in but also the "warm-up," shows, those which preceded it. Those statistics were formidable. And "Simon And Simon" gave us a chance to work the same kind of publicity concepts. And it was always damages in need of control that made it interesting. "Rosanne" was a crash course all by itself because the genius and daring of its eponymous star always courted controversy.

Some damage situations come at you so fast that you have only instincts to guide you. Most memorable of these for me was the indelible Oscar moment when the announcement of Marlon Brando's Best Actor win for "The Godfather" brought to the stage a beautiful young Native American woman, Sacheen Littlefeather, in traditional garb who had been asked by Mr. Brando to accept his award and to convey his protest at how Native American tribes were oppressed by U.S. government policy... and, perhaps by Hollywood portrayal. Since Guttman & Pam represented Roger Moore who would present the award, I was assigned to be the supervising publicist to take the winner and the presenting star through the media rooms. After Ms. Littlefeather's remarks in Mr. Brando's stead, Roger agreed with me that it was a good time for him to go back to his seat, and I knew that my obligation was simply to get her through the media as quickly as possible so as not to back up the press access to the Best Director and Best Film awards to come. It was not a time to trample Marlon Brando's and Sacheen Littlefeather's First Amendment rights to have his message heard. I was quite certain that the Academy's Board of Governors would agree with me on that. My job was clear.

A barrier suddenly appeared in the form of a two meter tall security guy who wouldn't let me take her since, as he sternly warned me, all of the show's participants were to be on stage for a grand finale tribute to John Ford. Mr. Ford was very possibly the greatest of all film-makers and arguably had brought more humanity to the screen and to his films than any other director. But he also killed more Indians on screen than George Custer did on the Great Plains. "Inappropriate" is a word inadequate to address the madness this security guy was demanding.

My greatest asset as a press agent has always been luck. At that moment, somebody backstage knocked over a huge flat, and six foot six security guys have a built-in compulsion to race toward such emergencies. I rushed her into the elevator, the doors of which were just closing as the security guy came running toward us yelling "Hey!! Where you going with that Indian?"

And there are times when you simply rely on media to understand and to cooperate with the restraint you need of them. When Guttman Associates executive Susan Madore was overseeing the victorious Dancing With The Stars participation of Olympic gold-medal gymnastic star Shaun Johnson, there was the perilous circumstance of the stalker pursuit of Shaun by an armed man who actually made his way onto the studio lot where the series is filmed. The nature of that development invited the most sensational coverage, but Susan's presenting the key media with the further dangers sensationalism might encourage found them most cooperative and conscious of what would be responsible handling of the story. There are many ways in which a press agent may have to protect a client, and a good two-way relationship with media often makes that possible. It was an impressive demonstration of media restraint.

Every opportunity and every challenge has it exigencies. There is no established press agent who is not the veteran of 1000 "skirmishes." Neither you nor your client will win if you permit one to be dragged into a war. They debilitate energy, and even in victory you're left with collateral damage.

There is no question that damage control sometimes brings out the best in one's imagination. There are times when a problem is not merely a solution in disguise, but rather an inspiration in disguise... a gift to oneself that keeps on giving. Such was the case with "The Artist" and the Made In Hollywood Honors.

Lisa Tayback and the Weinsteins' PR staff were running the very successful Oscar campaign for that silent black-and-white movie, "The Artist," which was threatening to grab Best Film in 2012. I was aboard for whatever I could come up with, and what I came up with was resentment when I opened one of the trade papers one morning before the nominations were announced. There was an article which was reporting five ways kicking about through which opposing films could head "The Artist" off at the pass, and one of them was to stress that the Oscar is an American award and shouldn't go to a foreign film company. "The Artist" was a French production. There was certainly a chance that such jingoism could derail an "Artist" victory.

I made up a list of the films I thought could get nominated, and, as I suspected, the only one with a real chance and which was actually *made in Hollywood* was "The Artist." I sent a note to that effect to journalists who would be reporting the upcoming nominations, hoping that this fact could be a salient element of announcement coverage. It got a little pick-up, but not real traction. It needed a bigger awareness. I called Los Angeles City Councilman Tom LaBonge, part of whose district is Hollywood. Tom has always been a politician working hard to counter the runaway production which is so all-encompassing that for that year (and the succeeding two years) only one of nine Oscar-nominated films was made in the film capital of the world. Tom agreed that it was an urgent problem and that a spotlight had to be thrown on it, something dramatic which created high-coverage news. He hammered out the concept and arranged for the City Council to establish the program. The City Attorneys determined it could be called the Made In Hollywood Honors which would henceforth be handed to any nominated film made here. Obviously, I specifically wanted to set up a home-team advantage for "The Artist." But Labonge and I wanted to extend that advantage for future films made here, a compelling appeal to all of the industry's local workers whose jobs had been outsourced. New councilman for Hollywood, Mitch O'Farrell, another staunch defender of the movie capital's past and future, quickly added his enthusiastic energies. We didn't want to fumble the opportunity to create something that, on a continuing basis, could be a jolt of awareness to help bring movies back to the town where it grew up... or at least to honor those producers who had kept faith with history. The establishment of this new honors program by the Los Angeles City Council was heavily announced... *along with the news that "The Artist" was the first and only qualifying recipient and would be so acknowledged.*

But we needed a big and inescapable break for the presentation ceremony, and this I accomplished by having the whole cast and crew… including, most crucially, the film's beloved canine star, Uggie… receive the honor. If Elvis had been in the building we wouldn't have had a bigger coverage. The idea of having crew members present and recipient was crucial, because it spoke to the concerns and needs of all film industry workers living in Southern California, many of whom were members of the Academy of Motion Picture Arts & Sciences. The sole qualification of "The Artist" for Made In Hollywood Honors recognition became a continuing theme of the post nominations campaign. Harvey Weinstein jumped on it. The film won the Oscar because it WAS the best film, but every little thing helps.

The next year, the only film made in Hollywood was "Argo," the film which would win the Oscar over the four I was working on. But a deal's a deal, and it was handed the Made In Hollywood Honor. Councilman LaBonge then bought into my idea that we extend the Made In Hollywood Honors to Emmy-nominated productions. Illustrating how imperative this bring-back-the-filmmaking effort is, only fifteen of the 45 Emmy-nominated shows that year (2013) were made in the town where it all began. None of those shows were represented by Guttman Associates, but I arranged that the well-covered presentations were made and will be held in perpetuity at the Heart Of Hollywood Terrace of the luxurious apartment complex 1600 VINE, held in a garden overlooking the street and town whose name still spells glamour around the world. A crucial validation that the Made In Hollywood Honors are contributive to the effort to bring Hollywood production back to Hollywood is that the respected California Film Commission and FilmLA, the official entity for both the county and city of Los Angeles to restore the primacy of Hollywood production, have joined as sponsors along with the LA City Council, 1600 VINE and the Hollywood Chamber of Commerce. A good and necessary idea does itself. Look what Uggie hath wrought.

Suitably, 1600 VINE is on the site of the historic Hollywood Brown Derby restaurant where stardom once glittered from every table, where flacks gathered every lunch with top clients for top interviews… It was as starry as the MGM commissary of that star-blazing time minus the matzah which, at the behest of Louis B. Mayer, garnished each table. Hollywood throbbed in those two places, as it did at their sister eateries all over town… in book stores and shoe stores. When my mother and I once walked on Sunset near the Beverly Hills Hotel (I had taken her to lunch at one of my most frequent interview sites, the Polo Lounge,) we stopped on the corner of Sunset and Crescent to observe the aftermath of an accident. My mother engaged in conversation about it with another lookie-loo and then, coming to surprised realization, said, "Oh, you're Ronald Reagan" Discovered in his stardom, he departed. He wasn't a politician yet. But that illustrates the degree of the town's star aggregation and integration and Hollywood's general star access in the mid-50s. Faces and names who were, at the same time, personalized friends in our lives and also our gods, moved through the soft palmy landscape as blood moves through your veins, healing and sustaining. Hey, industry, your Camelot awaits your return. Make movies that touch people's lives again, make stars again whom people will wish to relish rather than ravage, and the town's flacks will help you build legends once more. Give them the proximity and continuity to do what they do better than anyone else in the world.

Chapter 19

A Few Among the Many

The Lady in Lavender

It was quite a remarkable story. She came to Hollywood just to be one of the admiring and anonymous many… press agents among that number… who attend the handsome and talented few. Her writing was primarily for what were still called "fan magazines." The tabloids now pander to the lookie-loos of misery and scandal, people who plunk down their money at the checkout counter to see who's diddling or dying or starting to show cottage cheese. The fan mags merely babbled about the stars, making up silly stories to render stars intimately accessible to people who admired them. Her main job was running a fan club for one of the town's most pursued celebs. Then one day she chose to become a star, not a part of the retinue. She took off her sensible shoes and pulled herself up by the straps of her new Dolce Gabanas.

In doing so, Rona Barrett virtually invented one of the now inescapable subdivisions of television… entertainment news and gossip coverage as a genre distinct from general news coverage. And she invented herself. To pioneer a new glamour journalism, to launch the entertainment news revolution on TV, Rona had to undergo a most extraordinary make-over. With her weight loss and perfection of speech and re-molding herself from Brooklyn girl next door to glamorous diva, she amazed her friends, of which I was happily one. Rona first came upon the Hollywood scene in a form quite different from the sleek, slim, glamorous, witty and self-assured gossip queen who was to be the progenitor of TV's pre-occupation with entertainment news. She came to Hollywood from her humble Brooklyn or maybe Queens beginnings as a professional fan, but she climbed the high fence to the other side.

We first met when she headed the fan club for Eddie Fisher whom Rogers & Cowan represented during that time of change when the tepid 50s and the rambunctious 60s were blending together. The woman who became TV's queen of fashionable svelte, Rona was well-rounded in mind and body when she first plied her writing skills in Hollywood. She was, from appearance, only moderately interested in cosmetic enhancement and she had a defiant Brooklyn accent full of Jewish inflection. And all of it charmingly smart. She was funny and fun and very human, none of which did she forsake when the pounds came off and the fame went up. She saw that television was not addressing the public interest in entertainment news. To get there first, she did a crash course in slimming herself down and eleganting herself up. And she worked hard to achieve a clear, educated speech form that was both professionally journalistic and a-friend-in-the-know confidential to the public ear. Every aspect of her was refined and defined and remarkably changed. She and entertainment journalism on TV took off together when she moved her show to five minutes of entertainment news on Good Morning America. The flacks knew that a new day had arrived, and they were there for her with a flow of key news. She eventually expanded the empire to a nightly hour of late-night.

The most remarkable part of her metamorphosis was her speech transformation, her tongue-training as she once described it to me. When she treated me to the oratorical exercises she practiced daily to reshape and maintain her speech, it sounded like a Danny Kaye gatgitgiddelyveetvatsana scat-talk. She could drive that tongue a hundred miles an hour without missing a consonant. She broke major industry-shaping stories including one I booked with her in which a top show biz manager, disgusted with his own drug usage, out-ed the whole town on the growing instance and influence of substance abuse and how it was contributing to spiraling film budgets.

I was going to mask that tale, do it without names, but I bumped into Jeff Wald at the premiere of a lovely film produced by his client (and my friend) James Brolin and I told Jeff I was using the story. He thought about it half a second and then said, "Use my name," which was quite as brave as his original decision. Jeff was an aptly reputed tough guy who wasn't easy on Jerry Pam and me in our representation of his then-wife, pop singer and song-writer and feminist activist Helen Reddy. It was a labor-intensive and passion-intensive account in large part because it was the time of the fight to pass the ERA, the Equal Rights Amendment to the Constitution which would have secured for women the equality they'd never really been granted. Helen's theme song, "I Am Woman," was the anthem of the battle, and she was one of the powerful leaders of the parade. This gave Guttman & Pam a front row seat and some small hand in the effort. My own feminism was steeled in that fire.

Some time after the congressional blocking of ERA, Jeff asked me to set an appearance on Rona's late night show for him to blow the whistle on the woozy blues of Hollywood drug abuse. Rona was his friend, too, and he knew she would let him tell it straight. He'd come to this daring decision while under some a substance influence standing on a 12th story balcony of a Honolulu beachside hotel. Frustrated that he couldn't open a Pellegrino bottle, he tossed it over the side. He realized too late that the dolphin pool was just below and that he might have just killed one of nature's wondrous creatures. He watched it fall for a deliriously long time, and when it crashed, it killed nothing but his respect for his own sanity. It was, he said, the mind-muddled "grandiosity" of his action that terrified him. He decided to quit and to out a pattern of dependency that was harming his life… and Hollywood's. It was one of a number of influential sensations on Rona's series.

Rona was picking them up and mowing them down and setting the best and highest bars for TV entertainment reporting. She opened the door and established the ethical parameters for the TV entertainment news game and then she disappeared to live a rational and fragrant life growing lavender on a ranch near Santa Barbara and turning those flowers into delicious products… As someone in love with trailblazers, I always treasured Rona Barrett as a truly interesting person who changed things in Hollywood and as a friend you on whom you could count. A moving example of that was when she advised me that she was doing a story on wife-swapping between two couples with whom I was friendly. I went into one of my righteous snits, said I knew she was wrong and that our friendship was over if she used it. She didn't. A few months later, one of the stars, who happened to be a client, opened a what-have-you-done-for-me-lately conversation after what I thought had been a pretty good run of elevated status and visibility, and I told him of that false story I had suppressed. He looked at me in outrage and said, "How the hell did she know about *that*?"

Decades later I finally overcame my sense of embarrassment sufficiently to tell her how that incident had played out. She was no longer in journalism. "So, you were right," I said apologetically. "I knew that at the time," she answered, "I had all the confirmation I needed." "Then why didn't you go with the story?" "Because you said it would hurt our friendship," she said.

The King of Publicity Writers

By far and bar none, the most graceful , poetic and skillful writer ever to put his mind or pen to a publicity release was a Southern gentleman, in every sense of the word, by the familiar name of Jeff Davis... Jefferson Davis, no relation. I've encountered many good writers in my craft and I've certainly enjoyed those skills in the associates in my firms. It's easier if you have it in your blood, but even if you don't you can learn it. Ours is a communications craft, and how do you relate to writers if you don't know how to write? The email exchange between press agents and journalists often offers the daily rewards of clever phrasing, wordplay or witty spin... things that are not intended to be added to a story but rather added to a friendship. Notes are often graced with exercises in style for the sheer joy of writing, just as dancers may slip into a graceful pas de deux to glide to the other side of the room if the music is just right. But Jeff's writing was spun gold. This kindly son of Texas, cherubic even in the obesity to which his self-dissatisfaction had rendered him, had been at 28 the editor of the one of the Hearst Corporation's flagship papers, the San Antonio Light. How he could have been so open and courteous and empathetic to others and so unkind to himself just never connected for me. He had drunk himself out of that exalted position and others and wound up on the ragged shores of Hollywood in the late 40s seeking some place to use his typewriter. Perhaps because of the Hearst connection, he did some work for Louella Parsons for a while, but his drinking apparently undercut that. He wound up literally locked in a writing room at a one-man PR agency where his boss did the calls and Jeff poured out the writing, having to knock on the door for it to be unlocked so he could go to the bathroom.

I believe he wound up at Rogers & Cowan because Warren Cowan was quite an empathetic guy himself and he liked and knew how to use good writing. Jeff was not a client contact guy. He just sat at a typewriter... not cranking it out, but rather crafting flowing and persuasive copy. Good writing is always persuasive because good writers have to believe in what they're conveying. Jeff, to hear his sad confessions (he was another of the incredible people with whom I shared offices at Rogers & Cowan,) had a similarly abused private life, hen-pecked to hear him tell it and picked over not by his wife but by his mother-in-law. Jeff told every sad story with a laugh and an irresistible wit because he found himself so sadly amusing in his own estimation, perhaps too close to the picture to see what a charming and compelling human being he was, something that is quickly evident when such a person is your office partner. Gisela loved him, and he sent her haiku notes every day addressed to Missy Glee, which she scotch-taped to one wall. He was convinced his mother-in-law was trying to kill him. And, indeed, he certainly made a good case for it. The three lived in a very interesting old Hollywood home in Laurel Canyon, encouraging my guess that his wife enjoyed a good income. A Hollywood house, it had come with a cellar full of old silver nitrate film, about as stable as nitroglycerine. In those days instead of trash pickup, residents in LA burned their detritus in disposal units called, appropriately, incinerators. Jeff had warned his mother-in-law never to put any of the old film in the incinerator because it would explode, and he usually did the burning himself to be sure. One day, as he lit the fire and closed the lid, he dropped something, he said, and bent over to pick it up. At which point whatever was in the trash oven exploded and blew the metal lid over Jeff's crouching back and halfway into a car about thirty feet away. Jeff thought this was hilarious. He learned his almost-hard-won lesson, since after that he checked what was in it before he lit the incinerator,.

Jeff's softly ironic southern humor never failed him. On the other and sadder hand, it never really saved him either, but it did rally him through tough circumstance. One time he was in the hospital for some urinary problem and, as I was speaking to him on the phone, an orderly came into his room with what was apparently a length of tubing. Jeff excused himself from our conversation long enough to explain to the gentleman, "Sir, I'm sure you're a very nice man, but you're not coming near me with that thing until you show me your plumber's license."

Still, his life was oppressed, and he was an easy person to hurt. I believe it was a carelessly bruising phrase delivered to him one Saturday morning by Henry Rogers which really challenged my affection for Henry whom I knew to be brilliant, charming, quite elegant, a great press agent and a great executive and from whom I'd learned a tremendous amount. I hadn't minded that Henry had tried to get me fired off a film in Europe because a friend of his needed the job. He was that guy's friend, and that's what a friend is supposed to do. And friends come before people who are simply former employees, I suppose. And, on the very plus side, if it hadn't been for Henry's action, I would never have learned the dimensions of the ethics and humanity of Carl Foreman, how they matched even his extraordinary talent as a writer. But it was this Saturday morning incident at the office which stuck in my mind. Jeff and I were the only two people working in the rather large Rogers & Cowan offices on that weekend morning, Jeff turning out his reams of copy and I catching up on something. Henry looked in and said something appreciative of our being there on our own time and then he looked at Jeff and said, "Jeff, I see you here all the time, but I don't know what you do." He smiled and left. Jeff borrowed twenty bucks and went out to get drunk. Jeff was let go shortly thereafter because someone didn't think he made a good impression, which was true... but his writing certainly did. He struggled for a while and finally landed a job on the copy desk of the Los Angeles Herald-Examiner, a Hearst newspaper where his former eminence was respected. It was not a union shop, and there was soon a strike action to change that. The strikers all admired Jeff and cared about him, and it was conveyed to him that it was all right with them if he stayed on his job and he wouldn't be hassled crossing the line. But he was a gentle man and fearful as people who have experienced abuse often are, so he quit his job, and that was the last I heard of him.

Charisma 101

There was a who's-who of charismatic internationally overwhelming presences towering above you on the set of "Love In The Afternoon. That was especially the case when you were as unworldly a kid as was I when I worked on that film in Paris in 1956.... Billy Wilder, Gary Cooper, Audrey Hepburn. Maurice Chevalier. But the most charismatic personality on that set was the script girl. Olga Varenne came from a family of talented beauties. Her sister was one of France's top stars, but everyone said it was Olga who had the talent and the magnetism. She could have been rich, but she didn't want to act, so she was respectably poor. A gamine, the French would say. Everyone on the set either loved her or lusted after her, but she was much too old for me. She was 29 and she had a son. She spoke eight languages, and English was the only one that she loaded with a piquant and funny French accent, and she wasn't even French. She was Russian. Wilder and Coop teased her constantly and lovingly, and Billy would sometimes ask her to go get something for him just so that everyone could watch her walk away in her tight jeans. It was a kind of ritual on the set. She came to me once fuming. "What does eet mean een Eeenglish, cheat-TOES?" she demanded. "Cheat-TOES?" I puzzled, "where did you get that?" "Gareee," she said, pointing over at Cooper who was watching her, grinning. "See? Always he says eet, and the others they laugh." "But, cheat-TOES," I struggled, "put it in some context." "He always say when I go by.... Olga, he say, you are beeeld like a breeeeg cheat-TOES!" She didn't like the sound of my laughter. "Tell me!" she insisted. "Well, brick shithouse, it's... I don't know... what?... (I softened it slightly)... a pissoir." " He call me a pissoir?" she steamed and then headed toward Gary Cooper who had been watching us with amusement. "No, no!" I called, "it's a compliment." But she was standing over him giving him a French tongue-lashing, and he was laughing like hell, to the point of weakness, holding up his arms defensively as though she were beating him.

The French publicity complement on the film drew me into their social life. They all lived on the Left Bank, were shocked that I lived in the boring arrondisement of Ranlaghe, on the other side of town, and they forced me to move to the Rive Gauche, the Left Bank, where the personality and the freedoms of the City of Lights swirled in through your pores and you felt what it meant to be Parisian. It loosened the rigid constrictions of my background and personality. They were my teachers in my sudden immersion into whoever it was I was going to be. And no one more than Olga. One night ten or twelve of us had dinner at a cheap but atmospheric restaurant, and Olga asked if she could have my "so-word." I saw that she meant the little plastic sword that pierced the fruit in my Diablo... a drink of effervescent water and grenadine. I was, of course, the only one not having wine. She wanted the little toy for her son. Later Olga was driving me home in her Quatre Chevaux, her little Citroen. The evening and the joviality set the right traps and led me into my discovery of why the very air you breathe in Paris is romantic, why love there is an expectation, an entitlement and its charming little explorations mandatory. It was a very discreet but instructive flirtation... merely a flirtation... "ce n'est plus qu'un jeu" she said of it... a game. It wasn't going anywhere because she was older and with responsibilities and I was the poorest person on the company and the one with the least prospects and undoubtedly the least sophisticated. And she had her sacred sense of independence to think of. But she took pity and responsibility for creating my awareness and understanding that Paris was the only place that I should fall in love with someone. Had she not opened my eyes and my sense of life's grand potential, I might have missed the one opportunity of fulfilled life for which PR had led me to Paris.

A month or so later when my dating Olga had run its course, I met Gisela (thanks, again, to my PR fates) and on an occasion when I brought her to the set, Olga observed her from a distance with interest and then came over to me and smiled and said, "Wow." Actually, Gisela's visits to the Studios de Boulogne with me improved matters for me generally on the set. There had been a lot of resentment in the company from on high and from down low after it was understood somehow that Olga had smiled upon me. But then there was Gisela, and suddenly I was a fine fellow again. Later and on another film when I was studying German because I was going to meet Gisela's mother, I buried myself in an Asimil book from which one might learn German one chapter a week, but I had only two weeks so it was one chapter a day for me. Olga would look over my shoulder and give me the correct pronunciation. Once you get the soft consonant sound of the German "ch," particularly the correct pronunciation of the word "ich," you unlock the beauty of the German language. Olga's German was refined, and she was pulling for me. On "Love In The Afternoon" I'd arranged for Gisela to be an extra, first because she needed the money and the meal… Olga was curious about her but never made an effort to get to know her, I believe as an accommodation to me.

I worried about Olga from time to time because I felt she had far too kind a heart. Now, here's the sad part of the story… I mean sad because it does not speak very well of me. In 1976, Gisela and I and our daughter Danielle, then 15, were flying from Israel to the cold but joyous pre-Christmas time of Germany. At the insistence of Otto Preminger and through his arrangements, we had gone to Israel following the end of the Tehran Film Festival, and he had us stay at his favorite little hotel in Jerusalem, the American Colony, the former seraglio or harem of an Arab noble person. Otto, of course, had made "Exodus," the capture of the spirit of Israeli independence, and our company had had the privilege of representing Ernest Gold whose score for the film had won the Oscar and become a kind of second Israeli anthem. And now because of all that, Gisela and Danielle and I were on a Lufthansa flight back to Munich. At one point, I was simply walking the aisle and I noticed a woman in her late 40s absorbed in a book. There was a great sense of my past about her, and on the way back down the aisle I stopped to observe her, and of course it was Olga. She was, also of course, still beautiful and… this was of primary importance to me… she was exceedingly well dressed, the little fur cap (her Russian blood still insistent) on her head was most certainly haute couture. She was ok. That was really all I needed to know. I went back to my seat and debated with myself hard and long if I should inject Gisela and me back into her life. I wanted to know the details of her well-being and to let her see mine, Gisela and our beautiful daughters, all so lovely and like Olga, ebullient. Of course I should have, but of course I didn't. As we were disembarking in Munich, we to transfer to Stuttgart and she to go on with her life, I thought again of saying "hello" and "I'd like you to meet…", but I didn't.

The transfer flight to Stuttgart, a mere hour, was the worst ten hours of our lives. The weather, smashing the plane about, was so terrible that the stewardesses never were able to unfasten their seatbelts. As we were approaching our landing, the plane was lifting upward and dropping downward three or four stories at a time. I was assailed with a terrible sense of guilt that I and I alone had so endangered my wife and daughter and all of the other people frozen there as white-faced and wide-eyed as we. Certainly this was God's punishment upon me for my *crise de courage* on the preceding flight, my incomprehensible need not to visit my present upon my past or my past upon my present. Not saying hello to Olga was the most cowardly thing I had ever done, and now God was extending his wrath to all of the other poor people on this flight. As we lowered to the field… surging up, plunging down… I wondered at how readily agnostics capitulate to and accept God's micro-management of their lives every time there is danger blended with some accompanying assumption of guilt. Gisela was digging her fingernails into my arm and Danielle's hand. The ground was coming up to us. We rose suddenly like a well bucket being yanked up and then, it seemed, straight down as though someone had cut the rope. And that is how we met the ground with a mighty clang and clamor of sound… no, more like a metallic scream…. and a bone-pounding flinging and flailing about within the sure grasp of our seat belts. There was a calamitous scrunching roar… one hundred tons of metal trying to gouge its way into the earth. And then darkness and, remarkably, silence, then an awful protesting of various metals and then, again, silence. In about a quarter minute, the pilot's voice came over the still operative loudspeakers and he said in German, "For those of you who are going on with us to Frankfurt…." And everyone aboard burst into maniacal laughter. God had spared us… a joke… we were so improbably alive. I had just escaped responsibility for all those deaths. Then the doors were opened and we got down staircases hastily rushed to the plane. We exited into a raging thunderstorm, rain drops the volume of buckets smashing at us, a furiously cold wind literally pulling our skin. We were instantaneously soaked and we were freezing. It felt wonderful because it felt so whole-heartedly like we were alive. The plane was in the middle of the runway and we had to wait for busses to take us the long distance to the terminal. I looked back at the plane. The landing gear had gone all bow-legged under it. God had not spared us by much. Yes, what I had done was really stupid. Mea maxima culpa.

Months later, I told Gisela the part of this story that she did not know, about Olga's having been on the plane and my ridiculous decision. She literally did not speak to me for two days, maybe because she found it so unspeakably stupid… or even guilty. I just misguaged everyone and every thing on that one.

The Man Who Loved Ladies

Vernon Scott of United Press International was a vivid presence. He was fun and wrote funny articles and it was astonishing how many of his interviews with beautiful actresses quickly found their way to frank and revealing sexual discussion. Vernon was priapic, meaning not inured to sexual situation. Gisela and I spent a weekend in San Francisco with Vernon and Peter Ustinov, two more jolly companions you will never find. We were crammed in a taxi when Vernon saw a past sexual conquest walking on the other side of the street going in the opposite direction. Without saying a word, he opened the door and got out, even though the taxi was barely slowing for a traffic light. We watched him run up to her, and she turned to him, startled but then with a smile of enthusiastic welcome, Gisela said, "Now *that's* horny." And Peter seconded that with "Remarkable fellow."

It seems that Vernon had always been that way. In Detroit at the beginning of World War II, barely out of his teens, he found that women-without-men were looking, but he had a thing against dishonoring our men in service, so he chose instead to start an affair with the wife of a prominent Mafia boss. Such men usually discover such things, and this one did, so Vernon enlisted in the Navy and headed out to the relative safety of the South Pacific war zone. When he returned, he found that the coast in Detroit was clear because the cappo had been bumped off about a year before. But he headed for LA anyway where the high-living is easy.

No wonder I had no trouble getting him to interview Silvia Kristel, who had turned the town on its ear with the success of her film "Emmanuelle" and its successors. Not until that film did this town realize that soft porn had a profitable place in mainline theatres. And Vernon had a warm place in his heart, among other organs, for Sylvia Kristel He wanted to be the first to confirm and chronicle his fond fantasy that some of the sexual simulation in these films had not been simulated. "I've never seen an erection," she replied. "Well, I can take care of that right now," he offered. "No, I mean on a set," she said, doing a gentle side-step, "It was all acting. I've never met an actor who could actually be ready with all the cameras and gaffers around." "Lady," said Vernon incredulously, "did *you* have wrong guys!"

And if you've seen the "Emmanuelle" films or any of her other films, you know that if you can't do it with Sylvia, you flat-out can't do it. Indeed, she said, if an actor had, however improbably even in this time of Viagra-aggrandizement, unveiled such a condition for a scene, he would have been laughed off the stage. Even on porn films they employ "fluffers" before a scene to arouse an "actor" into that state of excitation.

One of the great wish-I'd-been-there longings of my life was the time that Vernon was sent by United Press International to cover a nudist convention somewhere in the Imperial County desert. He approached it with relish... until he discovered that Associated Press' beautiful correspondent, Aleene Moseby, had been assigned to go there, too. I would bet the farm that two editors had dreamed that coincidence up in delicious and diabolical conspiracy. It was the only time in his life that Vernon Scott felt uncomfortable in the presence of sex. When he told me about it, I mentioned having read some wit's report of a visit to a nudist colony and how frustrating it was not to be able to pay a beautiful woman the ultimate compliment. "I know what he meant," Vernon said, "I almost understand now what Sylvia Kristel meant. " Apparently for years after that, he and Aleene would only nod politely at events they mutually attended. .

Another interview at the Polo Lounge was with another European actress client of mine who was celebrated for intense relationships with interesting men. Vernon pursued the issue that she was currently romantically involved with a famous film personage and that they were frequently on different continents. "How do you handle that?" he asked. I felt the interview going in the wrong direction so I started to pull in the reins. But, no, she was very happy to pursue the line of discussion. "Off the record," I said firmly, as though anything I said at that point mattered. They shrugged me off. "So what do you do?" Vernon asked. "Well, we talk every night on the phone, and I tell him in detail any and all sexual experiences I'd had that day and he tells me his." She had Vernon's interest. He later described her unique arrangement to me as "a match made in Heaven… each of them gets to enjoy two distinct sex lives." He was, among his many other peculiarities and attributes, a good friend. If he felt you were under a gun, he would work with you on a story until you had an angle that worked for both of you. A conversation with him was a happy moment in any day until failing kidneys stole him from us.

The Glorious Battle-Axe

Florabel Muir, who had a west coast-based column for the New York Daily News, was another great character from the rough and tumble world of journalism. She'd been at it a long time. So long that her first editor had been Bat Masterson. I kid you not. The first assignment he gave her… I have the impression that this was in Utah in the still wild westness in the early 20th century… was to cover a public hanging. "I think he felt that would cut the green out of me fast," Florabel recalled to me once. There was nothing green about Florabel. She had covered so many killers and gangsters that her primarily Hollywood celebs column was kindergarten stuff to her. She was all rough edges and, I thought, big heart. She came on tough as nails, and a lot of people thought she was an old battle-axe, to use a phrase often invoked. I think that was an impression she encouraged and enjoyed. It meant that no one tried to flim-flam her. They were afraid to. Florabel had a sense that I was, at heart, a journalist, and so she shared journalist secrets with me, like her relationship with Mickey Cohen. People forget that Hollywood in the 40s and even the 50s had as many celebs who were tough guys and gangsters as it had actors who played them. Sometimes, as with George Raft, the two mobs, real and make-believe, interfaced. Mickey Cohen was one of LA's biggest stars, always in the news and in and out of jail. And one of the few journalists to whom he would confide was Florabel Muir. He knew a pro. when he saw one. But there were a few things she needed to learn, and he was willing to teach her. Early in her Hollywood stay she visited him in the pokey and he gave her some good information and then a good tip. "Keep your fingers clean," he told her. Coming from someone who was not only notorious but also, notoriously, a compulsive hand-washer, that could have a lot of meanings. So she said, "Be specific." "*Never take nothin' from nobody, you got it? Once you take a lollipop, you're theirs.*" I underline that mobster wisdom because their rules are the rules that keep your feet out of cement.

Florabel was, by nature more than by advice, incorruptible… and outspoken. I was still at Rogers & Cowan when I set her to interview the brilliant German actor Horst Buchholz at the Brown Derby in Hollywood. Horst was a big and fast up-coming deal. He had sprung to English language film heat in 1959 teaming with John Mills and Hayley Mills in the English thriller "Tiger Bay" and then had suddenly leap-frogged to stardom in films like "The Magnificent Seven," "Fanny" with Leslie Caron, "Nine Hours To Rama" playing Ghandi's assassin and Billy Wilder's "One, Two , Three" with Jimmy Cagney. So I wasn't surprised when Warren Cowan told me he wanted to join me in "covering" the interview. Warren hadn't been very directly involved with Horst, and because the very important Kurt Frings was Horst's agent, Warren was a bit more assertive than usual in making those little nudges a press agent slips in to keep an interview in the right vein. At one point, Florabel asked Horst a question, and Warren answered. Florabel looked at him and said, "Warren, we're old friends, but one of us is leaving this table. Now who's it gonna be?" Warren smiled and said, "Florabel, I learned a long time ago that it's futile to argue with a smart woman. I'll wait for you all outside. I'll take care of the tab."

In the movie capital, there was a trio of nationally syndicated columnists who cracked their whips over Era-Of-Glory Hollywood, celebrating or scolding stars at their whim. Earl Wilson, Liz Smith and other east coasters counted, but the town marched to the tune of these three ladies who "broke" in the local papers and who really got the gossip going each morning. Louella Parsons and Hedda Hopper were long-pampered queens. Sheilah Graham, whose syndicated column had fewer clout outlets, maintained parity because she alone of the three brandished a romantic coupling with a literary lion. She was famously the woman to whom the still-married F. Scott Fitzgerald had reeled after the institutionalization of his wife Zelda. It was an established great love, and it preceded her like heavy perfume when she entered a room. I admit setting interviews with her, mostly at the Polo Lounge, to get to know the woman whose romantic triage assisted a significant writer at the end of his own complicated narrative. The only insight I drew was that her beauty was quite compelling…

As columnists got decades into their syndications, they would, of necessity, bring on staff to assist or even co-write the daily writings. The associates would learn the style of the name on the column so well that it might be difficult to distinguish who had written a particular piece. I learned how to copy individual styles in my first year in publicity because it was not uncommon then to give some writers fully prepared columns. You see, the press agent's edge is that there just is never enough news, real news, to go around. There never was. So such prepped stuff gave overworked columnists a breather. I never had a problem writing to style… my own or anyone else's. There was one column in the LA Herald-Express (before it conflated with the Examiner) that was wide-ranging and well-read, a great outlet, and I would write at least two of her columns a month, sometimes a week. One of them was the article about Charlton Heston's big heart, for which I was so gently chastised. You could get in all of your plugs, squeeze other clients in. It was beautiful. The most amazing thing was that I actually wrote by-line columns for such clients as Milton Berle, Dick Shawn and George Burns. Mike Connolly, who had the gossip column in the Hollywood Reporter trade paper, liked to have comedians write guest columns for him when he was on vacation… a columnist doesn't want to let the editors get used to using that space for something else. So we set some of R&C's top comic clients for it, but what big stars had the time to do it?. Amazingly, they allowed me to pen them. It was "space" and space was awareness, and awareness fed the progression of careers. That's how simple it was then.

One of the top television comedians in the 60s was George Gobel, and I arranged for him to do a by-line for Pageant or Coronet, one of the pocket-sized format monthlies of the time. The thing was that George Gobel's comedy wasn't so much about jokes as about attitude, and I had to put in passages that you could imagine his acting out. The article was about Garry Moore, another top comedian with a leading variety show, and with whom George Gobel had something else in common. Each had a crew cut, the closely cropped lawn of grey atop their heads. You can see how intellectually challenging I made these things. The article was actually "Garry Moore Stole My Haircut." Today it would have to be Garry Moore Stole My Wife" or, if you want a cover line, "How I Lost 50 Pounds When Garry Moore Stole My Wife." How I ever got eleven hundred words out of that I cannot imagine, but I do recall that I had to copy the meter of Gobel's delivery style and the cant of his persona as well as get in a few laughs. But once you catch the jazz of it, the beat and the backbeat, it's not hard, and it was good writing training. A good press agent has to be able to write for different voices.

In The Company of Great Directors

Once you get the angle on a story, you're halfway there. That was particularly important in selling magazine stories on people who actually had no right to be the subject of magazines. One of the great thrills of working at Rogers & Cowan was that they handled so many of the great and classic directors... Frank Capra and Lewis Milestone among them... a pantheon of my heroes... including Mark Robson who had started with such low-budget classics as "The Dead" and "Bedlam." A star neophyte director on the Val Lewton RKO team which grew so many directorial greats, Mark then moved on to several of Stanley Kramer's early films which called the shots on American neo-realism, "Champion" and "Home Of The Brave," and then wound up directing many of the finest emotional films lapped up by female audiences. These included "Return To Paradise," "From The Terrace," Ingrid Bergman in "The Inn Of The Sixth Happiness," Susan Hayward in "My Foolish Heart," and he was working on "The Bridges Of Toko-Ri" with Bill Holden and Grace Kelly when I came into control of his publicity fortunes. You have to understand that for a film school student, this was walking with the founding fathers. These were my heroes. Mark and his wife often hosted Gisela and me at their home, elevating us with their collection of distinguished friends, while their remarkable collection of modern sculpture, encouraged Gisela into her own eventual accomplishments with chisel and stone

But the trade-out is that you have to imagine such people into magazines where great directors do not commonly appear. I postulated that, with his accomplishment in women's films, Mark Robson was a hero with that gender. He was, but they didn't know it. They just loved his films. The hero part was my job. How to get that into reality? I think it was Redbook to which I sold the angle...... What Makes Women Cry? Who wanted to know most of all what made other women cry was women, including the wives of studio heads. It created an awareness in Hollywood.... Mark Robson, the story established, is the top director with women audiences. From such perceptions good things flow.

The challenge of getting a classic director like Lewis Milestone ("All Quiet On The Western Front," "Rain," "Of Mice And Men," "A Walk In The Sun") publicity for what he had done without diminishing what he is doing is tough. What he was doing when I worked with him was the fine 1959 "Pork Chop Hill." Well, you start out by drawing connection between the then and the now. Here was a guy who had made THE definitive film about World War I, "All Quiet On The

Western Front," one of the great films about World War II, "A Walk In The Sun" and now he was making what became a definitive film about the Korean War. It's brilliance was confirmed in time, but in PR you have to advance "in time" to "now," and there are a lot of tricks a press agent can engage to do that. My effort was to establish "Pork Chop Hill" as "Lewis Milestone's new war classic." It put the film in the context of its two distinguished predecessors, and it was bringing the aura forward. History actually did come to that conclusion, and it also provided Gregory Peck with one of his most demanding dramatic roles and launched the film career of one of the most brilliant actors of the next fifty years and beyond, Martin Landau.

The film school background certainly was a bridge-builder in connecting with these greats, but the closest bond with Mr. Milestone came from a picture I had over my desk. It was a studio portrait of one of the greatest of silent stars, Clara Kimball Young, which she had inscribed to me when I did a taped interview with her for the UCLA film history archives. It was a powerfully beautiful and perfectly lighted classic of early film portraiture. Mr. Milestone and I were sitting in my office talking when he looked up and saw he photo and said "Oh, my gosh" and went up to look at it carefully. "Look at this," he said, "it's Arthur." I was a little perplexed, since it was Clara. He was pointing to the signature of the photographer placed in the border of the oval shot. It said A. Edeson, 1917. That had always attracted my interest, too. It couldn't have been Alva Edison... it was Edeson, but something had always told me that was important. Ms. Young had taken it from a treasured file in the little house in Hollywood just up the street from my parents' humble first home in California in 1945. My mother, who left no one unbefriended, had one day engaged in conversation the older lady she so often saw watering her flowers outside her own little house. When she learned that her new friend was one of the towering film stars and beauty idols of her youth, my mother was confounded with wonder, having slipped so unexpectedly through the looking glass.

"Arthur," Mr. Milestone said, "he shot 'All Quiet' for me. " Arthur Edeson, it turned out, was the first great Hollywood portrait photographer, the George Hurrell of his time, the only one Douglas Fairbanks chose to use and who Fairbanks then seduced into becoming a cinematographer who subsequently shot all of Fairbanks' films and many of the greatest films of both silent and talkie film history including "All Quiet On The Western Front." His close-up of the hand reaching for the butterfly at the end of the Milestone masterpiece is perhaps the motion picture art's most telling capture of man's aspiration to peace, one of the great film images of all time… Mr. Milestone and I were instant friends.

There were a number of filmmakers, like Lewis Milestone, who effected how motion pictures would be made forever thereafter. In a way, a press agent gets to touch movie history. Andy Keuhn was a master of his own art, the creation of film trailers or, as they said in my youth, the previews of coming attractions. These are the enticements you see in theatres before the feature or in shorter, snappier form in TV ads. Andy was a prince of that trade, introducing editing techniques for trailers in the 60s and 70s which compelled new ideas into film editing in general. We spent a concentrated weekend together filming a documentary at the Mojave Air Races which Gene Hackman had commissioned to illustrate that sport when Gene and I peddled our script "Snaproll," partly set against that lesser-known organized adrenaline rush enjoyed by thousands of fans atop their motor homes and pick-ups or the die-hard aficionados standing virtually under the racing Hellcats and P-51s, Spitfires and double-fuselaged P-38s. The noise alone would thrill you… and the action, should something go awry, could kill you. Air-racing pitted peerless World War II fighter planes and fearless pilots in short bursts around pylons. We developed the documentary around pilots from the Texas Air Force, one of the top groups of such airborne competitors, and their name was fitting. Taking decades-old fighters at speeds in the hundreds of mph at perilously low heights, these guys were cowboys in every sense of the word. Absorbing Andy's keen sense of how film would cut together, watching him virtually cutting it in his brain, was worth all of the editing experience in film school classes and as a documentarian. The ghost of his sense of timing, his sense of where the viewer's mind was, is evident in almost every action film in this action film era. "It's not what you make them see," he told me, "it's what you make them think."

The Greatest Free Lunch

Everyone who spends the most enjoyable part of his or her life watching old films on cable owes a massive debt of gratitude to a film historian named Jerry Harvey. Jerry was program director for the first cable movie channel to impact the part of LA where the movie business lives. His impeccable selections and thrilling booking schedule for Z Channel in the early 70s laid the groundwork and set the pattern for the wonders that await movie buffs at the click of their tuner every night after dinner. The dazzlement of the first five decades of movies was at our fingertips constantly, largely because of this guy Jerry Harvey whose heart beat in glorious black and white and who set the pattern for American Movie Classics, Turner Classic Movies and all of the others. He graciously made room on his programming for the Oscar contending films that Guttman & Pam played on the channel for years as our own exclusive playground for getting our client films nominated. *It was the greatest free lunch in movie promotion history* .

Jerry Harvey, very kindly, did nothing to upset our incredible apple cart, because he saw how our totally ethical scam was bringing attention to his channel and his glorious selection of the great films of the past. Every classic movie channel should air an homage to Jerry Harvey once a day. He was doing what he most loved. He was creating a living hall of fame for the films he loved, giving them a place to breathe and to be discovered by new generations. And then he committed suicide. I didn't want to learn his unhappiness. It was too late. I just wanted to celebrate what he had initiated.

The Arkansas Traveler

Press agents are frequently very original and memorable personalities, bright and sharp, innocent or ironic. One of the most powerful and enjoyable was Wally Beene, a journalist by trade and adventurer by nature. His drawling Arkansas charm was open and funny, and any experience, good or bad, was a rich delight to him. Wally had done tours of duty in the Pacific in World War II, a gunner on bombers. He was so eager for experience, that it seems inevitable that his bomber was the first plane to land in Japan after the capitulation, before the surrender, setting down among wide-eyed farmers who had no idea that the war was over. There were tensions and dangers, all of which Wally found great fun and recalled with treasured humor. He did his second tour of military adventure as a front-line reporter and columnist for Stars And Stripes in Vietnam, hitch-hiking on strafing fighter raids, sharing his goodies from home with kids on the frontlines. He celebrated tea bags and bottles of Tabasco sauce because they were the two most valued possessions under fire, able to turn meals-ready-to-eat into repasts that were actually edible.

Nothing nothing nothing phased him. Which is a pretty good body armor in publicity. One of the ten most indelible impressions of my career occurred one morning when I walked into his office while he was on the phone, smiling his energy into the conversation. At that particular time, Guttman & Pam was conducting business on the ground floor of a building up the street from the William Morris Agency and directly across from the Beverly Wilshire Hotel. So my office, Wally's and one other had huge floor-to-ceiling windows looking across the sidewalk and street to the carriage entrance of the Beverly Wilshire where we could see the elegantly gowned and tuxedo-ed crowds arrive each evening for the grand balls that illuminate every night in the entertainment business. On each movie town night fifty people are being named man of the year or woman of the year or something else of the year in each of four glittering ballrooms in each of at least a dozen of the great queen hotels. There are, it seems, more lifetime achievement awards than there are lifetimes, and all of this is the machination of press agents serving many worthy causes and many worthy clients. Money as well as awareness are raised at these events.

But this was morning, and El Camino Dr. was quiet with sparse traffic. Wally seemed at the end of the conversation, so I waited. I noticed that an elderly man in a very large Cadillac had initiated a u-turn in the middle of the block, directly in front of the huge window separating Wally's office from the sidewalk. It was the usual turn into the curb, back up, go in the other direction. But this took on a sudden and alarming energy when the man, instead of slowing himself into the curb, missed the brake and jammed down on the accelerator. Wally, still lavishing his personality on the call, caught this out of the corner of his eye and, as the Cadillac hit the curb at about thirty miles an hour and launched into a sweeping parabola towards the window, Wally rose from his chair, the phone still to his ear and his smile now a manic leer of crazed delight and intensity, and just as the car came rocketing through the window, he said with happy enthusiasm and insane calm, "Gotta GO now!" And he actually hung up the phone before he leaped past me and out the door, leaving me to stand frozen as the grill of the car crunched into his desk. I have never witnessed a film stunt of such audacious composure, and it captured and held my fascination much more than my own impending and narrowly averted death or injury.

As the years went on, Wally experienced and fearlessly survived an impossible string of horrific illnesses and disasters. He was told he would die in five years without a heart transplant which he refused and, sure enough, twenty-five years later he did die. He had the oxygen explode inside his throat and lungs during an operation and recuperated from that to the astonishment of modern medicine.

His endurance, amused spirit and sheer humorous delight in life was the stuff of legend, certainly among his acquaintanceship and his fan club headed by Steve Guttenberg and me. John Huston was a fan, too. I always insisted to Wally that his gravestone should say "Gotta go now." Which appealed to him, but Gisela wouldn't let me suggest that to his loving widow, Gerry, when Wally finally passed on recently, long after the Vegas odds had been left in the dust. "That stone has to be his family's memories, not yours," she said with outrage. But, Wally, this stone is for you.

Wally was the quintessential gregarious and unshakeable southerner, exploding with appetite. He was a fearless journalist, always more intent on locking up a good story than looking after his own safety. Unwittingly, I gave him one of his best adventures and then I never forgave him for my not having experienced it myself. During the 80s, we did a lot of business with top Japanese firms... Sanrio, Kadakowa... and for such Tokyo superstars as that Asian country's Frank Sinatra/Kenny Rogers, Hiroshi Itsuki (or, in Japan, Itsuki Hiroshi.) Kadakowa was the great Japanese publishing empire, and when its emperor... Kadakowa-san, decided to go into movie-making, he came to us to publicize it and to help deliver the stars he needed. The film was called "Virus," and it was, of course, about the end of humanity because of governmental and corporate refusal to address the spread of a species-ending disease. American stars who came aboard included Glenn Ford and Chuck Connors, and we brought Bo Svenson to the table and some other friends and clients, all of whom enjoyed significant pay-days. It simulated the "multi-star cast" then obligatory for any big disaster film. We were doing the unit on it, meaning that we were supplying all of the on-set publicity supervision and developing all of the copy (written materials) that would be needed. I did this personally for the portion of the film shot during a horrific Toronto winter, especially when we junketed in the full complement of Japanese media and key U.S. press.

But the film's location shoot in the Antarctic, with the film company based aboard the famous cruise ship the Lindblatt Explorer, posed too long an absence for me however much I longed to experience that. Wally was a skilled and facile writer and up to any adventure, and he jumped at the chance to unit the shoot when I offered it. It was a series of disasters from the start, all of which Wally folded into good-humored adventure. While the Antarctic in December is in summer, it feels like anywhere else' deep winter, and Wally's luggage never made it south of the equator. Chile was summery, with stores filled only with tennis togs. Between Chuck Connors, Bo Swenson and the wardrobe department, Wally, as usual, landed on his feet… this time in borrowed boots and coats. We were getting daily reports from him from the Lindblatt Explorer, filled with such lifetime memories as watching two killer whales hunt a seal on an iceflow by one whale's pushing up on one end of the ice and causing the seal to slide down into the second whale.

It was Christmas Eve and Gi and I were in Malibu preparing to head to our daughter's when I received a call from Associated Press which had fielded reports that the Lindblatt Explorer had sunk off the Antarctic coast. AP wanted confirmation, which obviously I couldn't supply, and so it then wanted cast and other information on the film. I knew that the size of the break depended in part on the size of the stars. There was a possibility that some of them had returned to be home for Christmas, however the question had been what stars were involved in that location, and I was able to say quite sincerely that Olivia Hussey and Connors and the others had been there for the shoot. I had only suspicion and no specific knowledge that they weren't there at the time of the disaster. I pumped the reporter for knowledge about the reports and was relieved to hear that there were no known injuries or fatalities. We listened avidly to the radio news as we drove to the party. All news stories are preceded with "datelines," identifying the geography from which the story originates. The Lindblatt evacuation (it never sank but rather was jammed solid into a reef,) understandably, was the lead story, and the dateline was…. Malibu, California. It quoted me as the confirming source, which I was not… I was a source of some of the pertaining details… but at least we got all of our plugs in big time. The next day we received a number of calls asking if I was OK.

What happened, Wally told me later, was that the boat had hit an uncharted reef, that they were in open boats with real questions about how long they could survive, but a Russian trawler picked up the may-day and was there in a few hours. The next day they were transferred to a Chilean destroyer, and they had to sleep in shifts on desks and other horizontal surfaces. Connors and the rest had, indeed, departed the ice a few days earlier, but I noticed that nobody diluted the story with the less glamorous facts and they became, since names make news, part of the legend. I still blame Wally for my not having been there. I could have owned cocktail parties with it for ten years. I don't drink, so I have to talk on those bubbly occasions. I read last year that the Lindblatt Explorer sank down there again, but there weren't any stars, so the story was a lot less prominently played, a footnote and with the prior and more starry sinking the essential reference. Ah stars. Ah stars stars stars.

Wally discovered Steve Guttenberg. Well, actually producer Walter Shenson did for his independent comedy "The Chicken Chronicles," but Wally was the unit on it for us, and he recognized the affable genius of this delightful seventeen year old actor. Steve, a joyous guy who loves people of like humor, called Wally religiously after Wally's health problems kicked in and honored him as he would family.

I had met Wally when I was at Rogers & Cowan. Because I had lived and worked in Europe, spoke a bit of the languages and could work well with European artists (well, actually, it was Gisela they really liked and related to, but I was allowed along for the ride,) it fell to me to set up and oversee the overseas offices for the company which kept getting bigger and bigger in size and reputation. We handled most of the continent's stars who flooded Hollywood in the sixties. I hired Wally as our man in Madrid, where he was then working for Stars And Stripes, and he later opened up Tokyo for us when Stars and Stripes posted him there as the Vietnam War heated up. Gisela and I and our daughters stopped in Madrid somewhere in the mid sixties because Rogers And Cowan had a lot of clients shooting there and because it had been a cherished stomping ground for us when we were just married. I had to drive up to the mountain town of Soria where we had Geraldine Chaplin and Omar Shariff shooting "Dr. Zhivago," and we also had Robert Shaw filming "Battle Of The Bulge" and Nicholas Ray preparing his next film. And James Mason hermitted in an old castle he'd bought in Estoril. Wally and I drove out to Robert Shaw's house for a meeting, and it stuck in my mind because I had always held to the belief that Wally could drink anything. Shaw brought out a beer sangria that he assured us he simply loved. You don't tell devoted drinkers that you don't drink, so I pleaded tourist's tummy, but Wally happily accepted a large mug of the stuff. Shaw was called into the house for a phone call, and Wally took a slug and then spat it out. He poured it onto the grass, a large spot of which then turned brown as we watched. Shaw came out, saw the empty glass and offered to refill it. Wally offered his ready smile of genuine Southern flim flam and said, "Nothing would tempt me more, but I like to savor the memory of a great drink." Shaw was pleased and raised his second mug of the toxic brew in toast to Wally's epicurean sensibility.

Lessons in Memory From Memoryman

I've always had an accurate memory for people or adventures which interested me, even rather precise dialogue retention because words and rhythms and thought construction fascinate me. But I've been assisted in the prodigious challenge of memory required for an omnibus book like this by my friendship with a remarkable Malibu character named Memoryman whom some of his friends call David. Memoryman can be dictated fifty double numerals (54,94, 35, etc) and then can repeat them to you forwards or backwards. He's the real life version of the memory guy in Hitchcock's "The 39 Steps."

Memoryman's methodology instructs you in the one-thing-leads-to-another school of recall. David and his brother had been abandoned or orphaned when David was four. They went into some rather brutal offshoot of the 1940s foster care system, but it seems in his telling much more an uncaring and restrictive orphanage. In a way, he and his brother were Holocaust victims. They were thrown on the cruel compassion of orphan life just as survivors of the Nazi persecution were being brought to America to have their ravaged little lives reconstructed. There is always only so much love to go around. David and his brother, charges of a most brutal state for 14 years, were sometimes tethered. David's brother went blind and then went mad and then died. David survived by figuring things out for himself. Why would a little boy with so few and fleeting moments of human kindness to remember become an expert at memory? He began by memorizing numbers. Numbers are neutral , numbers can't hurt you. He wrapped himself into a cocoon of neutral numbers and, in the process, ordered his mind to readily access everything he knew or heard. Feelings and relationships were painful. You would think he would have taught himself to forget, but he taught himself and the others to remember.

As I thumb through my decrepit telephone book, scribbled with acquaintances and intersections of four decades, as I look for this number or that, my eye is invariably caught by the glittery reminder of people I'm so happy not to forget. People I haven't called recently enough, people my telephone can no longer reach… My phone book, as disreputable as it looks, is a bouquet of forget-me-nots.

An Office at Goldwyn

Guttman & Pam was one of the few independent press offices on a major studio lot, and that was because Jerry had an association with United Artists, also on the lot, for whom we oversaw the release publicity for most of that distributor's films. This put us into the glory of association with the great talents ... directors, stars... of such films as "Last Tango In Paris" and "Sunday Bloody Sunday," of Bernardo Bertolucci and John Schlesinger. Who could ask for anything more? The UA association was a rich mine of opportunities. So was the office on that storied lot, across the street from the Formosa Restaurant where so much Hollywood history had transpired and where we took so many lunches. You could hear the echoes of historic lunches and dinners past from which great deals or great romances or maybe just flings took root. Our first next door neighbor was a director as classic as his films, George Marshall.

Need I say more than "Destry Rides Again?" "Destry," one of the greatest of westerns, greatest of comedies, greatest of aching romances... and one of the greatest films of that greatest year of films ever... 1939. Lunches and office stopbys with George Marshall more than matched my film school years in insights and pleasures. During one lunch at the Formosa when we were discussing "Destry," I suddenly remembered a momentary brush with a great talent which I had somehow repressed, perhaps because I was not totally sure of my assumption, perhaps because it was so sad. I put it on the table for George's verdict.

It was during my days of poverty in Paris when a hotel room costing more than a dollar a night was a little hard on the budget. I cherished George Orwell's recounting of impoverishment in my two favorite towns, "Down And Out In London And Paris" (35 cents at a bookstall on the quai of the Seine) and read it several times. It lent dignity and romance and a sense of luxury to my own scrimpings. I was staying at the Hotel du Bac, on the little side street Rue de Bac which bisects the junction of Boulevard St. Germain and Boulevard Raspail, leading from there one block up to Rue de Varenne where the studios, now museums , of two monumental sculptors, August Rodin and Aristide Maillol are near neighbors, across the street from the USSR Embassy. It cost, I recall, $1.38 a night for a dank little room with a wash stand, and where else could you have such neighbors for that piddling price? But that was Paris and that was 1956, God bless them both. There was a ritual noise each night at about eleven, the bumping and stumbling of someone lurching drunkenly up the dark, winding stairs. I happened to be going out for some late purchase one night when the author of those noises was struggling his way up to his room, and we had to pass on the stairs. "Pardon moi," I said, and he muttered something angry and unintelligible but in a distinctly Russian accent. I had the feeling I knew this man. I made a point of seeing him again, and, yes, I knew I knew him, but because of his always muffled appearance, I just couldn't place it. I asked the hotel's owner about him, and she responded, "Ah, l'ivre Russe." The Russian drunkard. Beyond that, she knew nothing about him. There was one stair passing when I tried to engage him in conversation and it flooded me with astonishment. This, it seemed powerfully apparent to me, was Mischa Auer, one of the most stupendously talented (I know, I talk like a press agent, but how can you not in regard to such an artist?) of the amazing character actors who contributed so much to Hollywood in the '30s and '40s. His manic, arm-swinging chase about a Park Avenue drawing room in "My Man Godfrey," aping a gorilla, bounding over chairs and bouncing off walls, is one of the classic moments of motion picture mime. With that realization or at least suspicion, I felt obliged to tell Monseur Auer of the reverence in which I held him. Revealed or, perhaps, confused by some madman's mistake, the man looked at me with horror and fled up the stairs. I never bothered him again, but felt deep admiration and sadness every time I saw him. Yes, it could easily have been mistaken identity on my part, since Auer did several other film roles in the few years after that. But those eyes.

This memory, buried undisturbed for almost 20 years, I shared with George Marshall who had directed Auer to one of his virtuoso comic/human performances in "Destry Rides Again." George let it sink in, reviewing some of his own memories through the filter of my sad discovery. Then he said, "Ah, Mischa," in fond tribute, and that was it. I told him I never was certain, but he thought I may well have stumbled upon the great actor in some sad interlude.

Later, I asked George if he knew what distinction Mischa Auer shared with Trevor Howard, a coincidence which I thought was my own exclusive intellectual property. "They each played a character who was constantly annoyed by being addressed by a mistaken name," he said, "... and it was the same mistaken name.... Callahan." I was amazed, and our friendship was tightly bonded in this shared perception. Joseph Cotten persisted in calling Trevor Howard's Inspector Calloway 'Inspector Callahan' in "The Third Man," and in "Destry Rides Again," everybody calls the quintessentially Russian Mischa Auer by the name of his wife's deceased first husband... Callahan. "I wonder if Graham Greene did that as an homage when he wrote 'The Third Man,' or maybe Carol Reed when he directed it," I said. "I've wondered about that myself," George responded with a smile.

With "The Third Man" somewhere up there in the top three or five of my all-time favorite movies, it was an incredible thrill in the summer of 1957 (when I was in Paris busily wondering "what next?") to get a call from Carl Foreman asking if I would like to be assistant unit publicist on his film, "The Key," which Carol Reed (not yet Sir) would direct with a cast of Bill Holden, Sophia Loren and Trevor Howard. Any one of those elements would have excited me, but all five? Carl was one of the brilliant writers squandered so ruthlessly by Hollywood when the House UnAmerican Activities Committee raced with a blowtorch through the American cultural and academic worlds in the early 50s ransacking art and sentencing some of our greatest talents to jail, exile or financial ruin, Their common crime?... they had, as empathetic and youthful human beings, each explored how socialist principals might alleviate the suffering and inequalities of the Depression. After all, many of these streams of political philosophy flowed into the river of change that was President Franklin Delano Roosevelt's New Deal. Many people of conscience in the 30s experimented with these possible remedies exactly as people experimented with social drugs in the sixties and seventies.

Gary Cooper Played Him in "High Noon"... Carl Foreman

Carl Foreman, the screenwriter of "High Noon" had been blacklisted and he elected to depart for England where he could write under pseudonyms. During the filming of "The Key," the 1957 Oscar race was shaping up, and interest in it flourished on the set of "The Key," because Reed's longtime associate David Lean seemed headed for a win with "Bridge On The River Kwai." And Carl Foreman was rumored to have secretly co-written the screenplay and was, decades later officially accredited as co-author with fellow black-listee, Michael Wilson, as sharing the Adapted Screenplay Oscar with the author of the original novel, Pierre Boule. Early the next year, I was back in London doing the unit PR for a Jack Palance/Anita Ekberg film "The Man Inside. " The head of Columbia PR in London liked my work on "The Key" and gave me my first and what turned out to be my last assignment as unit publicist. But I was there, and was able to augment my still meager salary by returning to Foreman's employ to help with the pre-release and premiere of "The Key." In this capacity, I was baby-sitting an interview with Carol Reed and some reporter, when an aide looked into the room and said, "Carol, David just won the Oscar for 'Kwai.'" "I'm very happy for David," Carol replied. The interview went on, and at some point about five minutes later with no reference to what was being discussed, this incredible creator, director of "The Third Man," producer of "Brief Encounter," one of the most magnificent contributors to film art, said "I'm very happy for David." I cannot tell you what special joy and relief I felt years later when Sir Carol Reed received the Best Director Oscar for "Oliver."

But of all the memorable acquaintance "The Key" brought, including the improbable friendship or at least kinship accorded me by Bill Holden, that most masculine of leading men... even his comedy had a kind of self-mocking masculinity.... the most compelling was Carl Foreman, a man so embittered by his banishment that many people found him cold. I thought he was just careful to whom he entrusted his friendship. He had been a writing king of Hollywood and everyone was his friend, and then he had been pursued and persecuted for having explored his conscience, and then nobody was his friend. He and Wilson had to stand by as Boulle "fronted" for them as the author of the Oscar-honored screenplay. If that doesn't make you careful with your placement of trust, I don't know what will.

But I knew even before I met him what a decent and honorable heart he had, and not just because his writing was enlightened with decency and honor. He had hired me, I'm sure, on the recommendation of Herb Stern whom Columbia had set as unit publicist for the film and who was the unit publicist for whom I'd worked on "Love In The Afternoon." A few days later, I got a call from Carl Foreman advising that Henry Rogers (Rogers & Cowan was handling the film in the United States) had telephoned Carl to say he wanted someone else, one of Henry's friends in England who had just lost his job, to have my position. I was crestfallen, because I had just turned down work on Kirk Douglas' "The Vikings" in Sweden, and the $125 a week for "The Key" had been my key to financial survival, to staying in Europe and, most importantly by far, to staying close to Gisela to make sure she did not slip my grasp and take my life with her. "I'm sorry to hear that, Mr. Foreman," I said. "Me, too," Carl replied, "because I don't give my word lightly. So you're on, and I'll pay you out of my pocket." At that moment, he stood as tall for me as he'd had Gary Cooper stand in "High Noon." The outlaw Frank Miller and his gang of desperados had come gunning for my job, but they wouldn't have a chance of facing down Carl Foreman and coming out of it vertical. I was determined to justify that trust, and I took it personally that a big part of my job was to establish in Hollywood's mind that Carl Foreman was back in business and casting aliases to the wind. Some of the media were still hewing to HUAC (the House Un-American Activities Committee) dictates, but I structured stories that required the use of his name.

For that reason, I regret having had occasion during the shooting of 'The Key" to be at least the partial author of one of Carl's most humiliating experiences. We had completed all of the location work on the seas outside of the South England port of Portsmouth, in and around Portsmouth Naval Dockyards and in the local streets still pitted with bombing ruins from The Blitz. The shooting of naval scenes off that coast was arduous because Carol was shooting in a section where the Atlantic and North Sea adjoined and where the conflicting currents made it always a perfect storm of high waves, Seasick City, we called it.

The first day I joined the company, I was given the choice of boarding the huge ocean-going tug that was both set and transportation and which left port at five AM, or catching a seven AM camera boat that went out to meet the company. Seven AM sounded better. Never trust the sound of better. I had to brace my leather soled shoes against a guy-wire and hold on to canvass packing to stay aboard as the little boat pitched and dove its way out to the set. Then, as we pulled alongside and the two crafts separated and then smashed together every twelve seconds, I had to leap for a rope ladder hoping not to slip and become a flattened buffer between the colliding hulls. Five AM sounded just great after that.

So it was a big relief to be back shooting at the Elstree Studios out in what was still the Hertfordshire countryside, where we had the luxury of setting up press agently promotions. This stunt I mention, the disaster of which still haunts, was the brain child of the British publicist, I swear to God. We'd started filming in September, but now it was wending its way towards Christmas, and the British PR guy, aware that Britain had troops stationed on Christmas Island, a half world away from the homeland in the gathering holidays, arranged for the British Bakers Guild or whatever it was called, to bake a Christmas cake resembling Sophia Loren and with the exact, famous and internationally panted-over dimensions of that remarkable lady. Again, I make the point that this was not my idea. I would compulsively tell you if it were. This writing is not short on reports of my idiocy. So, on the appointed day, the cake arrived at Elstree for the big unveiling by Sophia Loren, a truck deposited a massive crate… my guess is seven feet long, three feet wide, two feet high… on a huge table in the commissary. We had a very large press turnout, and I do plead guilty to that. With all of them set up in proper photo position, the door opened and Carl Foreman escorted Sophia Loren into the room. She took two steps in and then stopped and gasped.

The box looked like a coffin of a seven foot tall Viking. Carl placed one hand around her waist and gently took her hand with his other, helping her forward in a manner that added to the funereal sense of the moment. The day and the room were cold and grey. Many of the winter-bundled press wore gloves. With grave reservation, Sophia opened the casket… sorry, crate… and peered in… and then promptly let it crash back down. Only Carl's strength supported her. The British press agent, wishing to salvage (but actually managing to savage) the photo op, opened the lid and slid it off. Yes, the British Bakers Guild had used Sophia's goddess-like exact vital statistics, the amazing contrast of waist and bosom, but they had neglected to take into consideration one reality. If a woman is 38-22-35 in measurement, one must bear in mind that those are measurements of a circumference. But cakes, if you give it a thought, are notoriously flat on the bottom, so when you apply the dimensions of a rounded body to what is basically a semi-circle, the widths and protuberances of the finished form are greatly exaggerated, the width of hips spreading about two and a half feet, the chest area nearly a yard.

There inside was the most ghastly fat lady of a cake any circus sideshow could ever have offered… and with a slightly Sophia Lorenish kind of face. Sophia, that gracious, beautiful and normally gregarious lady, turned pale. Carl turned red. We all turned to God wishing that the moment could have been somehow rewound. I should have checked it out in advance. I can't help feeling with disgrace that that is how meagerly I had repaid Carl Foreman's gentlemanly kindnesses to me.

Why Photographers Are Fun

Jim and Julie Swarbrick were the unit photographers on Bob Hope's "Paris Holiday," the film which allowed me to stay on in Paris after "Love in The Afternoon." Jim and Julie were the most invigorating couple I ever met. He did the photography and she did his backup, occasionally wielding a second rollex when a scene demanded. They were the most vigorously in love couple, in love with each other and in love with the world-trekking life they shared shooting photos of movie productions all about the world. Jim was a kind of wild scarecrow of a guy, tall and scraggly and, for me at age 23, someplace up the mountain way past the clouds… maybe even sixty. And on one occasion which reduced me to paralytic fear, he indeed proved as agile and adventurous as a mountain goat. He also had lived the most romantic adventure of the many fearless adventurers I've been privileged to know. When he was a kid, probably about what I was when I knew him, he'd ventured into the world as a hand on a passenger freighter to the Orient. I understand that that word is now anachronistic and possibly even offensive to Asians, but it's the word that defined the exotic call of The East when I did my first yearnings and it certainly was the Orient when Jim first sought it out. Because of his charm and flair, he had been promoted to dining staff by the time they hit the China coast, paying a little more but, in his mind, lacking the vigor of shoveling coal and jack-of-all-trading about the boat. So when the ship arrived in Vladivostok in the newly scrabbled Soviet Union, this was about 1920, Jim had had it, and he wanted off.

The one thing he didn't have, however, was a passport. He did have a photo of himself that a passenger had taken of him in Shanghai (I smelled shipboard romance there,) and it wasn't hard for him to steal a menu. The ship's menu was leather, floridly embossed to the point of appearing official. He pasted his photo on the first page, wrote his vital statistics beneath and found a shipmate whose boot heel had a star on it. He imprinted that over his photo and then jumped ship. Confidently armed with his menu, he set off on an ad hoc crossing of the violent, chaotic, nascent Union of Soviet Socialist Republics. Think "Doctor Zhivago" during Omar Sharif's and Geraldine Chaplin's frantic escape east across the Urals. He learned Russian in the six month trek, supported himself God knows how, spent some time on an early farm commune which adopted him as resident sage. He had been hoofing it over farmland in western Siberia when he came upon a group of peasants beating an early tractor with sticks. It was the first farming innovation in the area since the advent of the metal plow. They were furious because this damned metal mule was too lazy to work. Jim found a gallon bottle of kerosene in a wagon, poured it in, and the mule leapt back to work. I can't even imagine the range of audacious adventures that trip afforded, but I have held Jim Swarbrick in awed and affectionate memory all of my life. I play scenes in my mind of weapons-bedecked commissars giving Jim's menu a thorough study, finally being seduced by the fancy calligraphy of the listings of pate de fois gras and benets de banana aux caramel and, most decidedly, by the confident smile of the bearer who knew that his rash self-belief would get him anywhere. Oh that Jim had put down his cameras for one year to write his tale.

But this fearlessness made heavy demand on my sense of self-preservation which was pretty tight-ass at that time. I'd spent the first 22 years of my life with my mom's having breakfast on the table every morning. What was I doing wandering the world, falling into the tender clutches of magnificent madmen like Jim Swarbrick? One of the key newspaper breaks at that time for any film being shot on exotic location was the assignment of a Sunday location story in the New York Times. It was usually adorned with a half page panoramic shot that sometimes decorated the top half of the first page of the Arts & Leisure section, the reading of which was part of the Sunday morning ritual of everyone who mattered in the entertainment business. We were shooting one sequence at a moated castle in the French countryside, a town called St. Germain en Laye, famous for the eponymous castle and cathedral which stood across a road from each other . The cathedral steeples thrust probably seven or eight stories high with steep-sloping slate tile roofs. It defied the imagination how any of this was accomplished five or six centuries before, what madness could have impelled any worker out onto that high, steep slope to install those slippery stone shingles. I was about to find out.

I got the assignment for the New York Times location story, but it was predicated on getting a great shot encompassing the magnificence of the geography and the film unit sprawled upon it. I'd done a good job of impressing the importance of this shot on Jim and Julie... too good.

When it came time to capture the shot I'd described, Jim elected to shoot the moated St. Germain en Laye Castle and the surrounding town and countryside from the slanted slate roofs of the cathedral. I thought it was too dangerous for Julie to do the backup shot. So did Jim. He handed me a camera, to hold for him I supposed, and then climbed out on one 45 degree sloped roof and then commanded me to do so on the other. I called out that I couldn't do it, that I had a fear of heights. He yelled back, "good, this will get rid of it... one way or the other." The photo he took of me doing it was one of the things I most mourned when we burned down. One positive thing about losing everything is that it gives you an accurate measurement of your attachments

Like Father, Like Son

Sifting through your past, you come upon surprises. In the process, I've been amazed by how much weight certain people or events had in my life. Exhibit A... Kirk Douglas has turned out to be a much more important and anecdote-rich person for me than I'd imagined. It was never a personal closeness, so the experience was always sort of one step removed. But looking back, I find that his integrity made a tremendous impression on me. I was standing with Michael Douglas recently waiting for our cars following a party Selma Hayek had hosted for Penelope Cruz on the road to her Oscar win for "Vicki Christina Barcelona." I was there because of that Oscar campaign. I mentioned to Michael my writing this memoir and that I'd been shocked to realize how pervasively his dad had been one of the stars of my life. "Great," he said, "he's an incredible guy. How do I come out?" "You do ok," I assured him.

Better than ok, actually. It was exciting watching him form and formulate himself while we were representing him during the early days of "The Streets Of San Francisco." He was one of Guttman & Pam's first clients, and I could see in him the same restlessness and intelligence and purpose as that of his dad, even though one had grown up in abject poverty and the other in wealth and opportunity. This was a case where the genetic trumped the experiential. That this culminated in our working for him on two of the most exciting film campaigns of my life, "One Flew Over The Cuckoo's Nest" and "China Syndrome," is reason enough for gratitude, The intoxication of film publicity is that sometimes when it's cooking, you feel you are at the center of the world. Michael afforded me that experience on a number of occasions. He has a sense of daring and never took a step back from a commitment or a performance, no matter how perilous or unprecedented the reach. His performance of an average Joe driven by an impersonal society to perilous dysfunction and disintegration in "Falling Down" was a dangerous chess move, but it captured the frustration and rebellion imposed by a dehumanizing society. It captured the times. His performance of D-Fens does (exploring and defining) for anger what his Oscar-winning creation of Gordon Gekko in in "Wall Street" did for greed. And was that not the greatest prognostication and warning ever accomplished by film, his roar of "Greed is good!"? He pre-saged nothing less than the battle cry of the greedy monsters of the money midway who, with their billion dollar bonuses and ruthless sacking of honest industries and the home-ownership dreams of those building their lives, short-selling not only our economy and our country but their own humanity, letting Bernie Madoff be the effigy of their own debauchery, planting the seeds of foreclosure and unemployment from the profitable security of great brokerage houses and hedge funds and from within the henhouse of the treasury department itself... that branch office of Goldman Sachs. Never has "don't trust authority" had clearer meaning. If anyone ever questions the relative honesty or morality of a press agent, I give you three words... Credit Default Swaps. And let not those bankers and brokers plead ignorance... no one is that stupid. It's in their blood to cast their lot with Gordon Gekko. Stop them before they steal again. All of this Michael and Oliver Stone powerfully predicted in "Wall Street."

You can't say Stone and Douglas didn't warn you. We still stand by and watch real world Gordon Gekkos, the architects of the 2008 crash, write themselves billions of our money in bonuses. Michael and Oliver Stone had told us the shape of things to come. What actor has better served his fellow citizens? In many ways, "Wall Street" may have been the flip side companion piece of his father's daring "Lonely Are The Brave."

Semper Fi

Daring is Scott Glenn's middle name. He is rarely as happy as when at life's peril. His sophisticated acting chops notwithstanding, Scott has ex-Marine written all over him. He lives his life *semper fi*, an intellectual and a spiritual seeker, but a tough guy who always looks like he just came out of boot camp, the steely stare of a drill sergeant and ready grin of the philosopher he actually is. He is an original. Of deep feeling he has plenty and of sub-cutaneous fat he has none. He never met an X sport or martial art he didn't want to conquer. When his role in "Vertical Limit." required decades of training in ice climbing, he accomplished it in months and became addicted to it just as he is addicted to any other sporting exercise that is life-threatening. He can disappear into a character he is playing, and given the kind of desperate characters he so often plays, that can be unnerving.

I have it from an eye witness that when he was portraying the ex-con cowboy antagonist of "Urban Cowboy," some extras, seeing him as a guy who gets things done, came to him and complained that the AD (assistant director) wouldn't let them use the Andy Gump porta-johns just off the set and that they had to walk a half mile to relieve themselves. Scott, who likes to stay in character, was carrying the shotgun that crucially defined his character in the film, the hair-trigger bad-ass Wes Hightower. He asked the AD to accompany him to the forbidden potty to explain why the extras couldn't pee there. The AD opened the door and pointed to the plastic roof that covered it. "See, a roof," the AD said, "extras contractually can only use johns that have no roof. They can't pee here." Scott raised the shotgun and blew the roof off the thing. "Well, now they can," he said.

That said, I've come to see him as a man profoundly of the spirit. When this Irish Catholic and part Cherokee renegade met Carol Shapiro and fell in love with her, he decided to find out what made her special. He studied her religion, found some connections there, and converted to Judaism, and this was long before she committed herself to him. When he got out of the marines, he started doing journalism in a small mid-western town. A better opportunity came up somewhere in the Caribbean, and on his way there he had a few months to explore New York. An actor friend asked Scott if he would rehearse a scene with him, a scene the friend would use as his audition for acceptance to the Actors Studio. Scott did it so ably that the friend asked him to repeat it at the friend's audition. It worked, but not for the friend. Scott was the one to whom Lee Strasberg offered Actors Studio membership.

Since his roles were more often rugged than romantic, one of our challenges in presenting Scott to industry and public was to convey that stylish sex appeal was part of his package. My associate, Rona Menashe, who was account exec on him, solved that by talking the ad agency handling Donna Karan into using him in an extensive ad campaign in key fashion magazines. She sold the masculinity, and the ads sold Scott.

One time after we'd had a publicity meeting on "Vertical Limit" with the Sony publicity department, we were coming out of the Culver City studios that used to be MGM and where I had starred in "Julius Caesar," and I offered to take him to lunch at a terrific Cuban restaurant irrationally named Versailles that was nearby. Fried plantains sounded good to him. Now this was precisely at the time of the furor over Attorney General Janice Reno's intention to repatriate to his father in Cuba the little boy whose mother had perished when she tried to escape Cuba in a raft with her son. The Cuban expatriates were rabidly going to the mat against that. As we started to dip into our beans and rice, I asked Scott, rather solemnly, if he thought I could make it to the door if I stood up and shouted, "Send Elian back!" Scott considered that and then said, "I don't know, but I can tell you this.

As I step over your cold and bloodied body, I'm gonna say 'I don't know who the sonovabitch is. He just sat down at my table and then started to yell.'"

A Key to PR's Past

Arthur Mayer may have assured the quality of post WW II American movie-making and movie-going as much as anyone. He was the distinguished New York exhibitor who launched the art house craze in New York (while Max Laemmle was doing it in LA) by bringing over the cutting edge Italian neo-realist, French *nouvelle vague*, Swedish Bergmanist films, dragging the Brits and Americans in their wake. In 1957, I was walking a street of Elstree Studios outside London on some PR task for Carol Reed's "The Key," and an older gentleman asked if I was American. He was in post-production on a western. They needed some American background voices for a scene of the bad guys a-comin' into town. "It's them... tell the sheriff... hide your womenfolk." Arthur Mayer was pleased that I'd consumed his "From the Long Chase To The Chaise Longue," the only book I've ever read detailing the fabulous and fumbled PR campaigns of times gone by. Gisela was supposed to join me in London as soon as she was twenty-one so we could marry, but illness held her in Germany. Mr. Mayer and his wife filled up my anxious nights with dinners at their home, the Chancellor of the Exchequer one night, the director of the Old Vic the next, joining them for all the top West End plays... but most importantly, the low-down on the early epoch of movie-selling and its carnival hype roots, something no one but he considered historic. As a youth when movies were in diapers, he'd had an eye on movie promotion as it was emerging and probably a hand in it, too. He filled in that gap in my knowledge of film PR's history.

The Incredible Michael Jeter

"Michael Jeter or... as we always called him... the Incredible Michael Jeter," was how Tom Hanks began his comments at the super-sad memorial for that great little actor and gigantic human being. Michael Jeter was so self-effacing and beloved that his "Evening Shade" co-star, Marilu Henner, a decades-long client of Guttman Associates, would ask what we had coming up for him but never what was coming up for her. Michael's agent and the head of Artists & Writers Agency, Joan Scott, had referred Roy Scheider, Henry Winkler (pre the Fonzie craze)and other terrific talents to us, but I had never heard her sound so excited as when she asked me to attend a sneak of "The Fisher King." "Who do you want me to look at?" I asked. "You'll know," she answered, "he stops the show... twice." It took only the first show-stopper, his desk-top delivery of a singing telegram, to confirm that this little hand-grenade of a talent was who she had in mind for us. Robin Williams and Jeff Bridges were terrific, but you left the theatre thinking Michael Jeter.

We actually had touched base with him before when Guttman & Pam did the publicity campaign for the film version of "Hair." He was the draftee at the Selective Service office who stripped along with the others, but wouldn't take off his socks. When two soldiers lifted him off the ground and his socks were pulled off, we discovered his toe nails polished bright red. Michael had show-stopper in his blood.

He certainly stopped the Broadway musical production of "Grand Hotel" every night when he, as the dying accountant out on one last fling, performed a dance beside and over and seemingly through a horizontal bar, making graceful grasshopper leaps that will never be equaled by any Olympic gymnast. Michael stopped the Tony Awards twice, once in the special performance of that dance and again when he won the award and recounted how he had come to New York at a time of such violent homophobia that he would be chased down into alleys by "real guys" and beaten into unconsciousness. It had not been much better in his against-the-grain growing up in small town Tennessee, but New York put a special spin on it. In spite of that or possibly because of it, he had gutted it out, and now he had just been handed a Tony... as he was later handed an Emmy and other honors and would win above all the hearts of millions of Americans and every person with whom he ever worked. His favorite role, of course, was Mr. Noodles on "Sesame Street" which brought joy and him to the tiny but all-encompassing hearts of millions and millions of children.

When a performer has show-stopped his way into the admiring awareness of industry decision makers, one of the most promotional techniques is simply to get him out to meet with them. These people formulate impressions, but they often do not act upon them until they make some direct contact. One of the best places for this is awards dinners. A lot of my clients have scored roles sitting, at our contrivance, next to the right person on the dais of a top awards ceremony. For such word-masters as Jimmy Woods and Richard Harris, making a presentation was a great showcase for their wit. For Jimmy, it was a key role in Clint Eastwood's "True Crime." Clint knew what a fine actor Jimmy is, but it was during an awards presentation that Clint realized Woods has the James Cagney rat-a-tat-tat eighty miles an hour word delivery he needed for that role. For Richard it was the Irish wit trucked out for a presentation to the recently knighted Anthony Hopkins... "and, Tony, how did a good Welshman feel kneeling at the foot of the English monarch?" A couple of offers followed that one.

I had Rip Torn present a special WGA (Writers Guild Of America) award to the universally respected producer Saul Zaentz. Rip had starred in Saul's (and director Daryl Duke's) first feature film, "Pay Day." After Rip's touching and awed introduction, Saul first gave a speech about how after first watching Rip's performance in the rushes, he realized the magic great actors would bring to his films and how that discovery lured him into a career which would include Oscar winners like "One Flew Over The Cuckoo' Nest." It kicked off a run of terrific roles for Rip.

Those lunches or dinners are full of introductions that stick. Carl Reiner, who awes us all, politely joined me and my diminutive friend Michael Jeter in the cocktail moment of the Writers Guild awards and then suddenly, jaw literally dropping, Carl realized who it was and said, "Oh, my God... Michael Jeter. You are the greatest dancer I've ever seen. 'Grand Hotel!' I checked afterwards to see if you were wired for levitation, and they said no. I thought they were lying." You can imagine Michael's epiphany in the glow of Carl's adulation. Michael was a great performer in part because of a childhood and a youth of pain and otherness. And now life was making it up to him. Good roles followed almost all of his award ceremony outings. His happiness had a way of making others happy, too. And then there was a great and deep unhappiness when they stopped the merry-go-round to let off the incredible Michael Jeter long before the ride might ever have been over.

The Courage of Their Convictions

There was a dark period at the start of HIV/AIDS awareness when even the most casual association with the disease took on a black list tinge in the entertainment business. Nonetheless, Michael spent all of his available time working with HIV/AIDS sufferers and helping in his own way the crusade Elizabeth Taylor was leading to break down the resistances to addressing it even within our fairly conscious industry. Her damn-the-torpedoes determination made the industry and the world acknowledge and address the affliction without social stigma, and Army Archerd's compassionate revelation of Rock Hudson's courageous confrontation with the illness further compelled it to our awareness. There was that moment just before Dame Elizabeth let in the light when just acknowledging the disease was like a contagion in itself. And that did not dissuade Michael Jeter from dedicating his life to assisting those who were afflicted and speaking up about his activities. Eventually, he became one of its casualties, but even that never diminished his talent or even his extraordinary athletic and artistic capabilities. I still wonder at the physical invention he brought to his role as the strange little stable owner in Kevin Costner's "Open Range," swinging through his domain of haylofts and stalls like Charles Laughton among the gargoyles and parapets in "The Hunchback Of Notre Dame." Even including the physical wonders of Douglas Fairbanks, Lon Chaney and such comedic geniuses as Keaton, Chaplin and Harold Lloyd, few actors ever displayed the physical grace and acrobatic athleticism in a film than those two great individualists, Laughton and Jeter, brought to those roles… Publicizing him, I never had to promote anything short of greatness.

I came to know the character called Radioman whom Robin Williams played in "Fisher King." His gambit was knowing where celebs would be in New York and following them about madly on his bicycle, usually arriving where they were going before they did. He is charming, always smiling and most affectionately regarded by the people he pursues. One of Radioman's favorites was Pierce Brosnan. Wherever Pierce went during hectic promotional raids on New York New York, Radioman was there. During the cluttered rush of New York PR for the Bond film which teamed Pierce with Halle Berry, the two stars were being welcomed to the city in a crowd-drawing ceremony in Times Square at which each was presented an extremely expensive Omega watch. As we got back into the limo, Radioman was suddenly there with his patented grin and happy greeting. "What 'd they give you, Pierce, a watch?" he said, happy for anyone else' happiness. Pierce took it off his wrist and handed it to him. "I was just keeping it warm for you, Radioman," Pierce said, and it was the only time I ever saw Radioman go wordless.

Unless you live in the southern, rural or small town parts of the USA, it's possible you have never heard of Earl Owensby… even though we did a pretty good job on him and had him featured in Esquire Magazine and had a "60 Minutes" piece on him in which he was profiled by no less than Morley Safer, who responded to him affectionately as an audacious and highly original self-made man of uncompromising convictions. Earl grew up as an orphan in the pretty-much-off-the-main-highway town of Selby, North Carolina. (As I wrote that, I wasn't completely sure of the name of the town and I made a note to call my Arkansas traveler buddy, Wally Beene, about it since Wally had done several unit publicity jobs for me and Earl there. And then I realized that Wally is gone. Some people just don't extract easily from the heart.) Earl fought for his country for several years and then returned to the town where he had toughed out his childhood and youth and started to sell on the road for a machine tools company there. In fairly short order, he owned the company and then very quickly became a multi-multi-millionaire. At that point, he invested in his first love… movies… building his own studio there and making and starring in action films well-grounded in the rural mentality and morality he knew so well. I, like you, had never heard of him until he showed up in my office one day seeking publicity. He was in LA for the film market where film-buyers from all over the world come to see what is available, Earl's films sold quite well overseas, although in the US they primarily played what was dismissively and quite ignorantly called "the redneck circuit." Earl's films and Earl were quite popular across the sunbelt and in places like the Illinois plains and California's central valley. Farm areas, small town areas. Earl was of and by the people. His fans included that greatest of all the country-rock singers, Elvis' acknowledged hero and inspiration, Roy Orbison. Orbison did the singing for Earl when Earl portrayed an Elvis-like character in the years of drug-afflicted decline in an Owensby flick called "Lady Grey." Orbison was a significant "other" whose convictions fired wide southern interest in Earl and his films.

Earl was and is in the best sense of the word, a character. In building his studio, he recreated his challenged youth, preserving the town by buying up the newspaper for which he had delivered and the movie house where he ushered and preserving them and each piece of his childhood by reconstructing them on his back lot. Pretty soon he came, quite literally, to own the town which had kicked him around pretty much as a kid on his own. Earl did not think small. When the south's top energy producer, Duke, gave up on the atomic plant they were constructing in South Carolina, just south of the border and not far from Earl's reconstructed Selby, Earl bought it. He'd heard that James Cameron was looking for a massive indoor water tank in which to shoot "The Abyss," and Earl showed him how he could convert the energy plant into that, and then the water and Cameron's huge Hollywood crew poured in.

"60 Minutes" did its piece on Earl for us when the first Hollywood film, a Burt Reynolds starrer, began to shoot there. Morley Safer, aware that Earl's sense of the appropriate differed dramatically from Hollywood's, asked Earl what would happen if there was any hippie behavior. "There won't be," Earl promised. "If they stick anything up their nose, it damn well better be their finger." I loved his adventurous southern drawl. St. Louis was south, but it wasn't really South. When I grew up there, It was poly-phonic, and the accents were German and some French and Jewish and various shades of black and south since the Depression had driven people of all creeds and colors up from the jobless Dixie. Since I sometimes bagged groceries for my mother's sister Blanche in her East St. Louis store where the clientele was exclusively poor white Appalachian and Ozark, I knew and enjoyed southern accents from hillbilly to plantation, and Earl had a special way with the tongue. We went to lunch once at the Red Lobster across from my office, and a family of fairly corpulent people sat at a nearby table. When one of the women began to choke on something, they just stared at her in horror, so I went over and performed a Heimlich and out it popped. Later when they left, Earl observed, "They certainly must of not valued her very much." "Why would you say that?" I asked. "a cause they never thunk ya."

There was another lunch, the day the Iranians took over the American embassy. The crisis must have made people hungry, because we couldn't find anything but waiting lists at any restaurant. I told Earl that I knew a place we could get in, and we walked about six blocks down Wilshire Boulevard to where a Persian bazaar and restaurant had just opened. Talk about timing. There were plenty of tables available… like ALL of them… but I puttered first through a pile of handsome Persian rugs which is one of Gisela's many areas of expertise and addiction. There was an unsual green one, beautifully knotted and perfect for her bedroom. I asked the price, and the dark-skinned salesman said, "Thirteen hundred dollars." "You have a deal," I said, starting to write a check. Earl grabbed my arm and said, "They just took over our Embassy. You gotta bargain him." "Earl, this IS a bargain," I said, handing the man the check. He looked at it and turned something approximating a shade of red. "No," he shouted, "thirteen HUNDRED!" Earl looked at the check and growled, "you said thirteen hundred, an' that's what he wrote

ya." "No," the man insisted, near tears, "thirteen HUNDRED! One more zero!"
"Thirteen hundred ain't got but two zeros," Earl snapped, "an' this rug's his." And
he started to roll it up. And there was a tug of war as the salesman started to pull
at it. I told Earl to forget it. "A deal's a deal an' you made an' concluded a deal,"
he insisted. "I'm not going to have him running after us down Wilshire screaming
'stop thief.'" I said, "I'll buy you some shishkabob." And we had a pleasant and
very solitary lunch, but Earl did make a fake pass toward the rug on the way out
just to give the guy an adrenaline rush. Take over our goddam embassy, will ya?!

Creating Your Own Niche

I find James Lipton, he of the penetrating gaze and penetrating questions on
his "Inside The Actors Studio" series, a fascinating figure... He is one of an elite
group (Bill Shatner springs to mind) who create their own marketable niche,
which translates into hallmark TV figures who can play themselves,, usually
self-mockingly... in TV ads. Jim found, polished and harnessed a distinctive personality, halfway between Noel Coward, George Sanders' disdainful superiority as
theatre critic Addison DeWitt in "All About Eve" and Monty Wooley's imperious
character of Sheridan Whiteside in "The Man Who Came To Dinner," modifying
their haughty attitudes to embrace and respect the originality and the talents of
the people he interviews. We have come to friendship in the course of the many
top-star client guestings I have arranged for his show, often talents I can't get to
do other TV appearances.

Gene Hackman did Inside The Actors Studio with Jim Lipton at my behest,
and then an illness prevented me from being with him in New York for the
taping. Lipton sent me a rough cut of the show, and I took exception to a question he'd asked Gene about some silly circumstance when Gene was a sixteen
year old marine (he'd lied about his age) in Korea. Jim likes to surprise guests
with arcane details of their life which he has discovered. I called him and told
him that I'd arranged for him to do one of the greatest actor/stars of our time,
and then he'd wasted 25 seconds with some meaningless gotcha question. "It's
already gone," he replied.

I'd proven my loyalty to him on the occasion of my setting Jay Leno to do
Inside The Actor's Studio with him. Jim said he wanted to kick it off with a
brief monologue of his own, and Jay and I both said fine. Jim's idea of brief
was eleven minutes, and he was sucking air by minute two. I had to break it to
him gently, so I told him I was going to do him the greatest favor anybody ever

would ever render. "What?" he replied, "I should cut it to six?" He didn't have any trouble filling in the nine minutes we cut out. Jay had given him an hour and a half of gems."

Jim made it clear to me that the booking of Barbra Streisand on the show was a culmination of his dearest ambitions and dreams. She was magnificently giving, extending by her own choice for an extra half hour her Q&A conversation with the audience of Actors Studio students. It was no surprise to us, since she has often described herself as "an actor who sings." Even Jim, with his profound appreciations of her, was unprepared for the uncompromising truth she brings to a conversation.

Pierce Brosnan made his singing debut during his trip to Inside The Actors Studio, the future "Mama Mia" star performing a number he rendered portraying a part-time pub singer in his company's little Irish film, "Evelyn." You usually have to find some coincident event to retain the specific dates of such promotions, but in that case it wasn't hard. Lipton and Pierce recorded that at the New School in Lower Manhattan on Sepember 10, 2002. It was the night before the first anniversary of 9/11. Following the taping we'd gone for a late dinner in Greenwich Village., We could have headed north for our hotel, but it was now, I announced, after midnight... It was September 11th. It seemed sacrilegious to head down to Ground Zero in the limousines we had for the evening. But it was only a few miles to the south, and how could someone not pay respects, not observe the occasion with remembrance. There were tens of thousands of people milling about in the late night, staring into the emptiness of the hole which had been our greatest national shock and loss, milling with constant flow of people among the folk art tributes piled along the fences, each demanding its toll of tears. And yet there was a strange, strange silence, an absolute people silence, with occasional distant sound of a taxi horn or a far-off siren, a far-off and then growing and then diminishment of sound. It seemed like the city was silently awake. And so I remained when we got back to the hotel. I had an early flight back to LA and was uneasy about flying on the first anniversary of 9/11, but I had Jimmy Woods guesting along with John McCain on The Tonight Show with Jay Leno" that anniversary night. I stayed up to write a letter to my family in case something happened, and the concierge mailed it.

By five AM I was walking the streets, trying to absorb the somber importance of that day in that city. But New York was still resolutely New York. Shortly after six thirty AM I saw that the doors of a deli were open, so I went inside and found everyone busily getting up to speed for the day. I asked a guy at the counter if I could get a cup of coffee. "Later," he said brusquely. "What time?" "Later." "Ok, but when later? A quarter to later? Half past later?" "Later." New Yorkers stick to their guns.

There were more security officers than passengers at the airport. I was the only one I saw who looked vaguely Middle Eastern. By the time we crossed over the Mississippi, we thought the fear would bid us adieu. But the ominous sense of how our nation's life had changed still hung heavy. Fear is hard ignore and hard to scare off. All the way to touch down, every one going to the bathroom studied each fellow passenger with suspicion.

Chapter 20

Sex Sells

This story has to do with intercourse and the absence thereof. The primary rule of practically anything is "a problem is a solution in disguise," right? Well that maxim came into sharp focus in how we resolved a little disturbance following the filming of a Joseph E. Levine production called "Tattoo." To have had actual coitus or not to have had it, that was the question. The film told the tale of a tattoo artist who kidnaps a beautiful woman for the purpose of tattooing her from top to bottom. The screenwriter, Luis Bunuel's daughter Joyce, utilized tattoo as a symbol of rape.

In an interview in Playboy Magazine. Bruce Dern, who portrayed the tattooist, was quoted as saying that the sex scenes had been realistic to the point of actual consummation... that he and his co-star, our client Maude Adams, had actually engaged in coitus before the cameras. Maude denied there was any element of truth to that and was understandably annoyed. It reminded me of the apocryphal story (which I, to the shallow depths of my soul, believe is true) of the voluptuous glamour actress Diana Dors who was besieged for the nth time by a diminutive actor professing that he *had* to have sex with her. To which she gloriously responded, "if you DO... and if I find OUT!..." Maude very much wanted to set straight the record that no such thing had occurred. They had, she told me, acted the scenes but definitely not acted them out. Two good actors don't have to actually have sex in order for the illusion to be drawn on the screen. It suffices that it is drawn in your mind.

As noted elsewhere in these pages but pertinent here, Sylvia ("Emmanuelle") Kristel, whom Guttman & Pam also represented, explained in an interview I'd set with Vernon Scott of United Press International (whose questions, on or off the record, were frequently sexual, a context never far from his really interesting mind) that she'd never seen an actor able to deliver an erection while nude on a set of a theatrical film in front of dozens of crew members.

The larger problem with "Tattoo" was that it didn't even have a distributor. It might never come before an audience so that people would be able to judge for themselves. A failed-to-release stigma would be an insulting and diminishing situation for both stars. Dern had ascended to major stardom in such films as "The King Of Marvin Gardens," "Support Your Local Sheriff," "The Cowboys," "They Shoot Horses, Don't They?," "The Great Gatsby "and especially in his Oscar nominated role in "Coming Home." Maude had, in only a few years, ignited a hot career in which she already had debuted as the lead Bond Girl with Roger Moore in "The Man With The Golden Gun," starred with James Caan in "Rollerball" and teamed with Vanessa Redgrave and Jane Alexander in the Holocaust-based television drama, "Playing For Time," speaking the words of a script by Arthur Miller. I give these brief filmographies for a reason. Careers feed on talent most definitely, but they are even more driven by heat. The extraordinary run of major films and honors which Bruce Dern was swinging when Joseph E. Levine drew him and Maude to "Tattoo" in 1980... and the stardom-building sequence of important projects which Maude had achieved, not to mention her amazing beauty... made the next film a key to continuity for each of them.

And making a film of this visibility for a top producer and then having it fail to get distribution would be a stumble for two important young actors. Maybe Mr. Dern was trying to drum up interest in the film when he made those comments. IF he made those comments. but I never read any disclaimer on his part. Either way, his assertedly true confessions were getting wide enough attention to embarrass Maude, alter perception of her or even possibly hurt her career,

Simulated intercourse scenes such as that contained in "Tattoo" were relatively new to major films then. Films were no longer simply cutting-away-to-the-roaring-fireplace or to the storm-lashing-the-window shots as they once did. But the explicit essentials of it were still left to the imagination. The actual act was.... and still, largely, is.... relegated to porn or to those show-all private moments that sometimes make it to Facebook and You Tube. Even a film about porn, "Boogie Nights," got down to the nitty but not quite the gritty of it. While the rumor that two hot stars like Maude and Bruce had been factually intimate in front of the "Tattoo" cameras would not necessarily be a career-stopper for a male star, it might take some of the serious actress shine off of a lady's career. Besides which, Maude didn't like that assault on her character, her professional integrity and her reputation. She wanted to answer the charges and to answer them furiously.

Which brings us back to A PROBLEM IS A SOLUTION IN DISGUISE. There was no question that I could drum up exposure for her on talk shows and in print interviews responding in anger and outrage to Bruce Dern's reported tales. But I remembered Kirk Douglas' dictum that a feud works only when you control both parties, and that definitely wasn't the case here. I told Maude that she should be very visble disputing the charge, yes, but not furiously so . Rather she should do it with humor. I wrote out a playbook of phrases like, "If Bruce Dern thinks that what we were doing in front of the cameras for 'Tattoo' was fornication, my condolences to his wife." Another was "There was no visual evidence that Bruce was prepared to do what he says he did" or "If Bruce actually brought the goods to the set, it's news to me. It was a tight shot, and I probably would have known." If she had answered angrily, then that would be the only thing discussed around the coffee machine the next day... her anger, her furor. And angry denial very often is taken as proof of the charge... the old "methinks the lady doth protest too much." A funny line, however, shows that the charge is so ridiculous that you have risen above it. Yes, you can laugh an allegation to death.

None of it was Neil Simon, but the alleged coital claim and its rebuttal were getting pickup, wide pickup because it was about the ever-popular subject of sex. I assumed that Mr. Levine, with whom I had worked sporadically when Carroll Baker was starring in "The Carpetbaggers" and "Harlow," wasn't enjoying the jokes, because some of the stories pointed out that the film had not yet been picked up by a distributor. No one, not actors, not producer, wants to have a film left waiting at the altar. So I was somewhat leery one morning when Joseph E. Levine was on the phone. "Mr. Guttman," he said, "do you represent Maude Adams?" "Yes, but..." "And are you the one who's been planting all this stuff about her and Bruce Dern not having sex?" "Yes, but. I... uh." "Well, I want you to know that because of all this crap you've put out there... (I waited, I tensed)... 20th Century Fox has picked 'Tattoo' up for distribution... and I want to hire you to handle the publicity."

And so the film did get distributed. At that time, a motion picture which didn't make the distribution cut didn't go DTV... direct to video... as it would now. It would just disappear and would become a whatever-happened-to embarrassment for the stars. So they were spared that, however little review praise "Tattoo" received. Dern went on to star in dozens of films including his recent Oscar nominate work in "Nebraska." Maude shortly thereafter became the first, possibly the only, actress to be the Bond Girl star of two 007 movies, playing distinctly different characters in each. The new one was the title role in "Octopussy" which had her sprawled across the ad pages and billboards of the world in one of the sexiest advertising images to grace a major film's marketlng. Two other comparable such splashes, in my mind, were Jane Russell's invitational sucking the straw while lying in the haystack for Howard Hughes' "The Outlaw" and Carroll Baker thumb-suckingly tucked in the crib or whatever it was for Elia Kazan's "Baby Doll." The three common denominators of each being a gloriously beautiful woman, direct and provocative eye contact, and our criminally excitable imaginations.

Because of Rogers & Cowan's vast and varied client list, I was a part of some of the most memorable what-it-boils-down-to-is-sex campaigns of the 60s. Two of the most memorable and dominant were Raquel Welch and Carroll Baker, two women and two careers and two sexualities which could not have been more diverse. Almost a decade before, Carroll's image in that short nightie in the "Baby Doll" ads, curled up in an oval basket thumb in mouth, had conveyed a vulnerable innocence that matched the controversial impact of the Jane Russell shot or Raquel's wide-stance pose in an animal pelt mini from "One Million, B.C., a poster I was told hung over the beds of half the nine year old boys in America. Carroll's pose was the injection of corruptible innocence into the equation which raised the stakes . Elia Kazan, the director who perhaps most powerfully introduced Actor's Studio/Method mentality in American films, had discovered Carroll among Lee Strassberg's Method disciples. He understood that Carroll's sexuality emanated from how she became the character. I was in Paris when "Baby Doll" arrived there, and the ubiquity of that provocative image of Carroll's thumb-sucking Baby Doll barely clothed in the skimpy short nightgown (which became known as "baby dolls.") was stopping traffic. Jaded Paris seemed caught up in this audacity which had so scandalized America, denounced from pulpit and the political bully pulpit.

The cinematic sexual revolution of the 60s may have started in1958 with Louis Malle's second film, "The Lovers." It had set the bar for how explicit a sexual scene could be in a film, with Jeanne Moreau's key encounter in her character's chain of affairs seeming to go on for nearly a reel, exhausting both her and the audience. The operative word there is "seeming," since it was not real hanky panky but rather the thing movies do best, illusion. It was largely inference. as when her lover's head slips down from the shot while the camera remains on her beautiful face to register her response to whatever is going on. It actually was quite reminiscent of one scene with the teen-aged Hedy Lamarr in the Czech film "Ecstasy" a quarter century before in which the camera focused on that extraordinary face and the audience read steamy worlds into the nuances of her nearly impassive response. A flicker of eyebrow made strong men sweat.

When Carroll Baker, in the heat of her early career stardom in such films as Kazan's "Baby Doll," George Stevens' "Giant," William Wyler's "The Big Country" and John Ford's "How The West Was Run"… and who has ever had a better run of classic directors and classic films to start a career?… came back from doing a film in Europe, I believe the year was 1962, I set an interview for her with Don Alpert who wrote many of the most important Sunday entertainment stories in the Los Angeles Times. This was during a period when sex was still all inference in American films, but Carroll during the interview at the Beverly Hills Hotel Polo Lounge, as polite a setting as one might wish, said that the powerful expression of love (meaning sex) scenes was becoming so common a factor in New Wave film-making in France that she thought that within a decade leading American stars would be simulating (acting, not acting out) actual sex scenes in major studio films. Alpert was a sophisticated journalist, but that assertion made him say rather incredulously, "Say that again?" However, he printed it verbatim, and it brought Carroll Baker a lot of outrage and suggestions that her sanity was lost luggage. Of course, in half her predicted time, such scenes became de rigueur for American stars in American films. The telling parody (and parody is celebration) of it was Meg Ryan's simulated protracted orgasms in the restaurant scene in Rob Reiner's "When Harry Met Sally."

They DO Shoot The Messenger, or at least they try to. Carroll was derided because she saw something clearly before everyone else did. It evoked that last gasp of Hollywood's feigned morality. People were or pretended to be shocked. But while Carroll took heat on one hand, on the other she *gained* heat. Shortly after her bold pronouncement, Paramount and producer Joseph E. Levine selected her to take the most sexual star role in the motion picture adapted from Harold Robbins' controversial novel, "The Carpetbaggers," and Robbins was the catchword for sexual frankness in American novels at that moment. "The Carpetbaggers" was being directed by another major filmmaker, Edward Dmytryk. The role of the frankly sexual Rina, Robbins' hottest heroine, cast Carroll in a new light, a specific kind of celebrity she had never before enjoyed. Seductress.

In that spectacular run of films which preceded it, the only one that was blatantly sexual was... "Baby Doll." And that was erotic rather than sexual. It wasn't about sex. It was about lust. However inter-related they are on occasion, sex and lust are two different things. The other three cast her as a willful girl-woman ("Giant," "The Big Country") or a strong and resilient pioneer woman, as Ford presented her in his portion of the multi-director "How The West Was Won." The controversy stirred by her comment in the LA Times seemed to have been a contributing factor in her consideration for "The Carpetbaggers." She was sexy, she was controversial, she was Rina. With the tireless effort and cooperation of the Paramount publicity team under the able Bob Goodfried, we turned up heat on Carroll's new sexual symbolism and we were able to attach a powerful "new sex goddess" identification to this beautiful woman and understated Method actress.

"The Carpetbaggers" lifted it all off the ground. A production shot of her sitting nude at a make-up table did the trick. Except that there was really no specific nudity. Her beautiful back of course and only a modicum of the upper -cleavage of her shapely derriere, nothing that isn't expected of any self-respecting plumber. Carroll and I each approved it, because the nudity was illusory. It became a shared national sexual experience, the biggest superstar nude photos since the Milton Green shots of Monroe... except that nothing was showing. It appeared on both the Time Magazine People page and the Newsweek Newsmakers page... safe sex, an unrevelatory nude. It's not like we (the studio, Carroll and Jack, I) didn't exploit it. When "The Carpetbaggers" was ready to premiere, Carroll was at full sex symbol status. We agreed that she would attend the premiere in a gown that, when backlighted, became very see-through. And backlight it we did, advising the paparazzi at the premiere to flash only her face (which we had lighted separately) if they wanted photos that would really sell. The coverage was vast and sexy.

Carroll Baker had been, from the very beginning, an actress to whom great directors were drawn. And the sudden "Carpetbaggers" aura of sexuality didn't change that. One of the immediate career events after "Carpetbaggers" was John Ford's casting her again, this time in "Cheyenne Autumn." Gisela and I met Mr. Ford only once, at a party Carroll and her husband Jack Garfein threw for him at the end of production on "Cheyenne Autumn." We hovered near him, our one chance to savor the authority of the greatest of American directors. As the man they called Papa sat there in his great eminence, patch over his eye, he beamed when he talked to us about Carroll. His endorsement established that the sexy exploitations of "Carpetbaggers" (and "Harlow" thereafter) did not strip from her the well-earned thespian bona fides. Carroll and Jack had met in their years with the Actors Studio, and they had a delicate balancing act integrating its values with those imposed by her sudden sex bomb fame. Shuffled into this, Jack directed her in a dangerously independent film called "Something Wild," a failure in its release and only now after 45 years coming into cult adulation among festivals, film schools and cineastes.

It was after the second Ford film and "Harlow" and "Sylvia" (another fine acting demonstration seen by few) that Carroll and Jack took their riverboat gambling instincts one step too far, taking on Paramount and Joe Levine. Carroll and Jack were fearless fighters. When Mr. Blackwell placed her on his worst dressed list, the Garfeins called their friend Christian Dior, and Dior issued a dismissive attack on the worst-dressed list compiler and his unmerited listing of Carroll. "What is this Blackwell?" Dior complained, "I've heard of an inkwell but never a blackwell." Carroll was no stranger to daring, having fought her way to stardom from a childhood of backwoods coal country poverty, entering show biz in bottom-of-the-barrel variety shows touring small towns in broken-down busses. "Sylvia" provides one window into this... To understand the mentality required for a woman's survival in prison, she arranged to be incarcerated in a tough women's prison for over a week, deglamorized, just another dame serving time, no one including the guards knowing who she was or that she wasn't a permanent guest. Sure, seven days is not seven years, but it was a brave learning experience of what desperation is. Even her challenging background as a kid hadn't prepared her. "That's why," she pointed out to me, "they call them 'desperados,' without hope, nothing left to lose."

In a still deeper context of desperation, Jack Garfein knew its terror during the long horror of his childhood in concentration camps, the lone survivor of his family. At one point, after he felt all were gone, a cousin suddenly was thrown into the camp, joining Jack in the forced labor in coal mines and the brutal nights in the camp. When the treatment softened slightly and they even once were granted a cup of chocolate, the word went around that they would be exchanged for German POWs. And one morning the 994 emaciated figures were lined up in front of the camp commandant who was outraged to learn that their number was now 997 because three new forlorn Jews had been added that morning. The commandant's order said 994, and that's what he would deliver. He demanded three volunteers. Two men raised their hands. Jack and his cousin exchanged a look, and then Jack, for no reason he could understand, raised his hand. His cousin began to cry. Jack and the other two were returned to the empty space of stacked board beds to wonder what they had invited, while the other 994 were marched to the gas chambers and the crematoria.

Can you doubt that fate had intended the partnership of these two survivors? And so it delivered Carroll and Jack to the Actors Studio where they met and fell in love. Two truly valuable people and artists. To evaluate this next part, you have to bear in mind that this was the 1960s and that movie stars did not get $20 million a movie. They didn't get $1 million a movie. To demonstrate how hot their clients were, press agents would use the catch-all phrase that the pay was "six figures," and sometimes, but not very often or accurately, "a high six figures salary." On one occasion when Frank Sinatra made a spectacular (for then) deal for his Vegas appearances, we proudly and widely announced that he was getting $100,000 a week... not a night, a week. The success of "The Carpetbaggers" put Carroll in the catbird seat, and Paramount made a generous... for that time... multiple picture deal for her. And the deal even designated at least one of the projects and its start-date. That last aspect or at least the interpretation of that part of the contract became a litigation between Paramount and Carroll. The project was to be the film version of Henry Miller's "The Tropic Of Cancer," one of the 20th century's most respected and revered novels of sexuality. It was a big deal, and Levine brought to its adaptation John Michael Hayes, who had scripted "Carpetbaggers." But Harold Robbins is not Henry Miller. Trying to honor the complexity of actual literature, the screenplay was moving forward haltingly.

Jack Garfein had set aside his own directing for years to manage the great opportunity of his wife's burgeoning career. They had also set aside the contractually-designated period of time for the filming of "The Tropic Of Cancer." They were vacationing in the South Of France waiting for the start of the film.

There was only one problem…. there wasn't any script. Gisela and I and the kids were in Italy while I overlooked Rogers & Cowans' Rome office en route to her parents in the Black Forest. I called Carroll and Jack to see how they were, and the information they supplied really shocked me.

They were very unhappy to feel jerked around by Paramount and they were planning to send a cable saying that Carroll demanded that filming begin on "Tropic of Cancer" on the specified date. I begged them, implored them not to do it. The desperations of their respective childhoods had taught each that you get what is yours only if you demand it. A contract is one thing, but reality is something else, and reality always wins that tug-of-war. Upon whatever legal advice or assumption, they felt that the cable would move things up. I applied the simple logic of Think-It-Through and saw only disaster. That cable not only would pass through various studio hands and be the subject of outrage and strategy with lawyers. It would leak out. Something that hot always leaks out. Jack thought that would up the pressure and expedite the filming. I saw only that it would embarrass the studio and Levine throughout the town. I made it very clear to both Carroll and Jack that the execs of other studios would take shadenfreude delight in Paramount's distress, but it was also clear that none of them would wish to be "next." They all would know Paramount was guilty of nothing other than not having delivered the script as speedily as had been envisioned. It happens to everyone.

Their cable of demand to Paramount crossed the Atlantic, and my fears were realized. A hot career ground to a halt, or at least ground to a paralyzing wait-and-see. Offers dried up, and Carroll and Jack were caught up in a law suit instead of a film. Their lawyers thought they had good legal ground, even when the studio sent Carroll not only an offer for the next film under her contract, but a directive for her to show up for work on the following Monday, or some other such specificity. It conveyed that she was to begin filming the title role in "The Billy Holiday Story." We all know that Billy Holiday… Lady Day… was a great blues singer… and that she was black, an African American as one would say today. It was no secret that Carroll Baker was blonde… in fact, she was, as had been Jean Harlowe whom she portrayed, the prevailing blonde bombshell. Paramount, apparently thought that this date with the absurd, would bring Carroll and Jack to a point of compromise. Henry Rogers joined me for a meeting about the matter with the Garfeins and their lawyer. With all of the cards on the table, Henry revealed his true brilliance when he said to Carroll… "Show up. It says 6:30 AM for make-up? Be there at six." Which she did. And of course there was no film waiting to be shot.

Showing up was the right thing to do, but it was already way past compromise. The case rattled its way to court, with the whole town watching, and devolved into a settlement in which Carroll was paid, as I recall, about $900,000 in lieu of the films remaining on the contract. I'm not sharing any private secrets here. This was all played out in bitter headlines and bitter reality. If it seems like improbable news now, that's because Hollywood memory is vague in the long run and stingingly unforgiving in the short run. These lessons fade as administration succeeds administration and are gone when nobody still has their own private parts in the wringer. But for Carroll and Jack it was a rest-of-your-life outcome. $900,000 was a lot of money for the time. But at what cost? It was still a studio town. She was the hottest actress in town, and nobody called. In the drought of Hollywood movies for her that followed, Carroll bravely and with bright reviews did a national tour of "Little Me" for David Merrick, but it was to Hollywood's active disdain. Carroll was a movie star, and that career was on stall by the shores of the Pacific. There was, I felt, an answer. I arranged for her to attend the Venice Film Festival in some official capacity because I knew that the Italians revered her still as the luminous movie star she was, as a beauty and as a talent, as did the rest of the European film community. They didn't care about Hollywood's little prejudices and revenges or its group sulk. I knew that Europe was still there for her from the press requests which continued to pour in from those nations, many of them drawn to the ordeal she was undergoing. The Venice visit led first to one Italian film and then to others there and all over that enlightened continent...

To demonstrate how silly film industry minds-made-up and prejudices can be, Carroll did not return to another significant Hollywood film for almost two decades, and that was because another brilliant Hollywood director... Peter Bogdanovich in this case... believed in her and in her talent. He cast her as Mariel Hemingway's mom in his "Star 80." The film was very personal to him, and he wanted a great Method actress for the role, so Hollywood's determination to neglect or punish be damned. Much later, Guttman & Pam represented her daughter, Blanche Baker, whose genes glistened in her lovely acting. But talent alone, as we've seen, is no sure path to Hollywood.

Sadly, I earned Carroll's life-long enmity when she and Jack divorced and, at that trial, I testified that Jack had given up or at least completely set aside a very promising directorial career to become his wife's full-time manager. I'd sworn to tell the truth. The truth is sometimes costly

I discovered another aspect of the super-salability of sex when we first handled the resort of Sun Valley and I was researching its past. Its launch was a paradigm of publicity success. In 1936 when Averill Harriman created the fabled go-to place, it was because he wanted to promote destination rail travel. It had given vivacity and glamour to the concept of destination resort. Of course, he owned the railroad which serviced the resort. He brought in that era's top PR genius Steve Hannigan to put a somewhat distant ski resort on the map. And their primary strategy, quite brilliantly, was that the sell would be all sex. Harriman, as one of the richest and most successful men in America, used the magic of his fame and power to lure the movie world's most sexual idols to his new recreational Camelot. But it wasn't the photos of Gary Cooper and Marlene Dietrich looking slim and sexy on the slopes that sold it. He purposely put in an open air steam-warmed hot swimming pool walled-in with glass in order to set up shots of famous and sexy bathing-suited bodies against the background of snow. It was the photo capture of that hot/cold sizzle of sex that really grabbed the minds of the wealthy sporting set by the throats.

How does Hollywood peddle sex in a compelling and yet socially responsible manner? Allusion and illusion. At our best, in the hands of our better angels and our better filmmakers, sex and desire can move a story and an audience without being explicit or exploitative. Part of this tradition is moral obligation and part is financial reality. Of course as public discourse about sex has widened and moral obligation has been redefined, what is permissible and salable has been expanded. Sex in films is always relative to the mood of the times.

We all aware that porn now proliferates, the slimey degradation oozing its way even into our homes and, certainly, into our commerce. It is a big engine of pay-per-view profit. We accept... reluctantly I would hope... that grunt-and-groan degeneracy is one of the highest profit engines on the internet and on some cable channels. We're held to the precept that this evolution is progress, an aspect of freedom of expression. If porn and vulgarity are free speech, and I suppose they have to be for everything else to enjoy that freedom, then we have to use our own informed taste as the filter. The public votes with its bucks, and the good news is that in mainline entertainment, with notable exceptions, it's the aura of sexuality that sells better than the overt portrayal of nudity and its explicit applications. Good examples abound in the film industry's history of the address of love and desire. Look at two of the most treasured scenes of sexuality. First, Rita Hayworth's sizzling sexual tease of Glenn Ford and the movie-going public singing "Put The Blame On Mame" in "Gilda." One remembers it as a kind of striptease, but what did she take off? Her gloves. She did it with such unhurried and confident entice-ment that it embodied everything we hold near and dear about sex. Second, Burt Lancaster and Deborah Kerr on that beach in Hawaii in "From Here To Eternity." Sex doesn't get any better or better celebrated, but that was Fred Zinnemann's tasteful genius. He told me once (on set of "Julia" in Paris) that the passion of the Lancaster/Kerr scene was in the sensuous swirl of the waves around them. It was a kiss, but it was the abstraction of all hungry, urgent sexual need. There you have it, two scenes that would be on anyone's ten best sex scenes list... no anatomy lessons, no need to cover your kids' eyes.

A sign of how values change is the fact that the Columbia PR department thought they had a big problem with "From Here To Eternity" because what was then considered the "overt sexuality" of that key promo photo of the Lancaster/ Kerr embrace was scaring off magazines and newspapers. Columbia press agent Walter Shenson was under pressure to "get it in" somewhere. My former partner Jerry Pam was, in 1952, the entertainment editor of the key Beverly Hills newspaper and, at risk of job, he printed it as a favor to Walter. That small break opened the dam gates and the shot was soon everywhere. When Shenson went on to produce a little movie called 'A Hard Day's Night,' he hired Jerry Pam to PR it.

Nudity is neither a career launcher nor a game-stopper. Nor are nudity and sexuality the same thing. Some time ago, Guttman Associates promoted the DVD release of Hugh Hefner's 1969-70 "Playboy After Dark" TV series, incred-ible time capsules of the best in music and comedy from a significant decade for music and for comedy. But how explicit were Hef's TV reflections of that over-heated moment of the convergence of free speech and free love? The only thing overt were the mini-skirts at the very top of all those long legs. If you recall Marilyn Monroe's sexuality in "Some Like It Hot" and "Seven Year Itch," icons of sexuality, her allure was naïve, innocent of its power... and yet it had far more to do with her erotic hold on our imagination then did the Milton Green nudes of her. The stark and blatant revelations of some of our current scandal queens on the internet, even including revelatory exercise of their sex lives, has brought them notoriety, but not film roles. The tabloids frantically chase their escapades to titillate our attention. The celebrity media scramble after all this sybaritic nuttiness and sadness, but these exhibitionists are only pathetic side-show acts. The legit world of entertainment and true sensuality is in another tent. Reality series don't count as acting, however scripted they might be…

The one act of nudity that arguably accelerated a screen beauty's career was Hedy Lamarr's *au naturel* amble into a lake in the Czech film "Ecstasy" in the early 30s. It scandalized America just as the Hays office was lowering the boom on overt sexuality in American films. Far more people heard of it and talked about it than ever saw it. The sensual impact was heightened by the actress' foreignness. When I was a kid, "Ecstasy" played occasionally at the Esquire Theatre, an early art house in the basically Jewish Fairfax neighborhood of 1940s L.A… We kids would stand outside wondering about the sexuality going on inside… Hedy Lamarr in the flesh… trying to read it on the faces of the people coming out, probably unnerving some of them that we might be midget spies sent by the Legion of Decency. "Ecstasy" plays occasionally on TMC, but usually so late that I fall asleep trying to stay up for that scene that so occupied my mind in childhood. Finally viewed, it is brief and neutral. The sensuality was in the lingering, almost watching-paint-dry studies of that perfect face as an adolescent Lamarr teetered on sexual awakening. It wasn't the scene that made Hedy Lamarr a superstar. It was the way the scandal steamed our awareness of one of the most hauntingly perfect beauties ever to appear on the screen, an underestimated talent in both comedy and drama. When, on the third try, I finally stayed awake long enough to see it, it was evident that the brief nudity was rather pristine and distant. The true sexuality was a love scene played solely in close-up on one of the most extravagantly and innocently beautiful faces of film history.

Before Hollywood made sex and nudity interesting by banning them, there were notable and largely innocent episodes of star nudity on screen, unremembered now because they were excised when Hollywood buttoned-up. Try to catch the unexpurgated print, sometimes seen on Turner Classic Movies, of the 1932 "Tarzan The Ape Man" with Johnny Weissmuller in his first go at the role that made him a film star and Mia Farrow's mom, Maureen O'Sullivan. It contained, in that time before the movie industry's self-imposed censoring antics rigidly overseen by its Hays Office and the Breen Office, a lyric nude underwater ballet. I'm not selling porn here. It was art, thoroughly innocent and thoroughly erotic in its sense of innocence about to be seduced. If there was any real perversion to it, it was that of pedophilia, such was Tarzan's innocence that Jane was about to dispatch. It is one of the most compelling and complex scenes of evolving sexual awareness ever, and the nudity was specific but muted and only ancillary. Even with that scene expurgated, it was the ensuing love story which raised that film to something well beyond the action hero genre. Tarzan went triple-G after that, and our moms happily shipped us off to its Saturday matinee performances, his earlier despoiling forgiven and forgotten. Hushed up, really. In the mid-20s, Tarzan was a Saturday afternoon serial offering with Elmo Lincoln as the ape man and there was incidence of what was then termed National Geographic nudity...

This information is not out-of-books for me. From time I was 11, I lived ten minutes from the great Silent Movie Theatre on Fairfax, admitted to the artistry of film before it could talk for an admission of one thin dime, some of the best dimes I ever spent. Silent films often demanded more of the audience.

And to what was the movie-going public treated 40 years before the raucous '60s freed America from oppressive fear of public nudity?.... an unembarrassed modicum of bare breasts as Hollywood took a shot at National Geographic-type authenticity and nudity. The 1925 version of Ben Hur starring Ramon Navarro, was basically a wraparound of the Christ story. The film was actually entitled "Ben Hur, A Tale of Christ," adapted from the best-selling novel of the same name. In the scenes set in Rome, when Ben Hur is exposed to the moral dissipation of that pagan Empire, the debauch is such that the spectacles of celebration parading in the streets are heated with inflammatory red tinting of the film with glimpses of bare-breasted beauties.

If a nude shot ever made a screen beauty a star, someone is going to have to prove that to me. When a press agent is trying to use revealing shots to establish a client's stardom, he or she is often embarking up the wrong tree. The star-making shot of Jane Russell lying in a pile of hay, the key ad art of her debut film, "The Outlaw," presented her disheveled but clothed. Howard Hughes knew the come-on was her challenging gaze right into your eyes. Marilyn Monroe was already a star when photographer Milton Green unleashed his studies of her nudity. The shot of her holding down her skirt standing over an air vent in Billy Wilder's "The Seven Year Itch" was far more star-making, and all it showed was legs and glee. Early nudes of Madonna became public long after she was a stratospheric star. The sexuality of photos in the star-blazing stage of her career often had a lot to do with costuming.

Guttman & Pam attended Jacqueline Bisset in her quick assent to lasting stardom in the mid-70s, and I've done so throughout her starry career. It was always obvious to me that the sensuality of her imperishable stardom was not the alluring figure, but rather the beauty of eyes and face, comparable in its perfection to that of Lamarr or Taylor and only a few others. It's the quiet composure and intelligence that emanates so subtly yet powerfully from those eyes. It's not the way the eyes *look*. It's the way they look *at* you.

The marketing people on "The Deep" almost forfeited the considerable promotional clout Jacqueline Bisset eventually brought to a film which became a noted box-office winner for its time. There are such things as contractually guaranteed rights, and one specifically granted to Jackie on that film was absolute photo approval. Because much of the film would be shot underwater, Norman Jewison costumed her in a tee shirt, not to show anatomy but to avoid precisely that. A wet tee shirt may cling on land, but in the deep, it traps air and blossoms out, defying specific revelation. It was a time when the "poster" culture put a high price on beauty, and one of the studio guys asked to come over and show me a poster on which Jackie, should she approve it, could make a ton of money. As soon as he unveiled it, I knew we had a problem. It was the famous poster, underwater, giving a very specific impression of her breasts. I knew that was not approved, and he admitted to it and made a frantic argument for her cooperation. It seems that shot was already set as the key ad art… the main visual element in most of the ads, and in a few days it would be a double truck (two adjacent pages) ad in Playboy and Penthouse.

In the film, Norman Jewison's promise to protect her was inviolate. The photo had been taken by a National Geographic photographer preceding her down to the set on the ocean floor, shooting up, and the circumstances of descent were such the air in her shirt ballooned up behind her, pulling the wet cloth against her. The ad guys had seen it, and contractual clauses be damned.

I asked Jackie to come in, asked her to sit down, and she did indeed start to cry when she saw the shot... not crying out of embarrassment at the revelation, but rather at the betrayal by people she trusted. She wanted to get an injunction against the upcoming ads featuring that shot in Playboy and Penthouse. I told her that she couldn't afford the fortune she would have to pay if she held up the issues, costing the magazines millions and millions in advertising and then did not prevail in court "In that case," she said, "I cannot in any conscience promote this film." The film that was certain to be the biggest box-office of her career.

And this film did indeed confirm her as a star for as long as beauty is cherished. Her stardom and talent still persist thirty years later, as witness her recent return to the winners circle at the Golden Globes. Following her decision to opt out of publicity for 'The Deep," I broke the news to the film's producer, Peter Guber. "We're screwed," he said, but I assured him that it was quite the opposite. Jackie would do plenty of publicity... to talk about how betrayed she felt by the failure of her friends and associates who violated her feelings and her contract. That would set the record straight... AND it would lay emphasis to the sensual aspects of the film. I knew this worked for the film, and I was very sure it worked for Jackie. It had always been clear to me that what the audience loved in her was not only her beauty but also her dignity. This approach established a strong awareness of the film and a reaffirmation of the dignity of a woman who refused to be exploited. It was a response on her part and a strategy on mine which sold the attractions of and critical response to the film in the most circuitous but effective of ways. After the film's success, Peter Guber called to acknowledge that it had been a powerful box-office factor. It was win-win times ten.

When Gentleman's Quarterly not too many years back very rationally included her in a layout of the 25 most sensual screen beauties of all time, the editors rather rudely selected a gotcha shot of her snapped on the set of "The Deep," a grab-shot of her sitting on the dock, the beautiful face obscured in scuba mask, the tee shirt wet and revealing. The magazine really missed the point by a wide margin. What is perceived in the mind's-eye is far more erogenous than what is perceived by the eye. Even in a diving mask, *Bisset was voted the sexiest performer of all those years.*

Unlike many actresses her age, Jacqueline Bisset's feminine attraction has remained a key element of many of the roles she has played as she and her career matured. The most recent film to emphasize this in its review response is "Death In Love." The controversial film deals with how a concentration camp survivor, whose affair with one of the death camp's brutal doctors, wreaks perverse pain on herself and her family decades later. Liz Smith concluded , "Bisset finally comes into her own, shaking off the spell her spectacular beauty always cast on audiences. After a long career with fine work throughout, she is only getting better." New York Magazine said of her work in the frightening film, "it is a role that's equal parts horrifying and fascinating, a line the actress walks with nearly predatory seduction." On the 30th anniversary of "The Deep," no actress could hope to do better than that.

Those who think sexuality is exclusively the province of youth have a very pleasant surprise in store as these stars progress decades into their AARP years. Jackie evidenced that recently when her Golden Globe victory for the BBC mini-series "Dancing On The Edge" illuminated her 69th year and fueled a surge of offers. It wasn't just the recognition of talent that brought her again to such currency. It was the charming confusion and stammer of her speech when she failed to hear that she had won and found herself being rushed to the stage for who-knows-what reason. It was a discombobulation that stole the evening… because it was so sexy. Beauty is in the eyes, and they never age. Sexuality is in the spirit, and that fire can burn forever.

If an idea works the first time, it will be twice as effecting the second. When Jackie was asked to star in "Class" for Marty Ransohoff, it was presented to her as a film about a woman ignored and discarded by a husband (Cliff Robertson) distracted by business and other attractions, who finds herself drawn to her son's classmate, her son being Rob Lowe and his friend Andrew McCarthy. It had purposes, she had felt in accepting it, other than being merely a sexy romp. She was promoting it enthusiastically… until, again, the first ad came out. It was a shot of her sitting with the two boys on either side of her, each appearing to be nude, but each wearing a necktie which hung down to cover their nudity. That was not the movie she had made, she felt, particularly because it suggested incest since Rob was portraying her own son, and the ad suggested she was having a relationship with both boys. I had to tell Marty Ransohoff that, again, she would not publicize the film when it was so advertised and he said the ads had tested well and wouldn't be changed. I told him the history of the selling of "The Deep"

and said that if the ads stayed, we would have to take the same tact, but that it had worked very well before. Again, she was speaking her conscience but it was also selling the film because it was acquainting the public with the narrative thrust of the film. Once again, I limited interviews to those in which Jackie lamented the shady ways of movie exploiters, and once again the campaign created awareness and interest for the film.

In the heated (and finally cooperative) phone conversations Marty Ranohoff and I had about this, I had the opportunity to ask him the validity of a story about a man who came to the UCLA hospital where the man's mother had just died. He was thanking the doctor who was consoling him and, realizing he didn't know the doctor's name, asked and was told it was Dr. Ransohoff. "Ransohoff?" the bereaved man exclaimed, suddenly very engaged in life once more, "Are you Martin Ransohoff's son by any chance? " Assured that this was the case, the man poured it on. "I have this script for him, I'm telling you he's going to be crazy about it." Marty assured me it was true in every respect. How could it NOT be? It was Hollywood-desperation nuttiness carried to its ultimate perversion.

The average active span of stardom or run of good roles for an actress is usually no more than 15 years. Jackie and many our other female stars have sustained several times that. The success of a career and of the publicity work that contributes to it may best be judged by how it long and how vigorously it maintains over the years. The first job of publicity is to get clients jobs. A great body or exuded sensuality doesn't automatically light an actress's fire among the people who determine who gets cast. There is a super-abundance of bodies and exuded sensualities in this town. What seals the deal on a sex-sell is how that has translated into popularity with the audience. Popularity is something that can be sold to the industry's decision-makers very well. Popularity is every press agent's meat. Since everyone has the courage of someone else' convictions, we confront the fact that there is no more persuasive someone else than everyone else... the buying public. A press agent sells an actress's (or actor's) sexuality as it is reflected in the public's eyes.

It is the *aura* of sexuality which can be a short cut to activated public awareness. The pin-ups of the 1940s, the posters of the 1960s... those validated quick fixes of fame and were the reliable publicity vehicles of their times. They were also the measure of their times. The '60s exhibited a much harder core of sexual sell. Howard Hughes may have tipped the scales in that direction with his provocative introduction of Jane Russell in "The Outlaw" in the late '40s. Hughes' key ad, the overtly invitational sexuality of his new star lying literally in the hay... available, disdainful, a long way from the bright enticement and innocence of Betty Grable smiling back at us in that bathing-suit-from-the-back shot that reminded World War II GIs what they were fighting for, or Rita Hayworth's kneeling-in-her-negligee photo nailed to so many bunker walls. Those photos were naughty-but-nice according to the indulgent phrase of the time, but there was nothing write-home-to-mom nice in Jane Russell's sullen, challenging availability. The road had made a turn. The press agent has to judge what kind of sex is selling at any particular time. And in this time of when rude blogging makes up a large element of communication, publicists must take care not to err on the side of blatancy.

In which regard, Guttman & Pam wound up representing some of the most sexually explicit films. In some, sexual experience was an element of great art, most notably Bernardo Bertolucci's "Last Tango In Paris." The blatancy of that film filtered through the dual genius of the Italian director and one of Marlon Brando's most daring performances. We made a trip to the other side of the spectrum when Penthouse boss Bob Guccione (his license plate was GUCCI 1) formed Penthouse Productions to make, as he advised us, accurate-in-every-detail historical epics, starting with "Caligula" with Malcolm MacDowell and a contingent of English acting greats. Rome's most morally bankrupt emperor times Penthouse... what could possibly to wrong?

At one point, Jerry and I represented both Penthouse Productions and Readers Digest Productions, which, if nothing else, proved us PR men for all seasons.

Chapter 21

The Wordsmiths

Everyone aspires to the ready wit and wordplay of a Noel Coward. What would each of us give to be able to respond as Coward once did when an actor of exaggerated reputation and even more extravagant self-perception came up to him at a reception for the noted playwright and actor, raconteur/composer/ad infinitum. "Noel," the fellow had said with confident self-importance, "I'm so-and-so." Coward patted the man's arm and said with a reassuring smile, "Of course you are."

A surprising majority of actors share Coward's way with the words. Actors are different from the mass of us who long for eloquence. They know the good lines and they know how good lines keep an audience on their side. This town is always looking for the best line or turn of phrase, in its scripts and, of equal importance, in its inhabitants… The sheer joy, utility and challenge of playing this game applies to actors and writers (for both of whom words are what they do) and even for most of the people who spend lives in their association. Producers and all of the other ancillaries of entertainment-making, strive to be and often arrive at being vivid in their speech. Perhaps it's because you tend to feel a wallflower if, in the give and take communication of the business, you articulate all of your thoughts and feelings in simple declarative sentences, sans surprising word conjunctions, sans imaginative metaphors, using the accepted vernacular and the figures of speech which come most quickly to mind, the ones we all have heard or said a thousand times before. Interesting flecks of speech don't all have to be home runs. Two walks and a single in succession count the same as a homer.

Actors work with words like shoemakers work with leather. They like the feel of words, they like the smell of words. They like how words fit together and sew together, how words can drip honey or how they can sting, how they blend seamlessly or clash jarringly as the case may demand. Actors love the smooth shape of words to both eye and ear. They keep utterable lines at readiness, not at the tip of the tongue, but at the edge of the mind. They have reference and reverence for what they themselves say. Whether it is conscious or not, they love the meter of good speech. I've enjoyed a life with people who are, as a tribe, well-spoken and inventively armed with vocabulary and literary reference.

Trained to the cadences and images of Shakespeare and Arthur Miller and Paddy Chayefsky, they think and speak with that affection for words. It can be fatiguing trying to keep up, but almost everyone gives it a try.

The Brits have a head start… it is, after all, their language. The U.K, with the rest of the Emerald Isle thrown in for good measure, has most eminently brought the beauty of the language to motion pictures. I have, all my life, collected great actors and actresses as friends or clients, usually both, in the hope that speech which honors both literature and language can be acquired by contact. It can't, but banter IS a contact sport in this town. The clear, expressive enunciations… some crisply British, some softly American… of James Mason, Gene Hackman, Martin Landau, Cary Grant, Rip Torn, Stacy Keach, Greer Garson, James Earl Jones, Maximilian Schell, Glenda Jackson, Tony Randall, Peter Ustinov, Michael Caine, Peter Finch… Finchie. Barbra Streisand, Audrey Hepburn, Bill Holden, Christopher Plummer, Jimmy Woods, Nicol Williamson and Richard Harris and the rest of the Gaelic tribe who could suffuse or refresh their Irish as needed, Jane Seymour, Jacqueline Bisset, Michael York kept me attuned to the sheer joy of utterance. Marinated in the dialogue of O'Neill or Mamet, Ibsen, Chekov or Shakespeare, actors are skilled as well in their own selection of words. Stage and screen writers and directors have the same relish of words. I was swept up in all of the passion and perfection of sound-shaping lavished with no hope of getting past my bland Missouri simplicity. But it's been a front seat in the antic gamesmanship of speech.

British actress Miriam Margolyes, small and spherical and perhaps the great vocal magician of them all, is a chameleon of speech who can be anyone, male or female, any accent, any age. When Warren Beatty was making "Dick Tracy" and fashioning characters of mad imagination for the town's most eclectic performers, I learned that Miriam was in town, and I asked him what he still had open. "All we have is the grocer," he said, "it's a guy." "So is Miriam, if you want her to be." "Oh my God," he said with sudden realization, and turning to a longtime associate, "do you remember Miriam Margolyes?... that incredible actor who played Emma Goldman's assistant in 'Reds?'" "Actor or actress?" "Whatever we need," Warren said. Unfortunately, the role had just been assigned, but it was interesting how she had impressed herself on his memory, She's an actor who is anything you need. She cultivated men's voices when she lived alone and didn't like unwanted telephone callers to think her a woman alone. In Scorcese's "The Age Of Innocence," he played her primarily reclined, Scorcese heightened the performance by showing her dominating the other extraordinary characters from positions of horizontal indolence. She incarnates the powers of the spoken word.

The U.K's greatest export has been speech. I've touched base with or at least observed Gielgud and Olivier, Richard Burton, David Niven, Trevor Howard, James Mason. I think most of all it was Laurence Harvey who loved and celebrated the beauty of spoken English, perhaps because it had been his lifeline out of a dangerous ghetto. Larry grew up speaking Lithuanian Yiddish and a stew of other Slavic tongues on the meaner-than-you-can-imagine streets of Johannesburg, South Africa. English was an acquired language for him, acquired first on the battlefields of North Africa after volunteering into the British commandos at age 15. He did it because he was an adventurer, because he was the toughest guy I've ever known, because immigrant Jews in those pre-apartheid days were a degree beneath contempt in the hate-filled streets, were a step below the Afrikaners' k-word for blacks. Larry survived the war and went to England to re-invent himself as the most perfect of all British dandies, the ultimate epicurean. Toast of the Old Vic, Laurence Harvey invented and lived a life as large as those imagined by Stratford's favorite son.

He was my first big star client and one of my most closely held friendships although we had almost nothing in common. Larry either could not endure or else had a lot of fun pretending not being able to endure my flat Missouri twang. Along the banks of the Mississippi and the Big Mo, we tended to turn horse into harse, forty into farty. It stung Larry's ears. "What do you think you are?... Irish?" he would fume. The Irish, too, A-R their O-Rs. "Horse," he would coach, fulfilling it into "hoarse," caressing the full richness of the rounded O, the soft sibilance of the S. He was bewildered that I could have language as the major tool of my trade without giving it the reverence it deserved. If you wish to hear the English language at its most exquisite, most soaring beauty, find... I beg you... that last copy on earth of Larry's reading of "This Is My Beloved" in soft conspiracy with Herbie Hancock's piano.

In spite of the survival mode ghetto jungle of his childhood... or perhaps because of it, Larry Harvey played the role of an English "dandy in aspic" (the title of one of his films) with absolute aplomb. After World War II, his commando service bought him a ticket to England where he somehow fashioned himself a new reality. "Manchurian Candidate," "Room At The Top" and all the others not-withstanding, Laurence Harvey's greatest role was Laurence Harvey. Laurushka Skikne, the skinny tough kid who had learned in the streets and in the commandos how to kill you thirty different ways, had transformed into Laurence Harvey. How he did it, I never learned, nor did he ever refer to that. By the mid-fifties when I met him, he was the Old Vic's brilliant young star, a renowned Hamlet, a revered Richard III. He was ecumenically well read, of perfect Oxonian speech but also with instant access to the meanest tongues of the vulgate. He was Prof. Henry Higgins and Eliza Doolittle all rolled into one. Adept at the best of English manners and rejoicing in the worst, he could become his Laruschka self at the mere glimmer of someone's bad manners.

Larry was in the make-up trailer for Hal Wallis' "A Girl Named Tamiko" on the Paramount lot one time, and I was waiting outside the trailer when Mr. Wallis, one of the rough-tough kings of the producing trade, saw me and asked me who I was and what I was doing on his set. I told him I was Larry's press agent, and he suggested that since he hadn't asked me to visit, would I please remove myself from his film set. Larry heard that, came out and said that if I was unwelcome on the set, he (Larry) felt unwelcome, too. "Please call me when Mr. Guttman will be here, and I will be pleased to join him. You can find me at home." Larry headed for his trailer, and Hal Wallis, maker of great films, collector of great art, watched each of us walk in opposite directions. When I got to the gate to drive off the lot, the guard said, "Mr. Wallis wants you to know that he would be pleased to have you return to his set." When I got there, Hal Wallis went to Larry's trailer to tell him. Larry was already in his street clothes. I was too far away to hear, but I could see Mr. Wallis point to me. Larry went back in and, after a few minutes, emerged in costume and walked by me to the set. He winked at me, that was all, but I saw he was happy as hell. He was back on the mean streets and he felt at home. I was sure he had made a point to Hal Wallis that had nothing to do with me, a point that was payback for a hundred other actors who had squirmed on command. Mr. Wallis was always polite to me whenever I visited his set after that. Well, more like indifferent.

When Larry was directing "Welcome To Arrow Beach," one of his last two films, Linda Lovelace, star of the notorious porn film, "Deep Throat," was brought by a friend to visit the set. I happened to be there. Larry told her that her talent could make her the queen of Hollywood. "Oh," she said, "You've seen my film?" "I'm sorry," Larry confessed, "I'm afraid I left after 27 inches." When an actress with whom he was to costar introduced herself at the start of the film with the advisory that she always slept with her leading men, he responded that he was "honored to be invited into such exclusive company" but he was involved. She accepted "exclusive company" as a compliment.

Gisela and I were at La Scala Restaurant with Larry one night when another of my Rogers & Cowan clients came in, the iconic film composer, Dimitri Tiomkin. I made what I soon had reason to believe was the mistake of introducing them. Dimi had just been nominated for an Oscar for his song "The Green Leaves of Summer" from "The Alamo," in which Larry had starred. Tiomkin was a dramatic man of sweeping gestures and richly and freely expressed sentiments in an imaginative version of English peculiar to him alone. A top-of-his-voice guy, his composing talent gave him something to be bombastic about. Dmitri Tiomkin was a genius.

Larry saw in Dimi's charming bombast its delightful originality of speech but also a bubble he deliciously and maliciously wished to pop. The two with Russian as a common tongue, each the émigré from a different oppression of Jews, had never met, and Larry told Tiomkin how much he esteemed "Green Leaves Of Summer."

"I love it, Dimi. In fact I have always loved it." Dimi glowed in the compliment and then, suddenly darkened. "What you mean always? I write that six months ago, There *is* no always," he said, indignantly. "Dimi," Larry said, "My mother sang me to sleep with that song, and she herself had learned it as a baby." Larry burst into a deep baritone rendition of "Green Leaves Of Summer" replacing the lyrics with a powerful outpouring of words of some Slavic tongue. It was slow and dirge-like, a 'Volga Boatmen" kind of lament. The assertion that he may even inadvertently have stolen the composition brought Tiomkin almost to tears. His outrage stood out with the veins on his forehead. Then Larry started making the same assertion about Dimi's Oscar-winning song from "High Noon," "Do Not Forsake Me, Oh My Darling." Again, it seemed very much a purloined peasant lament. And then some phrases caught in Tiomkin's ear, and he started to smile, I leaned later that Larry had been putting Slavic nursery rhymes to Dimi's lush melodies. Tiomkin started to laugh and grabbed Larry in a great Russian bear hug that finally stopped Larry's parody. Then they fell into a conversation of words we didn't know and into a delighted sealing of new friendship.

Tiomkin could also take the mickey out of himself, and wittily did so upon receiving an award at the must-attend annual Friars Club roast, an event heated up by Frank Sinatra's heading the group of top of singers and jokesters of live entertainment and the wise-cracking actors they admitted to their scalding company. Dimi, knowing that the gathered comics were going to hold fire to his feet, started it off by attesting, "And I would like to thank all of my collaborators... Peter Illytch Tchaikovsky, Sergei Rachmaninoff, George Friederick Handel, Franz List..." It worked so well that he trucked it out again in accepting his next Oscar.

Dmitri Tiomkin may have understood the business better than any other person I know. His angers were both explosive and evaporative. On one occasion I was driving him back from some interview when his excitability was engaged, some dispute over how we should proceed in a specific situation. I drove a little Volkswagen with a fabric sliding roof. We had pulled up to a light on Doheny just as it crosses Wilshire. Whatever the discussion, it had transported him into some passionate refusal of whatever I had suggested. He was yelling so loud that the fabric roof of my car, I noticed, was bumping up with each percussion, each wave of exasperation. He was literally raising the roof. This somehow was too much for me, and I commanded him to get out. Let me add that we were quite bonded, but this was an abuse I wasn't going to take. He was looking at me aghast. "I mean it," I insisted, "get out of my car... right now." "I can't telling you a disagreement to your idea?" he said in what he thought a kinder and more reasoning voice but which was still a roar. "Not in that voice. Get out." The light had changed and cars were honking behind me. He seemed bewildered and then exited the car.

As I drove off, I saw in the rear view mirror that the people in the detained cars were yelling at him as they drove by.

Well, that was one client down the drain, but I was still so furious… at Dimi but also at myself… that I didn't mention it to Warren Cowan. That would come the next day when he received the letter of dismissal. Nor did I mention it to Gisela who revered Tiomkin's music and his giant persona. That evening, I was busy trying to forget it when the phone rang. "Boychick," said the Russian voice, smooth and sweet as sour cream in borsht, intoned like the beautiful sustained note of a cello. "Eeet's Deemee. I was standing on a street corner today thinking there is much marit in your ideas… I come to the office tomorrow and we see how we make them work."

This following anecdote does not really have to do with words, but it does relate to the immaculate way in which Larry Harvey spoke them or even just thought them. People could read scathing judgment and comment even in his silence And it is a reflection of my friend that I would be loathe to omit. It came to me from Chill Wills who was in the cast of John Wayne's "The Alamo" with Larry and also part of the company who sometimes relaxed of an evening downing a few in a local Texas bar. They did so to the thrall of some of the customers but to the annoyance of other locals who were angered by the fame, wealth and general regard of being tough to which these Hollywood slickers pretended. There always was sense of a fight about to be picked. But which one of the star guys did they want to take on? With good reason, they figured it wasn't John Wayne, and Richard Widmark never lost the fear-making image of his "Kiss Of Death" debut. Richard Boone had an air of danger about him, too, and Chill himself, well no denying his good-ol'-boy credentials. But then there was this sort of skinny English dude with his fancy foot-long cigarette holder and what was he drinking? Not something long and cold and foam-topped or some real-man poison in a shot glass. Nope, this English snake drank white wine… some Frenchified stuff called Pooly-Fussy that the bar had to order special. And the way he talked… all elegant and better than anyone else, like the courteous way he'd converse with the waitress and leave her tingling like the last leaf on the twig. This guy was asking for it, and they knew easy pickings when they saw it. According to Chill, they sent the meanest looking one over to do the honors. I suppose they were too caught up in Larry's fine manners to notice the three foot wide shoulders on the slim body. The elected tough guy stood over Larry, said something menacing and Larry, raising only an eyebrow, said something infuriatingly polite… and that insulting little smile as if he were looking down on the guy standing over him. Wayne never moved a finger, Widmark sat there amused, Boone shook his head. The guy reached down and grabbed Larry's shirtfront to bring him to his feet. As Larry came up, so did his right fist which caught the guy just below the point of the chin and lifted him in an arc over and then down onto the table behind him. Larry flicked an ash on him from the foot-long cigarette holder that still extended elegantly from his left hand. Then he sat down and resumed his conversation. Nobody at their table even looked at the tough guy as his friends carried him out. I wasn't there, but I've enjoyed it in my mind's eye a hundred times. I can't think of another story which so perfectly captured Larry Harvey, the most interesting man I ever met.

How would you like to have to render the German adaptation of "Hamlet" back into English? Freidrich Schiller's rendering of "Hamlet" is one of the soaring achievements of German literature, and Gisela was as familiar with "sein oder nicht sein" as we are with "to be or not to be." But most of it, to meet the remarkable wealth of the German language, had been transposed from the original. How would you like to bend it back to Shakespeare's genius on the spot when you've never heard the Bard's most quoted work in its original tongue, when you don't know phrases like "This above all to thine own self be true" and "more than kin and less than kind" and "and flights of angels sing thee to thy rest" and when your audience knows them as old friends so that any variation of a word falls like a hammer on the ears? How would you like to do this when the audience is a gathering together in a tight knot of such acting greats as Marlon Brando and Montgomery Clift?

Maximilian Schell set up this murderous scenario when he followed his Oscar-winning performance in "Judgment At Nuremberg" by tackling Hamlet in German. Eddie Dmytryk, who had directed Max in his English language debut film, "The Young Lions," gathered most of that film's cast (Brando and Clift included) and many of the town's great young acting lions to see Max bring his genius to Shakespeare's indecisive prince. As Eddie set up the 16mm projector and the starry guests lounged on chairs or lay on the floor, Max made an introduction, inviting them to listen to the music of the language, as hypnotic in German as in English.

"And I'm going to leave you now, and my good friend Gisela Guttman is going to translate for you." This came as surprising news to his good friend Gisela Guttman, who knew the German version well but had never heard it in English, never heard "more than kin but less then kind" or "flights of angels sing thee to they sleep. But she struggled with it, looking occasionally at some of the actors to see if she was on course, and they would nod her on, About two thirds the way in, she was in a groove and most of them had stopped trying to correlate it to the English language version. Monty Clift, lying on the floor, overcome with Shakespeare's power in any language and particularly with the chilling reality Max brought to the role, started to sob. It increased and all attention was focused on his growing emotion. Finally, he scrambled to his feet and left the room and the house. Actually, what he blurted out was, "I'm getting out of this shithouse." I was reluctant to include that, perhaps because it was so painfully emotional and somehow so apologetic for his inability to restrain his response. No one spoke. The exquisite music of the German language carried the scene. Finally, somewhat shaken, Gisela resumed her impossible task until flights of angels sang the play and her stress to their rest. Less than year later they sang Montgomery Clift to his rest.

Five years later Gisela and I were at the superstar-studded party agent Kurt Frings held for Queen Soroya after she was cut loose from her royal job in Iran for reason of son-less-ness and was taking a brief fling at film acting. (Max Schell became her most intense romantic liason during her Hollywood period.) As mentioned in the chapter entitled "Starpower," Bobby Darin, Anthony Newley and a pick-up band of greats was making music, and Marlon Brando who had joined in on the bongos motioned Gisela to come over so he could instruct her in the instrument. I, for husbandly reasons, had approached close enough to audit any conversation. Finally he turned to her and said, "Hamlet?" She nodded, and he said, "You did good."

Actors love words and the fashioning of words, the tricks of them that you can play on other people's minds. Peter Ustinov possibly delighted in this above all. Peter and I had an on-going game… a viciously-played contest to be quite honest… of what we called verbalizations. It consisted of identifying nouns which could be used as verbs in arresting ways… the stipulation being that they had to be verbs of expression, of communication. Examples, "Don't harpoon that sea mammal, he whaled." Or "Mississippi, Massachusetts and Indiana, he stated." "Someone stole my Swedish car, he Saabed." I'd invented it as a way of passing time with him, and he relished it. We would be driving along, and one of us would suddenly come up with a verbalization, and, if it was any good, the other was deeply offended. The trick, again because it is too easy if you skip this rule… is that the verb borrowed from a noun has to be a verb of communication or expression, speech, utterance… like "You'd better find the missing piece from the train track, he railed." We had a big fight over "The sea, the sea, he mer-mered," because I insisted "mer mer" is not a noun, and he insisted it is two nouns if you are French. We gave five points to "Cut me a line of coke, he snorted." "This long, thin piece of metal is from your bicycle wheel, he spoke." But "I don't like cabernet, he wined" we gave passing marks. We had some delicious arguments, and it was always great to come up with a great one, because Peter's pout was like no other and his joy of victory infectious in its little harrumphs. In these battles, he was somehow the Peter Ustinov of "Topkapi." "There was a fifteen minute silence after I rejected his "She did *so* marry her brother, he incested." My point was that incest and insist are not phonic equivalents. He was pissed at my rigidity.

But generally Peter had great forbearance, and he did suffer fools well. At an Oscar show rehearsal, a male singer known for his smug air of perfection, came up to him and said, "Peter, I just want you know that I loved you in that spy film you and Melina Mercouri did in Morroco." For the record, the film, "Topkapi," was a jewel heist thriller set in Istanbul. But to the compliment, Peter politely remarked, "I'm pleased you got so much out of it." Peter was, for a man of such intimidating talents, a very good soldier. At that same Academy Awards, I had him presenting in some category and the "funny" pre-opening-the-envelope lines they gave him played off of his initials… P. U… I hated it and thought it unworthy of a great actor, but he wouldn't let me force them to change it. "Nobody will remember except you," he said, "and who cares what YOU think?"

One of the aspects of his work and his celebrity that Peter most enjoyed was the travel. Not just the stays in places like Turkey for films like "Topkapi," but the strange places his charity work and his international acclaim carried him. it was the reason he would accept, when his professional schedule permitted, being honored at festivals both famous and obscure. He readily said yes to being solicited as a lifetime honoree at a festival in Albania. At that time in perhaps the'70s,

Albania was a kind of secret society, a communist nation, Moslem and walled off from the rest of the world behind its own peculiar Iron Curtain and, apparently, far, far behind the times. It was not a glamorous experience, but one he enjoyed for its uniqueness. His treasured memento from it was a bill of Albanian currency of some denomination. Paper money and even coins most often celebrate some salient aspect of the nation's history or pride, and this paper money featured what appeared to be a 1934 diesel truck.

We rarely dined together other than in restaurants that featured the indigenous food of this culture or that. One time in a Greek restaurant, Peter ordered chicken souvlaki, a kind of Greek poultry kebab. As he poised above it, I asked if he knew from which country that dish actually derived. "Greece, I dare say," Peter offered. "No," I corrected, "Chickensouvlakia." He gave it the mild response to which its painful awfulness aspired, but a few months later he asked me why I had never arranged for him to be the lifetime achievement honoree at a festival in Chickensouvlakia. I took my beating like a man.

Words are a medium, one in which sound (and succession of sounds) is as important as meaning. That is why we all love the flow of Dylan Thomas even when the cognitive part of our mind gets lost in the forest of rich Welch metaphors and images. That is why we're transported by Robbie Burns even when the Scots idiom and vocabulary are centuries removed from our ken and must be intuited rather than understood.

The single greatest complement I ever received, and there haven't been many, occurred in Nairobi, Kenya, where Gisela and I had gone for me to polish the script for "The Last Elephant" which had begun filming as I was still conceiving my rewrite of a prior script and putting it on paper. Actually, we were there because the Writers Guild of America, in its incandescent wisdom, had proscribed that writers must be given two first class tickets to the location of a filming. And in its preparation, I had had the privilege of writing the character of the Kenyan police inspector for James Earl Jones who had committed to it after reading only the first two of the seven acts... not because of the script but because it was being directed by television's pre-eminent director, Joe Sargent who had directed Mr. Jones in the acclaimed theatrical film, "The Man." Because

I had only a few weeks in which to write the script, I didn't have time to explore the specific cadence and color of Kenyan speech, so I had proceeded on the contrivance that Kenyan English was rich in metaphor reflecting a culture so closely bound to and bonded with its nature.

Since I had been banned from the set... for reasons I may get into, but they paint a picture of me far more embarrassing than pretty... I had to arrange to slip onto the set of an autopsy scene in which Mr. Jones' character deduces the circumstances of the death of a woman murdered in the bush by ivory poachers. I had thrown in a number of indigenous phrases of my own imagining, and I was afraid the speech was too florid for even the genius of James Earl Jones to tame or give reality. Of course, the phrases flowed mellifluously under his magic interpretation, flaws reshaped as virtues. Afterwards, I introduced myself to him and explained I was there because I wasn't sure that dialogue was say-able. "I was afraid it was too consciously literary," I confessed. "On the contrary," he said, "it was literate." That was worth coming 12,000 miles to hear, and any other review I ever received was tepid in its shadow. Well, most of them were pretty tepid anyway.

The site they were shooting the scene was also the film's production office, so I took the opportunity to pick up my per diem pay for the prior week. It was paid to me in cash, lots of bills in small denominations of Kenyan money. It was a scorching day, so I had worn only slacks and a light short sleeve shirt. We had been warned of street criminality and the chance of robbery. Taxis were impossible to locate, so I stuffed all of the bills into my clothes and walked four miles in a shirt bursting with money through streets brimming with poverty and crime. What an idiot! For no logical reason, I wasn't robbed.

I have a special place in my heart for the lines I've heard that were so whacky and original no writer could have written them. Siskel's "I knew it was you guys" was one of them. I particularly enjoyed one which I encountered when Jerry Pam and I had gone to Glenn Ford's home to get to know him on the first of several occasions of our representing him. We were especially astounded by his incredible adventures in World War II. One could only grow dizzy as he told the tales. It was bracing just to contemplate the cool concentration and heroism some of them must have required. In the process of this conversation, we were standing near a window seat in the living room... wide and long and upholstered in bright and celebratory tartan. Covering the inset walls at the ends of the window were several dozen photos of exceedingly beautiful women, many of them very famous, actresses, each portrait inscribed with a message to Glenn. It was a gallery, no doubt about it, of common denominator.

"Does this mean what I suppose this means?" I asked him. Glenn nodded. The question which posed itself to me was why all of these women, all beautiful, some extremely famous, would wish to be initiated into this amazingly populous club under the watchful eyes of all the prior members. It occurred to me that that may have been part of the attraction. The complexity and perversity of our hunger for pleasure in its most extreme is, simply, incalculable. Incalculable, too, is the prospect of leaving for future awareness of others this signed photographic evidence of their membership in such a not-quite-exclusive band of sisters, not to mention that the bay window which semi-enclosed this nest of passion was by its very nature made of glass, making what transpired within visible to anyone who might wander the garden outside. "And was there…?" I ventured. "Yes," Glenn nodded, "one." "Wow," I observed, "a virgin?… in Hollywood?" "Only up to that point," Glenn qualified. "May I ask….?" I presumed. Glenn nodded obligingly and indicated the photo of a young actress who starred on a television series opposite one of our clients. "If you don't believe me," Glenn said, and pointed to the inscription. I looked at it closely. It read "Dear Glenn, you were the first. It was oodles of fun." As we went out, Jerry said to me, "Did you buy that thing about the bench? The virgin part?" "Are you kidding?" I replied in amazement that he should doubt it,, "It was oodles of fun? Do you think a grown man could make up something like that?"

And oh the tales to be told…. but how? That incident with Glenn somehow always reminds me of another… a told-to-me story, not personally experienced, but it is such a loving expression of human nature Hollywood-style that it would be stingy and unkind not to pass it on. I was fortuitously present when a major star of the golden age related a tale of having played tennis at the home of a star couple of that era… late '30s, early '40s…. the She of this story being the very last person of whom you might imagine the heroine of such a tale. The star/raconteur friend advised that when he'd finished an epic tennis battle with the husband and host, the husband suggested since the guest would be staying for dinner that he take a shower in the couple's bathroom. His wife wasn't home and the other showers were in some state of change. In the middle of this ablution, the naked guest heard the wife come into the bedroom singing, something for which she was exceedingly famous. Then, to his alarm, he heard her come into the bathroom. The steam-filled shower lent an obscuring of precise image, for which the guest was deeply grateful. But then, suddenly, the shower door opened and the hand of the mistress of the house reached in, felt around… and not for the soap… and then finding its prey, yanked gently on his private parts and she said chirpily, "Ding Dong, Daddy." And then she went out. Later at dinner when she had somehow realized her error, possibly through some consideration of tactile comparatives, not a word was mentioned and not an eye averted. How can this story not be true? "Ding Dong, Daddy" is as invention-proof as "oodles of fun."

I've thought long and hard about that last one, and since there is nothing dishonorable or embarrassing about it for any of its three stars, since it does in a way convey how human and civilized they were, I decided to reveal its interesting casting. The male guest was played by Ray Milland. In fact, it *was* Ray Milland. I'm also doing this because I enjoyed the circumstance in which I learned it and wish to honor the fact that it wasn't confided to me but only in my presence.

Edmond O'Brien, whose company I always sought because he was what being Irish and erudite were all about, was shooting a film (or maybe it was a TV series) at Universal. He had one of the very lovely stand-alone dressing rooms they had there. Whatever we were discussing, there was a knock at the door and then Ray Milland entered. He'd decided to pop in because this had been his dressing room on some film, and one of his favorite experiences had transpired here. I had a feeling this might have something to do with sex, and it did… not involving Mr. Milland but rather of anther prior occupant, Errol Flynn. Mr. Milland had been putting something up on a shelf in the closet when he found a very dusty reel-to-reel tape and somewhere else the tape recorder it fit. Who could resist? He wasn't prepared to hear the voice of Errol Flynn and even less prepared to hear Mr. Flynn doing play by play description of a vigorous sexual engagement of his friend and driver and a young woman whose name was not reported, although her sexual devices most certainly were. Mr. Milland was astounded, and on the set during the next scene he mentioned to his leading lady that he had discovered a tape of Errol Flynn, an actor he knew she admired. He was not prepared for her emotional delicacy and indignation. She had stormed out, and the only words they spoke to each other during the rest of the filming were those which were in the script. Eddie and Milland looked if the incriminating recorder or tape were still there, but they were long gone. When this encouraged mutual chat about dallliances, Mr. Milland said that his very favorite tale was the most innocent and delicate of all... and he proceeded to tell the shower story. I'm sure you've already concluded that the married couple were actor Gene Raymond and his glorious singer/actress wife, Jeannette McDonald. Makes you love her even more, doesn't it? As she so beautifully sang, "ah, sweet mysteries of life."

Top actors almost invariably have speech skills which go far beyond reading other people's words convincingly. Their best zingers came from that special part of the brain called "the top of their heads." Peter Ustinov, I'm sure it will surprise no one, was the master. We had a mild crisis... not crisis really but more like a flurry... when President Lyndon Baines Johnson through some of his emissaries complained about some really blistering things Peter, in a book of short stories, said about Johnson's conduct... or rather misconduct... of the war in Vietnam. The key complaint from the President was that Ustinov was "hitting below the belt." I asked Peter for a quote with which I could counter this assertion, and without a blink he suggested, "Tell them that I can't help it if President Johnson chooses to wear his belt as a crown." That kind of facility and precision makes you feel that you're not even in the game.

An American Classicist...

Edmond O'Brien, I have made perfectly clear, is one of the great actors Gisela and I most loved. His outrageous and varied talent was second only to his gracious kindness. He had that exuberant way with words and with friendship that is so distinctively Irish. Because he was such an essential and compelling part of the great American neo-realism and noir films... "DOA," "The Killers," "White Heat" going at it toe to toe with Jimmy Cagney, Ida Lupino's great direction of " The Hitchhiker," "711 Ocean Drive," he is perceived as a uniquely American and contemporary voice." Even his non-noir work as Frankenheimer's "Seven Days In May" and his Oscar-winning turn in Joc Mankiewicz' "Barefoot Contessa" cast him in quintessentially American voices... the two-fisted American with that great Irish mug. He dedicated his Oscar gold to Mr. Mankiewicz who the year before had given showcase to Eddie's skill with the classics by selecting him to portray Casca in "Julius Caesar." Eddie's contemporary and combative energy in most of his filmography too easily hides the fact that he was one of the great Shakespearean interpreters of the Broadway stage. Even though his teaming with Ronald Coleman in "A Double Life" focused on a production of "Othello," it left all the Shakespearean lines to Mr. Coleman. What an Iago Edmond O'Brien could have delivered.

One of the great classicists in movietown, his knowledge of literature and opera was second to none. Because of that, I came to know Mario Lanza even though I never met him. Eddie had made his Hollywood debut rather classically as The Poet, the romantic leading man in "The Hunchback Of Notre Dame" opposite Charles Laughton and Maureen O'Hara. World War II took him into the Army Air Force, and he wound up in that organization's marvelous propaganda play and film, "Winged Victory," the first film for a young actor with a pretty good voice, an Italian kid named Mario Lanza. You didn't have to have Eddie's sophisticated knowledge of opera to know that this was a voice of the century, but it was still a best-kept secret. Lanza was not yet acknowledged as a singer, and Eddie, recognizing a national treasure when he heard it, took the kid under his wing. They wound up one night in a famous New York Italian restaurant consecrated to opera. The owner, a man of prodigious voice, came to the table, and Eddie told him he was trying explain opera to this kid and asked the owner to lay a little Verdi on him... which the man did with gusto and skill. Eddie said to Lanza. "See?.... that that's how it's done. Now why don't you give it a try?" Lanza burst forth, and Eddie recalled that he was surprised that the owner, who was behind Eddie, wasn't screaming the "bravos" he usually did even for good amateurs. He looked back to enjoy the restaurateur's amazement and saw that he was lying on the floor in a dead faint.

He had an all-embracing love of people, and he and his wife, Olga San Juan, who blew Broadway away in "Paint Your Wagon," threw the most eclectically populated parties in town, always filled with great presences from the worlds of music, film and stage. One particular thrill for me was meeting his close friend, Billy DeWolfe, the agile comedic character actor, and I had a chance to tell him that one of my great film moments was a scene in "Blue Skies" in which he was talking to Bing Crosby or Fred Astaire, and he makes his exit by swinging one leg forward and over his head, executing a standing-start cartwheel in which his hands never touch the ground, just the feet one after the other performing perfect clrcles ending with his facing the other direction and then walking off. He said, "How sweet of you to remember that. With Bing and Fred up there, I didn't think anyone had noticed," at which point he executed the same amazing feat and walked off from us. I've never seen Gisela's mouth more agape. What a generous gift from a perfectly perfect stranger.

Eddie was the kind of person who invited us to dinner, and when I said we already had arrangements to dine with one of my sisters and her husband, he demanded that the whole gang be his guests at one of the top dollar eateries in town. On the other hand, before I knew him, he damn near ended my career in publicity. He had just won the Oscar for "Barefoot Contessa," which made him a very sacred cow in Warren Cowan's book. I was the office boy, and I had mailed some important press clippings to him special delivery. He called Warren and demanded to know what idiot had mailed that envelope. I had put two cents too little postage on it, and the mailman had rung the doorbell at six in the morning to collect the missing two pennies.

Even from this I learned another key rule of publicity. In "Shampoo" Warren Beatty's hair salon owner boss advises him "you gotta nickel an' dime 'em." Well, *you gotta two cents 'em, too. No detail is too small to overlook.* Two cents worth of double-checking can be the difference between success and failure.

A few years later, Edmond O'Brien was one of my most cherished clients and friends. He frequently awed me. He made a dazzling little noir thriller, "The Third Voice" with Laraine Day, allowing me to work with one of those actresses who were the inextricable screen presences of the late '30s (she started in "The Painted Desert" which ushered in Bogart's long reign) powering into the '40s and '50s, including starring roles in both the Tarzan and Dr. Kildare film series. She was, a great badge of Hollywood honor, a member of that most aspired to club in films, Alfred Hitchcock's gorgeous blond heroines. Her hitch with Hitch was in one of his the-Nazis-aren't-coming-they're-here thrillers, "Foreign Correspondent." The companion pieces were "The 39 Steps," (Madeleine Carroll as the blonde) and "Saboteur" with Priscella Lane handling the blond duties. Take away any one of those terrific ladies of whatever color tresses (they were mostly in black and white anyway) and the whole '40s-ness of movies tumbles like a tower of cards.

"The Third Voice" was Laraine Day's last film, and probably my favorite the-problem-is-the-solution-in-disguise campaigns for a film. It was a knife-edge thriller which hung completely on the you'll-never-guess-it surprise ending. When the reviews came out, I called O'Brien and he said "How are they?" "You don't want to know." "Bad?" "Good." "So?" "About a third of them give away the ending." He was as furious as I. We launched an extensive campaign of interviews not merely promoting the film, but expressing outrage that critics could commit such an unthinking and, truly, unthinkable crime. We managed to do it, Eddie with great passion, without further exacerbating knowledge of the film's ending. Eddie came out swinging, naming names and pointing fingers, and there were a lot of tails between a lot of legs. Offending reviewers probably thought they were getting roughed-up in an Edmond O'Brien noir thriller while an overhead lamp swirled ominous shadows. Eddie and I were having fun, and It proved a great way to draw interest to a very good suspense film that might otherwise have slipped through undetected. After that, the incidence of reviewers giving away the endings of films dropped to approximately zero. Or, at least, now they warn you that a "spoiler" is coming. Eddie was a great crime fighter, on screen and off. And sophisticated Irish intellect and passion can be very good company.

He loved the language, Edmond O'Brien did. Whether it was the clipped economy and metaphor of the noir genre or the graceful and elegant cadence of the classics, he brought poetry to all of the lovely tales he told. He spoke emotionally with a friend, unashamed of tears, and a night of shared confidences with him in Paris brimmed with that rarest coin of friendship, trust. Toward the end, meeting him and, separately, James Mason on a set or on a street and seeing bright eyes vacant and absent of recall, when fog closed in and fading memory had stolen poetry and humor and affection… those were ordeals which Gisela and I bitterly suffered and sorely regret.

Eddie and James were inextricable screen presences of the '40s and '50s and '60s and on. If you subtract their power and skill and speech and that of the other actors who loved the language and the art, those glorious movie decades would have been an unworthy heritage of that year of gold… 1939. It cast its bright light for decades. and Eddie and James and their brother actors and Laraine Day and her sisters-below-the-titles were part of the greatest-ever reservoir of acting talent which was the very grass root of Golden Age Hollywood. Every film was ten deep. Now that they've expanded best film to 10 nominees once more or even if the go back to five, let's see if today's filmmakers can fill it up with astonishment as 1939 did.

PR is a pressure business. Gisela once complained that I seem to enjoy pressure, and I answered that diamonds are created only under pressure. "Do you know the difference between a diamond and a lump of coal?" she asked. Before I had a chance at it, she asserted, "a couple million years… and you're not making diamonds, and I don't have the time to wait. "

Chapter 22

The Man Who Walked Away

He had a passion for taking each role as far as it could go and for helping make films of confounding originality. Then, in 2004, in his early 70s, at the height of his powers and of sound mind and body, Gene Hackman folded his tent like the Bedouins and stole away into the New Mexico night.

He'd given us a preview once before, also at a height of heat and acclaim, taking off for a year which became two years when nothing seemed worth returning for. Looking at his list of films, it's hard to establish when it was, but I think it was 1978 after the first "Superman." He'd shown himself a superb farceur. The offers rolled in, but Gene wanted to take a breather. There's no hole in his filmography because he'd done most of his work for "Superman 2" while filming "Superman 1." He finally leaped back in 1981 when his agent Sue Mengers wanted to deliver him for a film being directed by her husband, Jean Claude Tramant. Then his friend and earliest believer, Warren Beatty, pulled him in for a key role in "Reds," and Gene was back in the groove. The line related to "Reds" that I best remember was not in the film but on the night when I'd arranged for Gene to present the National Board of Review Best Director Award (it might have been Best Film as well) to Warren in Manhattan. Gene was there rehearsing a play, and I'd arranged to have a limo pick me up and then Gene and Betsy. The driver missed their address and it took 47 minutes to drive around the block for a second go at it, and, of course by then they'd left. They beat me to the theatre by a half hour. They'd walked... movie stars aren't supposed to do that. So in presenting this trophy, Gene recalled one scene that was particularly important, "I remember saying to Warren... I think it was right after the fifty-first take..." The laughter just didn't stop, especially from Warren When it finally subsided, Gene said, "So, in closing..." and then handed the award to its rightful owner. Gene was always good at finding the right exit line, and then in 2004 the line was, "Goodbye." That was ten years ago. Think what we lost.

If you want to sell a line, a product or a news story, you damn well better find something in it you can believe. That's what I drew when several co-stars at a location breakfast tried to get him join them in making fun of the day's dialogue. Gene pointed out that when they said those lines in a theatre, their faces would be twenty feet tall, so they'd better find something in those words they could believe. It's a never-fails rule which I fervently apply to everything I ever attempt or try to help someone else attempt. Gene brought it to everything he did... his truly skilled painting which he so incomprehensibly has given up... and now his amazing novel writing. His 2009 "Escape From Andersonville" won the Kentucky (Lincoln's birthstate) prize for the best Civil War novel of the 200th anniversary of Honest Abe's arrival on this planet.

Gene has applied that discipline to his political involvement, his aerobatic flying, his auto-racing. When he was into racing big time, he was... I learned from people on the same track with him... quite as determined and single-minded as the Popeye-Doyle-Gene was in his race with the elevated train. That thrill-ride was about Popeye's manic one-mindedness. Several race-drivers told me that they would hold back rather than accompany Gene into a turn. He didn't ease off the accelerator and he took out more than one protective pile of old tires.

A towering presence in acting for forty years, Gene loves the art of it but he hates the business of the business. That's why he said goodbye, withdrawing decades too early from the great roles and great money they continue to throw at him.

Over the years he toyed with the idea of direction. Some time before "The Silence Of The Lambs" was made, United Artists offered it to him to star in, to produce and to direct. He turned down this dream triple play finally because he felt he was too often identified with roles involving violence. People do tend to remember the Popeye Doyle of the "French Connection" films, Buck Barrow of "Bonnie And Clyde," his Sheriff Little Bill Daggett of "Unforgiven." Perhaps his greatest performance, in "The Conversation," was the antithesis of that, a man fleeing the horror of violence he may facilitated. But every film fan has a warm place in the heart for Gene's masterpieces of comedy and extremely human nature,

"Hoosiers," "I Never Sang For My Father," "The Royal Tannenbaums," Under Fire," "Scarecrow" or... you name it. The highlight for me of his Oscar-nominated performance in "Mississippi Burning?" is when, in a towering argument between the two FBI agent protagonists, Willem Dafoe's character invites Gene's character's anger that three steps too far, and we tense for a sledgehammer punch. that will surely come. But instead, Gene's character slaps him. I asked him if that was a writer's call or a director's call. Actually, the script designated the punch, and that's what director Alan Parker was expecting, as was Dafoe. But, in the heat of the performance, Gene realized that his character didn't want just to hurt the other guy. It went deeper than that. He wanted to humiliate him. What more insulting, more emasculating an assault than a slap? It defined the complexity of Gene's character in a simple gesture, all the more effective because no one else saw it coming... and Dafoe was so caught off-guard. But at the Oscars, when they played a clip of Gene's Best Actor nominated performance, it was a scene in which he smashes a southern bigot's face into a mirror. During the award show, when the camera cut back to Gene in his seat, I knew Gene was not going do "Silence Of The Lambs." It was the moment Gene knew that, too. He had endured the clip with a scowl. After the awards, as we walked out of the Dorothy Chandler Pavilion, discussing the clip, he said, "That's how they think of me." Goodbye, Hannibal Lector.

That sensibility almost cost movies one of the all-time most memorable performances, the terrifying blind and brutal justice he meted out in his portrayal of the sheriff in Eastwood's "Unforgiven." Clint gave me David Webb Peoples' extraordinary script for that western on a Warner Bros private jet that was bringing us back from Boston where Clint had received the Hasty Pudding Award at Harvard and the unrelenting roasting that goes with it. Clint was in that state of focused passion he has when he's preparing to direct a specific film. "I want Gene to do this with me," he said. Somewhere over Nebraska I finished it. Clint asked what his chances were of landing Gene. "Zero to none," I answered. Clint's eyes squinted as only Clint's eyes can squint. I explained Gene's aversion to further roles of violence. "But try him anyway," I suggested, to ease the moment. One Sunday morning a week or so later, Clint called and said, "You were right. He turned it down. But I can't soften the violence." I called Gene and tried. "The character is the soul of violence," Gene said. "Yeah," I agreed, "but let me ask you this... 'The Ox Bow Incident'"... is that a violent film?" "It's one of the great films about justice and humanity," he contested. "Three innocent guys croaking at the end of a rope?., the blood lust that got them there? A film with violence can't be a film about the insanity of violence?… a film about justice?" Hackman, obviously, concluded it could. And critics and Oscar voters agreed.

As much as Gene truly despised having to do publicity, he was damn good at it, telling the truth and telling it funny. He has the great actor's instinct for telling gesture. When "Royal Tannenbaums" was about to release, we were doing a major story on him for the Sunday Los Angeles Times. The key photo was being shot in the Beverly Wilshire Hotel's most luxurious suite, with Gene posed sitting on an opulent bed in cross-legged lotus position. He wouldn't do it with his shoes on. Being on someone's bed, even a hotel bed, with his shoes on was just too disrespectful for him. You have to be Midwest to understand. He pictured the setup from the camera's eye and then said, "It's a shame I don't have a hole in one sock with my big toe sticking out." I knew that wasn't a joke, so I handed him my key chain which had a scissors on it. The shot appeared full page, quintessential dignity, royalty even… with his big toe sticking out of the hole. It just perfectly captured a guy who can endure publicity only if he is mocking himself. It later was printed again full page in Vanity Fair, which almost never uses "previously employed" art. It was just too good to pass up. A true classic Hollywood photo… and a major tip of the hat to good PR instinct… Gene's not mine. I had a studio pr guy go up the street to buy Gene a couple of pairs of socks at Nieman Marcus for him, a miniscule gesture of gratitude for an inspired promo touch that captures the film's irreverence.

It took Hackman about two decades to discover how much he hated publicity. I think the final straw might have been the morning on which the stars of one film had to show up for a cast photo that was the key the ad campaign of the picture. Everyone was there, except for one of the two other male stars who sent his body double, stating that his head could be chopped in later. Right after the shoot, the bad taste still bright on his tongue, I told him that the studio needed him to do one of the top talk shows. As we were leaving the photo session, our separate cars were moving parallel up La Cienega Boulevard. At one red light, he got out of his car and came to my window. "Why don't you tell the studio to just send my body double?" I reminded him that he didn't have a body double. "They should have planned ahead," he said, slipping back into his car. I don't believe he ever did another major talk show to promote a film. When Gene was promoting his first authored novel, "Wake Of The Perdido Star," he agreed to do 20 minutes with Larry King, but not the full hour. They taped it and then threw in so many clips that it became the full hour. I heard about that in the morning, but I thought it was good exposure and and a savvy manipulation of Larry's part.

But when he did talk shows, Gene was resourseful, funny and self-effacing. As with any other performance, he brought to it his all. On one occasion on The Tonight Show with Jay Leno, Jay referred to Gene's passion for painting and the recognition of his work with a brush. Gene said that he didn't know about any recognition and told the story of having gone to a top Westwood art supply store and, when he was checking out, the clerk had said "We'll be giving you fifteen percent off on that, Mr. Hackman." Gene, embarrassed, said, "Thank you, but I don't want any special accommodation." "Oh, it's not special," the clerk assured him. "It's our standard senior discount."

On another occasion when he was supporting "Scarecrow," a film he really loved, he spoke of how he and Al Pacino, wanting to get into the sense as well as the garb of the two homeless and hopeless guys they would play in the film, went to San Francisco to absorb some of the down and out lifestyle. They went to second hand stores, suited themselves out in ill-matched hand-me-downs at the end of the hand-me-down line. Sporting many days of stubble and convincingly grubbed up and odorized, they hit the sad streets south of Market to get a feeling for it. Slipping into the mindset was what they did for a living. They wanted to get a sense of how these invisible men were responded to. At a first corner, Gene very deferentially asked some passerby for directions, which the fellow provided. "Thanks," Gene mumbled, "thanks a lot." To which the man responded, "You're quite welcome, Mr. Hackman."

There was a nasty happenstance when I visited Gene on "Scarecrow" location at the Colorado State Prison in Canon City, I believe. You don't go into a prison wearing suit and tie. This was the early 70s when everyone was a little into pseudo-hippie, and it was a fashion to wear thick belts with big exotic buckles, and I got into it, as is usually the case, just as everyone else was getting out of it. I don't pay much attention to my attire other than to make sure I get each foot into the correct pants leg. Gene checked out my belt as we discussed a new script he'd just received from Francis Coppola for a film called "The Conversation," a little piece Francis wanted to squeeze in before he left for Italy for his second

"Godfather" film. You could tell Gene's excitement even though the scheduling would be brutal. "Scarecrow" to "Conversation" turned out to be as good a back-to-back parlay as any actor has ever made. Toward the end of the day, someone from the production staff was escorting me out of the prison when suddenly I was pulled into an interrogation room. This wasn't going as smoothly as it was supposed to. I was being treated as though I was trying to escape. It seems my belt buckle said Colorado State Prison at Canon City. I was starting to sweat it until they began to laugh and told me the governor had given me a reprieve. I wonder how they happened to catch that nasty piece of serendipity. At rushes that night, Gene claimed to know nothing about it.

But Gene is an actor, and he didn't need funny confessionals to get laughs on those shows. He and Leno had a warm relationship because Jay, apart from his appreciation of Hackman's work, knew that Gene not only was a racer but that he and his son Chris also built racing cars (as well as an airplane that they flew for a while.) When Gene was promoting the submarine drama "Crimson Tide", on Leno's Tonight Show, someone on the production staff came up with a great idea for Gene's intro during the monologue. For major stars, the show sometimes cuts to a goofy visual of them when Jay is announcing the night's guests. This bright someone had discovered that there is a stark sewer-like tunnel which carries massive cables under the "midway," a wide street at NBC separating executive offices from the studios. When Jay gave the monologue promo of Gene's being on the show and said he was waiting in his special dressing room built to honor his role as a submarine commander, they cut to this sub-like space, a tube hundreds of feet long walled with electric cables, with Gene, the lone human element, sitting on a stool in the middle of it looking lost and abandoned. As they cut in on him, he had the expression of a kid who had been left at a department store… on purpose. It was a hilarious piece of acting. Gene later drew on that sense of lost-and-confused for big laughs in a scene of "Get Shorty." His character is tempted for whatever stupid reason to call and threaten a mobster, and he hangs up the phone still on his self- delusional high, which then melts away as he realizes with dull comprehension that he has just dumped himself on the doorstep of disaster. That forlorn look was sheer Preston Sturges, more than which I cannot say.

Another film, another location… Gene was doing an action film in Arizona, and I talked the studio into hiring a private plane to take me and six top journalists to the desert shoot for a lunch round-table with Gene. He wouldn't normally have done it, but maybe it broke the boredom. The lunch in his trailer went smoothly, and then he and I sat there to talk as the journalists went out to watch the filming of an action scene. A long silence and then Gene said, "If you were here last night I would have strangled you." "Really," I said, "and to what would I have owed that honor?" "I dreamt about the time you booked me on 'Hollywood Squares.'" "I've never booked anyone on that who didn't specifically request it." "Oh, yeah," he said, memory returning, "that was...," and he named another independent press agent. I knew there was a reason fate had me bring those guys down there.

Hollywood is a place where loyalty is either a natural consequence of character or an inconvenience to be avoided at all costs. Gene takes his loyalties seriously. He had been contacted by an Italian producer who wanted to do Ernest Hemingway's "Across The River And Into The Trees" with Gene on locations near Venice. The guy was trying to finesse the financing, and Gene, a lover of great writers and great writing, was there on his own dime trying to help make the thing go, and it was not on a fast track. An important big budget studio film was offered him, but he elected to stay with the Hemingway project because it was just reaching the point of go or no go. It didn't go, as it turned out, and the project Gene turned down even though the deal offered a piece of the action was a combination live action/ animation film that went through the ceiling, but I never heard him refer to that in regret. I don't mention the title, even though the story of his costly choice was fairly well known. Gene has never allowed me to mention films on which he had received the first offer, and they are a compendium of top 20 boxoffice films. I think he sort of enjoys the fact that six guys turned down "French Connection" before it made its way to him, but he doesn't want to embarrass any other actor with the suggestion that he'd been second choice to Gene.

Gene's compulsion to bring reality to every aspect of a character he portrays resulted in a rest-of-our-lives hobby on one occasion for me and in another instance for him. He, Nick Nolte, Joanna Cassidy and Jean Claude Trintignant were preparing to do "Under Fire" for director Roger Spottiswood. It was about journalists covering the right wing atrocities in the Central American civil wars during the 70s. Gene, with his rigorous instinct for perfection, determined to learn to play (or at least finger) the piano in a convincing manner because of one bar scene that plants him at an upright 88. His character's easy feel for the moody rolling blues was a very important window into who the guy was. Jazz says a lot about you. At Gene's request, we rented an upright piano and put it in one of our back offices. Gene came in every night for a month to practice that one song. I would go in from time to time during the days to touch the keys and was surprised to find that my fingers knew where some of the notes were. By the end of that period, Gene could play his tune with conviction, maybe not to the ear, but at least to the eye. He was able to convey the jazz sensibility that was such an important part of the character he was playing. That impressed me, A few years ago I thought of Gene and determined (since I don't have predictable time to schedule lessons) to teach myself to play the piano. Gisela bought me a baby grand, and I applied myself to it, figuring how to read music in the most cursory way, eventually getting to a point at which people could sort of figure out which song I was playing. "No," Gisela corrected, "you've just always been didactic." And the scene in the bar in "Under Fire?"… you never saw Gene's hands on the keys.

Curiously, it was almost two decades between Gene's nocturnal sessions with our office piano, and my doing anything more than occasionally tinkling out a melody. It was during a visit to the UCLA cancer center during my melanoma year that the impulse really took root. I was sitting in the waiting room with five or six dozen others. Not a lot of smiles. Many of those stories were not going to have happy endings. And then, drifting softly down the hall, the gentle, simple notes of Vernon Duke's "Autumn In New York." Duke also wrote "April In Paris"… he was a helluva tour guide and he knew his seasons. I followed the notes down to the atrium entrance where an old man was playing at an upright. About thirty people sat or stood about, their concerns set aside for the beguiling length of a few well-loved songs. I realized I wanted to come back some time and do that, too. On the many further trips to that building, there was often someone else… a little prodigy, an old woman with her walker beside the bench. And then one day there sat and played the elderly man who had first drawn me down the hall, and I wanted to tell him how he had stirred my life, but I wanted to be with Gisela when she got some news. And when we came back up, the man was gone. I once had a dream that we were playing a duet.

When Hackman was signed to star with Tom Cruise in "The Firm," he addressed the fact that one scene required scuba diving. He likes to do his own stunts, so Gene and his wife Betsy went to Hawaii and applied themselves to scuba lessons.

By the time of filming on "The Firm," Gene was more than sufficiently skilled to do the shot himself. The scene was so brief and filmed from such an angle that Danny DeVito could have done the stunt for him and nobody would have noticed. Gene's habit of handling his own physical scenes had, in this instance, a major impact on his life and on Betsy's. They became ardent divers, even going to the South Pacific to dive among sunken World War II warships which had become artificial reefs. They became active in the effort to protect threatened reef life, and Betsy became a noted underwater photographer, her work exhibited internationally (along with Gene's paintings) in a fund-raising exhibit organized by Steven Spielberg and Norman Schwartzkopf. And, in a way, it led to Gene's new career as a well-reviewed novelist.

That scube dedication definitely helped launch his sea change from actor to novelist His first novel, "The Wake Of The Perdido Star," was a pirate tale the historical sweep of which includes the origination of diving bells in the first decade of the 19th century.

Gene is someone who likes to ask you what you think of something after he has determined to do it and has no intention of reconsidering. Warren Beatty recommended he come with me after Gene had completed "The French Connection," and before it was seen. The expectations before the film came out were modest because Gene was, after all, the seventh choice for the role of Popeye Doyle, Jackie Gleason having been among the prior choices. People know these things, and it discourages positive anticipation. So, no one was inclined to speculate the kind of career launch that film actually afforded Gene. It arrived with question marks all over it and lowered expectations, but first screenings made clear that the film and Gene would be stars forever. To lock in Gene's new and exalted position I proposed that if he were invited to do something, he should first ask himself "would Robert Redford do this?" So one morning he called me and said, "I was just asked to play at Dodger Stadium in a celebs ballgame with former Dodger stars, and I asked myself 'would Robert Redford do this?' and the answer came back 'probably not,' but do you want to come down and watch me do it anyway?"

During the production of Stanley Donen's "Lucky Lady," a period comedy/romantic/adventure lark which teamed Gene with Liza Minnelli and Burt Reynolds, I was handling not only the actor-and-soon-to-be Oscar-winning producer Michael Douglas but also his name-sharer, the talk show host Mike Douglas. Gene was in the middle of his most intense period of flying, which prominently included learning, accomplishing and exhibiting aerobatic flying in his Pitts Special bi-plane. He also had a small (one airplane) airline which was contracted to fly stars and production staff to and from the location in Mexico.

He was also permitted to keep hls Pitts Special aerobatic bi-plane down there. As he once explained to me, "aerobatic flying is not something you do on Sunday" meaning one-day-a-week. On one occasion I had arranged on behalf of the Mike Douglas Show for Gene to take Reynolds on a flight demonstrating to Burt and to the Douglas viewing audience what a neat little aerobatic plane could do. A camera was affixed so that both pilot (Gene) and passenger (Burt Reynolds) remained with their heads always at the top of the screen but so that the earth and sky could be viewed swirling behind them… only sky during a dive or earth in a climb or jumbling around upside down and backwards as they tumbled through the sky. It made you dizzy just to watch. When Gene had the plane upside down, the earth was at the top of the screen.

At one point it all became a bit too much even for as inveterately courageous and daring a guy as Reynolds… or at least for his stomach. You could clearly see him throwing up… but in this one single case in the annals of stomach revolt, you could actually see him throwing UP. The plane was upside down at the moment. Since the camera was affixed in the same attitude as the plane, Gene and Burt were still seen with their asses at the bottom of the screen and their heads toward the top even though those heads were actually pointed toward the ground. So when Burt regurgitated, the resulting spew, naturally drawn by gravity, seems to fly straight up from his mouth. It was one of the greatest special effects in history. I have to say for Mike Douglas that even after having seen this footage, he still let Hackman take him up to experience aerobatic flight. And he properly kept his lunch down… or up, depending on whether or not the plane was upside down.

I never went up in the Pitts with Gene, and with wise caution. During our joint writing of "Snaproll" (a term describing a plane's sudden alteration of attitude from right-side-up to upside-down,) Gene described to me one of his favorite aerobatic tricks called the "lomshavoc" or however that inscribes in English. It is, he said, a Hungarian term for complete chaos, total absence of control. In this insanity, the pilot does something which sends the plane cart-wheeling through the skies, whirly-gigging itself and its passengers about, twirling, spinning, corkscrewing and agitating the air and challenging the pilot to find some way out of this mess. He recited it with such hand-wringing delight that I knew that if I ever was stupid enough to get behind him in those open cockpits, I would be lomshavocked out of breakfast, lunch and dinner, returned to the imposed drug-addled psychosis of my reckless youth, reduced to a state of zombiehood. And I, wisely, would never allow Gene that pleasure.

My favorite recollection relating to "Lucky Lady" however did not involve Gene. Gisela and I were in San Francisco one weekend visiting my aunt and uncle, and just by chance the rough cut of "Lucky Lady" was getting an afternoon sneak test screening at a prominent Bay Area movie house. I arranged for us all to attend. The film was in such an early stage of editing that it was being projected in what was called "dual system," meaning that the visual would be shown from one projector and the sound, held in sync with the image through some technology, would be broadcast from another machine. Normally this works, but in this case it didn't. And that was particularly disconcerting because, not by any device of the studio, that king of tough trade paper reporters whom I nonetheless enjoyed as a friend, Art Murphy, was among those in the audience. At one point the screening literally ground to a halt. The lights came up and someone turned on the musak to entertain an audience, serving only to further annoy them and make them feel trapped in a stuck elevator.

As I mentioned, the film was directed by Stanley Donen who had also directed "Singin' In The Rain," "Seven Brides For Seven Brothers," "Charade," "Two For The Road," "The Grass Is Greener," "On The Town," "Funny Face" and "Royal Wedding" among his many great gifts to us. In other words, a prince of the idolized filmmakers realm and someone I knew well and held in affection because he was married to Guttman & Pam's client,, the uniquely beautiful Yvette Mimieux. After about 10 minutes the crowd became restive-going-on-unruly. Hollywood great Stanley Donen appeared on the stage and began to extend an apology… the old if-you-will-just-bear-with-us, and you couldn't even hear it because of the musak. Some guy yelled out, "Either turn off the music or start to dance." Donen, a one time Broadway hoofer, recognized a great cue when it presented itself, and he began to do a delightful buck-and-wing across the stage, one that would have made his buddy Gene Kelly very proud of him. The audience erupted in a great ovation and delight and then, miraculously, the screen burst into image behind Stanley and the film resumed. You couldn't hear the first minute or so because the applause continued so enthusiastically.

The terrific post-script to this is that there WAS none. Murphy, witness to what was almost a Hollywood debacle which he could easily deride in Daily Variety, apparently admired Donen's return to dance performance along with the rest of us and he never wrote a word about it. That's class honoring class. Yes, I'm telling the story now, but it is, with the passage of time, an homage to an event in its charming resourcefulness and class.

Another time, during the contract negotiations for "The Firm," Gene called to report that although it was determined that Cruise and he were both before the titles on the screen, Tom had a contractual clause that only Cruise could be above the titles in the ads. "And you determined?" I asked, pretty sure what the answer would be. "I told them not to put my name in the ads." It was probably the only time a major studio film was released with key ad art not shouting the name of one of its headline players who happened to be an Oscar-winning superstar. Gene was perfectly content and actually found it funny. I loved it because it demonstrated how Gene is uniquely Gene, a guy of great humility and honor, the combination of which makes it impossible for him to allow himself to be pushed around. I witnessed the equally Gene flip side of that at the Golden Globe awards the night he won for "The French Connection." A woman came up to him holding out the program and asked him to sign on his picture which appeared on the top of a page above an already autographed picture of Alfred Hitchcock. Gene asked her if he could sign on the back of the program instead. She insisted, but he said "I could never put my signature above Alfred Hitchcock's."

The night he won the Oscar for the most relentless of cops, Popeye Doyle, a cordon of about thirty cops escorted him out of the Dorothy Chandler Pavilion as though he were the president, while all of the other stars made it out on their own. It embarrassed the hell out of Gene, but he was cordial with each of them because he knew they felt it was an award for cops, and he was very content with that.

While he was filming Robert Rossen's last motion picture, "Lillith," Warren Beatty called to tell me about this powerful stage actor who was making his film debut in that drama. That exposure got Gene his role in "Hawaii," and then a year later Warren knew with no second thought what Gene could bring to "Bonnie And Clyde," Gene's first Oscar nomination and a fast track to such films as "Downhill Racer" and "I Never Sang For My Father" which resulted in his second nomination. Warren declined the Sundance Kid role because he would do it only if Gene were Butch. It would have been a very different film, but no doubt still a helluva movie. Beatty has proven many times over that he is one of our great directors, film innovators and sage casting minds His instincts are solid gold. All Beatty-directed films resulted in Oscar gold for someone and well over fifty nominations in aggregate. And many of those for acting performances, his own included

Hackman certainly could have been/would have been as inventive and personal a director as he is an actor, and he was tempted to do it and was offered that opportunity many times, one instance mentioned above. When I surrendered to the reality that he was never going to do it, I asked him why and got that heh-heh-heh Hackman chuckle and then, "I'd kill the actors." That, I knew, was a joke, because I've never known anyone more protective of actors than Gene. When we were in New York for promotion of "Superman II," Gene and Chris Reeve and I were going out to catch Joe Williams in performance... I mean, when in New York, see the monuments. I'd spoken to a terrific actress whom Guttman & Pam represented and who happened to be there and I'd asked her to join us. She was beautiful, exceedingly talented and extremely serious and intense. In preparing Gene to meet her, I very thoughtlessly and inaccurately used the phrase "high strung," and he gave me that did-you-ever-pick-your-feet-in-Poughkeepsie? look of dire and dangerous irritation. "Don't ever say that about an actor," he growled. "Those are sensibilities. That's what she draws on."

During a break in the filming of "All Night Long," Gene had explained the Method concept of "sense memory" to me, and that dealt with the sensibilities on which an actor draws. What I took from it is how deep an actor has to go to bring real and sustainable emotional truth to a scene. The point I felt he was making (I don't claim to be very fluent in the language of acting) is that if you're reaching back to express anguish, you can't effectively do it by remembering seeing your dog run over. That access will fly for the first take, but it would be exhausted by take five. As kidding as he was about not directing out of concern for the physical well-being of the actors, I wonder if he really was constrained by the idea of making imperious demands. He's very respectful of other people's feelings and territory. However, on one action film, he also was concerned that the director wasn't fond of master shots to the extent that he wasn't doing them, and Gene told him he wouldn't do the constituent closer scenes until a master was in the can and the actors knew what the hell they'd done in the master. The producers quietly expressed to me their exceeding gratitude that Gene had done that. It had worried the hell out of them, too, and they were counting on Gene's pinning the director to the wall.

When we were writing "Snaproll" together, he hired an airline pilot to give authenticity to tha tower-to-cockpit talk of a scene in which the airline pilot character is landing at an airport. Gene wanted to capture the exact professional exchange. He told me this apologetically as if I might think it an invasion of a writer's space. I didn't, and it wasn't. Accuracy is always welcome. Gene has told me more than once that he's had it up to here with my urging him to get back to work. He asked recently why I kept bugging him, and I said it was because there's so little real gold around, why keep it in the vault? To which, also very Gene, he said, "Thank you." On another occasion of my pressuring him to return, he explained that he held back "because they'd pay me all that money, and I'd still feel angry." "Well, take half as much money and you'd feel half as angry." "No," he laughed, "I'd feel twice as angry."

Like almost all physically powerful men I've worked with in Hollywood, Gene simply never looked for a fight. So I was perplexed when I got a call from Associated Press one day with questions relating to Gene's having been in a traffic altercation punch-out on Sunset Blvd. I had no information to give them, so they gave me theirs. Gene was ok, but the two guys with whom he had the tussle, were sitting on a curb when the police got there, which seemed in the telling to have been a kind of recuperative posture. I gave AP some quote that Gene very specifically does not provoke a fight. Gene called the next day and asked where I'd gotten the quote I gave AP. "From you," I said, "you don't remember the time that (an actor not to be named) punched out (a director not to be named,) and it was going to trial and the actor's manager called to ask if you'd punched out the same director... that it would help his client's case if you had?. And you did this long pause and I marveled at the thought you couldn't remember if you punched that director, to which you said, 'It's not that. I was running it over in my mind, and I don't think I've ever punched anyone in my life.' *That's* where I got it." He thought it over and then said, "I told you I'd never had a punch-out?" "Yeah." "I must have been lying through my teeth."

There was only one thing about the Sunset Blvd. bout that bothered Gene, disappointed him, really. A lot of people who'd watched the fracas from inside Wolfgang Puck's restaurant there, came out to see if he was all right once the cops got there. And among these was a key executive at the Directors Guild, the offices of which were around the corner. He said to Gene, "Mr. Hackman, I'm with the Directors Guild…" and Gene anticipated he would continue to say, "and on behalf of the twelve thousand members of our Guild, I'd like to tell you that we're really happy you finally got your ass kicked." But he didn't say that. He just gave Gene his card and offered his witness in case Gene needed it. Gene felt cheated of some great cleansing experience. I asked if he'd taken any damage, and he showed me some scratches on his neck and jaw where the woman who was with the two guys had grabbed him from behind. "That was it?" I asked. He said, "No," and showed me his hands. His knuckles were really banged up. The incident had occurred after a car containing two guys and the woman had cut a right turn in front of Gene from the left lane. Gene got out to give them his business manager's card, figuring as most actors do that if you're famous, it's your fault. But these guys wanted more, and Gene got the fact that what they wanted was a piece of him, so he was ready when they tried to get it. They were in their thirties. Gene was in his seventies.

It was one of those phrases that you heard only in murder trial movies or watching that early hit series on American TV, the televised coverage of the HUAC (House Un-American Activities Committee) hearings into what the congressional right wing insisted was "pervasive" communist influence in Hollywood. "I take the Fifth" or "I refuse to answer on the basis of my Fifth Amendment rights not to incriminate myself." But, thanks to Gene, I actually heard it uttered in a federal hearing. You have to imagine a time (and, yes, it did exist) before the public use of video tapes not to mention DVDs. Even then there was a traffic in pirated copies of Hollywood motion pictures, and it was in form of 16mm films. It was not as endemic as the current illegal industry of DVD copies of current or even not-yet-released films which can be purchased on any street corner or bus in the world. It is a scourge which severely diminishes both Hollywood's profit margin and the public's supposedly firm commitment not to profit from a crime. But in the '70s and early '80s, the sale of 16mm prints was an early warning signal, and the Justice Department was holding Los Angeles hearings into it. Gene was called to appear because he alone or among very few stars always had a contractual clause to be provided a 16mm copy of his films. He wasn't fond of seeing them at public screenings, and this way he could watch them in his own home. I accompanied him, not a lawyer, because what he did was perfectly legal, not to mention contractual. The federal attorney, very respectful of this adulated Oscar-winning artist, merely confirmed his practice of receiving the prints. And then he asked if Gene was aware of illegal sale of other films. There was a pause before Gene said, "I refuse to answer on the basis of my Fifth Amendment rights not to incriminate myself." You could hear a chorus of "huhs?" throughout the room, general consternation…. Incriminate himself in what? They just dropped it and thanked him for his appearance. When we got to the car I said, "The Fifth Amendment? You weren't on trial. You had a contractual clause and you weren't guilty of anything." Gene smiled and said, "I know, but I flashed-back to the HUAC hearings, and I knew I could never say someone else' name in court. If they'd asked me to name our newspaper delivery boy, I couldn't have said Bobby." What his dramatic choice did say was a lot about who Gene Hackman is.

I've always had an affinity for people who, as I, look to the lyrics of the American songbook to describe their feelings. Those hundreds of wonderful tunes, America's greatest artistic gift to the world, gave us the emotional catch phrases for our lives. So I remember quite well a specific interview I set for Gene in the '70s with the Times of London. The final question of a very intelligent exchange was "And what do you wish for yourself?" Gene paused a moment to step around the quicksand of clichés which that invited. "Most of all" he said,, "I wish me love."

It's nice that it turned out that way.

Chapter 23

Oscar Fever

The Care And Feeding of Masterpieces

We came out of the big star-crunch celebrity premiere of "Reds" in Westwood, and Gisela said, "Well, Warren has you back in the masterpiece business again." That redundancy was intentional, underlining the déjà-vu-all-over-again-ness of it. Almost all of the films Warren produced or produced and directed were destined for Oscar prominence, always in the mix, constantly nominated, frequently winning. Seven films alone garnered well over 50 nominations, and his own nominations quickly went into double digits, which wasn't astonishing since two films all by themselves brought him eight nominations, a personal best no other artist has ever approached. "Heaven Can Wait" and "Reds" each resulted in Warren Beatty nomination for Best Director, Best Actor, Best Screenplay and Best Film. The only other such instance in Oscar history was Orson Welles for "Citizen Kane."

The promotional approach for a film should derive from what makes the film special. I've observed that every veteran flack of the Oscar game does this. I begin every campaign assignment, however much or little I will be expected contribute to the cause, by determining what that film has that none of the competition can claim. When I was invited aboard "Lincoln," it became apparent to me that what Stephen Spielberg's film had, alone of that year's crop, was that it was passionately patriotic in the historic sense. It touched on a moment exactly a century and a half before when the United States, under the determination of its greatest hero, did the right thing concerning slavery. "Argo," also of that year, was patriotic, too, in that it referred us back to an torturous time in which the Iranian revolution held our embassy staff and our country's pride hostage. Giving a version of the lone victory America could celebrate during that agony, it engaged our currently operative anger at the Ayatollahs' oppression. Iran was, at the moment of the 2012 Oscar campaigning, actively and boisterously seeking to build nuclear bombs. Anger, it turned out, trumped pride. It was "Argo's" year, no matter how many good minds Disney brought to "Lincoln" and Weinstein brought to "Silver Linings Playbook" and "Django." And, believe me, their campaign meetings were jammed with many of the top PR minds in town and electric with concentration and input.

What I'm going to do here is not do thumbnails on the well over a hundred campaigns I've touched, but rather look at a few specific decisions which illustrate the focus and excitement of Oscar season.

With "Reds," one of the distinguishing aspects of the film's originality was the inserted commentary of "witnesses," distinguished people then still with us who had actual personal experience with John Reed and other historical figures who populate the story of the only American buried in the Kremlin. Warren enriches his story with recollections by these fascinating people, historical in their own right. *Much of the determining element which will influence the degree to which a viewer will love a film is the after-taste, how he or she factors and savors it into memory.* Part of this depends on the clarity of perception. We often read the printed program of a play or opera after the performance, locking certain things into memory. For that "Reds" kickoff, we had the lobby mined with posters and other visual aids to clarify for the exiting audience of Oscar voters just who these witnesses were and to specify how they fit into the John Reed story. It helped viewers keep that aspect of the film straight. Paramount was, in effect, working the film's edge, being not only great romantic drama but also thoroughly authentic history. Paramount also made elegant color programs handed to the invited guests of special screenings of "Reds." I had Warren request added printings of these. This was 1981, before the advent of the mailing of screeners (videos and then DVDs) of contending films to Academy voters, so most of these people would view the film in its public run, often at their neighborhood theatres. We determined which movie houses were most likely to draw the attendance of Academy voters who were able to enter with a guest upon presentation of their Academy cards, the convenience extended by all aspiring films. We supplied these theatres with large quantities of the brochures so that when an Academy member signed in, he or she was given the program to read later at home, to ingrain the experience. It was not something other films did and it added a certain dimension to the experience of having seen that film.

The Power of Shaking Hands

When Columbia brought Guttman & Pam on to contribute to maximizing the Oscar prospects for "Kramer Vs. Kramer," it was agreed all around that for all its brilliance, it carried a strange cloud around with it. The Academy had a general feeling that Dustin Hoffman didn't much respect the award-giving process or care if he won or didn't win. He had made disparaging comment about the practice on one of his three prior Best Actor nominations, I believe it was "Midnight Cowboy." He had also been nominated for "The Graduate" and "Lenny." I was always surprised by Hoffman's widely reported and vehemently expressed indifference because at the Golden Globes at which he won something like Best New Actor for "Graduate," many of the award winners were absent, and all evening designated recipients had been saying "I'm sure so-and-so regrets that he/she/they couldn't be here tonight to accept this in person." So when Dustin was announced winner in his category and was an actual winner who actually came to the stage, he said, "I'm sure that I regret not being able be here tonight to accept this in person..." The rest was drowned out in laughter." You had the feeling that this was a guy who got the game and was OK with that. But then came his verbal rejection of a nomination, and a decade later when "Kramer" came to its heat, it wasn't at all clear how much he cared. Jerry Pam came up with a great solution... have Dustin be in town and showing up anywhere there was a minion of voters. The studio sold this idea to him, and Dustin Hoffman was by dint of his very presence... and presence and presence and presence... subtly getting the word about that he did not disdain the process.

And so the Academy cared, too. It cleared the road for "Kramer" to win Best Film, Best Actor for Hoffman, Supporting actress for Streep and direction and adapted screenplay for Robert Benton. Hoffman went on to win again for "Rainman." In Hollywood you have to not look like you expect and deserve an honor without disturbing the public perception that your not getting it would be an outrage against God's will. Of course that film did have clear artistic claim to these awards.

THE FINE ART OF GOING-FOR-IT: Talia Shire and I had our only argument after she'd arranged for me to see an advance screening of "Rocky." The question was which Oscar category she should target. I was insisting on Best Actress. She was dead-set on Supporting. She'd had no Oscar juice from the first "Godfather," and I wanted her to get maximum career push from "Rocky."

I'd had no professional association with "The Godfather," the first one, other than that my friend and film school buddy, Fred Roos, was one of the producers. He was also the casting genius who worked with Francis Ford Copolla to aggregate the great casts of stars-to-be for the "Godfather" films, the "Rumblefish" films and "American Graffiti" which Francis produced for this new kid George Lucas to get Universal to make it. Add in the other films Fred cast for Lucas, Sophia Coppola, Hal Ashby, Jack Nicholson and other actors, producers and directors and you soon see that he launched a whole generations of stars, perhaps THE whole generation. Suffice it to say that when Harrison Ford did his "Inside The Actor's Studio" with Jim Lipton, he did a call-out to Fred's discovery of him for telling character roles in "American Graffiti," "The Conversation," "Apocalypse Now" and then, quite literally, the rocket-ship to stardom in "Star Wars." Ford could have wound up being just a great looking leading man, but Fred gave him a body of work that spelled "actor."

It's what Jack Lemmon told Jerry Pam once when we were doing the campaign for "Save The Tiger"… that Billy Wilder had promised him to keep casting him in great roles until at least one established him as a star and at least one established him as an actor. And he needed that, his early Oscar notwithstanding. Jack had won the Supporting Actor Oscar for his third film, "Mr. Roberts," but for the next five years he was substantially just a guy doing good work and waiting for the right one to come along. It was "Some Like It Hot, " and just to make it stick, Wilder handed him "The Apartment" the following year.

Fred had commanded me to an early screening of the original "Godfather" and asked me to watch the performance of Talia Shire because she was his friend and Francis' sister. Fred Roos as much as anyone in town supremely understood great performance and he understood that I had certain skills relating to Oscar race handicapping and campaigning. Tali certainly looked like a Supporting Actress nomination lock to me, but I wasn't hired because she didn't have the money at that point. Her then husband, composer David Shire, had not yet become a millionaire for one song in the "Saturday Night Fever" score and album. The Paramount publicity department, with sound reason, felt it could handle the film's general Oscar promotion very well, which it certainly did big time. But Tali did not get a nomination which would have been hers with a bit more visibility. Here's how I arrive at that: She had delivered a standout performance in one of the year's two "big shoulder" movies ("Cabaret" was the other,) and all five nominated actresses in her category were for films that weren't nominated for Best Film and were essentially well-received but "smaller" films, the exception being Shelly Winters for a popcorn movie, "The Poseidon Adventure" (There's always an exception.) That may seem a kind of niggling analysis, but it's that kind of knowledge about how the system works that lets you have a good batting average in working on Oscar campaigns. Those were all factors which effect votes. Look at it this way... in theory they can't or won't vote for you if they haven't seen your work. Almost all of the actor members of the Academy (who alone vote acting category nominations) surely saw "Godfather," the film of the year, the ultimate Best Film winner. In a time when voters saw contending films only in movie theatres or at special screenings, not via their video players, they would have had to work very hard to have seen those other five films. Paramount flat-out did not work hard enough for Tali. She needed personal representation. Any skilled Oscar promoter would assure you that it was a fumble pure and simple. The Oscar trail is littered with such injustices, but this wasn't a mere injustice, it was a screw-up.

The upside to this history is that it provided the fuel for a campaign I did for Tali two years later that appeared to help get her a supporting nomination for "Godfather 2," a film in which she delivered well but in an infinitely weaker role. (A side-thought, here: Someone should do a book on the greatest performances never nominated. It would be a stupendous hall of fame. Start with Vivien Leigh in "Waterloo Bridge" and Gene Hackman in "The Conversation.") So when "Godfather II" came along, such things were not to be left to chance again. Fred and Tali and, I assumed, Francis wanted me to do the campaign. The problem, again, was that Tali's role in the second film was not nearly as fiery and operatic as were her protected sister/battered wife theatrics in the original. It didn't have what Gene Hackman calls "a scene," meaning a signature passage that conveys in concentrated spades the size and intensity of the performance in general. It had a strong character theme and a few scenes in which Tali was largely connective tissue for Michael Corleone with his brother Fredo (the brilliant Michael Cazale) and Michael Corleone's wife played by Diane Keaton. But the role offered nothing like her fireworks in "The Godfather." Charged with achieving justice for her this time, I was convinced that we had to reheat and put to use the general awareness among Academy members (particularly Actor Branch members) that Talia Shire was sadly (in discussing Oscar voting one never employs the word or concept "unfairly") passed over the first time around. I had a conversation about this with columnist (and close friend) James Bacon, and he agreed with me that her initial performance had been overlooked. He wrote a column from which I derived a key ad quote, "Talia Shire, who did not get the Oscar nomination she so powerfully deserved for her work in the first 'Godfather,' must certainly get it for her delicate and moving work in 'Godfather II.'" It was a quote that I took to the bank because it captured the double-pronged strategy we were working for the campaign. I used it in my ads for Tali, and the studio picked up on it, too, coming in with support for Tali in the Paramount campaign, which they hadn't for her more powerful work before. That kind of appeal to justice does work itself into the industry's mind, and it is an industry that has a great affection for justice. Every actor has been overlooked for some magnificent achievement as Tali had been for "The Godfather." It is not the letter of how the voting is described, but it certainly is the spirit. The nomination materialized for the second film.

Two years later there was another decision to be made, and that was the basis of Tali's and my disagreement. After that early screening of "Rocky" she asked me if I thought she could get another supporting nomination. I told her I thought she could *win* supporting but, more importantly, I thought she could get a Best Actress nomination, and that could lock her in as a lead actress. "The roles aren't necessarily better, but the money and the stature are." I insisted. She resisted, and I laid history on the table for her.

It's true that actresses like Eva Marie Saint and Goldie Hawn, Claire Trevor, Ann Baxter and Teresa Wright had gone on to become mainline leading ladies after early Supporting Actress wins, but there were fifty others who rather stayed top character performers. There is also the group including Ingrid Bergman and Vanessa Redgrave, Meryl Streep, Cate Blanchett, Rene Zellwigger and Angelina Jolie who won supporting Oscars *after* they were well-established as above-the-title stars. This kind of jockeying came to a head in the run toward nominations for 2008, when the Academy sent out an advisory that voting members need not feel obliged to vote for a contender in the category that the contender or distributor seems to have designated the category of choice. That may have contributed to

Kate Winslet's being nominated for and then winning the Best Actress Oscar for "The Reader," even after she had been presented in "Reader" ads as a supporting entry and had even won the Golden Globe and other awards for Best Supporting for "Reader" while also winning other awards for Best Actress for "Revolutionary Road. Harvey Weinstein and I had had conversations early on that the voters might defy the ads and nominate and possibly even award her as Best Actress for "The Reader." It was in the performance. Harvey had courteously acceded to the supporting campaign at her request. She did not wish to compete with her performance in her husband's film.

Tali's brother, Francis, had two director nominations for 1974's "Godfather II" and "The Conversation," but the Academy rules allow actors to have only one nomination in the same category in a given year. Winslet's "Revolutionary Road" performance very conceivably could have been or probably was among the top five nomination vote-getters but even so would have been disqualified for Best Actress nomination because it was exceeded by her "Reader" votes. Self-determination, however, was the case in 1976, and Tali discussed this with Fred and, I'm sure, her brother. They each concurred with me. She went on to be nominated as the lead actress in the film that won the Oscar. She was the female star of the film of the year. That had negotiating weight for her agents and paid off with films in which she played the lead opposite substantial actors.

It is *de rigueur* practice now during Oscar campaigning season to send out "screeners," DVD copies of each contending film, which assures that a voter has a chance to see each film at home, if not at one of the many screenings or the theatrical run. The first time I ever sent out a screener mailing, and this was video tapes since it antedated DVDs, was 1987 for "Innerspace." This was just selected scenes and it was a decision that occasioned great debate. Guttman & Pam was representing LucasFilm including George Lucas' special effects house, Industrial Light And Magic. Only two films were nominated for the FX Oscar that year, the other being an Arnold Schwarzenegger blow-'em-up movie. The ILM work for "Innerspace" was miniaturizing Dennis Quaid to be injected into Martin Short's cardio-vascular. The idea for the campaign was "it doesn't have to go boom to be special effects" since FX was not yet the inescapable must-have for most films that it now is. I had proposed sending out about ten minutes of FX clips to prove the point. The cost involved seems miniscule now considering what is spent on

Oscar ads and the mailing of copies of the full films, but it raised eyebrows then. Lynne Hale, the accomplished public relations chief behind the Lucasfilm empire, pushed it through, and ILM carried the award home. That is not to imply that it won because of the mailing. It won because the effects were exceptional work. But the voters have to see that, and it was unlikely that they had all seen that film. Some who may have seen neither of the actual films conceivably could have voted in that category, perhaps influenced by what they saw on that tape. There's no way to measure to what degree a specific promotional concept contributes to the vote count. You just have a sense if it's positive or negative, but in winning circumstances, I like to think that at least we didn't KEEP the client from winning.

Harvey Weinstein 101

Each year for at least the past forty years (half that time in partnership with Jerry Pam,) I've been contracted by various studios to consult on Oscar campaigns together with other skilled press agents in this competitive field. Working for a variety of companies on a variety of films, I attend many strategy conferences, and as "standard operating procedure" as are many of the recurring practices in this high stakes pursuit, it is amazing how often someone at the table comes up with an idea totally new and impactful. We wind up being each other's teachers, and you want to be at your best and most creative not only because you're being paid to do so or because you believe in the film, but because it is such an interesting competition as well as collaboration among equals. Another interesting given is that at some point in each meeting, someone will say, pointing out a promising approach, "this is "Harvey Weinstein 101." Harvey brought a don't-miss-a-base, never-give-up energy to the fine art of Oscar campaigning. His ideas are always flattered with imitation by his competitors, but he always has something he invents or greenlights for each new campaign. That's how he stays ahead of the game. Not only does he want to win, but It has the corollary benefit of assuring talent that he backs them to the hilt. That can be a compelling incentive when a great film is looking for the right studio at which to land.

A large part of the excitement and (in its *extreme*) challenge of working with Harvey is that he is, to the best of my personal memory, the only distribution company overlord in my experience who was personally on the job on the campaigns' strategy… and details. He cares. And he questions. And, when needed, he personally moves mountains, big ones. You feel like a member of Dwight D. Eisenhower's staff in those WW2 strategy meetings. Or a more apt analogy might be the strategy meetings conducted by General George S. Patton.

There are other producers of my experience who provide the same hands-on leadership… Warren Beatty, Robert Radnitz… Kirk Douglas, certainly, and Michael, too. They were fully involved stewards. But of studio chiefs, Harvey stands alone, although Freddie Fields at MGM loved "The Year Of Living Dangerously" and he was there for it all along, looking over shoulders, challenging you into ideas, but not imposing them. I never had the opportunity to work under David O. Selznick, Sam Goldwyn, Daryl F. Zanuck, Jack Warner, Howard Hughes or Harry Cohn… much to my regret and probably, in some of those cases, much to my good fortune. I'm sure they were at the wheel all the way through and would have been interesting to get instructed and buised by.

In "covering the bases," you have to know or intuit what influences people's opinions, and you have to isolate and target what particular information you are trying to communicate to the industry at each particular phase of the voting procedure. Your first task is to get the voters, accomplished artists all, to *see* it. Your second task to get them to see it *again*. Your third task is to make them aware how much everyone else loves this film. You can't talk (or, even more, argue) Academy members into liking or voting for your film. In the first place, it's forbidden by Academy rules. It's always the voter's deliberated decision, and that has to be respected. People in the movie business take this procedure very seriously and are very protective of the honor and integrity of their vote. But there are subtle and thoroughly proper ways to influence deliberation.

Heading Trouble Off at the Pass

Toward the end of the voting period, you make an effort to reach those who you know favor your film and to motivate them to cast their vote. Some simply do not vote or forget the deadline. Also, that is a period to re-validate and re-dedicate people's conclusions. And to keep them from being de-validated. This became quite crucial when I working for Clint Eastwood and Warner Bros. in championing the cause of "Unforgiven," which begot Eastwood's first Oscars for Best Motion Picture and Best Director. Going into the final days of balloting, we knew that "Unforgiven" was very possibly going to be the leading vote-getter, and we didn't want anything to take away from that. Johnny Carson, then still the host of The Tonight Show, was in the habit of having Gene Siskel and Roger Ebert guest at that particular time to discuss where they thought the votes would go. I knew that Roger loved "Unforgiven" and that Gene really disliked it. I booked someone else on that show so that I could be there. I wanted to talk to Gene about his possible launching into a diatribe about why he disliked Clint's film. However out of touch with popular opinion he was in this particular judgment, he was a guy whose opinion was justly respected, and I was afraid he could talk some industry viewers out of putting their X on the ballot next to " Unforgiven" for film and/or Director. I stopped by his dressing room for a chat before he and Roger would go out to chat with Johnny Carson.

I eased into the subject by saying "So, Gene, you're going to do an all-out attack on 'Unforgiven,' right?" "You have any problem with that?" he said, knowing full-well that I worked for Clint. "On one hand, no... freedom of speech. I'm a great believer in it." "And on the other hand?" he asked suspiciously. "My problem is that you're my friend and I don't want you finding yourself out on a limb ten days from now when 'Unforgiven' wins everything. You sell your opinion, Gene, but in this case you wind up looking like the only guy who didn't know." What I was telling him was true. He was my friend, I did care, and, as he well knew, I also had ulterior motive. Which of my motives should he trust? I suggested both. As I made my case for the inevitability of Clint's winning, he decided that he did come to trust that I had an honest concern deriving from our friendship. "Great!" he said angrily, finally surrendering to my reason, "That was the main thrust of everything I was going to say. I don't have time to construct a whole new position that has any punch." I remembered a conversation Jerry Pam and I had had that morning as we batted around the Academy possibilities, and I remembered a conclusion Jerry had made that seemed very solid to me. So I said to Gene, "You're going to predict that Marisa Tomei will win Best Supporting Actress for 'My Cousin Vinnie.'" Gene was a little taken aback. Tomei was sparkling and brilliant in that film, but so were the other nominees, all very distinguished actresses of long reputation in very important films. And they were each nominated for films which would seem to have more voter clout than the delightful "Vinnie." Gene made these arguments, and then I explained to him what Jerry Pam had figured out and how Jerry's rationales had a great batting average. All of the other nominees were Brits, said Jerry, himself a Brit, and that has divided-vote all over it. He was sure Marisa would win. Siskel was unsure, but a production assistant came in to give him the two minute count before he went on, and he had nothing else to go with. Gene walked out the door like a guy going to his execution, but he went out there and sold the Marisa Tomei idea like a sailor on the twenty-third hour of a twenty-four hour pass. Johnnie Carson and even Roger Ebert, who had been expecting the attack on "Unforgiven," were both surprised and more than a little skeptical. Gene gave me an uncertain look when he came off.

The question arises, would I have gone out to Burbank to warn Gene off the "Unforgiven" attack if I hadn't been handling the film? Would I have gone out "merely" to steer a friend right? I think the answer is that I probably would have made a phone call, but we'll never know.

That, shortly thereafter, became academic. Marisa Tomei did win, and the audience was as surprised... and, actually, delighted... as Carson and Ebert had been. Gene Siskel was one of the few seers who was on record as having seen it coming. When I saw him backstage at the Oscars while I was escorting Clint through the press rooms, Gene said, "Thanks." "Does it make up for the kidnapping at the O'Hare Airport?" I asked. And he answered, "No."

Anyone Can Be A Contender: The contender period of any Oscar race is the part I find most exciting. It's the time from early September (when Oscar anticipation starts to taint the industry's every thought) up to late-January when the nominations are announced. Until then, it's anybody's guess... and everybody's opportunity. ... A QUESTION MARK IS FAR MORE POWERFUL THAN AN EXCLAMATION MARK. The question mark engages us in a mystery, while an exclamation point is merely one man's opinion being shouted at you. The question of who will be nominated captures everyone's attention and a third of a year of nail-biting.

There is a prelude or overture and three acts to the drama of the Academy awards. The prelude is that time before a film's release when it is bragged all over the place for its "Oscar Potential." Jerry Pam captured the magic of this fertile prologue with his unchallengeable philosophy that *"Every film is fifty million dollars and five nominations until it comes out.* And that was when fifty million dollars was *a hundred* fifty million dollars. There is gold to be mined from such anticipation, careers to be impelled by such speculation, roles aspired-to which suddenly become possible for the prematurely anointed when they are talked up. Act One of this annual Oscar ritual is the "contender period." Lasting from September to late January, nearly five months, it is by far the most interesting of

The Three Acts Of The Oscar drama. It is during this wide-open electioneering period, that every good film and good performance is A Potentional Nominee. Act Two is The Time Of The Nominees. The nominees are for that five or six weeks princes and princesses of the realm, and this is where agents and managers run around turning that heat into next films. Act Three is the time of harvest, the time of glory for the winners. That is when the new movie deals discussed during the nominee period get nailed down and other fruit are plucked from the tree. Barry Fitzgerald was nominated both for Best Actor and Best Supporting Actor for "Going My Way," and won for the latter. But after that, with the Academy's tacit concurrence, the studios and the performers no longer left such things to chance. They spelled out the category of their election in advance in ads and in publicity. But every electorate has a mind of its own, and in 2008 the Academy urged its members to exercise that judgment to the exclusion of studio dictates. The voters and not the studios decide.

The over-riding opportunity of Oscar chatter is that for five glorious months a hundred press agents get to present three hundred clients as serious contenders. "He's/She's a top contender" is an oft heard battle-cry and the basis of many an interview or magazine story pitch. If the work on screen is good enough and the PR campaign creative and urgent enough, anything is possible. What is real and irrefutable is the value of being seen as a contender. You never want a client to reproach you with the line Marlon Brando so poignantly asserted to Rod Steiger in "On The Waterfront." "I coulda been a contendah."

"Rocky" was, by every judgment, a classic example of great Oscar campaign management, one with which I had no involvement except for Talia Shire's campaign, and then, through her referral, that of Burt Young. Burt, who played her brother in the film, is not only a fine character actor, but a compellingly great guy. A single and devoted father, a well-trained actor, a sophisticated guy with the charming rough edges of the ex-boxer that he was, he made me want to help him take advantage of a big opportunity. But I didn't want him to commit very precious funds to a campaign unless I was certain I could make it pay off for him. I guessed that "Rocky" producers, Bob Chartoff and Irwin Winkler, and United Artists were dedicated to a campaign for Burgess Meredith for Supporting Actor.

It made sense, with the added steam of a possible career-capping award for one of Hollywood's longtime greatest actors. The studio press guys confirmed that. I had almost no chance of scoring a nomination for Burt if he wasn't part of the studio's ad campaign. It's hard to make Oscar voters believe in a performance that the studio itself and the producers themselves don't believe in sufficiently to include in the campaign.

That was a rule that we were able to break for Jennifer Tilly for "Bullets Over Broadway" when Woody Allen and United Artists chose to bet all of their chips on Diane Weist who did go on to win the Supporting Oscar for that film. We would have gotten nowhere for Jennifer if we had been compelled to resort to ads that were evidently taken by her personally. Allen's producing partner, Jean Doumejian, was sympathetic to our effort, and we prevailed upon her to let us place ads which appeared to have been taken by Ms. Doumejian. Jennifer, with the producer's kind loan of her name, was nominated, and it didn't deprive Ms. Weist of her win.

But I had no such alternative for Burt Young's work in "Rocky." He could not afford an ad campaign of sufficient impact, and the media coverage would have been hard to come by if he were not visible in the studio campaign. I would have been forced to do a why-did-they-ignore-such-a-key-contribution? campaign, and that never gets you a nomination or even very much sympathy. I had an emotional stake in this because I really was touched by Burt's sweetness and devotion. He was a single dad following the passing of his wife, and he and his daughter Annie were a very moving bonding of love. A nomination could and would kick off his career as a character actor. I had to make this stick, so I called Irwin Winkler, the lead member of the producer team in regard to Oscar contemplations. He frankly acknowledged that they were going with Burgess Meredith and Burgess alone in that supporting category. I pointed out that even if that were to win them a Supporting award, it wouldn't bring a dollar to the box-office. The argument I played was that "Rocky" was definitely in a mano-a-mano with "Network," so Winkler's biggest consideration should be the number of nominations. Arguably, if "Network" were to get one more nomination than "Rocky," "Network" would win the Oscar. For a Best Motion Picture, the number of nominations counts. Not invariably, but often enough to be taken into consideration. And Irwin did precisely that. I asked him to total, subtracting a second Supporting Actor nomination, how many nominations he could count on for "Rocky" as opposed to how many "Network" might confidently expect. We did the math together. Without a Burt Young nomination, it would, at best, have been one less than a tie. And then Irwin Winkler enthusiastically embraced the idea of backing Young as well as Meredith. Both were nominated, giving "Rocky" ten nominations, the same number of "Network." Thus "Rocky," the classic tale of an underdog, didn't have to be an underdog in the final Oscar balloting. And the winner was… "Rocky." Although he didn't win the prize, Burt Young was a winner, too, because he was nominated in wake of which his career took off.

Once you get your client into the mix, he or she enjoys the status of "contender," and publicity opportunities open up. The press agent then plays his angles like a pool hustler. Burt Young was the only member of the cast of "Rocky" who was a former professional boxer, so we could play off that as well as the single dad aspect. *Humanizing your client is always a key factor especially going for an award or nomination.* And Burt had all the humanity any flack might need. He had the perfect qualifications to become what I think of as a "reversible mug," a category which can really keep an actor working. Our client lists have boasted several. A reversible mug is a character actor with a physical presence that works as well for a quintessential tough guy, as Ernest Borgnine (one of Jerry's and my earliest clients) did playing the sadistic stockade boss Fatso in "From Here To Eternity" and the quintessential lovable lug as he did in the title role of "Marty," which earned him the Best Actor Oscar, which campaign Jerry Pam conducted for him. Another Oscar-winning actor for whose victorious "Cool Hand Luke" performance Jerry tailored the sell was George Kennedy. George could be cast hateful or cast affable with equal affinity. That's what we wanted for Burt Young, and that's what he attained. The important thing was not that he drew a nomination. The important thing is that that heat helped him obtain a career

The annual pressure to produce an Oscar show of surprises and individual moments of unique showmanship was such that the producers were often open to ideas which were out of the ordinary, particularly in coupling presenters. When we were helping hype "The Man Who Would Be King" for John Huston, Jerry Pam sold the Oscar producers on a presentation pairing of the two stars, Sean Connery and Michael Caine. Then, unknown to Sean, we arranged to have Roger Moore, who had succeeded him as the reigning Bond, walk into the presentation. Sean's exuberance and surprise made it a great moment, upping the plug factor for both "Man Who Would Be King" and whatever the upcoming Bond film was.

The Oscars sell Hollywood. That's what they were constructed to do. During the production of Warren Beatty's "Dick Tracy," I'd explored with the Oscar night producers the idea of stunting the show with some combination of the extraordinary cast with which Warren had peopled the world of the famed detective. It didn't work out because Warren on that very night (Oscarnight always fell on a Monday then) would be shooting the key scene between Al Pacino as Big Boy and Dustin Hoffman as Mumbles. That opened the idea of doing a satellite remote from the studio during the Oscars to the shooting of a scene combining three of the most recurring stars of the nominations lists. The idea had enough spin to spark some deep exploration, but in the end the devil was most definitely in the details. I stopped off at the set afterwards to enjoy the rare privilege of watching Pacino and Hoffman do twenty takes of improv of the wonderfully goofy and slapstick scene, each take was a world separate from any of the others. Loving movies doesn't get any better than that. Warren glowed with every take, but wanted to see what else they could give. The miracle was that neither broke up during any take, while the set-siders struggled to contain their laughter.

My second favorite Oscar night promotional plan that didn't-happen came when we were unspecified PR handymen for George's Lucasfilm empire, serving still under the very savvy supervision of Lucas' talented czar of promotion and publicity, Lynne Hale. The first Monday of the Month early AM staff meetings at Skywalker ranch were fatiguing but exhilarating. Everything was so far ahead of the curve that you felt time-warped. I was bringing Guttman&Pam's two cents worth to the opening of "Indiana Jones And The Last Crusade," and Harrison Ford and Sean Connery were set to co-present on the Oscar show a few months before the big opening... that casting combo coup not being of our doing. But having seen a rough-cut of the film, I knew that a key visceral action scene was of the two of them hurtling in a vintage convertible through a tunnel with a small airplane speeding after them. The producer of that particular Oscar broadcast was an old friend, Allan Carr, and I interested him in an action arrival of Ford and Connery on the stage. It would require a screen on which the tunnel chase would play a full-on directly-into-camera shot of the two stars in the car with the plane crashing towards them from behind. The screen, I proposed, would be comprised of hanging slices of material, and, at a climactic moment of their near incineration, the actual car would roll through the screen, down a ramp and stop on stage, with Sean Connery and Harrision Ford then calmly getting out and moving to the mike to say "The nominees in the category of…etc. are…" Allan Carr loved it. George Lucas, (for whom we had previously promo-ed "American Graffiti") liked it a lot, or so it was reported to us when we got the green light to take a stab. But it was killed by some management figure for one of the stars who considered the idea not very dignified. Dignity rarely has anything to do with socko promotional ideas. Sometimes you have to be content with how much fun you had exploring an idea.

My very favorite and most regretted didn't-happen was the great vaudevillian inspiration which Warren Beatty and Jack Nicholson suggested to me after I had arranged for them to co-present the Best Film award. It was not my idea, and I believe it was my fault it didn't make the Oscar show magic it could have and should have. It was pure showmanship, and it wasn't even in promotion of any film. Their pairing was simply an existential riff on super-stardom. Each of them was a frequent party to the Best Film category moment, having each produced or starred in or participated through other hyphenations in a long list of films which had made it to that august moment. They knew that their participation would come at the end of an exhausting evening into which veins of boredom and aching butt would have long since infiltrated. The revelation of Best Film always comes after the passage of three-hours during which the resolution of only a dozen or so great mysteries had been resolved. It would come at a time when the audience is partially in a let's-get-this-thing-over mode. Jack and Warren wanted to wake up the audience to the important moment by coming out, doing the traditional comments about the utter world-importance of the contents of their envelope and then…… *dropping their pants*. Let me run that past you again… DROPPING THEIR PANTS. They came to me with this idea at the rehearsal for the show, and I loved it, but I said I had to tell the producer about it, that it wouldn't work if it came as a surprise not only to the audience in the Dorothy Chandler Auditorium, site of the show, but to the director, production staff and cameramen transmitting the show. Why? The why of this, which I explained to them, was that if the production was unaware, Jack Nicholson and Warren Beatty could be dropping their pants in a close-up of their faces and upper torsos, meaning that only the immediate live audience would know about the sudden southern exposure. And then the billions of people at homes throughout the nation and the world would be aware only that the Oscar-nighters had suddenly gone goofy with some unexplained hilarity. And then you cut to two guys in the tux tops and boxers. with a pool of black pants at the feet of each *Everyone* had to *see* it happen. Very reluctantly, Warren and Jack agreed that I should take it to the Oscar-cast producer.

The producer, Gil Cates who has overseen some of the Academy's most lauded evenings, did actually fully understand the inspired showmanship of the idea, but he begged me to talk them out of it. The Best Film presentation would be preceded by some massively staged "holy moment" of such august solemnity that the pants-dropping would be a sacrilege, he beseeched. I went back to tell them and found them in the craft foods area where an elegant line of heated braziers stood from which the celebrated gathering of rehearsal personages were ladling haute cuisine. I wasn't in a hurry to unload the bad news, so I started to fill a plate. "So how'd it go over?" Warren asked, approaching me. I tried to avoid eye-contact by continuing the food selection. I told him. He concluded that the reaction was nuts. "Maybe," I said, "Actually, certainly...but that's what he's insisting. This thing before, the show element you'd be following, it's supposed to be a historically holy moment." At which point, in some duress, I managed to knock the lid off one of the braziers, and as I reached to grab it, dropping my own plate, I knocked over the entire brazier, spilling hot food everywhere including on me. This brought a roar of welcome laughter to all of the gathered dignitaries and stars, and I mean tears-in-the-eyes hilarity with me as the stooge. And Warren said, "You see? Everyone loves dumb shtick."

Unfortunately, the producer's decision stuck. They didn't drop their pants. The holy moment which preceded their presentation bombed. The show was chugging to a close on a note of expired energy. Jack Nicholson and Warren Beatty in their BVDs were sorely missed. Amazingly, they never brought it up again. That's class.

Gil Cates, however, did bring it up when I saw him at the Governors Ball after the show. He came over and said, "I should have let them drop their pants."

I had one other bvd adventure involving Warren but this one not involving the Oscars. We were in New York shooting a cover on him for a women's magazine, the photographer being Calvin Klein's wife, Kelly. The shoot had gone late into the night, and I wanted the release Warren signed to be with Kelly and not the magazine, for certain reasons of control. We all went back to Warren's suite and I was, with their input, drawing up the paper. The problem was this... I am dyslexic. In consequence, at least for me, that means if some fact or factoid is either-or, black or white, this or that, I tend to reverse the actuality. And, aware of that proclivity, I'm never certain that my choice is right. I try to double-check. I have a pretty good memory, but not when it boils down to some arcane either-or. So I wasn't sure how to spell Kelly's last name. I kid you not. In my mind, her husband was either Calvin Klein or Kalvin Clein. I know that sounds ridiculous, but it's just how my mind works. I didn't want to expose this idiocy, so I excused myself, went in the bathroom, locked the door and, from waist down, stripped naked. I had to see what it said on my underpants. The label read: "Jockey."

Back in the world of jockeying for Oscar nominations, In the right situation, a "poor boy campaign" can be quite effective. It can work for a small independent movie if your ads and your publicity convey a "we can't compete with the huge ad campaigns of the studio films, but, wow, look how the critics loved us" thrust. We began working with director Dick Donner when he was set to direct the first "Superman" feature. He and the foreign producers did not see eye-to-eye, and he wanted to be sure that his take on the film prevailed in the publicity as well as on the screen. To give me more clout with the producers or maybe just because he believed in us, he brought Christopher Reeve, Margot Kidder and other talent from the film to the Guttman & Pam client list. Because I believed in Dick, I played a key role in getting our client Gene Hackman to reconsider the role of Lex Luthor which he had already turned down, possibly because he had the same misgivings about the producers' vision that Dick had. I knew they would love each other, so I arranged a meeting that resulted in marriage.

"Superman, The Film" certainly was not poor-boy in any sense of the compound word. It was a big bear that definitely came in the front door, knocking it down with a wellspring of imaginative new ideas... the emphasis on comedy and romance, for instance. For a long time, that was the blueprint on which films adapted from comics were predicated. As a well-needed change of pace, Donner chose to follow it with a privately (and stringently) financed independent film called "Inside Moves" a labor of love which gave him and us a chance to promo my Oscar-nominated friend John Savage and a terrific ensemble of great character actors. These included Harold Russell in his first major role since winning the

Supporting Actor Oscar in 1946 for "The Best Years of our Lives." Harold, who had lost both hands and forearms in World War II action, portrayed in the Wyler classic the similarly wounded vet troubled to return to the sympathy of his loved ones. The Academy, honoring his courage in undertaking the role, awarded him a special Oscar, and he went on to win the Supporting award as well. One of our key publicists, Wally Beene, shared Harold's combat experiences, and as part of our promotional effort for "Inside Moves," Wally mounted a powerful campaign for him that helped Harold greatly in his effort to obtain improved policy for physically challenged veterans.

When Oscar time rolled around, Donner and I determined that the one best shot we had for a nomination was Diana Scarwyd's supporting performance. Supporting nominations most often flow from huge front-runner films, films that are, themselves, major Oscar contenders and beneficiaries of big studio ad budgets. All of which "Inside Moves" certainly was not.

Dick put up his own money for ads for Diana. I asked him to cut back and *not* take full-page ads, just seven-eighths of a page to give a subtle sense of under-dog. It cost almost as much, but it also ensured that there would be news copy on the page, probably a carry-over from a key page one story. That copy would hold the readers' eyes to the page long enough to maximize viewership of the ad and awareness of a small, critically acclaimed film's belief in one of its performers. My personal conviction is that readers give an ad about three seconds to convince them that there is some reason they should read it. I structure ads around that. Maybe why-isn't-this-full-page? could stretch it to five seconds of discovery or create a sympathy. Dick is a great believer in the unconventional, and he went along with it. It may have not been a reason that Diana got nominated, but it certainly didn't KEEP her from being nominated.

She didn't win, but she'd had a helluva nominee run, and I'd arranged for the Los Angeles Times to cover her Oscar night ventures, so the next morning the top half of the Times' front-page-of-the-entertainment-section coverage of the evening was a shot of her and her agent, Mike Menschel, champagne-toasting in the back of a limo.

I have used the poor-boy approach with quarter page ads on a number of occasions. When Dean Stockwell made a smashing comeback with a small role in David Lynch's "Blue Velvet," I took a more dangerous tack and did a quarter page ad that didn't even have his name or the name of the film in it, no "for your consideration," no anything. The skewed-angle image from the film of his singing into a pretend microphone was so indelible and the film so indelibly controversial, that I felt the image alone would capture attention and that the identity of film and performer would be evident to anyone who had seen "Blue Velvet." Others might be intrigued by an ad of such cryptic nature, an ad that did not provide the viewer with closure, that made him or her work for what the hell it meant. The trades fought me on an ad with no copy, but ultimately went along with it, and it did trigger a media rush to interview Dean Stockwell about the smashing comeback return of "the boy with green hair," his huge hit as a child actor. Kicked off by a campaign of skeletal cost, the attention focused on his too-long-overlooked talent, and that put his career quickly back on track.

Another ad-with-a-twist campaign element was the strategy we had for Bruce Davison's tour de force in "Longtime Companion," the first HIV/AIDS related feature film to achieve an Oscar nomination. We knew the film's subject would resonate in the industry, but we also knew that a film of such modest release needed something bold to get any traction. This was June, long before Oscars are at all in view. To imbed it into the voters' Oscar awareness, we took the great reviews for Bruce, tied it to a strong visual from the film, and ran a strong headline… "The First Oscar nomination ad of the season." It locked him into the contender lists and then into the list of nominees.

I don't go "non-verbal" with ads often, but it works if it includes the right kind of clues. When Jane Seymour's starring role as the concentration camp internee in the "War And Remembrance" mini-series was about to air, I found two shots of her which seemed to be absolute documentary capture of Holocaust deprivation and persecution. One seemed, a trick of the light, to have lipstick, so we went to the other. Again with the exceeding misgivings of the trade papers, we placed the shot as a page 2 full-page ad. I had run all of this past the producer of "War And Remembrance," Dan Curtis, a friend and someone for whom I'd written a script. He wasn't enthusiastic, but he trusted my instinct. Astute readers either guessed the subject of the ad or, we found, they at some point in the day made an effort to find out. It was definitely fodder around the coffee machine. It is sometimes helpful to make the intended public of an ad do some work. We were told that someone from the office of the head of ABC-TV, which broadcast the mini-series, had called the paper to find out who had placed the ad and who the woman in the photo was. The sheer reality of the image conveyed the reality and aching veracity of Jane's portrayal. Her brilliant conveyance of the experiences of victims earned her Emmy and Golden Globe nominations on successive years and it achieved the Holocaust remembrance she so deeply sought to promote, having lost three members of her own family at Bergen Bilsen and having grown up with the painful knowledge of what her mother had suffered as an internee in Japanese concentration camps on the island of Java for many years.

In 1972, the year Jerry and I started Guttman & Pam, we had a pretty big Academy awards year, especially for a relatively small and brand new company. Warren Beatty guided Hackman to me to make the most of Gene's big opportunity as the star of "The French Connection," and we wound up with three of our clients going home with statuettes. For the other two campaigns, I believe the decision to do quarter-page ads was helpful. One was for Cloris Leachman, whose former husband, director George Englund, insisted she bring us on to create and execute the campaign for her wrenching portrayal of the pathetically abandoned and adulterous wife in "The Last Picture Show." There were so many great supporting performances in that film... hers, Ellen Burstyn's , Eileen Brennan's, Cybil Shepherd's... that I had to find a way to make her portrayal stick in the mind. How do I make that film about one supporting actress out of so many? My thought was to hijack the film's iconic image. This film's iconic image was so strongly the forlorn marquee of the little Texas town's lone movie house, the Royal that it was the title. So I reproduced that image with the words "Cloris Leachman, Supporting" on the marquee... no mention of the film, no illustrating photo of her, no category delineation, no quotes not even any character-depicting scene. That was the ad campaign, repetition of the single, enigmatic, simple image... evoking the sense of the film and boiling it down to the loneliness and despair of her little life lost in the great void of this time and place. Again, it's a technique that makes a viewer work to figure out what it's all about. That means that he/she has to stay with your ad a little longer, become part of it. Once you've put that much effort into an ad viewing, you've worked it into your brain. It has become a conclusion they own and think they uncovered. She earned a nomination and, of course, won the Oscar, in the course of which teaching me a terrifying lesson which should appear elsewhere in these pages.

That same year, Ernest Tidyman, the best-selling author of the "Shaft" private eye novels, had adapted the script of "The French Connection" from the Robin Moore novel. The film was a front-runner, but sometimes the fact that a film boasts such great imagery, that it functions on chases and action sequences as much as dialogue, can mask the ingenious nature of the screenplay. Ernie recognized this, and aware of the campaign we were doing for Gene Hackman, he asked Gene to introduce him to Guttman & Pam. As a top author, he certainly had the funds for prominent ads, but there was such a proliferation of ads for the film… all using the iconic images from the movie… Popeye Doyle shooting one of the villains in the back as he ran up the stairs to the elevated train, Gene's frantic determination driving maniacally in the key auto chase to the next el station, his freezing vigil while Frog One dined warmly and elegantly. I was afraid full-page ads for Tidyman would be lost in 20th's substantial ad assault, that they would seem redundant. So I decided to use the same images in quarter pages, to create counter-campaign ads that would call attention to themselves. I took 8X10 glossies of those shots and had each of them coming out of the roller of an old-fashioned Underwood hunt and peck typewriter, some of the finger pads missing… one of my old typewriters. This I photographed from above, and then finished the ad with (in old typewriter type-face) "The French Connection… Ernest Tidyman, adapted screenplay." As I expected, it seemed to remind people that these impact scenes had actually been written by someone. He was nominated and won the Oscar.

Peter Bogdanovich once quoted Orson Welles as having observed to him that an artist can steal from anyone but himself. But press agents can and almost always do steal from themselves. In publicity, such theft is considered a "signature" of the PR guy's style. But it's really just a case of getting a little more ride out of a good idea. When writer/director Robert Boros did a mini-series on the historic mano-a-mano between Bobby Kennedy and Jimmy Hoffa, I used the same Underwood and had a photo… featuring the two antagonists glaring at each other… rolling out of it. In that case and with Tidyman, I'd had to stand on my desk to shoot down from above to get the shot for the ad, having to do it barefoot each time for balance. In each shot, my big toe could be seen. If anybody noticed it, it must have seemed a cryptic touch… Or they might have thought it was Tidyman's or Boros' thumb, deformed from hard labor in the service of his art. Sympathy never hurts. Neither does simplicity.

Ernie Tidyman was a striking man with a signature full moustache. It was a look he shared with one of the great news photographers and film unit photographers of the time. One evening years later, Gisela and I were dining in the coffee shop of the Beverly Wilshire Hotel, and when I was paying, I saw this very familiar guy come in. If I am famous for anything, it is that I absolutely cannot recognize anybody out of context. One night at a party, I was having a conversation with a young couple and then I told Gisela that I was sure I knew them from someplace. She looked at me with disgust and said, "They're our next door neighbors, you idiot." Well, this causes a lot of problems, and so on that evening when Ernie came into the coffee shop and passed me, I said "John," the name of the photographer. And he said, rather gruffly, "No." I figured he hadn't heard, so as he came past me again, I said "John" once more, and he said no with even greater irritation. When I got back to the table, I came to anguished realization of the true facts of this encounter, and I said, "Oh my God… that was Ernest Tidyman, and I didn't recognize him." To which Gisela said, "So what else is new?"

Two days later, I got a phone call and a voice said, "Dick, this is Ernie Tidyman. I'm doing some new projects and I think we should get back together." He was so insulted that I hadn't recognized him that he had to hire me again. My embarrassment concerning the slight infused my work for him, made me want to make it up to him, and I personally succeeded in getting him the only film that he ever directed. Nothing energizes me like guilt.

Sometimes, while campaigning in the short subject categories where you are not working on high visibility films, you can base a campaign on a tangential aspect to gain an edge. For documentary shorts and short animation films, the vote,until that for the 2013 year was conducted on a single night when the five contenders, or sometimes less, are shown in succession at the Academy's luxurious Samuel Goldwyn Theatre, and only those members seeing all the films could cast a vote at the end of the evening. Publicity can help walk them into the theatre with some prior sense of the film's worthiness. And now that they can vote by mail after having (presumably and hopefully) seen all of the candidates via screeners or special screenings, publicity can mold their focus and their response. For a Canadian animation short, I based the campaign on the National Film Board of Canada from which it issued, getting the USC film school to honor that organization and the producer of the short we repped, with a retrospective of NFBC's great contributions to animation, dating back to the pioneer work of Norman McClaren. So that animation course I took at UCLA film school really did benefit my career. For Janus Film's documentary on the persecution of actor/singer Paul Robeson, I focused ads on Hollywood's and America's shabby treatment of that great artist, seeking to establish in the industry mindset that this might be a golden opportunity to right an old wrong. It was a flat-out *ad hominem* campaign, a campaign in which you seek to get the voting public to vote for the person who is the subject as much as for the film's excellence. *Voters still vote their sense of excellence, but they can be induced... perhaps "reasoned" is a better word... to come to the consideration with a certain empathy that can intensify response.* It falls in the general strategy of seeking to personalize a vote, to make it come as much from the heart as from cognitive judgment. Not that others don't employ it. In the successful recent Oscar campaign for "Twelve Years A Slave," with which I had no involvement, a key part of the campaign rested on the phrase, "It's time."

The producer was so astonished at the win for the Robeson film that, on the way to the Governors Ball, he left the Oscar in a taxi... which made for another big splash of publicity on the win. And, of course, he got it back. Another Oscar taxi tale recently came to my attention with great surprise. Shortly after the passing of Jennifer Jones, whose "Beat The Devil" and "Portrait of Jennie" and whose lustrous beauty and talent assure her presence in my pantheon, I was looking at her Oscar, the actual award, and discussing it with her son Robert Walker Jr. He told me that it was a copy which David Selznick, after years of pressure, had prevailed upon the Academy to provide. She had lost the Oscar handed to her that evening by leaving it in the taxi after the Awards. What astonished me is that Jennifer Jones and David O. Selznick went to the Oscars and returned home... in a taxi. Hollywood is a place of wondrous puzzlements. I also was taken by a beautiful photo of her signed "To mother and dad from your problem child, Jennifer."

Jerry and I were working for Lucasfilm and its various subdivisions when "Who Killed Roger Rabbit" came out. It was a film for which Lucas' ILM division had raised the bar on both animation and special effects, sending those two crafts into new orbit as arts as well as crafts. The new digital special effects gave a sense of three-dimensionality to the animation figures and objects to match that of the live action material with which it was so constantly paired in the film. This is a commonplace now, but then it was miraculous. So the expectation of Lucas' ILM (Industrial Light & Magic) tech geniuses' winning the special effects Oscar was a given. Disney and MGM and others had combined live action and animation before, but "Roger Rabbit" fused them. I talked Lucasfilm into letting me do a full page trade quote ad for the ILM effects. Every review of the film contained testimonials to that magic. For a big awareness hit, I had the USC film school sponsor an ILM seminar on that animation and effects fusion at the 1000 seat Academy Samuel Goldwyn Theatre and we were able to fill it to the gills with film students and industry members who comprise the Animation and SFX branches of the Academy whom we made great effort to invite, , the people who would nominate and drive the expectations for the special effects category.

Even "contention" can be a great career step for an actor. Pierce Brosnan was still perceived primarily as James Bond (following an earlier primary perception as Remington Steele) when he got an opportunity to prove his acting chops following John Boorman's casting him in a relatively low-budget production of the offbeat John Le Carre spy thriller, "The Tailor Of Panama." It brought good reviews, especially for Pierce and Geoffrey Rush, but it wasn't a film that was strongly presented, certainly not as a deserving Oscar nomination vehicle. At the end of that year, the Robert Redford/Leonardo DiCaprio espionage thriller "Spy Game" came out, and the New York Times review asked explicitly why "Spy Game" was being presented for Oscars while the vastly superior (in the Times reviewer's opinion) "Tailor of Panama" wasn't being mentioned. I got a leading columnist to pick up on this theme. I brought that kick-ass press endorsement to the attention of Pierce's agent, Fred Spector of CAA, and we conspired on a plan which, in all immodestry, I have to admit we executed to perfection... Fred's "bad cop" with the studio was as deft a piece of agent-promoting-his-star as I've seen. It's that kind of agent-star dedication that builds lifelong relationships in this business. I engineered press breaks reflecting the review's powerful case and took these to Fred with the idea that "Tailor's" distributor might seize advantage or avoid embarrassment by throwing a few shekels into an ad campaign. Fred accomplished this to great effect, advancing our agreed position that the "Tailor" distributors could lose street cred with actors if they didn't back up this kind of reviews with a campaign. Fred played his part to the hilt, did everything a dedicated agent should do and then some. The studio, to its great credit, didn't view it as blackmail, but rather as a good idea. The studio's PR people allowed me to work with them in selecting ad photos and quotes. This permitted me to select as the ads for Pierce's leading lady, Jamie Lee Curtis, photos and ad quotes which worked very powerfully for her but also worked for Pierce as well. The result was a significant Oscar contender exposure for Pierce in close association with an Oscar winner and perennial candidate like Geoffrey Rush. And it occasioned the Academy mailing of the film's "screener," benefiting everyone in the film and exposing one of Brosnan's best pieces of work to people who might never have seen it. It was an expensive mailing that otherwise would not have happened. It built a small but significant cult around that film. It's not something you, as an agent or press agent, do because you feel your client will appreciate the career spin but rather because you, as a trained professional, know that this is something which can... and therefore *must*... be done. That's the only gyroscope on which you need operate.

As they say, there is nothing that focuses the mind like being hung in the morning. Maybe that's why I enjoy Oscar campaigning. The result is either a tremendous high or a bottomless low. But either way, you get a verdict in only a few months. When you're promoting careers, there are highs and lows, too, but it takes years... lifetimes often... to see how it all turned out. And sometimes you don't know the real verdict until you read your obituary.

My all-time deepest Oscar regret involved the film my wife made as an expression of a mission that had driven her since adolescence... fostering a true remembrance and understanding of the Holocaust, the tragedy she saw in little glimpses as a war-baby in Nazi Germany. Although she was only eight when World War II slogged through its last bloody fields and ground to halt in Europe in May of 1945, right in her own backyard actually, Gisela carried an awareness of what horrors had been wrought in and by her country. Over the next decade, she witnessed the manner in which remembrance and guilt were swept under the rug, and she saw with what facility this history and guilt were shed and shred, the complacent national "who us?" which blossomed from Germany's new well-being and industrial prominence. As result, she collected her high school baccalaureate and left Germany at 17 to fend for herself in other countries, first as an au pair and college student in London and then, when I met her, as a student in Paris scraping by on baby-sitting and ironing work for communists who seemed to need a lot of both. This was only a decade after the war, and in each country she was disdained and even hated as a bloody *hun* or *bosche* for exactly the same reasons that she had left her homeland.

When we married and she came to America, she resisted American citizenship because she rejected the idea of nationalism as the determining definition of who each person is, and she wanted to make her statement about Holocaust remembrance as a German patriot and not as an expatriate. The opportunity came in 1988 when the famous painter/photographer Gottfried Helnwein, one of the prominent artists she helped or represented as art dealer and gallery owner, called her from Cologne, the city of her birth. It was November 9, the fiftieth anniversary of Kristallnacht, the official start of the eradication of Jews in Germany. There was not, Gottfried reported with anguish, a paragraph of acknowledgment of that anniversary in any German publication he could find, the culminating evidence of the subtracted history that had alienated each of them from their homeland (Helnwein is Austrian) however much the country's art and culture and natural beauty commanded their love. Gottfried determined to do a heroic art installation to make Germans take real and active note of the somber horror of a national policy under which the state could determine who was fit to live and who was fit only to die… Selektion. It would be giant paintings of children's faces, four meters high, one and a half football fields long, and the viewers would have to decide which children were Jews and should be sent to the concentration camps for eradication. The first night it was up, vandals slit the throats of the painted images they determined to be Jews on the basis of Hitler's Book of Races. Gisela insisted it be shown only with the slit throats to show that this was not the murderous sentiment only of the Nazi period but also rampant among neo-Nazis of the present, that it was not something that had happened long before but rather something that is happening now…

Noted presentations of the installation were arranged in Moscow, Berlin, Lausanne and other key art centers, but, even with the support of The Museum of Tolerance and the high praise and recommendation for the installation by Simon Wiesenthal himself, they couldn't get an American city to sponsor it. With the contacts and backing supplied by the Wiesenthal Center, Gisela finally got

Beverly Hills to commit, but the city's czar of art display censorship determined it was too horrifying for the public to see.... seventeen giant paintings of children's faces, not piles of bodies, not skeletons in striped pajamas behind barbed wire. Children's faces.

Gisela had obtained $40,000 to underwrite a prominent exhibit of the installation from the Austrian government, and she determined to use it instead to make a film about the installation and its reflection of how in Germany, and now in Beverly Hills, backs had been turned on the memory of the wanton slaughter of 12,000,000 human beings, half of them non-Jews, and the torturous persecution that attended it. That, she decided, would be the widest possible venue for the work. Gisela filmed our oldest friend, Maximilian Schell, reading Simon Wiesenthal's own words as narration and Sean Penn and Jason Lee, two Helnwein collectors, were brought in to give commentary. With her director, co-producer and composer Henning Lohner, who came to it with the same passion and who was as she a German Catholic, the film, "Ninth November Night," "Nuente November Nacht," came to powerful reality. I was only marginally aware of all this, and my help was never requested, although Guttman Associates did eventually put up a lot of the funding for the film. On the approach of the 65th anniversary of Kristallnacht, she arranged for the work-in-progress to be screened as the Museum of Tolerance' commemoration of that terrible night and the inhumanity which ensued. I was astonished, not only at the power and excellence of the film, but of those same qualities in the speech she gave before it. I'd never heard her do public speaking, so I was terrified for her until she began eloquently to improv her feelings. I don't know why my trepidations. I've always considered her the most compelling and persuasive conversationalist I've known, but public speaking? Imbued with her belief in her message and its wider meanings, she was inspirational. As she was on other occasions when her film was shown by the Academy, by the American Film Institute and by the Museum of Tolerance.

Over the next ten months I prepared for the most important Oscar campaign of my career. During that period, her breast cancer was discovered, and by the time we were preparing to enter "Ninth November Night" for Academy Award consideration, she had just completed her operation and her radiation but had, over her doctor's outraged body, declined to do chemo. The requisite (for Academy qualification) one week run we did at the Malibu Cinema in our home town, charging five dollars admission to the 23 minute film, all proceeds of tickets and sales of the art installation's catalogue book going to the Musem of Tolerance. Thanks to major coverage in the Malibu Times, Gisela was able to make a substantial contribution. One old man who had paid to see the film asked afterwards if he could buy the $25 book in five dollar installments, and when he reached for the book, she saw the numbers on his arm and said she would be honored if he would accept it as a gift.

There are hundreds of films submitted in the documentary categories each year. I knew the film had enormous power, because our premiere at the Malibu Cinema attracted an audience of major filmmakers, and at the end of the film, the last half of which is a cinematic walk through the art exhibit, the paintings of children, some of the canvasses with their throats slit... as the end titles finished and the lights came on, there was silence. No applause, just sixty people staring at the empty screen for about five minutes.

I thought Gisela had a chance. The film certainly deserved nomination, but that would be decided by a tough jury of professional documentarians. As is usual, there were some other excellent films having to do, in some way, with the Holocaust. This film broke a lot of rules and with blazing success. That's not always well received. It had a clear and consistent narrative drive, and so I was shocked to learn that she and the director had made it without a script. She said that I, as a writer, understood only linear structure, while she as a sculptor and Henning Lohner, as a composer, understood a structure that emanated from a core idea or theme, like the center of a circle with everything in the piece equidistant from that theme. I was convinced that if I could understand that, I would be a much better writer, but I'm not sure I ever did.

I knew we needed one thing to give it the distinction it deserved to call jury attention to it (the courage of someone else' conviction.) I called Jean Furstenberg, then president and guiding light of the American Film Institute. I knew that the fall AFI Film Festival was almost fully scheduled, but I asked her to see this film. She called the next day to say that she wasn't able to watch it until just before she went to bed... and that her mind was then so stimulated and her spirit so challenged that she never got to sleep. And, oh yes, it would be in the festival. That kind act allowed the Los Angeles Times to do a major story about the film and its makers, two German non-Jews creating a work about a non-Jewish Austrian painter who had made preserving the memory of the Holocaust his life's mission... just as had Gisela and Lohner. The article contained such laudatory description of the film that it almost demanded reflection in a trade ad, but I resisted that idea, knowing how important it was to those very serious jury members to make up their own minds.

I may have been wrong, but at the end of December, Gisela was informed that her film had been selected for "the short list," the eight films from which the three, four or five nominees would be selected. It was a tense month until the nominations were to be announced. I wanted this desperately for her, especially because of the salutary effect that could have on her battle with cancer. I wanted to err on the side of caution, not do anything that could cost her the nomination. And so I did nothing except leave it to the determination of the jury gods.

On nomination morning, having gone through the process of bringing good news or bad news to hundreds of clients, I suggested to Gisela that we just sleep through. If she were nominated, someone would surely call her. If we woke up and the sun was already lighting our garden, we would know that it hadn't happened. We woke up to sun. She came in and we hugged. She said, "I wish I'd been one of the hundred that didn't make the short list. This is like they select eight people, feed them a great meal and then take three of them out at dawn and shoot them against the courtyard wall."

That accurate observation notwithstanding, as result of the honor of having made the short-list honor, the film had many prestigious showings and many good things have flowed from it. Holocaust remembrance groups from all over the country request being able to show it on Kristalnacht anniversaries, one of them on the 70th anniversary when a gathering of members from the one synagogue and five Christian churches in a small Alabama town got together to watch and discuss it.

The Supporting Actor/Actress campaigns for great character actors are the ones I enjoy most of all. In the first place, they are more wide open. There are so many great supporting roles each year... these are brilliant actors who land brief roles that actually make or break a film... and writers often pour their most lyric lines into these characters because the dialogue of the leads often has to hew to the personas expected of them. You can't always get them nominated, but you sure can give them a terrific ride and career boost promoting a couple of months of "hot contender" talk.

A great example was Robert Forster's portrayal of the tough but humane bail bondsman in "Jackie Brown." The showy roles went to the star-studded leads...

Robert DeNiro, Samuel L. Jackson, Pam Grier and Bridget Fonda. With the exception of Grier's title character, the big stars were playing disgusting creeps. Robert was the film's slender thread of decency. It was a film that had Oscar breeding… Quentin Tarantino, Harvey and Bob Weinstein. The brutality of the other characters, I felt, put Forster's great performance onto a fast-track. It was the only time that the Weinsteins hired us for a film and then hired us separately to campaign one of the actors… Forster. I thought he had another big plus going for him in addition to a terrific performance in a very visible film… the arc of his career. Forster had come out of the starting gates with massive industry expectations. As a vitally handsome young actor, he was the discovery star in a John Huston film, "Reflections In A Golden Eye" as the third element in a triangle whose other two sides were living legends, Elizabeth Taylor and Marlon Brando. It gave him the scandal value of nude scenes before actors were doing nude scenes. But then something strange happened… nothing. The film just didn't score.

Robert's opportunities downsized for a few decades, except for his starring in Haskell Wexler's "Medium Cool," a film shot against the seething tensions of the 1968 Democratic convention in Chicago, a film far too painfully real to be more than a cult sensation. But a cult sensation it was, leaving a lot of actor-loving folks waiting for Forster's next big opportunity. It took over two decades. So when "Jackie Brown" fell into his lap and he ran with it, he was the perfect guy to be every-actor for the heavy majority of voters in the Actors Branch of the Academy, the only Academy members who nominate for the four acting awards… an accomplished actor who never got the big breaks and never made the big bucks, who stood for all of them and for all of their dreams and who infused hope into all of their talents. We drummed up sufficient key breaks to get that across. I told him that now came the heavy-lifting. He had to go to as many Academy screenings of other films as he could, not to see but to be seen. He pointed out he wasn't an Academy member. But I was. We hit the circuit. The one thing about Academy screenings… at least half the audience fills out ballots. And since actors are more often not working than working, a substantial percentage of attendees are from that branch. One night after a screening at the Academy's Samuel Goldwyn Theatre, practically the entire cast of "One Flew Over The Cuckoo's Nest" came up to him to shake his hand and congratulate him on "Jackie Brown." The hand with which an Oscar voter shakes with is the one that marks the ballots, and the press of two hands is a special kind of contract.

He was, of course, nominated, and slightly before the Awards, he called and said, "I suppose Harvey stops paying you right after the Oscar-cast," "Actually, he stopped right after the ballots closed. That's normal." "Well, let's say I start paying you personally from the day the ballots closed," he suggested. I knew he hadn't yet drawn any big paychecks from the nomination, but he insisted. Shortly thereafter, one of our clients was making a film independently on which one of the main stars had just fallen out. I'd suggested Robert for it to great response, and I was given the OK to offer him a million dollars for it. I rushed the script to him and called him for an ok to lock it up for him. "I'll set up a call for you with the director," I said excitedly. "Dick, I read the script. There's no point in my talking to the director. I can't say those words." "Can you say the words 'a million dollars?'" I asked with what I felt was more composure than was merited. "Yelling at me won't change my mind," he answered. A million dollars was much more than he'd made for a film since…. ever. He passed. A major star, an Oscar winning English actor, did the role. The film's distribution was frozen in a law suit and, to my knowledge, did not come out. Even if it had, it wouldn't have kept that Brit from winning his second Oscar which he collected the following year. Integrity comes with a price, but so does the lack of it…

We had done a pretty good job on "One Flew Over The Cuckoo's Nest," so Michael Douglas called on us to help out on the release and Oscar campaigning of "The China Syndrome." We had handled Michael as an actor during "The Streets Of San Francisco" and we knew he never did anything that wasn't special. His signature was that he was and is always ABOUT something.

Seeing "China Syndrome", we knew it had timely importance. We didn't realize quite how much, because a few days later the nuclear contamination of Three Mile Island occurred, and we were off to the races. "China Syndrome" proved to be possibly the most relevant Oscar campaign we've done this side of lending a hand to "Fahrenheit 911." Jerry and I really put our shoulders to it. The integrity of the film was startling, and Michael did not know and never COULD have known that nuclear meltdown would become all too real for the world precisely at the film's release. This drama involved the possible life and death consequences of nuclear power plants. He and director (and one of the nominated screenwriters for the film) James Bridges wanted the audience to understand in a cognitive manner as well as a viscerally emotional manner, that great risks require great caution.

And then Three Mile Island seconded the emotion. We didn't give a hard sell to that angle in the Oscar campaign. We knew the audience had already made the connection. Looking too opportunistic can be a turnoff. It can, in fact, appear cheesy. Don't, for Godsake, hit the keys too hard. Jack Lemmon and Jane Fonda received Best Actor and Actress Oscar nominations for this most immediately relevant film. Oscar voters respond to such relevance as long as you don't make that seem a contrivance... an opportunity too opportunely exploited.

We had worked with Jack Lemmon many times before. This was 1979, and we had done much of the campaign in 1973 when he won the Oscar for "Save The Tiger." It was a strange a-problem-is-a-solution-in-disguise campaign, because we did it not for the studio but for the writer. Steve Shagan, a former press agent and therefore a friend, was personally carrying a film that he felt the studio was not taking wire-to-wire, a film that was not getting an all-out campaign. So he was paying for extra screenings and other promotions, and that was the angle we pushed... a writer's very expensive thank-you note to an actor who had taken his words into orbit. We got media to hit that angle, promoting Steve's personally-funded private screening campaign and we got one top reviewer on a top television station, David Sheehan on the CBS TV local, to take this on as a crusade. The screenings were full and the word spread... and, finally, Jack won a Best Actor statuette to keep his "Mr. Roberts" Supporting award company. What was Steve's reward? His great script got an Oscar nomination and much greater viewership, and he went on to become one of the top best-selling novelists, proving that SOME good deeds go unpunished.

One of the things that helped get our new company off the ground was Fred Roos' pressuring Copolla to pressure Universal to hire us to do George Lucas' "American Graffiti." We were told that the studio had greenlighted the little (it was made for $600,000) independent film largely as a goodwill gesture to Francis. The studio hierarchy (again, hearsay) didn't get Lucas' loving comedic ode to the end of high school and evolving end of innocence of his own experience, set in the 'tween years of the late 50s, early 60s. Cindy Williams told me that when they were shooting it, they referred to the time setting as "nineteen fifty twelve." Someone up there in "the black tower" at Universal... that's what everyone called the studio's high-rise seat of power…, didn't get how Lucas had placed his comedy in that time context when disc jockeys were the guides into the new worlds of rock and altering consciousness. One major front office guy thought Wolfman Jack was a horror comics character. They had thrown that minor (even then) sum against the wall to keep Francis happy on other projects. Eventually, it set the record, held for many decades, of the greatest percentage difference between cost and gross. And when they saw the rough cut, they figured let's bring in the PR guys Francis designates, and then he can't complain about the film's failure. So it was dumped in our laps, and we thought that since it was about DJ-led society, let's let DJs lead the public to it… We got the comedy big time and set up screenings for all the top disc jockeys who, to the man and woman, went nuts over it. We set up radio promotion screenings, the only cost of which for the studio was five hundred dollars for pop corn for the promotional audiences. It was declined, even though the rush of attention for the film among young people was already apparent. Operation DJs was paying off big time. We paid for the popcorn ourselves, and soon it had a big hit buzz going for it… and Guttman & Pam was paid off and ushered off the film by the studio. Somebody had started reading the "cards," the test audience response, and they were beginning to get the idea that the film would go through the ceiling.

We had made close contacts with the young cast and eventually repped such of its members as Paul Lemat, Richard Dreyfuss (very briefly, but that's another story,) Cindy Williams, Candy Clark and Susanne Sommers. But the only one who came to us for representation after we were shown the door and while the "Grafitti" success was still in play was Candy Clark. I had a strong feeling that it was a film of such enjoyment that it could throw off Oscar nominations. And Candy was the one for whom I was being paid to initiate Oscar talk. It paid off, and she alone was Oscar nominated from that cast of brilliant newcomers and future heavy-weights. Cindy Williams was not happy that we hadn't talked her into a campaign, too, and in anger she hired us.

You don't win 'em all… that's all there is to it. Warren Beatty had brought me in to work with him on the Oscar-related promotion of "Heaven Can Wait," as I had done on all of his previous nominated films and most of his subsequent ones. Comedies are never open and shut contenders, even one as massively successful and unanimously acclaimed as his "Heaven Can Wait." When people are laughing their heads off, they can miss the artistic mastery and underlying emotional power that facilitate the laughter. Warren Beatty, all by himself, is a powerful provenance for a film's nomination prospects. His films… as lamentably few as they have been… have corralled over five dozen nominations. Several Beatty films have earned double figure nominations. Only three times has a filmmaker been nominated for all four key Academy Awards for the same film… Best Film, Best Director, Best Screenplay and Best Actor (or Actress, according to the artist's gender). One of them is Orson Welles for "Citizen Kane." The other two are Warren Beatty… for "Reds" and for "Heaven Can Wait." He won the Best Director for "Reds." I'm making a point of mentioning that a couple of times in this book because it is such an extraordinary accomplishment. In the entire history of film… two men.

Screenings made it clear that the Academy plainly understood that "Heaven Can Wait" was great filmmaking as well as great entertainment. So it was exciting and gratifying when the film received ten or maybe it was eleven nominations, quite extraordinary for a comedy. Proving that even Beatty and Guttman can guess wrong, we had an uneven number of ads budgeted for Best Supporting Actor promo to be divided between Jack Warden and Charles Grodin. They were both great, but Warden had several recent nominations for similar roles, and we gave the extra ad to Grodin on the supposition that it would be harder for Jack to do it again. Warden was the one who was nominated. It was clear that it would be a heady Oscar night for "Heaven," so I arranged for my wife and daughter Danielle (Moni was at Columbia… University, not Studios) to attend the ceremonies and then join me at Warren's table at the official post-awards dinner, the Governor's Ball. It began well. I saw that my family was happily seated in the presenters section between Ginger Rogers and Yul Brynner. One of the first awards was Art Direction, and that went to Warren's longtime collaborator Dick Sylbert for "Heaven Can Wait." A promising start. And then…. and then nothing. Art Direction was the only trophy HCW won all night.

Disheartened, I met Gisela and Danielle after the show and asked if they would mind if we skipped the Governors Ball, which was at the Beverly Hilton International Ballroom, and just went home. Gisela asked why, and I said that I just couldn't face Warren. All those nominations, all those other names in the envelopes. "Let me ask you a question," she said, "Is Warren going to the ball?" "Of course." "Well, since he has the dignity and grace to go there in good spirits, you're obligated to do so, too. Don't shame him." So we went to the Beverly

Hilton… and it was a terrific evening. With us at Warren's table were Warren, Buck Henry, Elaine May, Bill Fraker, Director of Photography on the film and one of Hollywood's great spirits. The Algonquin never gathered more wit and charm to a table. It was a victoriously hilarious evening.

One campaign that I enjoyed greatly because of the running battle I had with the client was my work for composer David Shire in 1979 when he had written two of the five nominated songs, the title song from "Norma Rae" and a song written for "Ice Castles." From the start, he and I disagreed. He felt the "Ice Castle" song was a far better composition and he stressed that it had been a very successful record. I told him that he was going to win for "Norma Rae." We battled back and forth. I was pushing the "Norma Rae" song, and the problem was that the only time the song is heard in the film is over the main titles. So whenever I got David a TV booking, the only clip I could show was the titles, which didn't please the producers of the shows. "So show the Ice Castles song," David insisted, "it's over a beautiful ice dancing sequence." I finally sat him down and spread the hard facts on the table for him. "Norma Rae" was a very popular film about a subject close to industry hearts, unionization, and the Academy members would have great sympathy for it. But it was going to win only for Sally Field as Best Actress, and members will want to vote for it in some other category as well. It was too good a film to be called out only once on Oscar night. "Why can't it win for Best Film?" David argued. "Because 'Kramer Vs. Kramer' is going to win." "How do you know?" "Because Jerry and I were hired onto that campaign a long time ago, and I know. I can see that film picking up steam. You're the Academy's only other chance to honor a union-positive film, and they're all union members."

David didn't like it. David didn't buy it. On Oscar night, someone opened an envelope and said, "And the Oscar for Best Song goes to…. for 'Norma Rae,' David Shire." The next morning at about 11 o'clock, I got a call from David. "Dick, I really want to thank you," he started. "David, you're more than welcome. It was my pleasure." "But you don't know how MUCH I want to thank you." "Yes, I do," I insisted. "No, really, you don't know…" "…that you voted for Ice Castles?." "How did you know that?" "I knew it all along. I just figured I had to scrape up at few extra votes to make up for yours."

I had worked with David previously on Francis Coppola's "The Conversation," which I still feel is the most extraordinary score ever written for one hand on the piano. It was such a neurotic, haunting and beautiful work that captured the frantic sizzle of Gene Hackman's trepidations as the surveillance expert Harry Caul who fears not only for his own life but for the lives of all the people whose conversations he steals for he knows not what purpose. It was a staccato chasing up and down of arpeggio scales on the piano, one hand, like taps on a typewriter. I loved it so much that I even wrote a lyric for it, just for myself, just to force myself to break down its synchopated clatter to understand the simple and yet complicated cadence. It was a fascinating exercise which crawled me into the complexity of a remarkable piece of music as I kept playing it over and over at different speeds. That became a key reason I finally wanted to learn to play the piano.

My handy fix-all adage "A Problem Is A Solution" comes into play quite frequently during Oscar campaigns, quite logically because when the top eight or twelve films of the year bang heads, a lot of people get headaches and every campaign faces its own specific problems. And in the kernel of each of those problems lies an appropriate strategy. We represented the accomplished director Martha Coolidge for many years. "Valley Girl" had been her breakout film, and then she presented herself with another in, "Rambling Rose." The advance screenings showed that the subtle and touching performance she encouraged from such topnotch actors as Robert Duvall, Laura Dern, Diane Ladd and Lucas Haas was going to give this gentle study of over-ripe sexuality and the beauty of first lust a good dark horse place at the table. Excellence and sexuality are a terrific enticement to bring the industry to its screenings. The producing/distributing firm was Carolco, and they were prepared to bring the right funds to the campaign. And then one morning, there WAS no campaign. The company suddenly hit some kind of hard times and the ad and screening money simply failed to materialize. There wasn't even any money for the "screeners." We couldn't send copies of the film to Academy voters who don't get around to seeing every contending film in the theatres. That left "Rambling Rose" rambling in the woods. They can't vote for what they haven't seen.

The reps for all of the "talent" - writers, directors, actors (you can imagine how that term, "talent," antagonizes the tech and crafts people on a film) got together in a strategy I developed for Martha to put forward, and it was agreed that the key agencies would try to carry "Rambling Rose" across the finish line. Each agency agreed to hold a certain number of screenings for Academy members. It was a voluntary and appropriate assumption of load by the agencies. But the situation... the producers having pulled the money and in effect the red carpet out from under the film and the artists... was something everyone seemed to want kept secret... like holes in your socks. I saw it in a very different light, and I slipped it to the single outlet that most kicked off industry talk. Suddenly, the grand gesture of the agencies was focusing attention on what must be a terrific little film that needed all the help it could get. It was an underdog story, a story of gallantry unexpected of agencies. The screenings were the news. It was *a-problem-is-the-solution-in-disguise* in action, and the word grew. The screenings were jammed. Actors particularly made the effort to see it, and we wound up with a Best Actress nomination for Laura Dern and Best Supporting nomination for Diane Ladd. It was the first time a mother and daughter had been nominated for the same film. For a director, it is as beneficial to be perceived as someone who directs actors to nominations as it is to be nominated oneself. Actors factor that kind of thing when deciding between offers.

The moral to this incident is that, contrary to common expectation, Hollywood can be a very caring and responsible place. An inequity occurred in which a deserving film would be deprived of the opportunity to be seen and judged. A group of agencies saw that they could help, and they did. Members of the Actors Branch of the Academy learned that they would have only this limited opportunity to see the film and they made the extra effort to judge their peers. I like what that says about Hollywood, and also about the responsibility with which Academy members exercise their votes.

The very best ideas for any kind of PR campaign, particularly campaigns to bolster consideration of Oscar contenders, are those that grow out of the achievement you are boosting. This paid off handsomely with several special events on behalf of the Weinstein Brothers' efforts to attract attention for director Rob Marshall's "Chicago." The essential truth was that it was a celebration of one of Hollywood's most cherished traditions, the big musical. So it was fun jumping aboard one splashy Hollywood Boulevard screening at the Egyptian Theatre, one of the lavish Hollywood premiere houses of the golden era. This one was in tribute to the great stars of the golden age of musicals. Once I got Mickey Rooney to host it and he got Margaret O'Brien to co-host, we started drawing a glistening crowd of stars from the 1940s and 1950s. This would have been a star-cluster red carpet forty or fifty years before, and we knew it would be similarly electric in the new millennium. Every so often an Oscar-worthy film came along to remind us… "Cabaret," "All That Jazz," "Chicago." The press turnout and enthusiasm was of a very high order, an evening in celebration of music Hollywood style. The biggest fan there was "Chicago" director, Rob Marshall. Each of the attendees was an icon for him., The media message was "Chicago's" homage to that glossiest and most entertaining of Hollywood eras when such amusements captured the American spirit. Mickey's energy powered the introductory moments, and then perhaps the most nostalgic premiere audience in decades cheered the new film. I never doubted it would be a big blast, because I'd escorted my wife when she shopped at Niemen Marcus, and I'd seen Ann Miller arrive, in her sixties or seventies, slim and bursting with starshine, an event. And salesmen went racing excitedly through the store spreading the word in whisper waves of "she's here, she's here." Ah, yes, the stars were so much brighter.

I've attended dozens of rehearsals for Academy Awards since we frequently arranged and arrange for our clients to be presenters. Quite apart from the close company and observation of the most noted artists in the industry, it is always an event filled with unusual experience. One of my favorite of these was the rehearsal I attended with Cher. Upon seeing Robert Altman's "Come Back To The Five And Dime, Jimmy Dean, Jimmy Dean," I was astonished by her first dramatic work and then discovered that she was without publicity representation. One of the reasons for this, I learned upon a call to her agent, was that she was in a period of money problems and couldn't afford it. "What if I were to defer payment?" I asked. Her performance in the Altman film and her upcoming work in "Silkwood" with Meryl Streep were the stuff of Oscar contention and career building if the PR was skilled. It turned out that "deferred" was the magic word, and I threw myself into the campaign, with several memorable moments in which her wit proved a spectacular reward. l set up a Q&A for her at UCLA, and over 1500 students crammed into the auditorium of the student union and with strong press coverage. The questions were lively and the answers more so. Cher's décor of her canyon home was quite famous for its Byzantine complexity, particularly the unique motif and furnishing of her bedroom. One question was, "Is it true that your bedroom is like a snake pit?" to which she answered, "Only on occasion." You can't do better than that. The campaign had traction, and Cher, for her work in the Altman film, was notably the runner-up for the LA Film Critics' Best Supporting Actress award

She wasn't nominated for the Oscar, but she was now positioned as a dramatic actress of importance, so I arranged for Cher to present a music score award at the Oscars together with Placido Domingo. The written banter was presented to her just before they moved out on the stage for the rehearsal day run-through, so I hadn't heard it. I was surprised and dismayed when, reading off the teleprompter, she was required to look up at the great tenor and say, "Gee, I always thought Italians are much shorter." It was, of course, a joke about her ex-partner/husband Sonny. I hated it because Sonny and Cher was her past, and now she was an actress. I went back stage where Cher was standing with Mr. Domingo and the producer, Stan Margulies. Stan was an old friend because he had written and produced "Paris Holiday," the Bob Hope film I'd worked on in Paris. As the three of them stood there, I told Stan that I really wanted the joke changed because it slighted the dignity of what she was now achieving as an actress. He responded, "Well, it got a laugh, didn't it?" I agreed that it had, and Cher who didn't mind the nod to her past said, "A big laugh." I acknowledged that but I requested permission to ask Mr. Domingo a question. That permitted, I said, "Mr. Domingo, I always thought you were Spanish." He apparently hadn't understood the joke, and he responded vigorously, "But of course I AHHM!!"

The joke went out the door...

And so, a short time later, did we. We had worked a substantial amount of time with payment deferred, which, considering the pleasure and honor of contributing to that crucial step in such a significant artist's career, was all right with me. One day, a young staff member who was working the account with me learned that Cher had prevailed in a court case with a tabloid newspaper she'd claimed had damaged her with false stories. She had been awarded and had received a large amount of settlement, so my associate had called her lawyer and received payment of the back fees owed us. I received a furious call from her agent angered that we had obtained payment. "You agreed to defer payment," he said. "Which we did," I said, "but her financial situation now permitted her to pay." "Defer means not get paid," he shouted. "I believe you have 'defer' confused with the word 'forego'," I suggested. We were fired by him on the spot. Or maybe we were foregone.

In a similar mode, I received a call from Kareem Abdul Jabbar's lawyer once when the great center was readying his retirement from basketball. As a UCLA basketball fan, I went to the meeting with excitement. To open the conversation, I asked what he wanted publicity to do for him. It was certainly not the mere accrual of more visibility since his awareness and regard couldn't be higher. "Acting," he answered. He'd made a notable contribution to "Airplane," but that was a comedy in which he was essentially playing… and playing off of… himself. And he'd been an antagonist to Bruce Lee in one of the classic martial arts films. But the prospect of his playing a wide variety of not-Kareem Abdul Jabbar roles was limited, and I told him so, startling and perhaps insulting him and his lawyer. "What do you think he should have publicity do for him?" the lawyer asked with understandable pique. "Produce," I said. "He's the one guy who can sit down with and excite any star in town. He can tie up with any producer who can make the deals and make the films once Kareem opens the door and brings in green-light talent, and he's a bright guy who can learn the moves of movie-making as they go along." I saw them exchange a maybe-he-has-something look, and then I left. The next day the lawyer called and said they liked my ideas. "What kind of fee did you have in mind?" I asked. "Oh, we have no intention of charging you for the association," he answered.

Of course there is great honor in associating with distinguished people, but there is no honor in "buying" someone onto your client list with free anything. Publicity is a skill with commercial value. The Oscar race is simply a very convenient metric of the value of publicity. But you can measure it as well in the continuity of many careers. The Oscar race is one place where not only the flacks' clients' talents and imagination are gauged, but those of their press agents are as well. It is an important corner of the marketplace where results are indisputable.

Backstage at the Oscars is a fatiguing but exciting place to be. The emotions run high there, and you have to be very deliberate of any move you make. It is a crucial time to apply that key press agent rule, *Firmly Understand The Priorities Of A Situation*. For some reason, I was in the wings of the stage near the end of the Award show in 1967 when Fred Zinnemann had just won the directing award for "A Man For All Seasons." Near me was a publicist who had been assigned to take the Best Director winner through to the press rooms, and he or the people who assigned him apparently had not considered the priorities. The creator of a dozen of the hundred greatest movies turned an anxious attention back to the stage. He was also nominated as producer of "A Man For All Seasons" which would shortly be revealed to be the Best Film winner. "Mr. Zinnemann, the press rooms..." the publicist reminded urgently. Never taking his eyes off the stage, the great director said, as though to himself, "I've waited four years for this moment. They can wait four minutes for theirs."

I believe that was when Academy Awards shows were presented at the Santa Monica Civic Auditorium, which was the location four years earlier when Sidney Poitier became the first African American male to win any Oscar... in this case Best Actor for "Lilies Of The Field." For some reason I was at the entrance to the press rooms with Sammy Davis Jr., perhaps he had been a presenter, when Sidney Poitier arrived with his Oscar to face the flashing bulbs and celebratory questions which awaited just behind the closed doors. Sammy leaped up on him... I mean up *on* him, his legs wrapped around the Best Actor's waist... and hugged him with uncontrolled delight. "I wanted to be the first," he roared, "but thank God it's you!" And they held the hug in exclamation mark to a turning point of history. Those moments of privileged witness do not fade.

The rules and observations reflected above are not my unique personal perception but, rather, they reflect the shared experience and privilege of the hundreds of skilled professional press agents who gather together each October through February to mother-hen the prospects of the year's fine films. If you want a visual metaphor, think of the winter Olympics sport of curling. The talented athlete throws that tea kettle or whatever that thing is that he or she slides down the ice, and then his/her compatriots slip and slide just ahead of it sweeping the ice with brooms. Somehow that conspires to take it as far and as accurately as it can possibly go. That's what Oscar press agents are... guys out on the ice with brooms. It is not glamorous, you might get cold feet, and it is very slippery work. And they don't earn a medal.

Chapter 24

The Wedding Planner

Nothing turns on media like a wedding. The more you try to protect it, the more they want in. The impossibility of the "get" (obtaining the rigidly protected key photos) turns up the prices stalkerazzi can demand for crashing a celebrity's nuptials, especially when it spoils the exclusivity for which some other magazine has paid a six or seven figure fee. Publicists do not select the gowns and the floral displays, but setting and servicing and protecting a contracted-out magazine coverage of a celeb vow-taking makes the press agent a wedding planner in a very real… and difficult… way.

There's one thing every bridal couple wishes their wedding to be. Perfect. With celebrities, that can be a tall order. Having the dignity, romance, privacy *and exclusivity* protected is a primary consideration. Its achievement is no easy task with the concerted photo resources of the world media clamoring for a piece of the action. Beyond the solemnity and delight of the ceremony, the newlyweds usually want the beauty of their ceremony to be captured in film and photos and conveyed to those interested in a fully deliberated manner. For most of us, that is friends and family. Fame changes the equation. For famous artists, the consideration widens to include millions of fans who celebrate and support the artists' work as well as the lookee-loo world at large.

A major factor is the commercial value of the exclusive rights to these images and the accompanying "insider" article. The press agent serves as auctioneer, dangling it among competitive media outlets. An astute press agent can make a big money difference. Most often in my personal experience and on the weddings

I describe below, I was negotiating vast sums to support my artist-clients' elected charities and causes. It's a splendid way to consecrate a marriage.

Concluding a media arrangement for a wedding forces the publicist to guarantee the exclusivity of the photos and to deliver the copy as the servicing publication designates, as the bridal couple has its heart set... and how you design its presentation to the world. The overseeing flack determines in which publications she/he wishes it all to appear, satisfying an interested public in a controlled manner, and accomplishing charitable goals. Making this all possible and harmoniously protected and accomplished is the part of the wedding planning which falls to the press agent. It's the hardest part of working a wedding because it's the only part that imposes upon the flack-in-charge a fiduciary obligation to anticipate... and thwart... the general media's need-to-get. You have to prevent a press free-for-all which would and very often does disrupt the ceremonies and then result in photo coverage from hell, not to mention possibly killing the deal on the fundraising. In the show-me-the-blood mentality of the tabloid media, ugly photos pay a prettier price then those which merely capture the happiness of bride and groom. You have to meet the purchasing magazine's or syndicate's contracted exclusivity, security demands and critical and very tight deadlines. Never ask a press agent if he or she enjoyed a wedding...

A wedding, a birthday, a christening as a fund-raiser? If you can, why not? Usually, you contract with one entity... a magazine, a worldwide photo syndicate. They approach international distribution aggressively to recoup the high costs. You hold back U.S. rights because you want to reserve that sale for the widest or most prestigious exposure, as we did with both the Brosnan wedding and for Barbra Streisand and James Brolin, holding each of those for covers of People. The purchasing publication then mitigates its costs by vending simultaneous cover breaks with the best and highest paying publications in all of the other markets, obtaining wider worldwide pickup and cover commitments than I would ever be able to do with ad hoc sales.

Not only does Guttman Associates demand publication approval and photo kill rights, but all overseas sub-purchasers have to adhere to the conditions I imposed on the main buyer, if such is the case, particularly printing approved text in exact and unaltered translation. You don't leave any wedding-spoiling mishap to chance. Public interest is gratified, since people do want to see stars' weddings, and your clients have the very best photographers preserving their memories in beautiful detail, while money is generated for their most cherished causes. It is one of the best win-win equations in publicity. But it's a back-breaker.

Jane Seymour and James Keach were married at a walled and gated estate in Santa Barbara. She reigned as the widely-acknowledged Queen Of the Mini-Series and was in the process of resurrecting Saturday as a TV night and returning family-worthy drama series to ratings respectability with the success of her "Dr. Quinn: Medicine Woman" on CBS. Beyond that, she was by accomplishment and by genes one of the most photographed women in the world and rarely took a bad shot. "Somewhere In Time," which teamed her with Christopher Reeve, was an achingly romantic story of love's defying the chasm of time which separated its lovers, and it became a cult classic joining millions of fans from around the world in its testimony to the power of romance. It has brought thousands of them back to Mackinaw Island in Michigan each year for decades, gathering where that love story was set and was filmed. When Christopher was signed for the film, he called excitedly to say, "I'm working with Jane Seymour... you know?.... the most beautiful woman in the world.?" Jane is one of the few actresses who actually enjoys photo shoots. The key magazines have always been happy to oblige, and she has long sustained as one of *UK* media's most pursued Brits in Hollywood even though now an American citizen.

So the bidding to purchase photo and coverage rights to her and James' wedding was vigorous. Her romance with director and actor James Keach began when he directed her in a television movie, and the press like a location angle to their love stories. The winning magazine's contract had to be protected with a full court press against the tabloid shutter-snappers. The estate where the marriage would occur was surrounded by high eucalyptus trees, unfortunately outside the property lines of the home. Stalkerazzi photographers, like buzzards, like to nest in high trees. I'm sure no neighbors sold bleacher seats, but there they were. Floral décor and other elements were placed to anticipate the most likely angles. Luckily, Jane, in tribute to her family members who had died in World War II because of their Jewish faith, created a floral khupe (arch or canopy) over the altar and bridal couple in observance of ancient tradition, and it served to protect the exchange of vows from an unexpected stalkerazzi ploy. What we didn't anticipate, because it was relatively new, was the fact that some of the most predatory photographers would engage helicopters, especially when they saw that their tree roosts would have lovely views of everything but the wedding. The khupe was great defense against airborne invasion, *but it wasn't soundproof.* You could barely hear the vows for the pounding chopper noise, a lesson I tucked away for later.

The wedding of Pierce Brosnan and former Today Show correspondent and media journalist Keely Shaye Smith became a particularly imperative must-get event for magazines and tabloids. Because Pierce was in the middle of his tour of duty as James Bond, I was able to negotiate a substantial fee with England's Hello Magazine for exclusive worldwide distribution of the story and art… comparable to that of David Beckham and his Spice Girl bride. There was ample reason the bidding soared. Keely and Pierce were hosting hundreds of distinguished guests for a wedding weekend of royal elegance at the historic and scenic Ashford Castle in County Mayo, Ireland, providing lavish visuals. They had already established themselves as one of the most admired and effective activist couples, particularly in the area of ecological and environmental protections.

With high price comes the obligation to provide a vacuum-tight exclusion of the stalkerazzi who would be there in record numbers, especially because of certain ease-of-access considerations. We had engaged massive security in order to protect the immaculate exclusivity of the wedding coverage There was a separate deal with People using the same art but with certain key shots reserved for the American weekly's exclusivity. There was a glorious ancient chapel on the gated and guarded acreage of the Castle grounds. I could have delivered bride and groom in a fancy horse-drawn coach the short distance from Castle to Chapel, easily defended against the lenses of photographers whom the security guys and I plucked out of trees in the Castle's forests the morning of the wedding. We also had to shield the events and the key participants from the armada of photographers' boats floating on the waters of the lake adjacent to the castle and which was perilously accessible to one and all. Unfortunately , the chapel was not an ordained Catholic place of worship, so the wedding would transpire in a 12th century abbey a 40 minute ride distant, constructed on the ground where Saint Patrick had in the 5th century first performed communion and introduction of the faith. The perfect choice for the consecration of their marriage it most certainly was, but protecting the Abbey from all of the lenses would be impossible. The problem was getting the wedding party in and out without exposure to the imaginative positions some of the hundreds of photographers had marked out for themselves. We had the windows of the Rolls Royces conveying the bridal party to and from the wedding masked in black velvet, while the vividly gowned and elegantly tuxedoed participants entered the church shielded within a covered hall of sheets held aloft by our tallest security guards. The light filtering through that glowing cloth onto happy faces and vibrant fashions provided some of the most beautiful wedding event shots I've ever seen and they were among the exclusive elements which the contracts with Hello and People demanded be protected. Miraculously, photo coverage was hermitically sealed, except for when their English press attaché decided to have private conversation with the bride while strolling the lawn of the castle in direct view of several hundred paparazzi floating on the lake. What is the Celtic word for "oy vey?"

Pierce's compelling sense of Irish tradition raised its Gaelic head. There was, he pointed out to me a week before we left for Ireland, a pub just across the road from the Abbey where the local males had gathered with wedding grooms from time immemorial to share a drink just before the ceremony. And this, he assured me, he firmly intended to do. I reminded him that we were selling this happy occasion for an amount that would make numerous charities extremely happy, and this required that none of the wedding party, particularly bride or groom, could be captured in ceremony attire by any photographers other than our own. "Are you telling me," he asked in high dudgeon, "that I can't raise a pint with the lads at me own wedding?" "I'm telling you that you can, but that each of those hundred or so glasses will cost your philanthropy about ten thousand dollars." The lads had to raise their own pints in absence of the groom to whom they related only by celebrity fascination, curiosity and Irish blood.

The day of that great bonding of a Bond and a bride arrived… the only wedding of a sitting Bond which gave it such a special clamor. And so we moved in a procession of elegant busses and resplendent Rolls Royces to the historic abbey, advancing at sedate speeds along narrow country roads and through narrow town streets which were lined with locals who cheered as Pierce's black-windowed Rolls passed by. I even had black cloth between the back seat and the driver. It was an amazing sight from the car behind. Every so often he would bring his window down a bit and stick out a fist with a thumb raised triumphantly skyward. You could practically read the lips of the enthralled women… "There it is, you see, his very own t(h)oomb!"

The entire wedding weekend was an experience of linked-elegances for all and of linked emergencies for me and the crew of the best security guards available in Ireland and England. The dinner was held in a great tent facing a fleet of photographers' boats. Hello Magazine locks in its issue on Sunday nights for their Thursday or Friday appearances on the newsstands. Other great weekly magazines deadline rarely more than a day later. I had had to insist on a Saturday rather than a Sunday wedding for precisely that reason. A stalkarazzi, on the other hand, could have his or her shot in the papers the next day. This was before the photo miracle of digital jpeg transmission of photos, so a guy on a motorcycle had to race hundreds of miles on curling two lane roads to get the shots to Dublin for development and returned to Ashford overnight.

Again, photography on actual film was the dominant challenging and inhibiting factor of both Keely and Pierce's wedding and, a few years before that, the no-less intense international media focus on the wedding of Barbra Streisand and James Brolin Each occurred before the present universal reality of digital photography, the modern miracle of photographs which one may view and even retouch or "photo-shop" in the camera or on a connected laptop, capable of being sent out into the world at the press of a button. How much easier the publicity would have been during those two weddings which echoed around the world. Everything has changed in that little-over-a- decade, so much for the better, so much for the worse.

When Barbra Streisand performed at a fund-raising concert with Barack Obama in the final weeks before the 2008 elections, it was very specifically not for publicity. So, as had long been the habit industrywide in such situations, we precluded press cameras. To what avail? Five hundred cell phones with the same camera capabilities the media enjoy were flashing it all over the internet five seconds after the downbeat of her first song. The book of PR practice had to be thrown out and rewritten.

The contractuals on the Brosnan-Smith nuptuals also meant that the accompanying wedding story, in all of its detail and delights, had to be ready for their reading, too, also by the morning-after's early light. For that impossible task, I had a secret weapon. Our daughter Monika is one of the best, fastest and most graceful writers with whom I have ever worked. Without her, I couldn't have ventured the whole wedding plan. That she could get the text of the Brosnan wedding story written, approved and on the editor's incoming email eight hours after the post-wedding party was no minor miracle. "Hello" was well aware of her work and reputation and happy to engage her and bring her over. She and Gisela were sharing a room, but she worked in my room through the night, pouring over her laptop to paint the extensive and photo-accurate word pictures of the wonders of the event, start to finish. That's the glory of real journalism… not only to convey what happened but to let you *experience* what happened. The most treasured memory of the event which remains etched in both Gisela and my hearts, was a week with our daughter, a week of constant companionship, co-workership, shared stress and the shared beauty of Ireland. We were grateful that her husband and children had loaned her to us for a difficult and (as it turned out) wonderful adventure. It reminded us of all the great world travels we'd had with our children, even when we could barely afford it, before college and life demanded them from us. On the downside, I was the only male wedding participant, other than Pierce, who could do the rigorous jigs and other Irish dances, and Gisela heartlessly pimped me out to all of the other wives. The next day I was truly hobbled by a knee which had gone on strike and I limped through the rest of our stay in Europe.

For two months before the anticipated but not-yet-announced wedding of Barbra Streisand and James Brolin in the summer of 1998, the media infrastructure in Los Angeles was gearing up for it. Media were pouring in from around the world. Barbra had designed the most elegant of evenings for the event at their Malibu estate, with a string ensemble serenading the guests through the gardens and into the main home and with Marvin Hamlisch at the keyboard conducting a chamber orchestra for the musical element of the wedding. We most certainly did not want the on-rushing media frenzy to intrude on a truly perfect occasion. Nor did we wish to compromise the exclusivity of the wedding coverage which had been sold for a record sum to augment the many millions of dollars the Streisand Foundation has long contributed to causes she supports. Again we faced water-based photographic coverage. The ceremony would be conducted in the great living room in front of windows giving out onto the ocean… where dozens of boats carrying cameramen floated in expectation. Yes, a long lens can get a true image from a distance of a quarter mile. Thanks to the ear-splitting experience of Jane Seymour's wedding, we were approaching this occasion with attention to media invasion by land, sea AND air.

The guests graciously observed the request not to reveal information about the date of the ceremony, but the day before the event, the tent beneath which the dinner would transpire started to go up, and the word was out. Unable to confirm it until the morning of the event, by which time it was general knowledge, and with the Seymour-Keach nuptials firmly in memory, I called every one of the media outlets I felt might have helicopters available for that day, confirmed the circulating details regarding the timing of the event... and then said that I fully understood that they would be doing coverage from above, but that Ms. Streisand would appreciate it if they would do so only from 1 PM to 5 PM. The ceremony and the following party would occur under roof and tent in any event, and it would be kind if they could arrange that the helicopter noise did not disrupt the vows. Every one of the news outlets respectfully complied.

Barbra understood and appreciated the kindness of that restraint, and the next day the executive producer of each show received a hand-inscribed thank you note from her. A number of the recipients called me to express their appreciation for that gesture. Ours is not a world absent of civility and respect.

Chapter 25

People Who Made Me Laugh

Early in his film success, Gene Hackman hosted a party at his home-with-a-view atop Coldwater Canyon, the ridge of which separates Beverly Hills from Studio City and North Hollywood on the other side of that mountain. The occasion was for an actor friend who had just made the jump from Broadway to Hollywood. The guy disappeared from the crowd for a while, and Gene went to find him, finally coming upon him standing at the edge of the patio looking over the shimmering light-spread of city below. "Joe," Gene said, "are you ok?" The friend turned to Gene, wonder in his eyes, and said, "Gene, it's just that... this party...all of those famous people in there... they're all here for me, Gene, for me!" He ecstatically swept his hand out toward the lights, "Some day all of that is going to be mine." To which Gene responded, "Schmuck! That's the Valley."

Gisela and I were at a foundry having one of her sculptures cast, and the proprietor, also a blacksmith, was working on a horseshoe. I asked if it didn't have to be red to be shaped. He said, "Nope, things can be burning hot and still not glow. Fellow came in the other day an' saw a shoe on that very same anvil, picked it up and let go real quick. I asked him if he'd burned his hand, an' he said 'No... just doesn't take me a long time to look at a horseshoe.'"

I suspected that this was a joke of the trade, but it demonstrates propriocep-tive behavior, something you do all the time. When you pick up a hot horseshoe, you don't have to wait for your brain to tell you to drop it. This is the emergency response which cuts the brain out of the equation. The spinal cord or even the muscle responds to emergency stimuli, and they don't seek a second opinion. They can initiate the requisite muscle and adrenaline response all by themselves. With great comedy, the brain is always involved. But some dazzling comic response is so fast that it seems to have erupted from the mouth, fully shaped.

One evening as we were walking to his car after a show, Jay Leno alluded with concern to the passing of the mother of another of my clients, asking if the client was ok. I said she was in pain, but that I thought she was prepared because her mother was 93. "Well, that's a good old age," he said. I answered that old is not always good, that my father was 96 and he'd told me that "when the indignities exceed the pleasures, it's time to go." Armed with which philosophy, he had stopped eating and passed away in a short time. Jay immediately tapped my over-indulged stomach and said, "Well, you could stop right now and *coast* to 96."

Recently, when we were in D.C. for Jay's acceptance of The Kennedy Center's distinguished Mark Twain Prize for American Humor, we were on our way to a run-through at the Center, and Jay asked if I was heading back to LA the next morning. "No," I said, "my daughter's driving me up to Gettysberg" "For the reunion?" he enquired.

Over the more than two decades that Jay owned the late night ratings, lighting up five hours a week for NBC, audience laughter evidenced that part of the fun is the written material like monologues which he pulled together with a staff of great writers and then delivered with such skill and verve. Another big part is the instantaneous wit… that proprioceptive stuff… his off-the-cuff response to the moment, his repartee with his band leader, his on-the-spot sculpting of the Jay Walk amusements, the comic truths of his conversations with guests, his comedy acting skills in the skits. Making people laugh is part inspiration and part hard work. He also works hard to keep others from knowing how smart he is. On one of the final shows, Morgan Freeman was describing the speed of his plane in kilometers per hour, and Jay said in instantaneous calculation, "Seven hundred fifty-six point five miles an hour" or some such on-the-nose specificity. And then he smiled guiltily at the audience as if it were a joke.

Also, while he's one of the kindest of interviewers, a laughter-seeking missile targeting the amusement rather than the embarrassment, Leno has a way of cutting to the bone of an issue… and not just his "what the hell were you thinking?" to Hugh Grant following the actor's misguided quest for companionship. That guesting, with its laughter and truthful address of the problem, took Grant gracefully over a very visible career bump and also locked in Jay's decades-long ride at the top of the ratings. Jay's own sense of outrage is often the crux of the laugh. This was apparent when he reported a news story that men who have sex with animals have a higher incidence of penis cancer. He paused and then blurted, "Good! It serves you right, you sick bastards!" It ended the monologue with a huge laugh of enthusiastic concurrence.

Gallup and Pew and all the other pulse-takers can take as many polls as they want, but the instant measure of where American sentiment hovered on most news issues was the laughter Jay's jokes got from his audience. Right after the invasion of Iraq, his zingers concerning W or Cheney or Rumsfield sometimes didn't get the response the sharp comic commentary really deserved. Sometimes part of the crowd would even show displeasure with the political jest. But just three months later, as Fathers Day approached, he had one to the effect that if the President's daughters haven't come up with a great gift for their dad, he really would love it if they could find some nice weapons of mass destruction. The laughs went through the roof on that one. The tide had changed in American opinion on what Bush/Cheney/Rumsfield had done… and patience had run out with the excuse the White House guys had given for having done it. Jay's audience was throughout a reliable measurement of the mood of the country.

We sometimes got requests from Make-A-Wish or the Dream Foundation when young people chose visiting Jay's show as the wish they most wanted fulfilled, getting to watch a taping, getting to meet him, often to visit his garage with Jay as tour guide… In those cases, I tried to be there to make sure the young person had the fullest possible experience, meeting the other people on the show, getting to see a studio from the inside out. One time it was an African American boy, about seventeen, who had spent five years in hospitals, and I was curious why this was his choice… why not going gliding or going on a safari or seeing a game in Yankee stadium and meeting the teams? He told me that during all of the years of fear and pain and loneliness (hospital rooms are lonely,) he always knew that he could watch Jay before he went to sleep and then close his eyes and go to his dreams with a smile on his face. I think that's the reason five million or more people chose the Jay Leno Show when they also had ten other top comedy shows to switch on instead. Every one is entitled to go to sleep with a smile on his or her face. I told that story to Jay recently, and he responded, "Great, another person I put to sleep." But I think that was to duck the depth of the compliment.

That blacksmith's joke is kind of metaphor for publicity. Things… horseshoes, careers… can be malleably hot without glowing red. A publicist's job is to supply the glow to assure that the people whom your client needs to reach do, truly and actively, appreciate that your client is red-hot. If your client has a sense of humor, it makes the job easier… and more fun.

I took personal pleasure in setting up the recent Kennedy Center's conferring upon Jay the Mark Twain American Humor Award. Apart from being able to share the distinguished doings with my daughter Monika and her family in D.C., it was so palably one of those occasions when, with the loving tributes of so many of his comedy peers, you could visibly place your client's horse-shoe of honor on the anvil burning bright red-hot, a heat his public had always bestowed in the form of record-breaking ratings…

Laughter Is a Many Splendored Thing

From observing the marital success of comedians, I sometimes wonder if "love" may not be the *second* most important L word in sustaining a marriage. "Laughter" is certainly of equal importance, if you play your cards right. Burns and Allen, Jack Benny and Mary Livingston, Stiller and Meara, Milton and Ruth Berle, Fibber McGee and Molly. Bob Hope and Delores stayed long and happily married, and each reached and passed the extravagant age of 100 in the process. Could there be some correlation? One could see and feel that these couples all had fun together, making each other laugh as much as they made us laugh. Edgar Bergen and Charlie McCarthy, his smart-ass, tuxedo-clad dummy, were the biggest thing on radio. Bergen's wife Frances was as classy as Charlie was sassy, but you always saw that this was a successful marriage full of kindness and, like the others one must suppose, buffered with shared laughter…

Once upon the time of the '60s when white bread and apple pie were coming unglued, I had a client at a Sunday morning interview show which was being shot at an outdoor flea market of hippie paraphernalia and clothes. While my client was getting made-up, I was strolling the booths with Anne Meara, another guest on the show. She stopped at one booth selling hippie togs and focused on a kind of free-love jerkin, a girl's leather bodice the center half of the front of which was open space minimally covered by inter-crossing leather thongs holding the two sides together. The bosom was covered, but the message was daring. Ms. Meara sadly commented how this reflected where fashion and youth were going and then enthused excitedly, "I have to get that for my daughter. She'll LOVE it!" Now how can a marriage fall apart when you're married to a spirit as free and spontaneous, as capable of double-think and, yes, as loving as that?

Fred Allen's biography, "Treadmill To Oblivion" (tied with Oscar Levant's "A Smattering of Ignorance"and "Memoirs Of An Amnesiac" for the all-time best don't-hate-me-because-I'm-smarter-than-you humor book titles) is less about Allen's own amazing wit than about his amazement at that of his wife and comedy partner, Portland, and her instinct for too-clever-to-be-an-accident malaprops. Jay Leno's rich and loving marriage to and partnership with Mavis reflects a strong foundation of his razor sharp humor and her powerful intellect and activism against injustice. The long and sustaining marriages of Red Skelton and Red Buttons, Danny Thomas, Marty Allen's rich and beautiful partnership with Frenchy and Eddie Cantor and his Ida-sweet-as-apple-cidah were relationships that spilled over into their *comedy*. *Tony Randall's loving one-ness with Florence stretched from their high school days until her passing and beyond.* And years later he built another *loving* culmination of his long and creative life with his second wife, Heather. We all look for secrets for long and happy marriage, and maybe we should study the longevity factor of love-times-laughter, the common denominator of so many couplings that worked. It's the element that held Gisela's and my relationship past the half-century mark. She found a way to end most of our arguments with a spin of laughter, most often cleverly intentional and, because a second language can occasionally play tricks on you, sometimes not. We're going out for a holiday lunch, and in no uncertain terms she made it clear that she wants me attired stylishly, or, as she put it, "in full regatta." That kind of thing can really regale-ya.

I had just finished a phone call with Jimmy Woods one Sunday morning, and Gisela asked, "What did Jimmy call about?" "He's just been offered a film that the Polish brothers are going to direct." "Oh," she said, "I love the Polish brothers." "You've never seen a film by the Polish brothers." "My favorite," she insisted, "George Clooney and the hair wax… 'Oh, Brother, Where Art Thou?'" "That was the Coen brothers." "Yes," she said with a smile as if that proved her point, "and aren't they Polish?"

Non sequiters and delightfully garbled metaphors sparkle like ornaments on the year-round Hollywood Christmas tree, and no one decorates that tree better than Gisela. Thank God I didn't marry someone whose first language is English. My perversity could not have withstood the absence of such delightful incomprehensibilities. I would have missed the laughs. I'm not making fun of it… she speaks three more languages than I… and she can follow the gist in several others including Yiddish and is absolutely scholarly in English. Her wonderful little lapses are mostly in confusions of the idom.

In refuting some answer I'd given her recently, Gisela snapped in furious rejection, "That's a load of CROCK!!!" "A load of crock?" I challenged. "A PILE of crock?" she corrected. "Well, that's more like it," I encouraged. It's like being *married* to the conjoined attributes of Angela Merkel and Gracie Allen with a little Barbara Stanwyck stirred in. OK, a lot of Barbara Stanwyck, the "The Lady Eve" Barbara Stanwyck.

I have to emphasize here that my German is pathetic. I learned the language in two weeks in preparation to meet her mother, and it never really improved. The fact that some of her German friends actually seem to think I'm communicating in that tongue makes her crazy. Apparently, when I don't know a word, I take an equivalent word in English or French and say it very emphatically with a strong Germanic inflection. These people, all far more linguistic than I, understand because they recognize the word from its mother tongue and then accept it as an arcane German word with which they are not familiar. When I forgot the word *unglaublich* (unbelievable) and improvised something, she fumed at her accepting friends, "Don't let him do that to you. There's no such word as 'ooncomprehensablich!!' She does the same thing to English. She's convinced the non-word "bonifiable" means certifiable or impervious to contradiction, and it's accepted as such by the people to whom she says it. "Reiterate' is invariably "er-iterate" which I, with dyslexic sympathy and evil enjoyment, never correct.

Most often she breaks me up because of style or attitude, and she plays these out with impeccable timing and perfectly defined character. Some of them become real performance art… truly superior improvs. One night recently I was passing the main board of our alarm system. It was 9PM and we weren't going out again, so I put on the alarm. The system, of course, announces that throughout the house. Gisela comes steaming out of the kitchen. "Did you just turn on the alarm?" "Yes," I reply with intolerable equanimity. "Well get this and get this straight, she says sternly, "*I* turn on the alarm and *I* decide *when* to turn it on." "OK," I say calmly, "but let me ask you this. Some night I hear noises outside, ok?. And you're not here. You're… oh, let's say you're spending the night with another man. May I in that circumstance turn on the alarm?" She puts one finger on the side of her chin, giving it due consideration. "I'm spending the night with another man," she ponders…. a pause of deliberation and then with great magnanimity and pointing the thinking finger at me. "Sure." Her timing is wondrous.

I would think that much of the joking and banter in most marriages is set in sexual context because sex is much too serious a business not to be joked about. It's like playing with hundred dollar chips. It ups the ante of the humor. Gisela and I were lying abed talking one Sunday morning, which beats Meet The Press by a mile, so I brought up a subject which truly measured the vapidity and idiocy of what was being talked up as the "newfound sexual freedoms" of the early/mid '70s. Wife-swapping. So I say, "What about this wife-swapping stuff? You think we should look into it?" And she says, "Why? Who do you have in mind?" And then the brightest and meanest light bulb of my life goes on above my head and I say, … "Sophia Loren and Carlo Ponti." "OK," she says, "I pick Sophia."

It was in the telling of that very Gisela anecdote that I first met Barbra Streisand. It was on a location shoot of "All Night Long" in some modest home in a modest suburb east of LA. I had run it past Gene Hackman, and she came over and said "What's so funny?"

I knew of Tony Randall's equally beautiful second love and marriage not only from the press items which were frequent because of the age difference, but also from seeing him backstage at the Tonight Show upon his occasional visits with Jay Leno. No one was more passionate or eloquent than Tony in expressing his deep pleasures. Nor was anyone more deeply engaged in language or more meticulous in studying its rules and eccentricities and fascinations… He loved to taunt people of other first languages by dropping some of the most outrageous words of those languages into casual conversation. I knew enough German to understand the borders of polite discourse that were crossed when he would greet Gisela with "Fik, fik, meine genadige Frau." She thought it hilarious, but whenever I similarly visited German expletives to gain some equal footing in our most heated battles, she was indignant and infuriated. She also loved it when Tony, he alone of all people, called her "Geeze." It sounded awful to my ears, but it enchanted her. 'How's Geeze?'" he would ask each time we saw each other.

I think my little splinters of broken German when I met her in Paris may have been an ice breaker. I wanted to write her a note in German. Everyone knows from those few lines of German in World War II films that "du bist" means "you are." You are what? What should I add to my two syllables of German? Obviously when Hitler wrote his life story and his mad philosophy of hate, he must have called it "my life." So I wrote "Du bist mein Kampf." Actually, it turned out to be more prophetic than I could have imagined. "Du bist mein Kampf" in fact means "you are my battle." I think the mad existential logic of that must have intrigued her. The last thing she was looking for was a flat and boring road. She'd never had one before nor would she tolerate any in her future. It may have been the nuttiness of my pigeon German that was buying me into her attention like a rock in her shoe.

But back to Tony Randall's urbane love of words and language. He studied them, polished them, honored them with meticulous enunciation and clever usage. I knew just enough Greek and Latin... a word, a phrase... to marvel at his passion for the etymology of words he seduced into conversation, tracing each to its roots. He infected me with that curiosity. He had a special place in his heart for the word "oxymoron," which means a word or phrase in which the component parts contradict each other (honest politician.) "The word," he said of "oxymoron" with the excitement of a guy whose team had just won, "actually IS what it deSCRIBES. Can you imagine THAT?" He went on to explain, lathered with wonder, that the Greek "oxys" means "sharp" or "acute," while "moro" means dull or blunt. "Don't you get it?" Tony enthused, "Sharp/dull, acute/blunt... the word oxymoron itself actually IS an OXYMORON! ... possibly alone among all words it personifies what it defines. Isn't that INCREDIBLE?!" his voice rising to that pitch of wonder that WAS what it deSCRIBED. That's all it took to make Tony extravagantly happy.

Along with the sweetly attendant Betty who secretaried his later decades, Warren Cowan's longest serving trusted and exceptional personal assistant was a pretty young girl, Sonia, who was very proudly Greek, and she had a kind of essential modesty one finds among Greek women... although I joyfully found Melina Mercouri a glorious exception to that rule. As Melina was courageously and beautifully outrageous, Warren's assistant was to the same degree demure.

On visits to our office, Tony, the scholar of all things verbal, would tease her, thankfully without her knowledge. He told her of his love for the Greek language and of how it had enriched our own. He delighted her with lists of fabulous words in English that came straight from her own mother tongue. He once confided to her that two of his very favorite words were adopted directly, unblemished and uncompromised from the Greek words, "I love them," he told her, "not only because of their expressive beauty of sound, but because they so wonderfully capture complex and essential aspects of human experience." "And what are those?" this young Hellenic beauty asked smilingly, unaware in her innocence of how Tony was setting her up. "Fellatio and cunnilingus," Tony answered with quiet propriety. "Oh, I'm sorry," the sweet maid of Athens said with gentle sincerity, "I'm not familiar with those." Tony nodded and said, "How sad."

Melina Mercouri was someone who could make you laugh and she also could make you cry. She was very responsive to and expressive of her feelings about all things. I was selling a story about her to a particularly acerbic female member of the press who, at one point, complained of Melina, "She cries too much." To which I said, more emotionally than thoughtfully, "Or maybe the case is that you cry too little." I paid heavily for that one. Irene Papas, another Greek actress of world renown, was also fun but a bit more controlled of emotions, as befits one of the chief interpreters of the classics, title star of the film "Elektra" and Clytemnestra in "Iphigenia." On one occasion I impetuously bought Gisela an expensive and exquisite antique Japanese wedding gown, perhaps because of its artistry, perhaps because she'd never in three nuptials (all of them with me) had a wedding gown. She didn't respond to it or to what I'd paid for it as enthusiastically as I'd hoped, saying, "I've married you enough." I showed it to Irene when she was visiting one of Gisela's art exhibitions, and she said, "I'd love to be married in that." She bought it from me, digging me out of a hole.

The person at whose expense Tony Randall most enjoyed having fun was himself. He took great joy and pride in his erudition, and great joy in mocking himself for its lapses. While he was filming something in Italy, he spent all of his free time becoming knowledgeable about Italian painting, visiting every museum he could, reading pertinent books, making notes. When he returned, he recounted all of this to me in glowing detail, including his incredible excitement about having himself discovered one of the greatest artists who simply was not given his due in art books or even any mention. He decided to make it his happy duty to bring to this long-deceased artist all of the fame he deserved, especially since this painter had such a varied sweep of styles and themes. Tony told me of going to a famous Italian art historian whom he wished to make his partner in the elevation of his uncelebrated master. He described the works and his devotion to them to the scholar. "And what is the name of this great talent?" the teacher inquired. "Ignoto," Tony answered with possessory pride. "Ah, yes, Ignoto," the expert repeated, "yes, extremely varied." "Can you tell me more about him," Tony asked eagerly. "It's not a him. It's a them. Ignoto means 'unknown.'" At this point in his story, Tony laughed unto tears.

One finely tuned marriage of wits I've studied close up is Renee Taylor and Joe Bologna. The incongruously perfect blend of his Italian street-smart wise-guy skepticism and her whacky, outgoing Yiddish lovability, this partnership hits its comedy marks as much in life as in their acting work together and their joint stage and film scripts. When they debuted their two character comedy "It Had To Be You" starring in it at the ninety seat Lee Strasberg Theatre in West Hollywood, we really turned out the star power and press for the opening, an audience of comedy talents and big event media coverage. When you're a hit and the audience is celebrated pros, the word goes out faster. We had two dozen big names and faces, and then the presence of political icon Bella Abzug made it seem to have left sane orbit. "Tell me again," Joe said to me by the sushi table at the after-party, "why are we doing this?" and he indicated the joyous crowd of funny people, continuing… "All the hoopla, stars, food?… a ninety seat theatre? We got more caterers than we got seats." "Because every time the male star of some hit hospital series and the female star of an eight year sitcom want to do a two character comedy in Warren, Ohio, this is what they'll do." "OK," he said, "you're on." "I've been on for two months," I said. "Yeah, ok, but now I might even pay you."

I was undertaking an Emmy campaign to get Renee nominated for supporting for her work in "The Nanny." I told Joe that I wanted to do an ad with a very new tact, an ad that was very ostensibly taken for her by him, a loving testament in which he would offer to send a clip reel to whoever calls a given number. An ad that personalized might jolt the attention of other actors. This was before the TV

Academy had a For Your Consideration website where aspiring nominees can post their clips. It was, in fact, before there were *websites*. The ad would be headlined with a note from him along the lines of "I want you to see the work of my wife of 25 years..." He changed it to "my wife and *girlfriend* of 25 years." I think it was the "girlfriend" that did it. We received an unprecedented response, and she was nominated." These comedy guys know what will touch the funny bone and what will touch the heart.

When Joe had to leave "It Had To Be You" for a film role, there was no comparable comedic actor available to replace him, and the show, which was selling out, faced the prospect of closing. I suggested Ed Marinaro, the "Hill Street Blues" star we repped, to take over. The tough cop role notwithstanding, Ed has a sweetness, and I knew he could be funny. He had to convince Renee, and he was nervous. "Marinaro, huh?" she started, "what is that, like Italian?" "No," he said, "it's not like Italian. It IS Italian." "You see?" she responded brightly, " Italians... they don't know how to *not* be funny?'' Ed got the role, great reviews and a whole new angle on his career.

When Renee auditioned for a key role in Todd Solenz' deep dark comedy "Life During War," the director's first words to her were "I don't want you to be funny." "I explained to him," Renee told me, "that the only time I'd ever heard those words before was from Joe, and that was on our wedding night. Todd laughed, but I still got the job"

She just called me from New York where she had watched a friend have laser liposuction and then decided to do it herself. She was so pleased that she was thinking about hiring out to do ads for it that would play during reruns of "The Nanny." I reminded her that she had always publicly opposed nips and tucks, that she was the only actress who hadn't even done the show "Nip/Tuck." "Oh, I'd incorporate that in the ad," she answered, "I'd start off by saying that I'd never wanted to change myself because when I die I don't want God's first words to me to be 'Who *ARE* you?'"

For a guy who set the NCAA rushing record... at Princeton, no less... and was a go-to star of one of TV's hit action shows and then other series, Ed Marinaro was a very unpretentious guy. Our offices then were opposite the Beverly Wilshire Hotel, and its Mexican restaurant, Don Hernando's, was our commissary. Ed and I and two other people came in for lunch one day, and the maitresse d', Peggy, had to make a table for us. Starting towards where she wanted to place it, she called out to the busboy, "Eddie, may I have four chairs in the corner?" When she arrived at the spot, she turned and confronted Ed Marinaro carrying four chairs, two in each hand. He was not only humble, he was strong.

Peggy is one of two women whom I credit as really having launched the reputation of Guttman & Pam. Even today, more than twenty years after I went solo (well, not really solo… my associates and I have a living partnership of effort, and their thoughts prevail as often as mine, hence the title of the firm) many people in the industry still are inclined to say Guttman & Pam rather than Guttman Associates. One reason is a that it has the beat of a comedian's rimshot… a drumroll…. Guttman and Pam… BOPiddyBOP.

The other reason for our reputation was Frenchy Allen, wife of comedian Marty Allen. Frenchy could match Marty roly poly for roly poly and funny for funny. She was the most beloved person in town. Frenchy loved everyone, and that just glowed, so everyone loved her back. One of her dearest friends was Sidney Sheldon, which is how we came to know her and Marty. Sidney was hardly an unknown when he came to us. As writer and producer, he'd turned out some of Hollywood's biggest hit movies, winning an Oscar for the script of the Cary Grant, Myrna Loy, Shirley Temple comedy "The Bachelor And the Bobby Soxer," making TV history with such series as "I Dream Of Jeannie" and "Hart To Hart."

Through well thought-out PR, we fast-tracked Sidney to the position of being a hot novelist before his first book was a hot novel. That, in turn, brought us Frenchy's extravagant admiration. Her generous acts of friendship and belief directly resulted in Guttman & Pam's becoming a fairly prominent PR firm. She loved the quick ride to pre-eminence as a novelist that Sidney had made with us at the wheel and his story-telling brilliance in the gas tank. "Guttman and Pam," she said to Mssrs. Guttman and Pam, "is the Tiffany's of the PR business." And then she went out and recited the same phrase to everyone she knew, and she knew everyone. Within days, it was coming back to me. "Guttman and Pam? I hear you guys are the Tiffany's of the PR business." It continued for years. I've never done as good a job for a client (and we're not bad) as Frenchy did for us. It was like the horse shoe on the anvil at the foundry…we already had a terrific client list and we were arguably hot. But we weren't glowing red. Frenchy made us glow.

When Frenchy died, the whole town turned out in black. And then the main eulogist, that unanimously and deservedly regarded splendid guy Michael Landon, stood up and said he wanted to read an article about Frenchy that Marty had written some time back for a fan magazine. And the snob part of me complained to my brain, "A fan magazine? Why a fan magazine?" But then Michael began to read elegantly and passionately, struggling to hold back sobs. The entire gathering did the sobbing for him. Not a dry eye in the house? There wasn't a dry *sleeve* in the house. Frenchy sailed off on the sea of her friends' love and tears.

Jerry and I knew Sidney could become a lynchpin account the moment he came through the door. He's in this people-who-make-me-laugh section because he could always make me laugh. He had the timing, instincts and irreverence of a good comic or, even more, of a song plugger which he had been on New York's Tin Pan Alley at the start of his career. He was as powerfully connected as he was powerfully talented. Since his first novel, "The Naked Face," wasn't doing it with its own bare hands, opening to only modest sales., we decided to project that Sidney Sheldon's first novel was in the process of becoming a major motion picture. "Soon To Be A Major Motion Picture" was a great come-on for a book even then. Jerry took "The Naked Face" to Roger Moore, Jerry's close buddy and one of our cadre of great British clients which Jerry brought to our partnership.

We announced that Roger was optioning "The Naked Face" for a film which would star the movie world's newly anointed James Bond as Sidney's protagonist. Sidney understood how these things worked, and he was delighted. And he understood that *sometimes something has to SEEM to exist before it can actually COME to exist.* The concept was: *make something BE by saying in a convincing way that it already IS.* The immediate publicity result of this was that Sidney was coming to his second book as a novelist who already, seemingly, was having his first book brought to the screen in an impressive circumstance. That would become the automatic actual case for each of Sidney's future works, but for the first one, we had to invent it... and keep postulating that invention *until it came to pass.* Everything about the story we planted was perfectly true. There was commitment on both sides, just no exchange of money. We never said "bought," we had said "obtained."

But this "action"... this active occurrence, this news, this news relevance of a book's acquisition for filming by a significant actor who was suddenly one of the top stars in the world… this gave Sidney a lot more traction and, strangely, "reality" (in the sense of active recognition) as a "happening" (an annoyingly popular adjective of that moment) book author. And, did the second book ever live up to its opportunity! It was a giant thriller called "The Other Side Of Midnight" which went to the top of the bestseller lists in every country in the world and refused to come down. It piled up sales statistics that we poured on the waiting world with a ladle. Sidney became the author who most readily was identified with the adjective "bestselling."

When Sidney came to us, he already had, as I said, a front row seat at the top of the world. But Oscar-winning screenwriter to best-selling author wasn't a slam dunk. He hired Guttman & Pam to launch his new career as a mystery novelist. Even when "The Naked Face" did not take off, we got him a lot of ink and TV "face time" as we in the fame game so elegantly call it. Sidney was a great interview, which certainly helped. He told an interview anecdote with the same sense of style and construction and building suspense as he told a novel. His experience as a song-plugger in NY's dog-eat-dog music world, where they sometimes listened only to the first eight bars, meant he knew how to sell something… and *fast*. Later on when some of the leading right wing evangelists were campaigning to get Sidney's novels pulled from libraries along with other such subversive works as "Huckleberry Finn," we really rode *that* one to glory! I arranged for Sidney to confront the most famous of these super-conservative oracles, Jerry Fallwell, in a debate on Good Morning, America. Sidney hypothesized a sizzling sexual narrative to the good minister and asked if that gentleman would also ban a book selling such a licentious tale of incest and out-of-wedlock conjugal visitations. And Fallwell's immediate answer was a resounding "of course." Sidney then revealed that the characters of that censorable story were Lot and his daughters, and the book was The Bible.

Roger Moore did get "The Naked Face" made about ten years later, starring as the shrink who had to clear himself of the murder of his patients. Or did HE actually do them in? That's what made a Sidney Sheldon book compelling. It was a film with substantial provenance, directed by Bryan Forbes and teaming Roger with Rod Steiger, Elliott Gould and Anne Archer. The point of this episode is that the initial announcement that Roger was going to do "Naked Face" as a film had given Sidney special position within the book-community. One of the measurements of a book's success is the defining phrase "headed to the screen." That edge gave Sidney footing to turn out a parade of gigantic best-sellers. Those best-sellers helped a press agent "dream-up" plant become a movie a few years down the line. *If that isn't veracity, I don't know what is.* Very possibly I *don't* know what veracity is, but at least I aspire to it.

What is the relevance of this recall in a chapter on people who made me laugh? Roger's dry wit, exactly the one which characterized his Bond films, made him the devastatingly handsome Peter Ustinov.

Another Roger Moore announcement became a film. Euan Lloyd was a producer client who was trying to pull together a gala soldiers-of-fortune saga called "The Wild Geese." He had the enthusiasms of everyone concerned except the people who had to write the check. We put out an announcement on the film, casting the story (with their advance approval) with a half dozen stars who were then clients on our list... Richard Burton, Roger Moore, Richard Harris and Hardy Krueger among them. We listed a few money sources Euan was in fact talking to, but not the one he thought he could rope in. In the glowing black and white of a trade paper headline, the story made the targeted foot-dragging money guys feel a good one was getting away from them. The check cleared a week later. And it DID star Richard Burton, Roger Moore, Richard Harris and Hardy Kruger, directed by a top action director, Andy McLaglen. And it added handsomely to the profits of those money guys who read that Variety story and then picked up the phone. PR WORKS.

Another announcement by Guttman & Pam for Euan (and Roger again) didn't turn into a film, but it did serve as a good luck charm for another client. William Shatner's jump from TV series to film seemed a sure thing when Paramount signed Robert Wise to direct the initial feature version of Gene Roddenbury's classic TV series, "Star Trek." However, the general feeling and resulting box office was that, even under the hand of a master filmmaker like Robert (Westside Story) Wise, the film was bloated. The continuing feature film future of Roddenbury's iconic property seemed bleak. Bill's managers who had brought him to us, Jay Bernstein and Larry Thompson, had charged us with solidifying the perception of Bill as a feature film star. Paramount had just announced that the second feature version of "Star Trek" would be a TV movie. That put Bill's big screen prospects in some peril, not to mention limbo. We went to Euan Lloyd with the idea of announcing the feature "Dien Bien Phu" about the tragic collapse of the French presence in Vietnam which presaged our own war there. The dream cast we gave Euan was Roger, Shatner and Alain Delon, who had actually served in the French Foreign Legion. And with that trio of Guttman & Pam clients, Euan was actually suddenly dying to do it. Except that it wasn't a script, it was just a title, a press agent dream-up. So, let me stress, we were announcing something of our concoction that was, indeed, actively being pursued. It had elements of reality because a top filmmaker was now really working to get such a film made with a very probable cast. He had everything but that script and the about $15 million he needed back when that was high-end budget. Consequently, the film never happened, but a week later Larry Thompson advised Shatner that Paramount had called to find out when "Dien Bien Phu" would shoot because now they wanted to go with the second "Star Trek" as a theatrical feature film rather than TV feature. Who knows what triggers such decisions? It didn't hurt that Bill Shatner had shown evidence in the trade papers of his continuity as a feature star.

The Power of Association

The Los Angeles Times was doing an article on "power breakfasts." That is to say a story about the limited number of restaurants where the truly big business of Hollywood was conducted over scrambled eggs and lox. That is where Peggy, maitresse d' at Don Hernandos at the Beverly Wilshire, enters the short list of two women (Frenchy Allen being the other) who materially shaped the power reputation of Guttman & Pam even though we were a rather small company in the scheme of things, albeit one with extraordinary clients. The selected crème de la creme list of power breakfast eateries was the Beverly Hills Hotel Polo Lounge, the restaurant at the Bel Air Hotel and Don Hernandos, since the Beverly Wilshire is within walking distance of most of the leading Beverly Hills-based super corporations and agencies. Peggy was asked which big companies did their power breakfasts over her huevos rancheros, and she said, "oh, all of the power executives from the huge firms here, the William Morris Agency, Merrill Lynch and Guttman & Pam."

We were merely an artificially gilded pimple on the butts of those world-conquering firms, but the association Peggy branded into the industry mentality had enormous legs... cross country legs, and they just kept running. We started getting a lot of corporate business, including the financially fortuitous and ethically compromising but (once more with feeling) high paying tobacco company-backed disco contests in which I, who oppose smoking on the grounds of sanity and humanity, worked for R.J. Reynolds or Liggett and Meyers or whichever firm it was whose product I detested. I asked them (three top guys) why they had come to us. When they said everyone knew we were one of the huge firms, I knew where it came from. They walked into an office that was nice enough, but it was fully evident we had a staff of no more than ten people. Nonetheless, their "huge firm" impression was unshaken because it was in print. We needed the money... it was a moment when we *really* needed the money..., and Peggy's quote had put us up as candidates for the job.

Great PR merely enhances and can never supplant talent as the reason for success, that's a given. But the story of how RJR or L&M came to our door illustrates the ultimate rationale for publicity and how it sometimes can help shape careers. It's true that Guttman & Pam handled such corporations as Faberge, Rolls Royce, Aston Martin (but only until Jerry drove one of their beauties through a tennis court and totaled it,) General Mills, Paul Mitchell Haircare Systems, kathy ireland WorldWide (correct spelling) and some others of stature. But at the time that the tobacco world beat a path to our door, it was Peggy's loving testimony that did it.

"It often is not what you do, but what people HEAR you do and,, therefore... THINK you do."

I'll make full confession on the cigarette thing. A sort of dry run before I have to explain it to St. Peter. Since we were projected as being in the Merrill Lynch, William Morris league, these tobacco peddlers came to us. It was the time of disco. They wanted to launch a new brand called Real Cigarettes by hosting big disco contests at the very top disco clubs, leading to a championship night at the biggest and most historic dance hall in LA. These new Real Cigarettes would be liberally distributed free to those attending. The tobacco guys insisted that only those old enough to smoke would be admitted. It was before the Surgeon General started a half-court (and half-hearted) press against smoking, but I wanted no part of a cigarette campaign, so I quoted a price that paled even these big spenders. As they headed for the door... my desired effect... I asked, out of press agently curiosity (which can be either a flack's Achilles heel or his leg up,) what they planned to call these contests. They said "The King And Queen Of LA Disco." Just because my mind thinks in campaign concept, I said, "Why don't you call it The REAL King And Queen Of LA Disco?" Well, they turned around and wrote a check or, at least sent a memo to some nicotine capital to draw up for us a check for that outrageous amount. The ludicrous fee I'd quoted bailed us out of whatever need so immediately imperiled our little company. When Jerry and I went to a strategy meeting with about twenty of these tobacco guys, we were the only ones not smoking and they all seemed to be smoking two or three cigarettes at a time. But I was embarrassed by the fee and the compromise of principle, and I determined to punish myself by covering all six events myself.

A half hour into the first one, I felt I was on the inside of a drum. The noise was beating me up. When I dragged into the house, my daughter Danielle saw I was in percussive shock, and I explained the disco water torture that God had chosen as my punishment. She said it was because I was fighting the beat and that I had to go with it. She taught me how to feel it going through me and not battering upon me. Then she taught me how to dance it. From then on I would bee bop to the music all night long and eventually became so convincingly capable on the floor that whenever I had occasion to dance with my daughters at some event, women my own age would come up to me angrily to tell me that I should be ashamed of myself.

In all truth, I justified the Merrill Lynch rip-off (accepting gelt by association) by doing a bang-up job. The first time I met Maria Shriver was when she came into town with a news crew from a Philadelphia station and I talked her into doing our disco promulgation of the nicotine trade. Jenny Agutter, Hollywood's hot new import, came down to step up the Fahrenheit of the event as the interview subject. Different things make you hot… Good actress?… very much so; Pretty?… of course; but Jenny had a kind of signature innocent sexuality that got a manic grip on the town's awareness. Her degree of unselfconscious nudity in such cutting-edge art films as "Walkabout" and in "Equus" with Richard Burton imposed itself upon the town's consciousness, not to forget libido, before everyone was getting naked in movies. Because she sought in no way to make the scenes sexual, they were very much so.

For our big championship dance-off, we scored a ten on the star scale by pulling in as our judges, Jacqueline Bisset (hot off simultaneous covers on Newsweek and People,) recent Oscar winner Jack Albertson, a former Vaudeville dancer, and top-of-the-charts disco composer Paul Jabara with whom we'd worked when we were hired by Casablanca do the publicity on the Donna Summer disco sizzler film, "Thank God It's Friday." The Real King and Queen dance-off wound up celebrated with several pages in People Magazine. I had more pressure from people who wanted to obtain tickets to that championship dance night then for tickets to the Oscars, and we jam-packed the biggest ballroom on the west coast, the Olympic. It was a preview of the dance fever now fueling TV. That treason to my principles and to the furthering of good health could buy me half a millennium in purgatory. In my defense, Real cigarettes never made it to market.

While I'm into confession, let me track G&P's brief and I-swear-to-God inadvertent toe-dipping into the porn field. I was contacted by a leading Canadian photographer who said he was launching a new magazine along the lines of Europe's Zoom, which was a very arty photo monthly that featured sexuality along the lines of the kind of nudity for which Helmut Newton and Mann Ray were famous. Class flesh, right? Not explicit anatomy in teasey almost-costumes or sterilized these-are-my-boobs centerfolds like Playboy, but nudity as studies of the human form along the lines of the masters. That's how it was presented to me, and that's how I bought it... My wife sculpted nudes. Sometimes at night I had to sit nude on a table in the kitchen simulating the position of some professional model for a piece she hadn't quite finished while he modeled for her and some other sculptors all day. She would complain that there wasn't the same space between my stomach and my thigh. The point is that I was, by reason of marriage and personal aesthetic, thrust into that cultural regard of the figure studies. It should have tipped me, however, that the magazine was called Eros. But if it was good enough for the ancient Greeks, it was good enough for Guttman & Pam right? To prepare the town and the media for this new outlet featuring the body as art, I had them make up gold necklaces for me in which the signet was simply the word Eros. I gave one to Danielle (I hope there's a statute of limitations on child endangerment.) She was working the window of a Malibu McDonalds, and suddenly the requests she was receiving had nothing to do with hamburgers. She told her mom about that, and Gisela quickly threw the gold necklace into the trash, and it appeared for a moment that she would do the same to me. Some promotional ideas are less good than others.

Before I acquired the good sense and threats of divorce to bounce the account, I apparently initiated enough good publicity for it that we started receiving calls from other entities in the world of sexual enticement, all seeking our representation of their products. I was blowing them all off, but one sort of intrigued me because it was so illogical and counter-intuitive. The gentleman came to the office and I gathered at first that he was a doctor, but that proved to be only the name of his company which made sexually related products. Once that was established, I told him I was out of that business, but he said he didn't need any help selling sex toys. They literally flew out the door. He needed advice for his "high-end" products. Apparently he did a large business in vibrators for women… don't get ahead of me here… which were sold in the leading, and I mean leading, women's department stores in the country. They were offered for such things as shoulder muscle massage, but it was apparent that their application was, shall we say?, other. That lucrative side business on the less-than-wild side was threatened by the fact that one of the top financial magazines was doing a story on the kind of companies that supplied this particular ladies' aid in the same aisles that peddled high fashion. Women, it turned out, didn't mind paying many times what these things cost in less fashionable establishments, because the bag in which they were carried out the door was not only respectable but enviable. The purchase of that commodity in that kind of haute coutour circumstance had that best of high end validations, provenance. The magazine was Forbes or Fortune, I think, something respected that began with an F, and the reporter was coming to visit him at his place of business where his other plastic pleasures and things like bubble gum whose bubbles appeared to be testicals were manufactured and shipped. If the shoulder massage devices were to suffer guilt by association, which certainly seemed in prospect, he stood to lose a great deal, not the least of which was a toe in the door of respectability. What could he do to prepare for the visit of that reporter?

It was, from the creative point of view and the psychological perspective, an interesting problem. Interesting mind candy. I told him that the best I could do for him would be to provide him with an hour of discussion and advice. I was really looking for a no. On the other hand maybe I could keep Gisela from finding out that I was making a quick trip back to the bottom of the barrel. I quoted him an outrageous price for that hour… well, outrageous by the standards of our reasonably priced boutique. "I could go to a shrink for three months of hour visits for that," he complained. "Sure," I said, but you still wouldn't know what to say to the reporter when he walks in your door," I answered. He said ok, and I did something illogical but, I thought, well-grounded. I owed him good advice for that kind of money, and I knew nothing about the milieu into which the reporter would be immersed. I told him I would meet him at his factory/shipping facility the next morning and that we would do the consultation there.

A substantial part of the nation's more perverse pleasures… the world's maybe… would be eradicated if someone suddenly vaporized the San Fernando Valley, particularly the part that is ground zero for US porn production and the inventive and in some cases comical devices purveyed by companies like the famous-in-its-field one that was engaging my advice. I was led to his office, and it was clean and spare, and, again, the ads for their frankly-freaky top-sellers abounded. He led me through the packaging area where dozens of Mexican women were stuffing plastic penises into plastic bags. There was a side room with a thick wooden door. "What's in there?" I asked. "Leather and discipline," he answered. "Ok, the morning he comes," I said slowly so as to be clearly understood, "that door is locked with a sign saying 'no entry, construction, exposed wires'… ok?" "I could say that's our research and development," he offered, and I said that I wouldn't use that phrase. He had mentioned something before, and I suggested he use that on the reporter when they pass through the penis packers. The company had close ties with a university hospital in Texas which used these things as prostheses. "When you go through here, drop that on him, and don't forget to use the doctor's name," I said. "And have the ladies wearing surgical gloves." We came to the high-end vibrator area, and I suggested making it larger for the reporter's visit, with more Mexican ladies putting those things into their elegant boxes.

He had mentioned that his vibrators were advertised in Cosmo and in key fashion publications, and I asked to see all of those ads. They were suitably classy and aesthetic, and I seem to recall they said things like "for that all-important relief." But they were definitely high end. I laid out the drill for him, telling him to take 20 of the high-end ads to a framers where Gisela had a lot of her framing done. "Tell them to frame these ads as they would do fine art pieces for Mrs. Guttman. They'll be classy. Then you take down the ads in your office and in the hallways and you put the elegant ads up instead. They sell elegant Currier and Ives prints and seascapes. Buy a half dozen in dark walnut frames, and then they should replace what you have in the reception room. Have three or four fashion magazines on the table there. When you're being interviewed, lay heavy on the work your company does with doctors on prosthetics… don't say dildos, just say prosthetics. Then I want you to get a guest's chair in your office that is very low. Have someone go to Crown Books and buy every sexual advice book that was ever number one on the New York Times best-seller list. It's ok to throw in the Kama Sutra. Put them on the edge of your desk so that when the reporter sits in the elegant but low slung chair, he can't see over those books when he's talking to you. You get up and say 'Let me move these for you,' and then when you do, you say, 'By the way, everyone of these books was number one on the New York Times best-seller list.' Before he gets in to see you, keep him cooling his heels in the reception area with the boating scene prints and the Vogues and Marie Claire, whichever ones contain your ads."

Apparently it all went as planned, and the interview went well and was printed with a slant that helped perpetuate his national Wilshire Boulevard/Rodeo Drive type shoulder massager business. He called and said he would really like us to handle his company, but I explained how busy we were. And that was the end of my slosh through the repugnant world of porn and sexual adjuncts. But it was an interesting exercise.

There are times in Hollywood when bright quips sink ships. I'm a master of that one. A strained reach for a laugh line has cost me dearly from time to time One hallmark of great funny people is timing… not just how you pace out a joke and nail the punchline, but knowing *when* to unleash a funny line or tale and when to not. That is not a subtlety I've mastered, and I've strained one marriage and numerous friendships with the wrong joke at the wrong time.

In one case, one of Gisela's best friends had suffered a detached retina on the tennis court. The whole gang of friends was tense because tennis was her life. At the celebratory party after the operation turned out well and because I'm supposed to know the right words, I was asked to deliver a suitable toast to express everyone's relief. "Harriet," I said, raising a glass, "here's mud in your eye." The shocked and horrified look on the group face was precisely the response that kind of gag begs, but I thought laughter would follow. It didn't.

I learned my lesson about one-joke-too-many when Candice Bergen graciously agreed to host one of Danielle's Revlon Run/Walks, this one held on the UCLA athletic fields. I knew Candy had other important business that morning, but she showed for a good cause, and I'd promised to get her out after about an hour. I'd neglected to consider that by the time she had to leave, Sunset Boulevard, where her chauffeured car would have to exit, would be jammed curb to curb with runners. My only recourse was to ask my friend Superior Court Judge Michael Harwin to obtain one of the attending police black and whites to get her to her home a few miles away. But it was up to me to tell Candy that she was going home in a cop car. "What? Dump me on the sidewalk in front of my neighbors like I'd just dried out from an all-night binge?" she so reasonably responded. I told her it was the best I could do. She shrugged and started to get in. Unwilling to leave such a tenuous well-enough alone, I stopped her. "Candy, I think that protocol requires me to push down on your head as you enter." The look she gave me made me grateful that she was in police custody.

Candy not only had the comedy genes of her father, Edgar Bergen, but she had the courage genes of ancient Viking predecessors. She was barely in her 20s when Sidney Lumet's "The Group" cast a glaring spotlight on her... her beauty, her father's prominence, and her brave undertaking of one of the first blatantly lesbian characters in a major film. That courage was further evidenced in her simultaneous prominence as an investigative writer/photographer, the career for which she had prepared at Ivy League Penn... and don't say Penn State. I was helping her (carrying the tripod) when Candy, a prized daughter of the very elite and proper mansion community of Bel Air, was writing and shooting an Esquire article called "Is Bel Air Burning?" documenting the locale's despised invasion by *nouvelle riche* hippies... *quelle scandale*. We were doing a gag shot of the very hippy Michael J. Pollard and his wife picnic-ing on the lawn of the sanctum santorum Bel Air entrance when she casually mentioned that she was already working on her next article, an *expose* of Scientology. This was a venture that a lot of sane people were trying to discourage. It was a first, and everyone thought a dangerous one. But... that damned Viking blood... she took an unsparing look at a very secretive society and opened a window of public interest which Scientology had kept locked.

This is a town where being too smart (something of which I've never been accused) and too funny is not always a good thing. I know one terrific actor with a sharp mind, a cutting sense of humor and good improvisational training. A friend, not a client, he was just the guy with whom you would want to share a relaxed evening, but not necessarily a "table read." A "table read" is when a cast sits around with the director and writers of some project and they do a cold read of the script, just so they can see where the natural laughs are and can get a feel of the pacing it requires. This usually comes after the casting is done. And, indeed, on this occasion, the actor in question was fully a done-deal for the film. Even though the script was good, with all his training and clever instincts for comedy he saw how he could in some instances enhance it. Accordingly, he changed or added little things and some big things, a couple of them getting good laughs. He was fired off the project. Writers don't want to hear how much better you can write than they can. And it's a matter of time and budget. The most expensive time is in front of the cameras, and some guy going off-script on the sound stage even to bump up the laughs is going to cut into the schedule and the focus and good humor of the director and the writers, who are often the producers.

Sometimes not only your ad libs but your whole campaign can be dangerously too good for your clients' best interests. We did such a good job for another corporate client… or at least our account executive Carroll Greene did… that we put him out of business. It was a lovely guy who had developed the toy called The Penguin And Her Baby. It was a lovable penguin who mechanically laid an egg inside of which was an even more lovable baby penguin. Carroll got it to a comedian, Stan Kann, who was a regular on most of the talk shows and whose routine was to do funny shtick with unusual mechanical objects. His routine with the Penguin And Her Baby was so hilarious and adorable that suddenly orders started pouring in to our client. It was shaping up as the Cabbage Patch Kid of that approaching holiday season, so much so that our client thought he could distribute it himself and that he did not need to go through normal distribution channels. Little did he or we know that those particular channels that our client was dealing with were controlled by some very strong and fiercely territorial interests who maintained rather intimidating defenses against the end run. Well, suddenly all of the toy store interest dried up. The old "careful what you wish for" strikes again.

It is not undue modesty for me to explain that even though Guttman & Pam represented some extraordinary talents, it was always a little firm. And so that continues even now. Mega PR agencies sprung up about us like the skyscrapers hedging in Willy Loman's modest home. The Rogers & Cowan template became the order of the day. The only thing sizable about Guttman & Pam then (and now Guttman Associates) was and remains the talent and reputations and accomplishments of our clients. The common denominator of our list was and remains the delight of representing great talent.

Gisela and I went to see Renee Taylor and Joe Bologna in one of their plays, "If You Ever Leave Me, I'm Going With You," and afterwards as Joe was driving us to a late bite at the Beverly Wilshire, I commented that the audience was a little long in the tooth, those who still had teeth. "You shoulda seen Thursday," he said in full grump, "the average age was DECEASED." A conversation with that couple is like a comedy writing session. I love doing Oscar season parties at their home where Joe had put in the world's greatest home pizza oven from which he extracts a tomato-dill pizza, wafer thin and crisp that makes you realize why the dish was once called pizza *pie*. In Joe's hands, in Joe's oven, it was a dessert. Renee and Joe were in the habit of getting married again… again and again and again… every five years, each time in the ceremony of a different religion. They haven't re-married for a while that I know of. Maybe they ran out of religions. Gisela and I have been married to each other on only three occasions. The mortar of our marriage, too, has been laughter. It holds things together or, in a truer sense, keeps them from flying apart. And she can make me laugh just to spite me and spoil a good snit.

I see Renee and Joe several times a week right now along with the other reliable attendees of the January jitterbug of screenings and parties studios hold to make sure that every Academy member is exquisitely aware of their contending films. It is the precious and pressured two weeks when the ballots for Oscar nominations are lying on desks waiting to be scribbled upon or emailed to the Academy of Motion Picture Arts & Sciences. At a lunch yesterday honoring the cast of "Lee Daniels' The Butler" before we scooted our gathered members up to a high tea for the nomination candidates of "Philomena," Renee was talking to Daniels, and he thanked her for gracing our event. "So many parties," she said, "so little time." Comedy is the trick of language that makes the ridiculous sublime.

The Decade of Great Comedy Albums: Story Tellers

The 1960s, even among all the other things that period launched, was the decade of the great comedy albums. During that era, the greatest challenge of press agentry was being able to laugh with unrestrained enthusiasm while listening to a comedy album under the watchful eye of its creator. It was a necessary survival skill for any entertainment frontline Hollywood publicist. It wasn't that it required the kind of over-the-top response you would witness from some inebriate at a comedy club. It was more subtle and demanding than that. You had to show amusement, concentration and *sincerity*. And you thought the SATs were tough. Vaughan Meader's comedy album parodying the Kennedy clan and the Kennedy mystique became a meteoric national bi-partisan sensation about a year into an administration that was celebrated or derided as Camelot. We of the liberal persuasion (and even some others) were under the sway of the Kennedy magic cloud, but we listened to the mocking album a dozen times, laughing harder on each spin. It seemed unbearably unfunny after the assassination of JFK. But it had opened the door for laugh albums, and comic talents like Bob Newhart poured through it. Of the guys who were straight up stand-ups, it was the ones on the outer edge who led the pack... George Carlin, Mort Sahl, Godfrey Cambridge, Dick Gregory, all with hard political slants, the Yiddish/nebblsh niche led by Woody Allen and Myron Cohen, with Orson Bean and Dick Shawn finding their own comic persona and Jonathan Winters taking it to the inspired edge of sanity. Bill Cosby's albums brought us wry humanity and observation. There was Don Rickles so rollicking and insulting, and Lennie Bruce freeing comedy in the same way that Bob Dylan was freeing rock. Richard Pryor was in his own orbit. You saw those guys in the coffee houses or in concert and you bought their albums. I was drawn to Mort Sahl because his anguish and anger were so human and intellectual. I still recall his lines I haven't heard for fifty years... "I hate movies... Every time things get tough, they go to a fade-out or dissolve. I don't have any fade-outs in my life. I have to live every bloody minute of it."

For some reason Mort didn't like R&C, but he seemed to exempt me from that. We had kind exchanges when I booked people on his comedy talk show. It appeared to me that the Borsch Belt comics, Red Buttons, Morey Amsterdam, Zero Mostel, Jack Carter were making their big impact with guestings on the TV variety shows, while the vaudeville and radio trained comedy superstars had their own shows, Burns & Allen, Benny, Hope, Berle, Red Skelton, Danny Kaye, Jimmy Durante, Danny Thomas. These really kicked into high gear because of the success of the Sunday night Colgate Comedy hour on which Hope and Jerry Lewis and Benny and a few other laugh royalty alternated. The supply of genius seemed endless and they kept restoring the stockpile. George Gobel and Gary Moore on their shows threw off other master-craftsmen like Harvey Korman and Tim Conway (whose license plate, I once noticed in the parking area at CBS was "13 weeks" meaning that none of his own shows, remarkably, ever went a full season.) Lucille Ball was a comedy movement all by herself and so was Carroll Burnett, who a decade before had been the comet across the sky of our theatre arts department at UCLA. They opened TV comedy up for women along with radio vets like Joan Davis and Eve Arden, but they didn't seem to make a big assault on the comedy album market which enjoyed that decade and which that decade enjoyed, the variety show guestings of Phillis Diller, Toby Fields and other stand-up ladies were welcome part of the comedy landscape. The successive waves of new TV-spawned comedy sensations like The Smothers Brothers and Flip Wilson rolled in like high surf.

The other great body of '60s comedy album stars were "story-tellers," with Bill Cosby at the head of the class. He connected on a very personal as well as comedic basis with the people who bought the tickets to see him. This was evident, at least on the one fairly intimate opportunity I had to observe him. It was the late '70s, and Guttman & Pam was repping Helen Reddy. I was on a private plane with her and her husband manager Jeff Wald heading for Vegas to pick up Bill Cosby with whom, beginning that night, she would share a bill at Harrah's in Tahoe, on the Nevada (which is to say the gambling) side of the state line. Consistent with his best comedy, on the Vegas-to-Tahoe flight Cosby was in a philosophical zone, and he was venting some very up-from-the-guts resentment he had for how much was charged for their shows. Every seat in the room, he said, would be filled by somebody who had paid thirty-five bucks (a lot of money then) to be there. Do you know, he was asking, how much that is for that guy? What can I give him that's going to be worth thirty-five bucks? This from the master... Bill Cosby! He and others were "priceless," but he was right. Even with priceless, you still have to be able to afford the thirty-five bucks. That night the room was packed with people who thought Cosby and Reddy was the best thing for which they'd ever saved up that amount. Maybe that empathy drives his need to entertain... the oldest inspiration for greatness in show biz... giving 'em their money's-worth.

Years later, I was hired by Carsey-Werner to help launch Crosby's lovely re-do of Groucho Marx' "You Bet Your Life" quiz show for the syndicated market. Cosby brought the show quick success with his easy warmth and evident connection with the audience. During the '50s I'd booked many guests on the Groucho version, so it was fascinating to see how much the two had in common, however unalike their styles, not going for big yoks but letting guests wander into funny remarks punctuated by Bill's sharing a look with the audience or Groucho's bounce of the eyebrows. The contemporary mastery of that rare art has been Leno's Jay Walking.

Another group of story-teller jokesters in the '60s emerged from the Sid Caesar's "Your Show Of Shows" school of comedy. That '50s show was the birthplace of comedians and comedy stylings just as Saturday Night Live has been for so long. My chance, decades later, to work with Imogen Coca on a Carsey-Werner sitcom was a delicious career perk. She was a comedienne of such gift that she could hold and even command her ground with the inspired Caesar. The immediacy and intimacy of their comic chemistry was new and fresh every time. This is a good point to note (and never too often) that, in my business, it is important to love and even adulate talent. It carries you through. Mel Brooks' and Carl Rciner's 2000 Year Old Man albums were the most direct descendants of Caesar's comedy maternity ward. The great class of the '60s comedy album story tellers was one of the brightest flowerings of the American comic spirit. And Mel's films were its second flowering.

As an anecdotist rather than a historian, the point I'm trying to make here is that it was a time when there were many comedy album stars to be publicized, the Golden Age Of Comedy Albums. So a press agent had to adjust to and prepare for the tough task of being examined under a microscope by these intense and not always secure creative artists while being observed by them as the first test audience for a new album. These story-teller comedians, watching someone listen to their work, were and remain people who do not like to hear the silence of serious contemplation. A gag teller can miss on a joke and hurry on to the next without missing a beat, but a story teller floats along on the continuous wave of your laughter. It was a rigorous task for press agents to serve this particular market. Jonathon Winters was setting bars in innovation that no one could dare, and Bob Newhart with his lovely understatement was the master of subtle and unpunched lines. I would love to have taken a first-listen test with them. But I'm being greedy. I had my share

No, there simply was no roller coaster ride to match the tensions of listening to the new album of a top comic of that period while under the heavy weight of

his challenging eye. You could hear his mind taking notes. Stan Freberg's "Stan Freberg Modestly Presents The History of the United States," was first presented in his office to an audience of two, Warren Cowan and me. Stan informed us that it was the first comedy album in stereophonic sound. When the voice came from the right, Freberg moved to join it, saying the lines along with the record, commanding both our eyes and ears to the ping pong aspect of his comic invention, and it was a brilliant device. The multi-directional sound really made you feel you were watching a play. It was aural 3D. With such great comics, it was not hard to listen and enjoy, it was just hard to do it while you were under forensic observation. Even with the pressures of my first audience of it, Freberg's history lesson remains one of my favorite comic experiences.

For Warren Cowan it was sheer hell because of his habit of falling asleep in such circumstance. We, however, had a plan for this. Warren would get my elbow frequently during this experience because there is nothing more destructive of client confidence than a drooping eyelid, and two is worse... and silence worst of all. The arrangement was that in such situation, upon the sharp intrusion of my elbow into his arm while he was in most transported nap, Warren would awaken with a convincing burst of laughter. At one point, a book on which my elbow rested slipped to the side, struck Warren and elicited a mighty peal of laughter at one of the few points when none was merited. Stan looked at him strangely and then smiled, attributing it, I'm sure, to Warren's general mood of merriment.

Gisela Gets the Laughter 101 Test

Take a press agent's complaints with a grain of salt. Coal-mining is tougher. But the pressures can be daunting, especially for the uninitiated. Gisela wandered into the line of fire once. We had flown to San Francisco where I had comedian Shelly Berman doing two-a-night at the Fairmont Hotel and Van Johnson doing one nightly performance starring in "Bye Bye, Birdie" at the St. Francis. When we got there in the afternoon, we stopped at Shelly's suite to say hello, and... just our luck... he had just gotten the first copy of his new comedy album. He didn't have to ask. Gisela, quite sincerely, said, "Oh, I'd love to hear it." I'd failed to warn her. The album was terrific, and Gisela and I were both laughing freely. Only when she realized she was doing this under a microscope did part of her spirit slip out from her body, pull back a few feet and start to watch and judge her response as she felt Shelly must be doing. What she also was not prepared for was that the comedians would grade the sincerity and rapture of your laughs, giving them marks from one to ten. If your giggle-morphing-into-guffaw was deemed appropriate, the comedian would smile and then nod approvingly… kind of a grateful and congratulatory "touché." Sometimes when you really got some subtle point of wit, the comedian would raise his eyebrows in pleasant surprise and shape his mouth into a delighted "oh" and silently join you in laughter chorus. Gisela did great and I'm sure she faked none of her laughter… Shelly was, let's face it, original and brilliant. But when we got into the hallway, she said, "That was exhausting."

Actually, we left the room with an assignment. Shelly, assuming we would be at both shows, had a front table for us at each. I had to explain that we would be only at the midnight show because I had Van Johnson in the musical at eight o'clock. His disappointment was superseded by his thrill at the mention of Van Johnson's name. "Oh, my God, Van Johnson… the red socks, 'The Last Time I Saw Paris'… he's a great, great actor… 'Thirty Seconds Over Tokyo,' 'The Caine Mutiny'… sing, dance, he does it all." "And a very sweet guy," I assured. "Do you think he…? no, I'm sure he wouldn't… but what if he could…"Shelly aspired aloud. "Come to the midnight show?" I assumed. "I'm sure he'll be drained, but they can't shoot you for asking,"Shelly said, as if he would take no for an answer. The very thought thrilled Shelly, and I knew I had to press. Van was worn out after the show, but I gave him "the red sox, 'The Last Time I saw Paris'" and the whole nine yards of Shelly's enthusiasm. "Van, he's not just a fan. He's an idolator." Van gave me one "aw, kiddee," but then caved in graciously as I knew he would with "sure, why not?" Shelly was thrilled with the news, and I passed on to Van that Shelly had put aside THE front table and I stressed that it was at midnight.

Midnight showed, but Van didn't . Seated at the front, just below the stool where Shelly would sit, we could see into the wings where Shelly waited, expending nervous energy until Van appeared. At about seven after, he had to start, but his eyes kept darting to our partially vacant table, The crowd roared its welcome. He started with his routine of calling a department store to tell them that one of their customers was going to jump from a window. The crowd was in heaven. Still more nervous looks by Shelly to our table, and then Van was there and Shelly relaxed back into the max delivery of his material. The waiter poured from the complementary bottle of champagne, and it was, so Van reported, flat. It was all Shelly could do to go on. Van Johnson had been given flat champagne… and then the second one proved to be so as well. The audience didn't sense Shelly's tension, but we did. When a sip from the third bottle was poured, Van started to bring the glass to his mouth, but Gisela reached over and placed her hand lightly over the glass. "If this bottle is flat, Van," she said, "I'm pouring it over your head." Van greatly approved the wine and enjoyed the show, as… from that point on… Shelly did as well. Gisela never gave me an opportunity to fall out of love with her.

Working with Milton Berle was a post graduate class in focus. In the first place, you were there as the gems were being dealt out, and you didn't want to miss one. A lot of his comedy was predicated on his insistence that he stole his jokes, but no one dealt out more zingers off the cuff than Milton. He worked every moment as if he were in a club, reluctant to utter any line that didn't reach for a laugh. It was a humor that was vaudeville and burlesque honed and incarnate. So some lines were cruel, but all were funny. In vaudeville, you needed the punch-in-the-gut one-liners at someone's expense to keep them awake in the back rows. I never saw American vaudeville, except when our client Mickey Rooney and Ann Miller exhumed the art form and made "Sugar Babies" the toast of Broadway. Fifty years after starting his Hollywood career, sixty-five after first waddling out onto a vaudeville stage as a toddler, Mickey was back on the cover of Life Magazine. Music hall seemed to have stayed alive in England longer than vaudeville did here, and that was the primary affordable delight Gisela and I had when we were nursing our shillings as newly married kids in London, lucky to live around the corner from the Edgeware Road music hall palaces where the comic, music and variety acts were still flourishing. We've never been part of more appreciative and entertained audiences. God bless vaudeville. That's where Milton and Bob Hope and Red Skelton, Durante and Kaye and so many others refined and defined the American comic spirit.

The frequent proximity to a comedian of Milton Berle's compulsive need to evoke laughter, of his ability to lampoon one and all, made a thick skin required armament. His friends and such entourageurs as his loyal press agent would gather in his dressing room after each of his show tapings, and one evening a young agent was there, a nice guy who like me was not very tall. Milton, who didn't know him, asked what he did, and he said he was one of Milton's William Morris agents, and Milton snapped, "Well, you're short enough." Comedy needs some basis in truth, and it was true that William Morris, headed by the legendary Abe Lastfogel who was diminutive only in height , did have a lot of agents who were not very tall. Both the agent and I laughed, not because we had to laugh but because it was funny, even though we were stooged by the joke.

Milton had a type of humor that loved stooges, of which I was often one. He used to have lunch frequently at the Polo Lounge of the elegant Beverly Hills Hotel, always dining in booth number one which faced the entrance. He would call out a laugh line for whoever came in and whom he knew. I used to do a lot of lunch interviews or meetings at the Polo Lounge, and many times when I came in, he would yell out, "Hey, Guttman... how's your (vulgarity alert) dick?" Well, that's what I get for not having stuck to the name Richard. Eventually I started spreading my lunch business to other watering holes.

Milton Berle invented TV like Al Gore invented the internet... no, not a joke, I mean that quite literally... in the sense that they each realized the power of a new medium before the world did and by spreading the word they fostered the phenomenon. They were there before our minds were..., those two guys made us aware and made us care. They were the messengers and the proof. They didn't call Milton Berle Mr. Television for nothing. He carried the medium on his back at the beginning. He was the barker outside selling curiosity and tickets and he was the killer act inside on stage. He was the first great addictive agent of television. Only more so. In the fifties he was most certainly Mr. Television, and on the night of his show, Wednesday or Tuesday... I forget because it was such a given that it was his night that his name superceded the calendar in our minds... some movie houses would close down, or you could go to one to be alone.

In 1958 I was bringing Gisela from Europe to meet my family. I'd never worked with Milton, other than setting an Art Buchwald interview for him in Paris for R&C. Driving across country, we stopped in Vegas before the last leg, and Milton was playing. I saw it as a chance to introduce my wife to American culture in one fell swoop. We had had less than $150 to get across America and now were on the tail-end of it, but you could go to a Vegas show then for the price of a fruit compote. Milton opened his show with the Metropolitan Quartet, the classical singing group that often appeared on his show. They began singing opera for real, but it was actually just a set-up for his comic nuttiness. The group goes into a Puccini quartet, and Gisela is very happy. Obviously, her new home is rich in culture. Then Milton comes out goofing it up as a bumpkin creating chaos with their act. Suddenly, Gisela stands up and shouts "Will someone please get that man off the stage?" It gets a huge laugh. Milton slips out of the act and starts to shoot laugh lines at her. She stands up to face it and yells, "You should be ashamed of yourself." "Why," he comes back with salacious leer, "you hear something good?" "Yes," she answers angrily, "until you got here." Milton and the audience loved it, and then he milked it with some shtick to the house and got back to the routine of the act. It dawns on Gisela and she gasps "Is my head red! I didn't realize he's a clown." She got up to go, and the people at the tables around us applauded, expecting some new exchange. She dropped back into her chair, intimidated, and it's not easy to intimidate her. At the end of the show, she tried to slip out quietly, but numerous people smiled their good reviews at her. "Sister," one guy said, "you were great."

Our anguish continued when we got back to our little motel on The Strip. The air conditioner had turned the room into a refrigerator, and we couldn't turn it off, nor could we stuff blankets into the blasting vents because the wind kept spitting them out. Finally I went out and, since there was no one in the office, I found the main electrical switch for the motel and shut it down. The big purple Santa Clara Motel sign above me died, and I stood in the only unglowing spot on the Strip. In the morning we came out to find people standing around the little lake of melt which now surrounded the ice machine. We said we didn't know anything about it and how terrible it was that our air conditioning had gone missing. Gisela vowed never to return to Vegas.

Of course we did return to Vegas many times over. Once was because there was some special anniversary relating to a particular Milton Berle opening, and Warren Cowan with Cowanesque dash, arranged to fly a plane-load of really quality Hollywood talents up. Warren Beatty (this was slightly post-"Bonnie And Clyde") came up with Gisela and me and we shared our limo ride to the hotel with comedy legend Georgie Jessel, the favorite wit of President Franklin Delano Roosevelt who had dubbed him Toastmaster General of The United States for his devastatingly funny lampooning at any gathering of the great. It wasn't an event in D.C. or in Hollywood without Georgie at the head table. I was impressed how Warren Beatty, the unchallenged King of Hollywood at that moment and many others, just listened and learned as Mr. Jessel expounded. The great gathering of stars was to be at the late show, so Gisela and Warren and I walked down the strip to see The Supremes in their early show, not hard to set up since Rogers & Cowan represented Motown and all of its acts and since Warren Beatty was… well, Warren Beatty. The word had been sent back to Diana Ross that we, meaning Warren Beatty, were in the audience. And she stopped the show at one point to direct the audience's attention to that fact and to comment on how unglued she and the other Supremes had come because of that presence. It was a gallant expression of how much stars love stars and how much women love Warren.

Rogers & Cowan also represented Frank Sinatra and the Rat Pack. I will repeat here as if it had not already become apparent to you… never before and never since has one entity, whether talent agency or management firm or law firm or PR company, handled the same tonnage of talent. None could match the constellation of super-stars Henry C. Rogers and Warren J. Cowan had accumulated. I enjoy stardom and its magic the way other people enjoy… well… magic. Because of that, I have on one wall in my office a framed copy of the famous shot of all the MGM stars in MGM's most MGM heyday. I glanced at it once and realized that even MGM with all of its accumen and its millions hadn't done it bigger or better than Warren and Henry had. When they talk about Camelot in Hollywood, they should give those two guys their due. But that Rogers & Cowan pre-eminence in the star-repping business… especially the kind of acts that were up in lights on the Vegas strip… brought Gisela and me back to sin city constantly.

The most memorable evening occurred when we went up to catch Ray Anthony who led one of the greatest of the big bands, for whom I was account executive. Then we were supposed to get over to the Sands to meet with Sammy Davis Jr. after his show. Gisela was putting dollar bets on the roulette wheel at Sammy's hotel as we waited, and then Sammy was there and excitedly hustling us out of the casino because we were meeting Dean Martin and all going to famed stripper Candy Barr's performance at some joint across the highway. She was going to jail the next day for having shown her all in one performance and this was her farewell show before taking a vacation in the slammer. As Sammy was explaining this to us, the roulette wheel had taken a few more spins. We started to go, but a guy next to her at the table took Gisela's wrist and said, "Honey, that was the coolest goddam thing I ever saw." We figured out that her number had come up just after Sammy joined us, and thus distracted and through no cognitive choice on her part, she had let the winnings ride. That number had come up again, and there were about a thousand dollars in chips on the table in front of her, but a croupier's rake was foreclosing on the take, swishing it back like autumn leaves as we turned to look. Evidently the number had come a cropper on its third go-round. Gisela, taking in the brevity of our wealth, said to the other gambler, "Easy come, easy go." Even Sammy was impressed. He mentioned her cool to Dino whom we joined at the Candy Barr show and Dean said, "What are ya, sweetheart, part Eskimo?" And then the show started and the audience was as wild and appreciative as Candy's strip was wild and appreciable. The twirling tassels bedazzled the crowd, and at no table more than our starry gathering. She danced and shed and exhibited with dismissive disdain for what the rest of the stupid world held dear. The audience was standing and screaming at the end as Candy went off to what we all imagined were handcuffs in the wings. It was an interesting night.

Another time we were in Vegas with Carroll Baker, who was, after "The Carpetbaggers" and "Harlow," the biggest sex appeal attraction in the world of cinema and at the same time one of its most trained and serious Actors Studio/Method thespians. There was common ground there because her sexiest attribute, apart from that once-in-a-generation face was that she was one helluva terrific little actress. She had a very sweet figure which had been amply seen in "Carpetbaggers." There was one shot of her in character sitting nude a a make-up table in which the only salient specificity of her anatomy was that pretty back and a barely plumber-like peek at the cleavage of her shapely derriere. Paramount thought I wouldn't approve the shot, but I didn't think it gratuitous and I knew what it would spin off. So it was printed in both the People section of Time Magazine and the Newsmakers section of Newsweek, and suddenly the panting by public and media alike began. One moment she was an appreciated Method actress with full bona fides from such stage and screen gods as Elia Kazan, Lee Strassberg and Harold Clurmon. And the next she was, well yes, Jean Harlow. She had a new film called "Station Six Sahara" and I'd launched it by taking her up the Sahara in Vegas and then holding a one AM screening for all of the show people on The Strip after all of the midnight shows. We preceded the event by all ceremonially catching Johnny Carson's show at the hotel. Those original Strip hotels meld in my mind. I connect this to the Sahara, but it was in any event a hotel or the hotel Howard Hughes owned because we wound up being put in his penthouse suite since everything else was sold out. When we got back to the suite at about 3 AM, the room was, again, freezing. I asked Gisela if I should go down and pull the main electrical switch again, but she suggested that I just take some extra blankets from any of the five bedrooms.

Each comedian had certain characteristics, either true or constructed, that he or she would milk for comedy. For Jack Benny, it was that he was stingy and wore a toupee and lied that his age was 39. One time, when Guttman & Pam was handling the Merv Griffin Show I was covering the taping of a show on which Jack Benny was guesting, Ribbing him about the age gag. Merv said, "Jack, everybody knows you're not really 39. How old are you, actually?" "Well," Benny said, "79, but people DO live a lot longer than that… " and then with that high voice and innocent, pleading look of his with which he milked or cued a joke… "…DON'T they?"

Comedy is a matter of taste as well as conscience. Every performer is bounded by the not very elastic rules of good taste, and, believe me, press agents are performers. And right out there on the high wire, too. But as in anything else, pay attention to your elders and you will learn. For a half century starting in the 1920s, George Jessel was one of the most famous comedians. The Toastmaster General of the United States had a television talk show that was well-watched within the industry, and I guested the great actress and acting teacher Nina Foch on it one evening. After the show, as we gathered to say goodnight to Georgie, he was talking to a young comedian who had been on the show. "You got a big laugh on that joke about the one-legged guy," he said to the fellow, "except somewhere there's a one-legged guy and you broke his heart. You can only break so many hearts." On the way out, Nina said, "It was worth coming here just to overhear that… what he said. *We have moral responsibility for what we do, all of us.*" A good lesson for a press agent.

Knowing Milton Berle was like being inside Damon Runyon's mind. Everyone who sounded like an escapee from a "Guys And Dolls" cast or from Sing Sing came up to him on the street or at a restaurant. His business, so often in mob-owned establishments, made him an acquaintance of many of them. He would introduce some guy to me by a recognizably normal Jewish or Italian name, and when the guy went off, Milton would say, "That's Jimmy The Ballbreaker, or Izzy Knuckles" or some other collegial nickname of a dreaded Mafioso. Some of them were superstars. I could name them, but I like my knees too much.

Well, Milton's main running joke was that he stole other people's jokes and that he had these vast filing cabinets in his office filled with these pilfered gags. I had one occasion to discover that this was absolutely the case. Milton had been on an airliner which suffered some mid-air problem and had to return to Idyllwild (or maybe it was already Kennedy) airport. Before it could land, it had to fly off a huge load of fuel, which left the passengers with a few very scary hours to contemplate whether or not the landing would be safe. Milton had stepped up to bat and talked the stewardess into giving him her PA microphone, and he then ad-libbed for two hours to the amusement and distraction of the tense crowd. It was a notable instance of humane hilarity. It made a big splash in the news, and New York Daily News contacted us about Milton's writing a two page byline story about the experience. I called Milton about it, and he said "sure." Obviously, he could have dictated the piece himself, but it was absolutely true that, even with his improv and ad lib genius, he had writers on whom he relied. So I went over to Milton's office at William Morris and met with him and one of his top writers, let's say Frank, to outline the piece which I, by general agreement, was going to ghost. There against one wall were the legendary filing cabinets filled with four decades of jokes, written by him or his writers or, as he freely celebrated, borrowed from others. Frank was already busy searching the files for jokes which could be used here. But, understandably, there weren't a lot of amusing-people-while-they-waited-to-die jokes.

Milton had no clear recollection of what he'd said for two hours to keep them laughing. He just remembered that "it was a hell of an audience. Everytime I said 'folks' they laughed." What the piece needed was one specific piece of business that truly pertained to a gig unlike any of the other thousands Milton had played. I asked him if there wasn't some special thing, maybe some annoyance. "Yeah," he said, "this kid that kept running up and down the aisle. Now I know why W.C. Fields hated kids. It was throwing the timing of every punchline," he said. "And so you said…?" I pressed, coaxing. "And I said 'hey, kid sit down.'" "No," I pushed… "and you said? Maybe you said 'Hey, kid, why don't you go play outside?" He looked at me as though I was crazy, and then so did Frank. "Outside was thirty-five thousand feet above Bayonne, New Jersey," he dismissed. "Isn't that what makes it funny?" I tried, but then I went back to getting the rest of the write-able details. At the end of an hour, I told him I thought we were still missing some big plane-about-to-crash yuk, and Milton turned to Frank and said, "Frank, what was that thing I said to the kid that got such a big laugh?" And Frank answered, "Miltie, you said 'Hey, kid, why don't you go play outside? is what you said." Milton turned to me and nodded, "Yeah, that works. Go with that."

By any test of logic, Oscar Levant should be in my section on artists who are larger than life. But I think people thought of him as darker than life, although I, in slavish admiration saw him as wittier than life has any right to be. In the early days of TV, when there was what was called "a special," usually a stand-alone one-of-a-kind musical production, there would sometimes be a panel discussion of it afterwards cast with imposing wits. Following the broadcast of a musical version of "The Legend Of Sleepy Hollow," Levant confessed to having found it "very sleepy and very hollow." In the same show, he alluded to his similarities to Judy Garland saying, "I'm one suicide attempt up on her, but she's two nervous breakdowns up on me."

Levant and his wife June had a talk-show on a local LA television station, and I used to book clients on it just to be in the same room with his brilliance. One time at a commercial break I went to make a suggestion to my client, the amazing writer Leslie Stevens, only to get to him just as Levant was confiding to him, "The bottom's falling out. The bottom's falling out." But whether it was larger or funnier or darker than life, Levant's genius… in wit as much as in music… was like unto no other. His autobiographical works are worth memorizing. I shared this obsession with Michel Legrand's manager who was similarly fixated on Levant. We were in a green room backstage when Legrand was performing as part of the AFI Lifetime Achievement Award show honoring Barbra Streisand. I mentioned to him my regret at having lost a ragged paperback copy of Levant's "A Smattering Of Ignorance" when our house burned down. He graciously sent me his own hard-cover copy of Levant's "Memoirs Of An Amnesiac." I was laughing out loud while reading it on a flight to Toronto with Pierce Brosnan, who, thus annoyed, inquired what I was reading, I shared a few passages to him and told Pierce how I'd acquired it. The next week Pierce sent me a signed-by-Levant hard cover of "A Smattering of Ignorance." Who says this is a cruel industry?

Considering the Witty People Hall of Fame through which my life has meandered, I keep coming back to the amazing fact that the person who has made me laugh most is Gisela. She always pretends she didn't intend the laughs, but her timing is too impeccable for me to fall for that. It is a humor predicated largely on the solid core of skepticism that follows in the wake of a war-baby childhood.

After our Malibu neighborhood burned down in 1993, a moment when laughter was sorely absent, the city of Malibu hired a geologist to establish the stability or lack of such for our hillside disaster area. He found that almost everything was an ancient landslide area, and for a while it was questionable whether any of us could rebuild. Eventually he was replaced, and building permits were issued... The next year we were purchasing our new home and Gisela hired the ancient landslide guy to do the geology on the house we were buying. She wanted the best and the toughest. He gave our new hillside good grades, and she was pleased. "Of course," he added, "it IS right over an earthquake fault line." "What?" she gasped. "1500 feet to the north..." "Are you kidding!" she exclaimed in horror, "when did it last go off?" "Sixty million years ago." She gave him The Look and said with unforgiving relief, "No wonder they fired you."

It is Gisela's incorrigible instinct for lacerating phrase and her ready-for-the-worst unquenchable spirit that permitted me to stay the impatient hands of time. It's rejuvenating to live with someone who can bring every argument to a screeching halt by making you laugh, not that there wasn't a lot of screeching going on before it arrived at its punch line... On the other hand, I'm not sure she would have made it 50 years with anyone else, her beauty and intelligence notwithstanding. She has star quality, and that's not easy to deal with. A press agent learns how to do it... mostly by relishing it. It would wear the rest of you into the ground. I love her honest self-perception. On the 40th anniversary of my high school graduation, I received an invitation to the class reunion. I don't know why I didn't want to go... I was doing ok, and I was certainly proud of my life partner. But I didn't. And then I received a lovely book they made with photos of everyone who was there. "Who were you in love with?" Gisela demanded. I explained that I had never loved before her, and she blew that off with, "Everyone was in love with someone in high school, even if you never talked." Ok, we stared at the pictures and finally I pointed to one woman. We were already nearing 60. "Diane Kestenbaum," I admitted. Gisela studied her and then said, "Well, I guess you've always had good taste."

My inability to resist making some stupid joke upon the invitation of a straight line cost me what would have been the adventure of my life. One day I received a call from a world renowned oceanographer... I'm going to guess Lucius Bebe or his son (I'm trying to do this thing on memory, not research... it is, after all, called a MEMoir) who was going to and then most certainly did make the first bathyscaph descent to the bottom of the Atlantic to visit the wreckage of the Titanic. With a great sense of showmanship, he felt the dive would get even wider attention if William Shatner, Captain Kirk and the most famous venturer into mythic outer space, were to participate. With my customary selflessness, I bargained that if I landed this for him, I would get to be aboard the dive, too. Agreed. I knew Bill to be an icy-nerved adventurer and I was sure I could sell it. My pitch was that since he, Captain Kirk forever, would never actually ever get to visit outer space, it would be a giant splash of publicity if he would go on the most important visit into oceanic inner space. There was a long pause, and then Bill said, "That sounds... daaaaaaane-gerous." This is a guy who fearlessly tackled many deadly dangers, facing off against a giant grizzly with only a bow and arrow, hurtling down an Olympic bobsled run at a thousand miles an hour, but we each have our own private "room 101," the one dark place we never want to go, and this was it for Bill.

But I didn't want to give up on my own adventure, so I called back my deepest-sea diver and worked the same offer for Jacqueline Bisset, predicated on her diving fame in, yes, "The Deep." He was thrilled. When I put it to her, I could hear real interest, and my hopes of great adventure soared. "But am I just there as an ornament on the tree?" she asked, her only resistance, "Am I just sitting there doing my nails?" There it was, a fatal straight line, and I leaped on it with, "Absolutely not. You have the most important job. You have to watch the seams and then, if the occasion arises, scream out, 'We're LEAKING!!'" After a few seconds of consideration, Jackie asked me to extend her polite decline and her wishes for a successful venture. I'm the only guy in the history of naval exploration who could torpedo his own ship.

It's hard to believe because he was so goddamn handsome and elegant, but Robert Stack was one of the funniest guys in Hollywood, usually making fun of himself. He and his stunning and equally funny wife Rosemary, as gorgeous and beloved a couple as ever trod the velvet paths of Tinseltown, were extremely sociable. When I offered him attendance at some major event, he said, "I think not. People are starting to feel Rosemary and I will go to the opening of a door." When Gisela and I first met him in 1958, Bob Stack was the biggest star in America. His "The Untouchables" series had taken the country by storm. Like

Milton Berle, he was firing the nation's addiction to its ten inch TV screens. He was on the cover of Time and Newsweek and Life and Look. He was everywhere and he was everything. It was shortly after I had brought Gisela to America. Because I had gained a close friendship with that one-of-the-greatest-songwriting-partnerships-ever, Sammy Cahn and Jimmy Van Heusen, during the filming of Bob Hope's "Paris Holiday." We were invited to a Sunday afternoon garden party the fabled columnist Louella Parsons threw for Jimmy. At that time, if Bob Stack was there, it was an A event... and this one was a very A event. We wound up sitting at a table with Bob, and he and Gisela were in engaged conversation for a while before she said, "I have this incredible feeling that I know you from some place." Bob was charmed as he suddenly realized that someone was exploring his mind because she found it interesting and not because he WAS the A list. We didn't become associated until I went into partnership with Jerry Pam who had handled him forever. I think Bob became a jester of his own fame not only because he was so easy-to-deride handsome, but because his first fame was as the actor who gave America's sweetest singing sweetheart, Deanna Durbin the only pretender to Shirley Temple's throne, her first screen kiss. But, for whatever reason, he was Hollywood's champion of self-effacement, and always doing so with great wit. He was the classy guy incarnate. Referring to some past event one time, he added, "But that was when I was Robert STACK."

I concluded on my first day as a press agent that the job was just pulling practical jokes and getting paid for it. Very little ever happened to dissuade me of that conviction. When I was in the television department at R&C immediately after my return from Europe, we were promoting a cop procedural show set in San Francisco, "Line-up," and it was one of TV's biggest hits. We did a lot of stunting for TV shows in those days, including, for "Line-up," sending a motor-powered Frisco cable car around America. A simpler promo was sending out a box of fortune cookies to each TV editor around the country. All of the cookies had fortunes that read "Good luck will be yours if you watch the 'Line Up" season kickoff September 14." Just as a joke, I had them put one cookie into each box with a fortune that said "Help, Help. I'm a prisoner in a Chinese cookie factory." Old joke, but apparently it perked up interest in the season start. I took some of these home, and when we went to dinner in Chinatown with my friend Don Lippman and his Chinese girlfriend, I slipped her one of the joke cookies when I distributed those end-of-the meal treats. She read her cookie and she tensed. She waved the waiter over, said something to him in Chinese and then handed him the fortune. He read it, and his mouth opened in gasp. Then he hurried with it into the kitchen. When we left, the waiter came to her and they had another brief but intense conversation. As we got into the car, she said, "Thank you for a most eventful dinner. It may have resulted in great good." I never found out what the cops had said when the waiter or the manager called, but they must have played along with the joke, too.

Hollywood Marraiges

When you're funny, you'll go for the funnybone wherever an audience is gathered, even at your own wedding. And Jocy Pantiliano... Joey Pants... is funny. The public may be too tabloid-persuaded to accept this, but there are a lot of strong, stable, loving and lasting marriages in Hollywood. There are no statistics, but, if there were, I believe the incidence of failed marriages would be about on a par with that of the general public... or, from another depressing point of view, that the public is now on a par with Hollywood. Gisela and I were discussing this once with Joey, and The Pants told us that when he and his wife were married, the priest at the appropriate moment in the ceremony said to him: "Do you, Joseph, take this woman to be your wife, to live together in the covenant of marriage? Will you love her, comfort her, honor and keep her in sickness and in health, and, forsaking all others, be faithful to her as long as you both shall live?" At which point, Joey turned to the assemblage and exclaimed, "Even on location?"

There was a period when I got hooked on "The Sopranos." It was, by no great coincidence, about the time that Joey was doing his arc on the show. Gisela, who watched very little TV beyond PBS and CNN, was passing by the family room just as Joey was in a climactic confrontation scene with Tony Soprano. I insisted she come in. "It's Joey. You have to see his blond wig." Gisela came in and got caught up in the argument between Tony and the blond Joey. "He's great," Gisela said, "is he staying on the show?" At which point Joey was bloodily assassinated, and I said, "Apparently not."

Hollywood weddings often incorporate humor. When one of Gisela's girlfriends got married in her mid-forties, the terrific trio supplanting the organ didn't play "Here Comes The Bride, " but rather "At Last," with the tenor/guitar player doing a great Etta James. And when the parson imparted the obligatory "anyone who has reason that this marriage should not... etc.," the bride turned and dared the room with a fearful glare that scanned and scathed us all. There were no dissenters, just a rousing applause…

Actors are often funniest when they are most insecure. At one of Marjoe Gortner's celebrity bedecked charity fund-raisers in Hawaii, I prevailed upon Pierce Brosnan to auction off his hosting a lunch at a famous Malibu eatery. At the start of the meal which preceded Marjoe's animated auctioneering to benefit the cause, Pierce (at that time pre-Bond but wildly popular around the world as Remington Steele) became convinced that he would go unbid upon and he authorized me to come in at $2500 to spare him that anguish, which decision he washed down with a glass of wine. Several others followed that down his throat, assuaging the dread of his impending humiliation. His anguish was much to the hilarity of his wife, Cassie. As beautiful within as without, Cassie not long after that was tragically lost to cancer, but on this night, Pierce's self-flagellation, self-mockery and Irish whimsy had her dissolved in laughter… As it turned out, I couldn't even get my $2500 bid in as the raises came in furious succession… Two bidders wound up tying at $6,000 and Pierce happily agreed to honor both. By that time he was anaesthetized to any result, good or bad. He stood to offer a toast to the successful bid, but luckily he was drowned out by the next bidding, which sent Cassie on another laughing jag.

James Mason was perhaps the funniest of my friends, and that in spite of the fact that he never tried to amuse YOU, only himself. The glee he took in this was hilarious… and sometimes humiliating, sometimes both at the same time. On this one occasion, I couldn't go back to eat at The Bistro for several months. It was the day after the night Gisela and I had joined him and his girlfriend, also known as somebody else' wife, for dinner, dancing and all around merriment at The Factory, a factory being what it had been before it became THE hot watering hole of the liberated '60s Hollywood night scene. Gone or almost gone were the nightclubbing '40s and '50s, Ciros, the Trocadero, the Mocambo, and now it was the era of the rock-the-night-away psychodelia, where people far too old for it went to act hip and look… well… ridiculous. At one point I was frugging — or whatever the flopping ragdoll movement of the moment was called — with James' borrowed lady while Gisela was dancing with James, or at least someone who looked something like her was. James had sprung the evening on us so late that she'd had to pin on a beehive blonde wig as was the prevailing last minute device of that period. A very charming gentleman with a tall beauty beebopping around him danced over to me and James' illicit friend and engaged us in very jovial conversation, making a very smiling connection before his lady beebopped away and he in her wake. As I escorted James' purloined pretty off the floor, Gisela and James slightly behind us, I noticed Abby and Vi Greshler staring at me angrily from a prime dance-watching table, one of those don't-ever-darken-our-door-again glares. Suddenly they realized that the Jean Harlow platinum blonde with James was Gisela, and they screamed "Gisela" joyously and sprung upon her with happy hugs that sent Jean Harlow's hair skittering across the floor. That was as close as Gisela and I, straying from our little valley domicile, came to participation in the wild '60s Hollywood scene.

The next day, James showed up at our offices shortly after noon, all full of himself with some delightful revelation he had to tell me. He said he would stand me to lunch at the Bistro next door. The Bistro was the in restaurant which Billy Wilder and friends had created and which quickly became the Must eating spot. Billy had it designed by Alexander Trauner, the adulated art director who had recreated Paris for Billy inside a Paris soundstage for "Love In The Afternoon." In the flush of excitement of my first foreign location, knowing no one and in love only with Paris for the moment, I'd had plenty of time to write copiously about everybody involved in the film, and Trauner and I had become friends. There was no Belle Epoque Paris bistro that looked more like a Belle Epoque Paris bistro than Trauner's The Bistro right there on Canon Drive. You felt like you needed to stamp your passport to walk in. The thing I had discovered about French bistros when Paris became my home in the mid-50s was that the city was still marginally in a state of post-war trauma. The vast middle-class was not really wealthy, and they lived for the most part in modest or small quarters so that much of their social pleasure and entertaining transpired in restaurants, brasseries, bistros and bars. And these all sounded and even smelled convivial. That's what Billy and Trauner had captured glamorously, expensively and trend-settingly with The Bistro. It was the flipside of Prince Mike Romanoff's erstatz (but oh so charmingly so) royal Russian splendor two blocks away. Romanoff's was all plush red leather booths where I scheduled many luncheon interviews just because it was the only place I had a good chance of seeing my hero, Humphrey Bogart.

The greatest culinary attraction of The Bistro for me was the gratinee… La Soupe de l'oignon gratinee… exactly the fabled onion soup consumed by the tub each late night in Les Halles, the round-the-clock meat-packing district of Paris which Wilder immortalized in "Irma La Douce." Les Halles lay just across the Seine and a romantic walk of darkened streets from Gisela's and my stomping grounds on the Left Bank during our getting-to-know-you time in Paris. It was worker food upon which the swells came to dine and where Gisela and I spent so many two o'clocks in the morning squeezed between people in satins and tuxes and meat packers in long white cloth coats sloshed with the blood of the slabs of beef they carried. We hung out there because it was a dollar for a bowl of that onion and cheese concoction, a full meal with all of the flavor-sodden chunks of baguette loafs and darkly burnt cheese. And we hung out there as other young Parisian couples did and because neither of us had a room where you could share a less public conversation or a caress, and because youth requires the wee small hours to explore the momentous possibility of love.

So, for me, Trauner's and Wilder's Beverly Hills bistro was my history. However, for a press agent, it was a terrible trap, so much so that I didn't like doing interviews there. Trauner had lined it everywhere with stylish period mirrors. Because of its shoulder-rubbing proximity to the Rogers & Cowan offices and because Warren Cowan and Henry Rogers had bought into the club Billy pulled together to finance it, we were at that point expected to do most of our interviews there. Now, a press agent has only three services to discharge at an interview. He is there to keep the chatter on track and the plugs flowing. He is there to "enthuse" it, keep it lively and full of energy so that the resulting story is positive and interesting reading. And he is there to pick up the check. It's the enthusing part that makes a mirrored ambience tricky for PR people. The attending press agent drives the energy of the interview with loads of appreciative smiles, like an audience forcing a laugh into a roar. You, the press agent, smile incessantly. Aye, there's the rub. At the Bistro, you were constantly catching mirrored glimpses of yourself in broad grin. Your constant smiles mocked you. It was like running the 100 with thirty pounds of concrete on your back. You felt like a hyena, but at an interview, one bump on a log can weigh it down. Your energy was much of the process.

It was, however, a pleasant place to lunch with a friend. So I walked in with James with innocent anticipation of joys unrelieved. Whatever it was he had to share kept escaping from him in little snorts of pleasure. He was rarely more charming than when he couldn't contain his glee about something. Finally, like a kid about to open THE package under the tree, he got to it. "There's something I have to tell you that I think you'll really enjoy." "Yeah?" "You know when you were dancing with my friend?" "Yes." 'And that very pleasant gentleman came up to you?" "Uh, huh." "And you conversed?" "Right." "Well," he said, and the mirth was bubbling out of his ears and his voice was rising with his delight, "that gentleman... was... her... HUSBAND." James had the knack of making each word, or even syllable, it's own universe. Another of his habits was that when he was very excited or very amused about something, he switched to his stage voice which could carry to the back row. I'm not sure he was aware of this, because he always seemed impervious to the scandalized looks this would draw from far corners of the room. In this case, each lovingly enunciated word clanged out like the tolling of a bell, spilling out across the restaurant. He now had the attention of one and all. "And HE..." James fairly shouted in the full thrall of his amusement... "HE... thinks.... you're.... FOCKING... HIS.... WIFE!!!" The room was silent except for the roar of James's laughter. I thought my agony could not be further ratcheted up, but I was wrong. "And here's the funny part," James added through his laughter... and he need not have shouted because the room was hanging on his every word, but he shouted anyway, "he's... a... gun... colLECTor! YES! He collects GUNS!" The rest of the lunch is muted in memory, but I do recall that when we left, people sort of treated me with a greater respect, or maybe it was just the intensified sincerity of handshakes accorded a guy on his way to the gallows. It all worked out all right. James was wrong about the gun collecting part, or maybe he just made it up to torture me. But the man eventually became Gisela's and my very good friend. Welcome to Hollywood.

A common denominator of people who made me laugh... and who make you laugh, I'm sure... is a vital truth-telling and audacity to the point of other people's shock. Angie Dickinson is a master of this, and it is a reason that any meeting or chat with her highlights the day, why she becomes a center of interest in any room into which she walks. We first represented her during her reign as "Police Woman," at which time it was already self-evident that the universal regard of her as ""sexual allure incarnate" came and comes as much from how she looks at things as it does from how she looks. Cut to the facts? That's Angie, and how outrageously, amusingly and charmingly so. At the jam-packed memorial for her "Captain Newman,

MD" co-star and friend, Gregory Peck, Angie's moving tribute included her direct comment to his widow, the beauteous Veronique Peck, about the great actor's unwavering devotion and fidelity to his wife, punctuated with, "And I tried. Oh, yes, I *tried*." Appropriate to a memorial? The loving audience thought so... oh, yes, it did... as witness the laughter and applause, most of all from Mrs. Peck. It was a glorious moment of Hollywood's letting its hair down.

I think "refreshing candor" is a key to Angie's unique humor and sexuality. It is sort of the spirit of the audacity these amusing people all seem to share. And it sometimes can create a gasping Hitchcockian tension in its audience. There was one such catch-your-breath performance that Angie and I survived, and perpetrator was my father.

My first television movie script which was produced, the first of several I did for CBS and Columbia Television, was "A Touch Of Scandal" (I still prefer my original title, "Somebody Knows") starring Angie and a group of great actors, Tom Skerritt, Don Murray, Jason Miller and Robert Logia. It had to do with sex, as do many things that actually get made in Hollywood. But it had more to do with gender inequality, which in politics is expressed by the fact that many male politicos are exposed in sexual hanky-panky and never miss a beat. But if a lady-pol were caught with her hand on someone's knee, she would be sent fleeing into the woods. So that was the dilemma of Angie's character, a prominent politician and candidate for higher office whom we first meet in a motel room in a scene steeped in the sense of sex-for-sale. Except that Angie's character isn't turning a trick. She's the john. And we know that somebody knows, somebody with a camera. What this all derives from is the fact is that her character's husband, her elegant and powerful career manager, portrayed by Don Murray, is asexual. And that fact, that word, became an issue of great battle between me and the director, Hungarian super photographer (as I first dealt with him) Ivan Nagy, not to be confused with the extraordinary ballet dancer of the same name. The producer, Doris Keating, called me to her office for a meeting with Ivan before production began. Ivan, she said, does not believe there is such a thing as asexuality, which he strongly affirmed, saying that he wanted the husband to have incurred an injury of war which deprived him of erectile function. I responded that Ernest Hemingway had beaten us to that one, and also that it would badly define our protagonist's character if she had gone into her marriage as a business venture with full intention of taking her action elsewhere. I prevailed, and the tension with

Ivan continued throughout the film. I understand how passionately Hungarians hold to their convictions since my father was born in Hungary. So I pretty much stayed away from the set, and Angie, who knew about the issue, thought that was a good idea. Why disrupt production?

But the day came when they were shooting a scene in the grand lobby of LA City Hall and Mayor Tom Bradley, a friend of Angie's, was coming to the set. I wanted my dad to experience that and decided to take him for a set visit. On the way down, I briefed him on the situation and suggested that he not say anything beyond "hello" to Ivan. He understood that the last thing I wanted to do was create a scene. Angie was relieved that I'd come to that understanding with my father. And so a moment occurred between scenes when the Mayor was there and photos were to be taken. Ivan was very affable, but, to Angie's and my aroused tension, there was that instant where I had to introduce my dad to our director. My father put his hand forward to shake and said to Ivan, "I hear you call yourself Mr. Big." I-hear-you-call-yourself-Mr.-Big was that Hitchock hanging-from-the-high-roof moment of terror for me and for Angie. Anything could happen next, and none of it, we thought, was good. Ivan was shocked… it was on his face. And then, with a great roar… hold on, a roar of laughter… he grabbed my father in a big bear hug and swung him around. Who knew that "nagy" in Hungarian means "big"?

Years later when the newspaper headlincs informed us that Ivan Nagy was somehow involved with Hollywood's madame to the stars, Heidi Fleiss, I could better understand how ill-prepared he was to accept the concept and fact of asexuality.

Gisela and I were once in at a charity celebrity ski event in Canada with Angie, and at a cocktail evening, Angie came over to say that a fan had just stopped to tell her how much he enjoyed the movie in which she was the politician who had to solve her lover's murder. She had asked him if he would like to talk to the screenwriter of that who was just across the room, and he answered, "Why would I want to talk to him?"

The Brits were always fun, to the man… and woman. Michael Caine brings as much fun to life as he does to his roles. He's a master of accents and can break you up in all of them. His machine-gun speed cockney is his best, possibly because it's his native tongue. Or perhaps it was Bermondsey which he spoke in "The Ipcress

File." I asked him the reason it always seemed to be exceeding the speed limit. "Because we, the poor and subservient, had precious little time to get anything across to our betters. You had to jam it all in if you got any kind of audience with them." That drawn out, slow motion disdain with which the upper crust communicated had the same root. They had to hurry for no man, because the very survival of those beneath them depended on understanding each syllable of their instruction from the privileged classes. To say that Michael stirred big-time interest in Hollywood when he exploded upon us in"The Ipcress File" in 1965 is laughable understatement. He was an overnight sensation. It was supposed to be a working-class Bond character, and it surely kept Caine working for well over five decades. Rogers & Cowan wanted him big time, so I stopped in London on my family's annual trip to take our daughters to spend a few weeks with their grandparents in the German Black Forest. The only chance I had to meet with Caine would be during the midnight "lunch" break of an all-night shoot on the banks of the Thames for a little film called "Alfie," which of course would turn Hollywood interest in him up to boil. I was delayed at a prior dinner meeting, and when I got to the set, I was told that Michael had departed to midnight "lunch" at a good and nearby restaurant, his knowledge of cuisine being epicurean, later resulting in his becoming a noted restaurateur himself... I needed to find a "loo," and I knew there was a public bathroom about a quarter mile up the river at Westminster Bridge, except it proved to be closed, not surprising since it was well-past the witching hour. No matter, the Houses of Parliament were right there, and they had lots of lovely bushes around them.

As I turned the corner, I saw that the building was well illuminated both without and within. There was a night-time session of Commons, and so the doors were open. I went in and found the much needed loo. As I faced the urinal, another gentleman came in and stood at one a few paces down. I was startled when he spoke, disturbing the amenities of the ritual, but doing so in a cultured British accent. "I see you're an American," he said. "I could understand," I replied, "if you could see that I was Jewish, but I didn't think these things had any kind of national identification." "No," he said, "your attire." As we moved to wash our hands, I realized it was British Prime Minister Harold Wilson. He explained that the session would go well into the night because there was some kind of atomic issue, I didn't get whether it was bombs or energy, but he invited me to watch a bit of it from the gallery since "these atomic things get a bit heated... some of the rhetoric can be colorful." He was right, and I enjoyed about 20 minutes of the vituperation and then walked back to the set where Michael had just returned.

I immediately was made to understand that he had already made another PR commitment, but he was cordial and funny. I felt obliged to explain why I was late. "It turns out I had an unscheduled meeting with Prime Minister Wilson." "Anything important?" "Well, it's a bit delicate to explain, but I got the feeling the Prime Minister was very much relieved. We both were." Warren Cowan's theory of "true lies" rides again. "Delicate to explain, was it?" Michael commented. "National identifications and certain atomic issues," I offered. "Right," Michael said, letting it drop. I didn't get to work with that new most intriguing actor in the business until seven years later. There was a hotshot British PR guy in Hollywood, a fellow named Jerry Pam, who was a close friend of Michael's agent, Dennis Sellinger and he had already locked up representation of Michael. When Jerry and I went into partnership, I had the pleasure of sharing his representation for over twenty years, and he was still in Jerry's coterie of close friends and clients another two decades beyond that. As was Roger Moore. Even after Jerry retired and moved to Portland. That's what you call relationship.

Michael and I almost went into production partnership when Natalie Wood wanted to film a script I had, "The Kindness Of Strangers," and she loved the idea of Michael's starring in it with her. Dennis Sellinger had set the deal, and then the tragedy of Natalie's drowning took from the world the great promise of what that quintessential little bright and shining star could have accomplished in the second half of her spectacular career. "The Great Race" is prominently in my mind, my having spent so much time on the set because Rogers & Cowan handled her and Tony Curtis, and one of my primary clients, Blake Edwards, was directing it. But you look at "Splendor In The Grass" and "Love With The Proper Stranger" and "Inside Daisy Clover" and "This Property Is Condemned" and "West Side Story" and "Rebel Without A Cause" and all of the other startling performances and the little girl enthusiasm she never lost and you think… well, you don't know what to think except of sadness and loss.

I had represented Robert Wagner at Rogers & Cowan, related to his beautiful wife somewhat because of that and did a bit of the work with Natalie who was also with R&C. Then Natalie and RJ divorced, and the next time I dealt with her was when she and her new husband, producer Richard Gregson, were guests at our first or second Celebrity Pro-Am ski tournament at Bear Valley. And then, as love sometimes devises, she was back with RJ, and that was very similar to the narrative premise of my script. And it was at that time of this starry couple's reunion that I received a phone call from her one evening and she asked if I had written a script called "The Kindness of Strangers," which I affirmed. And she said, "Well, you've written RJ's and my story." "I know," I said, "but, Natalie, I wrote that when you were married to Richard Gregson." "Well, it's our story, and I want to make it," she said angrily as if she thought I would give her an argument. "Natalie," I assured her, "this is one of the nicest phone calls I've ever received." And it moved ahead rapidly, with her even locking up her friend Sir Laurence Olivier to play her character's first husband. But tragic fate intervened.

Before I leave too far behind that quizzical conversation with Michael Caine on the wee-small-hours bank of the Thames, I want to note that one of the things I love most about actors is that they are very content to let a conversation have little unresolved mysteries, not all of the details explained to the point of asphyxiation. They know that good drama and good conversation enjoy their little elliptical moments, points to be pondered later or allowed to remain little puddles of incomprehension to be stepped over or splashed into without a second thought. Great actors in performance don't sit you down and explain every thought or emotion. They rely on you to draw your conclusions from the complex silent expressions they bring to a scene and a character... or to what they don't say. It's a way great actors and directors draw the audience into the narrative process. It's an element that gives wonks the right to love a film for their own and differing interpretations and to argue it passionately. "No... you're wrong. Didn't you see that look she gave him before she said 'I'll see you tomorrow?' It was because she knew she'd never see him again, the sadness she didn't want him to see." Things like that.

So conversations with actors allow you the pleasure of counter-intuitive statement which is allowed to be unexplained, enjoyed simply because it makes no sense, lingering only as a little mist of enigma, like a jazz note that takes you by surprise but then the music sweeps on. Many such conversations are little improvs. Here is a case in point, and it will be a kind of rambling one because it shifts from the Connaught Hotel in London to the plains of Soria in the Guadalarama Mountains of Spain to the historic penthouse of the Beverly Wilshire in Beverly Hills. Gisela and I were on our way to take our daughters to visit her parents in the Black Forest near Alsace-Lorraine. But we were hop-scotching our way there as I visited some of Rogers & Cowan's international clients in London, Spain and Rome.

In London, we had dinner with Larry Harvey who had just finished filming "Darling" for John Schlesinger, and what Larry wanted to talk about was a new young actress named Julie Christie. "She's the actress of our time, and you have to handle her. I've spoken to her about it and… you're going to the 'Zhivago' location in Spain, aren't you?" "To see Geraldine Chaplin and Omar." "Well, give me the date, and I'll make sure you two get together." It was a scenic drive from Madrid up to Soria, the mountain town which David Lean had chosen for the remote Siberian site to which Zhivago and his family flee the barbarities of the Russian revolution. But it was in its final spurt a torturous mountain road, made all the more so because my rented Seat started to smoke and jammed to a stop about three miles up the mountain. There was nothing I could do but back down the curving two lane road in neutral… youth is very handy when something foolhardy imposes itself. Perhaps because I was still slim enough to turn around to see out the back window, I somehow made it down and coasted to within one hundred yards of a gas station. The attendant knew nothing other than that it needed a mechanic which he was not. Where is the closest mechanic? About 30 miles back toward Madrid. I could take the train. I asked him to look at the car, begged him to. Wally Beene, our guy in Madrid then, had told me to rent a Seat because every shoemaker in Spain could fix it. I tried the starter for him. More smoke. He took the wires out of the distributor, cleaned each one with his tongue and lips and then re-inserted them. The motor sprung to life in a hum. He seemed happy with the tip. Not as happy as I was.

I reached Soria and saw Geraldine and Omar at the set of the Zhivagos' dacha, the scene with all of the glorious flowers. Julie Christie wasn't working, but the production office called her at her apartment in town, and she said yes, Laurence Harvey had told her I was coming, but could I please hurry because she had an appointment. The appointment was with a dentist because she had a tooth that was killing her. Not the perfect condition for a pitch, but as it turned out it wouldn't have been successful anyway. She told me how enthusiastically Larry had spoken of me, but what was it that I do anyway? Publicity. She hadn't the foggiest idea what or why that was. The Soria paper was lying on her coffee table, and on its front page was a giant photo of my client Carroll Baker, continuing inside where there was a full page shot of her. Julie thought it was very nice, but what did that have to do with her? I explained that Carroll was a very fine Actors Studio actress, but that because of publicity like this story which I'd set up and was appearing with similar prominence around the world and because other things she and I did together including covers of the top magazines, she was the hottest and most highly paid actress in Hollywood with the choice of many fine roles. Julie Christie, who was by force of her unique talent and beauty to get offers of all the best roles for the next decade, did not see the correlation. "And you would obtain stories like this for me?" She asked. "Well, in media that would influence the major directors and studios of Hollywood." "Oh," she said, "I would hate that." It was suddenly clear that she was not going to get a personal press agent, not then and very possibly she never would. I apologize if I'm wrong in that assumption. Studios would set the exposures, some of which she would reluctantly but graciously do. I was in charge of that for a while when I did the "Shampoo" campaign for Warren, and also on "Heaven Can Wait." More recently I had a small hand in touching the Oscar campaign for her marvelous performance in "Away From Her." Realizing that my pursuit of Laurence Harvey's grand plan for me had come to an end, I offered to drive her to her dental appointment, for which she was appreciative, graciously so because that's who she truly was and is.

Julie Christie, as briefly and sporadically as I came in contact with her, always made me laugh. It was, as I saw it, her incandescent embrace of the illogical. Several years after "Zhivago" and Soria, I had reason to note this charming innocence. Setting: the penthouse of the Beverly Wilshire Hotel, which accommodation was for so long the residence of one Warren Beatty. This was well into my Guttman & Pam period, so the Soria encounter would be far less than a distant memory for an actress in such star-glare. I had to go over something with Warren, and I'd stopped by just as he and Julie Christie were going out to dinner. Warren introduced me to Julie, and I remarked that we had met before. "When was that?" she asked with interest. "Perhaps you recall a day in Soria when you had a terrible toothache and had to see a dentist?" Suddenly her face lighted with glorious recall, "Oh, my GOD!" she exclaimed, "You were the DENTIST!!" I saw Warren's polite but passive interest in the introduction take on a mildly sharper focus, a minimally shifted gaze, a briefly reflected curiosity... I had been a dentist in a backwater albeit beautiful Spanish town? At the same time as I was doing his publicity at Rogers & Cowan? Even so tepid a disorientation must, by the pledge of practical jokers, be squeezed to the last drop. I responded with corresponding enthusiasm of reunion, "Do you mind if I....?" "No, of course not,," she said, opening her mouth wide and offering it to my inspection. I peered in with grave professional curiosity. "Very nice," I mumbled, "Very nice." Warren looked at us curiously and then let it go. We all empty our minds of such brief perplexities as we would our shoe of a stone. There are larger questions in life to address.

I love the mild amusement of watching unresolved mysteries play on other people's minds and faces. There were nine months between my resumed relationship in Paris with Gisela and our very humble first wedding. Our romance notwithstanding, I didn't think I had quite sealed the deal, and she had no intention of advising her parents of the potential new direction of her life, so we had to wait until she was 21. That August, just before I took off for England to start work on "The Key," she came into occupancy of an extraordinary penthouse in Paris' elegant 16th arrondisement, a residence filled with millions of dollars (it would now be billions) of classic art. It belonged to the Windschmits, a family of great artists who were primary restorers for the Louvre and also friends of her family. They were off for their (and tout Paris') annual August vacation, abandoning the City of Light to the sweating tourists. There was around-the-clock armed guard protection outside the door, but they wanted it occupied. This made a difference in our lives and, in fact, the lives of all of Gisela's friends, since they were all living, as was our own custom, in decrepit hotel rooms with one shower for every two floors. They could come and luxuriate in a bathtub. This happened to be around the corner from the 25 Rue D'Astorg headquarters of Artistes Associees, Allied Artists, which had employed me on my two Paris films. The head of Allied Artists in Europe was Fran Winikus, a lovely and elegant man, an epicurean, and I invited him to join Gisela and me for lunch in her humble abode since it was so nearby. We had just enough money for a good wine and her excellent wiener schnitzel. Fran, after avid examination by the attending cop, entered the penthouse fully mind-blown. He knew he'd paid me seventy-five and a hundred dollars a week, respectively, on my two films, and this was a penthouse in one of the most expensive parts of Paris. We had pleasant hors d'ouevres on the balcony overlooking the Sainte Augustine Cathedral, and then Gisela asked if he would like to see some of the art before lunch. She walked him through the atelier, the Windschmits' work rooms where sat, on easels, prime works by El Greco, Titian, Caravaggio and a half dozen other masters. The presence of the most exquisite tools of the painting arts which were splayed about heightened the mystery. Was she (or possibly I) a millionaire or conceivably part of the world's most adept counterfeiting ring? He had the knowledge, however, to know that this stuff was the real goods. Nothing was explained, only exposed. With great effort, he kept his composure, but his mystification was evident. The lunch was pleasant. He was a great raconteur. But every so often his eyes would drift back to the workroom as he had been seated to do, and the sizzle of his wonder was a palpable element of the lovely repast. As he departed, he upped my fee for the next proposed film job to one twenty-five.

Actually, Gisela and I had had other occasions of acquaintance with Julie Christie between Soria and the grand reunion in Warren's suite. I was handling Michael Crawford during his co-starring with Barbra Streisand and Walter Matthau in "Hello, Dolly" and for several years thereafter. Gisela and I enjoyed a number of social occasions with him and his wife Gabrielle, including a delightful trip we'd all taken to San Francisco for that festival's premiere presentation of Richard Lester's "How I Won The War," in which Michael teamed with John Lennon. On one occasion back in LA, we had scheduled an early weekend dinner with Michael and Gabrielle at the popular Westwood eatery, Madeo's, and Michael called about a hour before to ask if I would mind if Julie Christie, a very close friend of theirs, were to join us. I said, of course, that that would be lovely, and it had nothing to do with the fact that Julie Christie, having backed up her "Darling" Oscar with immortality as "Zhivago's" Lara, was at the apex of renown and admiration and definitely that very long moment's star of stars. I knew Gisela would enjoy her charmingly innocent company. I called the restaurant and gave Maddy the news, and he fully appreciated the significance and said it would be fine. When the five of us arrived at the restaurant, there was a large crowd outside waiting to get in. Maddy was waiting for us at the curb and joyously greeted us with a bright "Mr. Guttman, how lovely to have you join us," and swept us in past all of the lords and ladies in waiting. We were seated at what was rather conspicuously the number one table, the one most prominently viewed... and viewed we were indeed. There was a sense of occasion, and it was not lost upon Julie... merely misinterpreted. "Well," she said to me, "this is very grand. You must be quite important here."

As to her absence of recall of the actual circumstance of our meeting in Spain, how could she and why would she? Press agents are very comfortable in their cloak of invisibility and forgetability, or, at least, I am. We're an essential Kleenex of the entertainment business. But what would the world be like without Kleenex?

Among the many blinding talents with whom this business sometimes shuffles you, one of the most delightful for me was Mel Torme, The Velvet Fog. There were few performers even of African American blood who could sing jazz let alone scat like Mel Torme. And he had the comedy moves of a stand-up. His jazzy pop albums got incredible needlewear in our house, and when Gisela and I met him at a party at the home of Gene Hackman… talent seeks talent… Gisela told him she'd played his "Annie Doesn't Live Here Anymore" album over a hundred times. "Oh," he said, "so you're the one."

Gene's party was a "before" party. He had a passionate hobby of buying homes and then completely re-doing them, a precursor I think of his profound talents in painting which later blossomed. He had to design and to create. But then it was houses, and he had this "before" party so that his friends could have a good idea of the awfulness that he would later turn to surprising beauty and harmony. Amazingly, he would redo the houses while living in them. Gisela and I tried that once, and it was awful, but it offered a truly amazing grace in return. One night we came home with the kids, and I told Gi I couldn't go in, couldn't face a dinner with the sand on the kitchen floor crunching under our feet. So we drove a few miles to a favorite German restaurant, but it was Tuesday, and they were dark on Tuesday. It was around the corner from my parents' apartment, so we decided to stop by and surprise them for a few minutes, and of course my mother whipped up a lovely dinner for us. It was the last time we saw her before she died.

I saw Mel Torme again at a star-filled reception at the home of Tichi Wilkerson, widow and successor of The Hollywood Reporter owner Billy Wilkerson. Billy had once blackballed Rogers & Cowan clients from the paper for a month because he claimed Warren Cowan had given him a lousy table at some event we were handling. Tichi was gracious and good at running her paper, and her parties always abounded with the town's most welcomed guests. Curiously among these, I noted, was a European producer whose actress wife Guttman & Pam had handled. He had embarrassed me on several occasions, once yelling at some poor usher… an USHER… at a Berlin Festival screening where he felt his film wasn't being properly projected. I finally felt obliged to fire him and, sadly, his wife, whom I liked and admired. He'd called me at home that night to appeal the ruling. I insisted it was final, to which he asked, "Was it something I said?… something I did?" And I said, "No, it was *every*thing you said and *every*thing you did." So I cautiously avoided contact with him at the party and, to my dismay, wound up standing next to him as we awaited our cars. I was compelled to make charming chit chat that barely made it up from my craw, and then his car arrived and he departed. I noticed that Mel Torme had been standing near us the whole time absorbing the conversation. I was pissed about having compromised my true feelings about the guy. "So much for integrity," I confessed to Torme, "I actually despise that guy, and he is one of the cruelest and rudest people I've ever had to work with." "He just underwent one of the most dangerous and painful heart surgeries," Mel said in mild rebuke. "Oh, my God," I said, embarrassed yet again for angry remarks. "Two," Mel said. "What?" "Two... operations," "So now I feel worse." "Yes," Mel said, "his heart... they couldn't find it the first time."

The pun is held in low estate among the disciplines of comedy. Shakespeare didn't disdain it, but most people do, often excusing themselves with "no pun intended" after an offering one that was very much intended. A pun is best served raw, unplanned, of the moment. Peter Ustinov was a master, but my father could very easily make a race of it, and in his late eighties was still magically adroit. He had one other great friendship after my mother died, and after she passed away, I made an effort to take him to the films I had to see and most of the talk show guestings I had to cover, including an evening when I had Michael York on the Joan Rivers show. The other star guest, Cloris Leachman made a big fuss over my dad, and then we repaired to the green room to watch the show with other friends of the show's guests. There we heard Ms. Rivers announce that the third guest would be Norma Jean Almodovar, "the famous police officer turned call girl." Everyone in the room was a bit titillated at the prospect of a famous madame and dominatrix joining our number. Norma Jean was famous indeed, having run for Lt. Governor on the Libertarian ticket and having been a "60 Minutes" subject. I had in fact authored a movie of the week for ABC called "Cop To Call Girl" which never got a production order largely because I thought her story was a very touching and dramatic one, quite sympathetic, and the network was urging it be "Gidget Goes To Hollywood Blvd," which was pretty much how Norma Jean saw it, too. I had stipulated that I would do my interviews with her only when the producer, a woman, was my... I guess "chaperone" is the word I'm looking for. Gisela didn't like my lying on the floor listening to the tapes, which is how I work. This was exacerbated when Norma Jean sent a note to our home. "It's a letter from your dominatrix," Gisela said, handing me the opened envelope. "My *other* dominatrix you mean?" She ignored that with "She suggests that, and I quote, 'you have to track a lion to its den, so you should do the next interview at my house' ending it with the assurance, 'but don't worry, I'll be very professional'," She glared at me and then said, "And what's her *profession*?!" But she respected that I thought it was a worthwhile and very human story. Or at least I proceeded on that assumption.

That sets the stage for Norma Jean's arrival in the green room, wearing a tight floor-length red gown slit on one side up to the hipbone, emphasizing her rather dazzling beauty. She looked around the room and nodded to all, and then she saw me and smiled and said, "Dick, how *are* you?" My father, sitting in front of me said nothing, but later turned around and whispered, "Dick, how ARE you?" I told him I'd explain it to him afterwards. As I was driving him home, he finally said, "OK... Dick, how are you?" I rolled out the Dick-how-are-you connection, and he observed, "Well, she seemed a very charming and genteel person." "Which she definitely is, dad," I confirmed, "and she's led a brave and remarkable life, a story any good young actress could take to an Oscar. Her most remarkable quality is her candor. She told me that in three years on the force, she had intimate relations with scores of other members of the police department." "Scores," he said, impressed, 'that's a lot of (pause for effect) cop-ulation."

Why wasn't that passed on in the genes?

Some press agents think baby-sitting an interview is an auto-pilot gig. Introduce media member and client, think about something else, pay check. I've looked at it as hard work, because there always was a moment when it could take a wrong turn, and if you were off somewhere else, by the time you checked back in, some negative element was inextricably impregnated. You had to be alert to make that little tug on the wheel that would be required. But because the talents I've handled have been so unanimously bright and witty... my sheer luck, I guess... there was always some memorable comic moment to reward my attention. I was having David Niven interviewed at the Beverly Hills Brown Derby just before he took off for Europe to co-star with Brigitte Bardot, whose substantially unclad performances had become synonymous with delightfully salacious films. Today they would be soft PG13, but at that time she was a catchphrase for sex. "What do you play, David?" was the question. "It's a big role," he answered, "I'm the one who turns down the bed-sheets." Urbanity is a word one rarely hears applied to stars today, but that combination of dignity and subtle wit sure was nice while it lasted. Hollywood was lucky to have had Niven at the Oscar podium when one of the most stressful surprises arrived on the Oscarcast screen. Niven was in mid-speech when that uniquely sixties craze, "streaking," raised its ugly head and relevant body parts. As Niven spoke, a streaker, slashed into camera view, dashing across the opposite wing. It could have thrown the show off, but David simply got the genie back in the bottle by remarking, "Some people will go to great lengths to show their shortcomings." He knew how to meet a moment. Hollywood loved him, and more at that occasion than any other.

Dustin Hoffman is, from what I've seen, a non-stop show. And in various opportunities to observe or interconnect with him I realized that he's always at the top of that game. During the filming of Beatty's "Dick Tracy," I never really conversed with Hoffman. He was always too deeply buried in the character of Mumbles, his own diametric opposite. The one opportunity I had to study him being Dustin Hoffman (or *doing* Dustin Hoffman) was during the press junket weekend for "Meet The Fockers" during which he and Barbra Streisand did many of their interviews together during large parts of which Barbra was not only his partner in response but also his avid and amused audience. At the time of Guttman & Pam's Oscar campaign work for "Kramer Vs. Kramer," Jerry Pam did all of the contact with Hoffman.

A later Oscar campaign I touched for a Hoffman-involved film didn't turn out so equitably. It was one of those many years in which the Weinstein Company had a number of really fine films in the race. One I particularly loved was a gentle, touching and quietly uproarious film about opera and aging, "Quartet." A film about classic music and the people who devote their lives to it, it was directed with classic restraint and passion by Dustin Hoffman. It was full of lovely directorial touches and blended, orchestrated acting which always reflects the guy or gal wielding the baton. A superb cast headed by Maggie Smith delivered four very nominatable performances. And yet we couldn't get it the traction it deserved. That's the sad side of Oscar campaigns, the ones you coulda, shoulda and didn't get.

My only sort of one-on-one conversation (more of a riff, really) with him occurred when Gene Hackman and I were doing rewrites on our airplane script, "Snaproll." Gene thought his old Pasadena Playhouse classmate and New York struggling actor days co-survivor, which is to say Dustin Hoffman, would be great for the other half of that mano-a-mano comedy adventure. At the end of one writing session, Gene said he'd left word for Dustin that he'd like him to read the script, and would I mind dropping it off to him. It was a small rental home in the hills behind the Beverly Hills Hotel, and when I knocked on the gate, Dustin Hoffman called out that the latch was open. He was on a chaise by the pool reading some other scripts, and I waved ours and said that Gene was hoping he could read this. "Oh, yeah… yeah. What's your name again?" "Dick Guttman," I admitted, and he suddenly brightened and said, "This is so crazy. I used to play tennis with your brother Stan." "I don't have any brothers," I assured him. "No, no… Stan… he was a good guy, good player. Taller than you." "Most people are," I confirmed, "but all of my brothers are sisters." "No, no… Stan… say hi to him for me. So strange, you bringing me a script like this. And Stan being your brother…." I agreed with him that life is quirky. I was fully aware I'd just witnessed a master improviser doing his stuff, and I felt privileged.

Alan Arkin could always make me laugh. The bizarre thing is that he never really said anything funny, but he made you laugh with his dead-face takes. You have to go back to Buster Keaton for that. Not that he had Keaton's physicality… who did?… but the laughter always flowed from the characters he melted into, ranging from ironic to bewildered to outraged to functionally deranged, which is what finally got Alan his Oscar. We were doing the junket press for "The In-Laws," that great surprise comic hit teaming him with Peter Falk in which Alan portrayed the comfortably dull dentist drawn into the CIA antics of his daughter's prospective father-in-law. Alan was visibly into the promotional process for that film. Like Michael Caine at a certain period in his career, Alan had had a run of being very good in not very good movies. So at a press conference with Peter, the question/statement of one of the reporters to Arkin was that he really seemed to be enjoying the junket. "Yes," Alan answered, "it's such a nice change. I'm very used to the first question being 'tell me, Mr. Arkin, what induced you to do this film?'" It got a big laugh, particularly from Peter. Alan never cut a smile, a device with which he could always milk the laughter.

What was fun was trying to make Alan Arkin laugh. I was driving him to a talk show, and I asked if he'd ever had another press agent. "So and so." "He's pretty good," I said, "Why'd you leave him?" "Because he was always talking. He never shut up. Always the chatter. It drove me nuts. You know what I mean?"

I looked at him a moment and then said, "I have nothing to say on the subject." He accepted this with a dead-pan face. We drove on. About a minute later he let out one small guffaw.

But nobody can make me laugh as hard as Gisela does. We have this perfect secret of marital survival I do something to annoy her at which I am very good especially when I speak my stage German, and she in turn is volcanically expert and Wagnerian (Valkyrien, actually) in her responding annoyance, eyes flashing like the lightning of a perfect storm, talons fully brandished… and then she makes me laugh. It's true that I give her lob shots for her smashes.

It's also and perhaps shamefully true that when she first came to the country and had no familiarity with the vernacular or idiom, I did to some very small extent exploit that situation for my amusement. For instance, she heard the word "spooning" and I explained very helpfully is that was the euphemism for the sexual position in which a gentleman places himself behind a young lady, like two spoons in a drawer. "Is that what it is?" she asked in shock, having heard the phrase used casually. "I'm afraid so." So when a singer bursts forth with "by the light of the silvery moon, I want to spoon," or when in a sweet movie a small town mom catches her daughter sitting on a porch swing with her suitor, and the girl lightly chides her mother with "Oh, mom, we were just spooning," Gisela was aghast. It somewhat skewed her sense of American morality. So, too, the word "sidekick." She also had come… this time by her own device… to the conclusion that "sidekick" meant the object of a straying husband's affections… which is to say the kick he got on the side… which I very helpfully confirmed. This threw into curious light for her the references to Smiley Burnett's having been Gene Autry's sidekick and the same for Gabby Hayes and Roy Rogers. It brought a deeper psychological meaning to her viewing those otherwise straightforward cowboy films.

And, Finally, a Light Unto Darkness

My venture into film publicity began during that time when the McCarthy era still cast a long, dark shadow on the film industry, its tentacles threading through the entertainment world for years. So, please indulge a concluding anecdote relevant to that. It was an occurrence that won my laughter and admiration as a friend achieved a oourageous "last laugh" against an intellectual bully. I was privileged to witness a clear flicker of justice in a time of injustice… One of my buddies in high school and at UCLA was Jeff Blankfort whose father, Henry Blankfort was among the blacklisted Hollywood writers. Mr. Blankfort and his family were paying dearly for his humane concern for others after the employment of his screenwriting talents (he had written the excellent "Tales Of Manhattan" and several dozen other films) was terminated by the House UnAmerican Activities Committee in 1951 because he refused to name names. At that moment when Jeff and I were just starting at UCLA, Mr. Blankfort was trying to sustain his family by selling meat freezers. He eventually found his way into publicity and a noble life promoting education. At that time, UCLA was a crucible in the battle to restrict or preserve freedoms of speech, and there was effort from the right to compel professors in the California University system to take a "loyalty oath." Where you stood on that defined who you were. Jeff and I were taking English 1A from a teacher so committed to the anti-leftwing fervor, that he, a teacher, supported the loyalty oath. And knowing Jeff to be the son of a black-listed writer, he made Jeff a target of his zeal, embarrassing and redressing him with scorn whenever possible. One assignment was to read E.M. Forster's "The Celestial Omnibus" and to do a report on it as an illustration of what is now called literacy theory, the study of 20th century authors who wrote about reading and writing and the effect of wider literacy on individuals and society. Forster and Aldous Huxley were considered two of the leading authors in that branch of fiction. Of course the teacher, knowing that we were all bewildered, thanks in large part to his vague interpretations, elected to read aloud Jeff's paper, ridiculing it with voice inflections as he went along and then condemning it as utterly misinformed. Jeff took his beating and then said that he had to make a further confession. He had not, he admitted, actually written that piece. The teacher threatened taking this situation to the authorities. Jeff offered to facilitate that by producing a piece of paper and saying that this was the signed affirmation by the actual writer of the report that he had in fact composed it. "And I suppose your ghost writer is your black-listed father," the teacher smiled, delighted to unmask still one more link of the communist conspiracy. "No, the report was written by one of my father's friends," Jeff said, pointing to the large signature. And there inscribed was "Aldous Huxley." Checkmate.

The doors of perception are wondrous indeed. Laughter, especially a last laugh, often requires great courage as well as wit.

The End, Starflacker Part One

www.starflacker.com